Advanced Modern Political Theory

Advanced Modern Political Theory

Analysis and Technologies

S.L. VERMA

RAWAT PUBLICATIONS

Jaipur • New Delhi • Bangalore • Guwahati • Kolkata

ISBN 978-81-316-0170-9 (HB)
ISBN 978-81-316-0223-2 (HB)

Reprinted, 2017

Published by
Prem Rawat for **Rawat Publications**
Satyam Apts, Sector 3, Jawahar Nagar, Jaipur 302 004 (India)
Phone: 0141 265 1748 / 7006 Fax: 0141 265 1748
E-mail: info@rawatbooks.com
Website: www.rawatbooks.com

New Delhi Office
4858/24, Ansari Road, Daryaganj, New Delhi 110 002
Phone: 011 2326 3290

Also at *Bangalore, Guwahati* and *Kolkata*

Typeset by Rawat Computers, Jaipur
Printed at Nice Printing Press, New Delhi

Contents

Preface

This book fulfils a longstanding need to provide dimensions, methods, steps, scaling measures, and directions to develop an Empirical Theory for the discipline of Political Science. Till it is formulated, it proposes to work with the alternatives of Analysis and Explanation, and also to make out Political Technologies for use in democracy. Along with these goals in mind, the present text, *Advanced Modern Political Theory, Analysis, and Technologies* is written to meet the demands, callings and challenges of the Twenty-first Century. It shows the way to observe dispassionately the contents of politics as they are, and to explain, analyse, and evaluate them to reformulate prevailing 'political theory'. Most important among the phenomena considered for study are: Globalisation (13), Global Governance (14), Feminism (15), and Human Rights (18). All of them, alone or together, have been, in the context of forces emerging from Modernisation and Development (7) to Globalisation, reconceptualised State (10), Democracy (11), Political Ideologies and Political Cultures (12). Applied aspects of the *Advanced Modern Political Theory* have opened up new professions of Political Engineering (9) and Political Technologies (17). Accordingly, the study of 'political theory' has been made more worthwhile a venture. The Theory of Contemporary Terrorism (16) discovers the ways and means to deal with invincible *Jehadi* Terrorism, by law, persuasion, and force. For averting Contemporary Terrorism, the author pins his hope in Human Rights (18), but also highlights its limitations as a viable theory.

Till the scholars are able to realise the majestic goal of developing an Advanced Modern Political Theory, they are asked to make use of Analysis and Explanation (8). This the author has done after presenting substantive matters of politics in form of Political Behaviouralism (2), Power, Influence, Authority and Legitimacy (6), and by bringing Feminism and Feminine Political Theory (15) in the centre of the stage. The Advanced Modern

Political Theory (1) moves ahead by introducing Systems (4) and Structural-Functional Approaches (5) as theories in the making. This has been possible after resolving the inter relations among Fact, Values, Theory, and Methodology, striving to transform conventional *Political Science into Politicology*. Some of the topics have been illustrated with appropriate charts, diagrams and tables.

The present work concentrates largely on the past and present, but its goal is to prepare for the critical future. It tries to seek some consensus on Goals and Values for living a self-respecting social life. But we have to find out the means, methods, instruments and tools to realise those goals or values. It is natural that we have to foresee all challenges, risks, crises and demands – short and long term, and prepare a theoretical edifice to meet them. A political theory, as such, hardly supports the status quo or assures those in power to be unaccountable.

Apart from the Almighty, the inspiration to complete the present venture came from Professor Atal Bihari Mathur, former Director of College Education, Government of Rajasthan, late Professor S.P. Varma, University of Rajasthan, and Professor Rajni Kothari, Centre for the Study of Developing Societies, New Delhi. I was encouraged by a large number of friends, colleagues, and eminent scholars. In particular, I am indebted to Professors A.D. Pant, Allahabad, Raghuvir Singh, Gorakhpur, Vishwanath Pratap Singh, Patna, Shyamlal Jedia, Jodhpur, Mohan Lal Sharma, South Asia Studies Centre, University of Rajasthan, B.L. Arya, Divisional Commissioner, Jaipur, B.R. Purohit, Udaipur, Subrato Mukherjea, New Delhi, B.M. Sharma, Jaipur, P.C. Mathur, H.K. Rawat, Beawar, Rashmi Patni, Gandhi Bhawan, Jaipur, and many others.

But for paucity of time and energy, much more would have been included in the book. If that journey was undertaken out of academic philanthropy, it would have been too late. The political events and forces are running with jet speed, and very soon go out of reach. As usual, 'man' would have become 'victim' of academic apathy, indifference, and irresponsibility. Very soon, I hope, and imagine, treading on this path, incoming scholars would take up my unfinished and belated task. I am sure, in the larger interest, they would criticise, comment, and suggest the gaps, misunderstandings, and blunders which might have crept in this writing.

I owe a lot to the authors, thinkers, scholars, publishers and editors whose ideas and writings I have, directly or indirectly, upheld, or challenged, or redirected without giving them a wanting opportunity of exchange and discussion. Thought is free and has no walls.

In its present update form the book is likely to benefit directly the teachers, scholars, researchers, and students of political science, and other related Social Sciences. It would also prove fruitful to those who are earnest to get success in various competitive examinations held at regional, national, and international levels.

With this, I have fulfilled a long standing promise given to Shri Kailash Rawat, of Rawat Publications, Jaipur. My heartfelt thanks to him and his staff for publishing it in a nice, attractive, and enviable manner.

S.L. Verma

1

Advanced Modern Political Theory: Building Process, Role and Profession

The pivotal role of politics today inevitably requires formulation and making of a *scientific* political theory. Developed countries need it to avoid the holocaust of a nuclear war, solve problems arising from *affluence,* technological revolution, pollution and other human maladies. Developing countries, belonging to third and fourth worlds, necessitate it to organise their polity, get rid of illiteracy, squalor, disease and backwardness and find out a form of governance appropriate to their needs and requirements. We, in particular, want to know the way to provide for the minimum needs of our people, adopt both democracy and freedom, and reconcile the competing demands of peace, security and development. As a fast growing economic and nuclear power of the twenty-first century, India's responsibilities are global. In fact, the world as a whole requires an empirical political theory for its very survival, existence and progress. There is no way out. Let us not kill each other out of ignorance or be killed with our own weapons, violent or non-violent.

A discipline, unless it has its well-developed theory, cannot obtain the status of a mature 'area of inquiry'. David Easton is still right when he says that Political Science is 'in search of its identity'. According to him, theory alone accepts an overall responsibility for the coherence and direction of the whole discipline.[1] As a subject, it has a retarded, amateurish, parasitic and abysmal growth. The lack of an advanced and postmodern political theory simply reflects its internal state of affairs. It is still not *Politicology* or *Polilogy* but only Political Science and there is little harmony among its various segments or sub-fields.[2] Some of them enviously compete with each other to become autonomous disciplines even outside the periphery of Political Science. Few scholars of Political Science are in a position to explain and analyse political happenings scientifically, and/or guide policy-makers and citizens, and reasonably predict the coming events. They have no practical solutions to offer and bear no responsibility for them. Simple collection of facts and data cannot be enough. A scientific political theory is needed to deal with that and properly control and guide it towards a right direction.[3]

Need for Political Theory

A theory is an intellectual device to understand reality pertaining to a discipline. It offers a mental frame or a conceptual framework to pick up facts for study, analysis and evaluation. It is a kind of a ship to steer through the deep and high seas of complex social phenomena. In a theory, innumerable facts, having uniformities – concrete and analytical – are conceptualised. Further, concepts in them are, on the basis of observable reality, woven into generalisations or general statements.

A theory is essential for a discipline for:

(1) understanding the subject-matter;
(2) its existence, survival and recognition as autonomous discipline;
(3) developing the techniques and methods of study;
(4) evaluating existent knowledge and for expanding it further;
(5) finding out new areas of research;
(6) predictability, control over environment, and policy-making;
(7) integration of different branches, areas and sub-areas of a discipline; and
(8) prestige and status of a discipline among other sciences.

It may be honestly pointed out that Political Science as a discipline does not have a broad political theory as such. It has only a growing modern political theory which is yet to mature.

Robert A. Dahl also testifies that, 'In the English-speaking world, political theory is dead. In the communist countries, it is imprisoned. Elsewhere, it is moribund.' Karl W. Deutsch also accepts that 'there is no such theory today.'

Traditional Political Theory

Prior to World War II, political theory was traditional and related to moral philosophy in its various forms. Its first principle came from religion, philosophy, history and ethics. It was subjectively and selectively based on limited amount of data. It did not use the findings and methods of other social sciences. It did not have any general theory of its own and made little efforts towards the formulation of a general theory. Traditional political theory was mainly a theory of either state or government. It was concerned with 'ends' like justice, security, order, welfare, freedom, equality etc. Most of the political thinkers were political philosophers. Their main object was realisation of certain values. They did not use scientific methods. Their conclusions were based on unstable foundations of personal views and speculation. In a sense, they were universal social philosophers, though lacking in specialisation and division of labour. Controversies and contradictions among them were too many to solve.

In the twenty-first century, by the term 'political theory', we mean 'modern' or 'scientific' or workable political theory.

Meaning and Explanation

When seen in a simplistic manner, 'theory' is an essence of experience.[4] In this sense, everyone is a theory-builder or a theorist. Everyone himself or through others observes persons, groups, events, social phenomena, listens to their ideas and draws conclusions about them. When his findings are repeated again and again, his conclusions about them are tentatively confirmed. Thus, he is led by them to certain convictions, assumptions, propositions, rules of behaviour, or theoretical formulations. After some time, he stops making observations as a stranger and applies his findings on similar events. On finding newer facts, he automatically modifies his findings or knowledge about social behaviour, and acts accordingly. Such personal and subjective theory-building or 'abstraction' is undertaken by a student about his teachers' behaviour, by a candidate about his voters, or by a subordinate official about his boss and others. The whole society, more or less, operates on such accumulation of experience, anticipations, assumptions or derivations. Man faces his present and future on the basis of such findings. The more valid and systematic the observations are, the more reliable and usable his findings will be. He selects, sees and interprets the relevant facts through the medium of his own theoretical formulations. Without such formulations, the child or a stranger in a metropolitan city remains unable to understand the ongoings of society. He is unable to describe, explain and evaluate.

According to Caiden, theory is an 'intellectual shorthand' or 'the symbolic representation of the real.[5] As a tool for the progress of mankind, it enables man to communicate, saving their labour to relearn what has previously been experienced and discovered. 'From the chaos of observation and experience, man abstracts patterns of regularity, and probability, and gives these patterns symbolic expression and logical connection.'[6] It is a net to catch 'fishes' of facts. It is a 'mix' of our various conclusions about the 'world': a guide to guide us, an abstraction to make further abstractions, or an apparatus to explain and predict events. Obviously, this apparatus is analytical or a conceptual one which operates on the basis of our actual experience.

Percy S. Cohen cautions us that the word 'theory' is like a blank cheque, its potential value depends on the user and his use of it. Here it has to be taken as a group of derivations or findings based on careful observation of empirical facts. It is an achievement, and not an ascription or imposition deductively imposed from above. An empirical political theory is a set of generalisations derived from the observation of facts. According to Cohen, 'a scientific theory is, *ideally*, a universal empirical statement which asserts a causal connection between two or more types of events.' A theory is formed when facts are 'assembled, ordered, and seen in a relationship'. 'According to Sjoberg and Nett, theory 'refers to a set of logically interrelated propositions or statements that are empirically meaningful, as well as to the assumptions the researcher makes about his method and his data'.[7] Jack Gibbs improves upon this view and says, A theory is a set of logically interrelated statements in the form of empirical assertions about properties of infinite class of events or things.[8]

Eugene J. Meehan regards it as, 'a generalisation, or a set of generalisations, that explains general statements, or explains other theories'. According to him, theory is, 'an instrument for ordering and arranging general statements that man creates for his own purpose.'[9] According to Andrew Hacker, theory offers 'generalised descriptions or explanations of behaviour of man and political institutions.'[10] Whenever the emphasis of one's inquiry is placed on the understanding of what *is* or exists in politics in the nature of 'if ... then' relations that can be verified regardless of the preferences and values of the observer, one can be inclined to speak of political theory.[11] A scientific political theory, thus, is a system of interrelated explanatory propositions which identifies and describes relationship among facts discovered through observation. In fact, it synthesises the results of observation, experiment and comparison, and expresses in a coordinated and coherent manner all that is known or implied by a group of phenomena or events. Arnold Brecht, finally, defines theory as 'a proposition or set of propositions designed to explain something with reference to data or interrelations not directly observed or otherwise manifest.'

Most of the above mentioned definitions and explanations of advanced or empirical political theory have been subsumed under the category of *modern* political theory, and their chief characteristics can be enumerated below:

(i) It is based on the study of facts which can be directly or indirectly observed by human senses.

(ii) In the observation of facts, it uses accepted scientific methods and other reliable tools and techniques.

(iii) In the making of modern political theory, the researcher keeps his personal values separate from his studies, and tries to remain objective.

(iv) Often the researcher/scholar or political scientist adopts some *conceptual framework* or frame of reference or a perspective before actual commencement of research or observation of facts.

(v) The researcher interconnects his generalisations, findings or conclusions and prepares an explanatory device or apparatus, called a 'theory'.

(vi) Terms, procedure, methods, conclusions etc., are used in a definite, clear, technical and communicable manner; and

(vii) Such knowledge obtained in the form of a theory is reliable, useful, and predictable, and can further be verified or tested by way of replication or testing the procedure.

(viii) It remains under a constant process of transformation.

Theory-Building in Political Science

As given in diagram on next page the process of theory-building starts from persons, groups, their interactions or behaviour, events, ideas, activities etc. There can be several factors or causes for studying them which may arise from one's inner reflection, on demand or pressure, out of some profit or interest, or anything else. But a researcher is not interested in studying all the aspects of a given phenomenon or event. He selects the aspects relevant to his problem, hypothesis or conceptual framework. While studying 'youth politics', one takes little interest in knowing everything about a student's whole life. Hence, he takes up only facts for his study or observation, which means particular aspects, elements, traits, attributes or relations of that phenomenon or event. Thus, a fact by itself is an abstraction which must be an empirically verifiable observation. In the earmarking of facts, one isolates certain limited aspects of the concrete event, activity, group or phenomenon, at least provisionally or analytically from all its indefinite and infinite complexity. The facts are collected by using various tools and techniques of data-gathering.

Formulation of concepts is the next stage of theory-building process in Political Science. Events and phenomena belong to the world of common sense, but facts have their specific and selective aspects. A concept relates to the properties or attributes of a group of facts. It is a universal descriptive word itself. It is a shorthand definition of a class or group of facts, e.g., concept of pressure group, or anomie. A concept is an abstraction formed by generalisation from particulars which must have direct empirical reference. In other words, it is a result of abstracting or generalising our sense-impressions or perceptions, feelings, wants and behaviours. There are certain rules of explication and operationalisation of concepts. Concepts are empirically defined and applied to all phenomena or events falling within their import or ambit. Concepts are rarely isolated from each other. They

Diagram 1

Process of Theory-Building

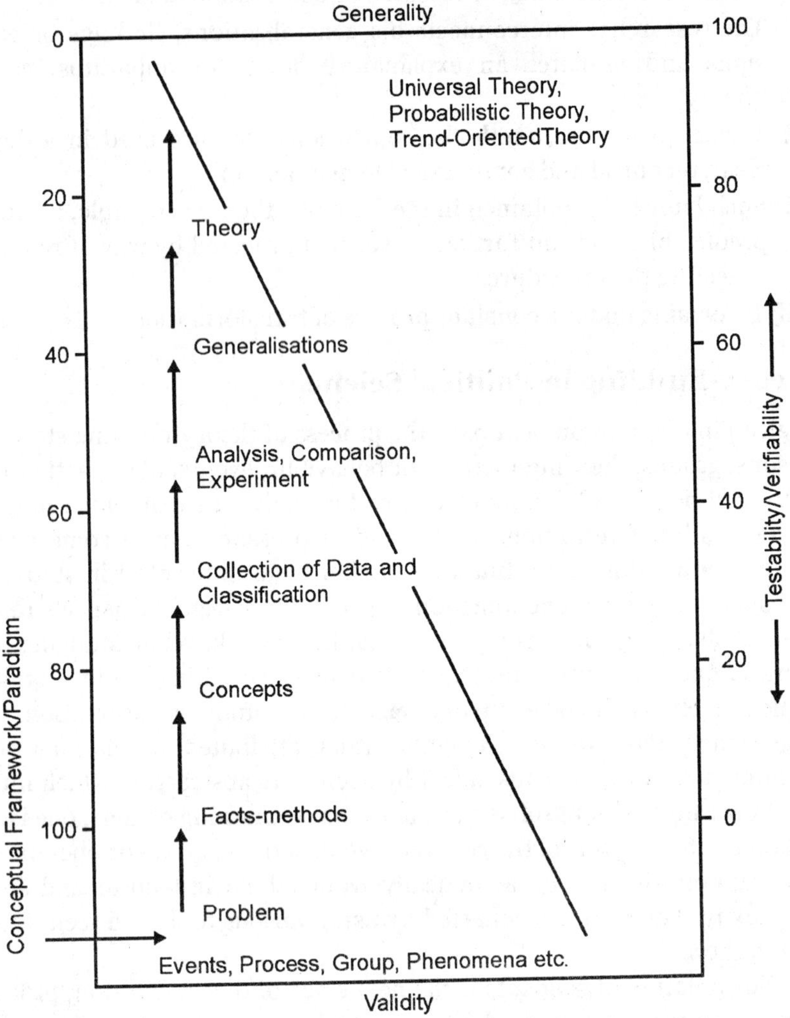

Generality

Universal Theory,
Probabilistic Theory,
Trend-OrientedTheory

Theory

Generalisations

Analysis, Comparison,
Experiment

Collection of Data and
Classification

Concepts

Facts-methods

Problem

Events, Process, Group, Phenomena etc.

Validity

Conceptual Framework/Paradigm: 0, 20, 40, 60, 80, 100

Testability/Verifiability: 100, 80, 60, 40, 20, 0

may have common or similar attributes in them. On the basis of their relationship or similarity, they are further classified. For example, persons coming under certain cluster of concepts are categorised as liberal, or certain activities having specific conceptual attributes are labelled as 'violence' or 'revolution'. Classification is the process of arranging the available data (relevant facts) under conceptual categories or classes according to resemblances or likeness of attributes. It provides the next stage for scientific analysis. It has been rightly observed that facts themselves do not speak, it is scientific analysis which makes them speak. Classification provides raw material to analyse and establish relationship, provisionally or tentatively, between two classes of concepts, events, attributes or phenomena. This leads us to the stage of generalisation. A generalisation is always conditional, definite and specific, and can be falsified or repudiated if newer facts compel us to do so. According to Meehan, 'A generalisation is a proposition that relates two or more classes of events so that some or all of the members of one class are also the members of the other.'[12]

Generalisations go beyond description of actual events and tell a lot about unobserved events and phenomena. They speak about innumerable events beyond the domain of immediate observation, though falling within the ambit of concepts, classes and their classification. Thus, they save a measure of labour, time, money and complications involved in repeated observations at each individual level.

The last stage in the theory-building process is the making of 'theory' proper. At this level, generalisations of similar or logically resembling nature are interconnected, and presented as a set of generalisations. It is ultimately a conceptual or analytical apparatus which enables us to explain and predict a particular phenomenon. Theories in Political Science again can be sub-divided as, (a) universalistic, (b) probabilistic, and (c) tendency statements. Universal theories, like laws, are applicable through all time and places, but in Political Science these are rarely available. Most of its theories are in the nature of probability and tendency statements. Political theories, empirical or scientific, can be limited to geographical area, particular segment of population, ethnicity, nationality or community made of some sect, religion, culture, sub-culture, language or specific level of development. So far, attempts have been made to evolve political theories applicable to the country and nation as a whole. Now, with the speeding globalisation operating on the processes of liberalisation and privatisation, political theories meant for the whole world, or its segments or super-powers are coming up. IT (Information Technology) Revolution has been facilitating their growth in different directions.

Many advanced modern political theories do not stop merely with the goals of 'understanding', 'explanation' or 'prediction', but go far beyond. Sometimes, having been based on a large amount of fieldwork, they present specific structures, processes, desirable resources and manpower with particular type of leadership to realise well-defined goals of peace, dominance, development and national and international security.[13]

Dimensions of Advanced Modern Political Theory

There are four dimensions of the theory-building process: (i) validity, (ii) testability or verifiability through scientific method, (iii) generality, and (iv) conceptual framework. *Validity* is closely related to the empirical reality of the attributes or traits found in factual events, groups and persons. *Conceptual framework,* discussed below, will help the researcher to sort out events for his study. In Political Science, they are mostly related to power, influence and authority. *Testability* or *verifiability* requires the use of scientific methods and standardised techniques, so that findings of the research may be either checked and tested, or, if need be, replicated by adopting the same procedure. The two dimensions of validity and generality appear to be antipolar. As we go up in the direction of theory-building, we gradually lose touch with actual empirical facts, and tend to apply our fact-based findings derived from limited range of observation to unlimited, unobserved or indirectly observable range of similar phenomena. *Generality* in our theoretical climb-up increases, but validity or empirical import decreases in inverse proportion. Hyper-factualism without a theoretic-thrust leads us nowhere. From this point of view the nomenclature of the discipline as Political Science is not proper, and needs appropriate replacement. However, throughout the whole process of theory-making, the link of empiricism or sensory observation has remained unbroken. Still, universal theories at the apex often lack much required empiricism, whereas the low-level descriptive statements do not make any theory. Therefore, scholars like Robert K. Merton have made a call to formulate middle-range theories.

Role and Functions

A *scientific* political theory is an ideal, whereas an *empirical* or *modern* political theory is the working model which Political Science aims at to build and develop. In its *ideal* form, as Meehan has summed up, a theory 'is an act of creation and a work of art. Good theories are things of beauty and aesthetic worth: fertile, suggestive, simple, productive and satisfying'.[14] Good empirical theories are rarely available. They perform functions as mentioned hereunder:

(1) An empirical political theory is a must for the growth of Political Science as a re-established discipline. Only an overarching or general theory can bring about integration, coherence and autonomy to its subject matter. In fact, it is an indicator of the health and youth of the discipline. No science can be fruitful or grow without having a comprehensive theory.

(2) Theory explains political phenomena and events, finding out cause-effect relationships. It helps us to understand the political behaviour of man and systems; phenomena of violence, war or development; problems like racism, casteism, regionalism, etc. Many a time, it predicts coming events, thus warning man against their evil consequences. In this sense, it becomes a powerful tool to defend oneself. A

theory based on empirical reality is a weapon to fight with false and motivated ideologies.

(3) Theory guides us to collect relevant facts and fill up the gaps or remove inconsistencies, if any. A science without a theory can be regarded as blind. Only theory enables a science to organise facts and give direction to research. Easton has remarked that without theory 'political research must remain fragmentary and heterogeneous'. It enables the researcher to face the avalanche of facts and draw relevant generalisations.

(4) A sound theory (not an ideology) evokes satisfaction, self-confidence and proper understanding among all concerned. It unites human beings, groups and associations, and infuses coherence in their activities. A scientific political theory often becomes a powerful weapon to win over battles or fight against enemies. Occasionally, it provides legitimacy to the system of government or its rulers. Attainment of legitimacy reduces the cost of government, and makes it acceptable, effective and efficient. The ruling class, time and again, can spread the information that its actions are based on a sound, scientific and all-acceptable political theory.

(5) Arnold Brecht has regarded a scientific political theory as one of the greatest weapons to defend humanity. On the one hand, it can provide the basis to solve problems like war, development, and abundance; on the other hand, it can expose the ideologies propagated as scientific theories which factually are subversive of the human values. In its applied aspects a theory can control, demarcate and direct the forces of violence, racism, nationalism, sovereign status of states etc. Unless this is done, science and technology are likely to devour its own maker – *man*.

(6) As theory presents political reality in brief and concise form, political actors – leaders, politicians, citizens, administrators and diplomats – can make use of this knowledge, and can take appropriate decisions. The adversaries and citizens can also raise their voice, if action is not taken in accordance with the scientific theory. In the absence of non-adherence to such theory, ruling or governance becomes subjective, secretive, and segregate, people causing immense damage or harm to humanity. If the rulers themselves learn the tenets of an advanced modern political theory or act on the advice of such theorists, blunders and wasteful cost in terms of man and material can be avoided.

(7) Even with the present state of developing a modern political theory, one can hope to reach higher levels of knowing political reality, and construct structures, systems and processes suitable to a collectivity. In view of the fast developing science and technology, the speed and

volume of empirical theorisation is likely to grow faster. In consequence, newer forms of postmodern political theory is surely to lead from micro to macro, even cosmic levels. In the way, man can use his discretion in approximating his ultimate values in the light of empirical analysis and observation of their consequences for man. The development of such modern political theory may not allow the rulers to run governments in the name of some mystic values or to operate it as their personal estate.

In this way, the main function of a theory or theorist is to anticipate events earlier than others, and to analyse, more profoundly than laymen, the immediate and potential problems of political society. Apart from studying problems, the theorist builds a solid block of knowledge (theory), and occasionally supplies better alternative in advance to the men of practical politics, and, thus, accomplishes his quest for reality or empirical truth. It is a powerful weapon which he prepares for the advancement of humanity by avoiding wasteful 'trial and error' method. Even a scientist should have proper theoretical orientation so that he may escape from hyper-factualism, untestable hypotheses, and erroneous predictions.

Features and Trends

As the modern political theory is still in the process of making, its nature cannot be anticipated or predicted with certainty and the required specificity. However, to make scholars aware of its growth and development, certain trends can be discerned below:

(a) *Openness:* Attempts to make a modern political theory feel free to pick up events and phenomena for study from everywhere, even if they belong to different disciplines like sociology, economics, geography etc., all types of persons and groups, various strata, patterns of activity or interrelations, forms of control or influence, psychological motives, etc. Even unconscious mind has come within its import or spread. With the avowed objective to regain an architectonic stature or status of a master-science scholars take up topics relevant to the making of a broad political theory.

(b) *Empiricism:* Great emphasis is given to knowledge obtained through human senses. All of them look for empirical, positivist, or experience-based understanding, so that it can be tested or verified. Knowledge thus acquired is subjected to observation, measurement techniques, and logical consistency. Observation and description precede explanation.

(c) *Methodology and Value Relativism:* Contemporary theory-building tends to be objective and value-neutral. Natural sciences are the main source of this inspiration. A large number of methods, tools and techniques have been borrowed from other physical and social sciences. But it can be said that in due course of time, Political Science would also evolve its own methodology. The researcher isolates his own values and ideology from his studies though ultimate values remain beyond the purview of scientific method, yet secondary values have begun to be empirically studied.

(d) *Close Relation between Research and Theory:* 'Theory seeks to march side by side with empirical research.'[15] Theory suggests new gaps and areas, and research confirms or verifies previous findings, and enriches theory.

(e) *Assertion of Autonomy:* The whole community of Political Scientists has begun to assert the autonomy of the subject, and engaged in bringing about coherence, unity, and integrity, mainly through the development of an empirical theory. Easton, Lasswell, Dahl, Catlin all have had been making Herculean efforts to achieve that goal. It can be claimed by now that they have been successful in establishing their all-acceptable identity among other social sciences. It can be assumed that Political Science is fast coming up as a basic discipline which can give direction and prove useful to other disciplines. As politics is directly related to control and regulation of society, its originality and predominance emerges automatically.

(f) *Interdisciplinism:* As its basic unit of study is either behaviour or interaction imbued with will, which instantaneously is related to almost all aspects of man and society, scholars seek lead from other disciplines. This necessitates an interdisciplinary approach, which means looking at the social phenomenon from the viewpoints of various disciplines. However, the task of integrating and accommodating these viewpoints is done by the political scientists who regard their approach as trans-disciplinary or pan-disciplinary. In consequence, the conventional walls of rigid departmentalism are pulled down. It does not mean that trespassers from other disciplines are free to cross over and claim the areas of Political Science as their own. Political Science continues to maintain its identity and crossable boundary lines.

(g) *Variety and Heterogeneity:* Theory-making efforts by various scholars at different levels and in unconventional areas have contributed to variety and heterogeneity to Political Science. A large number of models, paradigms, approaches, frames of reference, conceptual schemes, perspectives etc., have enriched the field of political studies. Some of them are either too wide and general, or too narrow to be hardly considered more than factual descriptions. However, their ultimate goal is to move towards or contribute to a general theory of politics.

(h) *Applied Aspects and Social Relevance:* In the early phase of behaviouralism, the goal of Political Scientists was to make out a 'pure science' of politics patterned after natural sciences. They cut off themselves from values, social demands, and problems. With the advent of post-behavioural revolution, they entered the field of applied research, and openly came forward to support societal values. They engaged themselves to find out solutions to emerging crises and problems. Their profession, to a large extent, became socially relevant, as it was in ancient times and recent or modern period.

Actual State of Advanced Modern Political Theory

Obviously, such a theory is not available in Political Science. Meehan observes, 'For the present, Political Science deals almost entirely with probabilistic generalisations and tendency-statements. Universal generalisations are rare, and perhaps non-existent.'[16] David Easton, Alfred Cobban, Mulford Sibley, and others have talked of the 'decline' or poverty of political theory.[17] Easton wrote that the American political scientist is born free but is everywhere in chains, tied to a hyper-factual past. The lack of more reliable knowledge flows directly from an immoderate neglect of general theory.[18] In his first book, *The Political System,* 1953, David Easton has argued in support of the need for the construction of an empirically-oriented general theory in Political Science. Later on, in his edited work, *Varieties of Political Theory,* he collected many external and adventitious approaches and called them as 'alternative strategies for theoretical approach' towards the ultimate development of such a theory. Yet the goal was not in sight. He himself presented a conceptual framework for the analysis of political life.[19] Still the goal remained elusive. According to Mayo, as none of these theories deal with entire social system, the goal of general theory of society remains unattained. Hacker predicts that the time is not yet at hand when all-embracing system by a single writer will be found satisfactory in major respects. However, awareness was there that 'the maturity of any science is indicated by the condition of its general theory and by the ability to discover formulae which will subsume the whole field, simply, demonstrably, precisely and in a manner that relates to other fields of human knowledge.'[20] Robert A. Dahl found, 'in the English-speaking world, political theory is dead; in the communist countries it is imprisoned; elsewhere, it is moribund.'[21]

It does not mean that efforts for construction of theoretical framework have all the time been wanting or nothing has so far been done towards this direction. From Plato to Marx, there has been a long line of political philosophers who have tried to evolve theories about politics, and have prescribed remedies for prevailing maladies. However, they largely failed in developing an all-agreeable empirical political theory. As such, among other social and natural sciences, Political Science, as a discipline, has lost its old status, coherence, and other avenues of growth and utility.

Conditions in developing societies like India and others are still worse. Most of the scholars here are culture-bound, tradition-loving, and ingrained in philosophical or religious schools of thought. A large number of them are unable to come out of the custody of western political philosophy and are utterly stupefied by traditional or classical political theories. They are unable to discover causes of decay and downfall of Indian polity or explain dispassionately the worsening conditions in various sectors of public life. Rarely, they study empirically the problems and crises of diversified Indian society. Barring a few scholars, almost all of them do not have any theoretical orientation to explain the behaviour pattern of Indian political system, or to offer alternatives to prevent ineffective palliatives. Almost all the departments and institutes of political studies are in an infant stage, sitting on the lap of their old god-fathers.

Scholars of Political Science in India, as also in the Third World, are teachers, nurtured either in the tradition of philosophy, history and culture, or are under the deep influence of foreign writers, ideas and institutions. Few have thought in terms of Indian politics, and are hopelessly wanting in knowledge of their national setting. Their teaching topics and techniques too are out of date, unrelated to contemporary realities, and totally atheoretical. Presently, Political Science is neither an *art* nor a *science,* and caters little to the needs of anyone, outside the teaching community itself.

Decline of Political Theory

The last one hundred fifty years till the Second World War have witnessed a steady decline, decay, and death[22] of political theory. On account of several factors, it could not remain an innovative, integrative and invigorating enterprise. It stood as a passive or spineless spectator to the two world wars and failed to save humanity from senseless devastation. These crises did not create any flutter in the hearts and minds of traditional political thinkers. Perhaps they were unable to react because of their old and anachronistic ideas or love of philosophic virtues to be realised in cloistered seclusion. It even did not cry against large-scale fratricide and senseless killings. They are still simply witnessing the events leading to a global war by nuclear weapons.

(1) Easton has fervently analysed the causes behind this sad state of affairs and has subsumed them under the concept of 'historicism'.[23] The latter term means a tendency to show that values and ideas are by-product of their milieu or prevailing circumstances. The writers adopt the role of historians and trace out history of values or institutions still surviving. They vividly describe the conditions which produced a particular set of

ideas. A 'historicist' political writer is little concerned with the problems of his times or finding out solutions or suggesting formulation of new values. He is, in brief, a prisoner of past, unable to peep into present or opine for a better future. As described by Easton, the contemporary writers were (i) living parasitically on century-old ideas, and (ii) remained unable to develop a new political synthesis. They loved and believed in speculation which again was found to a be product of history. They concentrated their minds in analysing the meaning, logical consistency, and historical development of prevailing ideas. Easton puts them into four groups: (a) institutionalists, (b) interactionists, (c) materialists, and (d) value-writers.

Institutionalists, like McIllwain, go into the history of ideas for past rationalisation or justification of particular political interests and institutions. *Interactionists,* like Allen and sometimes Carlyle, analyse the interaction between ideas and institutions, and its impact on the process of social change. The *materialists,* such as Easton, Sabine and others look into cultural and historical milieu which produced the particular political thinking. The *last group* represented by Lindsay, take up specific values, say, *democracy, nationalism* or *justice* and trace out their genesis so as to provide a strong support.[24]

(2) In fact, Easton wants a political theory containing also reformulation of values suitable to the present age; and theorisation about political behaviour and institutions. Apart from historicism, forces of moral relativism, hyperfactualism and lack of renovation have frustrated this goal. Moral relativism indicates one's faith in the absence of universal principles of morality and believing in morality related to prevailing milieu. Hume, Max Weber, Comte, Marx and others had advocated its tenets. They detached values from facts, and regarded them merely as individual or group preferences. These preferences were related, not with certain metaphysical or moral realities, but to one's own life experiences. Europe had evolved a common set of values like, capitalism, nationalism, and democracy, during the period of 1848-1918, and could afford 'moral relativism'. It continued to bask in the dreamland oblivious of the rise of a new value system in Russia, Fascism in Italy, and Nazism in Germany. The concept of 'sociology of knowledge' also brought forward the view that ideas in man are products of his social milieu, and related to his times. In this manner knowledge could not have a purpose or goal. The question of 'knowledge for what?' was raised, but remained futile in view of prevailing notion of value-free Political Science.[25] Few cared for the problems of society, still less led knowledge to political goals or values. Lack of a proper value theory, historicism, and neglect of causal or empirical theory led to this decline. Excessive concentration on the

study of facts, structures, processes, motives, attitudes etc., increased knowledge of *is* but not of *ought*, that is, destination and goals. Hyper-factualism or crude empiricism led to an avalanche of facts which was swaying away the whole discipline.

(3) Alfred Cobban found the contemporary conditions similar to those prevailed during the Roman Empire.[26] He looked at expansion of state power, bureaucracy, and huge military establishments as danger to the growth of political theory. The Communist world suffered from concentration of power and the party-machine, whereas the western world failed to reform its democracy as 'a living tool'. Abstraction of state as an engine of power keeps moral values away from politics. All this has resulted in the consequential decline of political theory.

(4) From the internal view of the discipline, Cobban opines that political thinking itself has become directionless, and lacks purpose. In the past, all great thinkers were passionately worried about the fate of society, and seriously wanted to reform it through their creative ideas. They had full conviction in what they wrote or said. Now that passionate commitment, he complains, has been substituted by the teaching of historical approach and the scientific attitude. Historical approach led to power as standard of success. Blind adoption of scientific method, borrowed from natural sciences, resulted in the loss of criteria of judgement, and merely produced cold-blooded passionless scholars.

(5) Dante Germino[27] discovers 'ideological reductionism' as the cause of decline of political theory. By this he means reducing political theory to merely an ideology, such as, Marxism. The intellectual and political movements during the last one hundred and fifty years have contributed to its eclipse. Positivisation of social science or a mad rat-race to become 'science' and political upheavals of democracy, nationalism, imperialism etc., have destroyed the environment necessary for the growth of political theory. Destutt de Tracy[28] the inventor of the term 'ideology', propounded it as 'science of determining the origin of ideas'. As usual, sense experience was the basis of his 'ideology' or 'science of ideas'. Positivism of Auguste Comte gave birth to a 'science of society' or sociology by discovering laws governing human behaviour. It was patterned on natural sciences. Marx went a step further. He claimed that he had discovered the laws of human development. With such laws in hand or with Marxist ideology of society, the existing class could be transformed into a classless and stateless society. There is no other alternative. Theory, to him, is but a weapon in the hands of the working class. All that evaporated with the collapses of Soviet Union in 1990.

(6) Another cause of decline found by Germino in the separation of *is* and *ought* or *fact* and *value or being* (reality) and *meaning*, brought about

by Linguistic Philosophy and Logical Positivism. The trend is best represented by Max Weber[29] who made a sharp distinction between empirical knowledge and value judgements. On the basis of this separation, he challenged the Marxian view. Although, he accepted the role and importance of values but put it beyond the purview of scientific treatment. As a social scientist, he stood for ethical neutrality which makes a political (value) theory difficult to grow. Therefore, Germino is convinced that, 'a full recovery of critical political theory within the positivist universe of discourse cannot be achieved'.[30] He regards Easton, Cobban and Waldo as axiological positivists who unsuccessfully tried to unite values with factual studies, and visualise the making of political theory.

(7) Consensus of opinion regarding values and objectives of society in the West and success in achieving them in practice have also weakened the desire to have any new political theory. People have got everything. Patridge observes, 'If classical political theory *has* died, perhaps it has been killed by the triumph of democracy'.[31] People in USA, UK and France, after settling down everything about ends are concerned mainly with means which is again a technical and scientific problem. Now, the West defends the status quo and is conservative, interested only in 'incrementalism', or 'piecemeal engineering' or accommodation and adjustment. Lipset, Dahl, Schumpeter and Berlin find little controversy over the goals.

Still, there is another view that political theory even in the traditional sense was never dead and continuity can be traced out. Plamenatz, Weldon and others do not accept that it has even declined or dwindled.'[32] It has merely changed its form. Even speculative theories, except spurious or utopian ones, are important as they have effected thinking, events and happenings. Formerly, political theories were embedded in philosophy, ethics or religion. Now, they are carving out their own fields, rather looking at the whole array of problems from their own perspective. Germino finds resurgence of traditional political theory, particularly, in the writings of Michael Oakeshott, Hannah Arendt, Bertrand de Jouvenal, Leo Strauss, Eric Voegelin and others. Similarly, Isaiah Berlin observes that without some general outlook or philosophy, there can be no human activity: political theory of some kind is never dead.[33] It is flourishing in newer forms with newer engagements. With the advancement of society, they say, people will need more theory to organise, justify and rationalise their actions. If there is no theory, they will invent it: beg, borrow or even steal. Man will always advocate some theory for himself and others. Apart from these views, there are some passionate ancients who claim that Plato and Aristotle are enough, for them. The world of theory has not gone beyond.

Revival of traditional theory has appeared in many forms. There are classical political theorists like Leo Strauss, Michael Oakshott, Hannah Arendt, Bertrand de Jouvenel and Eric Voegelin. John Rawls in his *Theory of Justice* (1971) revolutionised political thinking in the United States and outside. Besides liberals like Karl R. Popper and Isaiah Berlin, there are *libertarians* like F.A. Hayek, Miltan Friedman, Robert Nozic. On the other side stand *communitarian* political thinkers, such as, Alasdair MacIntyre, Michael Walzer, Charles Taylor, Benjamin Barber and Michael Sandel. *Neo-Marxism* has appeared in form of postmodernism or critical theory. Originating from Frankfürt School (1923), it appears in the writings of Antonio Gramsci, George Lukacs, Jheodor Adorno, Max Horkheimer, Louis Althusser, Eric Fromm, Jean-Paul Sartre, Che Guevara, Herbert Marcuse and Jurgen Hebarmas. Most of these political philosophers are rather concerned with philosophical issues than political crises and problems of today. One can regard their theories as non-political, even anti-political. They appear to reject basic and applied aspects of modern political theory.

Critical theory often challenges our common sense assumptions about the world and poses controversial questions. It is a way of thinking that encourages us to critically approach our assumptions about ourselves and the world. The Frankfürt School version of critical theory from the beginning focused on the role of false consciousness and ideology in the perpetuation of capitalism, and analysed works of culture, including literature, music, art, both 'high culture' and 'popular culture' or 'mass culture'. In the late 1960s Jurgen Habermas of the Frankfürt School, redefined critical theory in a way that freed it from a tie in with Marxism or the prior work of the School. In Habermas' epistemology, critical knowledge was conceptualised as knowledge that enabled human beings to emancipate themselves from forms of domination through self-reflection and took psychoanalysis as the paradigm of critical knowledge. Within social sciences, it included such approaches as world systems theory, feminist theory, postcolonial theory, critical race theory, and queer theory, social ecology, the theory of communicative action, structuration theory, and neo-Marxian theory.

Facing Postmodernity and Postmodernism

Postmodernism is a complicated term, or a set of ideas, it is one that has only emerged as an area of academic study since the mid-1980s. Postmodernism is hard to define, because it is a concept that appears in a wide variety of disciplines or areas of study, including art, architecture, music, film, literature, sociology, communications, fashion, and technology. It is hard to locate it temporally or historically, because it is not clear exactly at what point postmodernism emerges.

Postmodernism may be taken to refer to movements, philosophies or responses to the state of postmodernity, or in reaction to modernism. Many philosophers, particularly those seeing themselves as being within the modern project, use postmodernity with the reverse implication: the presumed results of holding postmodernist ideas. Most prominently this includes Jurgen Habermas and others who contend that postmodernity represents a resurgence of long running *counter-enlightenment* ideas. Postmodernism is different from postmodernity which can be said to focus on the conditions of life which became increasingly prevalent in the late 20th century in the most industrialised nations. These include the ubiquity of mass media and mass production, the unification into national economies of all aspects of production, the rise of global economic arrangements, and shift from manufacturing to *service economies*. Variously described as *consumerism* or, in a *Marxian* framework, *late capitalism*, namely, a context where manufacturing, distribution and dissemination have become exceptionally inexpensive, but social connection and community have become more expensive. Postmodernity as a condition ascribes to more rapid transportation, wider communication and the ability to abandon standardisation of mass production, leading to a system which values a wider range of capital than previously, and allows value to be stored in a greater variety of forms. David Harvey argues that the condition of postmodernity is the escape from 'Fordism', a term coined in reference to the *Brave New World* by Aldous Huxley.

Artifacts of postmodernity include the dominance of *television* and *popular culture*, the wide accessibility of information and mass and telecommunications. Postmodernity also exhibits a greater resistance to making sacrifices in the name of progress, including such features as *environmentalism* and the growing importance of the *anti-war* movement. Postmodernity in the industrialised core is marked by increasing focus on *civil rights* and *equal opportunity*, as seen by such movements as *feminism* and *multiculturalism*, as well as the backlash against these movements.

For *social*, *political*, *technological* and *economic determinists*, postmodernity is a major cause of the emergence of postmodernism and postmodern culture. For others, it is a mode of society which goes hand in hand with postmodernism. Postmodernity may be a reason for some to choose postmodernism as a way of life, *epistemological*, *ethical* or *aesthetic* position.

One position maintains that postmodernity is a condition or state of being, or is concerned with changes to institutions and conditions (Giddens 1990) – whereas postmodernism is an aesthetic, literary, political or social philosophy that consciously responds to postmodern conditions, or seeks to move beyond or offers a critique of modernity.

In the whole course of above discussion, political theory means 'traditional political theory' mainly related to goals, values, ultimate nature, and moral functions of political society and its institutions. They often tag political theory with political philosophy. The Greek word '*theoria*' for 'theory' originally meant 'deep thinking' or 'inward seeing'. Its aim was to search out intellectually the hidden meaning lying behind apparent reality. Germino regards political theory as the 'critical study of the principles of right order in human social existence.'

Thus, traditional political theory is different from modern political theory. The former emerges basically from philosophy, religion, ethics or history, and puts emphasis mostly on ends or goals of human life. Its theorists are mainly political philosophers, and they write with an attitude of a social reformer. Their interest towards actual political processes, events etc., is secondary, even peripheral. Being based on metaphysical or abstract entities, their basic tenets or principles, being subjective, cannot be tested or verified empirically. One may or may not accept them. The traditionalists widely differ on method, subject matter, and conclusions. The traditional political theories declined and went out of date, and no new political theory came from them. Even the rise and spread of critical theories and concepts of postmodernity and postmodernism have not served the purpose.

Evolution of Theory and Non-Theories

Lack of modern political theory or decline of traditional political theory has not discouraged scholars in their efforts for developing an empirical political theory. For the time being, in view of its growing nature and infancy, it is possible that it will not be hundred per cent 'scientific'. Till then, it would be proper to call it 'modern or advanced political theory'. The word 'empirical' as an adjective to political theory can also be used, but it carries certain amount of ambiguity, circumlocution, and controversy. It has also been used in the past. Till a better term is coined, the word 'modern' or 'advanced' can connote both 'scientificity' and 'empiricism'. It also bears the notion of objectivity and verifiability.

The impetus to develop modern political theory came from many directions. The failure of Weimar democracy in Germany and rise of Communism in Russia was a great challenge to the western political thought. The people of the West had given their consensual acceptability to the basic tenets, institutions, structures and processes of their political societies. The Marxist political theory was regarded as a great threat to them. Following sociology and economics, an emphatic attitude developed amongst political scientists. Another important event was the emergence of a large number of independent states out of debris of the Second World War. The conditions of

Cold War required them to be thoroughly studied and understood, a task which could not be performed with old concepts, tools and techniques of traditional political theory. The post-Cold War scenario is also a problem to both rulers and the ruled.

Political Science had attained the status of a sub-discipline as late as in 1840s. The first chair for the study of politics was established in the Columbia University under Francis Leiber in 1858. After the formation of the American Political Science Association in 1903, further steps were taken in this regard. Sarauf mentions four scholarly traditions: (1) *Legalism*: W.F. Willoughby, R.G. Gettel, J.W. Garner etc., represent this formal-legal trend; (2) *Activism and Reform*: it loomed large around Washington during 1930-40; (3) *Philosophical trend*: it is universal and motivates the scholar to become an all-around social reformer; and (4) *Realism*: it brought impact of science in the form of empiricism. It is represented by Bagehot *(The English Constitution,* 1865-67), W. Wilson *(Congressional Government,* 1885), James Bryce *(American Commonwealth,* 1888, and *Modern Democracies,* 1924), Arther Bentley *(The Process of Government,* 1908), Graham Wallas *(Human Nature in Politics,* 1908), Charles E. Merriam (*New Aspects of Politics,* 1925), David Truman *(The Governmental Process,* 1951) and so on.

However, from the viewpoint of its development, the whole evolution of political theory can be divided into seven break-ups: (i) unto 1850, the dominant nature of political theory was philosophical, deductive and normative; (ii) during 1850-1900, historical and comparative study of political institutions dominated the scholarly scene; (iii) the period of 1900-1923, was overwhelmed by empirical and quantitative techniques, like observation, measurement, survey etc.; (iv) in 1923-1945 break-up, psychological aspects of politics drew the attention of scholars; (v) by the end of the Second World War to 1949, early behavioural science emerged and created rupture and revolution in the study of politics. However, it was engaged more with facts and rude and crude form of empiricism; (vi) the period of 1949-1965 belongs to the formation of behavioural theories which also met with sharp reaction from traditional scholars; and (vii) 1965 and after saw the coming of post-behaviouralism or reform in the attitude and programme of hardcore behaviourists. Since then, a large number of political theorists have been working on the problem of theory-making. David Easton, Harold D. Lasswell, Gabriel A. Almond, James S. Coleman, David Apter, W.F. Riggs, Herbert A. Simon can be regarded as most prominent among them. But their ventures have also impelled scholars of traditional views to repudiate their efforts in usual manner.

Non-Theories

Efforts are being made to develop political theory at a number of levels:

1. Singular generalisations.
2. Segments of political life – of partial theories such as, theories of parties, leadership, administrative behaviour, decision-making, representation, cleavage etc.
3. Whole of subject-matter or general theory. They can be sub-divided, as:

Allocative Theories: They shed light on the way in which various processes contribute to the distribution and use of political sources, e.g., group approach, power theories, systems theory (when related to its internal operations) etc.

General Approach: It is available in two forms: (i) functional analysis, and (ii) systems analysis.

'Modern Political Theory' is one of the sub-fields of Political Science. Apart from being an academic or conceptual field, as discussed by Deutsch and Rieselbach,[34] it has an established structure. This structure of 'political theory' requires efforts towards its (a) pattern-maintenance, (b) adaptation with changing social, intellectual and scientific conditions, (c) goal attainment of explanatory power and prediction, and (d) integration to bring about coherence and harmony among various sub-fields. They studied 500 works written during 1955-1964. This period was divided into 1955-1959, and, 1960-1964. In the earlier period, most of the books were written on pattern maintenance. During the latter period, more attention was paid to adaptation and goal attainment functions. But very little work has been done, leaving Easton and Lasswell aside, on integration aspect of the political theory.

Earlier discussion on the causes of decline of political theory elucidates that it is different from modern political theory. Traditional political theory had its best days, and declined only during the last one hundred and fifty years. Modern political theory, as explained in the beginning, is yet to emerge and contribute its role to the re-making of human society. It can be recognised on the basis of some eclectic features, like, (i) objectivity, (ii) empiricism or sense-experience, (iii) scientific method and value-relativism, (iv) explanatory and cognitive role, (v) tentativeness or falsifiability, (vi) verifiability, and (vii) logical consistency. A theory, in the process of its making, may be found at a particular stage of its development (see diagram on p. 6), but has to be evaluated on the basis of these criteria. Taking them as features of an ideal-type political theory, it can be said, using the term from Meehan, that these formulations are 'quasi-theories', and not 'theory' proper. Some of various forms of these 'quasi' or 'non-theories' are given below:

1. A series of definitions, as found in the game theory.
2. List of factors – if it is not relevant and operational.
3. Approaches – such as, power theory, systems theory etc.
4. Classifications – as found in Almond Coleman's structural-functional approach.
5. Dichotomies – these are in the form of a polarity with two extremes and do not have any middle or continuum with no intervals – scaled or unscaled.
6. Analogies – may be formal-informal, or organic – mechanical (models), but are different from utopias.

Easton's Conceptual Framework

David Easton should be regarded as the greatest advocate of the need of a general theory in Political Science. From the very beginning, he has been contributing to it from all sources.

His own ingenuity to develop an empirical theory of political life is unique. Some of his works are: *The Political System,* 1953; *A Framework of Political Analysis,* 1965; *A Systems Analysis of Political Life,* 1965; and *Varieties of Political Theory* (ed.), 1965. Besides, he is editing *Contemporary Political Theory* series of books on theory. For his contribution to a general political theory, he has been rightly called as Talcott Parsons of Political Science. He has really redeemed American Political Science from fruitless hyperfactualism, speculative thinking, and valueless theorising. He wants an empirical grand political theory which would bring about integrity, unity and coherence in Political Science, and be able to give direction and set goals for society. Easton's concept of theory contains both values and empirical study of facts and events. His anguish concerning hitherto prevalent theories is that they are history-ridden, speculative, and unaware of contemporary problems of society. It is devoid of creative values and factual data. His eyes are mainly set on defence of values, a task which can be done properly by pursuing behavioural studies.

However, he himself has not been able to produce an explanatory empirical political theory. He has provided an outline or a theoretical framework which would guide and help scholars to produce a theory so as to provide an autonomous identity for the discipline. Easton calls it a conceptual framework. It is a set of mutually exclusive exhaustive categories. According to Easton, it is a system of working hypotheses, adopted and used only as long as it helps to orient political research in such a way that socially significant problems are better understood. Duverger observes that all scientific research 'is conducted within conceptual framework. This, in the first place, implies a classification of facts, and a more or less precise typology. This, in turn, supposes an accurate idea of the phenomena studied and the relations between them – in other words hypothetical 'theories' and 'systems'.[35]

In fact, Easton uses political theory for conceptual framework, and vice versa. Either of them (i) enables the researcher to identify the significant political variables and describe their mutual relations; (ii) provides categories for comparison and fills up the gaps where more empirical research is needed; and (iii) makes research more reliable and fruitful for other researchers. For interpreting the life processes of the political system, one requires a scheme of symbolic representation called by Easton as the 'conceptual framework' or the 'structure of analysis' which is different from concrete political system or structure of institutions, popularly known as government.

Conceptual framework is related to the formation of a broad-gauge theory for the whole discipline. It is a sieve to sort out, select or reject observed facts: a compass for indicating direction, a gauge reporting the state of development of a science at a particular time. It is a flexible conceptual apparatus, in a state of constant flux, and can be changed in the light of collected facts. One requires an analytical framework or a conceptual scheme prior to the collection or selection of facts, and to put them in order for drawing out empirical generalisations.

The key variable in Easton's frame of reference is 'politics', which consists in the interactions pertaining to authoritative allocation of values for society. He looks at these interactions in the form of a system which persistently performs the task of allocating of values. He likes empirically to observe the system and the way in which it persistently performs its task. For this purpose, he presents the concepts of 'input' and 'output' along with 'feedback' and others. As his framework deals with political processes, it is dynamic. The framework, on the one hand, keeps away the researcher from concentrating on too-narrow a field, while on the other, stops him from being lost into a field too wide. Along with disciplining the subject of politics to a higher level, it provides all important dimensions and parameters for the development of an empirical theory. However, it may be made clear that his conceptual framework is not a theory, and totally lacks explanatory power.

Aims and Scope of Political Theory

Protagonists of pure political theory or early behaviouralists do not agree that there can be any particular goals, aims or objectives of political theory. Catlin regards this problem as belonging to political philosophy, and limits the scope of Political Science to the discussion and analysis of 'means' only. Arnold Brecht (expired on September 11, 1977) repudiated this view, and maintained that it was the great tragedy of twentieth century.[36] A theory must have some ends in view or pursue certain goals.

Empirical political theory aims at presenting a coherent image of the operations of political reality. It may be conceptualised, as Easton and others did, as a system and subsystems. However, all aspects of politics are not systematic, and can be, more or less conflicting, as in case of contemporary West Asia or emergence of sub-nationalism in many parts of the Indian Union. It may take into account only processes or structures or functions, even groups or individuals. But as a general political theory, it would have to incorporate totality of politics, micro and macro. Similarly, it has to telescope political reality in such an analytical manner that it guides academicians to fathom further, and political actors to realise broader social goals, including the personal ones. As a publicly known weapon, it can be reliably used by all concerned.

However, the formulation of a scientific political theory is a general and long-term goal of theory-makers. But it has certain specific, short-term and practical objectives also. These are applied, utilitarian and humane aspects of political theory. Some of them are: (i) establishment of peace and harmony, so that there may not be any fear of extermination or extinction in a nuclear or conventional war. Various races, nationalities, groups etc., may live together in grace and honour; (ii) development of a political theory which may lead the developing countries to the path of freedom and prosperity, and save them from anarchy, stagnation, and tyranny; (iii) teach the self-transforming societies of the advanced world (popularly called as rich 'North' in contrast to poor 'South') to economise for greater affluence of all and to exercise self-control for the greater freedom of every individual; and (iv) finding out ready-made solution of problems and crises which often break out all of a sudden and cause loss, often beyond redemption.

In view of these objectives, scope or subject-matter of modern political theory can be ascertained. Its main topics are: political man, political behaviour, political groups; institutional, administrative or international politics; theory, ideology, parties etc. They are different from the contents of traditional political theory which puts emphasis on the study of values; origin, development, organisation and forms of state and government; institutions like political parties and local self-government, constitution, ideologies etc. It can be observed that some of the topics are common to both, but the perspective and objectives are different. Before 1967, the American Political Science Association had only six sub-areas, but later, it divided them into 27 which included, among others, areas like economics, sociology, military science, research methodology, statistics etc. In his article in the *International Encyclopedia of Social Science* (1968), Arnold

Brecht includes eight units: (i) group, (ii) equilibrium, (iii) power, control and influence, (iv) action, (v) elite, (vi) decision and decision-making, (vii) anticipated action, and (viii) function. Recently, it has started discussing and studying values like liberty, equality, justice, cooperation etc. Impact of sociology and anthropology has lent some new concepts like socialisation, political culture, political development, political communication, political symbols and styles, efficacy, and others. Research methodology and statistics both have been incorporated in the syllabi of some universities in India and abroad. Of late, there is a another trend also. Some university departments are going back to good old days when scholars used to sit and study politics in libraries, and through introspection. Such people tend to treat politics a mystic activity, to be comprehended by a few, and use knowledge to gain power. It leads to an elitist view of politics.

Classification of Theories

As there is not one general theory of politics, many formulations or theoretical constructions are claiming to be the prospective modern or scientific political theory. For rapid and proper development of modern political theory, these analytical formulations passing for 'theory' should be classified, studied, and analysed. There are several bases of classification of theories. On the basis of scientificity or science-ness, theories can be scientific or non-scientific. Scientific theories are value-free and use scientific method and techniques. Some theories deal with specific segments of political process. With this view, Stephen Bailey has divided them as (a) descriptive and explanatory theories which deal with 'what' and 'why' of the problem; and (b) normative or idealistic theories which discuss 'ought', 'good', 'good life', 'human values', 'ideal-society' etc. There are theories related to anticipated conditions and probabilities – they deal with prior conditions, or make predictions. The instrumental theories bring out 'how', 'when', and 'where' of the problems.

Other criteria of classification are time-order, generality, scope, and structure. Older theories that came up before the emergence of behavioural revolution are usually called as traditional or conventional political theories. Plato, Aristotle, Hobbes, Locke, Rousseau, Mill, Hegel, Marx etc., have contributed to this category. Most of the modern political theories have come up after the Second World War. Prominent among modern political theorists include David Easton, Lasswell, Karl W. Deutsch, Herbert A. Simon, Gabriel A. Almond, Coleman, Powell etc.

W.J.M. Mackenzie has classified all old and new theories on the basis of their generality: (a) *Overarching, grand or meta-theories*, such as (i) Marxist; (ii) liberal or radical democratic; (iii) pertaining to natural law; (iv) Parson's structural-functionalism; (v) David Easton's systems theory;

(vi) Oakshott's idealism, and, (vii) economists' theory of particularistic interdependence. Among them, the first three are old ones, and the rest have been developed during modern times. These theories have ample generality, but suffer from lack of validity (see diagram on p. 6). (b) *Partial theories* which deal with a part or segment of political life, such as, (i) communication theory, (ii) game and mathematical theories, (iii) decision-making theory, (iv) organisation theory, (v) power theory etc. The second category theories try to maintain a balance between generality and validity. Robert K. Merton calls them as 'middle range' theories.

From the view point of *scope,* Easton divides them as, (1) empirical generalisations, (2) middle-range theory, and (3) general theory. Empirical generalisations relate two or more concepts under a generalised statement. If their relationship is supported by observational evidence, the generalisation is accepted as 'true' or 'adequate'. The middle-range theory explains a particular aspect of political process, e.g., theories pertaining to psychology of voting behaviour. Sometimes it becomes difficult to draw out a dividing line between the middle-range and the general theories. General theories deal with the whole structure or process of political reality. Easton presents such a 'theory' (actually a conceptual framework or a theoretical paradigm) useful for the integration of the whole discipline, and analysis of political systems. An ideal theoretical structure contains axioms, calculus, and precise definitions. In other words, the set of generalisations therein is well-knit or closely structured. But in actual practice, such high-order relationship among generalisations of an empirical theory is usually not available. Under that ideal, relationship among generalisations can be of three types:

(i) *Functional* relationship pertains to association between two or more functions or their variables, for example, increase of education and increase of cognition. When they do not relate to specific structures, their relationship cannot be regarded as structured or stable.

(ii) *Causal* relationship is usually definite and more structured, but it may not be empirically observed or proved logically. In social sciences, causality in practice becomes *association* between variables. For example, at a particular level of stagnant economy, excessive increase in population leads to increase in poverty and consequent inequality. Such relationship is established in the form of a rule or generalisation.

(iii) *Tendency* relationship is often in the form of probabilistic claims. They are regarded as weak forms of generalisations. At the present stage of development, political theory contains mostly this type of generalisations. Factor theory contains such tendency statements. As they do not portray probability in concrete terms or as an empirical phenomenon, one cannot use them in making comparison.

Eugene J. Meehan,[37] adopting explanatory attributes, defines a theory as 'a set of generalisation, or a set of generalisations, that *explains* general statements, or *explains* other theories.' For him, theory is an explanatory device or apparatus. To be more specific, a theory is an engine for selection of facts, and for their symbolic storage, and for making probable predictions. An open theory undertakes search for new facts, as well as selection or rejection of old ones, reformulating, even replacing, existing theories. As a *scientific* theory, it would remain testable or verifiable by empirical evidence. Such explanatory theories can be (a) universal, (b) probabilistic, or (c) in the form of tendency statements.

Apart from the theories mentioned above, others come under the category of '*quasi-theories*' which lack explanatory power. They can be considered as theoretical structures, but remain deficient in explaining phenomena such as classification-schemes or typologies, dichotomies, or analogies. Meehan has not considered the undermentioned theoretical presentations as explanatory theory:

(1) *Definitions,* even if they are presented as a set of concatenated statements, e.g., as in game theory.
(2) *List of factors,* if they are not consistent and operational within the framework of a theory, e.g., information provided by census and statistics departments.
(3) *Approaches* are, in fact, attempts to make a theory, or at the most they can be regarded as partial theories, e.g., power theory or group theory.
(4) *Models,* usually, are more than classification schemes and represent variables observed in a particular phenomenon or event. However, they do not bring out any generalisation, proposition, or theory, e.g., Anthony Downs' *An Economic Theory of Democracy.*
(5) *Speculation* is Utopian by nature and woven around some abstract, unconfirmed and even impractical notions, e.g., Karl Popper's *The Poverty of Historicism.*

Easton, in order to develop a general theory, has classified the various forms of theory: (1) From the point of view of the discipline's boundary, a theory can be inside or outside. (2) On the basis of its scope or subject-matter, it can be 'micro' or 'macro'. (3) From functional viewpoint, it may be, (i) static, (ii) dynamic, (iii) time-structured, (iv) processual, (v) individualistic, (vi) systemic, and (vii) pertaining to comparative systems. (4) On the basis of structural consistency, it can be a well-organised, close-knit and inter-related set of propositions or definitions or otherwise. (5) Hierarchy or levels can also be the ground of classification, as (i) single generalisations or singular statements, (ii) intermediate, and (iii) broad-gauge or systemic theories. Easton is particularly concerned with the last category which deals with the whole subject-matter. It again can be subdivided in the form of two broad approaches: (a) allocative theories, such as, power or decision-making theories, the concept of equilibrium in the group theories of Bentley and Truman, and Lasswell's distributive approach; and (b) general approaches, again sub-classified as (i) functional analysis, and (ii) systems analysis.

Terminological Confusion

Political theory and Political Science, both are interrelated and supplementary to each other. However, some sort of confusion prevails over their interrelationship. According to one view, political theory is a generic term or major category which includes both Political Science and political philosophy. The second view maintains that Political Science is wider, which along with its scientific components, gives proper place both to political philosophy and political theory. Most of the Indian and Asian universities have adopted this view. The third view believes in a value-free Political Science, having no relation with unverifiable values or political theories. Most of the radical behaviourists uphold this view.

As regards their interrelationship, Catlin maintains a broader perspective. According to him, political theory involves common sense as well as value determination. He divides 'politics', that is subject-matter of politics, into (a) political practice, and (b) political theory. Political theory again is sub-divided into (i) Political Science, and (ii) Political Philosophy. Political Science deals with phenomena of control. All acts or units of control come under its purview and can be studied in a quantitative manner. Political philosophy discusses justification of values, motivation, direction, antagonism, change etc. He does not agree with Morgenthau that Political Science incorporates political theory. According to Catlin's view, Political Science is related to means whereas political philosophy concerns with ends, and, thus, both of them can be subsumed under political theory. In any analysis of politics, means and ends can never be separated from each other.

In this context, it is also very necessary to distinguish between *political thought* and *political theory*. Political thought includes political ideas and political thinking. Political theory in the modern sense is not identical with political thought. Political thought is a very wide term incorporating all forms of expressions pertaining to political entities, including Political Science, theory, ideology, opinion, ideas etc. Gettel, Doyle and several others belong to this school of thought. James A. Gould and Vincent V. Thursby[38] like to study subject matter of Political Science in form of political thought. However, one cannot agree with them. Political theory and political thought, despite their close relationship, are different in nature, scope and validity. The latter is much more subjective, speculative, abstract, transitory and ambiguous. Thoughts or ideas pervade every institution, structure, process and ideology. Political theory, as such incorporates political ideas of specific nature – empirical, communicable, valid and presented as a set of generalisations, A very small part of political thought can be regarded as political theory. Political theory is a long-term and painstaking enterprise, whereas, political thought is more related to the world of amorphous type – kaleidoscopic, imaginary, mystic, subjectivist and controversial. One should not equate political thought with political theory.

Andrew Hacker[39] is interested is studying 'political theory' only. According to him, a theory is 'an essay in Political Science if it seems to be the author's intention to offer generalised descriptions or explanations of the behaviour of men and political institutions.' According of him, every political theorist plays a double role, and is partly a scientist and partly a philosopher. There cannot be any 'pure' description or an 'objective' Political Science. The reality which is described is a 'selective' one, and the author's basis for selection is ultimately value-oriented or philosophical. An individual's moral sense gives shape to his perceptions and guides his interpretation of what he sees. Apart from these two categories, there is the third category of 'policy science' which tells that if you want these ends, then these are the means that you ought to use. Policy science is a kind of 'if ... then' prescription, found, more or less, in all theoretical writings.

Theory, in ideal terms, is dispassionate and disinterested. Science describes political reality without trying to pass any value judgement – implicitly or explicitly. Philosophy prescribes, on the basis of some visualised reality, rules of conduct to secure the good life for all of the society, and not for certain individuals or classes. A theorist does not have a personal interest in the suggested or existing political arrangement in a country, class or party. When a theorist becomes an interested party or develops a vested interest for his propositions, he converts himself into an ideologue. An ideologue is an interested party who defends things as they are or criticises the status quo in the hope that a new distribution of power favourable to him would come up.[40] The interest of an ideology is to justify a particular system of power in society. According to Hacker, only for analytical purposes it is possible to separate theory from ideology, otherwise, all political theorists are inevitably ideologues because, like other men, they are creatures of emotion and interest. In the hands of ideologue, philosophy is transformed into rationalisation for current or future political and social arrangements, and science into distorted description or explanation of political and social reality. Though theory and ideology are distinctly separate, yet all theorists are not aware of the ideological elements which enter into their writings. Some surreptitiously hide their real character and do not declare their interests. As most of these elements get mixed up, only a small minority can really theorise. In sum, political theory, according to Hacker, is a body of philosophical and scientific knowledge, which regardless of when and where it was originally written can increase our understanding of the world in which we live today and will live tomorrow. Obviously, Hacker's sense of political theory is different from modern political theory which invariably puts emphasis on its explanatory power and is of heuristic nature.

Political theory, in both its old and new forms, should also be separated from political philosophy. From older times, they have often been identified as one and the same. Political philosophy is a part of, or indirectly related to general philosophy, sometimes resting on the border lines of metaphysics. Concepts of political philosophy are subjective, abstract, mystic, general, and beyond empirical observation. A philosopher, such as Plato, Rousseau or Hegel, reaches his universal truths, axiomatic evidences or basic elements through speculation, imagination, insight, or abstract reasoning. He looks at political phenomena deductively on the basis of his unverifiable mental perspective, and asks the common man and institutions to rise up to that level. His assumptions and derivations are not necessarily testable or verifiable. Modern political theory, on the contrary, is quite distinct and related only to political reality, or objectivity which is worldly, sensory, empirical and knowable. It can be checked, studied, tested or verified, through standard methods, tools and techniques. By its very nature, it is explanatory, inductive and fact-based. Values and ideals put forward by various political philosophies are taken up by Modern Political Theory as propositions, hypotheses and hunches for observation and testing.

Political theory is also different from political analysis. The latter can be a part of the process of theory-making, political philosophy, Political Science, interpretations etc. In analysis, one looks for consistency of ideas, elements, factors or events, congruence with reality, coherence among statements, reconciliation between purpose and result, and cause-effect relationship. Analysis is a means, tool or instrumental activity to achieve a broader goal like theory building.

Arnold Brecht stands for *scientific* political theory only.[41] He points out that before the nineteenth century, philosophy, theory and science were used interchangeably. Still some such relationship is maintained. Theory attempts to explain phenomena in general and abstract terms. When scientific rules are followed, it becomes a scientific theory. But the latter is never a 'law' though it refers to some general 'law' or regularity. Law is rather a 'fact'. Similarly, not all theory is necessarily scientific, and not everything scientific becomes theoretical. Originally, philosophy was all-inclusive and coextensive with science, explaining everything – ideas about world, man, god, reality and truth. It is related both to *is* and *ought*, and is not limited or bound by the rules of scientific method. It goes beyond conditions and limitations of knowledge, logic and methodology. Now theory has moved towards science – its procedure, precision and control. Political theory, as such, stands in opposition to political philosophy, and accepts the latter, at the most, as its 'working hypothesis'. According to him, a theory 'is a proposition or set of propositions designed to explain something with reference to data or inter-relations not directly observed or not otherwise manifest.' In order to make political theory 'scientific', he has' elaborately presented his theory of scientific method and scientific value relativism. Through them, political theory can impart 'inter-subjectively transmissible knowledge enabling us to explain political phenomena scientifically.

However, under the prevailing circumstances, one cannot expect to make political theory so much 'scientific' so as to equate it with natural sciences. Brecht's concept of scientific political theory can be taken up as an 'ideal type' and theoretical constructions formulated within the borderline of empiricism. In fact, all 'modern' theory-building attempts operate in between the arena of science and empiricism. With gradual advancement of science and technology, and a neatly developed terminology, scholars of Political Science can hope to achieve their ultimate goal. For this avowed purpose, the meaning and application of the concept of 'political theory' must be comprehended only in modern or empirical sense, with emphasis on theory observable in almost all classical and traditional theories.[42] Classical theories deal with metaphysical realities, universal truths, whole human life, social structure, ideas and values. Their methods mostly are philosophical, speculative, historical, introspective, and conclusive. They do not stand neutral towards contemporary society and its prevailing environment. These theorists go beyond the obvious and dives deeper into social problems, institutions, events, and concentration of 'understanding' (*verstehn*). As such, they are often lost in the labyrinth of metaphysical and ontological realities which cannot be comprehended by laymen. They enter the field of political theory through analysis of 'ideas', often neglecting existing realities. Philosophy, therefore, dominated the field of theory, discussing primarily, reason, rational man, origin, purpose and nature of state, law of nature, future or goal of man, general welfare and others. Their quest as such led them to develop concepts of sovereignty, rule of law, nationalism etc. Subjectivity in theoretical formulations overwhelmed their theories with multiplicity, ambiguity, utter abstractness, and total lack of comparability, and attachment with empirical reality.

Problems and Limitations

A comprehensive and general theory is yet to emerge. Till then, scholars have to bear with available traditional theories, and engage themselves in building up a new empirical theory. Political scientists badly suffer on account of non-existence of modern political theory for the 21st century:

lack of coherence, direction, comparison, and empiricism in the discipline. Absence of a scientific theory hurts the status and self-respect of the academic community. English-speaking people have stopped their efforts to build a theory and live in their dead past like ghosts. Because of several constraints, it could not grow in past and present communist countries. Scholars elsewhere are unable to identify it. At many other places, some do not feel any need to develop it, rather oppose it. There are a large number of theoretical formulations masquerading as a general political theory, but none of them deals with the political system, both micro and macro, as a whole. Number of approaches is increasing and can be regarded as a sign of growing, health of the discipline. But some protagonists of these approaches, advocating them as 'theory', display rigid orthodoxy, conservatism, and parochialism. They fail to adopt an integrative and constructivist attitude. In fact, there is a great dearth of political scientists having interdisciplinary outlook, multimethodologism, and commitment to empirical research. All this requires intensive education, training, and facilities. A good number of scholars would have to work like Easton in the field.

Another difficulty in making the discipline autonomous and its study a 'science' is to determine the nature of politics, and find out its proper relationship with other areas of knowledge. Often its subject-matter is subordinated to ethics, religion, philosophy, sociology and economics. After committing such a mistake, it becomes almost impossible to develop viable political theory. The subject carries a long-standing boundary problem. Others trespass, meanwhile inmates of the discipline quarrel among themselves to own or disown their own field.

The problem of values is a key factor in the determination and growth of political theory. Some of them want to see Political Science as a pure 'science' keeping values at a distance. Others like Easton, Dahl, etc., are in favour of giving a proper place to values. Thus, there are two groups or academic cultures on methodological perspectives from the viewpoint of values in the study of politics. However, a synthetic view is also emerging. Karl W. Deutsch has supported this synthesis.

Some methodological problems have also put new challenges to the growth of advanced modern political theory. They pose the problem of generality versus validity, and holism versus reductionism. When a political theory is general, it usually has less amount of validity or closeness to empirical facts. If it is more factual, empirical or observational, it suffers from lack of generality. Easton's systems theory and Herbert Simon's decision-making theory illustrate this difficulty. Similarly, generalisations/conclusions derived from the study of a large entity or collectivity like a national political party cannot be easily applied to a small political entity or group. A microtheory remains unable to tell anything about a macroproblem. In the same way, the society or a particular collectivity wants solution of emergent problems and crises from the community of political and other social scientists. But, it cannot be reliably advanced unless some long-term basic research is undertaken which requires investment of huge manpower, finance, and energy.

Still the scholars as citizens and social beings have to devote central attention to the critical problems like war and peace, development of backward societies, elimination of hunger, poverty, illiteracy, parochialism, and disease, abolition of tyranny and racism, reduction of arms race etc. A little inattention or neglect can plunge humanity into darkness. Survival and existence of human beings is at stake. Every discipline, and Political Science in particular, has to renovate its concept regarding man and his behaviour – individual and social. But it cannot be done unless all disciplines come closer and develop interdisciplinary perspective. One single scholar, even an Aristotle, having that enormous knowledge may not be available. If we collect scholars belonging to different disciplines, the problem of coordination, accommodation and reconciliation remains unsolved. Within Political Science itself, political theorists have evolved their own peculiar jargon which obstructs communication even among themselves. Borrowings from other disciplines make the problem more difficult and beyond comprehension of average scholars.

The greatest difficulty is with regard to the changing, ephemeral, ambiguous, subtle, and coercive nature of politics. It cannot be comprehended easily by ordinary and even advanced minds. A political theory which once was regarded empirical and 'scientific' becomes unrealistic, historical and fanciful today. Political theories of today can meet the same fate tomorrow or a day after. In other words, every time, like armament industry, political theory would need constant renovation and rejuvenation. Political theory as such cannot be made only for the exclusive use of academics. Apart from gaining knowledge or knowing political reality, it has to be used for applied purposes. Otherwise, it would become an inhuman academic activity or a fossilised piece museum. For this purpose, the theorist, besides his own observation, has to come closer to political actors and activists, the movers and shakers of that knowledge. Still, close cooperation between the two – doers and theorisers, experience-holders and generalisers, is not easy and trouble-free. For the politicians political matters are directly involved with their existence. These are secretative and confidential by nature being related to power, influence and manoeuvring, and may not be divulged even to dispassionate academics. Even if it is told, many things remain untold, and only a naive would confide in them. Whatever be the stature and experience of a political scientist or a political theorist, he cannot substitute the actual experience of a grossly involved political actor. Still, the vision of theorists can be greater, wider, and more fruitful. It is desirable that both of them live together and develop mutual understanding and confidence. But the theorist has to escape from the prejudices and vested interests of power-wielders and their opponents. Sometimes, even dispassionate political theorists appear dangerous to the power-holders. If the political scientists actively stand opposed to the ideology of a ruling class, they would certainly be dragged before a firing squad or maimed by the mafia. In this area, both can play the sea-saw game of deceit, hypocrisy, and melodrama. However, in the absence of resources, power and support, a devoted votary of political theory has to fight his war unarmed and single-handed like a Christ or Socrates. Obviously, the solution of the above problems lies only with such scholars, whatever be the cost. In fact, there is no way out. If humanity has to be saved in advanced countries, and sub-humanity of developing societies has to be upgraded to human level, those who have some concern for man, have to come forward, and enjoy this masochistic adventure.

Future Prospects as a Profession

Let it be clear that political theory can be formulated and developed only by scholars having human sensitivity and passions. They should neither be god nor devil, but average human beings. Politics is made of emotions, rational and irrational ideas, sensory experience and interests, and human imagination. A man who has given them up would remain unable to appreciate and understand it. One may be a value-neutral, or value-oriented theorist, or a pure political scientist or an ideologue, even a traditional political theorist, political theory, in any case is built up by man for man. Such a theory may not be 'scientific' at the first instance, but would have to be '*empirical*' in order to be called 'modern', and stand upright among other theories and disciplines. Other exogeneous theories and approaches would have to contribute in the beginning, but in course of time, it would gain its own identity. Apart from performing the role of explanation and making prediction wherever possible, it can later on guide politicians to attain broader values and gather sustained support to them. In such a manner, it would become a common concern of all.

Advanced modern political theory, as such, apart from its academic branches and sub-branches, is likely to develop Political Science both as a discipline and a profession in several new directions:

1. *Science of Political Values*. It will study political values, their impact upon various collectivities, and methods to enact them.
2. *Pedagogical Political Science*. It will involve study, teaching, teaching methods, and research. Another cadre could be tutors, demonstrators and tellers.
3. *Political Engineering*. It would discuss the principles and making of various models of political structures and processes, and find out the

ways and means to repair and mend them. This can be regarded as an applied branch of the discipline which will be able to train and turn out its own consultants, engineers, technicians, doctors, observers, law-makers, repairers etc. They would be able to render or lend their services in various capacities to rulers, administrators, politicians, academicians, scientists, businessmen, and citizens.

4. *Training, Evaluation and Anticipation.* This branch will take up the specific task of training various categories of political actors on short-term, long-term, and refresher course basis. It would further involve the multi-perspective and interdisciplinary work of assessing or evaluating the form, nature and effectivity of various structures and their working procedures. For example, the form of parliamentary system as adopted in India or suitability of various Panchayati Raj models can be tested and evaluated. Anticipation involves scientific prediction to make the persons concerned aware of the possible consequences. Surely, it may lead to building up various utopias, and engage scholars in finding out various alternatives.[43]
5. *Power-Political Science.* It would work in the field in close collaboration with the field worker or political actor and the political scientist on the pattern of 'Chanakya-Chandragupta' model. The scholars working in the third branch, mentioned *supra,* operate in a value neutral manner. Here they would be aligned with the activists and frankly act as ideologues, propagandists, and value-supporters. The political actors wield power and authority, and exercise them to achieve their own ends, whereas their counter parts would help and guide them as staff agencies, sometimes acting and working for them. Both of them can suitably change or exchange their roles. In both cases considerations of power and authority remain the uppermost. Power-holders and activists can further be classified for specific purposes, such as, party organisers, policy-makers, mediators, orators, fund-gatherers, etc.
6. *Research Division.* It would concentrate on research activities, research methods, tools and techniques suitable for the study of politics, political structures, processes, motivations, behaviour, etc. It can undertake the job of preparing researchers, surveyors and other field workers whose services can be hired for specific purposes. Surely, they would not become part of any military or civil establishment which do have their own separate cells. Research work may go along with teaching or be kept separate.
7. *Interdisciplinary Intelligence.* It would be particularly diverted to the search for material, knowledge, theories, tools and techniques useful for the growth and efficacy of the discipline. In order to remake it an 'architectonic' or 'master' science, perhaps the undertaking of this

venture is unavoidable, though it would entail the problems of coordination. This would fill in the gap between study of politics and other works done in natural sciences, technology, humanities and social sciences.

Besides the above, the discipline can sprout in many other directions. The above mentioned classification is merely suggestive and the list is not exhaustive. So far, scholars of Political Science appear to have been working under the second branch. However, all of them can be put under some specific category, and their works studied accordingly. A few of them can belong to more than one branch. In any case, the classification would make the discipline more life-oriented, and realise the goals of knowledge. The world of politics always moves far ahead whereas the subject lags behind. Therefore, the discipline should come up with its general theory before it is too late. There is no escape or choice except to build up its own advanced modern political theory. Whatever be the cost, it cannot be greater than survival of mankind or progress of the Third World at par with the developed countries.

Some scholars have assessed the intellectual challenges to conventional political theory, such as post-structuralism and the scientific study of politics that have revitalised the field in the last 30 years.[44] They also broadened the perspective to take in non-western ideas and to reconceptualise political theory in the light of specifically global challenges.

Notes

1. David Easton, *The Political System: An Inquiry into the State of Political Science,* 1953, 37-52.
2. S.L. Verma, *Research Methodology in Political Science: Theory and Analysis,* 1989, Introduction.
3. Easton, 134-35.
4. At popular level theory stands for thought, idea, trend, tendency, conjecture, hypothesis, speculation, explanation, even interpretation of some kind.
5. Gerald E. Caiden, *The Dynamics of Public Administration,* 1971, 233.
6. Ibid., 113.
7. Gideon Sjoberg and Roger Nett, *A Methodology for Social Research,* 1968, op. cit.
8. Jack Gibbs, *Sociological Theory Construction,* 1972, 5.
9. Eugene J. Meehan, *The Foundations of Political Analysis,* 1971, 244.
10. Andrew Hacker, *Political Theory: Philosophy, Ideology, Science,* 1969, 2-5.
11. Deutsch and Rieselbach, 'Empirical Theory', in Hass and Kariel (ed.), *Approaches to the Study of Political Science,* 1970, 76-94.
12. Meehan, *Contemporary Political Thought,* 1967, 19.

13. The contours of such peace, development and spread of democracy have been, apparently, outlined in the speech of India's Prime Minister, Dr. Manmohan Singh, delivered on the occasion of 60th Anniversary of the UN, before the General Assembly on September 15, 2005, New York, Hindustan Times, 16.9.05.
14. Meehan, *The Theory and Method of Political Analysis,* 1965, 127.
15. David Easton (ed.), *Varieties of Political Theory,* New York. Englewood Cliffs, Prentice-Hall, 1966.
16. Meehan, *Contemporary Political Thought, op. cit.,* 20.
17. Easton, 'The Decline of Modern Political Theory' in Gould and Thursby (eds.). *Contemporary Political Thought, 307-327;* and *The Political System: An Inquiry into the State of Political Science, op. cit.* Chap. X; Alfred Cobban, 'Ethics and the Decline of Political Theory' in Gould and Thursby (ed.), *op. cit.,* 389-403.
18. Easton, *The Political System, op. cit.,* 47.
19. Easton, *A Framework for Political Analysis; and Systems Analysis of Political Life.*
20. George E.G. Catlin, *Systematic Politics,* 1962, 17.
21. Robert A. Dahl, 'Political Theory: Truths and Consequences', *World Politics,* (Oct., 1958), 89-102.
22. For the state of political theory, Easton has used the words 'poverty' and 'decline'; Alfred Cobban 'decline'; and, Dahl as 'dead'. For details, see, S.P. Varma, *Modern Political Theory,* 1975, 115-39.
23. Easton; 'The Decline of Modern Political Theory'; Alfred Cobban, 'Ethics and the Decline of Political Theory', in *Contemporary Political Thought,* Gould and Thursby, (ed.), 1969, 307-327, and 389-403.
24. W.A. Dunning, *A History of Political Theories,* New York: Macmillan, 1902; C.H. Macllwain, *The Growth of Political Thought in the West,* New York: Macmillan, 1932: G.H. Sabine, *A History of Political Theory,* New York: Henry Holt, 1937; A.D. Lindsay, *The Modern Democratic State,* New York: Oxford, 1943.
25. Robert S. Lynd, *Knowledge for What*? Princeton University Press, 1939.
26. Cobban, in Gould and Thursby (eds.), *op. cit.*
27. Dante Germino, *Beyond Ideology, The Revival of Political Theory,* New York, Harper & Row, 1967.
28. Destutt de Tracy quoted in, *Encyclopaedia of Social Sciences,* 1968.
29. Edward A. Shils and Henry A. Finch, *Max Weber on the Methodology of the Social Sciences,* Illinois. The Free Press of Glencoe, 1949; and, H.H. Garth and C.W. Mills (ed.), *Science as a Vocation,* New York, 1946.
30. Germino, *Beyond Ideology, The Revival of Political Theory,* 1967, 68 and 84.
31. P.H. Patridge, 'Politics, Philosophies, Ideology', in Anthony Quinton (ed.), *Political Philosophy,* Oxford University Press, 1967, 38-39.

32. John Plamenatz, 'The Uses of Political Theory', in Anthony Quinton, *op. cit.*, 20.
33. Isaiah Berlin, in Gould and Thursby (eds.), *op. cit.*, 343.
34. Deutsch and Rieselbach, *op. cit.*, 76-94.
35. Maurice Duverger, *Introduction to the Social Sciences*, London, 1961, 225.
36. Arnold Brecht, *Political Theory: The Foundation of Twentieth Century Political Thought*, Bombay, 1970, 4-10.
37. Meehan, *Contemporary Political Thought: A Critical Study*, 1967.
38. Gould and Thursby, *Contemporary Political Thought*, 1969, *op. cit.* Preface.
39. Andrew Hacker, *Political Theory, Philosophy, Ideology, Science*, 1969, 1-5.
40. See also, Karl Mannheim, *Ideology and Utopia*, New York, 1936.
41. Brecht, *op. cit.*, 14-20.
42. William Bluhm, *Theories of Political Systems: Classics of Political Thought and Modern Political Analysis*, 1965.
43. Rajni Kothari, "Environment and Alternative Development", *Alternatives*, V, 4 (1979-80), Jan. 80, 427-75.
44. Stephen K. White and Donald Moon, eds., *What is Political Theory*?, Sage Publications Ltd., 2004.

2

Behavioural Revolution and After

Political theory has always been in search of some basic material to build upon. It could be divinity, justice, desire, freedom, affluence etc. Goals of selecting particular material could be many, such as self-realisation, meeting the grace of God, carrying out directives of revelation, national unity, territorial integrity or expansion, domination, gaining specific power status, development, explanation or justification of events, prediction, legitimacy, mass-following, reform or restructuring of polity, formulation of ideology, and the like. Most of these goals prompt a theorist or thinker to pick up material on subjective grounds which others may nor may not agree upon. These grounds sometimes are so subjective and transitory that their choice either proves false or harmful. With the dawn of faith in 'science', one likes to prefer empirical material so that others too may accept its existence and validity. In this respect, institutions, entities like group and communities, orientation of cultures, processes of voting, conduct of war etc. were usually studied by scholars through institutional and historical approaches which were mostly subjective, partial and non-explanatory. In order to make the study of politics 'scientific', 'behaviour' was considered to be a neutral and universally available unit. Thus, a movement for studying politics or political phenomena on the basis of 'behaviour' started in the United States. Thus, the movement to study Political Science on the basis of or around 'behaviour' is widely known as 'behaviouralism'.

Behaviouralism, thus, is regarded as a turning point in the history of Political Science, thought and analysis. It has been widely acclaimed as a great 'revolution' which has transformed the goals, nature, scope, methodology, and theoretical formulations of Political Science. To a certain extent, it has distinguished Political Science from Political Philosophy and speculative political thought. Emergence of behavioural studies reflects the determination of new scholars to derive their findings on the basis of direct or indirect observation of human behaviour. It is to be regarded as a first real attempt to make political studies as a 'science of polities'. 'Behaviour' is a neutral phenomenon which can be dispassionately observed by all human beings. It can be measured and analysed empirically. Scholars were now hopeful to draw out an empirical theory on the basis of 'behaviour'. All political activity is constituted of human behaviour.

In a sense, we all are behaviouralists – living, dealing with, and interacting on the basis of our observation of other's behaviour. Courtesy, litigation, quarrel, leadership, riot etc. are names given to particular types of behaviour. Love attracts us, and misbehaviour generates repulsion. An intelligent man goes by actual behaviour of a person or groups. So is the case with other collectivities, nationalities and communities.

Man does not confine himself to the observation of human behaviour only. He has been studying since long the 'behaviour' of planets, sea, winds, plants, animals, etc., and, thus, augmenting his knowledge ceaselessly. Natural sciences have done a lot towards this direction. As a result, it became possible for man to emancipate 'reason' and 'being' from the clutches of church and other forms of superstitions. This enabled them to bring about industrial, technological and electronic revolutions. A chain reaction started there from. Behaviouralism can be regarded its natural outcome. According to behavioural tenet, politics also should be studied and analysed in the same way. Useful, scientific and purposive conclusions are derived from behavioural observation of politics. It can be possible to find out ways and means to make better and directed use of the achievements of science and technology. Politics, being a governing enterprise, is mainly responsible for using the products of natural and other social sciences. But, politics itself should be studied in a scientific or behavioural manner. If the study of politics itself is not scientific, it cannot guide us to make use of other subjects scientifically.

However, it does not mean that study of politics was never based on observation of behaviour. Both rulers and scholars of bygone ages have been keen observers of human behaviour. Plato, Aristotle, Chanakya, Confucious, Cicero, Machiavelli, Hobbes, Locke, etc., in one form or another have made subtle observation of the behaviour of the rulers and the ruled and other entities. However, their observations had often been overshadowed by metaphysical, philosophical, ethical, religious, and subjective considerations. They rarely agree in their conclusions and often make contrary claims and create confusion. The bulk of their writings belong to the category of political literature and history. In behaviouralism, empirical observation is the base, whereas ancient thinkers put behaviouralism at a lower level and indulge in higher and subtler realities of life. They liked to work with ideas, ideals, conjectures and spiritual attainments.

Behaviouralism: Explanation and Nature

Behaviouralism cannot be easily defined and explained. As there are many behaviouralists, so are the definitions. Both as an intellectual tendency and academic movement, it has so many facets: a revolution, a reform movement, a mood, an approach and an attitude. As such, convergence is lacking on the meaning and definition of behaviouralism.

The central theme or unit of behaviouralism is 'behaviour'. It has been adopted because of its objectivity, observability, value-neutrality and verifiability. Behaviouralism adopts 'behaviour' as its subject-matter of study and derives all conclusions therefrom. It aims, according to Dahl, 'at stating all the phenomena of government in terms of the observed and observable behaviour of men'. Its goal is to develop a 'science of politics modelled after the methodological assumptions of the natural science'.[1] Behaviouralism maintains that there are certain fundamental units of analysis relating to human behaviour out of which generalisations can be formed. These generalisations offer a common base on which a 'science of man' can be appropriately built. In the opinion of Charlesworth, behaviouralists assume that we can objectively and inductively discover what, where, how and when, but not why of human behaviour. David Truman long ago explained it as description of all facts of government in terms of observed and observable behaviour of man. Behaviouralism tries to understand, explain, and predict human behaviour on the pattern of natural sciences.[2]

In simple words, it includes:

(i) direct or indirect observation or sensory perception of the behaviour of persons, groups, and aggregates; and
(ii) deriving conclusions on the basis of that observation of behaviour.

Behaviouralism is a broader term. It is concerned with a scientific understanding of man in society regardless of the disciplinary umbrella. However, we are concerned more with political behaviour: Politics as a special form of human activity is not independent of social behaviour, rather it is related to all aspects of social relations. Political behaviouralism, apart from behaviour, is also concerned with its perceptual, motivational, and attitudinal components making for man's political identifications, demands, and expectations, and his systems of political beliefs, values, and goals. It includes all levels of the social system and culture as well as multi-dimensional orientations. In sum, it involves, external aspects of behaviour and the affective, contiguous, and evaluative processes engrossed through it. Kirkpatrick enumerates four features of political behaviouralism: (i) in place of political institutions, 'behaviour' of men in political situations is the basic unit of study; (ii) it looks at social sciences as 'behaviour sciences', and emphasises integrity of Political Science with other social sciences; (iii) it prefers quantitative or statistical techniques for precise observation, classification and measurement of facts; and (iv) it defines the goal of Political Science as the formulation of an empirical systematic theory.[3]

As Sibley has stated, scientific behaviouralism puts emphasis on formulation of scientific theory as well as process of verification.

Behaviouralism has many facets: an ideology, a revolution, a reform movement, an approach, a method, a mood or a tendency. Easton and other political scientists regard it a 'revolution' which has brought about overall changes in Political Science. Kirkpatrick does not regard it merely an approach. To do so is to mistake means for ends. Its aim is to make a 'science of polities' whereas approaches, methods etc. are only means. For many, according to Wasby, it is personal philosophy or lifestyle.

Some other scholars like Robert A. Dahl view behaviouralism as a method, an approach, a mood or set of techniques. He evaluates it as a protest movement which has been assimilated in full, saying, it will become, and in fact already is becoming incorporated into the main body of the discipline. The behavioural mood will not disappear, then, because it has failed. It will disappear rather because it has succeeded. As a separate, somewhat sectarian, slightly factional outlook, it will be the first victim of its own strength. Its two main characteristics are: dissatisfaction against the findings of traditional Political Science, and, need of methods and approaches to have empirical propositions and theories in Political Science. Dahl follows Truman in endorsing it as an approach. He, thus, appreciates various aspects of behaviouralism.

There are scholars like Leo Strauss, Alfred de Grazia and others who decry behaviouralism in toto. They are among its several critics whose arguments will be taken up in next pages.

Whatever be the way to look at behaviouralism, few disagree on some of its essential features mentioned below:

1. Its subject-matter is 'behaviour' of persons, groups, and other collectivities.
2. It is interdisciplinary in nature meaning that human behaviour can be properly understood by use of various disciplinary perspectives.
3. Behavioural studies are pursued on the basis of scientific methodology, standard techniques, and verifiable procedures.
4. Behaviourists keep their own personal values away from their studies.
5. The ultimate aim of behaviouralists is to develop an empirical, explanatory, and predictive theory.

Easton on Behaviouralism

David Easton in his essay on *The Current Meaning of Behaviouralism*[4] has pointed out important tenets of Behavioural Revolution: in brief, they are:

1. *Regularities.* If observed properly, some uniformities in human behaviour can be observed, discovered and found. These uniformities or regularities lead to generalisations or theories to explain human behaviour. Such as, repression causes rebellion everywhere.
2. *Verification.* These uniformities or generalisations should be valid, which means testable, at least in principle with reference to some relevant behaviour. It should be subject to checking and rechecking.
3. *Techniques.* There are some acceptable, public and standard means and methods for observing, recording and analysing behaviour. They are regarded as methodological techniques, such as sampling, interview, panel studies etc. which should remain available to all. These techniques are continuously reformed and refined to make data of observation more reliable and communicable among scholars.
4. *Quantification.* Uniformities obtained through observation should be precise, definite and measurable for this purpose; they should be quantified or expressed, either in numbers or symbols, as is done in natural sciences.
5. *Values.* The behavioural scholar does not start with any preconceived notions, or values because it vitiates his findings. Even if he believes in certain values, he either keeps them separate or announces them beforehand. He remains fully convinced that ultimate values or ends cannot be scientifically proved or disproved as their source of origin, form and ambit cannot be identified empirically. A communalist or a communist cannot, while remaining as such, become a dispassionate political scientist.
6. *Systematisation.* There should be close collaboration between theory and research, which are 'closely interrelated parts of a coherent and orderly body of knowledge'. Research must be theory-oriented, and theory should be well-supported by data. Systematisation means close relationship between theory and data.
7. *Pure Science.* Behaviouralists put great emphasis on developing a 'pure science' of politics and in conducting basic research. That knowledge alone can be rightly put to the solution of urgent problems of society. Understanding and explanation of political behaviour logically precede its practical application.
8. *Integration.* It believes in interrelatedness of all social sciences and aims to make Political Science 'interdisciplinary'. The 'political man' can be understood as a whole, by linking him with his other aspects:

social, cultural, economic, religious, psychological and historical. Such an outlook is likely to make political studies again a 'master science' or an architechtonic discipline.

In this sense, behaviouralism is not merely an 'approach', a mere 'mood' as Dahl says, or an ordinary reform movement, but 'a total commitment to the broad and essential requirements of scientific knowledge'. However, Easton's enunciation of behaviouralism as above involves both its early and later phases. Early behaviouralism neglected values completely, and was individual-oriented. Later, it moved towards macro study and incorporating values as 'facts' or 'givens'.

It would be quite clear that the main characteristic of political behaviouralism is not inherently different from Eastonian explanation, except that Eulau has confined his observation to political entities only. But it includes the preceptual, motivational and attitudinal aspects as well.

Evolution of Behavioural Outlook

Growth of behaviouralism[5] is the outcome of varied reasons marked mainly by a dissatisfaction with prevailing historical descriptive, legal-formal, and normative perspectives. In 1908, Graham Wallas *(Human Nature in Politics)* and Arthur F. Bentley (*The Process of Government*) advocated psychological and group-oriented approaches. Walter Lippmann (*Public Opinion*) in 1922 took up the study of public opinion and political

Evolution of Behaviouralism

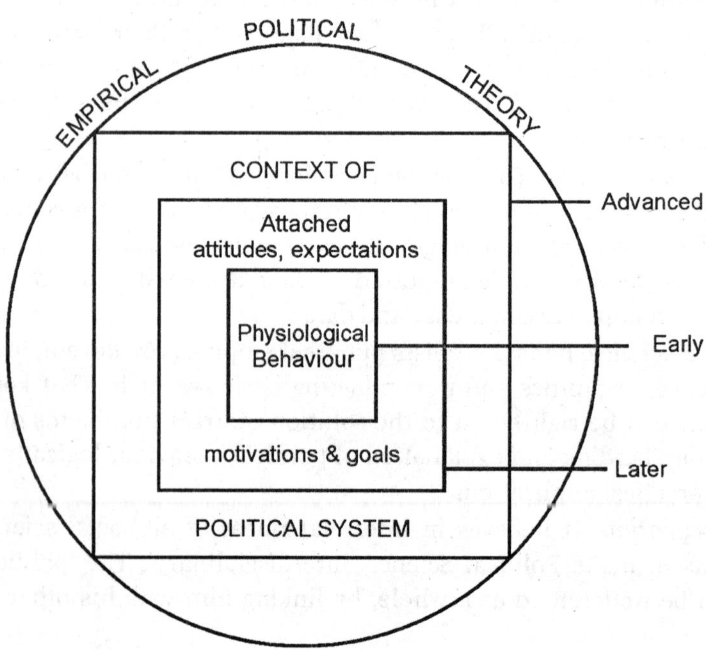

attitude-formation. In 1951, David B. Truman revived Bentley's neglected orientation in his *The Governmental Process*. But the pioneering efforts were made by Charles E. Merriam (*New Aspects of Politics*, 1925) in early 1920s. His efforts came out in the form of famous 'Chicago School' which produced a host of political scientists, such as Harold F. Gosnell, Harold D. Lasswell, V.O. Key, Herbert A. Simon, Gabriel Almond, etc. In 1928, Stuart A. Rice (*Quantitative Methods in Politics*) used statistical techniques in election and roll-call studies.

In 1930s, a group of European scholars like Marx, Durkheim, Freud, Pareto, Mosca, Michels, Weber etc., in view of rising totalitarian regimes and other crises, presented 'macro' or broad approaches. But Paul F. Lazarsfeld, Theodore W. Adorno, etc., remained interested in the 'individual' as the unit of analysis.

So far behaviouralism remained only a 'movement of protest' against traditional methods of analysis. After the World War II, the movement came out in the form of an academic revolution. It was the result of interest taken by the Social Science Research Council and the American Political Science Association, and other social scientists belonging to Europe and Japan. New departments, chairs, professorships, project studies, etc., were started in most of American universities. Behaviouralism very soon became an irresistible, pervasive influence everywhere. David Easton, Karl Deutsch, Robert A. Dahl, Heinz Eulau and others led the behavioural persuasion in almost every branch of Political Science. The discipline was soon thronged with new theories, approaches, paradigms, and methodological tools and techniques.

Evolution of behaviouralism has witnessed certain trends also. In its first phase (1920-30), it paid more attention to quantitative aspects and less on substantive and theoretical problems. In its second phase, upto 1950, behaviouralists moved in both substantive and non-substantive areas. After that, they began to specialise in various directions: multi-methodologism, behavioural theories, behavioural positivism and Watsonian behaviouralism. In the sixties, behaviouralists themselves were split as (i) theoretical behaviouralists, and (ii) positive behaviouralists.[6] The latter were enamoured of mathematical techniques, multi-variate analysis and other quantitative strategies. Theoretical behaviouralists criticised them severely as having been only interested in general properties of human behaviour, imposing irrelevant models upon reality, inventing a jargon, and were unable to advance solutions to human problems. Of late, both of them are gradually coming closer to each other. Behaviouralism can also be broadly divided as (a) pure behaviouralism, and (b) applied behaviouralism.[7]

Pure behaviouralism aims at contributing to theory and techniques of the discipline, and remains ready to study any problem. Its purpose is 'pure research', or knowledge for the sake of knowledge, seeking generalisations on the basis of technical judgements. It tries to gather all relevant facts for knowing the 'basic processes', and to say 'why things so happen.' The purists have their own technical language and a limited audience of their own persuasion. Applied behaviouralists take up problems of important social consequences and collaborate with several disciplines to solve them. Often they behave like social reformers, administrators or engineers and have some consideration towards persons and situations. They take up cases without any intent to generalise, and accept importance of the role of differences. Such researches are interested in 'how' can the things be changed; as such, they collect directly related facts. Applied behaviouralists report in common language, and have wider audience of practitioners and their clientele is large. Their aim is to solve practical problems and they regard their job as a useful profession. Though the two types of researches are distinctly separate, yet, in principle, can be mixed up in a person or a team of researchers.

All later developments, in the beginning, have made, behaviouralism, consequently, Political Science itself an 'Interdisciplinary' subject. It has gone from individual to groups and systems, techniques to theory, politics to social sciences, and outward human behaviour to ecology, biopolitics and genetics. Some of the scholars like Norman Jacobson are worried about the independent status of the discipline 'that politics is psychology, or it is sociology, that it is moral philosophy or theology, almost anything but politics.' Hence, tracing out the elements of 'polities' in human behaviour becomes an urgent necessity to make Political Science 'trans-disciplinary', meta-theoretical or overarching.

Stages in Evolution of Behaviouralism

But behaviouralists have not remained silent. They have, on the one hand, replied in a constructive manner, and, on the other, have countered their criticism by launching second post-behavioural revolution. They have transformed their 'pre-behaviouralism' into 'post-behaviouralism.' (John C. Wahlke). Overall behaviouralism now has five stages of evolution:

(1) *Individualistic pre-war behaviouralism (1900-1930)*: It was contributed by Graham Wallas. (*Human Nature in Politics,* 1908), Arthur F. Bentley (*The Process of Government,* 1908), Walter Lippman (*Public Opinion,* 1922), Charles E. Merriam (*New Aspects of Politics,* 1925), David B. Truman (*The Governmental Process,* 1950), Lasswell, Key, Simon, Almond etc. of the Chicago School and European contributions from Marx, Durkheim, Freud, Pareto, Mosca, Michels, Weber and others. More attention was paid to quantitative aspects of politics.

(2) *Collective collaboration after the World War II (1930-1950)*: Massive efforts were made by philanthropic institutions, academic associations,

university departments, and the governments of the United States. American Political Science Association, Social Science Research Council, Carnegie, Ford and Rockfeller Foundations came forward to forge it ahead. Journals like *American Political Science Review, Public Opinion, World Politics, Comparative Politics* etc. regularly appeared. Scholars like David Easton, Deutsch, Heinz Eulau etc. are thinkers of this phase. Behaviouralism appeared with its own methodology in both substantive and non-substantive areas.

(3) *Era of experts and specialists (1950-60)*: During this era, scholars finally separated themselves from behaviourism of E.L. Thondike (1878-1949), K.S. Lashley (1890-1959), Watson (1884-1952), B.F. Skinner (1904–1990) etc. and using the terminology of I. Pavlov. They evolved multimethodologism, new areas of specialisation, and micro and macro behavioural theories. Behaviouralists gained ascendancy in almost all universities and major academic institutions.

(4) *Pure and applied behaviouralism (1960-70)*: Behaviouralism appeared in two forms – (a) theoretical, and (b) positive. Theoretical behaviouralists are also known as 'pure' behaviourlists. Knowledge for the sake of knowledge was their goal. They devoted themselves to 'basic' or 'fundamental' research which contributes to empirical political theory as well as formulation of scientific tools and techniques. They conducted studies toward 'Why it so happens?' e.g., violence, casteism etc. They were interested in conceptualising basic processes of societal operations. During the course of conducting research they developed language or concepts of their own which sharply limits the number of audience. Positive behaviouralists criticise theoretical behaviouralism, and give priority to mathematical techniques, multi-variate analysis, model-making etc. Research into immediate and urgent problems of a polity makes them 'applied' behaviouralists. They take up empirical studies of governments, associations, institutions, groups etc. and seek help from other disciplines. Sometimes they appear as social reformers and have wider audience. They feel no need to generalise. Both varieties of behaviouralists criticise each other, but can mix up in any research venture. In this process, they tend to go from outward human behaviour to ecology to biopolitics to psychology to genetics. In this process, sometimes, Norman Jacobson observes the very existence of Political Science evaporates.

(5) *Post-behaviouralism and after (1970-2006)*: Post-behaviouralism appeared as a result of dissatisfaction with the nature, achievements and limitations of behaviouralism. David Easton himself (1969), along with other classicists, and all types of groups, criticised it. It became an end in itself, and lost touch with social reality and polity. It could neither produce any 'science of politics' nor any empirical theory.

Having discarded values as their central concern, they alienated society and the people who were more interested in the solution of immediate crises and problems, and reform social structures. At first, behaviouralists tried to remove misunderstanding and rebut criticism against them. Dissatisfied with their defensive explanation, another revolution emerged in the same direction.

Subject-Matter of Behavioural Studies

Directly or indirectly, all areas within the purview of sensory organs can be studied in a behavioural manner. Though limitations of time, resources, skill and technological advancement are there, yet according to Heinz Eulau, all segments of Political Science can be treated behaviourally.[8] Still, some specific areas preferred by the behaviouralists are:

1. Individuals engaged in face-to-face relationship.
2. Small groups and organisations.
3. Systems and subsystems like political parties, legislatures, pressure groups, etc.
4. Voting behaviour.
5. Concepts, such as the will, power, processes, decision, structures and functions, system, etc.
6. Processes.
7. Policies and values.
8. Comparative politics.
9. New tools and techniques.
10. Theories, approaches, and other frameworks.

Van Dyke has pointed out that behaviouralism (or behavioural sciences) is an all-inclusive term.[9] It includes all those sciences which study the behaviour of man or other living creatures. In 'political behaviour', we include all political activities of man. It is not only the behavioural aspect of politics, but all political behaviour. Simple use of the term 'behaviouralism' usually means 'political behaviouralism'. It involves all activities of man related to public decisions or distribution of power in society.

Behavioural approach aims at reaching empirical generalisations and developing a theory. Observation of behaviour leads us to certain uniformities or regularities of behaviour. Wider the uniformities, greater the validity of generalisations. These generalisations are to be testable or verifiable. In this sense, behavioural approach is more than a method. Political behaviour analysis has four important characteristics:[10] (i) it studies individual person's behaviour even while analysing groups, the elite, and movements, etc.; (ii) chooses a frame of reference, often taken from other disciplines; (iii) starts with theoretical propositions for the purposes of empirical research; and, (iv) adopts scientific methods and techniques. Areas of political behaviour analysis can be broadly divided into two parts: (a) behavioural studies conducted in situational or institutional contexts, such as voting behaviour, legislative, judicial, or administrative behaviour, etc., and (b) studies undertaken around specific organising concepts or the broader conceptual schemes. They are generally known as approaches, but do not rise to the level of a general theory, e.g., system analysis, group approach, decision-making analysis, communication theory etc. These centralising concepts obviously have two levels: (i) specific and lower, such as, group, power decision, conflict, etc., and (ii) general and higher, such as system, field, process, communication, etc.

Contribution of Behavioural Revolution

Behaviouralism has had revolutionary impact on Political Science. It has caused awareness to generate a general theory locating specific units of study. Its emphasis has been to understand man in society and bring about unity in social sciences. Scholars have learnt new modes of analysis and methods of data collection. There is a tendency of cross fertilisation or exchange of knowledge among scholars belonging to various disciplines. With a common macro theory or frame of reference, modern discipline of Political Science wants to develop a basic science of behaviour. In fact, it has given birth to many behavioural sciences, and has transformed the format of traditional disciplines. As already stated above, it has broadened the scope of Political Science itself.

Apart from heuristic and academic purposes, behaviouralism has a great practical utility, particularly, to bring about social change. It intends to develop modern political theory in a manner that it may be utilised for the purposes of 'manipulation' and 'policy formulation'. Human organisations, human nature, and interactional processes are transforming under the stress of fast developing technology, social growth, industrial and economic progress, cultural proximity in national and international fields, and possibility of human control over ecology. The transformation has taken place to such an extent that it defies all previous description, analysis, explanations, concepts, and generalisations. Simultaneously, it has to be accepted that in view of the interdisciplinary approach and mutual cooperation, progress of science and technology, capacity and competence of social scientists has also increased, so is their responsibility. They are being called upon to play the role of change-agents.[11] Solution of each problem is being demanded from them. They have to tell the way to implement the solutions. Behaviouralists have to direct everything about the speed, volume, content and control of change.

All such problems can be categorised for practical use of behaviouralism: (i) integration, (ii) social influence, (iii) collaboration,

(iv) adaptation, and (v) revitalisation. Behaviouralists have done a lot of work on the first three, but have to do much on absorption of fast coming changes as well as in growth and decline of various systems. Little has been done in bringing about planned change; changes are so fast that even available knowledge has not been properly utilised. Revitalisation of current knowledge, systems, processes, institutions, and norms is an urgent necessity. The behaviouralist accepts his responsibility to contribute his mite and implement his findings for better use. Through him, both creator and user of knowledge have to come together. Behaviouralism, seen with this perspective would appear as a vital scientific philosophy, and the only basis of human survival.

Misunderstanding of Traditionalists

It is most unfortunate that behaviouralism has not been properly appreciated by the traditional scholars. To some extent by the self-proclaimed behaviouralists have not even followed it. The conventional political thinkers forget that simply singing value-songs does not help anyone unless somebody studies their actual implications and the forms of implementation. Merely clinging to past or history does not solve the problems of the present and the future. Concrete ways and means are to be empirically sought out to serve and realise particular values. Unless the problems are dispassionately studied, blowing of imaginary trumpet proves futile. Superiority of values cannot be established by non-behavioural persuasion or by conventional methods, at least in the present age. In order to really strengthen universal and useful values, it is necessary to demonstrate and expose the actual implications or impact of values upheld by various theories, ideologies, leaders, and social reformers. Therefore, if the political philosophers, idealists or value-worshippers are really true to their profession, they should have opted and inculcated all tenets of behaviouralism so as to effectively visualise their dreams on earth. In fact, when they oppose behaviouralism, they tend to contradict their own aspirations and likings, out of misunderstanding and ignorance, if not by stupified mental make-up. Behaviouralism does not make a scholar an American or a capitalist. It is really deplorable that such scholars are ready to accept behaviouralism in other fields, but not in the study of politics, an activity very much related to world of senses, human passions and material calculations. Only that type of study can tell and demarcate the boundaries of ideas and ideals. Unless greater part of values touches the earth and the common man, their ethereal heights would surely put them into disappearance. History, if seen with dispassionate eyes, is a living witness to calamities and disasters brought about by the perpetrators of so-called ideals and super-mundane values. Modern idealists have led mankind to greater dangers of human annihilation. Behavioural studies would stand by in both cases – when an ideal must be accepted, or, not accepted.

Study of behaviour despite its limitations is the only alternative to know the extent of ideals which can come into actual practice and vice versa. Politics being related to worldly affairs belongs to collectivities and the common man and both are amenable to behavioural studies. Reality behind appearances or intentions underlying activities are too subtle to be identically looked into; they remain subject to myriad of interpretations, sometimes leading to conflicting directions. It may not be much useful in looking into the ultimate meaning (*weltanschauung*) of these intentions, aims and objectives. Man is mostly concerned with their actual impact and implementation and rarely goes to their original sources. He recollects his past to the limitations and requirements of his present and has concern for immediate future.

Political theorists and philosophers from earliest times have been talking of ultimate ends, or universal principles of life, often without learning whether they actually can be put into practice or not. They have cared little for the way to realise them. Few have fully looked into the consequences of visualising them. In fact, behaviouralism does not stand for or is not based against any particular set of values or goals of human life. Scientific behaviouralism in Political Science is totally neutral. Its purport is mainly to study human behaviour and find out observable propositions which would further throw light on whether it is conducive to the realisation of particular set of values. Owing to multiplicity of goals and values, behaviouralism scientifically remains unable to commit itself to anyone of them. Ultimately, all those values have to come out in the concrete shape of human behaviour which has to be analysed in an objective manner. Coloured eyes cannot study human behaviour along with its underlying set of values dispassionately. Committed scholars, who study socio-political phenomena, are, in fact, their own 'grave diggers' in the sense that, on the one hand, they remain ignorant of the real nature of human activities, while on the other, become unable to utilise objective findings to further their own ends. In this sense, behaviouralism is critical of all brands of ruling ideologies – Capitalism, Marxism, Fascism, etc. It tends to describe and analyse the actual behaviour of rulers, who rarely like to be exposed, even in a democracy. It tends to remain closer to the masses, who too should have a minimum level of culture so as to avoid the crime of putting some Socrates to death. Often open and liberal societies are regarded as closely affiliated or requisite for the behavioural studies for the simple reason that 'closed' or dictatorial regimes do not permit any inquiry into their tentacles of power. Even the vested or elitist elements prevailing in open societies do not like to encourage behavioural studies to their fullest extent. Consequently, several deaths and accidents of researches, surveys, inquiries, academic projects, etc. take place. Therefore, most of the charges against behaviouralism as 'pro-establishment' or 'status quoist' or 'anti-people' appear to be cooked up and are by-products of ignorant minds. By nature, true behavioural study cannot firmly stand for or against any existing order as it would be countermanded by another behavioural research, both being subject to open criticism, revision and verification. Too much energy should not be wasted over evaluating the activities of Don Quixotes fighting false giants. Few of these gladiators, including some behaviouralists know what behaviouralism is and how it has to be pursued under the given circumstances.

Obviously, competence and sophistication in behaviouralism is likely to increase with the progress of science and technology, and interdisciplinary close-up of various social sciences.

Political philosophers and other normative thinkers, like Leo Strauss, Eric Voegelin, are much worried about the defence of human values against behaviouralist persuasion which is regarded by them as amoralist, relativist, materialist and grossly ignorant. But ultimate ends, or universal moral principles or metaphysical values cannot be established or imposed by non-behavioural means like exhortation, divine sanctions, other-worldly allurements, acts of coercive church organisations or terrorists. Their utility or attractiveness has to be proved and visualised by human experience and through practical means and methods. They can be upheld and socialised into human lives, if maintained by courage and skill of a determined minority or majority of the people. Behavioural studies are very important for looking into the real meaning and implications of those values, ideologies or policies which are so sacredly upheld by them. Behaviouralism does not deny the existence of non-empirical values or metaphysical realities, whatever they may be, but is simply interested in their behavioural impact on social life. However, if anyone tends to hold metaphysical or esoteric values as the highest and desirable ones, without any reference to their temporal implications, or deny others to evaluate them on the basis of their behavioural aspects, it can only mean to perpetuate an inhuman system which, if treated otherwise, could be changed and reformed for the benefit of society at large.

John C. Wahlke has acceded to the view that so far behaviouralism has remained 'pre-behavioural' owing to (i) its unsystematic, atheoretical character, and limited range of research topics, and (ii) the erroneous conception of human nature.[12] It was evaluated that among 180 articles published in the *American Political Science Review* during 1968-1977, only 4 per cent were reckoned as 'behavioural'. Most of these studies took 'attitudinal' or 'mentalistic' approach as behaviouralism. Scholars had failed to bridge the gap between attitudes and behaviour, and use the findings of bio-behavioural sciences. Political scientists, according to Wahlke, should become bio-political scientists and adopt ethnological principles as working hypotheses. Real behaviouralists should study psycho-physiological responses. In different situations and to different stimuli, the basic premises and objectives of political behaviouralism are valid. But the need, under the circumstances, is that of more and real behaviouralism and not less or diluted behaviouralism.

According to Berelson, 'The scientific aim is to establish generalisations about human behaviour that are supported by empirical evidence collected in an impersonal and objective way … . The ultimate aim is to understand, explain, and predict human behaviour in the same sense in which scientists understand, explain, and predict the behaviour of physical forces or biological factors or closer to home, the behaviour of goods and prices in the economic market.'[13] Gunnell insists on 'action' and Wahlke on 'biobehaviour'.[14] Wahlke proposed that the bio-behavioural sciences must be recognised as 'basic' to the study of political behaviour, and what they tell us about mechanisms and principles governing human behaviour must guide our hypothesizing and theorising about political behaviour. 'I think the basic premises and objectives of political behaviouralism are correct. Indeed, I think the only way to move political research beyond its current pre-behavioural state is to make it much more genuinely behavioural. This is not to say that Political Science must become 'socio-biology', or that 'biopolitics' is the embodiment of truth about political behaviour. On the contrary, only genuine behavioural political scientists will be able eventually to answer the questions which are the real concern of Political Science.'

Impact of Behaviouralism on Political Science

Behaviouralism has given empirical methods, tools, and techniques to Political Science, and has made the latter more complete. Its inter-disciplinary nature has helped to understand the basic urges, needs, and demands of man in a better way. It has led scholars to move towards substantive areas and stable units of political life. Political Science is gaining the status of a hard core science, which bestows self-respect, confidence, and courage among scholars. Their findings are becoming more fruitful, more precise and more exact and ultimately leading them toward the cherished goal of a scientific political theory.

Some of the behaviouralists hope to evolve a 'Science of Politics' patterned after natural sciences. In it, they do not want to give any place to values or non-scientific methods. However, the tendency of 'scientificing' everything human at this early stage, called as 'scientism', could be avoided. The grace and utility of Political Science is not in becoming a prototype of Physics, but to go the other way, and remain a human social science. Till today, behaviouralism has not succeeded in achieving its mission of 'Science of Polities' or 'Science of Man', but its eyes are fixed on that goal. In fact, the growth of this discipline is in a transitional stage. It is moving from older sense of 'Political Philosophy' to contemporary status of 'Political Science', with an aspiration to become 'science of politics' in future. As such, Heinz Eulau affirms that Science of Politics is both a possible as well as a desirable venture.

Even traditionalists and traditional Political Science have come under its irresistible influence of quantifiable model of science. They have started recasting their subject matter, methodology, and conclusions. While studying human personalities, they make use of interview and questionnaire techniques, content analysis, and other statistical devices. Now they look favourably towards attitude measurement, scaling techniques, sampling methods and others. The traditionalists do not hesitate to learn and borrow from other empirical disciplines like Psychology, Sociology, Anthropology and others. A good number of topics, which previously belonged to the traditional areas, have been renovated to behavioural orientation. Similarly, many topics like attitudes, perceptions, values, and other motivations, previously subjected to speculative thinking only, are gradually coming out of traditional fields. The behaviouralists are taking them over, and producing brilliant empirical studies, and exposing actual realities to public eye.

Limitations of Behaviouralism

Heinz Eulau has regarded almost all segments of Political Science as susceptible to behaviouristic treatment. But Mulford Q. Sibley has vividly discussed the limitations of behaviouralism.[15] Behaviouralists, according to Sibley, regard themselves as value-neutral, but forget that their personality, limitations of knowledge, sources available with them, biases and prejudices and so on deeply influence their studies. These variables influence their choice of subjects, even methodology, and techniques. Leo Strauss remarks that pre-scientific and post-scientific knowledge play a key role respectively before and after their undertaking of behavioural studies. Polanqi has further observed that at all levels, knowledge is deeply coloured by personal participation of the individual.

As soon as one starts undertaking a behavioural venture, several limitations begin to appear, such as (i) human behaviour can be explained only under the given assumptions and the controlled situations; (ii) similar human behaviour can be repeated only under identical circumstances; (iii) it is difficult to develop concepts having similar meanings both for the observer and the observed, sometimes, concepts, not obtained by behavioural means, are applied and used, (iv) that facts, values, and observer or the behaviouralist are closely related. Even science has its own values. Karl Popper, Louis Althusser and others have vividly written about value-laden and ascientific aspects of science.

However these values do not tell upon the process or procedure of scientific method.

The behaviouralist as an observer conducts his studies with a particular framework or mental make-up which often is not behaviourally derived. Often his framework separates him from the prevailing milieu. As such, his findings may appear out of context, or can be related to actual politics only by non-behavioural means. There are many factors contributing to policymaking to the political actors which the studies might not have kept into consideration. The behaviouralist is also unable to help in making a choice regarding ultimate values. His predictions and other statements are often conditional and contingent, expressed in terms of 'if ... then', or 'either ... or'. Such predictions are rarely usable or dependable in normal social life.

Behavioural studies tend to neglect the role and impact of history, type of prevailing ideology and culture, geography, hierarchy of values and others. Sibley has suggested that their purist view must be enlightened on the basis of basic values and non-scientific judgements of history. Unless we know the past, one cannot understand the present, and further look into the future.

Behaviouralism and Behaviourism

Behaviouralism is something clear and distinct from 'behaviourism', which is a concept of a school of psychology originating with J.B. Watson, later vigorously revived by B.F. Skinner (1904-1990) in his *Beyond Freedom and Dignity,* 1971. Early behaviourists aimed at eliminating all subjective data, such as values, intentions, desires, etc., from research on human behaviour, and studied on the patterns of Physics and Biology. They analysed relationship between Stimulus (S) and Response (R) in human organism, which was regarded as a black box. Nothing was known about the black box. Later on, psychologists realised the role of subjective entities and experiences, and included Organism (man – O), reforming their paradigm as S-O-R. Skinner reiterates behaviouristic position that all psychological functions can be explained in terms of muscular reactions and glandular secretions, and *nothing more.* It is, therefore, the objective study of the stimulus and response aspects of behaviour. Man can ensure a safe future by controlling his behaviour redesigning the environment, for the environment controls man. Skinner has rejected the theory of 'inner man' or 'autonomous' man who, in fact, man is a creature of environment, and behaves accordingly. 'Choice', 'dignity', 'freedom', etc., should be considered from the view of controlling environment. Man can design or control his environment, and develop desirable patterns of behaviour.[16]

But Political Science can never neglect the importance of feelings, motivation, reason, choice, etc., and rather gives them the central place. Environment is important, but secondary to 'essentials' or essence of human personality. Therefore, behaviouralism, despite some methodological resemblance, remains totally different from behaviourism. Behaviouralism should also not be equated with empiricism. Empiricism is wider than behaviouralism, and includes evidence of history, prevailing culture and personal inner experience. It is partly scientific, whereas behaviouralism emphasises on cent per cent, direct or indirect sensory experience, and subjects it to scientific method, and inter-subjective communicability.

Tradition and Modernity

Behavioural Revolution triggered off a cold war between the traditionalists and the new political scientists.[17] It became both a 'hurrah' and a 'boo' term, so much so that each clique started removing others from departments, institutions and study centres. Somit and Janenhaus, (*American Political Science: A Profile of a Discipline*, 1969) has thrown light on the issues of the cold war. Of late, bitterness of the cold war has somewhat subsided and the contestants do not 'wash their dirty linen in public'. William and Joyce Mitchell have described their positions as 'stereotypes' who justify hostility toward another group. Traditionalists simply regard him an unfortunate victim of latest fads of numbers or statistics and jargon, having no interest in 'values', 'history', 'individual events and persons'. The behaviouralist deals with trivialities, common place observations, and jargoneering. His methods are ill-suited to elicit the truth. He seldom acknowledges his indebtedness to past thinkers. The behaviouralists or the 'Young Turks' are totally dissatisfied with the old-fashioned and unscientific theories of traditionalists. The latter, on the other hand, are unaware of the use of rigorous conceptual schemes, empirical propositions, and tests of validity and reliability. Both of them try to prove in some stylish manner that the other either does not know the correct meaning of a term or whatever he says has already been said earlier. One regards himself as a 'rebel' or 'revolutionary', and the other as a 'status quoist'. The behaviouralist finds himself as precise, neat, logical, systematical, theoretical and scientific. The traditionalist considers himself as and having an 'understanding' of human life and politics. In this war, though the behaviouralists have won, but there has been a 'successful protest' rather than a genuine full-scale revolution. The traditionalists too have not totally given way, and have reacted with full force. Some of their charges are summed up in the following pages.

Criticism of Behaviouralism

Behaviouralism has been criticised from several quarters. It can be divided into three parts: (a) general, (b) Objections from traditionalists, and (c) reactions from phenomenologists, Marxists and others.

General Criticism

(i) Behaviouralism suffers from lack of consensus and consistency. The behaviouralists are academically modest as they regard their findings and assumptions as relative. But in practice, they are immodest who refuse to accept the existence of a fact if it cannot be quantified, weighed, or measured. They declare themselves as purists and value-neutrals, but do have a set of values. Christian Bay has pointed out that they have a bias towards liberal democracy, and a liking for status quo and stability. Personally, they want to keep away from politics, and wish to remain apolitical or sit behind blue curtains.

(ii) Even if their achievements are 'scientific', they are trivial and unimportant. Rammey, Kirkpatrick, Dahl, Deutsch, Eulau, etc., have observed that despite expenditure of millions of dollars, the behaviouralists have not been able to produce a science of human behaviour. The making of a reliable, valid, and satisfying Political Science is still a mirage. They have yet to discover laws of human behaviour.

(iii) Behaviouralists overlook the simple fact that the subject matter of Political Science and natural sciences is different. As such, they should have different methods and techniques of study and evaluation. The subject matter of politics is comparatively much more complex, less uniform, more changing, discrete, intentional, and not directly observable. The methods of natural sciences, therefore, are not suitable to the study of Political Science. Unfortunately, there is the tendency to concentrate everything on the use of those methods. Either substantive areas are not taken up or unimportant matters are chosen to collect data and information. Some critics regard their methods and techniques as inadequate for the making of a scientific theory, and its verification.

(iv) Behaviouralism is ahistorical, and neglects the role of values. James A. Gould and Vincent V. Thursby exhort how can an act be 'political' without a purpose and value. Neglect of values simply leads to value nihilism. According to them, most of our present is deeply ingrained in or is the result of the past.

(v) The sole concern to produce a 'science of human behaviour' has resulted in running away from politics. Alfred Cobban considers the concern as a device invented by the teachers of universities to avoid controversies or politics without producing a science. The tendency to escape from immediate and urgent problems of society had made the behaviouralists arm-chair intellectuals or stooges and parasites living in high ivory-towers. Their 'pure' findings, away from dust and dirt of actual politics, cannot be considered useful for laymen and politicians.

(vi) Behaviouralism tends to substitute spiritualism and morality by materialism or sensory knowledge. Knowledge based only on human senses happens to be partial, limited, crude, segmental, and transitory. A part, a particular or a unit can be comprehended only with reference to the whole, the general, or the unity. The latter is provided by disciplines like Philosophy, Metaphysics or Religion. According to them, behaviouralism requires the control, guidance or supervision of higher, subtle and super sensory elements. The higher should govern the lower. The subtle and the abstract abounds the physical and the concrete.

Objections by Traditionalists

Traditionalists have repeated some of the objections mentioned above. They have not accepted all the characteristics or features described by David Easton. Their criticism is summed up below:

(i) Political reality is multi-variate and complex. It is utterly fruitless to seek regularities or a claim to study it objectively or dispassionately. As observations of political events cannot be replicated or controlled and experiments are almost naught, the findings cannot be regarded as testable. Any search for obtaining replicable generalisations is futile. Reality may remain hidden underground.[18]

(ii) As dynamic politics operates much below the surface, the techniques of interview, questionnaire, etc., do not help in knowing the reality. When reality remains unknowable through these techniques, there remains no room for verification. Behind every apparent behaviour there exists a social and cultural background, which can rarely be comprehended by behavioural tools and techniques.

(iii) Even the collection of facts, data or information cannot be fully objective. Quantification is closely related to subjective considerations. If we start following the behaviouralists, by upholding the methods and techniques over contents and problems, about 70-80 per cent of the subject matter of Political Science will go out of the discipline itself. Most of the subject matter of Political Science is not observable.

(iv) Data collected by the behaviouralists do not represent the political reality. They tend to observe the unobservable, and sometimes measure the immeasurable, or quantify the unquantifiable. Phenomena like liberty, equality, patriotism, peace, etc., cannot be put under the category of observables.

(v) It is impossible to claim oneself to be value neutral. Every scholar or researcher entertains his own value preferences, and cannot separate them even for a moment.

(vi) As the behaviouralists do not possess even middle range or low-level empirical theories, there is no hope for general or overarching theories. If the theory is general, it will not be valid, and vice-versa. In fact, theories with them, in terms of their own definitions, are not 'theory'.

Reactions from Critical Theorists and Marxists

Critical theorists like Habermas present the view that the modern industrial society can be understood only by a holistic and synthetic perspective. Each individual is an operating embodiment of his cultural and technological milieu, and of forces of economic production which make up his *praxis*. This praxis or learning from this milieu is the determining factor. Praxis inculcates legitimacy to the system. With this view, all attempts to develop an empirical theory appear futile.[19]

Under the influence of growing neo-Marxism in the United States, the student community and the young scholars have joined Neo-Political Science Movement. They want to free social sciences from the behaviouristic shackles of the status quo. They are closely related to the movement regarding Civil Rights for all, anti-nuclear war, rise of Black Power etc.[20] Their ideology is receptive to Marxism as well as Existentialism. According to them, behaviouralists stand for capitalism and military dictatorship and have led Political Science to a death trap. It has come in support of the affluent and self-contented American society. Its impact elsewhere also will be the same.

Bernard Crick considers it as undemocratic as it tends to treat man either as a machine or animal.[21] Conclusions derived from individual and micro studies cannot be applied at macro levels. It has led to so much specialisation and professionalisation that the elements of integrity and harmony are disappearing. The whole discipline is disintegrating. At the moral level, behavioural scholars appear to be ready to serve the dictators, monopolists, and power-hungry politicians. Another critic has remarked that the behaviouralists have so far not been able to say anything which had not been said before. Behaviouralism has triggered off a war and brought about anarchy in academics. It cannot show any path to humanity to march toward a desirable direction. It lacks even allegiance towards the autonomy of the discipline.

Scholars from Phenomenology, Philosophy of Science, and others have considered its emergence as 'end of politics'. It tries to justify improper as proper by transforming 'political' as 'non-political'. Irrationality becomes rationality, and vice versa.[22] Its value-neutralism can be treated as another kind of mischievous politics. This game of 'Scientificing' is being played through journals, articles, seminars and conferences, and research projects. According to them, it is useless to talk about 'pure knowledge'. Scientific method and ideology both are closely related. There is a great need to develop a Social Science which may bring about radical changes. It should understand and examine social reality while giving utmost priority to human existence. The problem is that of total change of contemporary society, much less of mere interpretation, still less of explanation.[23]

Most of the arguments advanced above pertain to early stage of behaviouralism; very soon, the behaviouralists prepared themselves in a positive and constructive manner. They concentrated their efforts in all seriousness and sincerity, and remedied several weaknesses, accepting the limitations and rescheduling their goals and priorities. Post-behavioural movement represents the culmination of this overall reform and reorientation amounting to another 'revolution' and 'change' in Political Science. Its emergence has to a large extent dispelled many of the above arguments and crudities of early behaviouralism. As such, reply to the remaining objections would suitably be taken after the discussion of post-behavioural revolution in Political Science.

Post-Behavioural Revolution and After

Post-behaviouralism is the next step or reform movement of behavioural revolution. Like behaviouralism, it was again propounded by David Easton in his presidential address to the American Political Science Association in 1969. It has two slogans 'action' and 'relevance'. It calls on the behavioural political scientists to study urgent and emergent problems, attend to crises and challenges of the contemporary society, and commit themselves to find out proper solutions. In other words, the behaviouralists should give up value-neutralism and irresponsible sitting on ivory tower. During behavioural heydays, they were neglecting, in the name of developing a 'pure science of politics', their responsibility towards society. Easton has discussed three main sources for the incoming of post-behavioural revolution:

(a) dissatisfaction with the efforts to make Political Science a natural science;
(b) utmost desire to find out solutions to the crises and problems of society; and
(c) a movement by a group of political scientists and an intellectual tendency.

This post-behavioural resurgence includes various shades of scholars – behaviouralists as well as traditionalists. Both had criticised orthodox behaviouralism, which was unaware of the problems like nuclear threat, civil war, undeclared war in Vietnam, etc., and had failed in (i) developing methodological sophistication, (ii) doing basic research, and (iii) alienating all values. Easton regarded it as a genuine revolution, not a reaction; a becoming, not a preservation; a reform, not a counter-reformation. Post-behaviouralism accepted the main tenets of behaviouralism but wanted to take Political Science towards new directions – making it more responsible and more utilitarian. It looks towards future both as a movement and an intellectual tendency; unlike behaviouralism, it is not related to any particular ideology or group. It included leftists, rightists, conservatives, classicists, methodologists, etc. However, it is a bit exaggeration to call it a 'revolution'. It is but a prolongation or strengthening of behavioural movement towards newer horizons. Some of the characteristic features of post-behaviouralism are given hereunder:[24]

(1) Substance must come before any consideration of tools and techniques. Foremost attention should be paid to the choice of purposeful, relevant and meaningful problems of the society. It is better to be vague than non-relevant, or precise.
(2) Social change, and not preservation of the status quo, should be its motto. Previously, behaviouralism mostly confined itself to description and analysis of facts, and overlooked broader social context. As such, in many cases, they could not understand the contextual meaning of facts.
(3) Scholars should take up social conflicts, deepening fears, and worries about the future as their subjects of study, and try to find out their solutions. They have to face hard realities of politics, and not to run away from them.
(4) Unlike the past, values should be given a central place and made the basis of choice of problems, research, and evaluation. Scientism, value-neutrality, sophistication, etc., has to be given up. They merely transform the scholars into technicians of Political Science.
(5) The main task of scholars was now to protect and defend human values and seek welfare of the whole world. Failing which they degrade themselves merely to mechanics, technicians and propellers of the mechanical structure of the present society. They should rise above bare behaviouralism, and labour to defend human values.
(6) To know is to bear the responsibility for acting and to act is to engage in reshaping society. In place of sheer contemplation, the scholars must come forward with *action to* actualise the contents of their knowledge.
(7) It pleads for the politicisation of the professions. In other words, the intellectuals must discover proper goals for the society and make it move to realise them. They have a positive role to play, and organise themselves to undertake the tasks.

Thus, post-behaviouralism intends to transform the academic, professional and valuational contents of Political Science. The latter has to cater both to the social as well as academic needs of society. Accordingly, the reoriented programme of the discipline imbibes a revolutionary change, namely: (i) immediate and urgent problems of the society have to be preferred to long-term or basic problems; (ii) 'adequacy' and 'not perfection' would be the criteria of the use of tools and techniques in research; (iii) behaviouralists remain publicly aware of the inadequacies and limitations of their studies, but they continue to keep up the behavioural perspective; (iv) going beyond description, explanation and understanding, the behaviouralist has to stand and support wider social values; and (v) post-behaviouralism recommends scholars to rejoin the ancients to stand and defend human values. They should take part in active politics in all or either of the three ways, as (a) a teacher, (b) a researcher, and (c) an activist. A scholar can perform his task either alone or in a team or group. A better programme than this cannot be available for the scholars of the Globalised World. All the tenets of post-behaviouralism suit to the requirements of the growth of discipline for all developing and developed societies.

But post-behaviouralism should not be regarded as a retrograde step or return to traditionalism. Post-behaviouralism is behaviouralism with its perspective of 'human behaviour'. It does not deny the importance of scientific tools and techniques of empirical study, but wants to give priority to applied research over basic research. It continues to understand the importance of basic research, but is much worried about the critical problems of society. The post-behaviouralist wants to see his discipline more purposive, more relevant, and more responsible. He calls for an action-oriented intellectual ready to make sacrifices for the good of society. But the goals of theory-making, quantification, techniques, regularities, etc., remain as they had been. Change or modification has been accepted only in case of its attitude towards values, pure science, and priority to basic research.

Post-behaviouralism brings Political Science closer to traditional or classical trend in the sense that it restores a central place to values and permits an active role to the scholar. Both agree on the integration and interdisciplinary approach in knowing political reality. Still, post-behaviouralism remains specific in its emphasis on scientific study, behavioural methods and techniques, and theory-orientation. Michael Haas and Theodore L. Becker have rightly found the evolution of behavioural process in a dialectical process. The traditionalists upto 1950 represent the long process of *thesis*, whereas quantitative techniques and early behaviouralism subsume *anti-thesis*. Post-behaviouralism, in a broad manner, reflects the stage of *Synthesis*.[25]

Criticisms Answered

Difficulties arise when limitations of behaviouralism are regarded as their weaknesses and shortcomings. Behaviouralists themselves have accepted that their approach and its attainments suffer from a number of limitations. Besides, other arguments and objections have to be analysed carefully. Replies and explanations from the behaviouralists are summed up below:

1. *Personal*: Some of the arguments from the traditionalists are personal, namely, that they are immodest, liberal, conservative, capitalist, status quoist, arrogant, etc. Behaviouralism as such has no relation with them. If some professors use it as a trick or device to avoid politics or making a choice, it cannot be regarded as a fault of behaviouralism.
2. *Inability*: Another line of criticism is about their inability or failure to produce a science of politics even after a long time. This demand and dissatisfaction of the scholars and laymen against them is justified. The behaviouralists have yet to produce a 'science of man' or discover the 'laws of human behaviour'.

   But the anti-behaviouralists themselves explain and remind them that the subject matter of politics being more complex and excessively intentional, the cause of delay or failure becomes too clear to need further explanation. Even Einstein had cautioned that the study of politics is more difficult than the study of Physics.
3. *Trivial and Micro*: The charge that they avoid larger and urgent problems of society and take up only micro or trivial problems to study as the latter are more useful in gathering data and other empirical information is true to a large extent. But, the selection of a problem depends on several factors like resources available at the disposal of a researcher, evolution of tools and techniques, availability and nature of data, etc. In the early stage, the behaviouralists had to fight for their survival and existence. They did not get adequate support from society. Under those circumstances, perhaps they could not do much. Now when behaviouralism has almost been accepted and endowed with more tools and techniques provided by ever-advancing science and technology, it can be expected that more important and macro problems would be undertaken for conducting behavioural studies.
4. *Inapplicability*: Another serious charge against the behaviouralists is that their studies are conducted under a given situation which may not be repeated or found anywhere. In practical politics, while taking decisions, political actors keep many things into consideration – history, culture, morality, power, caste, class, strategy, etc. A behavioural finding, howsoever scientifically derived, may not be at all useful. The argument appears to be cogent and formidable. In fact, Political Science requires higher type of qualitative research suitable for studying dynamics of politics. Tools and techniques, including concepts and findings, borrowed from comparatively static disciplines cannot fulfil our expectations, even if we formally adopt and learn all tenets of behaviouralism and post-behaviouralism.

Similar is the argument of uniqueness of events, persons, and processes. Their multi-variate nature makes the search of uniformities and regularities totally futile. But, the argument is true to a limited extent, as politics is concerned with uniqueness only in a limited manner. Man as man is gregarious by nature, and most of his behaviour is uniform, similar, and patterned. Existence of government, law, groups, associations, family, tribe, etc. is a proof to this concrete observation. Behaviour of aggregates and collectivities is, to a large extent observable, testable, and verifiable. Do not governments and their departments and other autonomous units maintain statistics on a regular basis? In practice, they have been working with them quite successfully. A few exceptions do not falsify their generalisations. These exceptions can be dealt with separately. Still, they generate some generalisations of specific or contextual nature.

5. *Problem of Values*: Post-behaviouralism has cut the Gordian knot on values. Their earlier position was more or less misunderstood. They were not against values as such. They had to remain value-neutral to make their studies 'scientific'. In case they could not do so, they had to expressly declare their values. Values always remain there, but they should not vitiate their research process and findings. Post-behaviouralism has added another dimension to the whole problem in the sense that the scholars should boldly uphold human values, and actively come out in support them. Rather, they should organise and fight for them.

   Now the problem before behaviouralism is that of what values and why? What would be their impact? What values do behaviour as such reflect? Which are the ways and means to realise them effectively? Which system, group or milieu is more congenial to a particular set of values? There can be several other questions. But now the problem does not remain unresolved. Arnold Brecht has developed 'scientific value relativism' for the understanding and analysis of secondary values in a scientific manner. He has expressed his faith that the ultimate values can also be empirically explained and analysed, though their sources cannot be ascertained scientifically.

6. *Higher-Lower*: Knowledge gained through behavioural means, being based on senses, has been regarded as *lower*. Experience obtained through extra-sensory means – imagination, meditation, introspection, intuition, divine inspiration, etc., is considered as *higher*. Acceptance of behaviouralism results in 'lower-governing the higher', whereas classicalists wanted the reverse. Leo Strauss talks of 'pre-scientific' and 'post-scientific' knowledge of the individual as the dominating factor in behavioural research. The whole set of argument is fallacious, and beyond context. A political scientist pursues exact, empirical, and

reliable knowledge which has to be limited, partial, and concrete. Arguments from the unknown and unknowable periphery of wholes has little relevance to his own venture. If one is really serious about the argument, the case is otherwise, the higher can prove its existence only on the basis and existence of the lower. If there is no lower, no higher can be upheld. Lower can exist without any higher. This 'lower' is the basis of 'inter-subjectively transmissible knowledge'. How can one, except with reference to the lower, prove that the 'higher' is really higher and is not self-delusion. Is there any unanimity of opinion or experience about that higher? How is that the 'higher' is always a monopoly of the few only? Why should the lower ones surrender to those possessing the knowledge of 'higher'? To sum up, everything 'higher' has to come down to the lower.

7. *Undependability of Techniques:* Political reality remains beyond the comprehension of research tools and techniques, like interviews, questionnaires etc. Indeed, these instruments are inadequate. But this observation merely proves a greater need to construct sophisticated, suitable and standard tools to know the yet unknown reality. While using them, the researcher should stand dispassionate. The tools cannot be the criteria of empiricism. The contents and nature of the subject matter must govern the quality and shape of tools. At a higher and later stage of their development, one would not have to say that the behaviouralists 'measure the immeasurable' or 'quantify the unquantifiable'. At the beginning, political scientists can develop micro theories which may lead to a general theory of politics.
8. *Capitalist Ventures:* Some scholars relate it to capitalism which stands for the status quo and exploitation. They want to free it and organise a social science liberation movement. Others do not want to tolerate the attempts of the behaviouralists to treat 'politics' as 'non-political' or lead it to 'end of politics'. But how can all of them do it. In fact, their attitude towards behaviouralism is itself 'behavioural', *viz.*, deriving conclusions after observation of the behaviour of the behaviouralists. And their demand and claim is to become greater behaviouralists. Their wishes and the credo of the post-behaviouralists appear to be identical: changing the status quo, anti-establishment, restoration of values etc. None of the behaviouralists, oppose the view of critical theorists that a holistic and synthetic approach should be adopted to study praxis and the system.
9. *Jargon:* Language of behaviouralism is technical, specific, and difficult. The behaviouralists one after another continue to coin new words and concepts which obstruct the way of communication among the scholars of Political Science. But this is being done to evolve a standard terminology to make observations precise and exact. Some of the

behaviouralists like W.F. Riggs make the language more difficult, but in due course of time, some usable, specific and acceptable language of Political Science would come up. Political Science, more than any other discipline, requires standard terminology. Even classicists like Kant and Hegel do have their own jargon, but that is not the goal or liking of behaviouralism. Behaviouralists want to have ultimately a smooth and effective communication system. As it would be closer to realities, it would soon gain currency among the common people.[26]

Problems before Behaviouralism

Behaviouralism as a mission and a programme for theory-building in Political Science has been facing many difficulties and problems:

1. The theory-building process is very slow and proving hazardous. It is difficult to maintain a balance between the requisites of generality and validity. Some theories have been appearing in the sub-field of international relations, which is not very suitable for the making of a scientific political theory, but others are lacking.
2. Lack of money, opportunity and resources, bias, fear, defective conduct of scientific enterprise, etc., are proving great hurdles to the behaviouralists.
3. Changing nature of the data of politics itself is a very big problem. All hopes are pinned on development research tools and techniques, increase of know-how, use of computers, information technology (IT), collaboration of other sciences, and cooperation of society.
4. Some of the dilemmas before them are: (a) relationship between old and new approaches, (b) conjoining of micro and macro researches, (c) inapplicability of data pertaining to group on discrete units, (d) discrepancy between the findings derived from system as a whole and from case studies.
5. Solution of some of the problems mentioned above can be found if researchers inculcate and develop interdisciplinary perspective, which obviously is another herculean task.
6. Post-behaviouralism has encouraged scholars to imbibe values and fight for them, but there is lack of consensus regarding choice of values. If there is politicisation of the profession, their findings would obviously be considered as biased and parochial. What would happen to the goal of building a scientific political theory? Still they can stand up for broad social values.
7. Scholars of the Third World countries are unwilling to accept the call and challenges of behavioural movement. They still like to cherish the age-old theories and goals, leaving politics in the hands of oligarchy.

It can be said that so far achievements of the behavioural movement have not been spectacular or epoch-making. The discipline has moved towards the growth and development of a scientific political theory, still there is a gap between quality and quantity, micro and macro, and, validity and generality. But there appears to be no other way out except accommodating existing theories with a behavioural perspective, at least, till the scholars reach their ultimate goal. From behaviouralism, as such, our expectations should be neither more nor less.

Notes

1. Bernard Berelson (ed.), *The Behavioural Sciences Today*, New York, 1963, 3.
2. David Easton, *A Framework for Political Analysis*, *op. cit.*, 33.
3. Evron M. Kirkpatrick, "The Impact of the Behavioural Approach on Traditional Political Science", in Austin Ranney (ed.), *Essays on the Behavioural Study of Politics*, 1962, 1-29.
4. Easton, "The Current Meaning of Behaviouralism", in James C. Charlesworth (ed.), *Contemporary Political Analysis*, New York, 1967.
5. C. William and Joyce M. Mitchell, "Behaviouralists and Traditionalists: Stereotypes and Self-images", in Stephen R. Wasby, *Political Science – The Discipline and its Dimensions: An Introduction*, Indian ed., Calcutta, 1970, 203.
6. Michael Hass and Theodore L. Becker, "The Behavioural Revolution and After", in *Approaches to the Study of Political Science*, *op. cit.*, 479-504.
7. Ibid.; and Heinz Eulau, Samuel J. Eldersveld and Morris Janowitz, (eds.), *Political Behaviour: A Reader in Theory and Practice*, New Delhi, 3-4.
8. Eulau, "Segments of Political Science: Most Susceptible to Behaviouristic Treatment", and Mulford O. Sibley, "The Limitations of Behaviouralism", in James C. Charlesworth (ed.), *Contemporary Political Analysis*, *op. cit.*, 31-32.
9. Vernon Van Dyke, *Political Science: A Philosophical Analysis*, London, 1-960, 158-62.
10. Heinz Eulau, "Political Behaviour", Vol. XII, *International Encyclopaedia of Social Sciences*, 203-14.
11. Warren, G. Bennis, *Changing Organizations*, Bombay, 1966, 113-14.
12. John C. Wahlke, "Pre-Behaviouralism in Political Science", *American Political Science Review*, Vol. 73, No. 1 (March 1979), 9-31.
13. Bernard Berelson, ed., *The Behavioural Science Today*, New York: Basic Books, 1963, p. 3.
14. John G. Gunnell, "Political Science and the Theory of Action – Prolegomena," *Political Theory*, No. 17, No. 1, Feb. 1979, 75-100; and, John C. Wahlke, "Pre-Behaviouralism in Political Science", March, 1979, Vol. 73, No. 1, *American Political Science Review*, 9-31, for more on p. 52; Ralph Pettman,

Biopolitics and International Values: Investigating Liberal Norms, New York: Pergamon, 1981.

15. Eulau, "Segments of Political Science: Most Susceptible to Behaviouristic Treatment", and Mulford O. Sibley, "The Limitations of Behaviouralism", in Charlesworth (ed.), *Contemporary Political Analysis, op. cit.*; *About Behaviourism*, 1974.
16. B.P. Skinner, *Beyond Freedom and Dignity*, New York, 1973/76.
17. William and Mitchell, "Behaviouralists and Traditionalists: Stereotypes and Self-images", in Wasby, *op. cit.*, 231-42; Albert Somit and Joseph Janenhaus, *The Development of American Political Science: From Burgess to Behaviouralism*, Boston, 1967, 3-13. See also, Raghuveer Singh, "Political Culture and Culture of Politics in India", Puntambekar Memorial Lecture at Indian Political Science Conference, at University of Jodhpur, 1984.
18. Raghuveer Singh, "Causality, Meaning and Purpose of Politics", Presidential Address at 38th Indian Political Science Conference, Patiala, 1978.
19. Jurgen Habermas, *Legitimation Crisis*, Boston, 1975; William M. Sullivan, "Shifting Loyalties and Critical Theory and the Problem of Legitimacy", *Polity*, Vol. XII, No. 2 (Winter, 1979), 253-72.
20. Charles McCoy and John Playford (eds.), *Apolitical Politics*, New York, 1967; and, Marvin Surkin and Alan Wolfc (eds.), *An End to Political Science: The Caucus Papers*, New York, 1970.
21. Bernard Crick, *The American Science of Politics*, Berkeley, 1959, 134-38.
22. Peter Laslett and W.G. Runciman (eds.), *Philosophy, Politics, and Society*, Oxford, 1967, passim; and, Sheldon S. Volin, *Politics and Vision*, Boston, 1960; and, John Plamenatz, *Consent, Freedom and Political Obligation*, Oxford, 1967.
23. Sudipto Kaviraj, et al., *The State of Political Theory: Some Marxist Essays*, Calcutta, 1978, 1-65.
24. David Easton, *The Political System: An Inquiry into the State of Political Science*, Calcutta, 1971, 323-77.
25. Hass and Becker, *op. cit.*, 479-504.
26. Robert A. Dahl, "The Behavioural Approach in Political Science: Epitaph for a Monument to a Successful Protest", *American Political Science Review*, Vol. 55 (Dec. 1961).

3

Facts, Values, Theory and Methodology

The basic material of science is valid and reliable facts. Even in daily life, one remains interested in gathering facts, and associates, most of his opinion, judgements and acts, with them. In the absence of facts, one loses ground and often encounters disappointments and failures. In natural sciences, most of the facts are tangible, specific, uniform, empirical, objective and measurable. In social sciences, facts are both tangible as well as intangible. The proportion of intangible or abstract facts is greater, such as, nation, state, caste, class, aggression etc. In order to make them scientific, all attempts are made to relate them with empirical observations. In fact, behavioural movement is a massive effort to provide an empirical base to intangibles of social sciences. A fact is 'an empirical verifiable observation' or a statement about it. Social facts are 'physical, mental, or emotional occurrences or phenomena, which can be affirmed with certainty and are accepted as true in a given world of discourse'.[1] A social fact is a phase of behaviour-thinking, feeling or acting which can be objectively observed. In the making up of a fact, we isolate certain limited aspects of the concrete process, activity, event, happenings or cluster of relations and interactions. Easton calls the totality of these activities or happenings as 'event', and particular aspects, according to the perspective of the scholar, as 'fact'. In this way, a fact by itself is an abstraction which later on is given a name, label, symbol or acknowledgement. Only a specific form of relationships is called friendship, or activities as war or election. Sometimes, it becomes difficult to know their exact nature and give an acceptable name or label.

Political Facts

Social facts are not so simple. People constantly remain curious about them – their exact nature, specificity or uniqueness, quantum, depth, intensity, transitoriness, association with other facts, etc. Facts are neither uniform nor universal. Persons concerned with the various aspects of a fact have varying perceptions and evaluate it in a manner different from others.

In politics, the problem is much more difficult, for a fact can have multiplying effects. In the political arena, everyone is running after actual facts. Political leaders like to know actual quantum of their popularity. Every super-power is spending millions of dollars to know everything about its rivals. India, like any other country, constantly collects facts about her hostile neighbours. Both the superiors and the subordinates want to know the fact of exact relationship existing between them. Scholars are engaged to study the rate and volume of progress made by society in various fields.[2]

Some countries, like India, which once were amongst most advanced polities of the then-existing world, do not know the exact causes of their backwardness. In spite of all planning, and adoption of socialism in India, the rich are becoming richer, and the poor are getting poorer. One may like to know how are two-third of the countries of the world living below poverty line, and failing even to have a North-South dialogue. Even South-South dialogue is not taking place. With all poverty and backwardness, the Third World is the biggest buyer of arms and active partner of arms race. Thus, all facts are so intermeshed with values and other factors that it is difficult to know their exact nature. Even when one reaches certain conclusions, he may soon find that others do not agree with him. In the field of politics, it so happens most often. On account of such varying perceptions, there are so much of controversies, quarrels, rivalry, and warmongering in politics. The only way to come out of this impasse is to resort to scientific or empirical study of facts as facts. One great hurdle in the way of understanding facts is that of values. At this juncture, scientific value relativism comes to our rescue.

Need of Scientific Study of Values

After behaviouralism, another basis of the formulation of modern political theory is the concept of scientific value relativism. Behaviouralism moves on the road of scientific method and tries to visualise political reality. While making use of scientific method, one comes across the problem of fact-value dichotomy. One can be value-neutral in the fields of natural sciences as their subject matter does not involve human consciousness, values or ideals. But social sciences including Political Science are directly enmeshed with human will and social values. Only a century ago, it was not possible to study social phenomena *scientifically*. But now with the help of scientific value relativism, it has become possible to study even political phenomena in a scientific manner. In due course, it can be expected that Political Science would be able to evolve a scientific political theory.

In fact, there is greater need of the use of scientific method in studying politics of the contemporary world. More than one hundred countries have attained independence after the World War II. But they are unaware of the nature of forces and the processes working within their political systems. People at large have faith in entities like God, church or religion, fate, caste, race and tradition without understanding the meaning and implications of these on their socio-economic and political life. Their leaders exploit their fond hopes and beliefs. In the name of God and religion, they monopolise power and use it for vested interests. Politics is made the concern of a few, with the vast majority left to obey what they say. At hustings, they raise up attractive and emotional slogans like 'Islam in Danger', 'Enemies of Nation', 'Democracy vs. Dictatorship', 'Remove Poverty', 'Unity of the Nation', etc., and easily reinstate themselves in power. Out of ignorance or otherwise, they do not have any scruples in making their countries as satellites of the superpowers. Instead of utilising the meagre resources for the good of their own people, the rulers enter into arms race with the neighbours to fight against false enemies. Only the rich benefit, while the poor become poorer.

Science and Scientific Method

Even before Aristotle, man has been pursuing scientific studies. But the meaning of 'science' and 'scientific method' has also been undergoing growth and change. Today, it is so different that few are ready to accept knowledge accumulated by the ancients as 'science'. Only that knowledge which is patterned after the methods of natural sciences is regarded scientific. Scholars believe that by adopting the 'scientific method', this discipline can also attain the status of science. Formerly, there was little difference between 'science' and 'philosophy' as both indicated special knowledge which was quite distinct from common sense. Even today, countries like France, Germany and Norway accept this affinity. Meaning of 'science' took a special form when study of physical sciences started using a particular method making their conclusions definite, objective, general, reliable and predictable. Knowledge thus obtained has revolutionised human life through technology. Social scientists somehow want to attain a similar status and have its utility for the society. As such, they prefer to imbibe 'science' in the narrow or limited sense only.[3]

Science relates to the world and worldly things. It concerns with what *has been*, or *is*, or *will be*, whatever be the *ought* irrespective of the person or his ideology. Science describes reality and is, therefore, limited by the conditions and constraints of observation. It does not claim anything beyond observation. Science involves three things: (i) verifiability, (ii) system, and (iii) generality. There are many sources of knowledge, such as, sense-experience, reason, authority, intuition and analogy. Science is related only to sense-experience, and reason based on the former. It is an accumulation of systematic and verifiable knowledge. Stuart Chase, George A. Lundberg and others have observed that science goes with method, and not with the subject-matter. Karl Pearson has observed, 'There is no short cut to truth; no way to gain knowledge of the universe except through the gateway of scientific method.'[4] The scientific method is one and the same in all branches of knowledge. The unity of science, according to him, consists in its method, not in its material alone. It is not the facts which make science but the method by which they are dealt with. It is not related to any particular subject matter, culture or country.

Scientific method is a mode of investigation by which science is built up. It is a procedure followed in determining and classification of regularity found in the political world. There is judicious and systematic use of observation, verification, classification, and interpretation of political phenomena. R.N. Thouless designates it as 'a system of techniques for attaining the end of discovering general laws'. These techniques may be different in many respects in different sciences but retain the same general character. It is a process or a set of interrelated and systematic activities for knowing an event or a thing in the form as it is, neither more nor less. The truth or validity of this 'knowing' depends upon its further 'knowing' by other interested persons also. In other words, that knowledge should possess the merit of verification or testability. Scientific method, thus, is simply a way of systematic study for acquiring reliable, precise and exact knowledge. It provides in the words of Arnold Brecht 'inter-subjectively transmissible knowledge'. Such knowledge is found among the individuals, and is communicable among them. The use and uniformity of scientific method throughout all branches of knowledge enables them to do so. When facts, concepts, and generalisations are obtained through scientific method, everyone accepts them, and the need to replicate, reproduce or observe them again is considerably reduced. In a sense, it is a way to save human energy, time, and money from being wasted on repeated observations of the same phenomenon.

Assumptions of Scientific Method and Its Goals

A method usually means the logical process or a systematic procedure used in discovering or demonstrating the truth. From a broader view, the scientific method also represents a particular attitude and a perspective to look at the world in order to obtain verifiable knowledge. It represents a philosophy, a theory and a programme to see the world in a definite, exact and precise manner. Underlying the scientific method, there are certain assumptions:[5] (i) *Knowability*: One can know man, group, society, institutions and the interrelations and processes operating among them. (ii) *Consubjectivity*: We get impression or image of a thing or event almost similar through our senses like any other man. (iii) *Regularities*: There are regularities in the forces of Nature. One can find succession, association or interconnection between various events. (iv) Man more or less enjoys freedom in understanding a phenomenon as true or false. The validity of this understanding cannot be demonstrated by scientific method. (v) A scientist investigates factual or empirical truth, which is different from moral, spiritual or philosophical truth. The form and contents of scientific truths change on availability of new facts. Some of the scholars regard these assumptions as values of science, but the word 'value' connotes subjectivity, choice or will which is not applicable in case of these assumptions. They are not ultimate, secret or subjective truths, but are merely instrumental in knowing the reality. By rejecting them or discarding the means, one cannot realise the end. These assumptions are objective and neutral in the sense that they do not influence the findings or conclusions.

Still, the scientists commonly believe in pursuing the truth. They do have certain values. As such, they have faith that the universe is cosmos and not a chaos. Various events, units, persons, and their behaviour can be subsumed under certain patterns. The aim of science is to discover these patterns. This work is done by science in open and public view. There are no secret processes, no predetermined diagnosis, no personal understanding and no bargaining. Everything is put before the public eye so that the whole world may see it and challenge its presentation.

Steps in Scientific Method: Arnold Brecht

There are certain steps for discovering truth through scientific method. But their number is not fixed. George A. Lundberg has mentioned four stages: (i) formulation of working hypothesis; (ii) observation and recording of data; (iii) classification and organisation of the data collected; and (iv) generalisation. Pauline V. Young has described them as six: (i) precise formulation of the problem in question; (ii) formulation of working or exploratory hypothesis; (iii) observation and exploration of the problem by a variety of scientific techniques; (iv) uniform recording of the data so obtained; (v) classification of the data into series or sequences; and (vi) scientific generalisation.

Arnold Brecht has enumerated them into eleven steps. They can be called as 'scientific actions', 'scientific operations', or 'scientific procedure':[6]

1. *Observation*: Events, things, and facts are observed through senses. That observation is tentatively accepted or not accepted till final confirmation. Sometimes many observations prove false. Hence a scientist always remains ready to change his ideas, experience or findings.
2. *Description*: Observed events and things are described, and that description is accepted or not-accepted till confirmation or availability of new evidence.

3. *Measurement*: It gives exactness and precision to observation and description. Measurable things and events should be put under measurement.
4. *Acceptance or non-acceptance*: After completion of the first three steps, we accept or not-accept the facts, things or events as a tentative reality. If later on, it proves otherwise, we have to reject it.
5. *Inductive generalisation*: Here the tentative acceptance or non-acceptance of reality (No. 4) is offered as a 'factual hypothesis'. A set of facts and events are associated with another set on the basis of similar properties. After making observation, description, and measurement of the election events, one could, on the basis of Lok Sabha Election of March 1977 in northern India, advance the factual hypothesis that 'where there were emergency excesses, the ruling party met with total defeat'.
6. *Explanation*: At this stage, either the tentative individual facts (No. 4) or inductively reached factual generalisation (No. 5) are advanced in the form of causal relations. They are offered as a 'theoretical hypothesis' which is used, till proved false, as a basis of explanation of related facts. In the above illustration, one can explain the loss or gain of a seat to the ruling party.
7. *Logical deductive reasoning*: Here we use the findings available to us either as factual generalisation (No. 5) or as hypothetical explanation (No. 6) as argument or basis of explanation to other observations, factual generalisations, or hypothetical explanations (No. 1, 5 and 6). We apply it as a mathematical formula in explaining similar facts or events not yet happened. For example, if any ruling political party of a developing country, in power for the last 25-30 years, is badly defeated, the logical deductive reasoning (No. 7) can be advanced in this or any case that it must have perpetuated excesses during emergency rule.
8. *Testing*: We apply inductive generalisation (No. 5) or logical deductive reasoning to newer facts and events of similar nature, and revise the steps from 1 to 4 if it comes out true, we treat them as tentatively proved expectations. In the aforesaid example, if our inductive generalisation (No. 5) or deductive logical reasoning (No. 7) is applied in similar cases of heavy defeat of a ruling political party, and testing (No. 8) proves it to be true, we can use our finding as valid in other cases also.
9. *Correcting*: Whenever there appear observations etc. from No. 1 to 4, or inductive generalisations (No. 5), or hypothetical explanations (No. 6) as incompatible or contradictory to our accepted findings, even at step No. 8, we have to correct them. In the above example, if there appears to be the cases, when even after indulging in emergency

excesses, the ruling party is not defeated, we have to modify our finding in the light of newer facts, i.e., the lack of unity among opposition political parties to the extent of merging into one party under a common leadership and programme.

10. *Predicting*: Prediction about events and conditions can be made on the basis of a finding, (i) if there is identity between (No. 5 and No. 6) factual hypothesis and explanation, and (No. 7 and No. 8) logical deductive reasoning and testing; or, (ii) it makes a scientific contribution by enabling to choose between several possible alternatives of action. The finding has to prove its validity on the anvil of practical experience.
11. *Non-acceptance*: All statements not obtained or confirmed in the manner described above, such as, *a priori* propositions, have to be separated from the collection of scientifically acceptable propositions. This is culmination of Brecht's scientific procedure. The factual hypothesis (No. 5) is further advanced as theoretical hypothesis, and sharpened as logical deductive reasoning (No. 7). This deductive reasoning or theoretical thrust is tested again (No. 8) and correction (No. 9) made. In the illustration mentioned above, for example, one fact of 'fear of establishment of dictatorship by a dynasty' was previously overlooked. As such, the finding would fail to make a proper prediction. It would also fail if the fact of 'unity among the opposition parties' is neglected, and, even after making the correction (No. 10), one would not accept the finding. Therefore, the last, step of 'Non-acceptance' is also a necessary part of the whole procedure. Like Brecht, other scientists have also regarded 'falsifiability' (Karl Popper) as an essential part of the scientific venture. In view of the nature of subject matter of social sciences, Brecht has not included experiment and comparison as part of his scientific operations.

Brecht has tried to develop a theory of 'scientific method', and regards it as the only one, using its first letters in capital form. It is not necessary that a researcher should formally start from first to last step. Instead, he can begin with a tentative working hypothesis. Brecht accepts the role of genius, goals of research, relevance of problem, etc., independent of the dimensions of scientific method. His goal is to enable the scholar to communicate his knowledge to another scholar, through standardised words, signs or symbols. Such transmissible knowledge has to be based on testimony and evidence.

Under those given situations, everyone would be able to acquire that knowledge. Still that particular knowledge is not last or beyond refutation, if facts prove otherwise. However, he does not put emphasis on verifiability as on transmissibility. The basis of science is communicability, and not systematisation or testability.

A proper use of other historical, anthropological, and psychological methods is permissible. He accepts importance of human inspiration and purposes, and does not disregard the role of religion or philosophy. He is not against those who take up 'science' in a broader sense if it is not used as a mask for real knowledge. As his scientific method goes beyond the verified facts and intends to explain them, Brecht regards it as a 'theory of theories'. As it is based on empirical observation, it is 'scientific', and is more than a method of approach.

Use of Scientific Method

It can be reasonably expected from the use of scientific method that it would generate inter-subjectively transmissible generalisations to Political Science which would further lead to the development of an explanatory 'theory'. It could discover laws of principles of political behaviour in a definite, objective, general, valid and reliable manner. Knowledge based on scientific generalisations gives power to control and direct the social forces, and makes it possible to predict coming events.

A careful analysis will demonstrate that such laws or verified generalisations of political behaviour have so far not appeared even in the advanced countries: Mosca's concept about the ruling class that there is a smaller governing oligarchy within a larger society, or Robert Michel's doctrine of 'iron law of oligarchy' cannot be regarded as a law of political behaviour. There have appeared some trends, tendencies, and causal-emotional insights, but no theory which can make reliable prediction or generate controlling power, has been evolved. Montesquieu's principle of 'separation of powers' is also controversial, dubious, and doubtful as a theory. The prismatic model of W.F. Riggs cannot be regarded a scientific generalisation, explanation or a theory. In the name of scientific study, Political Science does have: (i) some empirical studies, (ii) some practical suggestions on the solution of problems, and (iii) descriptive analysis of some institutions. Many of them cannot be put under the categories of cent per cent scientific studies. While describing important political institutions and systems, some attempts have been made to present classificatory schemes, general propositions, and frameworks of middle-range theories. Studies like *The Politics of the Developing Areas* by Almond and Coleman[7] also repeat the same performance without producing an explanatory theory. Meehan calls them as 'quasi-theories'. In a way, scientific method has enabled the studies of politics to reach the Political Science in matters of collection of data, description and classification, and formulation of working hypothesis; but the goal is still far away. Many factors are responsible for it: ambiguous relations between cause and effect, lack of uniformity in political events, problem of objectivity, impossibility of replication, changeable and qualitative nature of facts, etc. Most important problem among them pertains to values.[8] If this problem is analysed, understood and solved, a good number of difficulties can be removed coming in the way of achieving the goal of scientific political theory.[9] Dahl has rightly found both of them as antipolar views.[10]

Values

The word 'value' is used in two but interrelated senses. In the first sense, it is used by political actors for a desirable or undesirable things such as, democracy, justice, freedom, power, etc. Easton mostly uses it in this sense. In the second sense, it is a criterion or basis of evaluation which an individual, group or society uses it to accept or reject some goals, means to achieve them, procedures, ideals, etc. In the latter sense, values influence political behaviour. As such, origin, relevance, and interrelation among various values must be studied and analysed. Various values when put together make up the 'value system'. An individual carries them within himself either as a whole or in part. The value system can be consistent, cohesive, specific, latent or manifest. It can take the form of an ideology, policies, goals, laws, rules, ideals, and moral precepts. All of them can be directly stated as in a party manifesto. Otherwise, the values or value system can be known by studying behaviour patterns, value statements, culture-symbols or works, literary or artistic expressions, institutional presentation, or language formulations. A value judgement involves a statement which connects a transempirical value with an individual, thing or abstraction. As it is non-empirical, it cannot, therefore, be easily refuted by objective means. Most of the value judgements are the formalised expressions of sentiments and emotions derived from culture and invoke men to action. One can also reach values through observation of action or one's culture leading to value judgements. Values are major determinants of human behaviour. They become, thus, major areas of study for Political Science.[11]

Many things contribute to the making of values – intellect, will, sentiments, religion, ego, superstition, ignorance, tradition, etc. On the basis of values, a man regards a thing or activity as 'good' or 'bad', and may act accordingly. The individual may express them in form of his ideas, desire, act, will, goal, or opposition. It is difficult to validate the bases or sources of those values, but the latter, to a large extent, determine his attitudes, choices, activities, and aspirations. Therefore, the problem of values has to be studied, at least from the view of developing a science of politics.

Normally, the term 'value' is used in the following sense:

(1) All the economic or physical means helpful to achieve some immediate cause or purpose. They arc mostly called as instrumental values.

(2) Some express purpose or objective as aid to fulfil some other tacit or indirect purpose.
(3) Humans, things or tangibles for which there is clash, conflict, rivalry or competition to own.
(4) Pleasure-giving things, activities, ideas, purposes, or desires expressed to have them.
(5) Ultimate goals or ends which cannot be expressed through other aims, actions or purposes.
(6) Dispassionate actions involving no self-interest, such as making sacrifice for a general cause.

It may here be pointed out that all values do not influence an individual or group equally. The same value may have varying influence. There is lack of consensus among scholars about what place should be accorded to values. The problem is discussed below:

Study of Values

Early behaviouralists, with a view to developing a 'science of politics' by adopting the scientific method, stood for a 'value-free' Political Science. The traditionalists, on the other side, always talked of ubiquitous role of values and value preferences. They had them from religion, nature, philosophical meditation, axiomatic postulates, introspection, history, law and morality. The relationship of values with the individuals was based on faith, belief, confidence, intuition, superstition or ignorance. As such, few could claim to know them or understand their implications. The rulers could easily sustain themselves in power in the name of those mystic ideas or esoteric values. Against them, there arose a sharp reaction banishing all values from scientific studies. The latter group of behaviouralists tried to eliminate all emotional attitudes, particularistic fallacies, false idols, bias and prejudice, ethnocentrism, vested interests, moral values, and even ideals. They wanted to mould Political Science in the form of physics and chemistry.

Very soon, they began to face difficulties in developing a value-free Political Science. They confined themselves to mere description and classification of facts in the hope to realise a descriptive, empirical, operational and causal political theory. But their hopes withered within no time. It was pointed out that these adventures too had their own hidden values, ideals, and prejudices, which influenced their choices of problem, methods and findings. Thus, the whole discipline was split into two warring camps, and stood on a cross-road. Felix Kaufmann in 1944 had found that in social sciences, controversy relating to values was greatest among all the methodological problems. Values have a role to play before and after every research venture. No scholar can afford to avoid it. From the viewpoint of values, scholars of Political Studies can be divided into three categories:

1. Social scientists who keep their studies completely away from values. They can be named as '*value-neutralists*'.
2. Scholars who stand for values and regard safeguarding certain values as their main objective, are known as '*traditionalists or classicists*'.
3. Scholars who, while keeping themselves as value-neutral, regard study of values as possible and desirable. Brecht calls them as '*scientific value relativists*'.

Position of first and third categories is relevant to the discussion of values and making of a scientific political theory.

Value-Neutralism

Scholars belonging to this school of thought are also known as positivists, behaviouralists, or factualists. They want to eliminate all values that are personal 'preferences from the study of Political Science. The value-neutral political scientists want to study political events, activities, groups, and organisations in the way scientists study natural facts. They want to give social phenomena a specific, continuous and discrete shape. While doing so, they keep their personal value consideration away from the investigation. If human or social facts are treated in this objective manner, they hope, in due course of time, to develop a value-free human science.

August Comte, Emile Durkheim, Max Weber and other sociologists made efforts to develop a universal social science. Besides them, the idea received further fillip from logical positivists belonging to the Vienna Circle. This academic circle was started in 1922 by the scholars of Vienna University – Moritz Schlick, Rudolf Carnap and others. They severely criticised traditional disciplines like Metaphysics, Ethics etc. They accepted only mathematical and empirical statements as 'meaningful', and regarded all values as personal preferences. Nothing could be told about their superiority or inferiority. T.D. Weldon in his '*Vocabulary of Politics*' has enunciated this doctrine of preference: Determination of good or bad political institutions, like any other value judgements is made by individuals. They differ because of their biases, parochialism, selfishness, ignorance, etc. According to logical positivists, there can be no last or ultimate values, as science can prove no values as the highest or ultimate. Scientific method requires that values should be kept apart, failing which no social science, including Political Science, can attain the status of a 'science'. A social scientist has to remain value-free and value-neutral. Objectivity is the basis of scientificity.[12]

Consequences of Value-Neutralism

It is possible for the western scholars only to develop social sciences by adopting scientific method in the study of social phenomena. Underlying this venture, they had certain common tacit values.

Most of their values were almost identical, and a form of consensus had emerged. As such, they did not have to face conflict over values. While adopting value-neutral stance, very few were aware that they themselves had been standing on the ground of certain values. In this sense, value-neutrality became a part of their scientific method. But this closed approach has proved to be a great tragedy of twentieth century.[13] Some of the adverse consequences are enumerated below:

(1) Social scientists, on account of their scientific method based on value-neutralism, became unable to judge a goal or purpose superior to some goal or purpose in absolute terms.

(2) They could not speak on relative superiority of some values or purposes, used as means, in view of other ultimate values or purposes.

(3) All social scientists started deflecting from making any evaluations or criticising preferences in definite terms. In their view now, whatever was considered so far as good was non-scientific, amounting to some philosophical imagination or individual bias.

(4) For all these spokesmen of science, all values were equal, as they, like any other assumptions, were beyond the purview of scientific method. No value was final. All values were treated as impermanent, provisional, pre-scientific and relative.

(5) As all social scientists kept away from value-laden politics, they started living in ivory towers. Their output, being value-neutral, had no use for practical politics. They could now live and survive in any kind of regime, democracy or dictatorship.

(6) Between the First and the Second World Wars, humanity and human values reached the lowest ebb in the rise of Bolshevism, Fascism, and Nazism. But the social scientists tied to value-neutralism of their scientific method could not speak anything against them. They could not use their science in support and defence of democratic values. Their 'science' did not have any relation with values. Western culture stood helpless to defend its own values. Even John Dewey and Hans Kelsen were standing on crossroads. Albert Einstein, in 1940, had stated that even if one advocated the idea of eliminating all human beings from earth, it could perhaps not be repudiated on scientific grounds.

Thus, all values were considered as dogma, ideology or myth, and put beyond the scope of science. The main problem was not the presence of several ideologies, but to maintain that no choice can be made with the help of scientific method among various ultimate values. Every value-free social scientist considered all values as relative and dispensable.

Possibility of the Study of Values

Arnold Brecht has strongly advocated the need and possibility of the scientific study of values. Science is not in a position to point out the supremacy of specific ultimate values or throw light on the sources of those values. But it can analyse their nature and scope. It can also be known empirically which values are mostly preferred by a particular set of people. Non-observability or unverifiability of ultimate values does not mean that all attempts to analyse are futile, or, all values are equal. Scientific analysis of values opens many vistas: (i) we can know the exact and precise nature of our value judgements; (ii) we can analyse the consequences of those values and prepare a value scale; and (iii) by separating facts and values, we can understand the related problems and their reactions and implications.

Such value analysis involves the theory of '*scientific value relativism*' propounded by Brecht. It permits to study values and facts in relation to other values. Allotment of land by a government can be studied in relation to its value of equality. In fact, it enjoins a value-neutral position to the social scientist. While adopting it, the political scientist separates his own personal values from his investigation, and analyses the event or act from the viewpoint of its underlying values. The same act or event can also be studied from various angles involving different values. Such as, Gandhiji can be studied from the view of his own ideology, as well as from Muslim, Communistic, Congressite or Hindu points of view. Similarly, a social scientist can analyse and compare meaning, implication, and effect of 'liberty' and 'equality' with reference to a particular people. Any new country can learn a lot from such study.

Scientific Value Relativism

In scientific value relativism, the political scientist keeps his personal values separate from his study and does not permit them to influence it. He studies the problem, event, or phenomenon in a value-relative manner, or with reference to the stated values. While conducting a research or making investigation, one has to suspend his own ultimate values. Scientific Method merely leads to description and analysis of facts of political life. It has no relation with specific values. As such, it is not helpful in studying value-laden things, events or activities. This direct helplessness of scientific method has been, to a great extent, removed by scientific value relativism. Brecht has presented it in the form of a positive-negative formula:[14]

(1) The question whether something is 'valuable' can be answered *scientifically* only in relation to:

   (a) some goal or purpose for the pursuit of which it is or is not useful (valuable).

   (b) the ideas held by some person or group of persons regarding what is or is not valuable.
(2) It is impossible to establish scientifically what goals or purposes are valuable *irrespective* of:
   (a) the value they have in the pursuit of other goals or purposes, or
   (b) of someone's ideas about ulterior or ultimate goals or purposes.

In brief, analysis of values, ideas, and activities, by scientific method is possible only with reference to ultimate values or ideas expressed about those values. For example, voting for a person or party can be scientifically analysed only when a scholar knows the ultimate values or ideas about the values of the voter. Science cannot 'prove' the ultimate, highest, absolute, or standards of values. The latter are a product of mind, will, faith, inhibition, instinct or ignorance which is beyond the empirical 'eye' of scientific method. But it can clarify their meaning, and analyse consequences and risks involved in their pursuance. Scientific value relativism is the logical implication of scientific method; they are the two sides of the same coin. But it consistently refuses to take a stand on the choice of ultimate values.

After acknowledgement of ultimate values or ideas, the value relativist can discuss, analyse, speak on adequacy or inadequacy of all secondary values, ideas, actions, events and propositions. It can empirically know the contents of 'human nature and needs' which make up bases or sources of so-called universal norms or values. It can enlighten us on all moral or mental attitudes of man. Still they would be regarded, in view of the prevailing socio-economic and cultural level of development, as relative and contingent. Such analysis can point out human preferences, nature and need of man, and form of environment and social organisation required to sustain them. Knowledge thus obtained is transmissible, testable and valid.

Scientific value relativism is 'scientific' because it is based on scientific method. Regarding 'values', it adopts 'relativism', which means the scholar studies the values or purposes of an individual or group, keeping either the latter's ultimate values or some other given value system in view. The scholar or researcher, except in assumptions of scientific method, does not involve his own personal values or ideas. He can, if he likes, do so, but clearly expresses his values or ideas before hand. In that case, he appears more as an ideologue than a scholar.

Criticism of Scientific Value Relativism

There has been a sharp reaction to scientific value relativism. It has been criticised in two ways: (a) One group of scholars attempt to come closer to it without repudiating it. Brecht calls them as 'escapists'. Their view is that it is unworthy of scholars that they are unable to give any judgement or solve problems. Some of them find final solution in religion or God, or take ultimate values as general agreements, or working hypotheses. Some have favoured democratic majority or initiation as the ultimate verdict on good or evil. (b) Another group has tried to prove that scientific value relativism is false. Scholars like Leo Strauss, Eric Voegelin and others misrepresent and denigrate them by saying that they do not have faith in any absolute value and regard all values as equal. Dewey and Kaufmann do not recognise the difference between fact and value stating that scientific judgement is also a value. Other scholars like Saint Thomas, Jacques Maritain, Alfred Weber, etc., enlarge the meaning and scope of the term 'science'. According to them, science is not the only source of knowledge. Intention, religion and imagination are also dependable sources of empirical understanding. Some others believe in objectivity of values. Sociologists like Mannheim demand more relativity in the perspective of 'sociology of knowledge'. They relate knowledge to socio-economic and cultural contexts along with individuals' limited perspective and vested interests.

Brecht has refused to accept most of these objections which fail to disprove the position taken by him. His basic stand is that ultimate value cannot be scientifically validated. It does not debar anyone to have or cherish ultimate values. His simple claim is that the latter cannot be empirically proved. In order to undertake scientific study, one has to make observation in the light of its underlying assumptions or other expressed values. In the field of Political Science, he, at his own, cannot start with his own set of ultimate values.

Some scholars, in place of 'relativism', have proposed other terms. They like to substitute the term 'relative' with 'relational', 'dialectic', 'problematic', etc. But Brecht does not find them suitable to convey the underlying sense of relativism. Radbruch uses the term 'perspectivism' on the plea that values or value-laden things can be studied only with the perspective of ultimate values. But the term 'perspective' is ambiguous, and lacks specific meaning. However, Brecht, has regarded 'scientific value alternativism' as acceptable as it connotes the value as a choice among many other values. But, for historical reasons and clarity, he opts for 'scientific value relativism'. Scientific method is complete along with it. It has, thus, bridged over the long-standing gap between 'is' and 'ought' and removed the deadlock in the development of a scientific political theory. It has enabled scholars to study political facts which mostly are value-laden. In a sense, scientific value relativism pushed behaviouralism and scientific method ahead to the making of an empirical political theory.

Fact-Theory Continuum

Like facts and values, theory and facts also have a closer relationship. As in case of values, facts are the basic raw material of theory. Kant's famous adage may be rephrased as, 'fact without theory is blind, theory without fact is empty'. In fact, there exists a continuous relationship between facts and theory, popularly known as 'theory-data-continuum'. If theory is vital to every scientific advancement, facts are the building blocks of every science. Both remain in constant interaction. Development in facts leads to development in theory, and vice versa.

In fact, the researcher perceives the concerned or relevant aspects, properties or relations in an event or activity. Fact, as stated earlier, is a purposeful relevant observation. From the observation of similar facts, he goes to the foundation of concepts. A concept is a shorthand representation of a variety of facts. It is an abstraction formed by generalisation from particulars. It is a generalised term for a class of objects. As such, it helps in classification and measurement of facts. As a set of directions, or abstraction of certain properties or relation, it directs the researcher to pick out a particular kind of experience. After having classification of facts on the basis of concepts, the researcher analyses the various categories and discovers interrelation among them. From analysis, he goes to the stage of generalisation – making a general statement applicable to a large number of facts – both observed and unobserved. A good number of interconnected generalisations make up a theory (diagram on p. 6). A theory is facts assembled, put in an order, and seen in a relevant relationship. After coming to the stage of generalisation, one takes a jump or makes theoretical thrust and speaks for the similar, but hitherto unobserved, facts and events.

In a scientific venture, facts, concepts, generalisation, and theory should be based on empirical experience. When we go upwards from fact to theory, we move from validity to generality. Both rarely go together. As we go higher towards generality, which means speaking for a larger number of facts, we gradually lose validity or closeness to all actual empirical facts. Quantum of validity in factual statements differs in proportion to closeness to empirical facts. Scientific method keeps us close to observation of political facts. Theoretical movement takes us higher to generality of facts, but away from validity of observation. Theory simply means the putting up of the relevant facts under the umbrella of some relation, property or abstraction. This is done on the basis of actual observation of some facts which enables the researcher to include other unobserved facts. For this, he uses the tools of concepts and generalisations. However, the whole structure has to stand on the foundation stone of empirical observation or validity of facts.

On the basis of validation or validity, theoretical statements can be put at four levels:

(1) *Factual statements*: These are based on hundred per cent empirical evidence. Being observable, they are fully reliable.

(2) *Probabilistic statements*: These are based on empirical evidence, but are applied on similar objects or events. They are hypothetically applied to all of them, and are accepted as true till proved false. They lack cent per cent validity, but mostly are regarded as empirical.

(3) *Hypothetical statements*: Here we guess about facts. They are based on the interrelation of various variables which become a basis to prove them empirically. They help us in knowing the relationship between the change in one variable and the change in another variable. Lesser the ambiguity in the interrelation of variables, greater the precision. The mutual relationship makes hypothetical statements more fruitful and valid.

(4) *Theoretical statements*: This is the highest stage of theoretical movement made on the road to validity. At this level, all facts, probable and hypothetical statements are woven into a widening relationship. The theoretical structure at this level is more general and universal than the lower three. However, each higher level tends to lose more and more validity.

In the diagram below as the scholar rises higher towards the theoretical top, his knowledge about the facts gets more and more generalised. The area of his knowledge enlarges, but validity dilutes. As given therein, at the lowest factual level, if generality is 25°, validity is 100°. At the next higher probabilistic level, generality is increased 50°, but validity goes low to 75°, and so on so forth. To illustrate, if a vigilant citizen knows all the members of his ward, his knowledge about the ward can be counted valid up to 100 per cent. But his generality at higher level remains limited to a few hundred persons only, and validity about the people of his ward is not cent per cent. His factual knowledge, if applied to members of other wards, would only be

Diagram 1

Generality and Validity in Theoretical Statements

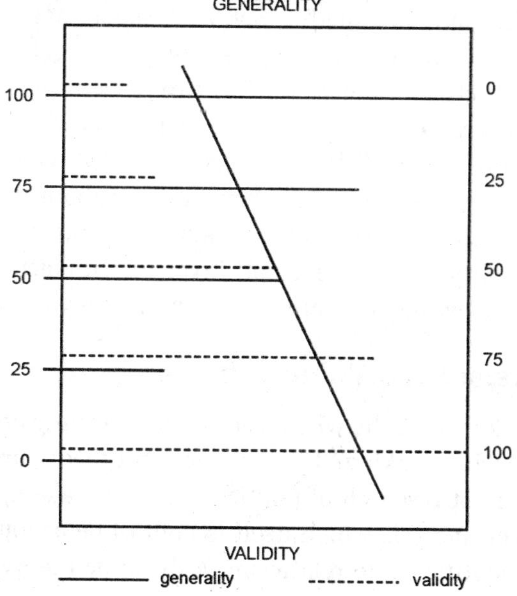

probabilistic, with increased generality and reduced validity. If he applies the knowledge of the results of his municipal council to the elections of other local bodies, such an attempt can roughly be called as the use of his hypothetical knowledge. In that case, generality will further be increased, but validity may go to a lowest ebb. 'If there is heavy polling in those elections, the opposition will be benefited' – can be a useful hypothetical statement. If more hypothetical statements are transformed into generalisations after empirical observations, and weared into a set or cluster, the latter will reach the level of a theory. Its validity will further be reduced.

All these levels of statements or knowledge are somehow related to or based on facts. A structure of knowledge originates from simple factual statements and ends in abstract and general statements. All such statements or generation of knowledge presents 'theory-data-continuum'. At the highest level of knowledge or theory, one is able to generate many new hypotheses, and predict unobserved but probable and important facts of political life. Without a higher and more abstract set of concepts and generalisations, one cannot know much about political facts and processes. A theorist cannot stand without a collection of empirical facts.

In all situations, knowledge of a political theorist is based on observation of facts, and their analysis in terms of scientific method. One has to constantly shuttle from facts to theory and theory to facts. But one may stop at the level of facts, their observation or analysis only. He is a political scientist, and not a theorist. He may even go a little beyond the facts and make some statements. Even this attempt does not amount to a theory. A theory emerges in the form of interrelated concepts and generalisations under a certain scheme. A theorist refers to relationship between facts by ordering them in some meaningful way. Each theory has to go beyond facts and events. Thus, a theorist has necessarily to be a scientist, but the two roles can separately be taken up by two sets of scholars. However, knowledge of facts can tell a lot about their 'what', 'how', 'when', 'where' etc., but remains empirically unable to speak on its 'why'. The understanding of 'why' relates to values. If ultimate values or ideas about them are known or shown, the researcher can scientifically study the lower level or secondary values also. As political facts are deeply involved with facts, a theorist has to know a lot about meaning and implication of various values also.

Policy Analysis: Fact, Value and Theory

Now, how to make use of the whole venture in the study of politics, analysis of policy, or decision-making? Facts, values and theory are closely interrelated in the study of research of politics. They all make up the structure of political or policy analysis which itself is built of behaviouralism, scientific method, and scientific value relativism. A dynamic theory is based on that

Diagram 2

Policy Analysis: Fact, Value and Theory

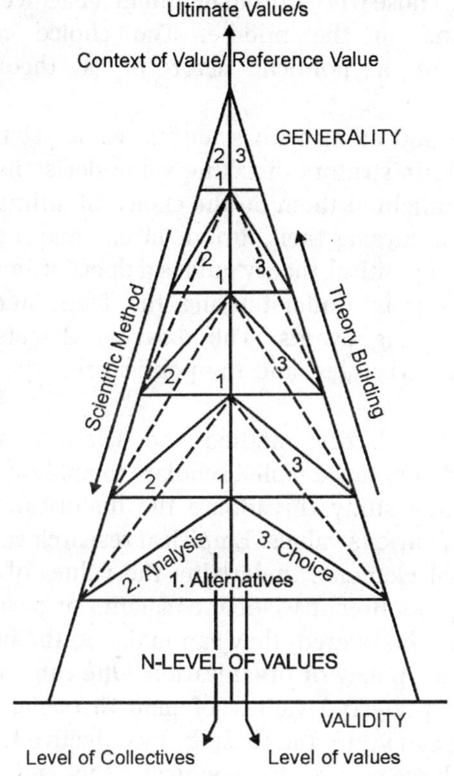

structure. A political actor or scholar analyses political decisioning or policy-making in a scientific manner. Diagram 2 above displays the whole process of analysis. Decision-making (or policy-making) process is shown by triangles. Every triangle consists of three arms: (i) multiplicity of alternatives, (ii) factual analysis of these alternatives under given constraints, and (iii) choice or determination of one alternative. The final decision taken by political actors or groups has been shown by number '1' put on the top of triangles. This decision-point, besides available facts, pertains to their values.

The decision-point of every lower triangle is taken under the decision-point of higher and bigger triangle. Lower decision-values follow higher decision-values. Sometimes, lower decision-points are taken directly on the basis of next higher decision-points. This non-hierarchical relationship is shown by triangles demarcated by broken lines. In the analysis of all political decisions, finding and observation of available facts through Scientific Method make up the basis. Every value-laden decision or event is analysed in the context of values upheld at the higher level.

As a political theory ascends higher, it tends to enlarge its scope or generality, But its attachment with the facts observed by scientific method leads it to validity. Those who want to maintain a balance between generality and validity stand in the middle. The choice concerns with the value-judgement of a political actor or a theorist interested in policy-analysis.

Scientific method along with scientific value relativism can help the politicians and administrators in taking value-decisions based on relevant facts. It can also enlighten them on the choice of ultimate values or higher policy matters by analysing their various facets, and implications for them and the milieu. The political theory guides a decision-maker, if the political actors seek its help in understanding the facts, and anticipating and controlling the coming events. The diagram depicts internal political decision-making by triangles, and the political theory by outer enveloping triangle.

Absorption of scientific method and scientific value relativism in modern political theory has enabled scholars to analyse values to a limitless level. They can now study threadbare the historical, personal, real and possible aspects of various values. Empirical research can do a lot in finding out some universal elements underlying the values of justice, liberty and equality. Similarly, as Brecht wished, constants or permanent elements of 'human nature' are discovered, they can make up the basic material of any political theory, law, policy or organisation. One can empirically know and analyse the 'most preferred values' of man throughout a country or the whole world. One can verify the findings by objective tools and techniques. In this manner, a large part of philosophical values and problems have come within the purview of modern political theory. Its scope is likely to expand still further.

Modern political theory, thus, has given up its impotence and silence over the problem of values, which was its hallmark during the two World Wars. It has arisen in an active and militant manner against the ideologies, which sell and propagate their claims and idiosyncracies as scientific values and verified facts. It can analyse their means, causes and consequences. The modern theorist, while remaining neutral towards values, can conduct dispassionate research and scientific analysis. He can analyse both 'is' and 'ought' separately, and also present relevant data in support of his preferences derived from empirical study of human nature.

Political Science as a discipline can now tell what type of political action can give greater guarantee for ensuing human welfare. A polity can realise what it wants, and escape from the results which it does not like. Scientific value relativism is in a position to expose the actual meaning and possible results hidden behind populist slogans and vaguely-written manifestos. It can make out where would their consequences lead a people. It can be regarded as a weapon against harmful political ideologies and for the defence of human freedom and values. Scientific value relativism and method (SVRM) does not prohibit any person or group to learn and adopt values from religion, nature, intuition, etc. What it wants is that they should be separately indicated. SVRM will explain them, and let all know their consequences in the prevailing context. This will enable them to maintain, reject or modify them, and take adequate steps for future. It can go beyond discussing meaning and implications to adequacy of means. Ideals like equality, liberty, culture, etc., also fall under these categories.

Both protagonists of values and value relativists accept the importance of values, and accord central place to them in their studies, but with a basic difference. Value protagonists begin and end with values picking up methods and techniques useful in support of their stand. Scientific value relativists stick to the scientific method from the start to end. They reach conclusions after making investigation and analysis through scientific method. They treat values as 'preferences', which are discovered on the basis of observation and objective inquiry. For them, SVRM does not and cannot advocate a particular set of ultimate values as true and valid for all human beings, except the assumptions underlying the procedure of scientific method which do not vitiate the findings arrived at or from debarring anyone to challenge, in part or whole, the venture itself. In fact, it is a weapon of truth and reason to fight against falsehood, superstition, ignorance, oppressive ideologies, and vested interests. If it is improperly used, it can disown the wielder of the weapon himself.

Ultimate Values and Political Philosophy

It has already been stated that the scientific method and scientific value relativism do not help anybody to make a choice on ultimate values. The way to seek direction in this regard rests with political philosophy. It studies political values, morality, 'ultimate' nature of political facts, human, nature, etc. Political philosophy often stands as a part of general philosophy, and goes deeper into the nature of political institutions, ideals, ideas, and others. Insight into political values can be obtained from Plato, Aristotle, Acquinas, Locke, Rousseau, Kant, Hegel, Marx, Laski, Nehru, Gandhi, Mao and others. The goal of political philosophy is to inculcate an intellectual commitment which may enable the scholar to provide solutions to all political problems. Importance and utility of political philosophy embody in its advocacy of the values which cannot be obtained by empirical research and scientific investigation. In actual politics, it sees no possibility of separation between 'facts' and 'values'. Therefore, it not much useful to separate Political Science and political philosophy. George E. Catlin[15] relates them respectively to means and values. However, in search of ultimate values one has to join the discourse of political philosophy, and leave the rest to the discipline of Political Science. After seeking guidance or enlightenment from political philosophy and ascertaining appropriate values for himself, the scholar or political actor has to understand scientifically their meaning and implication in concrete terms. In the context with prevailing milieu and socio-political structure, he would come to certain findings as to whether: (i) the latter would permit realisation of those goals or not; or (ii) if those values have to be realised what changes would be required to bring about in that society. For both one has to move along with other building blocks of advanced modern political theory.

Neglect of Intangible Reality

The goal of an academic discipline is to understand reality so that its knowledge may be used in the service of man and his universe.[16] In the context of man, this reality appears in two broad forms: tangible and intangible. It may be observable or non-observable. Human and social sciences have so far been dealing mostly with tangible, empirical, sensory or temporal form of reality, and have neglected its intangible forms. In order to maintain their status que as 'science', they avoid the latter. They overlook the simple fact that behind every tangible, there is ubiquitous presence of abounding intangibles. The intangibles may be explicit or implicit, express or hidden, known or unknown, causal, catalytic or neutral. This intangible reality broadly appears in three forms:

1. *Invisible objects:* These are subtle elements or abstractions of tangible things, e.g., air, electricity, nationality, race etc. which human senses normally cannot comprehend. Only sophisticated tools and devices can enable us to know them, and make that reality understandable.
2. *Mental and emotional phenomena:* There exists a vast area of head and heart, encompassing feelings, emotions, memory, habits and imagination which when internalised over a period of time tends to become a perceived reality. A major part of human life is usually and deeply immersed in them; and
3. *Spirituality:* It falls beyond the domain of human senses. Its experience or knowledge requires higher level of comprehension or consciousness and may not be perceived or appreciated by all in common with others. Experience of its existence is confined to the individual concerned. An individual may or may not be able to tell or explain it to others, but others or onlookers can witness it on the basis of change in his mode of speaking, living and behaving. This is only an individual proof of his experience of spirituality, supernatural, transcendental or metaphysical reality. However, one can himself verify its presence in some personal way through meditation, faith, reflection, revelation, identification, self-realisation, *samadhi* or *dhyan*. On empirical grounds, scholars can analyse, interpret, ascertain and

calculate consequences of such experience in individuals, communities and groups. At this level, its existence can only be argued, analysed and interpreted in some indirect manner. Every social scientist may not be able to appreciate or realise it at personal level. But it does not imply that it does not exist or does not condition behaviour, relations and interactions of human beings involved. Results and consequences of experiencing spirituality can, thus, be studied indirectly on empirical grounds.

These three forms of intangible reality have certain characteristics:

1. They have independent existence and are exclusive experiences.
2. Still in diverse ways, they are related and intensely associated with each other.
3. Understanding only one particular form of reality without knowing about and caring for the other related forms, often creates confusion, uncertainty and distortion of the entire research venture. By separating them, one may not know even partial aspect of that reality.
4. Means, methods, tools and devices to know these segments of reality are special to them and to researches related to those forms. Their use and application can vary from case to case.
5. Stop gap arrangements or temporary measures to deal with them or leaving parts of research ventures may not be treated as permanent solutions.

In Diagram 3 (on p. 93), Reality as a whole (shown as rectangle) is divided broadly as Tangible and Intangible. There are four levels of Reality – I, II, III and IV. The first ground level pertains to pure and simple tangible reality. It shows that all other levels ultimate are based on it and have to come down to prove their substance. Second level belongs to invisible objects, third to mental phenomena, and fourth to spiritual entities. Particular disciplines are closely situated at these various levels.

Intangibles Activate Tangibles

Both common man and elitist leaders mostly live around the tangibles. But in most cases tangibles are closely linked with, even made of and moved by the intangibles.[17] Social realities or phenomena in most cases are reflections and outcome of human non-observables/intangibles. It is sometimes difficult to classify forms of reality neatly either as tangible or intangible. It is likely that they may not be visualised without reference to the latter. Normally, these intangibles, or at least some of them, appear beyond the perceptional reach of our senses. But it is a fact that the fast increasing growth of science and technology has pushed more and more of these intangibles into the arena of tangibles. Intangibles are known through visible signs and indicators. They are connected with specific tangibles – speech, behaviour, acts and possessions. So far, it can be said, more than half of the areas of Intangibles remain uncovered or uninvestigated by social scientists. In future, the social scientists would, perhaps, deal more and more with the intangibles of the past as tangibles of the future. Therefore, the dichotomy between the tangibles and intangibles must not be allowed to appear as anti-polar, paradoxical or unbridgeable.

Elites Misuse the Cover of Spiritual Intangibles

People at large and in general live at temporal levels. They are often confined to themselves. Mostly they prefer to remain as creatures of their circumstances. Their fate is generally associated with the acts and doings of manipulating elites who happen to control, guide and direct them in many areas of life. These elites have their own world-views, both temporal and super-natural. Often they act on and operate the socio-political systems on the basis of supernatural world-views and other related intangibles made of feelings and emotions. The contents of the supernatural, directly as well as indirectly, are manipulated, explained and presented by them to serve and support their vested interests. Common man hardly knows anything about them, and mostly submits credulously to their exploitative presentations. There is great and urgent need to expose and explain them. All these subdued people need to be informed about these elitist propositions and convictions. Usually, on the basis of their abstract and esoteric supernatural ideology (indoctrinated as scientific theory or religion) elites tend to move and motivate the people at large. Their supernaturals or intangibles should be translated into concrete and understandable terms. It is the responsibility of human and social sciences to study them scientifically and explain their meaning empirically.

But scholars, social scientists and researchers of today are unable to do that. They suffer from their self-imposed limitations, unknown biases and opted concerns. Their methodology mostly concerns with the study of tangibles only. They are unable to cross over the boundaries of tangibles. Neo-Marxist philosopher Herbert Marcuse (1898-1979) has observed that all are trying to resort to specific form of tools, methods, and techniques, to evolve their own methodology of research to be more functional and realistic. So far they are simply trying to translate language of Social Science into 'Natural Sciences' and always talking of observation and measurement so that people think in terms of the status quo. Consequently, elites everywhere have turned into 'managers' of and are gaining more and more control over society.

Contents of Intangibles and Need of Advanced Methodology

All disciplines of Social Sciences, following natural sciences, try to stand on the ground of tangibles. But their subject matter is also enmeshed with intangibles in varying degrees. Relation with intangibles is greater in Sociology than found in Economics and History. Study of politics is involved with intangibles at almost all levels. In case there is greater quantum of the role of intangibles, greater would be the need of methodology relating to the study of intangibles. Disciplines which have greater scope for the role of three forms of intangible reality will have to require working more for the inclusion and development of trans-empirical methodology. Sociology, thus, would have to improve its methodology more than History and Economics. In this venture, Political Science would have to surpass them all. (See diagram below).

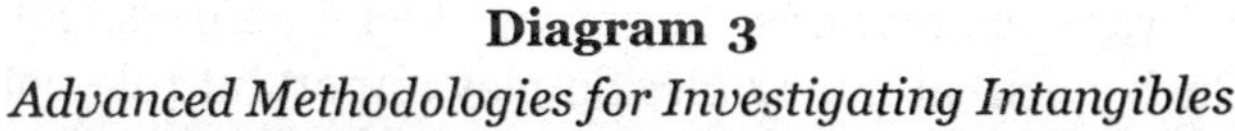

Diagram 3

Advanced Methodologies for Investigating Intangibles

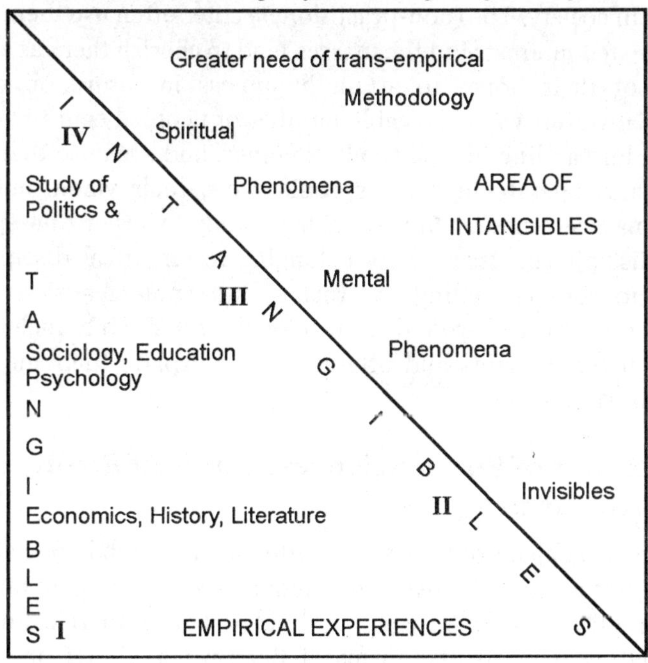

Even particular aspects of a perceived reality may require highly sophisticated tools and techniques which can be standardised only in a gradual manner. At times, one may take help from the tools and techniques available and meant for studying some other aspects of a given reality. Similarly, a developing discipline may supplement its existing arsenal of methodology by borrowing and adopting them from others. Naturally, particular disciplines and sciences have to resort to specific form of tools, methods, and techniques to study these Intangibles and to evolve their own methodology of research to be more functional and realistic.

Methodological Conversion of Intangibles to Tangibles

An academic discipline being closely related to some particular aspect of reality deals with a much narrower area of that particular reality. Yet it does concern with other aspects of reality also in some direct or indirect manner. For instance, disciplines centring on spiritual matters concentrate more on experiences of practitioners of faith, immersion, transcendence, salvation, revelation, reflection and other supernatural and transempirical attainments. Someone or many in succession trigger off secrets of intangible or spiritual reality. After sometime, a large number of people follow them in action, faith and institutions. In fact, role and importance of intangibles gains ground only in the context of their impact on various forms of worldly living and outward expressions, learnt by their admirers, followers and supporters. Such spiritual intangibles do play important role both for elites and masses in society. The (non-practitioner) elites often use them to rationalise their vested interests but the masses tend to cherish them as a source of realisation of their hopes to attain happiness in future on earth and elsewhere. However, when a sizable number of people begin to adopt such spiritual understanding in a particular manner, and organise themselves to live, work and operate in some specific ways, their whole outlook and behaviour may become a subject-matter of study by other non-spiritual or empirical disciplines. Researchers belonging to empirical disciplines find difficulties in comprehending spiritual or intangible realities. But these researchers on empirical grounds can widen their horizon to include various forms of spiritual insights and utterances and explain their meaning and effect in empirical terms.

Subject-Matter of Social Sciences, Levels of Reality and Research Strategies

There are many subjects or topics for conducting research in Social Sciences. The Table 1 'Interrelation between methodologies pertaining to tangible and intangible realities' given on page 95 divides them into 11 columns. They may be relating to particular forms of Reality – I, II, III or IV (col. 1). However, a piece of reality may be falling into more than one or two categories. In case, it relates to one particular form of reality, it would be useful to apply methods and techniques available for doing research in that area (col. 6). In the Table 1 each *level* of reality largely relates itself with particular category of research or *research design* (RD) (col. 2), *form* of reality (col. 3), usual *contents* (col. 4), and *subjects or disciplines* usually

Table 1

Interrelation between Methodologies Pertaining to Tangible and Intangible Realities

Levels of Reality	*Category of Research Design*	*Form of Reality*	*Contents*	*Main Subjects/ disciplines*	*Tools and Methods of Study*	*Some Topics of Research*	*Grouping of Methods and Techniques*	*Topics/ Areas of all Methods*	*Partial Studies/ Use of Restricted Methods*	*Neglect of Areas/ Personal-ities*
1	*2*	*3*	*4*	*5*	*6*	*7*	*8*	*9*	*10*	*11*
IV Subtle and Original	Analysis and synthesis	Spiritual/ Transempi-rical	Soul, self, conscience	Philosophy, Education, Religion, Political Sc., Literature	Meditation, faith, spiritual experiences, revelation	Direct experience, influence, reason, analysis**	Personal experience, informal interview, participation	Gandhian leadership, Hinduism, saints and others	Muslim League and participation in communa-lism	Buddhism, Jainism, Christianity, RSS, Marx
III Evaluation/ Abstract/ Conceptual/ Analytical	Interdisci-plenary and diagnostic	Mental/ Emotional/ Subjectively felt	Emotions, memory, imagination, culture	Political Science, Sociology, Public Administra-tion	Internali-sation, learning, empathy, introspec-tion	Backward-ness, poverty, nationality cultural traits etc.	III+ II+ I		Terrorism	
II Abstract intagible but mentally tanglible	Experi-mental and descriptive	Non-observable but objective	Race, state, nation, caste, personality, religion	Natural Science, Economics, History	Sophistica-ted tools and devices, indicators	personal traits, conditions of ST, SC, BPL families	II+I		Dalits, poverty and women	

Contd...

Contd...

Levels of Reality	*Category of Research Design*	*Form of Reality*	*Contents*	*Main Subjects/ disciplines*	*Tools and Methods of Study*	*Some Topics of Research*	*Grouping of Methods and Techniques*	*Topics/ Areas of all Methods*	*Partial Studies/ Use of Restricted Methods*	*Neglect of Areas/ Personal-ities*
1	*2*	*3*	*4*	*5*	*6*	*7*	*8*	*9*	*10*	*11*
I Tangible	Exploratory/ Formul-ative/ Survey	Observable and Empirical	Temporal world, goods, man, things, environment	All other subjects, Geography, Psychology, Economics, Behavioural Sciences	Observation, interview, participa-tion, calculation	Voting, census, behaviour, groups and community	I		Terrorism, Communalism, and law and order	

** Process on Preferable methods for the study of Fourth (Spiritual) Level:
(a) Self-realisation or experience in original or non-transferable manner
(b) Assessment of effect, process, revelation, utterances and introspection
(c) Outcome in form of behavioural changes, institutions, and forms of expression
(d) Knowing attitude, beliefs, opinion, likings, relations and responses.

dealing with them (col. 5). When an area of research, as in education, is related to two or three forms of social reality, it would require application of all (col. 8) methods, tools and techniques developed for studying those phenomena. Tangible studies, as on voting or student behaviour, have methods like observation, interview, questionnaire etc. *Second level* (col. I) studies on personality, nation, race etc. would include methods and techniques meant for the investigation of both first and second forms of reality (col. 8). Methods of internalisation, empathy, introspection, group discussion etc. would come into play when subjective entities, like emotions, aptitude, habits, culture, backwardness, poverty etc. (col. 3) are being put under investigation. It may be pointed out that study of the *third level* or form of reality, when existing at or connected with first and second levels, would involve means, methods and techniques available at these three levels (col. 8). By using these methods we would be transforming knowledge of the second and third category of intangibles into first category knowledge of tangible through specifying indicators, using process of operationalisation, drawing out generalisations, and replication.

The fourth level (col. 1) of spiritual reality is trans-empirical. It can be comprehended directly by specific individual only through meditation, reflection, identification, faith or transcendence (see the process below the Table). However, experience of knowing that reality would remain confined to the practitioner. It cannot be handed over or reproduced by him in a direct manner to anyone. It is non-transferable, non-comparable and unique, therefore, stands beyond the purview of empirical science. However, there are two other ways or categories of knowing its existence. One is either observation of the result or consequence of that realisation by some person or watching of the whole process by him in the form of physical indicators or statements uttered by the practitioner of spirituality. The other way is to make an estimate of his influence on individuals, institutions, conduct, acts and activities of his followers. A comparative study of influences earned by two or more practitioners of spiritual reality can also be made. One can also study them empirically by knowing attitudes, beliefs, opinions, likings, relations and responses of the believers concerned. While undertaking such a venture, the researcher would have to employ all the available methods and techniques of studying the three forms of reality to the extent that spiritual reality turns into some kind of empirical evidence (cols. 8 and 9).

There are many areas, such as, study of Gandhian leadership or impact of Buddha or Hindu culture on Indian democracy which demand application of all the methods, tools and techniques attached with the four levels of Reality (col. 9). While studying such topics one cannot stop either at first (tangible) or second (mentally tangible/non-observable) or third (analytical/conceptual) level. Unless one goes deep into 'spiritual' attainments of Gandhi, he or she cannot do any fruitful research in that field. So is the case with other topics of similar nature. Observing things belonging to Gandhi or looking into the working of the institutions founded by Gandhi, or reading about his emotions and feelings from his autobiography or knowing observations of Gandhi's followers about him may not lead one to knowing of reality. All such attempts may not reveal the 'truth' lying behind his leadership. Similarly, those who leave the spiritual or value aspects of Mohammad Ali Jinnah and other Muslim leaders or *jehadi* terrorists, and study the rest (col. 10) cannot comprehend these people in totality. The Indian National Congress, by neglecting this aspect, failed to understand why Jinnah and the Muslim Leaguers insisted upon partitioning India at all costs and rejected all persuasion, requests and concessions from Congress.

It is unfortunate that Social Sciences, as usual, have totally neglected the study of the role, experience, attainments and efforts of great religious leaders like Buddha, Mahavira, Christ and several others. They have conducted their studies only in known and usual areas of caste, tradition, hierarchy, family etc. The social scientists ignorantly forget that what the great founders of religions and other saints have attained and advocated, knowingly or unknowingly, did not remain confined to them only. The outcome of their spiritual heights, teaching and doings have been in forms of millions of committed followers, establishment of thousands of socio-religious institutions, generation of great traditions and generous beliefs, creation of art and literature, and many other things. Later, their influence has appeared in the form of empires and kingdoms. All this has revolutionised the lives of the poor, depressed, women and children. Their followers have also created as well as destroyed communities and kingdoms. All of them have been left untouched by the social scientists owing to their methodological blindness. Most of them still do not understand that there is a direct relationship between metaphysics and spirituality with politics, culture, education, wars and peace.

It has long been known that the scope, nature, contents and methodology of physical sciences is quite specific and unique to their subject-matter and desired goals. Still the social scientists have not given up their habit of adhering to an alien methodology. By blindly imitating them, they have suffered on all counts: credibility, status, utility and progress. Against all advice from David Hume (1711-1776), Jean Paul Sartre (1905-1980) and Karl R. Popper (1902-1994) they continue to confine themselves to the labyrinth of 'empirical science'. Max Horkheimer (1895-1973) had talked a lot about the dangers of 'technology' which is the gift of empirical (sensory experience and empiricism) sciences. Without normative basis, all revolutions have been converted into Bureaucracy or mere Technocratic Social Management. The liberal ideal has been routinised into election, media exercise and so on. In this manner, liberalism has been buried deeply.

Levels of Methodology for the Study of Politics

For historical reasons and a long tradition of conservatism, the normative thinkers have dominated the study of politics, pushing it to the domain of philosophy or poetry or literature. Its nomenclature 'Political Science' sounds misnomer. There is very little 'science' in it. Rather the suffix 'science' unnecessarily compels some scholars to adopt means and methods of natural sciences all the time without caring for the nature of the data, meaning or objectives of political studies. The literature of political studies is replete with many of the ideas, concepts and theories which lag far behind the contemporary world of science and technology, particularly, globalisation and the new economic order.

The dichotomy and separation between two types of methodologies (empirical and trans-empirical) have so far kept them apart, making each other's findings somewhat baseless, false and even misleading. Both of them have been claiming to accomplish what they should not methodologically claim to do. One cannot *see* any spiritual and mental phenomena without reference to concrete situations of human living, and empirical realities *rarely* exist without relation to human mind and spirit. To make out methodological horizons wider and the discipline more reality-oriented, it would be appropriate if the nomenclature 'Political Science' is abandoned in preference to '*Politicology*' or '*Polilogy*'. The new name may literally mean the same thing but it is likely to provide a new orientation and a wider coverage. The methodology *of 'Politicology'* or '*Polilogy*' as suggested above would be better able to deal with all type of phenomena in terms of human experience, and make knowledge public, open and 'inter-subjectively transmissible'. At the present level of methodological underdevelopment, it is quite difficult to explain a part of mental and spiritual phenomena relating to politics in empirical terms. The proposed politicological methodology would study reality as it exists. It would not negate, nullify or distort, but would honestly try to accept their influence on human mind and behaviour. Conscientious researchers should now no more remain one-way recipients of tools, adequate or inadequate, from other disciplines. The scholars in the past have been accepting and using them without questioning their basics, goals and utility. As such, their discipline has filled its store with a lot of deadwood, waste, rickety salvage, fossils and confusing hangovers during the last several decades. Any venture of research with this material is just groping in dark and leading others toward black holes. They should widen their horizons and ascertain reality by resorting to intangible methodologies. Transmissibility, reproducibility, verification and scientificity have to come after having substantial attainments. For this, scholars have to abandon their false egoism of calling their discipline as 'science' and avoid resorting to blind imitation.

Political Science as a discipline is intermeshed with all the four forms of reality. Study of politics should have means and methods to handle all these four levels of reality. Without applying methods appropriate to data, realistic knowledge cannot be generated. Methods of political studies must be compatible and vary with the nature of data. Lack of appropriate tools and techniques simply displays that the discipline falls short in adequate understanding of its own subject-matter. Research results or knowledge of politics cannot be better than the methods and techniques by which they have been obtained. Without suitable methodological weaponry, the quest for knowledge may prove an abortive venture. On the road of having appropriate tools and techniques of research, various forms of political phenomena can be studied in the following manner:

At the first tangible level, like any other social science, it has also a number of empirical methods of study and research. Politics is a worldly activity. It would make use of them.

At the second level of invisibles or mental tangibles, there are many sophisticated tools and devices available which enable us to know them, and make that reality understandable. These mostly are borrowed from natural and social sciences.

At the third level of mental and emotional phenomena, there are methods of psychiatry, linguistic and content analysis, experiments, black box techniques and the like. These methods may enable it to comprehend the phenomena of power, authority, legitimacy, nationhood, democracy, participation, deference, autonomy and the like. However, their study in Political Science would be more problematic and heuristic than obtained in other social sciences.

At the fourth and final level, there are abstract phenomena like spirit, faith, feelings, emotions, and other mental categories such as memory, habit, commitment, allegiance and sacrifice. It should be accepted that the means and methods of understanding the spirit and domain of faith would be studied only by experienced scholars and enlightened researchers. Till the categories of mental and spiritual phenomena remain in air or at mental level, and do not appear in the form of influence, power, organisation or group behaviour, they would be comprehended by scholars through empathy, introspection, analogy and meditation. Many times, people at large happen to act upon them when these phenomena are spelled out to them even on the basis of individual or divine experience of some highly respected or charismatic personalities. Scholars have to know and communicate all such mental and/or spiritual phenomena in an authentic manner. Till these come down to them in concrete form, they merely remain as potentials of politics.

When the impact of these mental or spiritual categories appears on human mind, behaviour and relationships among men and groups, their study falls within the purview of empirical and socio-psychological methodology. Till these non-tangible materials of politics do not come down to the social scientists in an earthly manner, or become somewhat susceptible in some form to their sensory perception, they have the choice of making use of the techniques of hunch, analysis and interpretation. The latter techniques stand in between empirical methodology and devices like empathy and introspection.

Relations between Tangible and Non-tangible Methodologies

As different disciplines stand on the ground of specific segments of reality, they are not at par with each other (See Diagram 1 on page 93). They are not connected with all the levels of reality. Some of them may be concerned more with particular form or level of reality. As such, they would be using only that particular form of methodology. However, their usual way of research-operation is found moving among levels – one to four or four to one in column 6. One may stop at the first or the second levels. Another may be concerned more with the third. However, in study of politics, all the three levels of intangible methodology are interconnected. They are complementary and mutually dependent on each other. In a way, empirical investigation comes first as well as at the end. Dissatisfied with the first, the researcher goes gradually from the first to the next level. If he is not content with the second and the third, he joins the fourth.

Reality known through intangible or trans-empirical methodology should not be considered as inferior to that knowledge which is acquired by scientific methods. Knowledge obtained through a scientific or trans-empirical means, both in theory and practice, normally covers a large ground and can be accepted quite useful for purposes of research. Both the masses and the elite acknowledge its existence and influence. They are moved and motivated by it. Though, in the present state of our knowledge, methodology of studying mental and spiritual phenomena, from empirical viewpoint, appears far less 'scientific' than the methodology of studying tangible subject-matter. As the knowledge of mental or intangible categories remains confined to a few individuals only and do not become visible or visualised to others, it is the task of users of 'advanced' methodology to get the individual esoteric experiences transformed and translated in empirical terms. Let it be accepted that the influence of faith in the mental and spiritual categories is greater than the so-called scientific knowledge. Hence one can neglect them only at its own peril.[18]

Empirical form of methodology is important and useful for communication and verification among fellow-scholars but it cannot be considered more important than its contents or subject-matter. Truth can be known or arrived at by several other means also. But all that coming down from level four to two or going upward from two to four, should be verified by tools and techniques of empirical sciences to obtain acceptability and consensus at all levels. Support of empirical evidence in some reliable form will save us from surrendering to subjectivism, elite monopoly and sorcery. Research conducted in such a manner would give it legitimacy, support and cooperation of the people concerned.[19]

We should not compartmentalise and isolate various forms of knowledge by reserving them for a particular category of scholars or groups of people to be denigrated by others. One fruitful impact of using trans-empirical methodology for the understanding of mental and metaphysical phenomena can be, in the form of transforming them into tangible terms. In the same manner, scientific methodology can also be enriched by seeking support of trans-empirical methodology.

It is possible to create or generate knowledge without crippling the knowledge venture into artificially isolated segments. Various aspects of knowledge of reality can supplement each other. A comprehensive view of knowledge should include both forms of methodologies, and make the scholar aware about tangible as well as intangible nature of things. It would have to make use of means, methods and techniques to know and support them on the basis of procedural adequacy and evidence. Hence, an attempt has to be made here to reconcile the empirical and the normative or the quantitative and the qualitative methodologies, and yet maintain the autonomy of their respective fields. Incorporation of knowledge of mental and metaphysical matter within the fold of the discipline would, make knowledge a total whole. It would also relieve the common man from the mystiques of the elites who claim to monopolise the secrets of mental and spiritual phenomena and deprive the rest from peeping into their preserves.

However, all disciplines have to prove their mettle on the anvil of empirical methodology at some later stage.

References

1. For details, see Pauline V. Young, *Scientific Social Survey and Research*, New Delhi, Prentice-Hall of India, 1975; John Galtung, *Theory and Methods of Social Research*, London, George Alien and Unwin Ltd., 1967.
2. S.L. Verma, *Research Methodology in Political Science*, Jaipur, Rajasthan Hindi Grantha Academy, 2005, Chap. 2 and 3.
3. Arnold Brecht, *Political Theory: The Foundations of Twentieth Century Political Thought*, Princeton, 1959, Chap. 3 and 4.
4. Karl Pearson, *The Grammar of Science*, London 1911, 1.
5. Vernon Van Dyke, *Political Science: A Philosophical Analysis*, *op. cit.*, 191-205.
6. Brecht, *op. cit.*, Bombay, 1965, 28-30.

7. Gabriel A. Almond and James S. Coleman (eds.), *The Politics of the Developing Areas*, Princeton, 1960.
8. Robert A. Dahl, *Modern Political Analysis*, New Delhi, 1965, 106-110; For details, see, infra, Ch. VIII.
9. Eric Voegelin, *The New Science of Politics*, Chicago, 1952; and, Leo Strauss, *What is Political Philosophy?* New York, 1959.
10. Dahl, *Modern Political Analysis, op. cit.*
11. T.S. Kuhn, *The Structure of Scientific Revolutions*, Chicago, 1970; and, James B. Rule, *Insight & Social Betterment: A Preface to Applied Social Science*, New York, 1978.
12. W.G. Runciman, *Social Science and Political Theory*, Cambridge, 1965; and, George J. Graham, *Methodological Foundation for Political Analysis*, Toronto, 1971.
13. Brecht, *op. cit.*
14. Ibid., 27-116.
15. Catlin, *Systematic Politics, op. cit.*
16. Verma, S.L., *Research Methodology in Political Science: Theory and Analysis*, Jaipur: Rawat Publications, 1989, Introduction.
17. Professor Raghuvir Singh categorically rejects 'scientific methodology' for its lack of metaphysical perspective; see, his D.P. Mukherji Memorial lecture entitled '*Methodology and Meaning in Social Science*'.
18. Author rejects outright the view of Professor Raghuvir Singh that the human discourse should spring only from the depth of Divine Logos, or 'the soul is all that it knows'. Singh fanatically declares that 'there can be no rationalist-humanist science of man and no empirical-scientific theory of the state and society.' op. cit.
19. The present condition of empirical methodology is neither satisfactory nor adequate. It takes into account only those phenomena or events which have had happened either in the past or are still persisting. It tends to study the status quo or as it is. It is unable to look at its change or engineering aspect. It remains silent on the aspect that what should be done or how should an appropriate mechanism be evolved to realise particular goals or values. Similarly, almost all its tools, techniques, goals and devices have been outdated in view of omnipresence of the power of globalisation in every walk of life: individual, social, nation, region and international.

4

Systems Theories: Systems Approach

It has already been stated that Political Science so far has not been able to develop an Advanced Modern Political Theory. However, there are many partial or quasi-theories, usually called as 'approaches'. Other constructions closer to them are: models, paradigms and methods. However, approaches are very important and useful for both analysing political phenomenon and also for building up an empirical political theory.

Need, Meaning and Scope

Every man or woman uses some approach to look at the events, activities, processes, persons and groups of one's milieu. On that basis he tries to make his opinion and reach some conclusions. He has some way or view of looking at them. Approach is just like an eye, intellect or mind. A man sees things which are relevant or interesting to him, and leaves the rest unconcerned. Things perceived by a smuggler or a policeman are different from that of a man of religion or a political leader. In the same way, political observers or analysts also look at the political events and activities from their own perspectives. If someone sees them from the angle of 'power' or 'law', the other scholar may view them as a particular 'group' or 'ideology'. As one sees only a part of the totality of an event or has only a partial vision of activities, he or she cannot tell everything about them. For understanding various facets of politics, we have to adopt various ways or approaches of understanding the whole event. David Easton for the development of a general theory of politics has recommended, besides Political Science, learning approaches and theories from other disciplines also.[1]

According to Vernon van Dyke,[2] an approach consists of criteria of selecting problems and relevant data. It provides standards governing the inclusion and exclusion of question and data. It denotes epistemological assumptions on which the search for knowledge is based. An approach determines the *way* of generalisation, explanation, prediction and prescription – *all* of which are among the main function of a theory. In this way, it is creator of a theory. When it goes beyond the selection of problems and data about the subject matter under study, it begins to transform into theory. Merton regards it as 'an ordering enterprise, focusing on definition, classification, and categorisation'. Haas and Kariel define it as consisting of 'a paradigm and conceptual scheme that has been worked out for handling aspects of one or more paradigms within a particular mode of analysis'. Young regards it as a new mode of political analysis. It is larger than a paradigm and is more empirical and analytical. In political analysis, an approach operates as a strategy for studying political phenomena.

It is narrower than a theory and broader than a paradigm. A theory is more objective, empirical and scientific, fully based on scientific method and techniques. An approach, on the contrary, is subjective and empirical in a limited way. All its methods are oriented to it. Numerically, in Political Science, there are few theories extending beyond the criteria of selection and the collected data. It has to be broad, holistic and explanatory. Approach does not go beyond its criteria of selection. As such, it is often descriptive, partial or segmental. A paradigm is a framework of ideas that establishes general context of analysis, combining mixture of philosophical assumptions and criteria of valid knowledge. A theory is a generalised statement summarising the real or supposed actions of a set of variables whether dependent or independent or intervening. It could be micro or macro, abstract, concrete or formal.

But approach is different from and broader than a method and technique. Method is a way of organising, building up or formulating a theory for application to data. It carries two meanings: (a) epistemological assumptions on which the search for knowledge is based, e.g., positivist and rationalist methods, and, (b) the operations or activities that occur in the acquisition and treatment of data. Method in the second sense may also be called 'technique'. Technique links method to the relevant data. It represents various modes or skills of recording empirical information, e.g., sampling, interviewing etc. It is more susceptible to routine or mechanical application and more highly specialised, depending less on imaginative intelligence. Model is also closer to it. A model is a simplified way of describing relationships. It can be constructed from a paradigm, a theory, a method and a technique. It can be typological, descriptive, formal mechanical, organismic or biological. Strategy is a peculiar way of applying one or any combination of the above type or model to a research problem. It requires that quality and integrity should combine in a strategy. A good strategy fits together with problem, theory, method and techniques in a systematic manner.[3]

Structure, Nature, Functions and Limitations

Normally, the structure of an approach consists of (i) a systematic orientation and perspective for specifying the area of study or observation; (ii) some statements concerning the central questions or types of questions or problem; (iii) criteria of relevance for mapping out and selecting data for analysis; and, (iv) some guidance for a hierarchical ordering of both questions and data in terms of significance. Approaches can be divided as (a) old, and, (b) modern. Older approaches have been many: allegorical (Plato), analytical (Aristotle), cyclical-historical (Polybius), empirical-pragmatic (Montesquieu, Tocqueville, Comte), realist (Machiavelli, Bodin) skeptical (Hume) and so on. Recent or modern approaches are also many: systems (Easton), structural-functional (Almond and Coleman), decision-making (Simon), communicational (Deutch) and the like.[4]

Approaches directly take up the problem for study without bothering about boundaries of the discipline. They stand between full-fledged theories and simple perspectives or points of view. They provide a general orientation as a framework for inquiry and a source of criteria of relevance and the base for selecting data, such as, process, political act, control, development, decision etc. Every approach suggests conceptual categories and hypotheses for empirical analysis. It is an ordering enterprise which leads toward concepts and categorisation and some generalisations. It is an intellectual organisation in the sense that it (a) establishes boundaries, (b) points out important variables, (c) helps in ranking them, and (d) supplies workable hypotheses. Generally approaches operate as interpersonal communication channels with a few minimum words with specific meaning, status of concepts and usable categories. They operate as bridges built between hyper-factualism and abstract theorisation appearing as checklists and typologies.

Approaches are preferred more for their fruitfulness instead for validity or accuracy. They provide new questions, new criteria and collection of new data. Overemphasis on methodology is avoided. The approach user catches up units of socio-political analysis. His insights appear into simplified models of realities, even as analogies and metaphors. There is no bar to adopting approaches from other disciplines. 'Because of their antecedent nature, approaches are a prerequisite of the development of full-fledged theory.'[5]

Conscious utilisation of well-formulated approaches is of crucial importance. But it rarely happens. Often the makers of approaches push them in the directions of full-fledged theories. Their opponents label them often as pre-theories or sets of concepts and questions having little value. 'No approach can be universal as it cannot handle all the tasks or problems of the political world. At the most they can endeavour 'constructive eclecticism'. Those who indulge in 'theology of approaches' have emotional attachment with their partial attainments. For them, their approach tends to become dogma, doctrine, tenets of ultimate truth. They consider non-believers as heretics. This kind of Puritanism 'becomes dysfunctional from the point of advancing the discipline of Political Science'.[6] Their efforts suffer from the problems of reification (treating concepts as real) and wastage. They go isolated and their efforts lack a sense of unity, coordination and utility. Such approaches hardly hope to reach horizons of 'theory'.

Young is right when he writes, 'the existence of a multiplicity of approaches is basically a healthy phenomenon and the appropriate response to this situation is one that emphasises the possibility of fruitful co-existence among a variety of approaches'.[7] Such attitude would lead to powerful structuring effects of language, acquaintance with the wide divergence of sources of concepts and symbolic forms. Individual approaches are most capable of handling specific tasks. Different approaches have different capacity in (i) richness and comprehensiveness of descriptions, (ii) fruitfulness in generating hypotheses, (iii) combinatorial capacity, (iv) usefulness in uncovering so far unthought out relationships, and (v) suggestiveness in selecting models for more detailed analyses.

There are three interrelated approaches or partial theories, namely, general systems theory, systems theory, and structural-functional approach. In the analytical sense, Young regards the latter two as derivatives of the general systems theory.[8] Some scholars consider general systems theory and systems theory as identical. Though they are closely related, yet should be considered as separate for analytical and heuristic purposes. General systems theory is overarching, all-covering and enveloping. It interconnects all systems and subsystems irrespective of the identity of various disciplines, whereas systems theory is specific to a particular set of variables, and mostly related to the study of political phenomena. The general systems theory operates as a perspective or orientation. But the systems theory has a goal to come out as a 'theory', and has its own conceptual scheme, and a programme to realise it. General systems theory emerged to help and guide various disciplines to benefit from each other at a higher level of abstraction, as there were many things in common. Their apparently varying findings could generate a general theory to the satisfaction of all.

'System' as Entity

A political system can be seen as – a set of objects together with relationships, between the objects and between their attributes, or, a whole which is compounded of many parts – an ensemble of attributes; or, a set of elements standing in interaction; or a group of objects or elements standing in some characteristic structural relationships to one another and interacting on the basis of certain characteristic processes. Even the society can be seen as a system of functionally interrelated variables or attributes. Robert T. Holt finds the social system as the system of interdependent roles and corporate structures of society. As such, a system involves some constantly cognisable processes underlying a set of persons, relations, actions, roles, structures or events. It is an operating 'whole'.

Every system carries some natural or artificial purposes, objectives, or goals. It can be concrete or abstract, empirical or transempirical, observable or abstract. The railway system is concrete, empirical and observable, but the ethical or Hegelian system is abstract, ideational, and non-empirical. Some systems can be both, semi-concrete or semi-abstract, as in case of political system. Each system consists of some actions, activities or interrelations. They can be natural, motivated or contrived. If ecosystem is natural, education system can more or less, be regarded as contrived. Attempt to bring in a socialist or Hindu system in India or elsewhere can be considered as motivated. Every system is built on certain basic material. This basic material is operated by and through its units, organs, subsystems, processes and activities. Each system, in due course of time, develops some specific characteristics, tools, means, and techniques. If the basic element of human physiology is life or consciousness, the religious system depends on faith in God. They have their own tools, techniques, methods, and styles to accomplish their goals.

However, it is not always easy to know the basic, elemental or key material of a system. One can easily know and recognise the means, methods, and instrumentalities of a concrete and empirical system like the water or light system of a city. But one often becomes helpless in the delineation of an ethical or a religious system. A man can know it only by observing its symbols, relevant expressions, and other indirect behaviour patterns. As regards their forms and goals, there are acute conflicts and controversies. However, most of the systems are related to each other in some direct or indirect manner. As such, their mutual relationships can take up hundreds of kaleidoscopic forms, independent, dependent, semi-independent, simple, complex, direct, indirect, etc. It is always difficult to measure and objectively evaluate the power, influence, capacity, capability, activities, and quantum and quality of relations, particularly in case of abstract systems. Cohen rightly observes a system as 'any ongoing set of recurrent and interrelated social actions'.

Political System

After the behavioural revolution, political scientists have replaced 'state' by 'political system,' considering the former as formal, inadequate and unsatisfactory. Still it is not clear which is the central element of political system. Classical political thinkers had found knowledge, reason, natural land, religion or conventional law as the basic element of state. Most of the modern political scientists find 'legitimate physical compulsion' as the key variable of political system. For Easton, it is 'authoritative allocation of values for society'. Lasswell and Kaplan regard 'severe deprivations' as the basic material of political system. Dahl relates it to power, government and authority. Catlin discovers 'control over wills' as the basis. Almond defines the political system, more or less, as 'the legitimate, order-maintaining or transforming system in the society'.

All the scholars have called its various organs and processes in varying terms. Easton has put them in the two broad categories of 'inputs' and 'outputs'. A 'political system' cannot be physically separated from its non-political aspects, and is, therefore, usually understood and studied in an analytical or conceptual manner. Society as a whole makes up the general social system, which contains many subsystems. Political system is one of these subsystems. When the political system is to be studied as a whole along with its intra-subsystems, then, it is treated as a 'system'. Besides that, 'system' can be considered as a part of environment. Thus, the concept of 'system' both in interlocking micro and macro forms, saves us from the error of considering 'systems' as isolated, separate, or independent entities. Besides throwing light on their interconnections, one can examine their discrete nature, and separate empirical existence. According to Almond, the political system in a society, is 'legitimate, order maintaining' or transforming system, Wiseman maintains that every political system involves political structures, actors, or roles performed by their agents, patterns of interaction existing between individuals or collectivities, and political processes. In the 'political system' of Kaplan also, there are recognisable multivariate interests. Instead of always being opposite, sometimes they are complementary to each other. There are regular structures and channels to reach the decisions and judgements related to particular interests. General rules are prescribed to govern the actors and activities relating to particular decisions and judgements.

Essential Features

A political system, according to Michels, has the following features:

(a) It is a permanent entity, existing amidst a broader environment and includes many other units.
(b) It consists of an identifiable and measurable set of interdependent elements or variables.
(c) It has boundaries which keep it separate from general environment.
(d) It is constituted around certain problems, objectives or goals, and builds up certain structures.

(e) Along with increase of specific problems and evolution of goals, it develops specific structures and processes, leading to more and more differentiation.

However, political scientists, sociologists, and political sociologists have analysed political systems with varying frames of references and different goals. More important among them are Talcott Parsons, David Easton, Gabriel Almond, and Morton Kaplan. Perspectives of Parsons and Easton are more conceptual. Almond and Kaplan have gone towards empirical research and theory making. Thus, there are many variations among them. Before we discuss it in detail, 'General Systems' would be taken up first.

General Systems Theory

General systems theory presents a general 'theory' for all the systems. It has developed a set of most abstract generalisations applicable to all systems. For this avowed purpose, the general system theorists try to develop concepts which tend to unify or interconnect various disciplines. They remain in search of highly abstract concepts relevant to all kinds of systems. They feel a need for having a solid foundation in general and abstract theory. For this purpose, they propose broad conceptual guidelines. Such conceptual framework is likely to reduce, (i) the rigid compartmentalisation of disciplines, (ii) duplication of efforts, and (iii) inefficiency due to lack of cross-disciplinary approach. General systems theory aims at meaningful integration of all knowledge. Its goal is unification of sciences and scientific analysis.[9]

The movement in this direction was started in 1920 by Ludwig von Bertallanfy, but it could flourish only after the Second World War. In moved from Biology to Physics, to Physical Chemistry, to Ecology and then Social Sciences. W.R. Ashby (*Design for a Brain,* 1952; and *An Introduction to Cybernetics,* 1956) represents this trend. In 1956, the Society for the Advancement of General Systems Research was constituted which published its year-book regularly. Social sciences took up this perspective through Parsons (1951-58), Homans (1950), Roethlisberger, Dickson, etc. Scholars, thus, began to looking for the concepts lending unity to studies undertaken in a variety of disciplines. Insights and theoretical contributions from various disciplines were made profusely available. All this was done around the concept of 'system'.

It is a departure from describing structures composed of units, parts and static conception of *equilibrium* based on mechanistic assumptions. Its basic principle is organismic with an attitude of 'open system'. According to Quincy Wright, in a prime sense, it is 'a way of thinking having the proportion of a world view'.[10] An open system continually exchanges 'materials' in its local environment and also with systems range of which is set, presumably, by organisational conditions. Each of these social systems has its own unique non-material characteristics, but all conform to the underlying character of living open systems.

The emphasis of General Systems Theory is more on uniformities underlying their principles of functioning and processes and less on structural similarities. It is in search of fundamental and highly orienting concepts relevant to all kinds of systems. It seeks isomorphism e.g. one-to-one correspondence between objects in different systems.

This theory is closely connected with the Systems Theory/Approach, and can be considered a concrete, logical and methodological expression of its principles and methods.

Some of the principles or limits of General Systems Theory are:

(a) organismic concepts as against atomistic and isolable concepts;
(b) components of the open systems are maintained constantly by exchanges in the environment;
(c) components lower in the hierarchy of organisation enter and leave the general system;
(d) there is dynamism, e.g., within the limits of its organisation, it tends to maintain itself and does not stick to any specific state of equilibrium. It can be viewed as a steady state;
(e) without any direction from above, its members eliminate disruptions, and try to restore order. This is an inherent, dynamic and unending tendency;
(f) its innate order is augmented by many other auxiliary components and resources, as part of homeostasis or feedback; and
(g) its final outcomes are not determined by initial conditions but by conditions of outflow and inflow over a period of time, called, 'equifinality' or adaptive dynamism.

Its assumption is: the more highly elaborated the system and the more complex its transactions are, the greater is its adjustive 'power'. Every system – a tribe, a nation or a regional organisation or world system avoids 'entropy', death or decay.

The General Systems Theory can also be viewed either as 'one general systems theory' or as 'general theory of systems'. The former is a broad conceptual category, perspective or orientation, seen as a hierarchy of systems and subsystems. The latter is an empirical theory applicable to all systems – common elements and processes found in independent and autonomous systems.

Main Concepts

'*System*' is the central and guiding concept of this theory. Other concepts relate to (a) description of system, (b) regulation and maintenance of that system, (c) changes occurring in the system, and (d) anomic and radical changes. The main thesis of this theory is to put all disciplines on some fundamental, uniform, and universal basis. Systems studied by various disciplines may be different in terms of size, time, volume, material etc., but can be similar from the view of their fundamental structure and processes. If basic uniformities found in various systems are discovered, a general theory of systems can come out. But this perspective does not stop with surface or apparent uniformity or analogous appearance. It looks for more than homology rather isomorphism. Its emphasis is more on uniformity underlying their principles of functioning and processes, and less on structural similarities. Therefore, general systems theorists explain the concept of 'system' at a higher level of abstraction. A system, according to Bertallanfy is 'a set of elements standing in interaction'.[11] A. Hall and R. Fagen defined it as 'a set of objects together with relationships between the objects and between their attributes'.[12] Colin Cherry found it 'as a whole which is compounded of many parts – an ensemble of attributes'. Others find it as 'a group of objects or elements stemming in some characteristic structural relationships to one another and interacting on the basis of certain characteristic processes'. For Easton it is 'a set of interactions'. There are many other definitions. These definitions involve two things: (i) The idea of a group of objects or elements standing in some specific structural relationship, and (ii) these objects or elements interacting on the basis of certain characteristic processes.

There are two approaches available from the viewpoint of empirical operationality of this generic concept. The first emphasises operationality of the 'system'. It would make use of the concept 'system' only when there are some empirical elements visible to the scholar; when those elements are inter-related in an important manner and the level of interrelatedness is sufficiently high. Such a system (1) should be observable in the context of time and place, (2) it should have its existence recognised by many disciplines, and (3) its structures and processes should undergo change over a period of time. One must keep analytic and physical systems separate and look into interdependence of their objects and elements.[13]

The second approach makes use of the concept of 'system' for constructivist and heuristic purposes, for data-gathering and analysis. David Easton, in his *A Framework for Political Analysis* (1965), adopts this perspective. (See, infra, p. 120) Such scholars decide about the existence of a particular system only at the end of their research. They regard the first approach as unattainable, even false. At the initial stage, 'system' is a guiding and directing tool of inquiry. Its reality or existence can be accepted only after verification and reaching certain empirical conclusions.

However, the main emphasis of the general systems theory is on the use of abstract concepts relevant to all systems. It moves around the concepts of *isomorphism* and *interlocking systems. Isomorphism* connotes one-to-one correspondence between the systems regarding the relationships existing among their objects. *Interlocking system* relates to correspondences across systems, and involves the existence of a subset of a broader system. Subsets of a broader system can be similar to one or more additional systems. There can be some basic similarities in the governing principles or processes of systems. Through these concepts all systems become interconnected: smaller subsystems look parts of a general system.

Other Concepts

Oran R. Young has divided these concepts into four major groups:

1. *Descriptive concepts:* These concepts are used in classifying large collection of data and giving the outline of the basic structure processes of various types of systems. On the basis of their subject matter, various sub-categories are suggested, such as, (i) concept that separate different kinds of system, such as, open and closed systems, or organismic and non-organismic systems; (ii) concepts concerning hierarchical levels, such as, subsystem, orders of interaction, and scale effects; (iii) concepts dealing with internal aspects of the systems, such as, integration, differentiation, interdependence, and centralisation; (iv) concepts relating to the interaction of systems with their environment, such as, boundaries, inputs, and outputs, and (v) concepts dealing with the various paths which the system may be following over time, such as, state-determinedness, equifinality, etc.
2. *Concepts relating to regulation and maintenance:* They relate to the notions of stability, equilibrium and homeostasis. Others concern processes, such as, feedback, repair, reproduction, and entropy. In sum, these concepts connote the ways and means by which systems maintain and regulate their identity over a period of time.
3. *Concepts pertaining to non-disruptive change:* They deal with the dynamics of systems. Change occurs either through internally generated processes or through responses to altered environmental conditions. These concepts include adaptation, learning, growth, and reversible or irreversible developments.
4. *Concepts pertaining to disruptive change:* These relate to the phenomena of disruption, dissolution, and breakdown. Other relevant notions are crisis, stress, strain, overload and decay.

All these concepts make up the body of the general systems theory, and can form the basis of studying each and every type of system – micro or macro. With the unifying umbrella concept of 'system', it can analyse all internal, external, regulating, and changing aspects of a concrete or an abstract system. That system can be either UNO or a political party or a club.

As a theory, it is an integrated and generalised set of concepts, hypotheses, and validated propositions (if any). From this viewpoint, it consists of an integrated set of high level principles dealing with all significant elements of a system often pertaining to many disciplines. Greater the number of systems and disciplines involved in it, greater will be the advancement toward its goal.

The second approach, as stated earlier, finds system as an apparatus or a set of techniques and a framework of a systematic process of empirical analysis. In place of specific principles and propositions of the theory, the interest is in the framework for analysing and organising data. Its utility lies in the usefulness of the framework for research purposes. There is no interest here in it as a theory; it is an analytic framework more in line with the scientific method. Easton has used it as a framework.

Uses and Limitations

General systems theory provides a source of concepts and working models for systematic empirical analysis. They can be applied to many substantive areas and generate empirically verifiable hypotheses. It has rendered service in standardising terminology, coding data, and storing information. Isomorphism and interlocking systems have provided a great attraction for empirical work. It has given ample scope for the use of mathematical and computational techniques. It has given a very useful framework for classifying and analysing macro systems. As its concepts, through the central theme of 'system', are common to many disciplines, it has a regulative role, particularly in an area where such concepts have remained alien.

Role in Political Science

General systems theory in its theoretical form has rarely been applied. Political Science lacks high level of theoretical consciousness as well as a programme of systematic abstract analysis. It lacks the basic conceptual and prepositional material.

Still some of its concepts have become popular and are used in a wide variety of contexts, such as, stability, feedback, entropy, etc. In practice, it is being used as a form of general orientation or a frame of reference. Such attempts help it to rise above beaten tracks. But it is not the proper use of general systems theory.

This theory can help in developing a set of basic principles applicable to a large variety of political systems. As its scope is broader and higher, its level of abstraction can envelope many disciplines, and accommodate multiple middle and lower range theories. At a time, when a general theory of politics is not available, it can serve as a blueprint for completing that long and arduous programme. It can put complementary qualities of various approaches to a workable integrated pattern for its use to political analysis. In that pattern, various approaches would have to give up or shed their crudities and redundancies. As it contains a rich storehouse of descriptive and classificatory concepts, it can sort out a large quantity of data and put them under manageable patterns and uniformities. Some of the concepts, such as stability, equilibrium, pattern-maintenance, etc., have been used in a loose manner. But political scientists have not been very clear about notions like systemic breakdown, decay and other political pathologies. Systems theory has facilitated communication among various disciplines, and it has been possible to borrow a lot from them. It is more useful for the analysis of macro-systems, providing a complete framework for the classification of large amount of data, it comes closer to political phenomena available at local, regional, national, and international levels. Concept of isomorphism helps in making use of our understanding one system to another, and of a subsystem to the system. Thus both micro and macro analyses can supplement each other. However, there is some inherent conservatism in the theory. For some areas, like political power, influence, conflict, etc., this theory does not appear to be very relevant. It studies control mechanisms of systems, but leaves out the questions of scope, depth, and weight of power. By its nature, it is unable to deal with questions concerning strategy and tactics of employing power, psychology of political behaviour, decision making, goal formation, and alternative sets of policy making.

Difficulties

It has been observed that the concept of isomorphism, observing one-to-one correspondence between systems, is abstract and deductive. There is a tendency to force things into the 'boxes' or isomorphic categories. A 'constructive' use of general systems theory can be permitted, but as a theory of empirical reality, it can be considered methodologically inadequate. It has an extremely elaborate and abstract conceptual structure which cannot generate viable hypotheses and propositions. A good number of its concepts lack empirical operationalisation, as in case of searching indices of 'open' and 'close' systems. However, most of the criticism of general systems theory is based on its conservative and pro-establishment nature. As most of the countries of the Third World are interested in making radical changes and throw off the status quo, this theory has a little appeal and use for them.

General systems theory offers little in the study problems of political power and influence, though deals with control mechanism – its scope, depth and weight of power. The unit of 'system' makes its difficult to conceptualise questions of strategy and tactics of employing power and influence. It cannot study perception, expectation, formation or cognition about power.

It has almost no use in examining the policy making processes pertaining to goal-formation or alternative sets of policy.[14]

Systems Theory

Systems theory, as it stands today, has only analytical or conceptual relationship with general systems theory. Historically, systems theory is prior, methodologically more empirical, and, practically more useful. But it relates, only to one discipline. Like general systems theory, it does not cover all political and non-political phenomena, and conjoins or does housekeeping for all disciplines. However, systems theory, too has not yet emerged as an explanatory empirical theory, and is still used for constructivist or heuristic purposes, and as a conceptual framework or approach for political analysis. It is particularly framed for the study of politics and its central conceptual apparatus is also used in a narrower sense. Recently, there has been a successful thrust by automation and computerisation programmes. Relevant data have been collected and set on computers, operated on the outlines of systems theory, and results read out to relevant segments of political life.[15]

Background

There is a lack of unanimity regarding conceptual relationship of systems theory with other approaches and theories. Easton regards it as applied form of functionalism.[16] Eugene J. Meehan identifies it with general systems theory and functionalism. Herbert J. Spiro disagrees with them and maintains that 'system' as a concept in Political Science is more than three centuries old. He has pointed out that Hobbes discusses the concept on chapter 22 of *Leviathan*. According to Kaplan, Aristotle was the first system theorist. But Almond and Powell accept the theoretical influence of sociology, economics, and cybernetics on the concept of 'system'. Their systems approach, while remaining in the tradition of political thought, has been adopted only as a conceptual apparatus. David Easton and Karl Deutsch have taken the concept from sociological and communication theories. From this view, Almond and Powell regard their systems approach as different from the concept of both Easton and Deutsch. Almond and Powell related it to the principle of separation of powers as given in the *Federalist Papers*, which came out of the changes released by the forces of enlarged franchise and industrialisation. They regard it an empirical concept.[17] Morton A. Kaplan has used systems theory in the analysis of international politics.

Thus, many scholars, both sociologists and political scientists, consider it a kind of functionalism. (For 'functionalism', See chapter 5) But 'pure' system theorists do not accept their view. Functionalism lays more stress on maintenance and equilibrium of the system. In the system perspective, attention is concentrated more on the system as a whole and its interaction with internal and external environment. Still both systems theory and functionalism, by their nature, origin, role and development are close to each other, yet for analytical purposes they should be kept apart. The concept of 'system' is not new to Political Science, still it has been invoked afresh by David Easton. In the elaboration and use of the concept, he is much influenced by Ashby, Parsons, Merton and others, but it is novel in presentation. However, he has developed it as a conceptual framework for political analysis, but he himself has not used it. Mainly A. Almond, Apter, Coleman, Eckstein, Kaplan, etc have undertaken its use as a 'theory' for conducting empirical investigation. Gabriel A. Almond has applied it in the studies of development and comparative politics. Morton A. Kaplan has used it in the field of international politics. Systems theory is indebted to general systems theory, but at present, it is more interested in its application to political system only.

Perspective of 'Political System'

System theorists in Political Science adopt the perspective of 'system' in their study of politics. In comparison with general system theorists, they like to define it in a narrow and restricted manner. As such, the latter are interested in 'political system', and not 'systems' in general. A political system can be seen as a set of objects together with relationships, between the objects and between their attributes, or, a whole which is compounded of many parts – an ensemble of attributes; or, a set of elements standing in interaction; or a group of objects or elements standing in some characteristic structural relationships to one another and interacting on the basis of certain characteristic processes.[18] Even the society can be seen as a system of functionally inter-related variables. Robert T. Holt finds the social system as the system of interdependent roles and corporate structures of society. As such, a system involves some constantly cognisable processes underlying a set of persons, relations, actions, roles, structures or events. Every system carries some natural or artificial purposes, objectives, or goals. It can be concrete or abstract, empirical or transempirical, observable or abstract. The railway system is concrete, empirical and observable, but the ethical or Hegelian system is abstract, ideational, and non-empirical. Some systems can be both, semi-concrete or semi-abstract, as in case of political system. Each system consists of some actions, activities or interrelations. They can be natural, motivated or contrived. If ecosystem is natural, an education system can more or less, be regarded as contrived. Attempt to bring in a socialist or secular system in India or elsewhere can be considered as motivated. Every system is built of certain basic material. This basic material is operated by and through its units, organs, subsystems, processes and activities. Each system, in due course of time, develops some specific characteristics, tools, means, and techniques. If the basic element of human physiology is life or consciousness, the religious system depends on faith in God. They have their own tools, techniques, methods, and styles to accomplish their goals.

However, it is not always easy to know the basic, elemental or key material of a system. One can easily know and recognise the means, methods, and instrumentalities of a concrete and empirical system like the water or light system of a city. But one often becomes helpless in the delineation of an ethical or a religious system. A man can know it only by observing its symbols, relevant expressions, and other indirect behaviour patterns. As regards their forms and goals, there are acute conflicts and controversies. However, most of the systems are related to each other in some direct or indirect manner. As such, their mutual relationships can take up hundreds of kaleidoscopic forms, independent, dependent, semi-independent, simple, complex, direct, indirect, etc. It is always difficult to measure and objectively evaluate the power, influence, capacity, capability, activities, and quantum and quality of relations, particularly in case of abstract systems. Cohen rightly observes a system as 'any ongoing set of recurrent and interrelated social actions'.

Similar is the controversy on the nature of 'political system' in the field of Political Science. There are sharp differences over the nature of state organisation even among traditional thinkers. After the behavioural revolution, political scientists have replaced 'state' by 'political system', considering the former as formal, inadequate and unsatisfactory. Still it is not clear which is the central element of political system. Classical political thinkers had found knowledge, reason, natural land, religion or conventional law as the basic element of state. Most of the modern political scientists find 'legitimate physical compulsion' as the key variable of political system. For Easton, it is 'authoritative allocation of values for society'. Lasswell and Kaplan regard 'severe deprivations' as the basic material of political systems. Dahl relates it to power, government and authority. Catlin discovers 'control over wills' as the basis. Almond defines the political system, more or less, as 'the legitimate, order-maintaining or transforming system in the society'.

All the scholars have called its various organs and processes in varying terms. Easton has put them in the two broad categories of 'inputs' and 'outputs'. Almond and Coleman have classified them into seven functional categories, putting four under 'inputs' and three under 'outputs'. Lasswell has analysed them as seven processes. There is a total lack of unanimity regarding form, structures, organs and processes of a political system. Almost all, Bottomore, Weber, Binder, Shils, Almond and Coleman, Almond and Powell, Eisenstedt, etc., have classified political systems in different manner.

Systems Theory (Approach) in Political Science

Considering the development of an all-inclusive and universal or abstract theory as unattainable by empirical methods, political scientists have adopted the limited perspective of 'systems theory'. Several disciplines have contributed to its making and development. It represents interdisciplinary nature of modern Political Science. 'Systems' concept makes empirical and comparative study possible even of those political institutions, apart from the state, such as, international political system, city, political party, etc. The concept is helpful in studying changes like transformation, feedback, exchange, tension, conflict and development. Besides Easton, Gabriel Almond, Talcott Parsons, Karl Deutsch, Morton Kaplan and others have made such studies.

Systems theory analyses interactions, structures, institutions, and processes pertaining to politics. Politics involves power, authority, physical coercion, and allocation of values for society. In all shades of politics, political processes, and structures are enmeshed with several other elements, factors, and considerations. As such, a 'political system' cannot be physically separated from its non-political aspects, and is, therefore, usually understood and studied in an analytical manner. Society as a whole makes up the general social system, which contains many subsystems. Political system is one of these subsystems. When the political system is to be studied as a whole along with its intra-subsystems, then, it is treated as a 'system'. Besides that, 'system' can be considered as a part of environment. Thus, the concept of 'system' both in interlocking micro and macro forms, saves us from the error of considering 'systems' as isolated, separate, or independent entities. Besides throwing light on their interconnections, one can examine their discrete nature, and separate empirical existence. According to Almond, the political system in a society, is 'legitimate, order maintaining' or transforming system'. Wiseman maintains that every political system involves political structures, actors, or roles performed by their agents, interaction-patterns existing between individuals or collectivities, and political processes. In the 'political system' of Kaplan also, there are recognisable multivariate interests. Instead of always being opposite, sometimes they are complementary to each other. There are regular structures and channels to reach the decisions and judgments related to particular interests. General rules are prescribed to govern the actors and activities relating to particular decisions and judgments. Easton, therefore, regards the political system engaged in decision-making and implementing the authoritative allocation of values for society. A political system, according to Michels, has the following features:

(a) It is a permanent entity, existing amidst a broader environment and includes many other units;

(b) It consists of an identifiable and measurable set of interdependent elements or variables;
(c) It has boundaries which keep it separate from general environment;
(d) It is constituted around certain problems, objectives or goals, and builds up certain structures;
(e) Along with the increase of specific problems and evolution of goals, it develops specific structures and processes, leading to more and more differentiation.

Still political scientists, sociologists, and political sociologists have analysed political systems with varying frames of references and different goals. More important among them are Talcott Parsons, David Easton, Gabriel Almond, and Morton Kaplan. Perspectives of Parsons and Easton are more conceptual. Almond and Kaplan have gone towards empirical research and theory making. Thus there are many variations among them.

Systems Theory: David Easton

David Easton's 'systems theory', though developed for 'constructivist' purposes and is a conceptual framework for analysing politics, yet it is useful for constructing an empirical theory of Political Science as well as using it in understanding actual forces operating in a political system. The political actors and citizens can know 'what', 'where' and 'how' of political operations, and take remedial actions. Third world countries can gain a lot from its study and actual use, avoiding many risks, crises, and difficulties. Advanced countries already make use of it in one form or other.

Easton presented his conceptual framework in his *The Political System* (1953). He elaborated it further, in 1965, in his two books, *A Framework for Political Analysis,* and *A Systems Analysis of Political Life.* In the first, he has presented an outline of the conceptual framework of systems analysis. In the next, he has further developed it in detail, but its title is misleading as he has not done therein any actual empirical analysis. Besides, he has written a large number of articles, and edited many books. He is a proclaimed spokesman of two academic revolutions – behavioural and post-behavioural. The centre of his attention is in bringing about disciplinary integration in Political Science through the evaluation of a general theory. He believes that systems framework can serve his purpose. Later on, it has come out in form of input-output analysis which has proved useful for empirical and practical purposes.

Easton's input-output analysis is also known as the 'flow model'. It can be regarded as a form of functionalist analysis. Young finds his framework as 'the most inclusive systemic approach so far constructed specifically for political analysis by a political scientist'.[19] It is a product of an original insight of a political scientist. It is neither borrowed nor smuggled from other disciplines. Easton, according to Meehan, is the most consistent and systematic functionalist of Political Science, though he may not agree to that categorisation. He attempts to provide a 'general' functional theory of politics. 'System' is the broad unit of his analysis. But his 'system' is intermeshed with many 'inter' and 'intra' systems. In this matter, he comes closer to the general systems theory. But he is interested in the 'constructivist' aspect of the approach, as he does not make its use in conducting empirical research. His concept of 'system' is conceptual, analytical, and abstract. He wants to explicate a conceptual framework which may ultimately emerge as a general theory of totality of political life. Thus, he is the Talcott Parson of Political Science. He is committed to stability, order, and persistence of 'systems' but his perspective is political. The concept of 'system' takes on towards integration of various disciplines.

Main Concepts

The basic unit of Easton's system analysis is 'interaction'. Interaction is generated from the behaviour of the members of the system when they play their role as such. When these myriad interactions, in the perception of the scholar, become a 'set of interrelations', they are considered as a 'system'. Easton's subject matter of analysis is only the set of political interactions.

There are four major premises or broader concepts of his flow-model or input-output analysis: (i) system; (ii) environment; (iii) response; and (iv) feedback. In the analysis of politics, one has to make use of these concepts.

System

His system is a 'political system', the basic unit of analysis. It is a 'system of interactions in any society through which binding or authoritative allocations are made and implemented.' Easton is interested in studying political life which is seen as a system of behaviour operating within and responding to its social environment while making binding allocations of values. The making of binding and authoritative decisions distinguishes the political system from other systems (existing both within and outside the overall society) that form the environment of that political system.

Within this political system, there are many political groups and organisations, called para-political systems. But he is more concerned with 'political system' standing as the most inclusive unit of political life. Political system, as such, is found everywhere. It is the inclusive whole of all political interactions. Easton analyses the nature, conditions, and life processes of political life operating in form of an analytic system.

By adopting the concept of 'system', Easton has free Political Science from its traditional, legalistic, institutional, and formal moorings, and proposes to view it as it really is. This 'system' is made of interactions of those persons who take part in public life, and are related with making and implementing of public policies. Easton is not satisfied to see 'political activity' merely as 'direction of man by man' (de Jouvenel), or as 'relating to control or will' (Catlin), or 'relation between influencer and the influenced' (Lasswell). It is also not adequate to see politics related to authority, power, government and rule (Dahl). His concept of system is more inclusive.

In a sense, his concept of 'system' is integrative involving values, culture, authority, governance, implementation, participation, process, etc. 'System' is a very wide term, which includes all forms of formal and informal processes, interactions, functions, structures, values, behaviour, etc. The political system allocates values for the whole society and its decisions stand obligatory. A 'system', thus, can be any set of variables, whatever be the form or intensity of interactions or interrelationship operating among them. A political system is a subsystem of the societal system, but it has a binding power of its own. Even within a political system, there are many subsystems.

Easton's political system is both open and adaptive. Exchanges take place between a political system and its environment which is made of many systems and their subsystems, including even para-political systems. All these, and other various events and influences make up the conditions under which members of a political system act and react. The latter can find these as favourable or obstructive to its survival. As such, it must have the capacity to face those obstructions, and adapt itself to those conditions. Most often, a political system has a trait or capacity to adapt itself to changing environment. Political systems contrive mechanisms to regulate their own moves, transform internal structures, and even reformulate goals.

A political system, like any other system, has boundaries. These boundaries relate to the formation of political interactions and go on changing. The political system, somehow, tends to maintain its systemic boundaries, and boundary conditions. In other words, it has to carefully look after and protect its life-processes or capacity to respond effectively to external environment or internal influences. It has to operate as an effective transforming process. In case, it is unable to maintain its boundaries, it may lose its identity, even merge into other systems.

It may be reiterated that Eastonian framework of systems theory is conceptual and analytical. His 'political system' is born of concepts, and is conceptual or 'constructivist', used as a set of variables selected for description, explanation, and research. It is different from, and not, a concrete or natural system. An actual, concrete or natural system, also called as membership-system, consists of human beings or actual individuals. Easton's analytic system is made of abstractions that focus selected elements of human behaviour. His system, thus, is a set of particular interactions, which is related to allocation of values that are binding for society and their implementation, within that membership or concrete system, called society. Binding nature of the set of interactions is another quality separating political system from other systems. This abstract analytic system interacts with its environment, converting its inputs into outputs through processes or withinputs, and feedback as shown in the following diagram:

Diagram 1

Dynamic Model of Easton's Political System

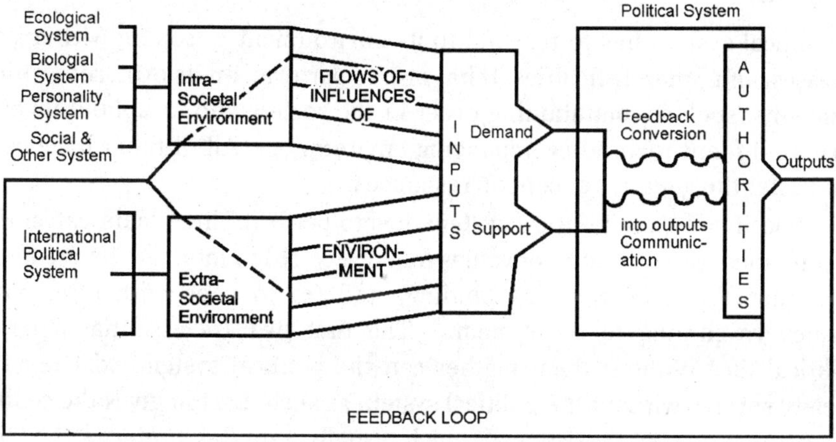

Environment

Easton's political system is a complex set of certain processes or interactions which transforms particular inputs into outputs of authoritative policies, decisions, and implementation. This conversion takes place in some environment. As an open system, it must have the resilience to respond to that environment, facing all obstacles, and adjusting itself to conditions. Only by doing so, it can survive or exist over a period of time. Analytically, environment can be of two types: (i) extra-societal, and (ii) intra-societal. As given in the Diagram above extra-societal environment involves international political systems, like various political systems, alliances, UNO, etc.; international ecological systems; and, international social systems, as cultural, socio-structural, economic, demographic, and other systems. Intra-societal systems include ecological, biological, personality-oriented, social, cultural, socio-structural, and demographic systems operating within the political system. Conflicts, strains, and changes emerging out of environment can prove functional or dysfunctional to that political system. Therefore, the latter should have, for its survival, persistent capability to respond to that environment. Easton rightly puts more emphasis on the *capacity* of the system to cope with the environment. Countries of the Third World can find a lot of useful material in Easton's concept of 'environment', and required 'capacity' to deal with it.

Easton has pointed out that system theorists have spoken a lot on the first two concepts – 'system' and 'environment'. As regards the third and fourth concepts of 'response' and 'feedback', he can be said to have made his own contribution to systems theory. In fact, the latter concepts, instead of being singular ones, are clusters of many concepts. So is the case with the first two concepts also.

Response

A political system has to respond to its environment in coping with crises, stresses, and other difficulties. It has also to perform, on its own, some other functions, such as, maintaining order in the society and to uphold its own form and identity amid everchanging environment. All of them have been put under the generic concept of 'response'.

Specifically, the political system, has to perform three main categories of functions: (a) allocation of values for society, (b) to motivate its members to accept the allocations as binding, and (c) to cope with stress and challenges coming to the system.[20] The first two are essential parts of political life. Without them neither can the political system exist nor the society survive without the political system as such. Easton gives the central place to 'systemic persistence' which usually remains under 'stress' for several factors. The system has to look into the sources of stress and modes or processes of regulating stress. A political system is a set of interacting essential variables which fluctuate within a certain limit or range. It cannot go beyond its 'critical range'. The system is considered under 'stress', if the essential variables push it to cross over the critical range. The system tries to remain within critical range, but at times, it is compelled to go beyond. For its survival and persistence, it has to respond in many ways – at the level of demands or support, or at output or feedback levels. The political system collapses in case it is unable to cope with coming stresses and crises. Therefore, it is always necessary constantly to evaluate the nature of stresses, capacity of the system to cope with, and the means and methods to do so. The political system is driven by: (a) 'demands' and challenges made on it, and (b) 'support', it gets from its members. It meets the challenge of demands with the help of supports, but it can manipulate and regulate both. It receives them in form of 'inputs' from its environment, the society at large. These inputs are converted into 'outputs', but the system also keeps a watch over effects and consequences of its outputs through 'feedback', which helps it constantly to modify its inputs as well as outputs. Easton's political system, in a way, is a conversion process in which inputs are transformed into outputs, helped and guided by feedback. All the systemic responses are broadly divided into two categories: (a) inputs, and (b) outputs.

(a) Inputs

Inputs are responses entering into the system. They consist of: (1) demands, and (2) supports. Demands put strain or stress on the system, whereas support provides energy to sustain it. Though the two are of different nature, still they make up one category of 'inputs' to be converted into 'outputs' through withinputs or the conversion process. Easton does not discuss the nature or form of withinputs. The political system receives both demands and supports from society or environment. It is driven by demands, and sustained by supports.

(1) *Demands:* Demand is 'an expression of opinion that an authoritative allocation with regard to a particular subject matter should or should not be made by those responsible for doing so'.[21] It can take the form of stress, effects, demands, agitations, crises etc. all coming from environment. They all intend to influence, move, modify, or change the political system, and can be undifferentiated wants, articulated recognizable demands, or specific issues. Mostly, they are of collective or public nature. Demands are, after their determination, satisfied through 'allocation of values'. Demands can take several forms, such as, provision for certain things, services, and conveniences; regulating public behaviour; participating in the political system, for making symbolic expressions, etc. A system may not be in a position to convert all demands into outputs. It looks into quantity, nature of contents, source, kind, volume, intensity, etc. Only a few demands reach the output stage. Excessive demands put stress over the system, and cause 'overload'. Overload may be due to the volume, intensity, velocity, urgency, and contents of the demand.

In order to deal with the problem of overload or excessive demands, the political system can make use of several 'regulatory mechanisms':

(i) *Structural mechanism*: It is located at the boundary of the system and regulates the flow of articulation of demands. Unimportant demands are scrutinised and regulated by and through various gatekeeping roles. They may not even be allowed to enter the system.

(ii) *Cultural mechanism:* On the basis of prevailing socio-cultural norms, certain demands can be designated as incompatible with them, thus, lessened in considerable manner, if not rejected altogether. Sometimes they become the basis or constraints of political demands.

(iii) *Communication channels:* Through the use of TV, radio, correspondence, press, etc. demands may be strengthened or weakened or diluted to a considerable extent.

(iv) *Reduction processes:* Demands may be reduced to a limited number through a process-selection, scrutiny, grouping, etc. Some criteria, general or restricted, may be added to it.

(2) *Support:* A political system also receives support from its environment. After subtracting demands from inputs, we get supports which operate between the system and its environment. They are positive responses towards specific objects or level of a political system. Support can be towards (a) the *political community* which means the acceptance of political division of labour; (b) the *regime* which embodies basic values, political structures, and norms underlying the political system; and (c) the political *authorities* or persons holding power in the given context. Support can be given at some particular or all levels. Support to political community reflects paying regard to the general form and arrangement of power in the society, and acceptance of the demarcation between the political and non-political. Support to a regime broadly means legitimacy of the system, its constitutionality, basic structure, and inherent values. The last level invokes holding of respect, loyalty, and obedience to the particular persons wielding political authority. It includes administrators and officials.

The support can be rendered in many ways – by paying taxes, obedience to law, participation in the form of voting, discussion, comments, and constructive suggestions, or deference towards public authorities. The form and style of expressing support can be overt or covert, positive or negative, diffuse or specific, and so on. Often the political system obtains support by and through allocation values and implementation thereof, manipulation of outputs, socialisation, and other political means. Without support at a certain minimum level, no political system can persist. There can be many causes of failure, as is the case with some Third World countries for not getting support from their populace, such as inadequate use of regulatory mechanism, non-generation of support, and neglect of outputs.

(b) Outputs

Outputs are the decisions and actions of the authorities. They produce effects and consequences which have direct relation with the members' attitude and behaviour for the system. Easton calls them as 'authoritative allocation of values', 'binding decisions and actions', or 'exchange between the system and its environment'. Output is turnout or production made by the political authorities. It is the flow of those responses which go from the system to environment. Outputs are converted inputs or finished goods prepared from the raw material of inputs. Even the political authorities themselves can also take initiative in the making of outputs. They are the results of the transformation process of the political system.

Outputs reveal many forms – realisation of taxes, regulation of public behaviour and conduct, distribution of honours, goods, and services, allocation of values, display of symbolic outputs, etc. They are reflected in verbal or written statements from the authorities as well as concrete actions. They can be the effects or results of immediately authorised decisions.

If they relate to decisions taken in distant past, they would be called as 'outcome'. In case they are not binding, they would be named as co-outputs. Outputs can be inter or intra systemic. In all cases, they release support-stress. They can be regarded as a primary source to get specific support, but a satisfactory flow of output over a period of time tends to produce all-out or diffuse support.

Outputs have several aspects – economic, social, cultural, political, etc. From the viewpoint of political system, political aspects of the outputs are more important. They influence the broader society or environment, and also determine the need and form of each succeeding round of inputs. Even the form, need, and quality of support depends on it.

Feedback Loop

'*Feedback*' is another important concept in Easton's systems theory. Capacity of a political system to persist over time depends on feedback. It is a dynamic process through which information about the outputs and the environment is communicated to the system which may result in subsequent change or modification of the system. Information about demands and supports may enter the system as inputs in usual manner. When information relating to converted inputs, or outputs comes in, then there is a kind of re-communication of information, or re-inputation of inputs already converted into outputs. By doing so, the political system gets an opportunity to modify or transform its behaviour conducive to that feedback. In this manner, it can make it more effective or persist in a better way. In the absence of feedback, it is likely to operate in the usual unresponsive manner, and lose support. Information about environment reaching as inputs in usual manner may enter the system too late. It may reach there in a distorted form, as it happened with Indira Gandhi Government (1977) and the Shah of Iran (1979). 'Loop' means a curve that rejoins the main line farther on. 'Feedback Loop' connotes a process wherein information is obtained; actions, reactions or responses are made on it; then to see the result, and re-collect the same; and, to be benefited by it to achieve the goal. It includes the arrangement and linking of information channels for the aforesaid purpose. Feedback involves a continuity by linking of obtaining information, reacting, and knowing the effects further to improve upon Systems behaviour and responses. It is a 'output-information-reinputation-recommunication-reoutputation' process.

Feedback process, in this way, is concerned with input sequence, demands and support emerging out of environment, conversion processes, outputs, and feedback mechanisms. Feedback mechanisms carry effects and consequences of the outputs into the system again as inputs. They make the system dynamic, purposive, and goal-oriented. Interactions and their various forms within a system confront the problems of stress, maintenance, etc., by counter-balancing, by reducing, or by removal. But their interaction-circuits may remain incomplete or breakdown at any point, e.g., stoppage at the level of demands. A demand has to go alongwith the long conversion process. Its shape, size and content may considerably change till it reaches the output-stage. Sometimes, the demand dies out by then completely. Similarly, information coming from the environment may not be considered as a 'demand' by the authorities. Ultimately, the latter have to decide whether some allocation of values should be made to meet that demand or not. But reaction or response to every such breakdown of the circuit has to be taken into consideration for further action and implementation by the system.

Easton presents the concept of 'feedback loop' as the basis of the capacity of the outputs to generate specific support. It connects the consequences of the outputs with the inflow of inputs: demands and supports. Thus, it establishes a circulatory relationship between inputs and outputs. There is all-round impact of this dynamic process – on support, stress, survival and persistence. It completes the political circuit through its input – conversion – output – feedback process. In a political system, several feedback processes operate at various levels. But Easton relates the feedback processes pertaining to the whole political system.

For analytical purposes, there are two forms of feedback: (1) negative feedback – it relates to the information regarding the system and the regulation of errors; and (2) goal-transforming feedback – it is concerned with the purposeful redirection of the system. In all conditions, feedback is a regulatory demand of political systems. However, feedback itself can suffer from many pathologies, regarding accuracy, responsiveness, time-lag, etc. Several mistakes can take place in the process of communication. Even delayed information can cause great harm to the survival of a political system.

The feedback loop can be analysed from several angles. From the view of system-maintenance or gaining specific support, its operation can be divided into four stages: (1) There are *situations* of feedback, which can come out of authorised direction, associate outputs, or outcomes. They all are part of the political system. But its estimation depends on its perception or observation. (2) There are *feedback-responses* which can be in the form of satisfying the demands, or positive or negative support. (3) In the third stage feedback-responses are communicated to the political authorities.

(4) In the last stage, after completion of the feedback-circuit the authorities deliberate, discuss, and arrive at certain decisions. Much depends on variables like responsiveness of authorities, time-lag, availability of information-resources for decision-making, etc. Here, resources of the system as a whole are involved. The feedback loop, in Easton's input-output analysis, interlinks authorities and its members in a manner that the former may take steps soon after they get information through the feedback.

Goal of Persistence and Flow Model

The goal of Easton's political system is to maintain 'persistence' and not 'equilibrium'. He is a critic of equilibrium-approach. His system converts demands and supports into outputs through feedback mechanisms. It is not a routine operation, but a complex cyclic process with a dynamism peculiar to it. The system has its own goal which it tries to reach by facing problems of stress and maintenance. His analytical framework is based on two critical variables: (i) sources of stress and persistence of the system, and (ii) regulating processes or mechanisms of regulating these stresses. Persistence stands for continuity of the capacity of the system to allocate values to the members in a binding manner and implement them. In Easton's words, it is 'the continuation of the capacity of a system to make and execute binding decisions of allocations on its members.'[22] It is a unique trait of political systems. It maintains the system with all modifications and changes entering into its environment. It transforms inputs into outputs, which influence the environment, and creation of inputs. The feedback mechanisms communicate reactions and responses to the outputs of the environment to the system. The latter are interlocking cycles within the systematic cycle, and there is endless, interlinked, and interactive flow of operations which constantly change, and subsequently change the behaviour of the system. Thus, Easton presents a *flow model* of political system. It has an extraordinary capacity to adjust to, and sometimes even to transform the environment. For this, there operate so many processes and mechanisms, unlike other systems. Apart from regulating its own behaviour and maintaining itself amid changes, it transforms its own structure, even reformulate its goals.

In equilibrium approaches, scholars, mostly sociologists, give all importance to: (i) stability or maintenance of the system as it is; and (ii) neglect the environment or processes bringing about change in the system itself. They overlook the system's capacity to cope with the problems coming from environment. A system, beyond the assumptions of these scholars, can have goals other than maintaining its equilibrium. At times, it may like to destroy an already existing equilibrium or wish to acquire a new pattern of equilibrium. It may, as Easton opines, like to change its environment so that transactions between the environment and the system are not stressful. It may seek to insulate itself against undue pressures from the environment, and, the members 'even fundamentally transform their own relationships and modify their own goals and practices so as to improve their chances of handling the inputs from the environment.'[23] Easton's system has the capacity for creative and constructive regulation of disturbances. It is both open and adaptive to environment and liking of its own members. Thus Easton's model is different from equilibrium models which neglect their changing environments. Their goal is survival or maintenance of the status quo. Easton's political system does not operate merely to face stresses, crises or change for maintaining itself. It is creative, innovative, forward-looking, persistent, goal-determining, and capable to cope with crises. However, the goal of persistence is bound up with problems of systematic survival and the preservation of essential variables within the critical range. Goal-attainment is restricted by the needs of system's maintenance. As such, the theory contains little beyond the question of persistence.

Evaluation

Theoretical Contribution

Easton has developed his systems theory as a conceptual framework for empirical political analysis. His approach, as such can be considered as a brainchild of behavioural revolution. It can be regarded as a blueprint for developing an empirical political theory. His input-output analysis presents a flow model of political system. He goes beyond stability and equilibrium as goals of political systems and finds them as dynamic systems capable of coping with not only the stresses and crises arising from the environment, but to transform even itself and the goals themselves. He looks not only into the system, but also other systems and subsystems, and the totality of environment. As his 'theory' is analytical or conceptual, it is not attached to any particular ideology, system or culture. The 'Systems theory' gives a complete set of categories which can be utilised for the analysis of any particular system as well as for making comparative study of political systems. Easton, in order to develop a general theory of political life takes up the basic unit of 'interaction', and sees persistence as the goal of a political system. The latter is an interaction system, conceptually devised by a scholar. It is separate from actual or concrete system. So is 'political' analytically separate from 'non-political'. Oran Young regards it as 'the most inclusive systemic approach so far constructed specifically for political analysis by a political scientist'. Meehan also considers it as 'one of the few comprehensive attempts to lay the foundation for systems-analysis in political science and provide a 'general' functional theory of politics'.[24]

The approach is particularly useful for analysis of political life and its process. It is different from other systems in the sense that a political system has its own dynamism and its operations are purposive and goal-directed. Each segment of a political system is susceptible to its own special types of stress and maintenance-difficulties which are counter balanced by the typical regulatory mechanisms peculiar to that segment. It is based on a combination of deductively derived categories and generally accepted empirical material.

However, the theory has had a promising future in the field of international relations, international politics, regional associations and unions, world-systems and the like. Kaplan has used Systems Approach with mechanical and engineering perspectives.[25] He has proposed structures of six global or international systems: (1) Balance of Power System; (2) Loose Bipolar System; (3) Tight Bipolar System; (4) Universal International System; (5) Hierarchical International System; and (6) Unit Veto International System. He could empirically test only the first two till the seventies. With the spread of LPG (Liberalisation, Privatisation and Globalisation) and global economic reforms, time has come when scholars can make use of even General Systems Theory on empirical grounds.[26]

Criticism

Easton's 'systems theory' is not a 'theory', and lacks explanatory power. He intended to develop such a theory and made a start, but remained at where he was. Even in 1965, he could not produce a general theory of politics.

His theory is unable to deal with fundamental, basic or revolutionary changes, such as, revolutions, growth, decline, disruptions, breakdowns, etc. His political system is confined to deal with variables which seek persistence and remain within 'the critical range'. It has various mechanisms to cope with stresses, like overload, lag, and others, at the most marginal or incremental changes. His approach is more interested in systems maintenance, and has little material to go beyond its persistence.

His approach has no room for problems concerning power, the elite, leadership, mass politics, representation, etc. As input-output analysis has not been put to empirical investigation, actual utility of the approach cannot be anticipated beforehand. It has not generated any general political theory which Easton has wished to obtain. His concept of 'persistence' also does not appear to be logical or inclusive. In fact, he mixes the two aspects of 'political system', as an analytical concept, and, as a membership system. He could not stick to his original conceptual scheme. While elaborating his system's analysis, he has before him a concrete national system, though he tries to use it in abstract sense.

Even while taking up the problem of 'allocation of values'. he left the distributive aspects like who gets, what, when, and how? He does not discuss the problems of attaining and retaining the values. In fact, concrete entities like persons, groups, roles, etc. find a secondary or no place in his scheme of analysis. He has neglected actual political facts for an abstract scheme of political analysis which suffers from reification, rationalism and formalism. His categories of concepts of a certain extent have distorted the reality of politics. Easton has not been very successful in separating political system from non-political systems. He could not explain how allocation of values in a club or a firm is separate from that of a political system. He is vague about the meaning and scope of the term 'political'. It is difficult to understand how, after standing for persistence of political systems, it is possible to develop a general theory of political life. Political interactions are not restricted to the allocation of values and their implementation for the society. His attempt to narrow down the political system to 'roles and interactions relevant to the authoritative allocations for society as a whole' is simply and empirically not true.

Easton, like other functionalists, has committed the error of using members and their behaviour in a concrete political system for abstract political interactions. He proceeds on the basis of some self-made definitions which are related to each other. In consequence, he has a conceptual framework from which he wanted to get empirical relevance of a high order; this has resulted into an abstract structure which, according to Meehan, is logically suspect, conceptually fuzzy, and empirically almost useless.[27] His approach according to Hannah Arendt is Archimedean wherein one thinks everything 'in terms of processes' and is not concerned with single entities.[28]

Paul Kress, Runciman, Gvishiani, etc. have severely criticised Easton's conceptual framework. According to Kress, Easton's analysis lacks empirical basis, and is empty of facts. Runciman regards it as a shield against Marxian analysis to protect western capitalist society. Gvishiani regards it a symbol of bourgeois attitudes to maintain the status quo.

Easton is not interested in knowing the impact of a political system 'on individuals who constitute the system'.[29] In his claim to move from the institutional to the behavioural approach, he, because of his interest in the 'interactions', really hangs somewhere between the two. He has dissolved the traditional political action in the acid of interaction,[30] 'men are without qualities, lacking all essentials, and remain as containers'. Kress describes Easton's theory as 'an empty vision of politics'.

Implication for the Third World

Easton's system theory, though not an empirical political theory, provides a useful conceptual framework to analyse, understand, and compare politics of the Third World countries. It gives them a systemic perspective to know their environment and relationship with other inter and intra systems. Mostly these countries are passing through a transition, and are not interested in maintaining the status quo. They have certain goals, which they want to realise without confronting major crises, conflicts, or breakdowns. Rulers are relatively new to politics, and have limited knowledge of understanding the forces underlying the political system. Concepts like feedback, output, and support can prove very fruitful to them. Equilibrium approach, obviously, could not serve the purpose. Systems approach enables them to know the sources of stress, and finds the way to remove them. It makes necessary that the rulers get some minimum support at all the three levels. It permits them to modify their internal structures, and other regulatory mechanisms to achieve desired goals which too may be reformulated to cope with the prevailing environment.

Still it is useful for them to a limited extent only. Some of the developing countries are interested in bringing about major political changes: social, economic, cultural, and political. They even prefer radical changes. For them, persistence is not enough. The countries look for basic and fast structural changes, though they do not know the direction. There is internal turmoil and conflict, even violent struggle between various segments of society.

Some of them are not so 'open' and 'adaptive' political systems. Political power is confined to the elite – traditional or modern. The elite sometimes fear that 'if they loosen their hold over the power-structure more backward and conservative forces may take over the system. Even their administrative system is in the making. With a backward economy, the people are unprepared to live with the prevailing socio-economic structure.

Moreover, Easton's theory is not an empirical theory, and hence unable to generate confidence, guidance and support to the ruling elite to deal with actual politics. It is merely a conceptual framework for doing research and analysis. That too is born of the experience of advanced countries like the USA. The elites play a critical role which finds no place in his systems approach. There is neither consensus on available scarce values, nor on their acceptable or binding allocations, nor on their proper implementation. Sometimes, para-political systems or subsystems appear to be more powerful than the political system. When the environment to them appears more compelling than their own political system, what sort of help or explanation can Easton's theory render to them? Often the problem for them is to find out ways and means to adjust under the umbrella of a super political system, yet claim survival and independence. Obviously, Easton's systems theory has a limited and restricted capacity to speak on their problems. But it certainly paves way to them for making their own political theory.

In recent years Easton has turned to structural constraints as a second major element underlying political systems. He has recently completed a book about the influence of political structure on various aspects of political life. He has also been associated with a project inquiring into the effects that variations in the structure and organisation of democratic political systems have on the effectiveness of their public policies.[31]

Notes

1. David Easton (ed.), *Varieties of Political Theory*, Introduction.
2. Vernon van Dyke, *Political Science: A Philosophical Analysis*, Stanford: Stanford UP, 1962, 114.
3. All this is done by making a Research Design using appropriate Methodology. Research Design converts strategy into an operational plan for field work, study or experiment or an experiment. It is prospectus or outline from which research is carried forward. Methodology includes (1) those relating to personality, motivation or purposes of the researcher in brief along with his orientation; (2) problem of concept-making, that is, organising ideas or tools of analytical thought; and, (3) problems that are often exclusively denoted by the words 'method' and 'techniques'.
4. Sociological approaches are put in three categories: evolutionary, cultural and structural. Yogendra Singh, *Social Stratification and Change in India*, New Delhi: Manohar, 1977.
5. Roland Young, (ed.), *Approaches to the Study of Politics*, Evaston, Ill.: Northwestern University Press, 1958, 99.
6. Ibid., 105.
7. Ibid., 99.
8. Oran R. Young, *Systems of Political Science*, Englewood Cliffs, New Jersey, 1968, 14. See also Ball and Young (eds.), *Approaches in the Study of Politics*, Evanston, 1958.
9. Ludwig von Bertallanfy, '*General System Theory*', *General Systems*, Vol. I, 1956, 1-10.
10. Quincy Wright, *The Study of International Relations*, New York, Appleton-Century-Crofts, 1955, 230.
11. Bertallanffy, *op. cit.*, 3.
12. A. Hall and R. Fagen, "Definition of a System", *General Systems*, Vol. I, 1956, 15.
13. Roland Young, *op. cit.*, 16.
14. Ibid., 17-19.
15. L.V. Blauberg, V.N. Sadovsky, and E.G. Yadin, *Systems Theory: Philosophical and Methodological Problems*, Moscow, 1977.
16. Morton A. Kaplan, "Systems Theory", in James C. Charlesworth (ed.), *Contemporary Political Analysis*, New York, 1967, 151 58.
17. Almond and Powell, *Comparative Politics: A Developmental Approach*, New Delhi, 1973, 12; ed., *Comparative Politics Today*, Fourth Edition, 1988, Passim.

18. Most of these definitions have been taken from Oran Young.
19. Meehan, *Contemporary Political Thought*, Illinois, Homewood, 1967, 111.
20. *Stress* include 'activities that threaten the capacity to execute such binding decisions'. *Capacity* relates to location of values among the members and the latter's acceptance of these values.
21. David Easton, *A Systems Analysis of Political Life, op. cit.*, 17.
22. Easton, *A Framework of Political Analysis, op. cit.*, 85.
23. Easton, "Systems Analysis: An Example of Functionalism", in Gould and Thursby (eds.), *Contemporary Political Thought, op. cit.*, 202.
24. Meehan, *op. cit.*, 169.
25. Kaplan, *System and Process in International Politics*, 1957; *The Political Foundation of International Law*, 1961; *The Revolution in World Politics*, 1962, passim.
26. David Easton on his visit to the Department of Political Science, University of Rajasthan, Jaipur (Rajasthan-India) Jan. 28-29, 1980, had pointed out that he preferred to take up political system, only as a transforming system, and make analysis, and avoid theory-building. Presently, we are confined to only political aspect of reality, and it is not possible to work with a single discipline. It is difficult to find scholars with many disciplines and to conduct research as a team. Under the prevailing circumstances lack of reliability and integration, it is improper to guide and advise the decision-maker with such inadequate knowledge. We should take up only analysis and proceed with values. More resources are needed to do basic fundamental research.
27. Meehan, op. cit., 173-174, 185.
28. Hannah Arendt, *Between Past and Future: Six Exercises in Political Thought*, New York, Viking Press, 1961, 61.
29. S.P. Varma, *Modern Political Theory*, 1975, *op. cit.*, 185-86.
30. Paul F. Kress, "A Critique of Easton's Systems Analysis" in Gould and Thursby (eds.), *op. cit.*, 226-27.
31. David Easton, *The Political System*, Knopf, 1953, 1971 (2nd ed.); re-issued, University of Chicago Press, 1981; *A Framework for Political Analysis*, Prentice-Hall, 1965; *Varieties of Political Theory*, (ed.), Prentice-Hall, 1966; *Children in the Political System*, (with J. Dennis), McGraw-Hill, 1969; re-issued, University of Chicago Press, 1980; *A Systems Analysis of Political Life*, Wiley, 1965; re-issued University of Chicago Press, 1979; *The Analysis of Political Structure*. Routledge, 1990; and *Divided Knowledge: Across Disciplines, Across Cultures* (ed. with C. Schelling) Sage, 1991.

5

Structural-Functional Approach

The structural-functional approach has been specifically evolved and used for the study of the countries of the Third World. The latter are also called as transitional or modernising societies, developing countries, or new states. The need of developing such a 'theory' or approach arose because of the inadequacy of traditional Political Science to examine and explain the phenomena occurring therein. The United States and her associates also wanted to know the actual stage, nature, and volume of their development, so as to provide their aid and assistance suitable to their own policy-requirements amidst an atmosphere of cold war. Though the cold war ended in 1990s, still they need and work up it to deal with them during the era of globalisation. These countries too are in need of a theory or approach to understand their own political systems for various purposes. In brief, the Third World countries provide a laboratory for the development of a general theory of transitional societies. It is likely to serve the demands of twenty-first century.

Promise of a General Theory

This approach is a major attempt to develop a political theory on the basis of actual empirical studies of the politics occurring in various developing societies. It provides a framework to look at society as a whole, and describes social reality in terms of structures, processes, mechanisms, and functions. It aims at a consistent and integrated theory applicable to all such societies, and provide explanatory hypotheses relevant to all aspects of a political system. William Mitchell (*The American Polity*) finds in the approach 'the best possibilities for eventually developing a general theory'.

Gabriel A. Almond,[1] who developed it in collaboration with James S. Coleman and G. Bingham Powell, has formulated it as a 'functional theory of politics'. He is interested in all political systems changing from 'traditional' to 'modern'. But as a functionalist, he is like Talcott Parsons, David Easton, and others. Orang R. Young regards it a derivative of the general systems theory as it studies 'system' from the perspective of 'function'. But others do not agree with him. They regard systems theory rather than general systems theory much closer to it. The latter has merely given to it a general orientation, and some useful concepts. Systems theory has greater affinity with structural-functional approach. The latter is associated with systems theory or functionalism because of their common focus on system-maintenance.

Main Concepts

Structural-functional approach is a holistic perspective which studies society or system as a whole and with a view to its maintenance. It is a variety of functionalism involving the study of both functions and structures of a system. It describes the order of determinate relationships of structures and functions of a system, including its processes and mechanisms. Certain patterned and recurrent processes keep up the functionally integrated system in equilibrium. Society is conceived as 'a system of functionally inter-related variables'. According to Robert T. Holt, 'the social system is the system of interdependent roles and corporate structures of the society'.[2] Scholars may put emphasis on either functions, or structures, or both. Structural-functional approach involves that:

(1) every society is a well-integrated system consisting of relatively persistent and stable structures;
(2) the system or structures perform certain requisite functions; and
(3) functions contribute to the balance, health, or equilibrium of the system.

In this approach, a scholar analyses what functions are being performed by what structures to maintain the equilibrium of a political system. Its main concepts are: system, function, and structure.

System

The concept of 'system' has been explained earlier.[3] A system, according to Cohen, is 'any ongoing set of recurrent and interrelated social actions.' The system is primary. Functions maintain the system. Structures, such as, limbs, habits, organisations, groups, etc. perform functions. The essence of functional approach is the system maintaining activity while structures performing this function remain secondary. In the structural-functional approach both are viewed from the point of their contribution to maintain the system. For studying maintenance or equilibrium aspects of a system, most of the scholars have elaborated a set of 'functional requisites' for all systems. Functional requisites are conditions necessary for the operation of a system. For example, Talcott Parsons has put them under four categories of (i) pattern-maintenance and tension-management, (ii) goal-attainment, (iii) adaptation, and (iv) integration.

Function

'Function' connotes many meanings, such as, conditions or needs or basic processes or activities or necessities required for the maintenance of a system. For Merton, 'function' is observed consequences. Radcliffe-Brown describes it as recurrent actions. Levy explains it as 'any condition, or state of affairs resultant from the operation of a unit in terms of a structure through time'. 'Function' can also be considered as persistent relationship or its influence on the unit or system. It is the contribution of some elements to the system or its maintenance at a given state. It relates to operations pertaining to persistence or a situation wherein more than one actor or event may be involved. Function, in brief, subsumes activities or actions operating in a system, or influences thereof. Functionalism, according to Eugene J. Meehan, is a particular mode of inquiry. Functionalist explanation requires (a) a phenomena to be explained, (b) a system in which the phenomenon occurs, and (c) a stipulation of the consequences of the phenomenon for the total system.[4]

Thus, 'function' as such has many meanings. Particular meaning and its use depends on the functionalist himself. However, as effect, activity, consequences, influence, or contribution toward a system, 'functions' by nature are general, transitory, varying, and abstract. It is different from its popular use. It is used in place of 'basic needs or conditions or necessities' of a system, being organismic and value-laden. 'Function' is a neutral term which frees a system, its structures, and activities performed therein from assuming an essential or traditional relationship, interdependence, or teleology. Functions resulting from structures like bureaucracy or courts may or may not be proving helpful for the persistence of a political system. A functionalist scholar looks into the consequences or effects of events, acts, and operations upon the equilibrium of a system.

Structure

Diehard or orthodox functionalists study a system only as a set of certain functions: operations, acts, effects, or consequences. They neglect structures, even the system. This attitude makes the analysis confusing and undependable. Many functionalists have reformulated their functional concepts, and give importance to structures. Joseph La Palombara felt that ambiguities can be removed if we give importance to the structures of a political system at par with its functional aspects. Sometimes structures prove more important than functions.

'Structure' is a pattern of ordered relationship, operations, interactions, or actions. Over a period of time, recurrent functions, activities, or processes convert themselves into or generate structures. Levy finds it as a pattern or an observable uniformity in terms of which action or operation takes place.

Recurrent activities concerning adjudication generate the structure of judiciary over a period of time. Structures like legislature, army, college, etc. also come out in a similar manner. Structures, thus, are made of roles and their functional relationship. Parsons has called it 'a system of patterned expectations'.

Structures in due course of time begin to influence the operations of functions and the system itself. They acquire the capacity gradually to delimit, direct, constraint, even operate the functions of the political system. Bureaucracy, political parties, judiciary, etc., illustrate this observation. They evolve characteristics of persistence, regularity, continuity, increasing size and influence, and normativeness. Their 'is' transforms into 'ought' which means people take their existence as given, and begin to think that they 'ought' to exist and should be complied with. Structures are concretised, patterned and stable forms of specific functions. Unlike functions, they are more qualitative, uncommon, stable, specific, effective, and useful in making comparison with similar structures belonging to other systems. Their role is unusually important in revolution, war, development and other forms of major change. Riggs has pointed out the major attributes of structures:[5]

(1) They survive despite change of functions, even adopt the form of institutions when they inculcate some elements of norms, culture or value, e.g., the institution of the Crown in Great Britain. Structures are outcomes of constant functioning, and appear as 'patterned functions'. Once they adopt the form of a structure, they continue to exist despite small or marginal changes in the form of functions. Sometimes they exist even after the fulfilment of their initial goals.

(2) They usually perform their assigned roles, but it is not necessary that they would continue to perform them. Sometimes they stop or decrease their functioning. Developing countries borrow or adopt structures from developed countries, but fail to obtain their functions or functioning.

(3) There is no essential relationship between structures and functions. Still in specific social setting, some particular functions are operated by specific structures. In order to obtain those functions, one has to create structures related to them. However, existence of these structures does not mean that they would always result in functions having the same quality and quantity.

Riggs puts more emphasis on structures to render analysis more empirical and fruitful. He prefers to use the concept 'function' in a much broader sense, and does not delimit it to cause-effect relationship or consequence. Riggs likes to go from structures to functions, regarding the latter as hypothetical. A legislature is an elected body of the people but its assumed law-making role should be treated as a proposition to be proved on the basis of empirical observation.

Other Functional Concepts

As a result of using of both 'structures' and 'functions' in a balanced manner along with the enveloping concept of 'system' there emerges structural-functional approach. But there are other useful concepts also. Functionalists use the standard terminology developed by Talcott Parsons for describing the functions whether they lead toward equilibrium of the system or operate against it.[6] They are presented in the form of 'ideal type' concepts, or orientation of absolute or extreme quality, also called as pattern-variables. Actual operations or functions stand in between the two dichotomous situations. On the basis of orientation towards equilibrium, these traits have been put into two broad categories:

1. Universalistic	1. Particularistic
2. Diffuse	2. Specific
3. Achievement-oriented	3. Ascribed
4. Affective-neutral	4. Affective
5. Collectivity-oriented	5. Self-oriented

Most of the structures in developing and backward societies, such as, bureaucracy, political parties, etc., operate in an anti-equilibrium direction, i.e., particularistic, specific, ascribed, affective, and self-oriented manner. Some of them may be operating in between the two, whereas, structures like universities can be similar to the advanced countries.

Robert K. Merton,[7] who regards 'functions' as 'observed consequences', stands for the development of a middle-range theory. From the viewpoint of their contribution to equilibrium of a system, he divides functions as, (i) eu-function, (ii) dys-function, and (iii) non-function. *Eu-functions* like paying taxes, contribute towards adaptation and adjustment of a system. *Dys-functions* obstruct adaptation and adjustment of a system, such as, smuggling activities or hoarding operations. *Non-functions* are redundant operations, as beggar-brand 'sadhus' roaming about the countryside. Merton does not accept the teleological concept of 'functional-integration of society'. All events, operations, or activities may or may not be contributing to systemic equilibrium. In some cases, observed consequences or functions might be fully known, but in many cases, one may not be even knowing anything about accommodative or obstructive functions. Thus, according to Merton, *manifest function* is that which is intended by the participants and its consequences are recognised as in case of introduction of TV or '*panchayati raj*' (scheme of decentralisation at the local levels). In *latent functions*, the consequence, as in case of increasing unemployment, may not be intended and recognised. Merton also draws attention towards collateral consequences of functions. He does not believe in the concept of functional universalism propounded by Malinowski. He puts forward the dynamic concept of 'functional alternatives' implying thereby that a function can be brought about by many structures, and many functions can lead to one specific structure.

Marion J. Levy has put more emphasis on structures, and pays attention to development of system.[8] He has formulated the concepts of *requisites* and *prerequisites*. *Functional requisite* is a generalised condition necessary for the maintenance of the type of unit under consideration. *Functional prerequisite* is a function that must pre-exist if a given unit is to come into being in a particular setting. Similar statements can be made for *structural requisite* and *prerequisite*. There are three conditions necessary to analyse functional or structural prerequisites: (i) initial, (ii) transitional, and (iii) resultant. If any two of these three are known, the rest can be predicted. They can be: (i) the constitution, (ii) the legislature, and (iii) the law-making. Levy has cautioned the functionalists to be aware of reification, that is, mixing up of concrete and analytical structures, i.e., considering 'system' as a concrete structure in Political Science.

Application of Approach: Almond and Coleman

Gabriel A. Almond and James S. Coleman have together developed this approach for the analysis of the politics of the developing societies. Lucian W. Pye, Myron Weiner, Dankwart A. Rustow, and George I. Blankstein have made use of this framework, and have studied these societies on empirical basis. In the work[9] referred above, Almond has elaborated the approach, and Coleman has drawn conclusions on the basis of these studies. Their book claims to be the first effort to compare the developing political systems according to a common set of categories. They have aimed at (a) a theoretical framework for a comparative method of analysis for all political systems, and (b) a theory of change or development for explaining how political systems transform from traditional to modern. To some extent, they have succeeded in formulating a probabilistic theory and a typology to measure efficiency and capacity of various political systems. It can be regarded as a landmark in the direction of making Political Science a 'science' properly so-called.

Conceptual Apparatus

Almond and Coleman's conceptual apparatus is made of political system and its seven functional requisites described in Parsonian pattern-variables. The basic unit of Almond's political system is 'role', and not 'interaction' among individuals. Almond's political system performs the functions of integration and adaptation by means of employment, or threat of employment, of more or less legitimate physical compulsion. Legitimacy of the physical compulsion governs the inputs and outputs of the political system, and separates the latter from other social systems. Almond's concept of political system involves: (i) a concrete whole influencing, and, in turn, influenced by the environment and the ultimate presence of legitimate physical force, (ii) interaction taking place between roles adopted by individuals, and (iii) an open system engaged in a continuous communication with entities and systems beyond its own boundaries. Thus, the political system, more or less, is the legitimate, order-maintaining or transforming system in the society. 'Political' relates to 'politics' which is interaction among roles related to legitimate physical compulsion.

As a 'system', political system has three characteristics: (i) comprehensiveness, (ii) interdependence, and (iii) existence of boundaries. *Comprehensiveness* includes all interactions and structures, differentiated or undifferentiated, in their political aspects. Interdependence involves a change in one subset that produces changes in all other subsets. *Boundary* is the conceptual line where other systems end and the political system begins.

Outline of Almond-Coleman's Paradigm of Political System: Performance Style

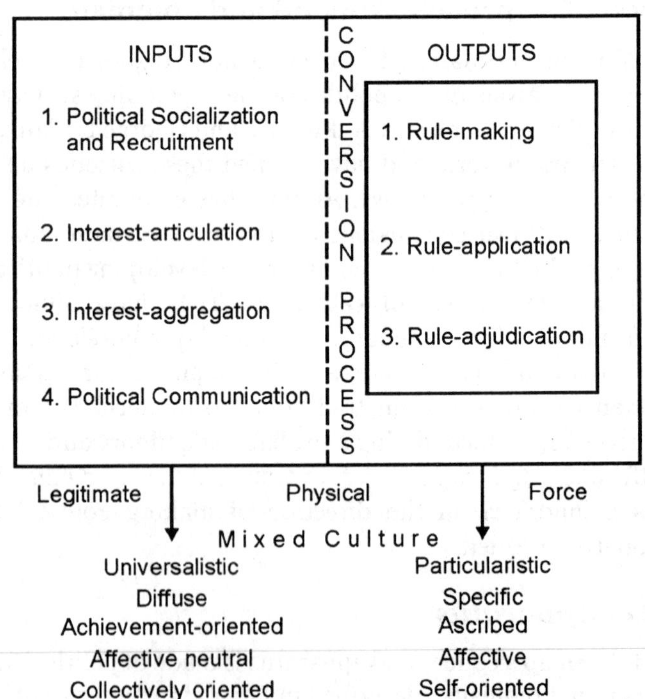

Like all other systems, a political system has also a tendency to move towards equilibrium harmony, stability or balance.

Apart from conceptual characteristics mentioned above, political systems have four operational properties: (i) all have a structure, (ii) all perform similar type of functions, (iii) all political structures perform more than one function, and (iv) all political systems are 'mixed' in the cultural sense. None is all-modern or all-traditional. Functions are the mainstay of this political system. Almond approaches structures through functions. For maintaining itself, a political system has to perform certain essential functions. Much depends on the efficiency of performance of these functions. Political development relates to the proportionate measure of that performance-efficiency. Functions are much more necessary. In maintaining order, functions may spill over here and there into other structures. They may be less observable, intermittent, dysfunctional, etc. If functions are to be there, structures must there be. Structures can be multifunctional and also belong to other systems. In comparison with structures, functions are more important and their analysis leads to accurate representation of the dynamic processes of a political system. As functions or processes are responsible for the maintenance of a system, he has worked out a list of seven categories of functions, called functional requisites, found essential for the maintenance of a political system. The basis of their efficiency depends equilibrium or development of that system. Greater the efficiency, more will there be political development.

Functional Categories

Functions required for maintaining a system have been classified into seven categories. They are known as 'functional requisites'. In the analysis of the requisites one has to look for which or what functions are being performed? What is their orientation or style of functioning? Are some functions related to particular structures or which structures contribute towards particular functions? Is there some specialisation of functions available in some specific structures? Are there some patterns or levels of efficiency in the performance of functions? In the last, the functionalist looks for the theoretical direction which these patterns display.

Almond has divided the seven functional requisites into two broad categories: (a) Inputs, and (b) Outputs. Both have functional sub-divisions in the following manner (see diagram on p. 142).

(a) Input Functions
  (i) Political socialisation and recruitment
  (ii) Interest articulation
  (iii) Interest aggregation
  (iv) Political communication

(b) Output Functions
- (v) Rule-making
- (vi) Rule application
- (vii) Rule adjudication

In the context of developing areas, Almond finds greater role of input functions. They are also called by him as 'political' functions, and are mostly performed by non-governmental structures, relating to society, culture, and others. But they are not performed in a specialised, recognised, and orderly manner. Output or 'governmental' functions are performed by governmental structures. Consequences or effects of the operations of these functions-inputs and outputs can prove eu-functional or dys-functional to the system. Their performance may lead toward the maintenance of equilibrium or cause maladjustment or decay. In the latter eventuality, functions operate in a particular, specific, ascribed, affective and self-oriented manner. Agrarian societies described by W.F. Riggs contain all such traits. In Western societies formal structures are more differentiated, effective, and powerful, than informal or primary structures, whereas reverse order is found in non-Western societies. However, such arrangement is rarely available in 'pure' form.

(a) Input Functions

(i) *Political socialisation and recruitment*: Political socialisation is the process of 'induction into the political culture'. Members of the system inculcate values, goals, norms and attitudes pertaining to the political system. Political socialisation can be undertaken in manifest or latent manner, and can be universalistic or specific. There can be some specialised or differentiated structures for this purpose. It can be left to chance or to voluntary agencies. It can be planned leading to accelerated pace of development and efficiency, as in case of former USSR, China, and other countries. India presents the 'mixed' pattern, partly planned and partly voluntary.

The main agencies of socialisation with varying forms and effects are: family, school, church, peer-groups, work-groups, office, service associations, political parties, governmental structures, media etc. All tend to prepare individuals for appropriate roles. These roles interact, and make up the political system. Socialisation expands the cognitive maps of individuals and groups, and can be drawn out and measured to a certain extent. This can be done on the basis of measuring one's responses, reactions, and behaviour. In view of its impact on the present and future course of system, it becomes important to know who controls the socialisation process and with what purpose. It may aim at maintaining the status quo (as in Pakistan and Bangladesh), development (in India), revolutionary change (in Cuba), or military grandeur (in China). Obviously, except in a democracy, the ruling elite controls the form and content of socialisation. But at the family level, it is latent, informal, and affective. Later, it becomes manifest, formal, and intellectual. One can study it from many angles, of form, content, style, impact, scope, and volume.

It is political socialisation which determines the form of political recruitment. It decides who would take up what roles. Some of the people, by law or otherwise, may be debarred from undertaking particular political roles. Recruiting individuals to appropriate political roles bears a direct relationship with the maintenance of a political system.

(ii) *Interest articulation*: Interest articulation determines the boundary-lines of a political system. It is the process of joining issues and problems, or making of common interest among small scattered groups. What interests would enter the political system is conditioned by its political socialisation, which, again, is controlled and directed by the political culture. The demand of establishing an agricultural university or an industry may not become the 'political interest' of a populace. In a different context, many people may not be ready to accept that demand as their political interest. Articulation of interest can take place by and through many structures:

(i) Institutions, e.g., legislature, services, army, etc.
(ii) Non-institutional interest groups, e.g., tribes, racial groups, priests, community, etc.
(iii) Anomic-interest groups, e.g., spontaneous rioting, demonstrations, etc.
(iv) Associational-groups, e.g., civic, cultural, and other commercial associations, trade unions, etc.

Interest articulation maintains the boundary-line between society and the political system. Anti-equilibrium style of functions, according to Parsons, tends to be particularistic, specific, affective, and self-oriented.

(iii) *Interest aggregation*: A political system can cope with innumerable interest or diversities if they again are aggregated or grouped at higher levels. Various interests, demands, pressures, wants, etc., have to be combined and expressed in the form of broad policy decisions. Aggregation can be realised in two forms (a) by accommodating various interests into wider policies, and (b) by recruiting persons belonging to various particular interests into the decision-making body. Interest aggregation enables the system to operate in a simplified, acceptable, responsive, accountable, and efficient manner. It becomes easy for it to jump from input to output stage. Aggregation makes it possible to act in a measurable and calculated way. However, distinction between interest articulation and interest aggregation is subtle and flexible. Sometimes, the ministers in a coalition cabinet, begin to act and perform articulation functions. In tribal, traditional, and developing societies, some of the functional categories are and often get mixed up.

Structures specialised to perform aggregation-functions are political parties, council of ministers, bureaucracy, national convention, etc. The political parties are particularly suitable to do this job. They can be classified on the basis of (i) type of organisation, and (ii) style. From the viewpoint of *organisation* the political parties can be (a) authoritarian, (b) dominant non-authoritarian, (c) competitive bi-party system, and (d) competitive multi-party system. Their *style* can make them (a) secular, pragmatic or bargaining; (b) absolute-value oriented or ideological; (c) particularistic, and, (d) traditional. In fact, they can be further sub-divided in many other ways. Aggregation of multiplicity or myriad of interests by political parties generates effective control by the system over groups, bureaucracy, and other associations. Their demands can be selectively met and channelised.

(iv) *Political communication*: Communication is the medium through which all other functions are performed. Almond equates it to circulation of blood in human body. Its scope and form is wider than conventional terms like public opinion, mass media, press, etc. It is sharing of ideas, information, and values by various means, and expressions thereof. Communication when revolves around 'legitimate physical compulsion' takes the form of political communication. It performs the function of boundary-maintenance by deciding on the issues as political or non-political. Political communication interconnects society and polity directly and through feedback, and saves the latter from man-made calamities. Communication ferets out the secrets or underworld happenings to come into the open, making the latent manifest. If communication system has specialised structures, and operates in an autonomous and neutral manner, it can compel other functions to confine themselves in their specific spheres. If it has evolved its own vocational ethics, it may not allow aggregation-structures to dabble in articulation-functions, and vice versa. That way, though it is one of the seven functional requisites, yet it becomes a 'regulator of regulators', by disallowing structures to transgress their boundaries.

But communication itself can prove obstructive to the maintenance of a political system. It is always necessary to find out the decontrolling of the communication system. They can be money-bags, ruling elites, press lords, and dictators. In closed systems, minds are moulded by these elements, and communication transforms into propaganda, indoctrination, or interest articulation, for a group or clique. Every form of non-official communication is forbidden by law. In open or democratic societies, communication, to a large extent, remains free. Its structures are multi-dimensional, neutral and their functioning is smooth, speedy, flexible, and expanding. Open communication system strengthens inputs of the system towards equilibrium.

However, as a process, it can be studied and compared on the basis of (a) homogeneity, (b) mobility, (c) volume, (d) cost, and (e) direction. It can also be related to levels of education, literacy, language, class, caste, and values. In such analysis, roles of interpreters, analysts, spokesmen, and intellectuals cannot be neglected.

(b) Output Functions

Almond has analysed input functions in detail owing to their dominating role in the developing countries. They have also been called political functions. The political system converts them into outputs. Because of their transformation through formally recognised mechanisms. They have also been designated as 'governmental functions'. Though they have been classified into three in a traditional manner, yet he separates them analytically from traditional structures, namely, legislature, executive, and judiciary. The three outputs – rule-making, rule applications and rule adjudication – are functions which can be performed by any formal or informal structures. As their content-part is widely known, they can be discussed in brief.

(v) *Rule-making*: The concept of 'rule' is broader than 'law'. Interests after being articulated and aggregated have to be given formal recognition, and legitimate expression. In ancient times, it was divinely ordained or oracled through some godly person, priest, or saint. Religion and religious persons expanded it further. As the people had faith in them and their divine origin and destination, they accepted and obeyed them almost unthinkingly. Traditions, taboos, usages etc. along with divine laws left little room for 'rule-making' by man. Later, kings and lords, took over this function. With the rise of democracy and expansion of state activities, specific structures like legislature, legislative committees, executive, higher bureaucracy and judiciary began to perform this job, i.e., rule-making by man. Rule-making too has two levels – higher, and ordinary. At the higher or governing level, there is superior law or Constitution or unwritten rule of law embodying the basic elements of values and culture. The lower house, which is directly elected by the people on the basis of adult franchise legislates ordinary laws. All laws or rules actually represent human interests, which operate through political parties, pressure or interest-groups, elite, and other vested interests. Functions performed by some of them may go against the maintenance of a political system, as in case of committed party leaders or money-bags, who operate through costly election system in India and other such countries. Rule-making formalises the accepted part of the demands or claims made by the people through their representatives. At times, rule-making or its specific part can be dysfunctional or non-functional.

(vi) *Rule application*: After making of rules, or formal recognition of the will or interests of the people, the next category of functional requisites is 'rule application'. It is putting of rules into actual practice. In modern times, it is the biggest part of outputs. In olden times, most of these functions were performed by society or community, and various religious bodies. Functions left with the political system were performed by army or aristocracy. Citizens or subjects themselves were responsible for many operations. With the increasing role of the political system, more and more functions are made over to it. It requires specialised and expanded structures to deal with the situation. State's monopoly over coercive power appears in the form of rise of bureaucracy. Originally it was a sub-structure, but, later on, has became a formidable autonomous structure or system. Its functioning requires an independent study. To what extent is it carrying out the rules or wishes of the people in practice? Does it serve the purpose for which it was instituted and developed? Does it have its own interests and purposes to serve? Rules, it may be noted, unless implemented faithfully can cause much frustration and decay in the system.

(vii) *Rule adjudication*: Rule application functions broadly apply rules or will of the people equally to all in equal situations. But there can be individual or specific situations wherein it is difficult to apply or if applied, it can cause injustice or grevious injury to some persons. Such difficult situations require specialised functioning by expert, experienced, intelligent, neutral, and independent structures. Apart from individual cases non-application or improper application of rules, it has to be observed and analysed whether other functions – both inputs and outputs – are operating in accordance with the basic rules formulated and accepted by the political system. It is necessary that rule adjudication structures – courts, tribunals, popularly selected judicial bodies etc. – remain free from the influence of other structures, and are able to do their job well. Their function is to keep structures and sub-structures within the given confines, and see that the system operates on expected lines. However, functioning of the rule adjudication structures itself is hypothetical, and can prove dysfunctional to equilibrium of the system, on account of its incapacity, favouritism, inexperience, cost, delay, lengthy procedure, and non-implementation of their decision.

Typology of Political Systems

Almond and Coleman have studied the developing countries in accordance with their conceptual schemes of seven functional requisites essential for maintaining a political system. In their presentation of these seven functional categories, they have resorted to the Western model, based on British, American, and French political systems, as their 'ideal type', considering them as successful in maintaining their equilibrium. They have used these seven functional categories to make a comparative analysis of the politics of the Third World. They have studied them from the view of maintaining equilibrium. For this purpose, they have analysed:

(1) Whether functions, required under seven categories to maintain a political system, are being performed, or not? Which categories of functions are playing what part to maintain the equilibrium? Equilibrium is the focus for analysing the functions.
(2) What structures are performing these functions? Are there some specialised structures for performing these functions?
(3) What is the style of their functioning? That style is depicted in the Parsonian language of pattern-variables, on the basis of available data and information.
(4) In view of performance of functions – its efficiency and autonomy, availability of specialised structures, and style or orientation towards equilibrium-political systems have been categorised in accordance with their patterns or stages of development.

They have put the Western model at the top of developmental scale. Edward Shils has pointed out that no non-Western political system has been able to follow it completely. As such, everyone of them remains in the transitional or developing stage. Shils has evolved six patterns or models, but Almond and Coleroan have adopted, by the year 1960, only five of them:

1. *Political Democracy*: These countries – Japan, Israel, India, etc. have all seven-category-functions, and specialised structures too. But their style of working and values have non-democratic orientation.
2. *Tutelary Democracy*: Formally, their 'political systems perform all functions and have structures. But the structures of rule application dominate the rest of outputs, assuming the role of conducting democracy. That time (1960) Ghana and Nigeria were put under this category.
3. *Modernising Oligarchy*: Under this pattern, the elite as a class or coterie rules to modernise the country so that democracy in the long run may win over. Democratic constitution is either postponed or suspended. Army or bureaucracy or both dominate the political scene controlling operations of functions for their own purposes. Actual style of their working is anti-equilibrium. Pakistan, Burma, Turkey, Sudan, etc., had been categorised in this manner.
4. *Totalitarian Oligarchy*: An oligarchy grabs power and operates the whole system on the basis of coercion. The distinction between society and polity is obliterated. The ruling coterie controls and conducts all inputs, as well as outputs. Almond and Coleman have quoted North Korea, Nazi Germany and Fascist Italy in this context.

5. *Traditional Oligarchy*: There is no evidence of democracy or modernisation. Most of them are traditional monarchies which rule in the name of God, Religion, or Tradition. Political rules depend on status and ethnicity. Functions concentrate in the hands of its rulers, and the level of their efficiency and autonomy is very low. Saudi Arabia, former Nepal under monarchy, etc., come under this category.

In the present context, except India, Japan, Ceylon and Israel, most of the developing countries belong to second, third, and fourth categories. Several other scholars, such as, Cohen, Lasswell, Finer etc., have also advanced their own classificatory schemes. But none is exhaustive. Even Almond and Coleman were not satisfied with this typology, and had attempted to improve it further. Even functions and structures operating in the developed and the developing countries are different. In developed countries, informal and primary structures are acculturated and penetrated by secondary and formal structures. But, the case is reverse in the developing countries, when even 'political' functions are sometimes performed by governmental structures.

Probabilistic Theory of Political Systems

Almond and Coleman have expressed the belief that their structural-functional approach, if studied empirically, can generate a probabilistic theory of political systems. It can tell a lot about them in a probable manner. It can explain their present operations, demarcate stage of development, and show path for future course of action. Use of formal logic and mathematics in collecting relevant data can make the studies even more valid, precise, definite and factual. Till then, we can make or formulate probabilistic statements. David Truman in his studies of groups, and V.O. Key for political parties have also used words like, 'by and large', 'in general', 'if ... then', 'with greater-frequency', 'more or less' while making their theoretical statements.

In their probabilistic theory, they have begun with seven functional categories requisite for the maintenance of a political system. Assuming a system underlying all functions, they have divided them as inputs and outputs. Their approach *separates political structures from political functions*. The two are not essentially related to each other. Still, the functions are more important. They can be empirically known through indices and indicators which can further be validated by observable data and information. Analysis of functions leads to certain structures, which ultimately take us to specific structures performing specific functions. Such finding is a mere *probability*. Probability of *association* between specific function and structures can indicate another probability of particular *style* of functioning, and implications for the maintenance of the system. Thus, we can analyse political systems, and compare them empirically on the basis of seven categories of functions, specialised structures, and their styles of functioning. Eventually, certain probabilistic statements can be made about those systems. They can further be tested and verified with the help of a wide range of available data and information. Though the value of such probabilities is not known and exact prediction cannot be made, still comparative analysis can be made on the basis of frequency of functions performed by particular structures, and their style of working.

On these three bases, Almond and Coleman who accept the influence of Parsons and Shils on their approach, point out that innumerable patterns or matrices of political systems can be discovered, compared, and empirically verified. However, in the light of these matrices or theoretical hypotheses, in a limited manner, some performance-indicators of functions performed by structures can be selected. These performance-indicators can further be supported by quantitative evidence. But they believe that everything can be proved by statistical or quantitative evidence in due course of time.

The empirical analysis on the basis of structural-functional approach has marched ahead towards the formation of a probabilistic theory. Equilibrium, on the pattern of advanced political systems, is maintained by efficient performance of functions categorised under seven functional requisites. This requires specialised structures, along with their style conducive to equilibrium. At the lowest in *traditional oligarchies*, there is no autonomous operation of functions under seven categories. The system in many cases performs little functions. Dynastic monarchy along with other feudal elements is only immutable structure operating in a primordial style. At the next stage, comes the *totalitarian oligarchy* with its structure dominating the whole societal system by force. Such structures, if not shattered by other forces, breakdown under their own weight. Functions and structures lose their interconnections. Functional requisites lose their identity in that system.

In the *modernising oligarchy*, there are structures, but some structures, like the army and the bureaucracy, in the name of paving way to modernisation or democracy, monopolise all-important functions. Rest of the structures lose their validity, legitimacy, and influence. Their declarations claim to be system-oriented, but in reality lead to a dead end. When one rises higher on the path of political developments and observes *tutelary democracy*, he finds structures of democracy exist there but are unaware of its own functions, or 'appropriate style'. Some one like the director of a drama or film teaches and exhorts the roles to operate, but, under the weight of primary and informal structures, remains unable to move. The next highest stage of development is *political democracy*, which has both structures and functions but lacks style. They operate in a formal manner, and remain deprived of appropriate socio-economic, and cultural base. Most often, their orientation is anti-equilibrium.

Thus, their probablistic theory implies the path of political development on the basis of seven functional categories. Political development relates to efficiency of these functional variables. It goes from functional requisites to specialised structures, which have to operate in favour of maintaining systemic equilibrium. Greater the specialisation or differentiation of structures regarding various functions, and their appropriate orientation towards systemic equilibrium, greater is the likelihood of political development. Even modern political systems are afflicted with multifunctionality of structures as well as quality of culture. They can get rid of them (a) if they have specialised autonomous structures, which should have their own boundaries and regulate the performance of their function: these structures should have the *capacity* to maintain their boundaries; and (b) 'traditional' idioms of particularism, specificity, ascription, and affectivity are penetrated by 'rational' idioms of universalism, achievement, neutrality and diffuseness. Indicators relevant to such functional regulation and cultural penetration can be discovered. In that case, a formal theory of political modernisation can possibly be developed. It can be used in making prediction for developing countries regarding their direction of political development. Formulation of such a probabilistic theory is difficult, but not impossible.

Developmental Approach: Almond and Powell

Almond (with Coleman) was not satisfied with his structural-functional approach as propounded in *The Politics of the Developing Area*, 1960. He found the concept of equilibrium, harmony or maintenance as static and conservative. The developing countries do not opt for the status quo, but seek change, even rapid and radical transformation of their societies. He realised that their scheme of seven-functional requisites, was enough for describing systems, but does not explain 'how and 'why' systems change. The approach paid little or no attention to conversion processes or withinputs. It was unaware of the interaction of a political system with its international environment. Treating Western political systems as 'ideals' or 'models', they kept themselves away from ground realities.

Objectives

As usual, Almond, along with Powell, aims at developing a comprehensive and empirical theory of political systems explaining how and why do they change. For this purpose, Almond with his co-author improved upon his previous approach incorporating concepts from Easton's systems theory, Deutsch's communication theory, and the perspectives of other development-theorists. Their new or modified framework can be called as systemic-structural-functional approach. Almond and Powell[10] have designated it as 'developmental approach' and also called it 'probabilistic functionalism'. Their purpose is broader as they realise that fuller understanding of political change requires to know its 'how' and 'why'. Simple knowledge of 'what', is not enough. In his new perspective, Almond replaces 'equilibrium' by the concept of 'interdependence' or 'interactional functions'. He analyses political systems from three directions: (a) inside, (b) outside and (c) adjustment and maintenance. In other words:

(i) How are *conversion* functions being performed?
(ii) What is the *capability* of a political system, as an 'individual' and its environment?, and
(iii) How is the system *adapting and maintaining* itself amidst various pressures for bringing about change?

The ground basis is the transformation process-conversion of inputs into outputs. Its operation involves the capacity to do so, enabling it to survive as an 'entity' or 'individual' amidst changing environment. This is what the system does by performing adaptation and maintenance functions. The first explains 'what' and 'how', and, the second and third processes 'why' of political change. These questions are separate but related to each other. The focus of approach, therefore, is on 'interdependence' of the various parts of the system.[11]

Concepts

As usual, the concept of 'political system' is associated with the use or threat of use of legitimate physical force in society. Their central theme is the interdependence of structures and parts, and a boundary between the system and its environments. Interdependence involves change in the characteristics of a system and its parts when there is change in one of its parts. Boundary is the line where the system starts or stops. Boundaries of political systems go on changing. Functions of political systems operate at three stages: inputs, conversion, and outputs. In his reformulated conceptual scheme, Almond has given more importance to '*structures*' and '*culture*'. Structures consist of roles, institutions, subsystems, etc. Structures are analysed on the basis of specialisation and differentiation. Recruitment and socialisation functions provide roles to operate the structures. Socialisation functions involve inculcation of political culture. Political culture provides values, faith, motivation, cognition, emotions, criteria, attitudes towards participation or apathy, etc., to the individual. Political culture can be rational or traditional. Rational political culture imbues secularisation or secularism. Secularisation or rational culture is directly related to specialisation and differentiation of structures. Reason or intellect demand specialisation for efficiency, and differentiation for better division of labour in the functioning of structures. Individuals assimilate political culture through socialisation process. Thus, political culture, through socialisation of the individuals and their roles, influences all the structures and the functions of a political system.

Levels of Analysis

Though Almond and Powell have given more attention to structures and culture, yet their basic approach is functionist. Functionalism thinks of social structures and roles as performing functions in the system. A system can be analysed at three levels: (i) system maintenance and adaptation level, (ii) conversion level, and (iii) capability level. The analysis can explain its operations, process of change, and factors operating underline the change. In a way it speaks about the whole theory of political change. At these levels, political systems can be fruitfully compared which can further explain and validate interrelations among these levels.

All these levels are specific aspects of systemic functioning. The basic operation of the system is conversion-function. Through it, the system attains its capability to maintain and adapt itself and reach its goals. However, we can begin with any one of the three processes.

System Maintenance and Adaptation Level

At this level, conversion functions are seen from the view of maintenance of the system and its adaptation with the environment. This is done through recruitment and socialisation processes.[12] All of them operate through structures. Structures are patterns of observable activities. They are made of *roles*. The political role is one of the basic units of a political system. Sets or roles are called as structures. Interrelated roles and structures together make up a subsystem. Role, structures, and subsystems of various systems may differ (i) to the extent of their differentiation or specialisation, and (ii) on the basis of their quantum of independence or subordination to each other.

Differentiation refers to the processes in which 'new type of roles and structures are recreated and adapted to the old'.[13] It is a process by which roles change and become more specialised or more independent. Sometimes new roles are established, or new structures and subsystems emerge or are created. Political recruitment is the process by which the roles of political systems are filled. It may be on the basis of general or specific principles, by election, nomination, hereditary, or otherwise.

Structural differentiation, independence of roles and structures, and their capabilities are interrelated specialised role, if autonomous, result in better performance. Relationship between roles and structures, is, therefore, important. Autonomous roles happen to be more responsive. Controlled or directed roles are often inefficient, ineffective, and apathetic.

Interaction among Political Culture, Structures and Functions

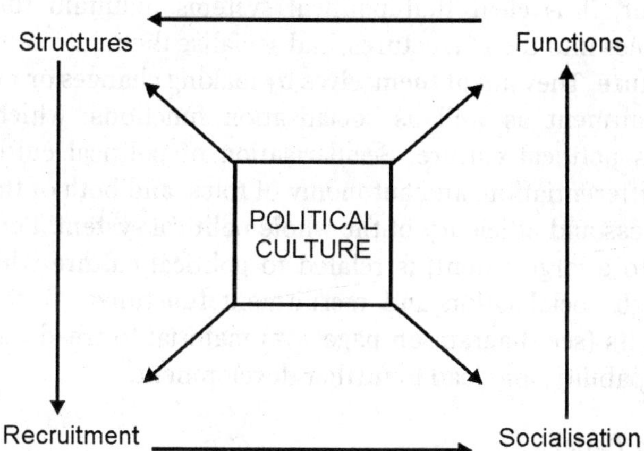

Political culture is the psychological dimension of the political system. It consists of attitudes, beliefs, values, and skills prevailing at a particular time or imbibed by bulk of population. However, there can be many patterns of culture or sub-cultures, related to region, class, language, or historical background. Culture to a large extent motivates the roles, structures, and subsystems, and therefore, influences the whole system. It can accelerate or obstruct the process of role-differentiation and independence. Political culture is maintained and changed through the process of political socialisation. It is a process by which political attitudes and values are learned by individuals. Through the function of political socialisation, individuals are brought into a particular political culture, As there are many sub-cultures and means and methods to realise them, it may take many forms. Rational political socialisation leads to secularisation or secular culture. Secularisation is a process by which individuals increasingly become rational, analytical and experienced in their working and behaviour. Traditional or parochial attitudes, beliefs and habits are substituted by rational ones. Thus, through socialisation process, political culture is maintained as well as changed, and the latter ultimately influences the working of structures and therefore, the system as a whole.

Political recruitment is another important function. It is a process whereby the roles of political systems are filled. It may be on the basis of general or specific principles, by election, nomination, hereditary, or otherwise. Political systems recruit individuals into political roles. Structures function through roles. Recruitment function cannot be separated from socialisation process. Recruitment inducts individuals with different cultures, interests, attitudes, and values. The background of these people has a great impact on the performance of their roles. Therefore, their socialisation into appropriate political culture becomes an urgent task for every political system.

However, it is clear that political systems maintain themselves by recruiting roles into their structures, and socialise them into some pattern of political culture. They adapt themselves by making changes or modifications in the recruitment as well as socialisation functions, which ultimately influence its political culture. Secularisation of political culture leads to structural differentiation, and autonomy of roles, and both of them result in responsiveness and efficiency of the whole political system. Performance of structures, to a large extent, is related to political culture which operates them through socialisation and recruitment functions. At this level, the system gets its (see diagram on page 155) material to tread on the path of attaining capability, and lead to further development.

Conversion Level

Almond, while making use of Easton's input-output model, improves it further as *input-conversion-output model.* His focus is on conversion process, which transforms inputs as outputs. It responds to the question 'what does a political system do for maintaining itself?' Inputs and outputs mostly relate to environment, but their transformation-process is an inside matter. As functions are performed by and within structures, the inputs and outputs are also operated through their structures. Almond has classified conversion functions into six categories:

1. Interest articulation.
2. Interest aggregation through political parties, bureaucracy, etc. in form of policy proposals.
3. Rule-making by transformation of policy-proposals for the purpose of implementation.
4. Rule application by political and permanent executive.
5. Rule adjudication by specific structures like judiciary.
6. Communication function.

The first two functions are 'political' inputs and the next three are 'governmental' outputs. Political socialisation and recruitment has now been considered as a separate level of analysis. It has been set apart to explain the 'why' of systematic behaviour. Communication function has also been accorded a higher role, and dealt with separately. In fact, it conjoins all the levels and involves all functions. Conversion functions cannot be performed without communication. It is a meeting ground of all functions. Almond, therefore, has found it difficult to put communication functions exclusively under any particular level. As most of these functions have already been discussed, there is no need of giving details again.

The conversion process is internal to the system and is a continuum: (1) demands are formulated, (2) demands are combined in the form of alternative courses of action, (3) authoritative rules are formulated, (4) these rules are applied and implemented, (5) in case of dispute, rules are determined by law in individual cases, and (6) there is constant communication within and outside the system. These categories provide the basis of comparing various political systems also.

Capability Level

At this level, the political system is observed as a 'person' or entity acting in its domestic and international environments. The political system consists of interacting roles, structures, and subsystems, and of underlying psychological inclinations which affect these interactions. As a process, it converts inputs taking from the environment or from within the system into outputs, which are sent into the environment thereby changing it, and in the process, the political system also changes. Capability analysis describes its entire performance in the environment. It involves five aspects: (1) extractive capability, (2) regulative capability, (3) distributive capability, (4) symbolic capability, and (5) responsive capability.

Extractive capability represents the extent of material and human resources to which the political system can draw out from the environment – domestic and international. This provides the basis for other capabilities to become more effective. It is similar to Easton's concept of *support*. There is difference between actual and potential extractive capability. There can be many ways to procure extractions : force, patriotic appeals, incentives, rewards, etc. It is always important to look for who provides support, why and to what extent.

Regulative capability refers to the exercise of control over the behaviour of individuals and groups. It is done on the basis of legitimate physical force. Its actual use shows decreasing politicality of the system. One has constantly to investigate what individuals and groups, in what areas of life, and with what frequency or intensity, need the actual employment of legitimate force. Often mere threat to use it or demonstration of that threat becomes operative. Both regulative and extractive capabilities are interdependent. In the absence of proper balance, one can result in destroying the other. Regulation requires resources and vice versa.

Distributive capability involves provision of services, goods, statutes, and other facilities to the individuals and groups. Distribution can be considered on the basis of variety, areas, quality, quantity, segments of population benefitted by it, impact, and cost involved. Distribution has to keep some relationships with extraction and regulation. *Symbolic* capability is the rate of *effective* symbol flow from the political system into the society and the international environment.[14] It includes statement of values and policies, display of flag and forces, visits by leaders, celebration of functions and festivals, etc. Cost of these symbolic expressions is small but they are effective when respond to popular attitudes, beliefs, values, expectations, and situations. Both distributive and symbolic capabilities can support and reinforce one another, making up for mutual deficiencies. The last *responsive* capability relates to the relationship between inputs and outputs. Much depends on the responsiveness of the system to handle various demands, pressures, and crises. The system as a whole, or its parts or the elite can display its activeness to respond. There can be structures and processes to channelise the inputs in an efficient manner. If the structures and subsystems are autonomous, responses to demands and pressures become, more or less, automatic. Sometimes they have to be immediately met with, and any delay can cause immense harm to the system itself.

There is interrelationship between these capabilities. Dictatorial systems are more extractive and regulative, and less distributive. Communist systems are more distributive, but also extractive and regulative. Democracies are highly responsive and distributive. Their regulative and extractive capabilities remain subordinate to them. Capability analysis, thus, speaks about the flow of activity into and out of the political system, telling how is it performing in the environment, shaping it, and being shaped by it further. The analysis also enables us to classify and compare political systems on the basis of these capabilities and their indicators. For example, distributive analysis would spell out which system is allocating what items to which sectors and with what effect. Performance of capabilities explains the phenomenon of political change or development. It can come about from elites, social groups, or international environment. Change coming from any one of these sources causes change in the flow and conversion process of inputs and outputs. Everything depends on system's capabilities to deal with inflow of inputs, their conversion and effect of outputs, and understanding them all with the help of its communication network. Outputs influence inputs or domestic as well as international environment. Capability analysis deals with system's role to change its environment as well as getting changed by it.

Political systems interact both with their domestic societies as well as political systems operating in the international environment. Their performance at that level can be analysed through capability analysis. It is input-conversion-output process seen from the international angle. There is some relationship between the pattern of domestic capability and pattern of international capability. Various patterns can be analysed, discovered, and compared. Factors affecting capability of a system are: political elites, material and human resources, organisational apparatus, and the level of support. All can be, more or less, improved upon. Capability analysis can also tell us a lot about the path of development. Adequate extraction and regulation capabilities enable a system to distribute resources. Structural differentiation and secularisation increase the former capabilities. It can also suggest several possibilities of dealing with a crisis – increase or decrease its distributive and symbolic activities, restructure its conversion system, or actualise its potential capabilities.

Dimensions of Comparing Political Systems

As stated above, Almond and Powell have shown the possibility of comparing political systems at three levels: (a) maintenance and adaptation, (b) conversion, and, (c) capability – and their patterns of relationship among the three levels of functions. The concept of political development, according to Almond and Powell, involves these levels of functions. However, their comparison scheme dwells upon three major criteria: (i) structural differentiation or multifunctionality; (ii) secularisation; and (iii) the stage of political development. The first two relate to the basic concepts of 'structure' and 'political culture'. The third is the interrelationship among the three levels of analysis. The theory of political systems consists of 'the discovery of the relations among these different levels of functions, and of the relation of the functions at each level.'[15]

Political development denotes some significant changes in the size and substance of the flow of inputs into a political system. It results in further structural differentiation and cultural secularisation. There are many problems or challenges which lead to changes in the size and substance of the flow of inputs, and put the system or its structure and culture under stress. The problems or challenges have been broadly categorised as:

1. *The problem of state building*: When the political system fails to 'penetrate' the society, the political elite create new structures and organisation to regulate behaviour and extract resources from the system. It is generally associated with the development of a centralised and effective bureaucracy and other structures. It takes much time and efforts to evolve appropriate state-mechanism and build structures there upon.
2. *The problem of nation-building*: When the system lacks adequate development of attitudes of obedience and compliance in the population, the elite redirect socialisation and recruitment processes by which people transfer their devotion and loyalty from smaller tribes, villages, sects, caste, colour, etc., to larger central political system, It may be called as an enveloping we-feeling.

3. *The problem of participation*: It arises when there is rapid increase in the volume and intensity of demands for a share in decision-making by various groups and levels in the society. Participation results in the making of political groups and factions, election, and legislative bodies. It calls for understanding these forces, political competence, and responsive attitudes, among the elites.
4. *The problem of distribution*: It emerges when there is a sudden increase in the volume and intensity of demands for more distribution of resources or values among various segments of population. The system can face this challenge if it is able to extract more resources from its environment, and regulate the behaviour of demanding individuals and groups. At this juncture, its symbolic and responsive capabilities may come to its help. Distribution-problem subsumes all welfare functions.

A political scientist has to analyse the ways in which the system operates at three kinds of maintenance and adaptation, conversion, and capability to perform their functions. A study of these ways gives out certain patterns of challenges and responses, of political systems. Challenges and responses to them cause political development in political systems. Almond and Powell have studied, analysed, and compared various political systems prevailing from primitive age to modern era, and have prepared a *typology* of these patterns of political development. They have done it by relating conversion process to capability functions. Their developmental classification of political systems leads to '*a theory of political development*'. The basis of various levels of development has been threefold – differentiation, autonomy, and secularisation. In other words, political development means occurrence of more and more differentiation in structures, their operation in autonomous manner and rationality throughout the system. Almond has made these three variables as the basis of description, explanation, and prediction regarding the behaviour of political systems, and yet he regards his developmental approach as 'probabilistic'.

Types of Political Systems

Dahl based his typology of political systems on number, subsystem autonomy, and legitimacy. Almond puts forward the criteria of (i) structural differentiation, and (ii) cultural secularisation. In his classificatory scheme, he endorses the influential ideas of Aristotle, Max Weber, Karl Friederich, S.N. Eisenstedt, Edward Shils, Robert A. Dahl, James Coleman, David Apter and Lipset. He has incorporated sociological and systems perspectives, particularly, from Talcott Parsons, Marion J. Levy, and Karl W. Deutsch.

Almond, along with Powell, has divided all political systems into three broad classes. He classifies them according to the degree of structural differentiation and cultural secularisation. They are:

1. *Primitive Systems*: These are intermittent political structures and a minimum of structural differentiation, along with a dispersed and narrow culture. They can further be sub-classified as:
   (a) Primitive nomadic bands, as, Ouagadougou (old)
   (b) Segmentary systems, as, Nuer
   (c) Pyramidal systems, as, Ashanti
2. *Traditional Systems*: These consist of differentiated governmental-political structures oriented toward a 'subject' culture. These have further been classified as:
   (a) Patrimonial systems, as Ouagadougou
   (b) Centralised bureaucratic systems, as, Inca, Tudor England, Ethiopia, etc.
   (c) Feudal political systems, as the twelfth century France
3. *Modern Systems*: These systems mainly consist of differentiated political infrastructures, such as, political parties, interest groups etc., and have some form of 'participant' political culture. Among them there is a large variety:
   A. Secularised city-states: Limited differentiation, as in Athens.
   B. Mobilised modern systems: High differentiation and secularisation.
      1. Democratic systems: Subsystem independence and participant culture
      (a) High subsystem independence, as, in Great Britain.
      (b) Limited subsystem independence, as, in Fourth Republic France.
      (c) Low subsystem independence, as, in Mexico.
      2. Authoritarian systems: Subsystem control and subject – participant culture
      (a) Radical totalitarian, as, in the former USSR.
      (b) Conservative totalitarian, as in Nazi Germany.
      (c) Conservative authoritarian, as in Spain.
      (d) Modernising authoritarian, as in Brazil.
   C. Premobilised modern systems: Limited differentiation and secularisation
      1. Premobilised authoritarian, as in Ghana prior to February 1966.
      2. Premobilised democratic.

Almond and Powell have analysed the above political systems in the light of their conceptual framework and have reached a set of empirical propositions.

Towards a Theory of Political Development

A theory, according to them, designates relationships between variables in such a way that predictions can be made about the consequences of their interactions. It can be tested and further reformulated. They believe that their approach enables us to lay a basis for prediction as well as for description and explanation. It is aware of restrictions and limitations of political systems. These are inherited from the past, and influence their future, limiting as well as excluding certain alternatives. The developmental approach claims to know about a set of important variables among other properties of a political system, and also their limits or potentials. All systems at different levels of differentiation and secularisation or subsystem independence encounter different sets of limitations, pressures and potentialities. Developmental approach not only describes, compares, and explains, but also predicts political changes and developments occurring in political systems.

Political development is related by Almond to political structure and political culture. In the development approach, political development is measured by role differentiation and subsystem independence, and political culture by secularisation. Political culture also involves socialisation process. The approach moving towards the direction of a scientific theory analyses political systems at three levels and by interconnecting them draws out certain important theoretical conclusions. Almond spells out these three levels as that of (i) conversion, (ii) capability, and (iii) classification of political systems. All these have been discussed on the basis of structural differentiation, subsystem autonomy, and secularisation. They respectively deal with 'inside', 'outside', and 'comparative' view of political systems. The development-aspect reflects the syndrome of political structure, subsystem independence, and secularisation, but the analysis at each level goes along the path of their conversion functions, capabilities, and system-maintenance-patterns.

Almond and Powell have described and analysed political systems indicated in their typology or classification scheme. They have found that there is a tendency for the interrelated variables of structural differentiation, subsystem autonomy, and secularisation to vary together. But their relationship is not necessary, direct or unchanging. Almond's classification is based rather on its utility and meaningfulness in comparing political systems. It simply shows how the structural and cultural characteristics of political systems are associated with their processes and performance characteristics. Political systems, as stated earlier, face four types of development problems: (i) state-building, (ii) nation-building, (iii) participation, and (iv) distribution. All of them influence the development variables of differentiation, secularisation, and subsystem independence. They make up the turning points of the path of political development. In other words, a political system has to encounter the problems of unification and control, group identity and loyalty, involvement of members of the society in the decision-making processes, and distribution of goods and services to its people by gradual increase of the three variables.

An emerging theory of political development, according to Almond, has to connect the ways in which particular political systems have encountered and solved these four problems of development with their prevailing patterns of structure, culture, and performance. In the event of conversion, capability and adaptation processes of a class of political system juxtaposed have to face these problems. One has to relate their past experiences with the contemporary performance, and see its impact on the future also. Political development, to a certain extent, can be predicted by:

(a) describing and comparing (i) performance of political systems as 'units' or 'persons' in their environments; (ii) their input-conversion-output pattern; and (iii) their system-maintenance and adaptation processes;
(b) classifying and comparing political systems according to basic structural and cultural characteristics related to different levels and performance patterns; and
(c) relating various types of political systems to their historical experience about solving four development problems.

In case, relationships between fundamental variables are determined, the way to predicting limitations, pressures, and potentialities shaping the future of a political system becomes clear. All explanation and prediction of political development is based on the following theoretical assumptions:

1. Development of higher levels of system capabilities is dependent upon the development of greater structural differentiation and cultural secularisation. For example, the rise of rational bureaucratic organisations carries over the system to a higher level of regulation, distribution, and extraction. Similarly, the development of political structures like interest-group or party-system increases responsive capability of political systems.
2. There is a close relationship between subsystem autonomy and responsive capability. In the absence of subsystem-independence, despite highly differentiated political structures, responsiveness of the system would remain low and limited.
3. Political systems have to face the system development-problems of state-building, nation-building, participation, and distribution. All the pre-mobilised and traditional and primitive and pre-mobilised

systems, along with expansion of communication and technology, tend to suffer from development-problems in a cumulative and pressing manner. Owing to their inadequate level of differentiation and capability, alternatives before them always remain severely limited.

Political Investment Strategies

A great hurdle in making prediction relates to our ignorance about the attitudes and intentions of a given leader or of a small decision-making group. The above generalisations or theoretical statements are not specific, and the presence of a particular leadership can make a vast difference in the volume, speed, time and direction of the development of a political system. For this purpose, various alternative courses of leadership strategies – planned or unplanned – should be independently studied and conclusions arrived at. These strategies can be viewed as *political investment programme.*[16] Given the prevailing conditions of the system and its environment, the development theory can explain and predict the results of those various alternative programmes. Main problems before political development planning, or investment relate to state building, nation-building participation, and distribution. Analysis of political investment strategies lead us to make a rational choice from among the available alternatives. At first, we would have to specify its structural, cultural, and conversion characteristics, and also its capabilities. Next, we would have to spell out the properties of the type of political system which we would like to have. Rational choice would mean predicting an investment programme among the alternative programmes. It would guarantee to take us most probably from the present to the desired system with less cost and risk. It would enable us to predict the outcome of alternative investment programmes for goals like democracy, welfare, and stability.

A study of the historical development of political systems would take us closer to '*a theory of political development planning*'. Examining the various patterns of growth of historical political systems would enable us to make risk, cost, or benefit predictions more precise. There can be some scheduling of priorities in the sense that at one time a system may prefer to develop regulative and extractive capability to responsive and distributive capability at an early stage of state-building, which go in reverse direction for conducting its distributive and welfare activities. The political development programme will put stress on (i) proper scheduling of the system's development problems: state and nation building will be given priority to participation and welfare; (ii) holding investment choices open: the development of the regulative and extractive capabilities must stop where it threatens the destruction of pluralism; (iii) making compensatory investments to face disruptive consequences of development processes by divising broader investment programmes; and (iv) relating non-political development-programme to political development programmes by making investment in education, industrialisation, family structure and organisation, etc., as they affect the inputs of political systems.

The development programmes appropriate for developing political systems are likely to differ from one another. They would have to look into their different starting points both at structural and cultural levels. The rate and volume of investment will reflect differences in resources as well as in the ability of these societies to absorb that investment. Development theory, incorporating those strategies and programmes would increase our ability to calculate the risks, cost, and benefits of different development programmes in secular 'probability' terms.[17]

Criticism

Almond's early approach has been severely criticised on several grounds: (1) The assumption regarding functional unity of society, concept of equilibrium and stability, etc., have been considered as conservative, status quoist, and empirically false. (2) It supports the teleogical misconception that there is a certain fixed number of functional prerequisites. It is a form of universal functionalism. (3) The approach is normative in the sense that it stands for the maintenance and adaptation of the system. (4) It remains unable to deal with important variables like power, policy-making, role of the elite. Almond and Powell have included the role of the elite in the preparation of political development strategies, but their suggestion does not constitute an essential part of their developmental approach. (5) Having once adopted the approach,. it is rather futile to talk of the generation of a political theory, since they have already applied it in advance: a form of *ex-post-facto* judgement. As such, it is not an explanatory theory. It is, in its first form, at the most a classification, scheme or a model, which can guide a scholar to make observation or collect data under certain categories.

Their second or improved form too is not a very advanced approach, making a move toward the formation of an empirical theory. (6) Some of the concepts used by them are not defined clearly and have been applied in varying manner, such as, system, interaction, function, etc. Meehan considers the approach as functional only by designation. Almond goes little beyond description and convenient classification.[18]

Cohen has criticised their analysis on ideological and logical grounds. He finds its goals, scheme, and contents as beyond the purview of sociology but not Political Science. Holt and Richardson object to explanation of structures from functional point of view. Most of Almond's concepts are circular, being based on each other. They fail to develop a probabilistic theory of political systems. Almond himself has been revising his conceptual scheme off and on, and a final formulation perhaps has yet to appear.

Evaluation

Structural-functional approach, after its exposition by Almond and Coleman, became very popular in the field of political analysis and comparative studies. The approach raised high hopes to develop an empirical political theory. Morton A. Kaplan applied it in the field of international relations. Karl Deutsch, Holt and others spoke of its fruitfulness, in a large number of fields. In Political Science, it has been one of the most popular and empirical approaches. It has given a standard category of comparable concepts which help us in collecting data, events, activities and processes relevant to develop a political theory.

As this approach emphasises interdependence or interaction as the basic unit of a political system, it counterbalances the prevailing trends of atomism and radical individualism. It is empirical in its orientation, and has further been enriched by Merton, Levy and others. Concepts like enfunctional, dysfunctional, nonfunctional, functional and structural requisites and prerequisites, intended and recognised functions, unintended and unrecognised functions, pattern-variables, structural differentiation, subsystem autonomy, etc., have proved very useful in the conduct of empirical research. They have provided a standardised terminology for developing a middle-range theory.

Some of the charges raised against early structural-functionalism of Almond and Coleman have also been done away with. Almond and Powell have reformulated their functional perspective as a 'developmental approach', aspiring to make an empirical theory of political change. They have gone beyond their early classificatory scheme of functional requisites of developing areas. They have adopted systems perspective in full, and put more emphasis on structure and culture. Their development syndrome involves the variables of structural differentiation, subsystem autonomy, and secularisation which enable them to describe, explain, and compare all political systems at the levels of maintenance, conversion, and capability. The analysis is spread over to all types of political systems – both developed and developing. They have classified political systems at their performance levels associated with role differentiation, subsystem, independence and secularisation.

In his later exposition, Almond does not suffer from excessive ethnocentrism or Anglophobia, as he accepts that there can be several paths of development, and a system can go back in reverse order. His perspective is now much wider as it enables him to compare capability of political systems at international level. His approach, even while acknowledging its limitations, is able to deal with, what, how, and why of political change. Almond is able to earmark a system's development-problems of state and nation building, participation, and distribution, and point out how structural and cultural changes are made at the three interrelated levels. By and large, his classification-scheme can be empirically analysed and supported by factual data.

His most important contribution is his concept of 'political investment strategies' or 'political development planning', which would prepare various alternative development programmes keeping leadership patterns and prevailing conditions and environment of the political system in view. Investment programmes in political development would give preference to various goals and system development-problems, and be able to know the outcome of all available alternatives. It would certainly be helpful in the development of Engineering Branch of Politicology or Political Science.[19]

Notes

1. Gabriel A. Almond, "A Functional Approach to Comparative Politics", in Gabriel A. Almond and James S. Coleman (eds.). *The Politics of the Developing Areas*, Princeton, N.J., Princeton U.P., 1960, 3-64; Gabriel A. Almond and G. Bingham. Powell, J., *Comparative Politics: A Developmental Approach*, Boston and Toronto, Little, Brown & Co., 1966 (Bombay, Vakils, Feffer and Simons Ltd., Adaptation by Current Thought Series used).
2. Robert T. Holt, "A Proposed Structural-Functional Framework" in James G. Charlesworth (ed.), *Contemporary Political Analysis, op. cit.*, 88.
3. *Supra*, Chap. IV.
4. Meehan, *Contemporary Political Thought: A Critical Study, op. cit.*, 113.
5. Riggs, "Systems Theory: Structural Analysis", in *Approaches to the Study of Political Science*, edited by Michael Hass and Leroy S. Kariel.
6. Talcott Parsons, *The Structure of Social Action*, 1937; *Essays in Sociological Theory: Pure and Applied*, 1949; *The Social System*, 195; *Social Structure and Personality*, 1964.
7. Robert K. Merton, *Social Theory and Social Structure*, New York, Free Press, 1949, 1957.
8. Marion J. Levy Jr., *The Structure of Society*, Princeton, Princeton U.P., 1952; *Modernization: Late-Comers and Survivors*, New York, Basic Books, 1972; See also, *International Encyclopaedia of Social Sciences*, 1968.
9. Almond and Coleman (eds), *The Politics of the Developing Areas*, 1960, Introduction.
10. Almond and Powell, *op. cit.*, Indian ed., New Delhi, Amerind, 1966, 1972, passim. Hereinafter the name of Almond in the present context includes Powell.
11. Almond, "A Developmental Approach to Political Systems", in Finkle and Gable, *Political Development and Social Change*, New York, John Wiley and Sons, 1966, 101-116.

12. Almond and Powell, *op. cit.*, 12.
13. Ibid., 13.
14. Ibid., 131.
15. Ibid., 191.
16. Ibid., 215.
17. Ibid., 220.
18. W.G. Runciman, "Functionalism as a Method in Political Thought" in Gould and Thursby (eds.), *Contemporary Political Thought*, New York, Holt, Rinehart and Winston, 1969, 188.
19. See chapters 3 and 9.

6

Power, Influence, Authority and Legitimacy

Power

From the very beginning, power has been regarded as the most important element in the organisation of society, groups, and institutions. However, in politics we study it as the phenomenon influencing public behaviour of man affecting a political system. Politics is inseparable from power. Catlin regards Political Science as the 'science of power'. Russell has also regarded that 'the fundamental concept in social science is 'power'. According to Bierstedt, 'power' is a universal phenomenon in human societies and in all social relations.'[1] For Morgenthau, politics is nothing but 'the struggle for power.'

Despite its praise and appreciation as a key phenomenon, few people understand it clearly. Statements like 'power tends to corrupt, and absolute power corrupts absolutely', 'state is sin', 'power is violence', 'classless and stateless society', 'withering away of the state', 'total disarmament', etc., simply evince this ignorance.[2] In some cases, such moral aphorisms merely demonstrate ill-conceived notions. With such misunderstandings, some very important cultures, countries, and civilisations have lost their existence. Mottos like 'Truth Always Triumphs' cannot help, as they hide real source of 'triumph', keeping the people in dark. India's pursuance of Panchsheel in this context illustrates the irony of her credulous faith. All other disciplines have spoken of its role, but few have been able to do justice with this very important subject – matter of Political Science. Often rulers, politicians, and administrators claim to know it without understanding it in a proper manner. In consequence, they and their people have to suffer immensely.

Negatively, politics is the art of avoiding the use of legitimate force for society in larger interest or common welfare. Greater the legitimacy lesser would be the need of force. Greater the role of politics, lesser would be the requirement of police. Violence, in non-Gandhian sense, is use of force and coercion. Violence or force in not end of politics but is its concomitant or variant. Force is an important guard of politics for the latter involves use of power and authority. As politics mainly operates on identification of values and goals, force stands subordinate to it.[3] Wolin is right when he says: politics is both a source of conflict and mode of activity that seeks to resolve conflicts and promote readjustments'. Force is punitive, but also reformative and foundational. Without force politics tends to become ethics or religion. It is a worldly affair involving material goods and interests. Therefore, politics without force or violence cannot survive for long. However, there should be proper mixture of force with politics. Politics without violence is suicidal for the politician as well as for a political party or a society. However, it is exercised more through the agency of state.

Evolution of Power Approach

The concept of power and its importance is not new. Socrates, Plato, and other political philosophers have written a lot on it. Most of them have been normative thinkers. Thrasymachus, Aristotle, Hobbes, Machiavelli and others have seen it from a realistic angle. While Trietscke has studied it from historical angle, Nietsche analysed it on philosophical basis. Merriam, Catlin, Russell, Dahl etc., have confined themselves to domestic aspects. In the field of international relations, Hans J. Morgenthau is regarded as the chief spokesman of realitist theory. Catlin, Lasswell, Dahl, Shils and others are democrats. But German thinkers like Carl Lowenstein, Clausewitz, etc., have oriented their thinking on power toward militarism, war, and conflict. Scholars like Hiennemann, Vernon van Dyke, Kaplan and others are interested in conducting academic analysis of power. While studying the concept of power, we should keep the perspectives of these various scholars in mind. They guide as well as mislead.

Concept of Power

As usual, there is lack of consensus on the meaning, scope, and nature of the concept of power. Power broadly, can be seen, (i) generally as a phenomenon found in the whole social order, community, or nation, or, (ii) in particular, in individuals and other macro units. Weber defines power (macht) as 'the probability that one actor within a social relationship will be in a position to carry out his own will despite resistance regardless of the basis on which this probability rests.' Therefore, he conceives the state as a compulsory political association, if, and in so far as, its administrative staff successfully holds a claim to the monopoly of the legitimate use of physical force in the enforcement of its order. According to M.G. Smith, power is the capacity to take autonomous action in face of resistance (contraposition and confrontation) from persons, groups, rules, or material conditions. It is 'the ability to pursue one's will effectively, if necessary by imposing it on others'.

Catlin explains his 'power hypothesis' that everyone wants to execute one's will. Through the execution of one's will, a man wants to realise his particular wish or end. Conditions or freedom to realise one's wish or end is power. Power, therefore, is 'ability to be free in effecting one's own will and to control, whether exercised or not exercised, but potential'.[4] It is the potentiality of effective action which imposes one's will upon the behaviour of others even against opposition. Catlin regards influence as a potential power. *Force* is a kind of guarantee of control. *Violence* is the force we morally condemn. Control lies in the success. For him, unsuccessful power is no power. George Schwarzenberger also regards it as 'capacity to impose one's will on others by reliance on effective sanctions in case of non-compliance'. Catlin puts emphasis on actor's *potentiality* of effective action, and is not satisfied with Weber's 'probability' or possibility. *Potentia* is actual power. To him, mere *potestas* or legal power does not suffice. Political Science studies the phenomena of control or control relationship of human wills. It is study of the science of 'power' or of 'government' which for him means control.[5] His Systematic Theory places 'power' in the central focus.

Rowe includes power and authority under the generic phenomenon of 'influence'. But he finds vital difference among them. According to him, the basis of power is might. Sanctions exist behind the gamut of power. These sanctions pertain to exercise of force or coercion. When authority or influence becomes ineffective, coercive sanctions are used. Both power and coercion are closely related, but are not identical or co-extensive.

Lasswell along with Kaplan has tried to analyse power in a detailed and scientific manner.[6] The concept of power, according to them, is perhaps 'the most fundamental in the whole of Political Science. Political process is the shaping, distribution and exercise of power. Power in general should be distinguished from its specific form as applied in politics. Political power is power over other men. Differing from others, Lasswell puts power under the generic concept of 'influence'. According to him, the study of politics is 'the study of influence and the influential'. He subsumes power under 'influence'. He is interested in studying influence related to the distribution of values in general, and the influential persons or elite in society. Influence is the value position and potential of a person or group. Power, according to him, is 'participation in decision-making'. Power is a value in its own right as well as a means in the realisation of other values. Exercise of power and influence can be based either on coercion or persuasion. Lasswell connects power with severe deprivations: 'Power is a special case of the exercise of influence.' It is the process of affecting policies of others with the help of severe deprivations for non-conformity with the policies intended. Catlin is not satisfied with Lasswell's conceptualisation of influence. Influence is not government. It is control which makes power effective. Control looks to the results, not to modes or processes. But power does not include the whole matrix of social relations.

Bierstedt explains it from a broad sociological perspective. Society is ordered relationship among individuals, groups, and organisations. Interactions among them are structured and organised. 'The element,' he observes, 'that underlies these systems of organised interactions is power.'[7] It supports the basic order of society and the social organisations operating within it. Without power, there is no organisation or order. Where there is organisation or order, there is power. According to him, power is always latent. It is 'ability to employ force, not its actual employment'. Power is the capacity to apply sanctions, not their actual application. It is ability to introduce force in a social situation. From this point of view, it is the predisposition or prior capacity which makes application of force possible. Unlike force, it is always successful. When it is successful in the form of the exercise of force, in principle, it ceases to be power. Power is latent. Force and authority are its expressed forms. Force involves exercise of sanction, such as, reduction, or total elimination of alternatives to persons or groups. Therefore, power is neither force nor authority, but the latter two are intimately related to power.

Several German thinkers like Heinrich von Treitschke, Friedrich Nietzsche, etc., related power to the state, and developed 'power theory of the state'. The essence of the state is, according to Kauffman, development, increase, and display of power with the will successfully to maintain and assert itself. In war, according to such scholars, the state reveals itself in its true essence. For them, naked display of force was power.

A. Khoshkish, in his book *Power or Authority? The Entelechy of Power*, 1991, examines it as 'entelechy' or actualisation of potentials. This potentiality is in flex or is 'potentio-kinetic'. It is akin to the Hobbesian definition: "The power of a man is his present means, to obtain some future apparent good."

Bertrand Russell and many other pacifists have decried the role of power. Russell, using in its widest sense, has stated it as 'production of intended effects upon the outer world, whether human or non-human.'[8] Concentration of political power in the state is destructive of human initiative and freedom. He is opposed to all organised life, and regards authority in any form as anti-thesis of liberty. Power harms those who hold it as well as those on whom it is exercised. It intensifies the passion of rivalry making one more bellicose. His arguments though based on psychological analysis of human nature, are yet ethical and philosophical in nature. It is impossible for man to lead a social life without organised society.

Older thinking on sovereignty, leaving its legalistic and juristic aspects, can also be seen from power perspective. According to Laski, the study of politics concerns itself in relation to organised states. The basis of state-sovereignty is the contingent power to use the armed forces of the state to compel obedience to its biddings. He accepts, that there are many limitations on the exercise and sources of power. These limitations belong to history, tradition, need to secure assent, methods of securing assent, influence of political evolution, pressure of groups, religion, ethics, etc. Dorothy has also dealt with 'sovereignty' under the title 'The Problem of Power in the State'.

Power: Nature, Scope and Forms

The phenomenon of power can be seen from two angles: (a) broader, and (b) narrower. Machiavelli, Hobbes, Graham Wallas, German thinkers, the ancient Indian school of '*danda*'[9] etc. belong to broader view of power. They regard power as an independent variable or element of political life. Catlin does not regard it as an end in itself. But others regard all other variants of influence as different forms of power. The narrower view demonstrates popular approval and commonsense. Accordingly, it is related with severe sanctions and is coercive by nature. It is often identified with violence, fear, terror, force, coercion (see, the following Diagram).

Forms of Power

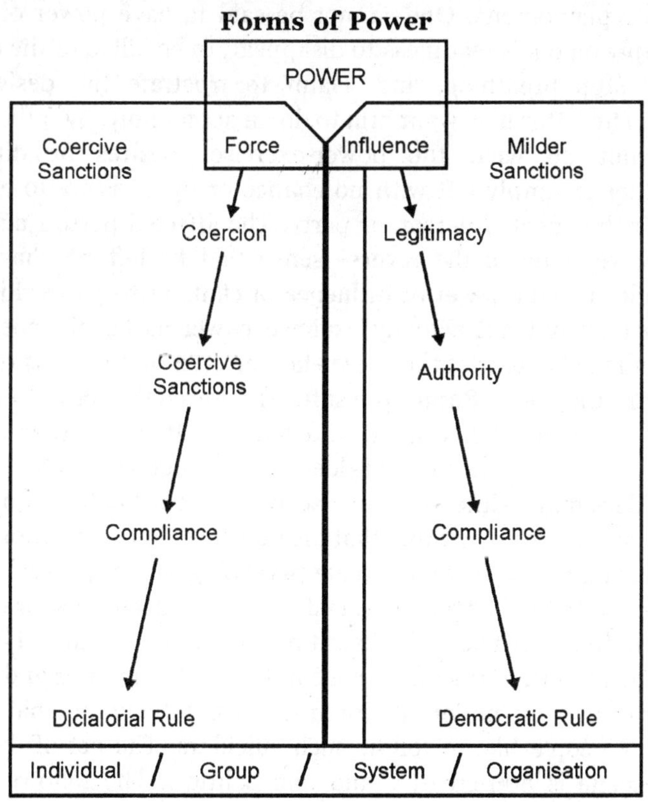

Whatever be the forms, this author holds the view that power is the capacity to produce intended results. It may produce required behaviour either by coercive or non-coercive means. When these means – force, authority, or persuasion – come out, power is transformed from latent capacity to concretised forms. Power may be exercised without requiring the actual use of force or persuasion, but the latter always remains attached with it. The diagram displays power as an over-arching phenomenon. It has further been divided into 'force' and 'influence'. Force involves severe sanctions, or deprivations. Influence inbibes softer or acceptable sanctions, expressed in the form of leadership, legitimacy, and authority. Force or coercive power, unlike influence, is related and can lead to dictatorship, or authoritarian rule. Dominance of influence, leadership, persuasion, etc., is the hallmark of democratic rule. However, in practice, both are used, as they happen to supplement each other. They tend to weaken in the long run, if allowed to operate independently.

Status of Power of Soul and Morality

Often people claim to find highest power in soul or morality. But power is exercised only in empirical and material terms. Politics and society are this-worldly phenomena. One cannot be said to have power or prove his power simply on one's readiness to disappear, to be killed or die out of long fasting or stop breathing, and, claim to frustrate the designs of his adversary. The latter may want him to do an act forcibly, by inflicting pains. He may not do what the power-exerciser desires or directs. The power-holder is simply left with no chance or opportunity to exercise his power over the affected person or party. The affected person may claim to exercise power only in the reverse sense that he left no chance for the power-holder to gain power or influence or claim victory over him. But the affected person did not actually exercise power as he did not make any change in the behaviour of the power-holder even on the basis of removing himself from the scene. Rather the sufferer allowed the former to vindicate, dominate or reinforce his stand and survive. It was rather a walkover granted by the victim to the evil-doer. The number of such evil-doers or power-holders may, witnessing such scene, go on increasing. Sometimes, a masochist or suicider may think that his sacrifice, non-opposition or selfless act of resorting to death would create psychological or spiritual 'change' in the heart of the actual or potential evil-doers. But such hope or expectation appears childlike, myopic and frustrating. It is more a removal of that very man of good intention. It leads to consolidation of the power and position of the powerful persons under all circumstances. Actually no change of heart occurs. Few people like to follow such suiciders. The act of disappearing from the scene is non-creative and non-political. The followers of many faiths or religions may not accept the underlying philosophy, faith and understanding of such suiciders despite their show of extraordinary determination in ending their own lives for a cause. Thereafter, such persons are usually venerated and worshipped like a god by a large number of people. But their followers hardly follow them in practice.

Their followers usually remain peaceful till they remain connected with their non-violent leader. However, they do not have any soul-force or moral power. Direct or actual physical power resides only in the large number of people sitting around the leader. In this way, so called spiritual power of the departed soul translates into *Actual Physical Power* (APP). This is actually the power of the people. Besides them, power also rests with the people who do not take part in the event, and appear apathetic, dormant and inactive. It is probable but irresistible, and can even compel any adversary to relent and concede. Every group, community or organisation invariably possesses *probable potential power* even without showing up its actual physical power. It is a condition precedent in all sorts of power including assumed or actual power. Spiritual power (?) stands powerless when it is not supported by either Actual Physical Power (APP) or Probable Potential Power (PPP).[10] It is this '*probable potential power*' of the people which an adversary keeps in mind. To him, there is no soul-power.

Thus, the power of soul or spiritual power empirically is not power. No soul power can fight or compete with other soul power. In fact, only the persons or collectivities having either *actual physical power* (APP) or *probable potential power* (PPP) can organise themselves or fight. Souls even when existing in body or having left the human bodies do not and can never fight. In order to subdue them, some other persons or collectivities must have either *actual physical power* (APP) or *probable potential power* (PPP). However, they fight with power as a total phenomenon or its variants – put under its coercive and non-coercive forms. This they do in view of the prevailing situation arising at the moment.

Moral power or power of moral values is different from soul power. Moral values broadly belong to outer form and following of religion. They can stand apart from it, and go with tradition, history and habits. They remain active in a people, community or collectivity. Often people stand organised around them, and act and react for maintaining them. Moral values carry actual physical power embodying in persons who happen to oppose elements opposing, decrying or crushing them. In this way, their power is different from soul-power which, in fact, is no power at all. Often people, including some scholars, falsely take *actual physical power* (APP) or *probable potential power* (PPP) as soul power. To some extent, this may be true in case of moral power, but is utterly false in case of soul power.

Power in Action

Power, in a *broader* and empirical sense, includes both coercive and non-coercive power. It directly involves persons, groups, organisations, and systems. A person or political system operates on various forms of power. Max Weber defined a political system as 'a human community that (successfully) claims the monopoly of the legitimate use of physical force within a given territory'.[11] Lasswell and Kaplan use the word 'power' and attach it with severe deprivations. Almond combines concepts of Weber, Parsons, and Easton. He defines a political system as 'that system of interactions to be found in all independent societies which perform the functions of integration and adaptation by means of the employment, or threat of employment, of more or less, legitimate physical compulsion.'[12] Thus, he distinguishes political systems by 'legitimate physical compulsion' from other social systems. It is the essence or base of politics and political systems. Almond is concerned with 'legitimate physical force'.

Power is the *fundamental basis* of politics. It has been described as a common urge or inclination of mankind. As Catlin opines, none sacrifices his freedom to do whatever he chooses or his long cherished liberties: 'None yields his power except from fear, from a conversion of his desires to other ends, and for the particular power to attain these new ends.'[13] Hobbes wrote, 'I put for a general inclination of all mankind, a perpetual or restless desire of Power after Power, that ceaseth only in Death.' Power over men and material is a means to specific security and control. His is the concept of *homopoliticus* or the political man, who demands the maximisation of power in relation to all other values. He believes in power to determine power, and incessantly strives to attain it. According to Michels such a man 'will almost always endeavour to consolidate it and to extend it.' However, it is an 'ideal type' or 'pure' concept, which, when applied in practice, has to be modified substantially. At times, people sacrifice power for the sake of non-political values, but they do so in individual or exceptional cases. But that aspect of power has also to be kept in mind.

Power is *social* and *relational*. It is sociological in its origin – always attached to a person, a group, or an association. Power is power because of prevailing values, interaction patterns, and procedures or modes of attaining them. It lies in specifics and particulars. One can have power over others in particular areas, that too in varying degrees, and intensity. Power can differ with other powers in its *domain*, *weight*, and *scope*.

As stated earlier, power is the latent capacity to apply force. It is not expressed or made visible. Force, authority, domination, etc. are its expressed forms. They are action-aspects of power. Force is employment of sanctions whereas authority is the institutionalised right to employ power. Power has two main forms *Coercive* and *non-coercive*. Coercive power is mainly related with force. Influence is non-coercive power. Influence does not require coercive power, as in the cases of Christ, Buddha and Gandhi. Power as force may dispense with influence, as was done by Chenghiz Khan, Adolf Hitler, Yahya Khan and others. But Napolean, Lincoln, Nehru, and Indira were persons of both power and influence.

Power against Power

When two or more powers stand parallel to each other, the power confronting the other for a longer period over the larger number is considered as superior. This superiority, besides time and number, can also be gained on the basis of use of specific forms, like use of force, manipulation, persuasion, influence etc. of power. However, force proves to be the ultimate mainstay of all other forms. Force has to be most modern, tactfully used, highly motivated and resourceful. Force has to be met with force. Hardly, there is any substitute to it. Neglect of force and its proper use and organisation leads to the end of a polity. For example, present day spread and success of terror is the result of neglect of its proper use to face it. If non-state terror kills innocent people, authorities of the polity must be held criminally accountable to the justice who too must act with greater speed, effect and activism. Failing which the judiciary too should be restructured by the organs of civil society.

Dimensions of Power

There are many other *forms* of power. *Dominance* is a psychological concept as its locus is in the individual. It appears in interpersonal relations. It is a function of personality and temperament. Dominant individuals play roles in powerless informal groups. Power, on the contrary, is a sociological concept. It appears in statuses which the people occupy in formal groups or organisations. *Force* involves application of sanctions. Force is manifestation of power and not power itself. Power is the ability to employ force, not its 'actual employment. Power is *latent* force. Force is *manifest* power. Unlike force, power is always successful. Power that fails is not power. It has to accumulate, aggregate and augment. Force and influence are its operational and manifest aspects, and provide base to use power.

Power can be *formal* or *informal*. *Formal* power is known as authority. Power is transformed into authority through the formal organisation of human associations. The right to use force is attached to hierarchical statuses in the organisations. Power is formally allocated not to persons but to positions or statuses by specified norms, rules and laws. Power, thus, is institutionalised as authority which can be exercised by any man occupying that position. As there are informal organisations and groups, informal power and *informal* authority also exist. Power remains uninstitutionalised in informal organisations. It does not take the form of authority. However, authority itself cannot exist without the immediate support of power and the ultimate sanction of force.[14]

Herbert Gold Hammer and Edward A. Shils have stated three major forms of power on the basis of *extent* to which behaviour is influenced. It is (i) force, (ii) domination, and, (iii) manipulation. In *force,* one influences the behaviour of individuals by physical manipulation like assault, confinement, etc. In *domination,* he influences their behaviour by making explicit to others what he wants them to do, such as, by command, request, etc. In *manipulation,* he influences the behaviour of others without making explicit the behaviour which he thereby wants them to perform, such as, by utilising symbols or performing certain acts as in propaganda. *Legitimacy* is the 'right to rule'. When the subordinated individuals recognise that right, the power exercised by the weilders of power is regarded as legitimate power. In case, it is not recognised by them, but exercised, it becomes *coercion*. Legitimate power further appears in three major forms. It is *legal* when the subordinated individuals recognise it on the basis of a belief in the legality of the laws, decrees, and directives given by the power-weilder. When the recognition of legitimacy rests on a belief in the sanctity of traditions by virtue of which the powerful exercises his power and in the traditional sanctity of the orders which he issues, it becomes *traditional legitimacy. Charismatic legitimacy* rests on devotion of subordinated individuals to the personal qualities of the powerful.[15] A weilder of power whose authority is recognised as legitimate can exercise any form of power, such as, force or domination.

From the viewpoint of the *flow* of power-relationship, power can be unilateral, bilateral, multilateral, and bargaining. It is *unilateral* if only one party to that relationship exercises power over the other. When two parties exercise power over each other, it becomes *bilateral,* as in case of a bargaining event. In *multilateral* power-relations, many parties mutually try to influence each other's behaviour. When the power-weilder alters the behaviour of others without bringing in any intermediary, the exercise of power is called *direct*. When it is exercised through subordinates or intermediaries, it is regarded as *indirect*. From the point of view of control or autonomy, power can be *concentrated* or *diffused*. When power is exercised through a large number of subordinate units, it tends to become diffused as the power-weilder is rarely able to exercise control over them. The subordinates begin to exercise some amount of independence and take initiative. Power is concentrated when the power-weilder exercises ways and means to have control over it.

Geographical areas also shape form and extent of power. Power spreading over the whole globe or dominant among nations is known as *international* power. Power of a country may be dominant in some region, and get the status of *regional* power. Power limited within the territory of a nation is popularly designated as *national* power. Extent of influences rule, and their comparative weight make powers of various nation-states as *super, major, medium,* and *ordinary*. Consequences of the behaviour of power-weilder can be intended or unintended.

As power is social and relational, it is also *distributive*. Political Science is interested in knowing who gets it, how much, in what way and the bases of its distribution. It cannot be possessed like a thing or commodity. It arises out of relations existing among human beings, called by Lasswell as 'inter-personal'. If we go deeper, it would appear that ultimately, it, belongs to the areas of human mind – psychological, pathological, even neurotic. Power can be generated even by withdrawing from it, thereby generating a sense of veneration, loyalty and personal commitment to the powerless power-weilder. In this sense, both Buddha and Gandhi wielded power. When analysed further, we would find that such power is based on similarity of ingrained *values*, directly or indirectly, operating in the minds of both power-weilders and their followers. In this sense, power requires cooperation or non-cooperation, as the case may be, and the inculcation of certain values which may not be fully understood by them at all. They should some how feel and acknowledge those values and some faith in them. Ultimate acknowledgement of the will or capacity of the superior power-weilder to influence others is final arbiter of power. *Acknowledgement*, which may be given in a direct or indirect manner, is more important than the possession of power as a material thing. The acknowledgement, according to Hacker, can be based on the consideration of power-weilder's knowledge, skill, physical powers, property, personality, fear, etc. When a person acts in deference to the wishes of the power-weilder, it implies acknowledgement of the superiority of the will or capacity of the power-weilders. If there is no obedience to his wishes, and the affected party is ready to undergo all the consequences, no power exists. Power very much depends upon proper assessment of the contours of obedience. A power-weilder has to keep an eye on them.

To make power effective, it is necessary to *use* it. Its non-use renders the powerful powerless. Power is concreticised in action or activity, which must have some aim or *objective* in view. As such, power instead of being an end-in-itself, is instrumental to gain other objectives. Politics understood as 'struggle for power' does not convey its proper meaning. It is rather a struggle to launch certain *values* through power over others. These values may include narrow self-interests or broader social interests or a mix of the two. These values also have an intimate relationship with the needs and demands of human nature. Man wants both liberty and social order. Therefore, conflicts as well as cooperation become ingredient of power. In order to realise those values or objectives, power mainly depends on *organisation*. One may have knowledge, Divine grace, ideology, manifesto, ideals, etc. but cannot realise them without organisation of a church, a political party, or other a band of followers. Political power comes out of an effective organisation and by adopting tactics appropriate to sustain it. It requires great skill and refined techniques to keep organisations attached with pre-determined goals. There can be many goals of power, such as, (i) collective good, (ii) conscious pursuit of self-interest, or (iii) pursuance of unconscious motives. These goals can be modified or reformulated in view of change in leadership or prevailing circumstances. Either the weilders power, or subordinates or clientele can bring about change in goals consciously or unconsciously, even by procedural set-up. It requires unusual statesmanship to realise these goals. Power has to be restructured, applied, augmented and allocated in a proper manner.

In sum, power can be visualised in many ways. Felix E. Oppenheim has summarised various views on power, as (i) exercise of control; (ii) exclusion of rational persuasion; (iii) inducements; (iv) intentional control; (v) relationship between preferences of the powerful and respondent's behaviour; (vi) involvement of conflict with respondent's intentions or interests. But Terence Ball is not satisfied with Oppenheim's conception of power as 'all relationship in which one actor determines another actor's behaviour by almost any means and for any end whatever.'[16] Ball finds it as unduly broad, as all instances of influences are not instances of power. Not all instances of power are instances of influence. Oppenheim makes his conception of power as coextensive with social causation, and renders it too broad to be useful for empirical analysis.

Force is different from power. The latter is ability to employ force. Force and other manifest forms of power remain invisible in the lap of power like electricity in clouds. To make power or one's capacity effective, one has to develop all traits to employ, force properly along with adequacy and availability of all means of power, such as personality, influence, force, organisation, etc. Power has to be supported by sanctions. A sanction is a power-act initiated primarily as a reprisal for non-conformity with a prior act of power. It results either in the deprivation of values already possessed or an obstruction of values which otherwise would have been realised. There are several forms and levels of sanctions. Military power represents the apex of coercive sanctions, socialised and trained in an effective organisation.

In fact, there are several sources of power: brute force, position, connection, persuasion and influence, self-confidence, charisma and reputation, consciousness and will, and coefficients of power.[17] Through legitimising processes, it transforms into Law and Authority. About non-justified Power, Lord Action, long ego has said, "Power tends to corrupt and absolute power corrupts absolutely." In fact, it corrupts both, those who exercise it and their victims. Power, in general, is what make things go, wheels to turn, ships to sail, man to move in particular ways. It is energy. Energy becomes power only when it is harnessed, guided, and controlled. Out of control energy is not power. Negative or out of control power is negative and destructive. In order to be usable, it has to be made creative, constructive and directive. Power in human affairs involves the control of human behaviour for particular ends through the express or implied threat of punishment for those who refuse or fail to comply. But this can be done through education, indoctrination and influence. Power is the ability to take and enforce decisions – laws, decrees, rules or regulations. Power serves as a protection against the danger of feeling or being regarded as insignificant. There can be public or private power systems. Public power claims jurisdiction other over all persons who reside in a given territory. Political power, says, Locke, is the right of making laws with penalties of death and consequently all less penalties for regulating and preserving property and of employing the force of the community in the execution of such laws. Persuasion is more common than the use or threat of force. It is more effective and enduring. Therefore, we talk of will, consent, consensus or deference. All this makes the power system legitimate, investing it with authority. Without authority, political power appears as naked force. This is accomplished by political socialisation through family, schools, churches, other voluntary groups, political parties, pressure groups, media, charismatic leadership and symbolism. To keep power away from being corrupt, constitutional limitations through laws and courts are imposed. Its scope and domain is made limited and fixed. Its operation can be liberal, conservative or authoritarian. It may or may not come under the influence of outside forces.

Political Power and Military Power

From a broader view of power, both political and military powers are forms of power. But in politics, military power finds a secondary or background role. Power is not actual exercise of force but a capacity to make use of it. Political power is mainly psychological whereby man controls minds and actions of other men. Military power is actual exercise of force in an organised manner. Whenever there is actual exercise of military or para-military power, it means political power has been rendered ineffective and has abdicated its role in favour of organised coercion. Politicians tacitly accept their failure when the military takes over. The latter can be used for short-term, limited and immediate purposes.

However, Vernon van Dyke puts military power within the arena of political power. Karl von Clausewitz regarded war as continuation of politics by other means. For him, both peace and war are a continuous process – a historical continuum.[18] He regards military power as a sub-division of political power. Conflict underlies all politics. It may be conducted by means of either words or violence. However, the two remain forms of manifest power, as political power pursues non-coercive means whereas military power represents the highest and organised form of force. Establishment of order by force or military power is remnant indication of old primitive societies, at times necessary, even desirable. In a developed society, military, power remains in the background of political power. Political power operates through the processes of influence, leadership, legitimacy, persuasion and authority. Only politicians know and use it. It is the anti-thesis of force.

Empirical Theory of Power

All political interactions, domestic or international, involve the phenomenon of power. But its concept lacks precision. Scholars have attempted to analyse sources, goals, instruments, and effects of power, but lack unanimity over its referents. The concept of power must be explained in the context of various political systems and subsystems, and in a manner that empirical generalisations are derived therefrom. Along with them, it is desirable that a scientific theory is developed which is able to explain power in its various forms and their specificity and uniqueness.

Power as a relational phenomenon to produce induced behaviour presents a unifying and centralising principle. To make the concept empirical, two things must be kept in view: (a) power is behavioural, and (b) relationship between elements of power, and power-behaviour must be established in a manner that it may form the basis of explanation, prediction, and empirical experiment. This is what an empirical theory does, Power is a relational, interpersonal, and interactive process. A man or a nation can exercise power only if there is someone else to act upon. Power is not a thing or commodity which can be possessed without exercising it. Weapons, wealth, property, organisation, etc. are important elements, bases, or sources of power. They are considered important as they provide opportunity to exercise control over others. It is improper to treat them all-important, and forget to relate them with actual power-behaviour. Empirical power goes to the extent a political actor influences the behaviour of others. Power does not exist or remains ineffective if a nation is unable to change or modify the behaviour of other nations. When we say a *nation* is militarily more powerful, it simply means that it alone has more weapons and a bigger army to change the behaviour of nations concerned, and also has a will to do so when an occasion arises.

Often the analysts of power have not tried to compare the variables or elements of power with power. For this purpose, an adequate concept of power must be developed. It can relate power-behaviour with elements of power, and evolve appropriate hypotheses or suggest propositions. A behavioural approach to power is justified on two grounds: (a) As power involves influence or control, it is an observable empirical activity. The power-weilder must be in possession of relevant elements of power. He must comparatively be free from obstructions or restrictions, and also have capacity or ability to use them. All of these things can be subsumed as 'capability', (b) The power-weilder must have the will or resolution to control others. Power-setting requires both – capability as well as the will. Or as a potential power, it should be ingrained with credibility, so that it may be empirically observed.

The need to *measure* power also directs us to adopt the behavioural approach. A scientific power theory aims at comparing and measuring power. Elements or cases of power do not provide standardised units (like currency notes, weights, etc.) for measurement and quantification. A millionaire cannot be compared with a highborn man. Scholars like Quincy Wright have also found this difficulty that political and social power, because of qualitative variations, cannot be uniformally measured like physical power. Solution of the problem lies in making activities of political actors as basis of measurement. We can measure the behavioural consequences of wealth and status, jointly and separately, observing the number of persons a power-weilder controls over.

For this purpose, power has to be *defined* or translated into behavioural terms. According to Robert A. Dahl, A has power over B to the extent, A induces B to do acts which otherwise he would not do. Goldhammer and Shils define it as a person having power to the extent he is able to influence others behaviour according to his own intentions. Dahl's explanation, thus, overlooks internationality of political actors, leaving aside power-acts like manipulation, propaganda, etc. A nation, even after doing an act under the influence of another nation, can claim that it has done it at its own will. The clause 'according to his own intentions' makes the conventional statements, as, 'against his will', 'despite resistance', 'which otherwise he would not have done', etc. redundant. But if Goldhammer and Shil's clause is accepted, should all acts pertaining to fulfilment of one's will or wish be regarded as acts of power? Should a small nation's wish to live in isolation or neutral be regarded as indicator of its power? Isaac suggests that (i) such acts of power-behaviour should be performed both by the influencer and the influenced; and (ii) there should be some contact or communication before the actualisation of power relations between them. Without some form of contact, power relations cannot exist at all.

In accordance with the behavioural explanation of power a political actor influences the behaviour of others in terms of his own intentions or will. But there arises another difficulty. Unilateral or causal relations do not exist in power-settings. Many acts of power trigger off feedback or mutually influencing operations. If nation A influences the behaviour of nation B, there is an opportunity that B also influences the behaviour of A. Of course, this analysis, in addition, makes the comparison of their power, at least more difficult, if not impossible. In case there is interval of time, the personal behaviour of the actor must be put under observation. Quantum of power and direction would also tell which side has more power.

Thus, influence on the acts of behaviour of the actors is regarded as the main unit of observation and measurement of power. There are various forms of political acts by which an actor can influence the behaviour of others. They can broadly be divided in three forms: (i) force, (ii) domination, and (iii) manipulation. In *force*, there is exercise of physical acts, namely, empirically observable physical sanctions. In a situation of *domination*, the actor expresses his intentions to the other party and realises that situation or intended behaviour. Often force and domination go together. Force is used to make domination effective. In manipulation, the actor does not let others know the aims or objects of his behaviour, namely, exercise of power. It includes actions, which cannot be easily understood or observed. However, techniques are developed to know latent intentions and observe and measure relevant influence. Rest of the acts are open and manifest.

Power theory requires that power-acts must be clearly defined and fully comprehended, who is influencing or controlling by what acts. Variables included in a two broad definitions usually are very difficult to be analysed properly. Only those acts can be understood and empirically analysed which are performed against the wishes of a person or a nation. In power relations, such acts among actors often take place. A strategy is required which may empirically link these stimuli and responses, and produce generalisations. If a set of a activities is regulated before another set of activities, a correlation between them or probable association can be established. After visualising an observable contact between the two nations, if we find a form of some activity from out of their total behaviour, it can be assumed that power relations exist. Many members of parliament change their public statements after having a meeting with the prime minister. Sometimes, the principle of 'anticipated expectations' is also used and applied. Only after bringing power into observable dimensions, it becomes probable to measure it.

It is clear that a scientific power-theory cannot consider the state as the sole repository of power. Trietscke, Nietsche, Kauffmann etc. regarded the state as embodiment of power. Such an extremist view subordinates all activities, organisations, groups, etc., to the state. In modern times, state has monopoly over the exercise of legitimate power, but power, both in coercive and non-coercive forms, also operates beside the state. There are non-state actors of power, such as the terrorists like Al-Queda. The power-principle, or theory in a loose sense, enables us to perceive political activities in an organised and meaningful manner, and is useful to understand the behaviour of nations and other political actors.

Steven Lukes in his book *Power: A Radical View* (1974) discusses three ways of exercise of power: decision-making, agenda-setting and thought control.[19] The postmodern thinker, Michel Foucault (1926-84), discovers a link between power and systems of thought through the idea of a 'discourse of power'.[20]

But, it may be pointed that power is not the only sole material making up a political systems, and its legal organisation known as state. There are many other factors and contents which constitute political systems and subsystems. If the concept of power is confined only to force or coercion, the theory would prove misleading and too narrow to be of any use. Along with power, we have to study its other forms also. Most important of them are influence, authority and legitimacy.

Influence

Power is the capacity to produce intended behaviour. This capacity can be exercised on the basis of coercive or non-coercive sanctions. Force is based on coercive sanctions. Influence is related to non-coercive sanctions. Both are the two main forms of power. However, some regard power as a form of influence, and other treat influence as a form of power. They appear different when power is identified with force, and influence as unrelated to power. Influence and force, both are treated as variants of power.

Influence is persuasive. One submits voluntarily to influence. Influence does not require coercive power. It is attached to an idea, a doctrine, or a creed. It has its locus in the ideological sphere.[21] Christ, Buddha, Marx, Gandhi and the like had influence. By 'influence' is meant ability to get others act, think, or feel as one intends.[22] From this point of view any cooperative activity – any organisation, formal or informal, ephemeral or lasting can be looked as a sphere of influence.

Lasswell uses the concept of 'influence' in a generic sense: 'The study of politics is the study of influence and the influential.[23] He is aware of the distinction between power and influence. According to Lasswell, 'influence is the value position and potential of a person or group.'[24] It aims at affecting the policies of others by persuasive means. Rowe includes power and authority in the concept of influence.[25]

Political influence is the power sought for by politically active persons like legislators, ministers, leaders, etc. For some persons it is a source of enjoyment for its own sake, while for others it may be a means to determine or affect a policy. It intends to decide what interest it shall serve, of what value, and with what form of expression. Political influence is unevenly shared. Often a vast majority wields very small influence, whereas a small minority, known as the elite can rule over a whole political system. Catlin has observed that influence contributes to building up a control system, especially of a consensual, habitual, or cooperative order. It is distinct from 'command' and 'coercion'. It has potentiality, but remains on the verge of power as coercive force. It is rather potential power, less than actual control. *Potential power* appears in persons or groups when someone evokes their attention on some just and suppressed cause. Such causes often stand in suppressed, secondary or unconcerned manner. They are not immediate but mediate or next to currently conflicting causes. *Probable potential power* (PPP) exists among a very large number of unorganised people. It belongs to masses. It may erupt in an organised or unorganised manner. Even state power may stand helpless before its avalanche. Successful influence is a form of mental control: authority, leadership, political party, legitimacy, etc., are its various manifestations.

Two Views

In a general sense, as 'capacity to induce behaviour', both power and influence are identical. In order to conceptualise both as one, we propose to use it as 'Power' (with capital 'P'). Analytically, 'power' as capacity is a noun while influence is both a noun (fact) and a verb (process or activity). In the elaborate explanation of interrelationship between power and influence, both views can be adopted. The *power view* regards influence as a form of power, which is largely indirect and unorganised. Some scholars like Weber, MacIver, Bierstedt, etc., take wider view of power. Morgenthau views all politics as struggle for power. Others distinguish two variants of power, as coercive and non-coercive. In politics, non-coercive power is more important than coercive power. The *influence view* observes influence as an all-pervading phenomenon. The second view also involves two perspectives. One finds all behavioural changes as related to influence. Rowe finds it an umbrella concept covering power, authority, etc. According to him, power is coercive influence. The other view is specific, and acknowledges both power and influence as independent variables. Influence is different from power in the sense that man voluntarily submits to influence, whereas power requires submission. Karl Marx and Gandhi had influence, not power. Influence in this sense does not require power. Power can exist without influence. In politics and political organisations both are found in a mixed form, as in actual practice influence also has power and vice versa, though consequences differ in nature and impact.

Power and Influence: Dissimilarities

Here, 'Power' has been used in a popular coercive sense. It is separate from Power in general sense. Power as 'force' is indicated by the small first letter: power. It is force, based on physical sanctions or severe deprivations. Influence is non-coercive power, mainly persuasive. Both power as coercive force, and influence as non-coercive power, can be distinguished in the following manner:

1. 'Power' (as force) is coercive. It carries severe physical sanctions which can probably be applied in power-situations. When power is exercised on a person or group, there remains no alternative available to him except complying with it. Influence is psychological, persuasive and voluntary. A person or group under influence always has alternatives while accepting a particular compliance. It is pursuasive and imbued with milder sanctions.

2. 'Power' remains with the power-wielder in an independent manner and makes him autocratic and undemocratic, as it is exercised against the will or wishes of other person. If not legitimate, it invites counter-action, either in the form of counter-power or counter-force. Influence is dependent, being relational. In a way, the influencer plays a greater role than the influencee. As it is accepted voluntarily, its legitimacy is implied and is totally democratic.
3. 'Power' is based on fear of pain or deprivation, as the power-wielder stands against the values of the other party. When it is exercised, influence ceases. Influence comes out of similarities of values or ideological commonness. When influence operates, there remains no need of force or coercion. Both are antithetical to each other.
4. 'Power' has greater limitations from the point of cost – money, energy and time. Still it may or may not be successful, as the other party may not yield to threats, manipulation, etc. In comparison with it, scope of influence is unlimited or broader. It is largely inexpensive. It is often successful and its output in the form of cooperation or compliance is greater.
5. However, power has the quality of being definite. It is general by nature, in the sense whosoever holds it will be fearfully effective. Nevertheless, influence remains indefinite, fluid and fuzzy. It is interpersonal, and not-transferable.

As both can bring about change and control of human behaviour, there are certain *common* features observable in them. Both become effective when they are legitimate. Otherwise, force as power can operate, but influence cannot. In a general sense, both are relational, rational, and relative. Though there is no demarcating line existing between them, yet both need each other. Sometimes, influence does not operate on whom power activates. If, it is seen seriously, it will be found that influence generates power and power influence. Certainly, influence coming out of power is qualitatively different from power generated by influence, being persuasive, democratic and emotionally attached. But the ultimate effect of influence is power, as it can be at any time transformed into coercive force. Non-coercive aspects of influence continue to make it more effective, but it also augments its power as a potential force so much so that sometimes influence may have greater effect than power as such. In this sense, at one time or other, Gandhi, during freedom movement of India, and Mujib during war of liberation in East Pakistan (Bangla Desh) had greater effect in view of their influence over the masses than the adversaries on the basis of their power. During the middle ages, the Pope was more powerful than the Emperor.

However, at the analytical level both have been regarded as independent variables. Influence is preferred because cost incurred on it is always less than on exercise and accumulation of power as force. Consequences are almost identical when influence is transformed in forms of power, and exercised in actual practice, but such occasions rarely arise, particularly, when it is already widespread, enveloping a large number of people. Influence can prove ineffective in the last resort, when a diehard adversary finds that the influence is determined to stop its conversion into coercive power. When situation goes beyond the control of influences, it becomes obvious that influence can take the form of power in its various aspects. Power as force is occasionally used when influence fails to influence the diehards, fundamentalists or rebels.

Role of Influence in Politics

In democracies, influence has a greater role to play. In ancient times, with limited functions, the state perhaps could do with small power, though it had resorted to many other means to supplement its stock of power. Modern state with its ever-increasing functions cannot confine itself within the boundaries of limited power. Therefore its politics relates to the phenomena of influence or non-coercive power. In international field, nations, and national politics, individuals, groups and parties remain engaged in spreading over their influence. For them, it is a question of life and death, particularly in democratic and civilised politics. So far, there is no theory or developed apparatus to measure one's influence. Scholars have failed to come to their rescue. Leaders largely depend on their own subjective evaluations and other half-baked notions. Limitations of power necessitate the support of influence. As influence denotes a kind of 'voluntarism', it can be treated as 'heart of democracy'. However, a small minority or the elite can attain much influence in democracy, while the vast majority may remain dormant and without influence.

Influence: Nature, Process and Sources

Influence, or enveloping power, is a relation among individuals, groups, associations, organisations and states. In lieu of this relation, one actor induces other actors to act in a way they would not otherwise act. Bachrach and Baratz explain, 'one person has influence over another within a given scope to the extent that the first, without resorting to either a tacit or an overt threat of severe deprivations, causes the second to change his course of action.'

There are limits on the use of power (force) everywhere. Exercise of coercive powers saps all sources of enthusiasm, initiative, etc. Under these circumstances, such power-wielders themselves resort to various ways and means of influence. Rarely does a person solely act on the basis of his own knowledge or judgement. Often he relies on information, suggestions, reactions from other persons. The more effective one among these persons influences his behaviour. Influence does not require coercive power.

There are many *sources* through which influence emerges. Political influence depends upon the possessions of wealth, health, education, personal charm, etc. Apart from them, skill with which they are employed is also important. In political resources, Dahl includes money, information, food, threat of force, jobs, alliances, social status, right to make and implement laws, votes, etc. They are not available to all. Distribution of these resources follows the changes in economic, social and political set-up. Changes can occur through rules or otherwise – violent or constitutional. Political influence is sought by the politically active. Some seek it for pleasure's sake, while others treat it, as a means to determine or affect public policies. All are not equally skilful in making use of their political resources.

Uneven Distribution of Influence

There are many reasons for the uneven control of political influence: (a) some acquire specialisation in specific functions and have more information about a particular subject matter; (b) others inherit a lead or lag in their socio-biological attributes, physical strength, social status, political standing of their parents, forbearance, etc., (c) variations in socio-biological inheritance together with their acquired experiences produce differences in the incentives and goals of their work; and (d) variations mentioned above happen to create differences in values and resources. Everyone does not go to politics or becomes a political leader. Different persons seek different resources. Such variety is good for the health and life of a political system.

Briefly, differences in one's endowments and experiences lead to differences in political resources and motivation. The latter push people towards varying political skills and the extent to which they are able to make use of them. All that results in uneven distribution of their political influence which has an overall effect on the starting points mentioned earlier. Uneven political influence does not mean that there are permanent political elites or newer elites will not emerge. Older ones may disappear with the emergence of newer ones.

Measuring Political Influence

Everyone related with politics is interested in measuring his adversary's political influence. Influence in politics largely depends on political sources and skill to use them. Political resource is a means by which one can influence the behaviour of other persons. For measuring influence, one can rely on Dahl's notion that A influences B to the extent that he gets B to do something that B would not otherwise do. We can notionally measure A's influence on B when the latter does x when A does not influence B. When A does influence, B does x_1. Thus, the influence of A on B would be $x_1 - x$. We can determine direction, volume, scope, weight and durational effect of a person's influence under study. Dahl has suggested five ways of comparing influence.[26] They can be taken as the basis of measuring influence:

(1) the amount or extent of change occurred in the position of the actor influenced;
(2) subjective psychological costs of the influences while complying with an order or undergoing a hardship;
(3) the amount of difference in the probability of compliance, especially when the influencer puts the influences under his act of influence;
(4) difference in the nature and extent of responses. Some may respond in all general matters while others may react to specific stimuli; and
(5) the number of persons responding to the situation, act, or influence.

These steps are not at all foolproof. In order to arrive at better and reliable results one has to make use of maximum number of measures. The paradigm given by Dahl for comparison would make it more specific: '... is more influential than ... with respect to ... as measured by ... and ... .'

Rowe opines that influence owing to secrecy and other factors can rarely be measured. It can only be approximately assessed in terms of (a) extent, (b) duration, (c) certainty, and, (d) fecundity. The last relates to policy-sustaining effects. He rightly observes that political influence is unevenly shared. It is a fact of life. But this unevenness is ever-changing. None can peacefully sleep over with what one has at a particular point of time. Though a small minority rules over a particular system, yet its influence continues to change over time. Fortunately, computers and automation have come to their rescue.

Actual and Potential Influence

It is always necessary to distinguish between the past or current influence of a particular actor under a given situation, and his probable or future influence. Both of them can be different from his maximum potential influence if he could make a bid to use all his existing political resources with utmost skill and wit. A politician's present influence always falls short of his maximum potential influence The influence of an actor in a given situation always fluctuates, but it rarely reaches the apex of his maximum potential influence. Only a few actors acquire the required degree of political skill, they feel it worthwhile to use their resources to the full to maximise their political influence. Political actors often stop and begin to rest at one of the many points of scale of vertical political life. They often get tired and are never sure either of their own or opponent's political influence. In politics, we are mainly concerned with actual influence which should be constantly analysed, measured, and accounted for. Measurements of one's potential influence is a luxury and can be undertaken in a leisurely manner, but it is a task not to be dropped altogether.

Authority

Often influence and authority are wrongly construed as identical. We have already discussed influence as an independent variable. Political leaders constantly endeavour to magnify their influence but they know well that it is highly flexible, fluid, dynamic, indefinite and uncertain, though at times more effective than power itself. It is personal, relational and relative, depending much upon the nature of influences themselves. Therefore, they remain in search of stabilising their influence by way of transforming it into authority or acquire a hold over institutions and structures of authority like state, law, presidency, judiciary and others. Apart from political actors, society and its various segments too desires stabilised, accepted, known, and described or formalised patterns of power and influence. Such patterns usually are conducive to individual liberty as well as efficiency and effectivity of political systems. However, it takes years and decades to carve out recognisable authority structures.

Concept, Nature and Process

It must be remembered that neither force nor influence is authority. But all the three are manifestations or express forms of power. Power, in a sense, is the predisposition or prior capacity which makes application of force, influence and authority possible. Power is the ability to employ force or sanctions, but not its actual employment. Authority is 'the institutionalised *right to* employ power'.

Authority has been conceptualised in various ways, such as,

1. a property of a person or office;
2. a relationship between two offices, one superior and the other subordinate;
3. a quality of a communication by virtue of which it is accepted; and
4. an interdependence between two segments of authority – one issuing orders, and, others receiving and complying with orders.

There is a lack of unanimity over the meaning and use of 'authority'.[27] Authority as a phenomenon is older than the 'state' itself. According to Bertrand de Jouvenel, it is an outcome of the natural ascendancy of some men over others. Michels regards it as 'the capacity, innate or acquired, for exercising ascendancy over a group'. But Biersted disagrees with him. In his view, authority is not a capacity. It is a relationship of exercising ascendancy. It is a sanctioned or institutionalised power.

Authority is also regarded with deep suspicion, even open hostility. It can be a threat to an individual as it calls for unquestioning obedience. Therefore, some celebrate the decline of authority. It is also a threat to reason and critical understanding. It demands unconditional and unquestioning compliance, and can generate a climate of deference, and abdication of responsibility, and an uncritical trust in the judgement of others.[28]

In the field of management and public administration, authority has been regarded as 'a right to command'. According to Simon, authority comes into existence only when the subordinates postpone or give up their own freedom to choose one of the various alternatives available to them, and take up the formal order or indication as the criterion of their choice. Beach puts it as the legitimate authority to direct or influence others' behaviour.[29] UNESCO report (1955) maintained it as that power which is recognised, respected, known and legitimate. Tennanbaum finds it as interpersonal relationship between the superiors and subordinates. The subordinate grants 'authority' to the decision-maker and puts himself in the position of the latter's subordinate. According to Simon, authority relations exist only when there occurs actual change in the behaviour of the subordinates. The superior person takes decisions and communicates them to his subordinates with the expectation that their subordinates will accept them. Authority relations involve (i) expectation of obedience, and (ii) willingness to obey. This concept of authority goes against the traditional view, which regards it, a 'top-down' command; the boss has right to issue orders and the subordinates have their duty to act on them faithfully.

There are two theories regarding nature of authority: (a) The Formal theory maintains it as right to issue commands. Authority flows from superior to subordinates, making up the organisational hierarchy. (b) The Acceptance theory relates to behavioural and human relations schools. According to it, the former theory explains authority only from legal or formal point of view. In actual practice, successful authority depends on the acceptance of the orders by the subordinates. In view of Chester I. Bernard, four conditions must be fulfilled: (i) the subordinate must be able to understand the order or communication; (ii) after getting it, he must have belief that it is not against the goals of the organisation; (iii) he must consider his compliance in conformity with his own individual interests as a part of whole set-up; and, (iv) he must be, mentally and physically capable of complying with the order.

According to the latter view, authority flows down-up. In the absence of acceptance, cooperation, willingness and ideological similarity, authority becomes nominal or formal. It is no more real authority. Under the acceptance theory of authority, the subordinates tend to make room in their mind for receiving the orders or communication from their superiors, and comply with them without arguing and opposition. The subordinates invariably accept orders falling within this area. Bernard calls it, 'zone of indifference.' For Tenanbaum, it is 'sphere of acceptance' whereas Simon has named it as 'zone of acceptance'. This zone tends to increase or decrease in proportion to ideological relationship found between the superiors and the subordinates.

It would be observed, there is some exaggeration in the acceptance theory. There is a great need to bring about a synthesis between the two. The subordinates in an organisation do not have so much leeway to accept or reject orders coming from above. Authority, in order to be made effective, is organised in a deconcentrated manner, and various sanctions are attached at various points. A chain of delimited quantum of responsibility and accountability interlinks these points in the hierarchy. Acceptance of authority by the subordinates cannot be the ultimate criterion of compliance. The general support and consent of the society propels up the authority of an organisation.

Bachrach and Baratz opine that while authority is closely related to power, it is not one of its various forms.[30] In fact, it is *antithetical* to it. They reject the traditional view that it is 'formal power', and also criticise that it is 'institutionalised power'. According to them, the concept of authority as a form of power is not operationally useful. If it is so, who possesses formal power, when the superior is actually helpless. It is also not useful for those who believe in limited or constitutional government. Its prescription by law does not bestow all legitimacy to it.

Friederich defines authority as a quality of communication that possesses 'the potentiality of reasoned elaboration'. A possesses 'authority', because B regards A's communication as authoritative. It means B recognises compliance or command as reasonable in terms of his own values. B defers to A, not because he fears severe deprivations, but because A's decision *can be rationalised.* It is not essential that A's decision is expressly supported by reasoning. It is sufficient that it has potentiality of such reasoning and is so recognised.

If B believes that A's communication allows for reasoned elaboration when actually it does not, it is 'false' authority. When the source of compliance shifts from 'genuine' to 'false' authority, and B realises that communication cannot be elaborated effectively, then, relationship initially involving authority has been transformed into one involving power. Compliance, thus, commanded is an exercise of power. Authority operates in terms of similarity of values. It is both a source of and a restraint upon exercise of power. It both justifies as well as limits the use of power. But authority itself has to be grounded upon reasoning that is meaningful to a majority of the people.

Authority can be transformed into power and vice versa. In human and healthy societies, it can perform the valuable function of limiting the behaviour of persons, especially those in official positions, impelling them to confine to legitimate acts. But their actions must be potentially justified by 'reasoned elaboration' in terms of values of the same society. If the value pattern of that society itself is pathological, authority, then, is simply a tool in furthering that state of pathology. Unfortunately, politics itself emerges, evolves, grows, and activates on the basis of those prevailing values. But it is only politics that can put a challenge to those outworn values, and inculcate newer ones. In their own limited way, scholars, philosophers, poets, etc., also do that, though they operate only at the mental level.

Authority, to sum up, is accepted not because it has been given by superior authorities, but on the basis of the consent of the subordinates, who often accept orders considering them right and proper. Authority of the superior person is accepted only when he issues orders in the aforesaid manner. Its basis is not sanctions, but rightness – rather similarity of the goals, values, and norms existing between them. It is direct and institutionalised right to influence the behaviour of the subordinates.[31]

Authority is exercised almost mechanically within the network of clearly defined hierarchical roles: parent-child, teacher-pupil, employer-employee. Authority-relations are institutionalised. Duties and obligations are clearly demarcated. Behaviour under them is reasonably predictable. Relations continue over time and become part of normal life. Under a system of well established authority, men of great ability are less in demand. Under authority, even mediocre persons holding positions in a regular manner can run society or an organisation.

Forms and Functions of Authority

Thinkers since ancient times have discussed nature, forms and functions of authority. In modern times Max Weber (1922) has discussed it quite thoroughly. His forms of authority are based on sources of legitimacy:

1. *Traditional authority*: Subjects or subordinates accept commands of their superiors on the basis of precedents, past history or divine origin. Under this form of authority, delegation is ad hoc and arbitrary. Subordinates are treated as personal servants, who render services to the king as embodiment of symbols and traditions.
2. *Rational-legal authority*: Under this form of authority, subordinates accept a rule or directive on the basis of its being in conformity with some higher universal principle which they regard as legitimate. Modern bureaucracy operates on this principle. Delegation is rational. Legally established impersonal rules constitute the basis of compliance.

3. *Charismatic authority*: When the subordinates defer to the orders of their superior on the basis of his personal qualities and put themselves under their impact, charismatic authority occurs. There is no delegation as such. Subordinates are treated as disciples and followers. As Weber regards rational-legal authority as fragile, he considers other forms of authority as correlates and complementary to it.

Authority may appear in some other forms also, such as, (i) national and international; (ii) in relation to organs of government, namely, executive, legislative and judicial; (iii) constitutional or statutory; (iv) national, regional or local; (v) political or administrative; (vi) single, plural, corporate, commission or board form; (vii) economic, social, religious, technical etc.; and (viii) formal or informal.

Authority in general sense has unlimited functions. It is responsible for the determination and execution of systemic goals. It performs the functions of coordination, discipline, growth, and delegation. Systems attain pattern-maintenance, goal-attainment, tension management, etc., through establishment of appropriate authorities. Communication, decision-making, improvision of procedure and evaluation are the means and methods by which systems operate and persist over time.

Legitimate power is the basis of authority of an organisation. Authority does not indicate superiority of an individual. He is only a living symbol of mechanism. This is the 'magic of government' that enables a man to command, even if he is less intelligent, less able, and below average than his subordinates. Orders given by man in authority have to be carried out. In formal organisation, authority is rationally distributed among various persons making up the hierarchy of an organisation. But an informal organisation can also have authority, authority-positions, and authority-persons or authorities. Formal organisations, therefore, often try that informal organisations either do not grow or if they are unavoidable or required at all, they are kept within bounds. The military does not permit their existence but trade unions are allowed to operate by law. Still very rarely they are one with each other. Informal organisations often grow underground, if not permitted to operate openly. Man does not live along with formal lines, and moves beyond the blueprint. This adds elements of sociability, cooperation, voluntarism to the bare bones of hierarchical organisations.

Authority operates on the road of values. Values, alike power, also impose restrictions on the exercise of authority. Often the constitutions begin with their value-preambles. Democrats do not cherish the exercise of authority. Power bereft of values is also not meaningful to the people at large. Values which may slowly change and gradually accepted by the ruler or the ruled help in transforming power into authority and authority into power. Kings and emperors in the past forcibly occupied other principalities, and in due course of time were accepted by their subjects as legitimate authority. Power without authority remains indefinite, situational, instrumental, and uninstitutionalised as brute force. Authority, built on the ground of accepted and institutionalised power, is specific, definite and limited by its nature. Its directives are considered binding being based on certain underlying norms. At least, the subordinates or people concerned have faith in their being based on those norms. Authority wields all rights to execute a proposed plan, scheme or policy. It operates through a binding set of rules, regulations, procedure, conventions and established norms. Authority itself is bound by them, for, by nature, it has to appear definite, unambiguous, specific, and limited. It carries on the burden of responsibility and remains accountable to some higher one. It can be delegated to various points of organisational structure. Thus, many subauthorities come up which are adorned with many indicators or insignia for the convenience of recognition, distinction, ego-satisfaction, effectivity, and discipline. Sometimes authorities are known by dress, crown, stars, seal, staff, locus, building and others. They are given certain discretion, immunities and positions or status. They have to be in consonance with the exercise of rights given to them. Parts of authority lying with the wielders are coordinated with integrated hierarchies through various means and mechanisms. Authority is known by its compliance. But every time this does not happen. For its constant and effective compliance, and in view of its possible non-compliance, authorities are equipped with power and sanctions, occasions of influence and leadership, and other similar tools. In the absence of power, authority loses its influence. In a sense, authority is the last expression of institutionalised power. Without power, it is merely goodwill, which is often subjective and exceptional. Politics connects power and authority at various levels, and with various devices.

Role of Authority

In point of fact all studies of government or the state are really examinations of the nature and working of political authority. No system of rule could survive long without exercising some measure of authority. To rule through power alone involves such a great expenditure of coercive resources as to be unsustainable. There are recurrent debates about the role of authority and its value. Liberals and socialists tends to view authority as instrumental, believing that it arises 'from below' through the consent of the governed From this perspective, authority is rational, purposeful and limited. This view reflects a preference for legal-rational authority and public accountability. Conservatives, on the other hand, see authority as arising from natural necessity, being exercised 'from above' by virtue of the unequal distribution of experience, social position and wisdom. Those who exercise authority do so for the benefit of others, but this does not set clear limits or checks upon authority. It blurs the distinction between *authority* and *authoritarianism*.

The justifications for authority include, most basically, that it is essential for the maintenance of order and is the only means of escape from the barbarity and injustice of the 'state of nature': a society without political rule. Authority also establishes common norms and values that bind society together, and thereby gives individuals a social identity and sense of rootedness. Critics of authority, including, particularly, libertarians and anarchists, point out that authority is by definition the enemy of freedom. It threatens reason and critical understanding by demanding unquestioning obedience. It is psychologically, and perhaps morally, corrupting in that it accustoms people to controlling or dominating others. In the long run, they lose the sense of 'freedom'.

Limitations of Authority

Under the umbrella of authority, a person accepts the communication or directives of his senior without any discussion, deliberation or reasoning, making his decision as his own decision. Authority, thus, is the highest stage of legitimate power.[32] It is legal, objective, organisational, specific, and limited. It operates through established procedure, express rules, and definite manner. However, in itself it is not much effective. Authority is effective only when imbued with power, influence and leadership. Influence fills in the gap between power, force and authority. Technology of making effective organisations keeps in mind that authorities have appropriate room for exercise of power, influence and leadership. They are purposely equipped with discretion, titles, sanctions, salary, privileges, immunities, and other paraphernalia. Power as force has a limited role, and can be exercised only in exceptional cases, that too with high cost. Hence, influence comes to its rescue, but it is fluid, flexible, instable, uncertain and unspecific. Therefore, its liquidity has to be poured into organisational vessels. Authorities, in the organisation, then, can perform functions assigned to them. But the main task of acquiring legitimacy for all of them remains to be earned and acquired by politics. Even power and influence cannot be much effective without legitimacy.

Legitimacy

Authorities exercise rights, sanctions, and other immunities and privileges, not because 'authority' originates in them, but owing to people's belief in the source of base of their rights. The base or source of these rights is called 'legitimacy'. Alike authority, power and influence also, in order to be effective, require legitimacy. If there is no legitimacy, power and influence both are opposed and counteracted: authority is totally disregarded. It is legitimacy, which makes them effective and operational. Individuals, organisations, and institutions cannot have power and influence without having legitimacy, though all the three mutually may be reinforcing, even oppose each other. Dahl regards it as necessary and economical. Leaders in democracies, usually espouse a set of, more or less, persistent and integrated doctrines, popularly called as 'ideology'. It purports to explain and justify their leadership in the system. Leaders develop 'ideology' to endow their leadership with legitimacy and convert their political influence into authority. As stated earlier, it is far more economical to rule by means of authority than by means of coercion, power, or influence. Moreover, it is legitimacy which distinguishes coercion, force, and power from influence, persuasion and leadership. But exercise of force can be 'legitimate' against criminals, miscreants and rebels.

Conceptual Explanation

Legitimacy, according to Dolf Sternberger,[33] is the foundation of governmental power. It is exercised both as consciousness on the part of government that it has a right to govern and with some acknowledgement by the governed that the government has a right to do so. Etymologically, 'legitimacy' is from Latin 'legitimus' which means 'lawful'. During medieval ages, it meant constitutional role or order, conforming to ancient customs, traditions, and procedure.

Etzioni finds it as a source of satisfaction derived from participation in the organisation: the ability to justify. It is a belief that the structure, procedures, acts, decisions, officials and leaders of government possess the quality of 'rightness' property or moral goodness. They should be accepted as such irrespective of the specific contents of the particular acts, orders or communication.

The concept is as old as politics itself – from Plato down to Max Weber and Habermas. But the concept is not very much clear. It is opposite of usurpation, though all usurpers try to legitimise their usurpation as rightful occupation. Revolution or *coup d'etat* may not necessarily be illegimate. If it is successful, it introduces a new principle of legitimacy superseding the older one. Any means can be employed to acquire legitimacy. Recognition is not very necessary. Internal consolidation and acceptance by the people are, by and large, more helpful. However, even existing government may lose legitimacy by violating its principles of legitimacy. Leaders in every political system try to ensure that their decisions are widely accepted, not out of the fear of violence, punishment, or coercion but from a belief that it is morally right and proper to do so.

About obedience to the state, David Held proposed a continuum of seven types:

1. Coercion or following orders
2. Tradition
3. Apathy
4. Pragmatic acquiescence
5. Instrumental acceptance
6. Normative agreement
7. Ideal normative agreement

He likes to reserve types 6 and 7 for legitimacy. A legitimate political order is normatively sanctioned by the population. People follow rules and laws when they think they are right, correct, justified or worthy.[34] There are some other explanations of legitimacy like 'end of ideology', 'the one dimensional society' and so on. By 'end of ideology' Lipset means a decline in the support by intellectuals, labour unions and left-wing political parties to 'red flag waving': end of class politics. It means ideological issues dividing the western societies are no more important. Like Almond and Verba, Lipset affirms that there is a general consensus on political values, such as, equality, achievement and procedures of democracy, stability etc. Herbert Marcuse rejected it and propounded his thesis of 'one dimensional society'. But both start with the appearance of political harmony in Western capitalism in the post-war era. In his book, *One Dimensional Man*, he finds that the cult of affluence and consumerism has created modes of behaviour that are adaptive, passive and acquiescent. All this is sustained by ideological and coercive forces. Then, political order is not based on genuine consent and legitimacy.

Differing from Weber, David Beetham in *The Legitimation of Power* (1991) develops a socio-scientific concept of legitimacy. Weber and others have emptied it of any objective reference and in effect acquiesced in the very manipulations of the powerful. One should go into its actual characteristics as a system of power. He highlights how legitimacy is brought about?[35] Accordingly, power can be legitimate if it fulfills three conditions: (i) power must be exercised according to established rules; (ii) these rules must be justified in terms of the shared beliefs of the government and the governed, and, (iii) legitimacy must be demonstrated by the expression of consent on the part of the governed. Non-legitimate power, therefore, suffers from illegitimacy (breach of rules), absence of shared beliefs and delegitimacy or withdrawal of consent. It must not be the result of 'ideological hegemony'. Otherwise, liberal democracy would turn into what Ralph Miliband calls a 'capitalist democracy'. Education must not be reduced to a process of ideological indoctrination or mass media turning into a propaganda machine. Antonio Gramsci drew attention to the degree to which the class system, as upheld by bourgeois 'hegemony', that is the ascendancy or domination of bourgeois ideas in every sphere of life. Thus the masses are deluded by bourgeois theories and philosophies. The proletariat remain incapable of achieving class consciousness and unable to realise its revolutionary potential.

As an alternative to the Marxist belief, 'sociology of knowledge' believes in thinking that the people can be traced back to their position in society and the social groups to which they belong. Each one of these groups has its own distinctive way of looking at the world. Ideologies are, according to Karl Mannheim (1893-1947), 'socially determined' and reflect the social circumstances and aspirations of the groups they live in. Berger and Luckmann find in *The Social Construction of Reality* (1971) that everything that passes for 'knowledge' in society is socially constructed. Not only they see the world as it is but as they *think* it is, or as society tells them it is. Legitimacy is always a 'social construction'.

Legitimacy can also be manufactured. Noam Chomsky and Edward Herman in their book *Manufacturing Consent* (1994) have developed a 'propaganda model' of the mass media. They explain how news and political coverage are distorted by the structures of media itself. It operates through a series of 'filters' and at sources, advertisers, sponsors, agents of power, business-backed think-tank and the like. Mass media can subvert or deter democracy. They overlook the fact that the people have their own values and can resist media messages.

Legitimacy is essential for the maintenance of any system of political rule. Attention has been given not only to the machinery through which it is maintained but also upon the circumstances in which the legitimacy of a regime is called into question. This is popularly known as 'crisis of the state'. There are two views: one, of 'overloaded government', and, two of legitimation crisis. The first is held by Huntington, Nordhaus, Kind and Rose and Peters. Jurgen Habermas and Offe stand for the second. The former calls for measures of containment and control. The latter see dilemmas difficult but also look for decisive, progressive, and radical change. Habermas in his *Legitimation Crisis* (1975) points out that within liberal democracies there are crisis tendencies which challenge the stability of such regimes. There is tension between a private-enterprise and a democratic political system. Capitalist economy inherently makes democracy instable. But David Held does not agree with them on three grounds: (a) there is no empirical evidence that there is progressively worsening crisis of the state's authority; (b) state power is not eroding as its capabilities, resources and apparatuses remain intact; and, (c) the state is not vulnerable to collapse or disintegration. Political order is the outcome of a complex web of interdependencies between political, economic and social institutions and activities that power centres around. They create multiple pressures to comply. State power is important but is not the only key variable.[36] State is deeply implicated in the creation and reproduction of systematic inequalities of power, wealth, income and opportunities. It enjoys sustained legitimation by groups other than those whom it directly privileges. However, only a political order that places the transformation of those inequalities at its centre enjoys legitimacy in the long run.

Nature, Forms and Process

In the context of organisations, Etzioni writes that they set norms, enforce rules and regulations which have to be complied with. For compliance, they rely on power and try to get it through the system of rewards and punishments, even manipulation, indoctrination, and training. In such a situation of power, it is not necessary that the recipients of order or subordinates agree to it, or accept it as morally justified. But exercise of power in this manner keeps them alienated. They will conform only to those actions which are backed by power. The subjects would not volunteer information, show initiative, or cooperate. In case, power weakens or is rendered inadequate, the recipients would start following their own norms or replace the former power-wielders from positions of authority. When orders are issued or rules set in conformity with the accepted values, compliance is much deeper and more effective. The subjects 'internalise' the rules, and voluntarily act and cooperate in executing the policies. They find order and discipline less alienating. Rather, they would continue to follow rules and orders even when an organisation's power is lessened and weakened.

Legitimation does not increase the material interest of the subordinates or make the order or rule more 'pleasant'. But it serves a need – to follow norms that conform, and do not conflict with their values. There is distinction between normative satisfaction of the need for justice or legitimacy and the need to find opportunities to gratify other needs. Some orders are legitimate and gratifying whereas other orders may be legitimate, but not gratifying, still others may be illegitimate but not gratifying. Organisations require legitimacy, that is, conformity with values. It is closer to conformity with a higher sense of morality.

In the context of governments, legitimacy can be classified into two broad groups: (1) numinous legitimacy which is based on faith in the divine origin of rule; and (2) civil legitimacy which exists when a system of government is based on agreement between equally autonomous constituents, who have come together to cooperate toward some common good. Weber relates his typology of authority to sources and kinds of legitimation as (i) traditional, (ii) rational-legal or bureaucratic, and (iii) charismatic.[37]

Sources of Legitimacy

Besides Max Weber's typology of legitimacy, the need and feeling for justice can be regarded as another source of legitimacy. In fact, ideology of the people, and not of the rulers, is the main source of legitimacy. In democracies, legitimacy is indicated by its ideals, popular consent, representativeness, elections, rule of majority, civic liberties and similar privileges available to the people. Grace A. Jones, with reference to the British political system, has mentioned certain sources of legitimacy in the following manner:

(1) Past visible in political and social institutions;
(2) Tradition of non-violence;
(3) Numerous symbols and rituals;
(4) Belief in the value and validity of existing political procedures, e.g., conventions;
(5) Election-procedure, freedom and consensus justifying laws;
(6) Homogeneous and integrated society, continuity of traditions in family from father to son, e.g., party allegiance; and
(7) Political culture with some degree of adaptability.

Dahl has also indicated various sources of winning legitimacy or earning compliance:

1. To encourage compliance:
   (a) by increasing rewards for compliance,
   (b) by decreasing disadvantages of compliance,
2. To discourage non-compliance:
   (c) by decreasing rewards from other alternatives,
   (d) by increasing disadvantages of other alternatives.

He has suggested that internal sources of rewards and deprivations are always better than external sources. More and more internalisation gradually replaces the need of external sources. When the political system is widely accepted as legitimate and its policies are regarded as morally binding, the cost of compliance reduces. When legitimacy and authority are in low key, it has to make more use of money, police, privileges, weapons, status and other political resources. Obviously, democracy requires more legitimacy and authority than other systems.

Still legitimacy is not some high level abstract feeling, but a phenomenon existing underlying the whole system. It is related to whole system and its governance. It is not a moral feeling or subjective conceptualisation. It is a belief of the people in the rightness of the activities of the government. But it comes out in concrete form also. In the words of Easton, it relates to the allocation of authoritative values for the society. Who, in what form, when, how, in what manner, and where are also the questions related to its legitimacy. At the *interval* level, it is related to praise, honour, affection, etc., or their reverse forms like dishonour, anomie, alienation, etc., At the *external level* it is connected with material things like land, money, licence, status, privileges, immunities etc. They may not actually be given but expectation of getting them or the fear of losing them also works a lot in motivating each form of legitimacy. Material goods, in any system, are never unlimited; therefore, political leaders always try to economise them. They do so by (i) preferring internal or abstract awards, and (ii) using means like leadership, influence, and propaganda. With the help of these, they are able to get compliance simply on the basis of communicating to them. Material rewards, apart from being limited and scarce, their distribution can also prove dyfunctional. But these internal and external sources should not be treated as separate. They are related with each other. In sum, internal resources are less costly than material resources. Non-material resources of legitimacy are less expensive than running the political system on the basis of power as physical force. Democracy requires the first two sources, whereas dictatorship mostly operates on physical force. Therefore, cost of running a system on the basis of force is very high, making the system still more fragile, instable, and alienated.

Apart from the consideration of cost, it must be pointed out that authority is the most efficient form of influence. It is legitimacy which enables political actors to transform influence into authority. Power, influence, and authority, standing on the ground of legitimacy, do not require to spend much political resources. In the context of Third World countries, it can be stated that legitimacy plays a key role in getting along with their political system. They have scarce economic and political sources. They have to telescope centuries into decades, and attain modernisation as early as possible. Only an attitude of 'rightness' or belief in the legitimacy of their structures, functions, procedures, leaders, and decisions can come to their rescue. Even, with less amount of power or a weakened government, a developing society can attain its goals. It keeps majority as well as minority communities bound to each other. No majority can keep a considerably big minority under coercion. It has to win them over by propagating values, ideology, and role-expectations. So is the case with the minority groups and communities, as they too have to stand at par on the common levels of legitimacy. Within the bounds of this legitimacy, political leaders, parties, groups, and individuals are allowed to compete among themselves. As legitimacy is deeply entrenched into cultural values, secession or separatism cannot burst out so easily.

Legitimacy and Democracy

Legitimacy is the life of democracy. But it does not mean that all should invariably believe in identical set of values or creed. Democracy does not believe in ostracising the people having opinion different from prevalent ideas or beliefs. The modern trend, instead of concentrating on consensus, in all matters, stands for consensus on procedure. It believes in the existence of a commonly acceptable procedure and maintaining its purity so that all members of the system may cherish their own goals and values and realise them, and also reach an acceptable settlement of their disputes. From that point of view, legitimacy can be treated as the basic fundamental structure of culture or value-consensus of the social system.

Democratic ideas and legitimacy also cannot be considered as identical. So is the case with legality and legitimacy. As they operate within the boundaries of legitimacy, non-democratic structures like bureaucracy, army, police, and organisations of heavy industry and other concerns, are allowed to exist and managed by rules in a democracy. Heads of state and other top officers are allowed to have privileges, immunities and other amenities during crises, and for special occasions. Similarly, even limited use of violence, here and there, is also permitted. Certainly, the basis of the modern state is neither Platonic Justice or Reason nor Rousseau's General Will, which can at the most be regarded as ideational notions. It is not possible for big nation-states to have uniformity of faith in all intellectual, cultural and political matters. Such uniformity is considered even not desirable. Existence of differing opinions is often regarded as an indicator of legitimacy and necessary for the health of democracy. The task of democracy is rather to bring about harmony and cooperation amidst various diversities. Legitimacy is concerned with the consent and consensus about the procedure by which people and parties concerned get what, when, where and how of the cake, and by remaining close to it feel a sense of satisfaction. Adoption of procedural consensus, which is often available in the main parts of democratic constitutions, is more important than who rules and what and how much. This procedural consensus indicates 'value of values' or 'basic living culture' of a democratic polity. Such procedural consensus enables legitimacy to maintain proper relations between freedom and restrictions. The latter are obviously placed on the former to enjoy greater freedom for people at large. Such legitimacy is often reflected by the existence of free and regular elections, consent, representativeness, adult franchise, civic liberties and others.

Compliance and Political Accountability

Practically, legitimacy in the context of political systems means public or *political accountability*. Need of a satisfactory solution to public accountability is greater because of its legal mechanism. The State is a compulsory organisation having monopoly over the exercise of coercive power. As all citizens and subordinates, and their non-adult dependents have a faith in the legitimacy of its structures, processes and functioning, its responsibility to operate within the confines of 'rightness' increases manifold so as to respond to their hopes and expectations. These expectations must be accomplished more with the exercise of influence, authority and leadership than force, coercion and violence. Though after attainment of legitimacy, exercise of power or force cannot be treated as coercion or violence, yet it should primarily resort to persuasion, propaganda, and deference to the moral susceptibilities of the people. Authorities do have the right to exercise force, domination, manipulation, and other sanctions, but their use should strictly conform dispassionately to the accepted procedure as shown below.

Power, Influence, Authority and Compliance

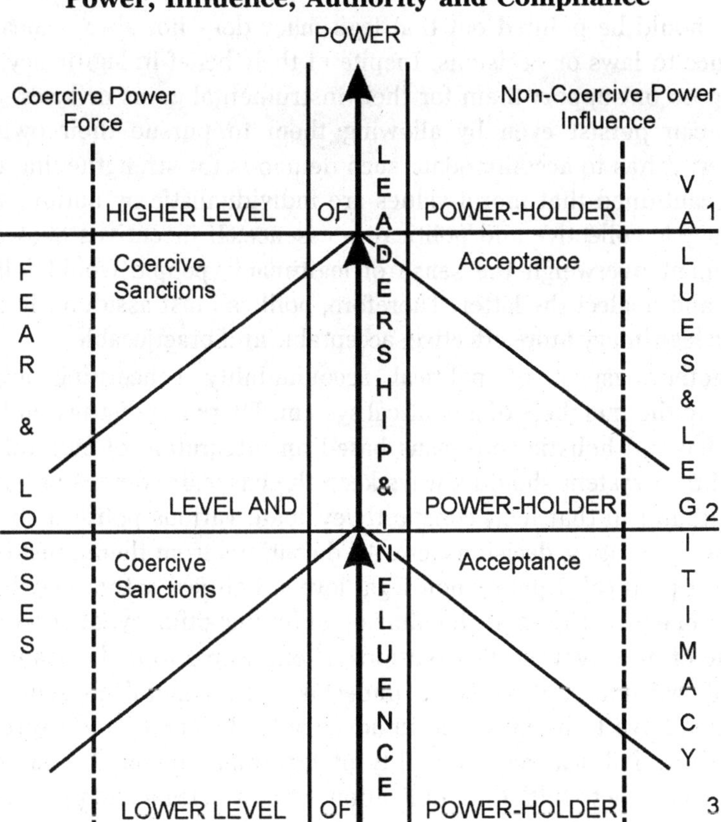

Obedience to rule is necessary to maintain and sustain a society and its polity, but it should base itself on the following:

(1) *Legitimate authority*: It bestows 'right' to issue orders and directives, take decisions, make policies, and run administration through various authorities, subject to rational higher principles of social life.
(2) *Incentives:* They can be positive as well as negative, external or internal, instrumental and non-instrumental. They can be functional, if used with discrimination and proportion to cases under consideration.
(3) *Sanctions:* These can be used in a direct or indirect manner, and their consequences can be intended or unintended.
(4) *Ideology and leadership*: In democracy, they play a dominating role, as discussed earlier.
(5) *Participation and cooperation:* When people are involved in the process of decision-making and implementation of policies, compliance, despite difficulties, increases. Cooperation of persons representating communities and sets of opinions, makes compliance increasingly ensured.

It should be pointed out that legitimacy does not always mean blind obedience to laws or decisions. Inspite of their belief in legitimacy, people can oppose or support them for their instrumental gains or loses, and the former can persist even by allowing them to pursue their own goals. However, it has to accommodate such demands for strengthening itself. It can be cautioned that moral values are individualistic by nature, whereas legitimacy is collective and political in essence. If incentives of award and punishment overweigh the sense of legitimacy, people would follow the former and neglect the latter. Therefore, politics must assiduously contrive to make legitimacy more effective, acceptable and practiceable.

Another aspect of political accountability concerning legitimacy belongs to the members of a political system. There is a distinction between legitimacy and holistic consensus based on integration of cultural values. The political system should always keep the bases or sources of legitimacy before it, and in that light constantly evaluate various political structures, processes, activities, decisions, etc. All deviations from them must be taken care of at political, legal or non-legal levels. Political actors may be called upon to make sacrifices at the altar of gaining legitimacy, as it happens at the time of upheavals and revolutions. If one wants to make change in the basis of legitimacy, it must be undertaken by general consent, and all concerned have to be informed in advance to deliberate and express their views on it. Political accountability of legitimacy demands that political leaders continue to fulfil their obligations at moral, legal and political levels.

The countries belonging to the Third World have scarce means to spend and have constantly to face the 'revolution of the rising expectations'. Their storehouse has limited political and economic resources. As such, they cannot afford to operate on the basis of naked power or sheer force. If they do so, their energies and scarce resources would be dried up in replacing one rule by another, increasing forces, and purchasing of arms. Therefore, it is very necessary that they try, first and foremost, to earn legitimacy for the whole political system, and begin to work on influence and authority. Politics, not power, is the direction to which they must move to tread on the path of development. Politics must acquire legitimacy first, then it should proceed to convert influence into authority.

Notes

1. Bierstedt on "Power", in *Human Relations in Administration*, 1960, edited by Robert Dubin, 172.
2. Dahl on "Power", in *International Encyclopaedia of Social Sciences*, 1968, 12, 405.
3. Richard Bellamy, ed. *Theories and Concepts of Politics: An Introduction*, Manchester, UP, 1993.
4. Catlin, *Systematic Theory*, 1960, 6.
5. Catlin, "Political Theory: What Is It?" in Gould and Thursby (eds.), *Contemporary Political Thought: Issues in Scope, Value and Direction, op. cit.*, 28.
6. Harold D. Lasswell and Abraham, *Power and Society: A Framework for Political Inquiry*, New Haven and London, Yale University Press, 1950, 75; Lasswell, *Politics: Who Gets, What, When, How?* Cleveland and New York, World Publishing Co., 1958, 13.
7. Bierstedt on "Power", *op. cit.*, 172.
8. Bertrand Russell, *Power: A New Sociological Analysis*, London: George Alien and Unwin, 1937; *Human Nature in Ethics and Politics*, 1954, and *Principles of Social Reconstruction*, 1920.
9. K.P. Jayaswal, *Hindu Polity*, 1948, Chap. III and IV, passim.
10. When Gandhi started 'individual satyagraha', the British rulers remained unruffled for it lacked both APP as well as PPP. According to Gandhi himself it was no more than a 'token protest'. According to a Government report, in some areas it was limping along, in others it was moribund and in others again it seemed to be dead. File No. 4/8/41, NAI, Home Political Files, Nos. 18-10-41. See, S.L. Verma, also chapter 17 *infra*.
11. Max Weber, "Politics as a Vocation", in Gerth and Mills, *From Max Weber*, New York, 1946, 78.
12. Almond, *The Politics of the Developing Areas, op. cit.*, 6.
13. Catlin, *op. cit.*, 7.
14. Bierstedt, *op. cit.*, 180.
15. See, for details, infra.

16. Felex, E. Oppenheim, "Power Revisited", *Journal of Politics*, Vol. 40, No. 3 (Aug. 1978), 589-608; See, comments on it, Terence Ball, "'Power' Revisited: A Comment on Oppenheim", *op. cit.*, 609-18.
17. A. Rhoshikish, *Power or Authority: The Entelechy of Power*, Lanhan: University Press of America, 1991, 35-63.
18. Hans J. Morgenthau, *Dilemmas of Politics*, University of Chicago Press, 1962, 256.
19. See, also Andrew Heywood, *Political Theory: An Introduction*, Third Edition, Palgrave, 2004, 122-28.
20. Discourse is a system of social relations and practices that assign meaning, that is identities, to those who live or work within it. Discourses are a form of power in the sense that they set up antagonisms and structure relations between people who are defined as subjects or objects, as 'insiders' or 'outsiders'.
21. Bierstedt, "An Analysis of Social Power", *American Sociological Review*, XV, 6, 710-738; and also, Felix E. Oppenheim, "The Concept of Power Revisited", *Rivista Italina di Scienza Politica*, 8, 1, (April, 1978), 57-75.
22. Edward C. Banefield, *Political Influence*, New York, Free Press of Glencoe, 1961, 3.
23. Lasswell, *op. cit.*, 13.
24. Ibid., 55.
25. Rowe, "Political Influence", *op. cit.*; Peter Bachrach and Morton S. Baratz, "Decisions and Non-decisions: An Analytical Framework", in *Political Power*, edited by Roderick Bell, David V. Edwards, and R. Harrison Wagner, 1969, 100-110.
26. Dahl, *op. cit.*, 41-44.
27. Herbert A. Simon, *Administrative Behaviour*, Preface.
28. Andrew Heywood, *Political Theory: An Introduction*, Third Edition, Palgrave, 2004, 141.
29. Dale S. Beach, *The Management of People At Work*, 1970, 565.
30. Bachrach and Baratz, Power and Poverty, 1970, 100-110.
31. M.G. Smith, *op. cit.*
32. Dahl, *op. cit.*, 19-21.
33. Dolf Sternberger, *International Encyclopaedia of Social Sciences*, 9.
34. David Held, *Political Theory and the Modern State: Essays on State Power and Democracy*, Cambridge: UK, 1989.
35. David Beetham, *The Legitimation of Power-Issues in Political Theory*, London: Macmillan Education Ltd., 1991.
36. Held, Ibid., 151.
37. *Supra*, Chapter, VI, 194-95.

7

Modernisation and Political Development

Theories Studying the Third World

Problems, aspirations and activities of the countries belonging to the category of the Third World[1] are being studied here under the broad concepts of Modernisation and Political Development. All of them represent 'dynamic political changes'. With the dissolution of the second world by 1991, the term 'Third World' should have become outdated, but it still continues owing to its long use and popularity. These countries still constitute a vast majority of world's population and if they act in unison, they can play decisive role in this age of globalisation.[2] Therefore, for different reasons, both the developed as well as the developing countries have been interested in studying them. In the context of Western civilisation, Karl Polanqi called the nineteenth century as the age of 'Great Transformation', but the twentieth century in view of these new states had proved to be of still 'Greater Transformation'. Now, the New World Order or globalisation is facing challenge from them in the twenty-first century. Advanced countries were interested in them because most of them (i) lacked concepts, tools and techniques to understand them, (ii) wanted to woo them by giving aid in proportion to their needs and requirements, (iii) for strategic reasons drag them into cold war, (iv) found in them rich areas for economic exploitation, and (v) also to exercise influence and control over them. These countries too started studying their own political systems because of their (a) interest in making rapid socio-economic progress and come at par with the Western standard, (b) wish to survive, and maintain their independence amidst cold war, (c) desire to conserve their identity, (d) programme to tread on the path of modernisation and political development, and, (e) awareness to play an effective role in world politics. For both of them the Third World provided big human laboratories to study 'political change' and societal transformation, and, thus, formulate new theories, perspectives, concepts, and models, thereby enrich the discipline of Political Science. Millions of dollars were spent by affluent countries to make best use of the opportunities, and serve all ends.

Countries of the Third World were also in search of a theory or perspective of modernisation and/or political development, which could enable them to understand their own system – their own societal forces, aspirations, choices, goals and values. What would be the direction, factors, programme, and stages of change? What form of polity would it be suitable for them leading them to continuous growth and political development? They also wanted to avoid evils, crises and difficulties while treading on the path of development. They wanted to live in environment of freedom, peace, security, self-respect and affluence. Therefore, most of them were eager for working out a theoretical perspective for themselves. No final theory for them has come out as yet. Riggs has observed, 'there is no such theory, although there is a host of speculations and even hypotheses. Nor is there any consensus on the meaning of the word *development* in this context, or even, for that matter, of the word *political*.[3]

These countries have been variously called, as, emerging nations, new states, backward, underdeveloped, new developing countries, transitional societies, the Third World, modernising polities, group of 77, South, LDCs (Least Developed Countries), etc. Previously, under the colonial impact they were categorised as Anglicised, Gallicised, Europeanised, Westernised, Russianised, or socialised countries. During the last quarter of the twentieth century, all had, in a way, adopted the ideology of developmentalism.[4] Economists and sociologists like to call them as 'modernising' countries, but political scientists prefer the term 'developing' societies or polities.[5]

Societal Change: Modernisation and Development

Both modernisation and political development are forms of societal change. Change is some kind of break in continuity, and is found and felt everywhere: natural or contrived. Man is always influenced by changes, therefore, he, by nature, remains curious to know them. He is more interested in those changes, which can come under his control. Changes, in general, can be either (a) natural, involuntary, and slow, or (b) artificial, planned, and fast. They can be revolutionary,[6] evolutionary or developmental. The latter can be political, and non-political. Economic, technological, industrial, and managerial all fall in the area of non-political changes. Political changes often are man-made, planned, collective, purposive, dominating, contrived, and effective. They tend to control, coordinate, direct and evaluate other changes. Countries of the Third World are interested in political changes in order to bring about changes in socio-economic, cultural, and industrial fields, known as *modernisation* and *development*. They want to transform polities from 'tradition' to 'modernity'.[7] We shall take up 'modernisation' first.

Modernisation

The concept of 'modernisation' is ambiguous, and needs to be explained again and again. It is transformation of societies from the old to the modern. C.E. Welch views it as 'a process which involves rational utilisation of resources, which seek to establish a modern society.' He identifies it as 'any societal culture that allows individuals to develop a critical view of man in his relation to nature and society, which enables him to see life as involving different kinds of choices – personal, social or structural and moral.' According to Benjamin, it means 'systematic, sustained and purposeful application of human energies to the rational control of man's physical and social environment for various human purposes.' William H. Friedland explains it as 'a society's capacity and ability to accommodate the need for change'. Halpern sees it as 'the transformation of all systems: political, social, economic, intellectual, religious, psychological and so on'. Karl Deutsch conceptualises it as '*social mobilisation:* the process in which major clusters of old social, economic and psychological commitments are eroded and broken and people become available for new patterns of socialisation and behaviour.' In the Indian context, Myron Weiner, explains it (1) industrialisation (2) programmes to change the Hindu social structure, and (3) a unified national state. In this sense, we do not want to be 'modern' but 'modernised', and like to have modernisation, and not modernity. 'Modernisation does not', says C.H. Dodd, 'necessarily result in modernity.' It is the effect of the new on the old, not the eradication of the old and its substitution by the new.

Modernisation, sometimes called as social and political development, refers to all those social and political changes that accompany industrialisation. Among these are urbanisation, changes in occupational structure, social mobility, development of education as well as political changes from absolutist institutions to representative and responsible governments, and from a *laissez faire* to modern welfare state.

The above explanations indicate the 'classical' view of modernisation. They are ethnocentric and oriented toward the West. Some of the features of classical modernisation can be enumerated as: (i) increasing control over nature and environment; (ii) as a result of this control, maximum exploitation of natural and physical resources, or use of machine and technology; (iii) industrialisation; (iv) urbanisation; (v) widespread literacy; (vi) increase in national and individual income; (vii) increasing participation in the activities of government; (viii) development and extension of means of mass communication; (ix) social mobility; (x) commitment to national unity; and (xi) faith in equality.

The other is the 'contemporary' view of modernisation. S.N. Eisenstadt finds, historically, modernisation as the process of change towards those types of social, economic, and political systems that have developed in western Europe and North America from the seventeenth century to the nineteenth. Willbert E. More, Chandler Morse, Lucian Pye, etc., also think in similar terms. Therefore, V.R. Mehta has criticised it 'as a teleological concept which proceeds along a fixed route as a result of certain demographic changes.'[8] It is considered as a process of 'catching up' with the advanced nations in terms of the latter's framework. Unlike the 'classical' paradigms of modernisation, Eisenstadt does not assume that 'development' or 'modernisation' constitutes a 'unilinear demographic, social, economic, or political process which extends to some plateau, whose basic contours will be everywhere the same.[9] Processes common to modernisation are growing differentiation, social mobilisation, weakening of traditionality and cultural parameters. A problem attendant on it is the ability to develop and maintain an institutional structure capable of absorbing changes beyond its own initial premises and dealing with continuously new and changing problems, while also developing qualities of participation, liberty, and some degree or type of rationality. In the Indian context, Wilfred C. Smith explains it as a process by which a country becomes 'conscious of itself and of its processes and of the kind of country that it is possible for it to become, and by which it finds or constructs technical means for executing such choices as it consciously or unconsciously makes.'[10] Mehta finds it as 'a process whereby a society becomes increasingly aware of itself, its identity and aspirations, and seeks to concretise its awareness into practice by seeking equivalence with other nations.'[11] According to him, all new ideas and processes must meaningfully relate to the needs, resources and aspirations of the society in question. The process is to be grasped not in terms of the process that has taken place elsewhere, but in terms of a particular society's own achievements, its history, customs and social relations; the tools and material with which people have lived and worked. Thus, according to him, to modernise is, first, to know one's own society in terms of its historical experience, and second, to act in such a manner that its potential as revealed by the historical process and contemporary aspirations is fully realised.

Modernisation is an all-pervading phenomena which can be studied at many levels. Some of them are: (i) psycho-cultural, (ii) demographic; (iii) social; (iv) economic; (v) intellectual; and (vi) political levels.

David Apter on Modernisation

David E. Apter in his book, *The Politics of Modernization,* presents a typology of governmental forms and some theories about how they change, demonstrating the relationship between these forms and several functional categories. He makes use of structural-functional analysis taken from Parsons and Marion J. Levy. According to him, modernisation 'is bound to be too complex for any theory to remain suitable for long.'[12] He looks towards three things: (i) moral-political problems of modernisation; (ii) the boundaries of a system and demarcation of the nature of the subsystems within it; and (iii) abstract basic structural properties of the system and its relevant subsystems.

According to Apter, all modernising societies are in the process of transition or in the process of becoming. Politics, in a large measure, is the business of coping with role-differentiation while integrating organisational structure. He sees 'modernity' as choice, a non-economic process, an attitude of inquiry, moral (normative), social (structural), and personal (behaviour). Choice demands rationality, debate, discussion, attitude of experiment, invention, and innovation. Modernisation provides an opportunity to develop a critical attitude to the individual towards relation between nature and society. After that, individual begins to adopt various choices and alternatives. Government, as a generalised membership structure, bears the responsibility of adaptation and maintenance of the social system. Its choice, in the long run, assumes a moral authority as a result of their acceptance by the society.

Some forms of government are more conducive to achieve social ends. But forms of government, instead of natural consequences of structural conditions of society, are more the outcome of desired choices of individuals. These choices relate to ultimate goals of human life. Political systems, on the basis of the moral attitudes can be classified as (i) secular libertarian, and (ii) sacred-collectivity. Apter stands for, besides scientific techniques of study, on moral perspective of the analyst. Political actors provide meaning to their activities. This situation has a great influence over the whole setting. Therefore 'moral insight' is also necessary for any political analyst. In fact, Apter is closely related with the influence of the process of modernisation of social structure on the process of politics and the evolution of various forms of government. He, in particular, wants to analyse to what extent authority is capable of making choices and judgement.

Apter distinguishes modernisation both from development and industrialisation. Modernisation is an aspect of development. Development is increased specialisation of functional roles in society. In that process, secularisation of society takes place. Industrialisation is a part of modernisation process in which specialisation of roles related with production comes in. Modernisation brings forth industrialisation as it provides perspective and necessary social apparatus for it. Innovation increases manifold, social system continues to differentiate. All these processes lead to many political problems or politics of modernisation. An endless and unknown path of fearful newness starts. Apter's chain of thinking runs as:

Development (of choice) – Modernisation – Industrialisation – Politics of Modernisation – Development.

Forms of Political Change

In view of the needs and requirements of developing societies, we are mostly concerned with political aspects of societal change. Political change[13] as a phenomenon has been the subject matter of all major thinkers. Some of the theories and perspectives related to political development have been highlighted in the last part of this chapter. Here, we are concerned with the two close but different phenomena of *political modernisation* and *political development*.

Political Modernisation

Eisenstadt observes it as a continuous spread of modern forms of political organisation and process.[14] This process is more ubiquitous and general than that of economic growth. It also serves as a basic prerequisite of economic development. Almond and Powell link it with socio-economic changes. In its comprehensive perspective, it includes: (1) increase in the capacity and capability of the political system to tap the resources of the society, both by increasing such resources and by creating a higher potential for effective operation of political administration; (2) increase in the need for coordinated social action in order to solve new problems; and (3) likelihood of increased political participation and political demands from members of the society. Welch finds the goal of political modernisation as the development of an institutional framework that is sufficiently flexible and powerful to meet the demands placed upon it. According to Richard Sisson, it involves 'an institutional imperative – the capacity and will to create, staff, manage new institutions and to engage in new forms of organised collective efforts.'[15] Daniel Lerner in his *The Passing of Traditional Society* proposes the sequence of urbanisation, literacy, extension of mass media, wider economic participation (per capita income), and political participation (voting) as the natural order of political modernisation. Eisenstadt broadly categorises general traits of political modernisation as: (i) continuous development of a high extent of differentiation, unification, and centralisation of the political system, and (ii) continuous development of a high extent of 'free floating' (i.e., non-committed to any ascriptive groups) political power and resources.

In a more concrete manner, these traits mean:

(a) a highly differentiated political structure in terms of specific political roles and institutions, of the centralisation of the polity, and of development of specific political goals and orientations;
(b) extension of the scope of the central, legal, administrative, and political activities and their permeation into all spheres and regions of the society;
(c) the continuous spread of potential political power to wider groups in the society – ultimately to all adult citizens; and
(d) the weakening of traditional elites and of traditional legitimation of the rulers, and by the establishment of some sort of ideological, and, usually also, institutional accountability of the rulers to the ruled the holders of the potential political powers.

Patterns of Political Modernisation

The transition from 'traditional' to 'modern' is not an easy and smooth process. Each political system aspires to pursue it in its own specific context. Political systems differ from each other in terms of historical background, social system, economic growth, industrial output, educational level, infrastructure of politics, national characters, political culture, etc. Political modernisation in the western Europe was characterised by feudal absolutist background and by strong urban centres. East Europe had autocracies, but less urbanisation. Colonisation, immigration, religions, ample economic opportunities, natural resources, etc. made up the background of USA, Canada, and Australia. Backgrounds and starting points, similarly, of Latin America, Japan, China, Asia, and Africa were different from each other. Some of them were conscious of their early differences while others were not.

These political systems also show differences of pattern and process available within themselves. Priorities, time-span, instrumentalities, techniques, and modalities also vary. Conflict between 'old' and 'new' or 'continuity' and 'change' is faced by the leadership in three ways: (a) by radical and revolutionary change; (b) by legislation, and, (c) by adopting a long-term policy of reconciliation with tradition. Turkey, Russia, China and other countries represent the first category. India predominantly stands for the second. Japan illustrates the third. Thus, political modernisation does not take the same methods, speed, strategy, time, and energy in reaching its goal, and has to face consequences or achieve success in varying measures. In Great Britain, it was a gradual and long-drawn process. In the USSR, it was compressed, telescoped, and quickened in a surprising manner. It was revolutionised in China by a determined, dedicated, and pragmatic leadership. Japan presented a miracle in the field of cultural mix, industrial and scientific advance, and faster economic growth. In some cases, it has demonstrated its 'segmental' or 'partial' character, as in Afro-Asian countries, appearing in some sectors of social life while leaving the rest almost where they were.

Besides these variations, there is common urge for political modernisation – hastening steps in the direction of socio-economic and systemic viability. As can be expected, most of these countries undergoing modernisation have been facing many problems and difficulties also. Some of the political areas in which they occur are: (i) unity and consensus; (ii) stability and effectiveness of government; (iii) political communication between leadership, and masses; (iv) articulation of interests and organisation of political masses; and (v) psychological strains and tensions. They can further be elaborated separately.

Development and Modernisation

Scholars like Ferrel Heady do not find any distinction between development and modernisation. Both are concepts related to each other, and use to refer to major social transformations involving a complex of social, economic and political changes. However, Huntington regards them separate: modernisation as social change, and industrialisation as economic change. He relates development to institutionalisation or the process of building institutions.

Obviously, the two concepts reflect societal transformation in general, and are closely related with each other. Still they can be distinguished from each other in the sense that in modernisation, there is more emphasis on intellectual, cultural and economic, or inner aspects of societal change, whereas development is external – social, political, and structural. The former is an ongoing continuous *process,* the latter has some end in view, and is a goal-oriented term. Modernisation is more ethnocentric, value-laden, oriented to the West than development which appears leaning less on particularism, and leaves wider scope to the countries concerned. Apparently, if one goes deeper, without and within, the other relates to the outer and narrower milieu. Still both are ambiguous, having much in common and confusing to a great context. From the Indian point of view, both are material and secular concepts built on the western paradigms and have apparently little concern with spiritual or mystical values.

Dilemmas between Modernisation and Development

As of 'modernisation', there is no agreement over the meaning of the term 'development'.[16] Some of the earlier definitions show as if there had been no political development in non-Western and non-American World. Dodd, by the term 'development', simply means, 'change'.[17] It is progress towards largely indefinable ends, or towards ends determined by some agency, or by ourselves. For the Marxists, its end is the establishment of communist society. Much confusion has been created by the use of this term, observe Riggs, Ferrel Heady and others.

Economists were first to define it as economic growth. Political scientists, like Joseph La Palombara, view it as 'the capacity of a political system to handle or manage changes in demands that confront it over time.'[18] Controversy lies in the priority to be given either to modernisation or development. Advocates of modernisation, economists in particular, regard it as a prerequisite to and a wider process than development. Political scientists and others give priority to political development as a basic infrastructure of modernisation at large. Their views on a time scale can be put as:

Economists' View: Development – Modernisation

Political Scientists' View: Modernisation – Development.

Concept of Development

The term 'development' should be distinguished from 'progress'. Progress is concerned with moral judgement applied on normative criteria. Development is a process in which a system or institution is transformed into stronger, more organised, more efficient and more effective form. It implies a conscious effort for the attainment of a specific goal. For J.H. Mittelman, it is 'the increasing capacity to make rational use of natural and human resources for social ends.'

There are other definitions of development which try to compound all types of changes into one. Accordingly, it is a major social change from one state of national being to another more valued state. It involves a complex of mutually related economic, social and political changes. Economic factors are only one aspect of the total process. Changes are the result of both past history and current[19] experience, and in turn provide the basis of further changes. Scholars mix up development with growth: social and cultural change with economic growth. The former presenting qualitative and the latter quantitative changes. Riggs unnecessarily regards the two as distinct and separate. Development, according to him, is not merely quantitative. He refers to changes in the basic structural arrangements of a society and economy, not the degree to which these structures are productive or non-productive. The term 'growth' can be used for a different variable from 'development'. According to Esman, development denotes a major social transformation, a change in system-states, along with the continuum from peasant and pastoral to industrial organisation. The assimilation and institutionalisation of modern physical and social technology are crucial ingredients. The qualitative changes affect values, behaviour, social structure, economic organisation and political process.

Development, broadly, is a combination of both techno-economic and socio-political changes. Bendix explores it as (i) a change for better; (ii) never-ending process of change; (iii) gradual change; (iv) a combination of qualitative and quantitative changes; (v) change in all spheres – political, social, economic, etc.; and (vi) not necessarily a copy of the 'western' countries.[20]

Development takes place when an index of what is deemed desirable and relatively preferable, increases in magnitude. It is increasing the ability of a system to shape or reshape its environment: ability to make decisions.

According to Riggs, the central variable in 'development' is increasing differentiation of structures rather than any particular consequence of that differentiation, whether it be productivity, capital formation, income distribution, personal security, or some associated political, social, or administrative variables.[21] He invents a technical term 'differaction' for development, which can be both negative and positive.

Development is not a natural process. It is a planned and induced change. It is a change which is positive, all-round, balanced, qualitative, and contributes towards making the life of man.

Unplanned changes can also contribute to 'development'. But in order to avoid waste of resources, particularly in developing societies, planned changes or induced development is always desirable. At this juncture, it can also be explained as a state of mind, a tendency, a direction. Without it, no change can be initiated or realised properly. All this, to political scientists, means modernisation, which is regarded as an antecedent to development. Still the two concepts or processes should be analysed in a specific manner, at least for analytical purposes.

Political Modernisation and Political Development

It is still more difficult to distinguish political modernisation and political development. Much is common to both within interlocked processes, as given in the following diagram of modernisation and development.

Close-up between Modernisation and Development

Modernisation
Development
Political
Political
POLITICAL
DEVELOPMENT
Modernisation
Development

The concept of 'political modernisation' has been explained earlier. It is less vague, more open-ended, and includes notion of development. On the basis of Lucian Pye's syndrome and others, political modernisation can be explained as political transformation undergone in Europe. It can be related to four processes: (i) a general attitude towards equality which allows equality of opportunity to participate in politics and compete for official positions; (ii) the capacity of a political system to formulate policies and to have them carried out; (iii) differentiation and specialisation of political functions though not at the expense of overall integration; and (iv) the secularisation of the political process – separation of politics from religious aims, goals, and influences. Packenham relates it to rationalisation, participation, and integration.

Problems coming out of political modernisation, mentioned above, have to be solved. At this stage, political development comes to our rescue. It is the political system's *capacity* to solve these problems. The essence of political development is the capacity for or capability to solve developmental problems.[22]

According to Almond and Powell, political development takes place if a political system successfully copes with the challenge of developmental problems of the state and nation-building, distribution, and the like. Its significance lies, in general, to increase effectiveness and efficiency of the performance of the political system, and also its capabilities.[23] A system, according to them, must have adequate sources of extraction and regulation before it can begin to distribute resources: structures first must be differentiated and specialised. Diamant conceives political development as a process, which aims at a particular condition, specially the one which creates an institutional framework for solving an ever-widening range of social problems.[24]

It is quite clear that both embrace one or more notions involving political change, and use them to explain either of the two concepts. They discuss:

(1) Political changes necessary for the achievement of a specific objective, such as liberal democracy in USA or Great Britain.

(2) A general process of change in the political sphere, closely related to other areas of society, supposed to comprise (a) the expansion and centralisation of governmental power, and the differentiation and specialisation (and subsequent integration); of political functions and structures; (b) increased popular participation in politics; and (c) increased popular identification with the political system.

(3) The political system's capacity (a) to solve problems, developmental and others, and (b) to initiate (and sustain) new policies for the society in which it operates, and to set up new structures or reform older ones, to carry out such aims.

(4) The ability to learn better and how to perform political functions and to set up political structures.

Political modernisation mostly refers to processes mentioned in (2) above, while political development includes, (1), (3) and (4). From this point of view, India in 1980s could be said to have, in a rough manner, political development (infrastructure and capability), but not political modernisation (deeper, inner, and wider commitment to politics). Political modernisation is a process within, it may not come out in structural forms, and vice versa. There can, thus, be political development, owing to borrowings, historical legacies and adaptation of political technologies, in a country without political modernisation, and the latter without flowering itself into infrastructures of political development. There can, thus, be to some extent political development without political modernisation, and political modernisation may remain unable to fructify itself into political development, when both concepts are used in a specific sense.

Political Development: Conceptual Explanation

Political development is a more elusive concept than economic development.[25] It is more controversial in normative terms and more difficult to measure in empirical and operational terms. It is used frequently by both normative and non-normative or existential thinkers. Normative theorists stress that a political system develops as it approaches the good political order. They devote less attention to systematic statement of conditions which give rise to and maintain political development, and are more concerned with specifying ends and justification for having such political development. The existentialists spend more time on specifying the characteristics of what they regard as politically developed systems and the conditions and processes which give rise to them.

Lucian W. Pye has vividly examined diversity in the explanation of the concept of political development.[26] Political development has been variously explained as:

1. political prerequisite of economic development;
2. the politics typical of industrial and advanced societies;
3. political modernisation under which advanced nations are regarded as pace-setters;
4. the operations of a nation-state;
5. administrative and legal development, it includes all colonial practices and authoritative structures;
6. mass mobilisation and participation involving new standards of loyalty and demagoguery;
7. the building of democracy;

8. stability and orderly change;
9. mobilisation and power; and
10. one aspect of a multi-dimensional process of social change regards it unnecessary to isolate political development from other aspects coming under the total process of modernisation.

There are other interpretations also, such as, national self-respect, attainment of dignity in international affairs, etc. But according to Pye, most of them create confusion. According to him, these various interpretations share some broad characteristics, which can provide the basis of agreement. He categorises them under three aspects and interlinks them in the form of *development syndrome:*

(a) Spirit or attitude towards equality: it includes participation, universalistic nature, standards of achievement etc.;
(b) Capacity of political system: it is related to outputs: economy, performance of government, effectiveness and efficiency, rationality in administration, and secularisation of public policies; and
(c) Differentiation: it involves increase of structures, institutions, division of labour, specialisation, followed by ultimate sense of integration.

Thus, political development, according to him, is a three-dimensional process of equality, capacity, and differentiation. He admits that these do not necessarily or easily fit together. Rather, acute tensions and problems are generated by them. Pressure for greater equality can challenge the capacity of the system, and differentiation can reduce equality by stressing the importance of quality and special knowledge. His development syndrome is also unilinear. Problems of equality relate to political culture and sentiments about legitimacy and commitment to the system. Capacity-problems involve the performance of authoritative structures of government. Problems pertaining to differentiation strike at the performance of the non-authoritative structures and the general political process in the society at large. In any case, political development revolves around the relationships between political culture, the authoritative structures, and the general political process. Mehta opines that Pye interprets development by incorporating almost every conceivable feature of the American political system.[27] Pye finds the development-process as evolution of society from incoherent homogeneity to coherent heterogeneity, with capacity to solve developmental problems.

Alfred Diamant conceives it as a 'process by which political system acquires an increased capacity to sustain successfully and continuously new types of goals and demands and the creation of new types of organisation.' For this process to continue over time, a differentiated and centralised polity must come into existence. It must be able to command resources from and power over wide spheres and regions of the society. Almond visualises it as the acquisition by political systems of a new capability, in the sense of a specialised role structure and differentiated orientations, which together give a political system the possibility of responding efficiently, and more or less, autonomously to a new range of problems. Both Almond and Powell reiterate that political development shows the formation of new capabilities, with specialised role-structure and differentiated orientation which enables the political system to deal with new challenges.

Hagan also finds it as 'the formation of new structures and patterns which enable a political system to cope with its fundamental problems.' Samuel P. Huntington characterises political development as 'institutionalisation' which can be applied both to past and present. For him, it is the development of institutions to meet people's demands. According to him, this process of institutionalisation can go forward and breakdown, and can decay as it has happened many times in the past. He wants to use it as a 'value-free' concept, applicable to all types of societies. However, Pennock and Smith put a caution that it should not be measured in terms of the ability of political systems to survive only but also to satisfy the demands of those who are subject to its rule. The system has to satisfy them with 'political goods'. Riggs also concurs with him and observes that political development opens a number of choices to satisfy political goals.

Political Development as a Research Variable

Robert A. Packenham observes that 'political development' has received varying attention at the hands of scholars. Upto 1965, it was treated as a 'dependent' variable. Political development, thus, was based on political modernisation (rationalisation, participation, and integration), and political democracy. Various approaches use it as:

1. a function mainly of the legal-formal apparatus of government, prescribing features like equal protection of law, rule of law, election by secret ballot, separation of powers, etc.;
2. a function of a level of economic development;
3. a function of administrative capacity ;
4. a function of a social system that facilitates popular participation at all levels and helps bridging over various diversities; and
5. a function of political culture reflecting fundamental attitudinal and personality characteristics among members of the political system.

However, these approaches did not study political development deeply and comprehensively. They could not weigh each other comparatively and free themselves from their normative notions. They also lacked data to prove their assumptions. They neglected variables like the will, skill and capacity of political development.

After 1965, political development was visualised as a continuous process, and not some fixed-end-state. Helpern defined it as 'a persistent capacity for coping with a permanent revolution'. Various terms were used for this conceptualisation, such as, the will and capacity, problem-solving capacity, institutionalisation, ability to sustain new goals, etc. Scholars of post-1965 era treated it as an independent or intervening variable. Huntington is his article, 'Political Development and Political Decay' defined it as 'the institutionalisation of political organisations and procedures.' Almond and Powell explained it as, 'the increased differentiation and specialisation of political structures and the increased secularisation of political culture.' A political system is said to be developing, according to Diamant, 'where there is an increase in its ability to sustain successfully and continuously new types of social goals and the creation of new types of organisation.' Halpern observes it as the relationship between 'the structural changes and demands set loose by uncontrolled force of transformation' and 'the will and capacity of political authority to cope with these changes and demands.' Eisenstadt finds it as 'an institutional framework capable of continuous absorption of change.'

This perspective also uses concepts like skill, capacity, etc., in imprecise manner. Huntington's concept of 'institutionalisation' is also not very clear. Diamant, Eisenstadt and others have an overlap between definition and explanation. They arbitrarily treat it from independent to dependent or intervening variable.

Political development has some normative aspects also. Its goal is said to be 'modernisation' which has not been operationalised and explained properly. Scholars leave such aspects open to others. Statements like 'the capacity to cope with changes', 'problems arising out of political development', etc., are not properly explained. Often they overlook short-range aspects in favour of long-range aspects. Western scholars generally regard cost of violent revolution more than cost of flow and piecemeal modernisation. Thus, in these studies of political development, various important aspects have been either neglected or overemphasised.

However, political development, finally, can be explained as a generic process of successfully sustaining new demands, goals, and organisation in a flexible manner. In view of the developing countries, it also means meeting of particular goals and demands. In these countries, it is simultaneously a cause for other types of social changes.

Nature and Scope

There are three views on the nature and process of political development: (i) unilinear, (ii) multilinear, and (iii) dialectical. Now, the second and the third views have found general acceptance. Some of the general characteristics of political development can be mentioned below:

(1) It is a multi-factor and multi-dimensional phenomenon occurring in the countries of the Third World;

(2) It is both a cause and consequence of socio-economic change in developing societies;

(3) It is a process of induced political change involving, according to Pye, equality, capacity and differentiation. Almond and Powell have found it to be a compound process of (i) role-differentiation, (ii) autonomy of subsystems, and (iii) secularisation of political culture. Others have analysed and defined the process in a different manner.

Political development is related to almost all sectors of societal life. However, it is more concerned with (i) socio-economic changes influencing political settings of the society; (ii) forces affecting the path, nature, speed and volume of political development; (iii) roles of various political structures; (iv) political participation of the people at various levels and segments of government; (v) the elite, leadership and their ends and style of functioning; (vi) role of army, bureaucracy, and mass media; and (vii) nationalism, ideology, political culture, and socialisation.

Stages and Problems of Political Development

Another important step is to know and determine the various levels or stages of political development. Brian Berry maintains the concept of 'level' as static and cross-sectional. Comparatively, the concept of 'stage' is more dynamic and result-oriented. Idea of stages of development has come from economics through W.W. Rostow (*Stages of Economic Growth*, 1968). Rostow suggested that alike economic growth, there might be stages of political development. But he stopped short of studying regularities, crises, and order found in economic development. A very successful attempt in this respect was made by Almond and Powell in their book entitled '*Comparative Politics: A Developmental Approach*' (1966). All have agreed with Pye regarding his three-dimensional approach on political development. But none could properly coordinate them at the level of various relevant stages of political development. Pye somehow was successful in indicating six crises in the development-process of England.

Kenneth Organski's *Stages of Political Development* (1965) relates national development with political development, and points out that the combined process operates in an orderly manner. Neglect of any particular stage can be the cause of serious consequences or problems. Some stages can proceed in an overlapping or parallel manner. Using his economic perspective, he has mentioned four *stages* of political development: political unification, industrialisation, national welfare, and affluence. But he could not evolve any 'theory'. One follows another. The third and the fourth stages are concerned with participation, integration, distribution etc.

Pye in his *Aspects of Political Development* (1966), pointed out six crises in the development of England: (i) identity, (ii) legitimacy, (iii) penetration, (iv) participation, (v) unification, and (vi) distribution. One can treat them as six stages of political development. Pye's first three crises can be equated with Organski's political unification. Rest are almost similar to the stages of Organski's process of political development. But, it must be reminded, they are related to the developmental process of advanced countries. One cannot legitimately expect developing countries to follow the same order. However, Edward Shils did make another empirical analysis of transitional political systems and classified them in five categories: (i) political democracy; (ii) tutelary democracy; (iii) modernising oligarchy; (iv) totalitarian oligarchy; and (v) traditional oligarchy. These patterns of transitional societies can be taken as stages of political development. In fact, they can display political development in ascending order with the western model as his 'ideal type' though, not expressly mentioned.

John Kautsky, in *Political Change in Underdeveloped Countries: Nationalism and Communism* (1962) has studied both traditional and modern societies and categorised them in five classes, as, (i) traditional aristocratic authoritarian system; (ii) transitional system dominated by national intellectual elites; (iii) totalitarian system of aristocracies; (iv) totalitarian system of intellectuals; and (v) democratic system. He has classified that there can be many other mixed forms or subsets. He has also made up his classification on the basis of social classes, and, has not analytically related them with each other.

Almond and Powell have discussed four problems related to political development. Every political system endeavours to face them: *First,* There is State-building. In the first phase, the political system has to face the problem of penetrating into every part of the system, and integrate its various segments. *Second,* Loyalty and commitment. After overcoming the first problem, it has to strive to make itself a nation, by a we-feeling or belongingness to it. *Third,* Participation. This problem compels the system to invite its various groups, classes, etc. to take part in the decision-making process. *Fourth,* Distribution. This relates to the demand of welfare. There is domestic pressure on the system to redistribute income, money, opportunities, honour, etc. All these problems can be looked as interconnected stages of political development. All the developed countries have passed through them, and the developing nations too will have to undergo them.

As discussed earlier, after 1965, scholars of political development freed themselves from the influence of economists and sociologists. In the place of regarding government and development as outcomes of societal forces, they started giving higher status to government, politics, political leaders, the will and capacity. They stopped considering political development as a by-product of the world-wide phenomena of modernisation, nationalism, or democracy. Helpern, Eisenstadt, Huntington, Diamant, etc., have treated 'political development' as an independent variable. For them, capability, competence, skill, effectivity, etc., appeared to be more important.

Samuel P. Huntington (in his *Political Order in Changing Societies* (1968), in the chapter an 'Political Development and Political Decay') has sharply criticised the proponents of stages and unilinearists. He pointed out that (i) they regard modernity and industrialisation as the top most values, and do not think over the possibility of *decay* of a political system; (ii) they create confusion, by including social, economic and cultural matters in modernisation, even if they remotely or directly concern with politics; (iii) it is wrong to treat everything happening in the Third World as political development; and, (iv) political development is not an irreversible process. According to him, there are many instances of political decay. He urged to understand political development in terms of 'institutionalisation'. Institutionalisation consists in existence of properties of adaption, complexity, autonomy, cohesion, etc., in the structures and processes of a polity. It can be observed both in past and contemporary societies. He has also mapped out three levels or stages of political development: (i) Centralisation – at this stage, one central authority takes over a numerously existing local authorities; (ii) Differentiation – thereafter owing to increase in functions of a political system, there is differentiation in existing structures. The political system begins to perform many new functions; (iii) Participation – later on, groups, sub-groups, individuals and so on begin actively to take part in decision making. According to him, all these, stages should appear in order, otherwise, there can be functional consequences of the system. In order to avoid such mishap, either slow down the speed of concentrating authority or the mobilisation process itself, or alternatively, the institutionalisation process may be accelerated. By relating political development with institutionalisation, he has been able to apply the concept both on ancient and modern societies.

But Riggs does not agree with him. Old polities, whatever be the degree of their institutionalisation, cannot be equated with modern political systems. Huntington has not explained the meaning of political decay or breakdown. He was expected to elaborate problems attached with it. In fact, he could not rise above his parochial structural-functional approach, despite his high talk about dynamic equilibrium found in the systems.

S.N. Eisenstadt in his *Breakdowns of Modernization* (1964), *Tradition, Change, and Modernity* (1973), has stated that in early stages as a result of industrialisation, modernisation, or structural differentiation, numerous political problems raise their head. Governments may or may not overcome them. When control and coordination utterly fails, system becomes standstill, and political development stops. Many developing political systems are confronting with such obstacles and difficulties. There is breakdown of modernisation in various systems. For him, political development and political modernisation are identical.

Some discussion regarding problems of political development in the Third World has already taken place. Pye has called them as crises which are six in number: (i) identity, (ii) legitimacy, (iii) penetration, (iv) participation, (v) integration, and (vi) distribution. These crises are usually the developmental problems of all transitional societies. They can come all together or one by one in an orderly manner. But there is no limit on the number of problems. Some of the problems have not at all been considered by development-theorists, such as, political succession, choice of development strategy, procurement of resources for development, intervention of superpowers, cold war or military pressure, population explosion, etc. None of them, in fact, could set among the various stages, crises, or levels of political development.

Theories of Political Development

Theories of Political Development consider polities of the Third World from underdevelopment to development. The process which facilitates their efforts to achieve their social ends, is 'development'. The factors which hinder them in this direction are responsible for their 'underdevelopment'. For this the Marxist and neo-Marxist scholars have advanced 'dependency theory' to explain the phenomenon of underdevelopment. Liberal and Marxist thinkers give different accounts of the factors of underdevelopment. Various attempts have been made to develop theories, approaches, paradigms and models of political development, which rid polities and societies of underdevelopment.[28] More important among them are briefly discussed below.

Dialectical Theory of Political Development

W.F. Riggs is one of the greatest authorities on political development.[29] Though he calls his formulation only a 'paradigm', yet it can be regarded as a 'dialectical theory of political development'. According to him, increased structural differentiation is the key variable of political development. He is mainly a structuralist, and maintains that governmental or political structure can be borrowed or transferred independent of cultural considerations. He regards governmental institutions and practices as 'technology'.[30] It can be transplanted anywhere across political systems and political cultures.

The key to political development is the ability to shape and be shaped by environment. Men or societies want political development to enhance their freedom of choice and pursue goals, called 'political goods' by Pennock. The ratio between the two variables – ability and environment, provides one

Dialectical Theory of Political Development: Paradigm of Riggs

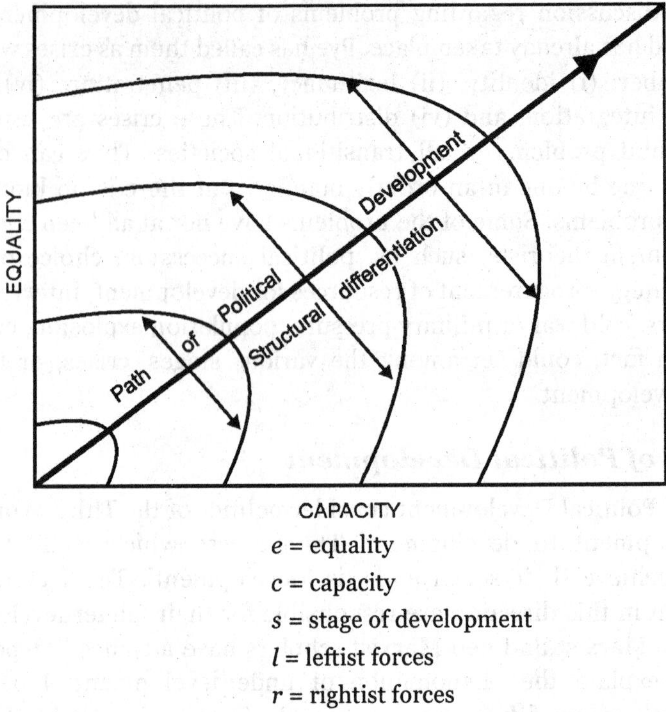

of the many tests of the level of development attained by a system. Political development involves a system's capacity to absorb and utilise more and more information from its environment. Its goal is to respond to this information and to bring about change to satisfy its needs, and to enhance the range and diversity of goals that can be satisfied.

With a view to explaining the phenomenon of political development, he makes use of the contributions of developmental scholars. He presents them in form of a few theoretical propositions. According to Riggs, a set of operations governs the phenomena of change among dependent variables. It appears in response to inputs generated by the independent variables. The system has to stabilise at different levels of development leading to an equilibrium necessary for a system to go ahead. If a system has higher level of differentiation, it could absorb basic changes. More differentiation means more capacity to absorb changes and face challenges. There are three independent variables: (i) challenges posed by environment, (ii) efforts to be made by the existing system to work better, and (iii) efforts to change the existing system. Dependent variables available to the system are – (i) performance level, (ii) level of differentiation, and (iii) degree of 'integration', absorption. Political development is interaction and interplay among these variables. But he prefers the use of the term 'political development' in plural like 'polities'. He regards 'development' as merely a label for a cluster of activities, operations, and changes.

Riggs adopts the three criteria or properties of Pye's syndrome of political development: differentiation, capacity, and equality, with a typology of developmental stages based on key governmental technologies. These governmental technologies are transferrable cross-culturally or systems can have another functional equivalents. These governmental technologies or structures are important and independent of any cultural sway. They can be possessed, used and operated like telephone, radio, TV or camera irrespective of political cultures.

According to him, technological changes in politics and administration do have sudden qualitative jumps or thrusts, and create *structural differentiation*. They do bring in problems in the wake. Other functional categories, besides structural categories, can have quantitative measurements. Political development can be explained by technological (differentiational) advances in government. Of course, increased structural differentiation, while solving some problems, also creates new difficulties in the direction of proper coordination and integration of the system. This structural differentiation and its advance has to help maintaining a balance between 'capacity' *(c)* and 'equality' *(e)*. *Capacity* is the ability of a political and administrative system to adopt collectively authorised goals and to implement them. *Equality (e)* is extent of participation and sharing of benefits available during the course of implementation of goals. Thus, differentiation, caused by technological structures is related to equality *(e)* and capacity *(c)*.

Diagram (on p. 228) presents paradigm of dialectical theory of political development. System treads on the diagonal path of political development. This path, made of structural differentiation, is cut at various points or stages (S_1, S_2, S_3, ...) when the system arrives at certain balance or equilibrium between forces of equality *(e)* and capacity (*c*). The balance or equilibrium between the two provides a developmental thrust or leap forward on the path of structural differentiation. The system moves ahead. The two legs of political development are *capacity* (or rightist forces) and *equality* (leftist forces). As such, the system advances further on the two legs of structural differentiation. If the lines show more area covered by them towards right, the equilibrium will be disturbed. There would be imbalance and the system would be in favour of rightist or capacity (elitist) forces making arrowed crosscutting line longer towards right or capacity. So will be the case with leftist or equality (mass) forces. If the system moves towards left, it would mean there are much more demands on the system to participate in the decision-making or for sharing of benefits, and the forces of capacity thereby have reduced strength to check them from putting more pressure on the system. Structural differentiation is the key to deal with both the goals of equality and capacity. 'Conflicts between these goals are most acute in transitional stages', Riggs observes. There is hide-and-seek in attaining either of the two goals. Hence, maintaining equilibrium is necessary to move onwards along the path of political development which can be possible only by and through structural differentiation attached with governmental technologies. The equidistance shown by arrows $r - 1$ at S_1, S_2, S_3, ... is rarely maintained in actual practice. Like *thesis* and *anti-thesis,* both equality and capacity oppose each other. Structural differential is created out of their conflict or struggle and appears in form of *synthesis.* Therefore, it has been called as 'dialectical theory of political development.' As soon as synthesis appears, the system begins to take strides over the long and tiresome path of political development.

The developmental process of thesis – antithesis – synthesis continuously goes on both in developing as well as developed countries. The environment or ecology of the whole political system presents the background for inventing or developing appropriate governmental technologies. Once such governmental technologies are in hand, reproduction or existence of circumstances in which they were made and developed is not necessary. These technologies can easily be imported, and they bring about qualitative change in the political system. As a result of import of these governmental technologies, radical changes are taking place in various countries of the Third World. Impact of foreign aid, loan, transfer of technology, training, etc., can be seen in this perspective. Although, Riggsian dialectical model deals with the processes of internal differentiation, yet it can also explain a lot of changes taking place outside of a political system. Both leftist or rightist forces can make use of these governmental technologies. For example, bureaucratic apparatuses can be used both by a ruling coterie or a popular government monocracy or democracy. But development ensues only on creation of an equilibrium. Structural differentiation appears, only at balancing or midpoints, and generates development by bringing about an equilibrium between forces of equality and capacity. In the absence of balance, political system often fall into *development-trap.* It means the political system hands over itself either to the forces of capacity or equality, at the expense of each other.

To sum up, an increase in the level of differentiation *(d)* makes it possible to achieve higher levels both of equality and capacity. But such an increase can be generated endogenously only when a balance between capacity (c) and equality *(e)* prevails. The system falls into 'development-trap' when it resorts to either of the two, and stop all structural differentiation. Only the balance between the two enables the system to heighten the level of structural differentiation, and realise higher degree of capacity and equality. Western countries so far had endogenous development, but non-western countries resort to exogenous form of development. They can go right or left, and also maintain a balance between them for their people as a whole. Each position, obviously, has problems peculiar to it.

Thus Riggs has been able, to a large extent, to coordinate various studies on political development. With the help of his developmental paradigm or theory, crises, observed by Pye, can be explained. It can also explain Huntington's 'political decay', or Eisenstadt's 'breakdown'. Halpern's 'will and capacity' also can stand closer to it. Huntington's 'institutionalisation' can be taken as a form of structural differentiation. Various explanations over political development can also be accommodated within the perspective of W.F. Riggs. However, Riggs appears too much dependent on the variable of structural differentiation. His theoretical paradigm requires empirical verification at the hands of scholars and political actors. Surely, it has potential of empirical verification, though it also raises several other issues and questions.[31]

Developmental Approach: Almond and Powell

Like Riggs, but on a larger and wider empirical level. Almond and Powell (*Comparative Politics: A Development Approach*, 1966) also have formulated a developmental approach for studying modernising societies. They have made much more use of concepts like political system, political culture, secularisation, socialisation, subsystem autonomy, environment, etc. In the presentation of an exhaustive typology of political systems ranked on a scale of political development, they have gone quite close to the formulation of an empirical theory of political systems. It has already been discussed alongwith structural-functional approach in Chapter Five.

Communist Model of Political Development

The communist model of political development is based largely on Marxist-Leninist ideology. The source of motivation for political development, accordingly, lies in industrialisation, monopoly over forces of production, exploitation of labour, class consciousness and organisation of the working classes. Lenin is more important than Marx regarding political development. He led the Russian revolution and had to confront problems of development in backward countries. Lenin showed the path of development for Russia by the establishment of dictatorship of the proletariat by resorting to revolutionary means under the leadership of a disciplined political party. After him, Stalin succeeded in industrialising the Russian society by repression and violent means. Thus, Russia attained modernisation within 30 years which the Western countries could achieve after the end of about 200 years, and became a superpower. Stalin concentrated his attention on the making of Russia alone, and did not take interest in the development of other countries. Many other countries turned communist, but they did not blindly follow the Russian path of development. But the blueprint of political development was almost common for them all. The political set-up of all communist countries remained similar.[32]

In colonial and backward countries, Lenin gave support to bourgeois-national movements so that after attainment of freedom they would have economic and political development under Russian direction. But many countries, including China, did not do so. In fact, within the communist camp, there were many models of political development, such as, Chinese, Yugoslav, Cubaic, Rumanian, etc. Thus, before developing countries, there were two broad patterns of political development – western and communist. Often these countries, due to lack of resources, skills, time, etc., and role of politics, opted for the Russian or Communist model, but, they found themselves unable to pay the cost in human terms, and also were not ready to give up nationalism and democracy as a matter of faith. This model collapsed with the collapse and fall of the Soviet Union in 1991. Only a few countries now claim to follow it.

Dependency Model

The exponents of 'dependency theory' argue that third world countries had remained underdeveloped because their social and economic development was conditioned by external forces like colonialism and exploitation. Uneven political development is a universal phenomenon. Scholars have tried to explain it in two forms: (a) dependency model, and (b) centre-periphery model. Andre Gundre Frank *(Comparative Government,* 1969) in the context of Latin American countries raised the fallowing three issues:

(i) Why is there uneven development in the world?
(ii) Why are the now underdeveloped countries suffering from failure of internal market?
(iii) Has the phenomena become a fundamental feature?

Frank is aware that Great Britain and the USA took respectively 183 and 93 years in attaining industrial development. But the developing countries are eager to have it in about 30-40 years. Many factors can be attributed to it. Mercantalism held its sway from 1500 to 1770, industrialisation took another hundred years from 1770 to 1870, capitalism ruled over from 1870 onwards. But it does not mean that emerging nations should undergo the same process. Paul Baran, Frank Curzy, Gultang, etc., have sharply criticised the Western model of development. Andre G. Frank rejects the classical explanation that the poor are poor because they are vice versa. The fact revealed to us is that the West started developing from 1550 to 1770 at the cost of Latin American countries. There was no mercantilism in favour of these countries. They were fiercely and fully exploited, and trade went against them. Walter Rodney and B. Cuings confirmed Frank's conclusions in the context of Africa and Asia. Thereafter, industrialisation took place in Europe. It made possible for these countries to have capital accumulation. They established their political authority over them, and had a free hand in their total exploitation. After the World War II, they were politically free, but remained still under the yoke of neo-colonialism. Thus, inequality and exploitation, which had already been existing, continued to prevail unabated. Two reasons can be attributed for it:

(1) There is unequal exchange between the owners of production and producers of raw material. The imperial or colonial masters exploited them in their own way, and also compelled the producers to produce raw material required by them. Thus, all benefits went to the owners of production.

(2) The world was assumed to be one economic order. As such, the under-developed countries were forced to produce raw material and were not allowed to manufacture finished goods.

All this led to dependence on imperialist and neo-colonial powers. It caused formerly rich Latin countries to grow poor and the poor European countries to become rich. So much so, that rich countries like Brazil (and India) became poorer, their natural resources were exploited by countries of trade and industry, with less and less return to the producer. Frank observes that USA, Canada, and Russia were also colonised, but came out of exploitation-net of European countries earlier, and joined the same forces of exploitation. Russia and later China became communist. Paul Baran also finds that the developed countries are taking away all economic surplus, making the developing countries still more dependent. A large number of these countries are politically and juridically free but not 'developed' as yet. They are actually under neo-imperialism – politically free but economically still under their tight control. The gap between the developed and these developing countries is increasing every day at the rate of 14 per cent. The rate of development in these countries is 3-2 per cent only. Frank adduces three major causes of their plight:

(a) Economic aid is another form of exploitation, given at wrong time for a wrong sector;

(b) Technical aid is second rate, outmoded and rejectable. Goods produced as a result of this aid cannot be sold anywhere; and

(c) Multinationals are creating havoc everywhere, taking all profits, and encouraging conflicts in the host countries.

Das Sandoz further adds that besides economic dependency, there is evidence of political dependency because economic superiority provides clout to have high hand in political decision-making, both at national and international levels.

Centre-Periphery Model

Dependency model has not fully satisfied scholars of economic and political development. It has taken into account only external factors and conditions of underdevelopment. Internal causes too contribute to the underdevelopment of these countries. Frank and some others appear to have adopted a fatalist and pessimistic approach in the sense that these undeveloped countries can never hope to become developed. It appears that they have readily applied their findings taken from Latin American countries to all developing countries of the world. Some of these countries may have different reasons for their underdevelopment, such as, explosion of population is consuming all of their surplus, profits, etc., and nothing is left for making further investment. Wastage and heavy cost of administration can be extra reason for their plight.

However, another plausible explanation has come in the form of centre-periphery relationships (see the following diagram):

Centre-Periphery Model of Under Development

Exploitation Linkage

PERIPHERY

CENTRE

Flow of Profits

Flow of Profits

CENTRE

A. Every developing or underdeveloped country has a centre and its periphery. Main cities and trading towns are called as centre, and villages which produce raw material are treated its periphery. In them, the centre exploits the periphery as usual.

B. Besides above, in the field of international relations, the advanced or developed countries form the centre, and the developing countries constitute the periphery. The developed countries or the centre exploits the periphery or the developing countries.

C. The centre of centre (developed) countries enter into contract or collusion with the centre of periphery (developing) countries, and the drain of continuous exploitation goes on. The periphery (producers of raw material) of periphery countries is doubly exploited. First, the centre of developing country itself exploits the periphery. Second, the centre or advanced countries exploit the centre of periphery countries. Collusion takes place owing to profit-motives of the centre of periphery (developing) country. The centre of the developed country brings the centre of the periphery (under developed country) on their side by giving them greater advantage, as multinationals give more profit to them, but in fact consume all of their scarce resources. Samir Amin in *Accumulation on a World Scale: A Critique of Theory of Underdevelopment, 1974,* has pointed out that the industrialised countries and the less developed countries are integrated in a manner that capitalism fails to perform its role of development. There is unequal exchange in the international trade. The West is playing the same role through WTO, IMF and others. Advanced countries invest their capital in the former colonies and use them as suppliers of raw materials and labour at throwaway prices. They are potential markets for their manufactured goods at the market prices.

Still, the Centre-Periphery model lacks a fuller explanation. It is not necessary that the periphery always cooperates with the centre There can be contradictions between the two, and they may not cooperate at all. It tries to explain the tentacles of neo-colonialism, but much of political development remains to be accounted for.

Kothari-Mehta Perceptive

Few are satisfied with the present models of political development. Rajni Kothari has found the various models of development as highly dangerous and suicidal by nature. Modern science, modern technology, and modern communications are all based on fragmented approach to human problems. Conflicts have become global. Inequity has increased, and very little has been done systematically to solve it. Particularly, 'thinking in the Third World is bereft of systematic inquiry into the fundamentals of life.'[33] Man has virtually surrendered his freedom at the altar of new religion called modernity. Kothari believes in presenting a wide and all-embracing framework that wears together the concerns of science, philosophy, culture, and religion from alternative civilisational perspectives. His is a holistic approach, leading to a larger process of self-realisation or certain basic values. He rejects relentless consumerism as indicator of development.

There are certain basic postulates of the alternative model of development proposed by Kothari, such as, (i) removal of poverty, (ii) equity through local self-reliance entailing plurality, (iii) self-reliance and decentralisation, (iv) development takes the form of liberation, (v) endogenous science and its use for man, (vi) building of a new road to prosperity, and (vii) restoration of original symbiosis between science and nature which has been disturbed as a result of making science an instrument of exploitative technology. In fact, these postulates make up the action plan of his environmental perspective. But the basic features of his approach are following:

1. It adopts a holistic view of development.
2. It is concerned with a structure of equity that ensures autonomy and self-reliance of diverse entities in place of a structure of dependence that is sustained by the promise and transfer of technology to enable others to catch up.
3. It puts emphasis on participation.
4. Its main accent is also on the importance of local conditions and the value of diversity.

Kothari rejects the prevailing alternatives of liberal democracy as well as state socialism. The former is dominated by machine-politics whereas the latter is actually dominated by a small bureaucratic elite. But both are found authoritarian. Nobody is really ready to come to rescue the developing nations. The number of underdeveloped and developing countries was 77 (known as group of 77) in about a decade ago, but increased to 120. The internationally accepted target of 0.7 per cent of GNP to be given by the developed countries to developing countries, has fallen below 0.35 per cent of GNP achieved in 1975. Few are really ready to appreciate that 'lasting peace and equitable prosperity are really two sides of the same coin.'[34]

Mehta also finds various developmental approaches as 'vulgarisation of what was a typically European experience into a universal experience.'[35] According to him, change always takes place against a background: 'it is a result of an interaction of the subjective, objective and the ethical conditions, and cannot transcend its temporality.' Each society has a peculiar genius and distinctive nature and temperament of its own. Therefore, only those forms of modernisation are likely to succeed which spring from a fuller and holistic understanding of the process of change inherent in that society. In his concept of modernity the old subsists side by side with the new. There can be no denial of the past, rather the socio-cultural should prevail over everything else. The process of modernisation, for Mehta, is in fact a search for and development of one's own identity. In sum, only those forms of modernisation are likely to succeed which spring from a fuller and holistic understanding of the inherent process of change in society.

Welfare Model of Development

Welfare state model is a modified version of the liberal view which had have originally been supporting the market society model.[36] The idea of welfare began with Prince Bismarck (1815-98), the German Chancellor (1871-90), and, Herbert Henry Asquith (1852-1928), British Prime Minister of Great Britain (1908-16). Fuller expression to the idea of welfare was given by the Beveridge Report (1942).[37] Implementation of this report turned England as be a model welfare state. It resorted to the policy of progressive taxation. Those who had higher income and wealth were required to pay higher rates of taxes. In effect, it is a method of redistribution of wealth in society. Eventually, France, Italy, Germany, Sweden, Australia and New Zealand followed the model in degrees only. Other countries owing to shortage of resources adopted it on a subdued scale. The functioning of the welfare state was adversely affected due to bureaucratic inefficiency and rampant corruption.

Gandhian Model of Development

Mahatma Gandhi (1869-1948) was primarily a moral philosopher. He did not advance any theory of development. He gave precedence to morality over politics. Politics for him was an instrument of achieving moral goals and self-realisation. His role in the independence movements of India was aimed at securing moral regeneration of India. He never wanted India to emulate the ways of the Western civilisation: consumerism, materialism, competition, arrogance, selfishness, concentration of wealth, and exploitation. He stood for self-control, renunciation, moral strength, bread labour, truth, non-violence, and compassion. This model is highly appreciated and eulogised, but has hardly been practised.[38] His techniques of mass mobilisation and struggle are a great contribution to the philosophy of social change.[39]

LPG Model of Development

This is the currently prevailing market society model of development. It has revolutionised economies, cultures and communities the world over.[40] It has created the problems, which the advocates of sustainable development and environmentalists claim to concentrate on and solve them.

Sustainable Development and Environment

Development is a man-made positive phenomenon. It stands for the improvement of human life in all spheres. But higher production under various forms of development involves exploitation of natural resources. Gigantic machines consume huge energy resources, and cause pollution, disease and shortages. In a sharp reaction to them, there is demand of 'sustainable development'. Its idea was floated earlier during the Earth Summit held in Stockholm in 1972. It expressed a serious concern over the rapid depletion of the exhaustible natural resources. Later it was elaborated in the *Bruntland Report,* entitled *Our Common Future,* published in 1987. The issue of 'sustainable development' was warmly supported and upheld by the environmentalists.

Environmentalism or ecologism[41] appears to be a natural outcome of the demand for sustainable development. It redefines relationship between man and nature, and among human beings. It insists that man is no more the 'master' of nature. Man is one of the partners with all other living organisms.

There was no problem at the beginning of human civilisation. With the increase human population from merely 20 crores to over 5 billion, rise in the level of consumption, superiority of science and technology, and limitless demands of man over and from nature, the equilibrium between man and nature has been completely lost. There is fast depletion of natural resources. Man has to follow what E.F. Schumacher has said in his *Small is Beautiful* (1973). Otherwise man would be digging his own grave. Shumacher has warned that the earth and its non-renewable resources should not be confused with the conventional concept of 'capital'. Advanced countries, particularly, the USA and others, are inflicting great harm on the earth. They have to change their lifestyle, transport system, consumption of energy, food habits, and the like. Reacting to them, millions of people in the advanced countries are now connected with 'Green movements' and 'Green politics'. They want to save mankind from imminent catastrophe – green-house effects, global warming and ozone depletion. Man has to dismantle large-scale manufacturing system and change over to smaller-scale manufacturing systems to be supervised and controlled by self-governing local bodies. Population, consumption, concentration of wealth etc. have to be reduced sharply. They all remind the UN slogan that, "We have not inherited this earth from our forefathers; we have borrowed it from our children." For this, all have to be: "Neither left nor right, but forwards." We have to prepare ourselves for a better future of mankind. From time to time, the UN and other world bodies discuss these matters, but advanced countries fail to comply with directives and recommendations.

Criticism and Contribution

It is quite clear that few scholars are satisfied with the various theories, approaches, and perspectives of political development. Both Kothari and Mehta, in their criticism of political development, appear more ideational philosophers than as political scientists. They talk of culture, values, and ideals, but are less concerned with the ways and means of realising them in actual practice. Narain and Mathur have found almost all the Princeton exercises of studying political development in the Third World as futile.[42] The developmental theorists have not been able to stick to their proposed concept of 'political development'. Western Scholars, according to them, have simply extrapolated their present as the future of the non-western world. These critics are very much concerned about 'under-development of political development' studies. In a different direction, Daya Krishna suggests political socialisation and political communication as indicators of political development.[43]

Some of the studies on political development have prescriptive character, deeply ingrained in ethnocentrism and oriented towards Western values. There is unnecessary entanglement of political development with modernisation – controversy between 'tradition' and 'modernity', a misguiding scholarly dichotomy. The Western model as goal of development-theorists is pernicious. All the models as such often prove unsuitable, harmful, unattainable, even undesirable. Such studies are mostly conducted by scholars alien to the culture, ends and aspirations of the people. Their search of indicators of development is not comprehensive. It causes misunderstanding. Their tendency to raise the limited range of findings at the highest or universal level of generality is equally debatable. Scholars heavily depend on public funds and official pleasure as well as favour. Officials feel themselves insecure in permitting such studies. Either there is no collaboration between decision-makers and political scientists, or if there is collaboration, it turns into a tacit form of collusion. In many cases, development-scholars lack training regarding the use of proper techniques, direct access to information, essential concepts and methodologies and public support.

Besides above, observes Packenham, these scholars have relatively neglected many important variables, data and perspectives relevant to political development.[44] They have totally neglected role of violence, revolution, ideology, political rights, and international environment, particularly pressure and manoeuvre of the super-power. Often they have overlooked role of political leaders, and side-tracked policy-relevance. Riggs quotes La Palombara, 'the concepts and propositions that go into 'theories' of political development are so abstract and obscure, so shot through with unfortunate neologisms, or so clearly static – rather than dynamic in their final implication – as to make empirical testing either a very risky enterprise or downright impossible.'

Still, it must be straightforward accepted that these studies had created revolution in the field of empirical research methodology, and could see new states as potential laboratories where controlled and semi-controlled experiments were being conducted. Political science could come out of its traditional shell, and discover realities as they were. In the process, most of the theorists have smashed the old West-oriented and ethno-centric subject-matter of Political Science, and have built new academic structures, suitable even for cross-cultural transfer and adjustment. Though a large number of them stood for the status quo or equilibrium or in favour of the Western hegemony, yet others could expose them in full. In the international field, one can find the rise of new states as the demand for 'equality', whereas the pressure of the superpowers for dominance and influence is a demand for enhancing their 'capacity' or hegemony, in the name of world peace or a new world order.[45] As most of the advanced countries are not willing to take up preventive and reformative measures towards 'sustainable development', the whole earth is moving toward suicide. They are worried more on global Terrorism and Nuclear Holocaust, than on slow but sure exhaustion of wherewithals of human survival. Only a democratic world order, if it emerges, can save mankind from extinction.

Notes

1. Alfred Sauvy had coined this term in his article published in 1952. Countries included in the 'third world' number over 120.
2. See, infra, Ch. 13
3. W.F. Riggs, "The Theory of Political Development", in James C. Charlesworth, (ed.), *Contemporary Political Analysis*, New York: Free Press, 1967, 317.
4. David E. Apter, *Introduction to Political Analysis*, New India: Prentice-Hall of India, 1978, Ch. XIV.
5. Irving Louis Horowitz, *Three Worlds of Development,* New York, Oxford University Press, 1972, 271-420.
6. Calvert, Peter, *Revolution*, London: Macmillan, 1970; Johnson, Chalmers, *Revolutionary Change: An Adaptation*, New York: Feffer and Simons Inc., 1966.
7. S.N. Eisenstadt, *Tradition, Change, and Modernity,* New York: John Wiley & Sons, 1973, Chap. 6, 9, 10 and 11; See, 'modernity', chap. 1, supra.
8. V. R. Mehta, *Ideology, Modernization and Politics in India*, Delhi: Manohar, 1983, 48-49.
9. Eisenstadt, *op. cit.*, 210.
10. Wilfred C. Smith, *Modernization of a Traditional Society*, Bombay: Asia Publishing House, 1965, 22.
11. V.R. Mehta, "The Concept of Modernization", *Political Science Review,* June-Oct., 1977.
12. David E. Apter, *The Politics of Modernization,* Chicago: University of Chicago Press. 1967, x.
13. See, various issues of *Political Change,* 1970, 80 and 81, Rajasthan University, Jaipur.
14. Eisenstadt, *op. cit.*, 73-74.
15. Richard Sisson, *The Congress Party in Rajasthan: Political Integration and Institution-Building in an Indian State*, Berkeley: University of California Press, 1972.

16. Alfred Diamant, "The Nature of Political Development", in Jason L. Finkle and Richard W. Gable, *Political Development and Social Change,* New York: John Wiley & Sons, 1966.
17. C.H. Dodd, *Political Development,* London: Macmillan. 1972, 9-15.
18. La Palombara, "Alternative Strategies for Developing Administrative Capabilities in Emerging Nations", in W.F. Riggs (ed.). *Frontiers of Development Administration,* Durham: Duke University Press, 1970, 175.
19. Soul M. Katz, "Exploring Systems Approach to Development Administration", in Riggs, *op. cit.,* 110.
20. Reinhard Bendix, *Nation Building and Citizenship,* New Delhi: Wiley Eastern, 1969, 5.
21. W.F. Riggs, *Administration in Developing Countries: The Theory of Prismatic Society,* Boston. Houghton, 1964, 419-22.
22. Gabriel A. Almond and G. Bingham Powell, *Comparative Politics: A Developmental Approach,* Boston, Little Brown, 1966, 104-05.
23. For details see Chap. V. supra.
24. Alfred Diamant, "Political Development: Approaches to Theory and Strategy", in J.D. Montogomery and W.J. Siffin (eds.), *Approaches to Development,* New York: McGraw-Hill, 1966, 16.
25. Daya Krishna, *Political Development: A Critical Perspective,* Bombay: Oxford University Press, 1979
26. Lucian W. Pye, "The Meaning of Political Development", in Finkle and Gable, *op. cit.,* 83-85.
27. Mehta, *op. cit.,* 49.
28. Apter, op. cit., Ch. XV. Apter analyses these 'Theories of Development' in the light of Almond-Coleman's Structural-functional approach which has been discussed in Ch. V, supra.
29. W.F. Riggs, *Thailand: The Modernization of a Bureaucratic Polity,* Honolulu, East-West Centre Press, 1966; *Administration in Developing Countries, op. cit.*
30. Riggs, in Charlesworth, *op. cit.,* 338-39. See, also, chapter 9, infra.
31. Riggs, Fred W. and Daya Krishna, *Development Debate,* Jaipur: Printwell Publishers, 1987; and Dayakrishna, *Political Development: A Critical Perspective,* Delhi: Oxford University Press, 1979, 179-205.
32. I.L. Horowitz, *op. cit.*
33. Rajni Kothari, "Environment and Alternative Development," *Alternatives,* Vol. V, No. 4 (Jan., 1980), 427-75.
34. P.V. Narasimha Rao's Address to the Twelfth Special Session of the UN General Assembly, *Hindustan Times,* Aug. 26, 1980.
35. Mehta, *op. cit.,* 49-50.
36. Spiro, Shimon E., and, Yaar, Ephraim Yuchtman, eds. *Evaluating the Welfare State-Social and Political Perspectives,* New York: Academic Press, 1983, Ch. I.

37. It was presented to the Parliament as the Report on Social Insurance and Allied Services by William Henry Beveridge (1879-1963).
38. For details, see, Ch. 17, infra
39. Verma, M.M., *Gandhi's Technique of Mass Mobilization*, New Delhi: R.K. Gupta & Co., 1990, 208.
40. For details, see, Ch. 13, infra
41. Smith, Ian, "New Radicalism-The Green movement", *Political Ideology Today*, Manchester: Manchester University Press, 1993, 311-22; Kenny, Michael, "Ecologism", in Robert Eccleshall, Alan Finlayson, Vincent Geoghegan, Michael Kenny, Maya Lloyd, Iain Mackenzie and Rick Welford, eds. *Political Ideologies: An Introduction*, Third Edition, London: Routledge, 1994; Mathew Festensten and Michael Kenny, *Political Ideologies: An Introduction*, Oxford, 2005.
42. Iqbal Narain and P.C. Mathur, "Political Development: A Theoretical Construct without Research Implications", *Indian Journal of Political Science,* Vol. XLIII, No. 2 (April-June, 1982), 1-11.
43. Daya Krishna, op. cit., 156-74.
44. Robert A. Packenham, "Political Development Research", in Hass and Karial, *op. cit.,* 182.
45. Riggs, *op. cit.*, 348.

8

Analysis and Explanation

Meehan critically observes that the vocabulary of politics has changed little since Aristotle wrote the *Politics*.[1] The concepts that political scientists employ are vague and loose, or even wholly meaningless. Mysticism, magic, and ritual have held their sway, not only in the practice of politics but in its study as well. The literature of Political Science is heavily loaded with uninterested and untestable propositions, and place bad arguments or conclusions that do not follow from premises, often couched in a language that is most dogmatic or sententious.[2] The failure of political scientists to conform to even the elementary rules of logic is notorious. Meehan writes, much of the inherited body of political 'knowledge' is worthy only of destruction; it is counter-productive rather than merely worthless, worse than useless because it creates the illusion of capacity and misdirects the young in their work.

Much of the output of Political Science even today, is indifferent in quality, erratic in focus, untestable, trivial, or meaningless, aimless institutional descriptions, pointless typologies, and trivial data cummulations. They are too common for comfort. Their generalisations have failed to produce a foundation on which the contemporary scholar can build with confidence, and that despite the enormous number of persons gainfully employed in the profession and the immense sums spent on 'research'. Political Science is still unable, and in many cases unwilling, to provide guidelines for either the governors or the governed, whether the question pertains to the goals of social policy or the invention strategies expected to produce particular results.[3] In normative matters, pious platitudes about liberty, equality, democracy, and the like are interspersed with vague ideals and aims; both are useless as guides 'go action', because they are unrelated to human purpose, or because they are compatible with any and every purpose. Such a state of Political Science presents the best case for destroying it. Social scientists have managed to keep their professions, at the level of witchcraft, magic and folklore.[4]

As the goal of making a scientific political theory has not been realised, it is advisable to deal with acceptable substitutes or 'theorisation-in-practice'. These are analysis and explanation.

Analysis

Conceptual Clarification

Analysis is logical examination of a problem or subject matter by using some formalised or non-formalised means and methods of study. It is an attempt to know reality with a specific perspective.[5] A perspective allows us to *select* and *organise* our perceptions, and guide our actions.

Analysis can relate to old or new approaches. Older approaches move around reason, law, laws of nature, values, institutions, and are mostly non-empirical. Modern approaches are conceptual, empirical and theoretical. But there is no reluctance or reservation on the part of an analyst when he undertakes to study ideas, ideals, and other metaphysical realities by following philosophical method; or background of events, traditions, culture and ethos adopting on the basis of historical method; or reality of pychological phenomena by adopting psychological methods including introspection. It is freedom from methodological formalities which makes analysis amenable to all aspects of non-empirical areas of Political Science. It has grown over thousand of years, both in the East and the West, and has thrived in all cultures.

To narrow the focus, analysis is the process of mental or factual breaking down of a whole into its component parts and elements. It is a method of obtaining fresh knowledge, separating the essential from the non-essential, and reduce the complex to the simple. The breaking down of the object into its component parts reveals its true structure, form or pattern. It is used in all mental operations such as, abstraction, conceptualisation, generalisation etc. It appears differently according to the nature of the object or problem of study. As a developing process, it reveals various stages which may be cohesive or contradictory. The analyst proceeds from the complex to the simple, from the fortuitous to the necessary and from multiformity to identity and uniformity. The purpose of analysis is the cognition of the parts as elements of a complex whole, particularly less observable, less empirical and too big and too subtle for measurement and comprehension.

Analysis is the use of reason in an understanding of a problem or an issue. In the absence of a general theory, it can be regarded as a workable device to obtain knowledge. It is an action-frame of inquiry with a purpose.

From that point of view, it is not so value-free or scientific. Every analyst adopts his own intellectual posture or has his own conceptual priorities. This is his privilege. This can be regarded as an underlying assumption that precedes his analysis. It may not be deduced from his analysis of the phenomena he undertakes to describe and evaluate. In this sense, analysis is different from a theory, approach, ideology or explanation. It is an intellectual process to know reality in a limited manner. Often analysis in Political Science is circumscribed by given historical conditions and prevailing circumstances. It caters to know specific problems and feels free to make use of any method and seek counsel of any discipline or source of knowledge. An analyst may take micro or macro problems and conduct his enterprise at any level – higher or lower. It has imprint of its user in matter of purpose, style and strategy. Each analysis attempts to yield some conclusions in the form of propositions, working hypotheses and generalisations that may not be regarded by others as valid and general.

Forms of Analysis

Analysis is a much-used mental activity in academics. Still it is not uniform. It appears special in three areas: (i) empirical research, (ii) elaboration, explanation and drawing conclusions, and, (iii) in submitting individualised statements. In a way, all of them are sub-theoretical attempts made by individual scholars. However, we are more concerned with second area, i.e., elaboration, explanation and drawing conclusions as actual form of theorisation.

Analysis, in the first area of *empirical research* is used when the whole body of the gathered data is at hand. It is also known as 'data analysis'.[6] That comes after data-processing. It involves scrutiny of the assembled data, outlining the major aspects of the data, classification, coding, tabulation, statistical analysis, inferring cause-effect relationship and formulating scientific law.[7] It begins with hypotheses, concepts and variables developed around some research questions.[8]

Coming to the second area, it can be said that all politics is not amenable to observation or sensory treatment, therefore, may not be scientifically studied. No doubt politics is largely temporal, human, relational and oriented to big and small groups, still, all of its subject-matter is enmeshed with and moved by non-empirical forces like values, ideals, ideas, ideology, tradition, faith, myths and ignorance. If we confine ourselves only to empirical or behavioural part of organised life, the discipline would be able to retain only a small fraction of presently available subject-matter. We may broaden our outlook by adopting 'scientific value relativism'[9] and feel free from the charge of apolitical scientism. But still some of the real source and forces of politics are left over. Some of them have been mentioned above. They do reflect in behaviour, thought and communication, but their abstract, subjective and ephemeral nature prompts pure science scholars either to isolate them or treat them as givens. This is an scientific attitude towards them. Some of these forces are responsible for the generation and germination of all types of politics. Therefore, even if they do not appear in concrete or semi-concrete forms, their study should be made part of Political Science.[10] Without knowing them, concrete structures, institutions, behaviour-patterns and other isolated political activities may not be properly comprehended. Their force continues to operate in air, changing sometimes, the very meaning, goal and purposes of popularly known political activities, institutions and structures. At times, scholars and politicians are taken aback on sudden turns of political events only because they happen to neglect them and fail to appreciate them in a suitable manner. Their knowledge does not stand on empirical grounds, but their force and potency is unparalleled, subtle and unique. However their task of knowing them fully may not be left to the field of analysis. In this sense, both scientific method and analysis stand complementary to each other replacing and removing their limitations and weaknesses by mutual strength.

This is not a concession to analysis, as till today, there is little 'science' with Political Science. A large part of the knowledge of politics is produced by Analysis. Most of politics continues to operate on the basis of analysis, and there is little of it with Political Science. Till Political Science assumes all over responsibility, there is no alternative to resorting to political analysis.

Art As Well As Science

Robert A. Dahl,[11] while discussing the nature of analysis, finds it both 'art' as well as 'science. As an art, it is skill. Skill in political analysis can be acquired by practice, training and experience under the guidance of some skilled analyst. But skill in analysis is different from skill in practice of politics. As science, analysis can provide testable generalisations and theories derived from the data of experience obtained through meticulous observation, classification, and measurement. It is scientific to the extent it actually yields tested propositions of considerable generality. In the context of analysis, analysing politics and practicing politics are two different things. James Madison was a brilliant analyst while Franklin Roosevelt was an astute political leader. But both skills can go hand in hand as in case of Woodrow Wilson. Jawaharlal Nehru can also be put in this category.

In the light of value-position of the analyst, there can be two types of analysis: one, value-free political analysis, and, two, value-laden analysis. Scholars belonging to the first view conduct a value free or value neutral political analysis. Robert A. Dahl has calls them as 'empiricists'.[12] Empiricists do not go beyond sensory perception and stop at 'is' or 'pure' facts.

Dahl calls the other view as 'transempiricist'. In popular parlance, the can be called as traditionalists or classicalists. They have sharply opposed the view of 'empiricalists' or empirticists. They argue that (i) only in trivial and unimportant matters, facts and values can be separated; (ii) behind the facade of neutrality and objectivity, the empiricists smuggle values in an unacknowledged and subtle manner; (iii) language of politics itself is value-laden; (iv) they neglect human purposes and relevance; (v) they use jargon which is very much difficult, complex, and incommunicable; and (vi) their observation or study is more often rationalisation of what they do and believe.

Eric Voegelin and Leo Strauss are the main advocates of the transempiricist view. According to them, it is neither possible nor desirable to separate values from facts. They believe in fact-value congruence or conformity. Voegelin opposed the view of the empiricists that (i) to attain scientificity, mathematical models and methods should invariably be incorporated, and (ii) methods of natural sciences are useful in developing a general theory. Leo Strauss has severely criticised the view of empiricists that they neglect human values and find very little difference between man, machines and animal. Facts should be analysed in the light of values. Importance of values lies in man himself, his soul, or supreme reality residing in him. Their realisation is the ultimate goal of man. A value-free analysis is impossible. The word 'political' itself is value-laden. In every political act there lies certain purpose. It aims at either preservation or change of existing system. In both these cases, achievement of the better is involved. This is directly related with the idea of good life. Good life is closely connected with good society.

Strauss regards fact-value dichotomy as unscientific. Even the empiricists do entertain truth as their value. Scientific positivism brings about conformism. Relativism is such a facade which is used by behaviouralists to smuggle and justify certain values. Even the distinction between political and non-political is based on prescientific knowledge. Activities of all citizens and politicians are value-oriented.

Robert A. Dahl rightly finds both of them as antipolar views. Both of them are theoretically right. Transempiricists talk of generality and supremacy of values. They argue that the empiricists too entertain certain values and their analyses are not completely value-free. In practice their views are not so divergent. Both are in search of truth or reality. But the empiricists put greater stress on 'intersubjectively transmissible' or 'testable' knowledge. The values (actually assumptions) which they entertain are secondary and instrumental and do not vitiate their research. The transempiricists also do not wish to neglect facts. But they like to see them in the light of their universal values. Both move around facts and values. They stand parted only in case of ultimate values and their need and utility in analysis. The classical political thinkers too had been studying both facts and values. Value-relativism also puts great emphasis on the study of values.

Dahl has opined that analysis should not be value-neutral. A value-free political analysis is neither possible nor desirable. Empiricists or transempiricists both agree that (a) the scholar keeping himself value-neutral, should scientifically analyse the facts in the light of given values; and (b) while upholding liberal and broader values, and making an express mention of them, the scholar should study facts and other values. Without scientific analysis of facts, one cannot make proper value judgements. One should not be worried if some values enter while doing analysis of facts. But those values should not vitiate the findings or understanding of reality. We should move ahead in the direction of more and more empirical analysis.

We study politics, to use the words of Aristotle, 'for the sake of good life' – to choose the best, realise it and to change or maintain the status quo. From this point of view, the place of factual knowledge instead of being a substitute of value-judgement, is rather a prerequisite, so that our decisions are proper, useful and fruitful. The charge of bias towards the values of liberal democracy should neither disturb us or our ways nor means be sought to escape from it. Only in popular and liberal democracies, one can find congenial environment to develop an empirical political theory. There is no need to apologise even if these values influence our choice of problem, alternative policies, and evaluation of the system. However, precaution should be taken that these values do not influence our findings. Our 'ought' must not corrupt our base – 'is'. This much is enough.

Dahl feels that the failure of social scientists in making objective evaluation of empirical aspects of politics itself is another argument for making more efforts to uphold an empirical political analysis. A scholar needs to study the impact of social, material, and psychological variables of politics. It would help him to gain technological means to realise agreed objectives, to apply normative principles in concrete situations, and to know the justification of various moral precepts. An empirical political analysis would guard him against confusing ideologies and conflicting values. One does not lose the status of being a 'Scientist' simply by keeping relations with values. Dahl regards factual knowledge as a prerequisite to ethical judgements. Harold Lasswell also adopts this perspective in his support to policy sciences. Arnold Brecht differs from them in the sense that they stand for the defence and implementation of fact-based 'values' while he puts emphasis to realise, not 'values', but *preferences*, derived through the Scientific Method.[13] Brecht is aware that he stands for preferences, but he does not deprive anyone of cherishing his 'ultimate' values.

Dahl highlights the following grounds or sources of values, of an analysis: 1. Political values ultimately rest on God's will. His will may be known through a direct revelation to an individual or agent or indirectly by means of reason, or intuition, or experience; 2. They ultimately rest on natural laws. Natural laws may or may not be laid down by God. Knowledge of natural laws can be acquired through reasoning; 3. Political values can also be derived, as John Dewey had attempted, by methods of empirical sciences; 4. Political values can also be seen as *preferences*; and, 5. Though values are seen by some scholars as *preferences*, some of them find them as *universal*. In sum, all have given place to values in their analyses.

The two views agree on the following propositions:[14]

1. The values, interests, and curiosity of a scholar influence his choice of topics;
2. It is impossible to establish criteria of importance and relevance *entirely* from empirical knowledge;
3. An objective analysis of politics presupposes that one values truth, as distinguished from falsehood;
4. All empirical sciences rest on assumptions that cannot themselves be established by the methods of the empirical sciences;
5. Biases of a researcher may induce him to misread his observations and evidence;
6. Objectivity, neutrality, and the capacity and opportunity for scientific detachment are impossible without certain social and political prerequisites, such as, rulers' willingness to tolerate freedom of inquiry and the like.

With this perspective, the empiricists refute the charges of the transempiricists, and clarify that (i) while striving for neutrality and objectivity, they do not indulge in trivial matters irrelevant to human purposes; (ii) they have criteria of relevance; (iii) they do not regard all values equal; (iv) their studies are not mere rationalisations for values and practices of liberal democracy'; and, (v) they do study problems like stability, change and revolution.

Scope and Problems

In political analysis one can include almost all things belonging to politics even if they formally relate to other disciplines and faculties. Its main subject matter is politics, political institutions, political values, norms and goals, power, authority, legitimacy, and political behaviour. As analysis is applied and topical by nature, it looks towards conditions of stability, change and revolution in political systems and groups. Liberal scholars look after viability of democracy, basic civic and political rights, and sanctity of democratic procedures. Political analysts constantly endeavour to compare various political systems and try to discover the best one. They frequently analyse the nature of basic values or goals of a polity and discuss ways and means to realise them. Besides questions of war, peace and development, their attention remains centred on the implicit and explicit activities of governing and non-governing elites. They criticise and evaluate various available alternatives regarding decisions and policies.

Forms, Levels and Kinds

Broadly, analysis can be visualised in four *forms*: (i) full analysis: all areas that are not susceptible to empirical research and theory fall under the purview of full analysis; (ii) background analysis: all broader concepts, major constants, covering laws, conceptual frameworks etc. analysed before the actual conducting of inquiry belong to this category; (iii) data analysis: data collected during the course of survey, investigation or research is put under this category; and, (iv) end analysis.

There can be many *levels* of analysis ranging from specific aspects of social reality to its hierarchical levels: (a) aggregate analysis – survey sampling belongs to this category; (b) relational or group analysis – it is concerned with interactional patterns between individuals and groups found as networks of mutual relations. In this analysis, a group characteristic is analysed without any reference to individual properties as in bureaucratisation or professionalisation; (c) institutional analysis – it attempts to compare relationships within and across the legal, political, cultural and economic institutions of society. Relevant properties, attributes or elements may be compared within institutions; (d) ecological analysis – it is concerned with large, all-covering and contextual explanations as done in field studies of crime and delinquency; (e) cultural analysis – it concentrates on the association of norms, values, practices, traditions, ideologies, technical objects and other artifacts of culture; and, (f) societal analysis, which typically uses societal or sociological gross indicators as done in urbanisation, industrialisation and the like. Sometimes these levels overlap.

Analysis can be classified on the basis of number of variables used, and, transformation in the nature of phenomena. On the basis of number of variables, it can be (1) univariate, (2) two-variable, and, (3) multi-variable. Dynamic or transformation study analysis can (a) trend analysis, or (b) panel studies.

Explanation

Explanation is different from 'analysis'. It is closer to 'theory' than analysis. Theory stands on the solid foundation of explanation.[15] However, analysis also seeks some explanatory law and moves towards theorisation.

Explanation is the final stage of research. The goal of every scientific process is to arrive at an explanation of the phenomena under study. To explain is to elucidate the process which exhibits a certain phenomenon. It is discovery of a relationship between one phenomenon and another. It makes it possible to understand the way the phenomenon in question was caused. Presenting of explanation is Political Science is not an easy task. There is a crisis of explanation in social sciences. It is not very easy to discover and isolate the explanatory factors which could give an account of the situation under study.

According to Meehan, explanation is an instrument that generates anticipation about the environment. It makes possible to have control over events in the environment by linking changes in the values of two or more variables according to rule. It seeks reasons how and why changes occur.[16] An explanation focuses on the record of change that appears in descriptive accounts of the environment, seeking the reasons how and why changes occur. There are seven stages in the process of explanation: (i) concept, (ii) indicators, (iii) measurement, (iv) description, (v) classification, (vi) forecast or expectation, (vii) explanation, and (viii) control or change of environment. Structurally, it consists of a set of symbols or variables and a set of rules. The set of rules relates those symbols to empirical observations. It is a closed logical structure or calculus consisting of rules for manipulating the symbols.

Structure

Meehan enumerates five problems in the basic structure of explanation:

1. the phenomena to be explained;
2. the logical apparatus required for explanation,
3. the transformation rules that link the logical calculus or apparatus to empirical observation;
4. the isomorphism between the loaded calculus and the situation; and,
5. the problems involved in the use of well established explanation to deal with a particular phenomenon.

Selection of events or phenomena for explanation is closely connected with evaluation. The formal logic underlying an explanation is known as *calculus or logical structure.* It generates justified expectations within its prescribed boundaries. The calculus has the power to force a conclusion or compel acceptance of specified expectations relating to the effect of changing the value of one variable in an interrelated set. The key to the process of explanation is the transfer of expectations from within a formal calculus to the observed environment. But the calculus or the logical structure must be closed and finite. Only empirical observations or research methodology determines its shape, form, and validity. Calculus should be loaded with concepts having empirical relevance and have isomorphism or identity with essentials of the situation or event.

The size and complexity of the calculus depend on the purpose and capacity of the user. His conceptual framework requires him to select a set of factors or variables from the environment to be accounted for. Much depends on the way in which he conceptualise and explains the event. The formal calculus must fit the situation. Its symbols should be assigned empirical meaning underlying the event or situation. The calculus or logic of explanation, in this manner, would be able to show significance of the event by making its implicit logic express and explicit. If the description of the situation and the rules of transformation or interaction are applied correctly, the venture would succeed in its purpose. Explanation, according to Meehan, provides justifiable expectations with reference to the environment and suggests ways in which man can intervene to alter the course of events to conform to his own desires. It would, thus, be able to prove compatible with existing knowledge and also with past experiences of his history. Wherever possible it can be applied and experimented in some laboratory or situation on the pattern of natural sciences.

Logical Forms

Explanation, in a narrow sense, is based on logic, which is study of the methods, and principles used distinguishing the valid from invalid reasoning. Besides sense-experience, every science is based also on the principles of logic or reason. Science involves the rules of reasoning or use of arguments. Arguments are sequences of sentences in which some sentences (premises or antecedents) are claimed to be the justification or support for another sentence (conclusion or consequences). This justification or support offered on the basis of connection, relationship, association, property, common variable or attribute found between things and activities mentioned in the argument. Their source, ultimately, is sense-experience or empirical observation made by man in his social environment.

Logic is interrelated set of arguments. Arguments relate to validity and truth. Arguments can be (i) deductive, and, (ii) inductive. It should be pointed out that validity and truth are two different things. Validity means that the premises of an argument are related to the conclusion in such a way that the conclusions must be true if the premises are true. Validity is the property or attribute of arguments. It says nothing about the truth or falsity of individual statements. It the premises of a valid argument are true, then the conclusion must automatically be true. Truth is a property of individual statements which can be either premises or conclusions. It is meaningless to call individual statements 'valid' and also to call arguments 'true'.

Arguments can be valid or invalid. Similarly, only individual or single statements can be true or false.

Deductive argument is one whose premises provide conclusive evidence for the conclusion. If all the premises are true, the conclusion must also be true. Deductive arguments proceed from general premises to more specific conclusions. The truth of the conclusion is implicit in the premises. It makes the information contained in the premises explicit. Inductive argument derives a generalised conclusion on the basis of particulars, often empirically derived premises or observations. The premises of an inductive argument make the conclusion probable, not certain. The inductive approach relies on scientific discovery of facts. One characteristic of inductive argument is that it establishes a conclusion whose content goes beyond its premises. From the observation of a sample, an inference is made about a whole population. This is called the 'inductive leap', jumping from the premises which relates to an observed sample, to the conclusions which concerns the entire population. The greater the number of representative units in the premises observed in the sample, the smaller is the inductive leap. The smaller the number of representative units observed in the sample, the greater is the inductive leap. The premises of an inductive argument do not establish the conclusion conclusively. The premises of a valid argument, here, may be true, but the conclusion can still be false. Its premises only support or lend weight to the conclusion, as they do not make the latter certain.

On the basis of two types of arguments or reasoning, explanations fall into two categories: (a) deductive explanation, and, (b) inductive explanation.

Explanations are, basically, answers to 'why' questions. In fact, there are many other styles of explanations: *genetic, rational, dispositional,* and *functional. Genetic explanation* gives the history of an event by presenting the event as the final stage of a development of a developmental sequence. The event may be described as happening through the hands of many specific individuals or agents directly or indirectly connected with it. In fact, historical description of events cannot explain why that event took place. However, the events forming the historical sequence are selected on the basis of what the scholar assumes the cause of the final event. These assumptions form his tacit generalisations. The description of preceding events may be regarded as statement of particular facts or initial conditions.

Rational explanations take into account the agent's calculation of means available in a situation for the attainment of his objectives. His actions are explained by listing the reasons that motivate him to act as in decision-making and communication theories. A decision-maker's behaviour is explained by calculating the utilities or pay off under different conditions and circumstances. Rational explanations like genetic explanations, contain tacit generalisations which can be treated as covering laws.

But they suffer from two shortcomings: their generalisations actually are hypotheses or conjectures, and are not confirmed regularities, and, they often assume that the required initial conditions obtain without independent evidence. *Dispositional explanations* take into account person's dispositions, tendencies or attitudes making them to behave in some particular manner. It can be assumed that man happens to be authoritarian, civic-minded, peaceful, violent or non-violent owing to them. Frequently such orientations are used to explain why peoples and groups behave in a particular manner. All such assumed dispositions can be reconstructed as covering-laws. Only research or empirical observations can confirm whether man actually carries those dispositions under the given circumstances. *Functional explanations* take into their consideration the recurrent activities, behaviour-patterns or roles of persons in maintaining a system or in realising a particular goal. Functional analysis examines a system that requires certain conditions or requisites to remain in adequate working order and particular persons or groups behave to maintain those conditions. It seems that the behaviour of these persons or groups satisfies a need or a functional requirement of that system. Here the functional explanation takes the form of extended affirming of the consequent arguments, affirming or not affirming the antecedent conditional arguments. The antecedent conditional is placed in the form a covering law. It leaves little scope for 'functional equivalents', and does not properly define the terms, and assumes antecedents without empirical examination of facts.

In essence, they all are of similar nature, and can be subsumed under two aforesaid categories. A scientific explanation includes a set of laws or generalisations in the premises. As they cover the situation or event to be explained, these are called 'covering laws'. Explanations that use covering laws are called 'covering law explanations' or nomological explanations.

They appear in *two* forms: *deductive* and *inductive*.

Deductive explanation is very powerful because it makes use of a valid form of deductive argumentation where the *explanandum* must be true if the *explanans* are true. Both individual and general events can be explained with certainty as the covering laws and the initial or given conditions are true. But such explanations have limited applicability to political and other social sciences. In Political Science we do not have universal covering laws. Understanding of deductive explanation helps us to understand even inductive explanation because of their similarity in a number of respects. However, political scientists cannot give up the search for universal generalisations or covering laws. In some areas deductive explanations have been evolved and achieved. Analysis of deductive explanations is necessary because of their employment by ideologues and spokesmen of various causes, interests, and power-patterns. Analysts should remain ready to challenge validity as well as truth of deductive arguments and explanations.

Inductive explanations, like deductive explanations, also have *explanandum* and *explanans*. Political Science abounds in inductive explanations which contain statistical generalisations in their *explanans*. *Explanandum*, therefore, cannot be deduced from the *explanans* with certainty. The *explanandum* is generally probable. It is implied by the *explanans*. The *explanans* confer support or evidence for *explanandum* but does not make the latter certain. The *explanans* can be true and the *explanandum* can still be false in inductive explanation. Inductive explanations explain either the probability of individual events or statistical generalisations.

Major difference between deductive and inductive explanations is that one negative event can falsify a deductive explanation, but one negative event cannot falsify an inductive generalisation. Deductive explanations usually employ universal generalisations. Only some negative mass events or a high frequency of negative events can falsify inductive explanation.

It may be pointed out that explanations both in social and natural sciences are rarely presented in formal or standard logical form. Generalisations and initial conditions are not explicitly specified. In most cases, they are either assumed or treated as implied or understood. Demand of readability too compels scholars to do away with formal forms. Many explanations presented in paragraph style conceal unspecified and untested generalisations or initial conditions. They can be reconstructed in proper manner and presented systematically exposing their logical errors and limitations. On the basis of degrees of explanatory completeness, there can be (a) *complete*, (b) *elliptic*, (c) *partial*, and (d) *sketchy* explanations.

In *complete* explanation all relevant generalisations and initial conditions are completely known and completely specified. But in Political Science, such explanations remain as 'ideals'. In *elliptic* explanations, all the generalisations and initial conditions are known but all of them are not specified. The scholar assumes that the reader already knows them all and does not mention. But this omission is harmless and can be recouped easily. In the *partial* explanations all the relevant generalisations and initial conditions are not known. Only the known ones are specified. As the relevant generalisations and facts or conditions are not given, the claimed *explanandum* cannot be deduced from the *explanans*. In other words, the *explanandum* appears to claim more than what appears in the *explanans*. The *sketchy* explanations or Explanation *Sketches* do not contain all relevant generalisations and conditions. Arguments are advanced on the basis of some hypotheses or stray incidents or conditions. Explanatory completeness is negligible in them.

Explanation and Prediction

There is a debate over proper relationship between explanation and prediction. One view regards them basically the same, while other view finds them fundamentally different. But there cannot be a valid prediction without having a proper explanation. Despite several hurdles, prediction remains the basic goal of social sciences. In a way, capacity to predict events indicates scientific development and growth of a discipline, including a theory. Prediction enables us to apply knowledge involved in a theory or science to solve practical problems of organised political life. It enables politicos to anticipate and avert negative events that might occur in future.

Structurally, predictions are identical with explanations. They have, like explanations, covering laws and initial conditions with the difference that in explanations the conclusion already occurs, and the *explanans* are sought, but in predictions the *explanans* are given and the conclusion is sought. Every adequate explanation is potentially a prediction, and every adequate prediction can be treated as a potential explanation. But there are situations when a scholar is able to explain but not predict, or able to predict but not explain.

Prediction about individual events can be made if the covering law generalisations are universal. But such universal covering law generalisations are rarely available in Political Science. Only limited or partial prediction is feasible in Political Science as it has to be based on statistical generalisations and sets of initial conditions. Statistical generalisations do not allow prediction in individual events. They can permit only probability of an individual event, that too in proportion to the degree of frequency.

When relevant information in the *explanans* is missing, it is not possible to predict the event or *explanandum*. Sometimes prediction takes place without being able to explain. The statistical prediction of election-results is far better than explanation of those results. Prediction without explanation may take place when only some initial conditions are known but none of the covering laws are known or specified. But such prediction cannot be considered as informed or scientific prediction. An event can be explained and predicted when covering laws and initial conditions are discovered and made known.

Explanation requires knowledge of necessary and sufficient conditions. But Social Sciences have only limited measure of that knowledge. A successful theory stands on its explanatory power. There are two criteria of evaluating this explanatory power: (a) making of scientific prediction, or (b) providing understanding or *verstehen*. Earlier we have discussed limitations of scientific predictions. Prediction can be scientific only when we are able to know all causative factors or have knowledge of all necessary and sufficient conditions making an event. Till we are able to do it, political scientists cannot make scientific predictions. As such, they cannot talk of 'control' over human events. Therefore, we cannot accept Hempel's proposition to evaluate theories only on the basis of their 'power of making predictions'.[17]

Dilthey, Wildenband, Weber and others put emphasis on the power of man in determining their environment. Therefore, 'understanding' or man must be the basis of adequacy of explanation. They put analysis of data as secondary. Man often thinks in terms of prevailing societal structure or ideology. This makes historical perspective much more important. Often they grapple, in their analysis, with the search of ideals and norms of society. Sometimes they indulge in vague historicism.

Thus, both views suffer from severe limitations. The first one fails to reach its height of scientific prediction; second one, makes its 'understanding' subjective, changing and captive of past. Whatever be the 'scientific' prediction, man begins to falsify it, as in case of Marxian prediction of Future Society. Man himself is an independent variable. Automation, IT, LPG etc. have increased his power beyond all calculation or prediction. Analysis and Explanation do not stop at any destination of making 'scientific prediction'. Explanations are always problematic, always imperfect, and always uncertain. Their quality depends on logical coherence, compatibility with other accepted explanations in the field, experimental evidence, of course, use to achieve the purpose. There are various grounds for criticising explanations, but all of them cannot be properly justified.[18]

Explanations are in some respects analogous to maps. Using conventional symbols and transformation rules that link them to the environment, maps produce a record of particular observations that tells us what to expect when certain landmarks are sighted. The five basic points for testing maps or explanations are: (i) internal consistency, (ii) the relation of selection of variables to the stated purpose, (iii) accuracy of data incorporated in the structure, (iv) compatibility with accepted structures used in analogous situations, and, (v) the test of use in achieving the purpose applied to maps or to suggested explanations to evaluate their quality. There are three major forms of testing. It is done by probing into the explanations on the basis of their compatibility (a) with existing knowledge, (b) with historical illustrations, and, (c) use or application in laboratory or natural experiments.

Interpretation

Social investigations involve three conditions: (i) they are conducted in certain social set-up; (ii) they regard their facts identical with all other similar facts; and, (iii) their conclusions or findings are applicable only in their specific culture. Despite these limitations, 'interpretation' enables us to obtain some generalisations. In this sense, interpretation is explanation, clarification, enlightenment, exposition or arriving at some conclusions. Interpretation presents knowledge of relevant causes, bases and intentions of the doers. It can also be looked at as intellectual auditing, rationalisation or justification. It enables a researcher to expose underlying relationships and processes. On the basis of interpretation, one can prove or discard a given hypothesis or some highlighted proposition. While doing this, the interpreter, by linking his conclusions with the conclusions of other similar investigations, contributes continuity to knowledge, and propounds explanatory concepts. With such findings, social scientists can move further. Interpretation enables them to discover underlying principles of societal change which in some way lead to prediction of specific events. Explanatory concepts attract scholars to work for expansion of new knowledge. Only interpretation enables us to 'understand' a particular research, and arrive at some working generalisations. However, it should further be confirmed after consultation with some expert having worked in these fields. Haste makes waste, and leads to all kinds of blunders.

Scholars often refuse to criticize their own works and of others on mutually acceptable grounds. Teachers have trained teachers to train teachers, and so on *ad nauseum*.[19]

Data-collection becomes useful only when it is properly interpreted. Unless that is done there can be no utility of the data collected. It is essential that its interpretation is objective and unbiased otherwise the results are bound to be misleading. Interpretation comes after collection and analysis of data. The scholar must ensure that all the collected information has been scientifically analysed with the help of appropriate methods. There is a tendency among scholars that they lay too much stress on drawing vague generalisations. One should not try to generalise everything. Generalisations of social sciences can easily be challenged. Interpretation is a very specialised technique and as such the whole work should be very carefully and consciously done so that the conclusion drawn are rational and verifiable. They should be largely acceptable to the society, and not look ridiculous.

Notes

1. Evron Kirkpatrick, "From Past to Present", in Freeman, Donald M. ed., *Foundations of Political Science-Research, Methods, and Scope*, New York: The Free Press, 1977.
2. Meehan, Eugene J. *The Foundations of Political Analysis: Empirical and Normative*, Illinois: The Dorsey Press, 1971.

3. Ibid., 8-16; See also, Roseman, Cyril, Mayo, Charles G. and Collenge, F.B., *Dimensions of Political Analysis, An Introduction of the Contemporary Study of Politics,* 1966.
4. Ibid., 25.
5. Fitzgerald, Jack, and Cox, Steven M. *Unraveling Social Science: A Primer on Perspectives, Methods, and Statistics,* Chicago: Rand McNally College Publishing Co., 1975, 1-5.
6. Merritt, Richard L., *Systematic Approaches to Comparative Analysis,* Chicago: Rand McNally & Co., 1970, 45-59.
7. Phillips, Bernard, *Social Research-Strategy and Tactics,* New York: The Macmillan Co., 1967, Third Printing, Part Two, Three and Four; also, Geoffrey and Edwards, *A New Dictionary of Political Analysis,* London: Edward Arnold, 1991, 89-90.
8. Johnson, Janet Buttolph, and Joslyn, Richard A., *Political Science Research Methods,* New Delhi: Prentice-Hall of India Private Limited, 1989, Ch. 3.
9. See Chapter 3.
10. Ibid.; also, Howard Ball and Thomas Lauth, Jr. *Changing Perspectives in Contemporary Political Analysis,* 1971.
11. Dahl, Robert A., *Modern Political Analysis,* New Delhi: Prentice-Hall of India (Private) Ltd., 1965.
12. Dahl, supra, Ch. 3.
13. Brecht, Arnold, *Political Theory, The Foundations of Twentieth Century Political Thought,* Princeton: Princeton University Press, 1959.
14. Dahl, op. cit., 102; also *Who Governs? Democracy and Power in An American City,* 1961.
15. Cole, Stephen, *The Sociological Method,* Chicago: Rand McNally College Publishing Co., 1976, 227; also Harvey, David, *Explanation in Geography,* Indian Repring, Rawat, 2003.
16. Meehan, 4.
17. Carl G. Hempel, *Aspects of Scientific Explanation,* New York: Free Press, 1965.
18. Ibid., 64-71. See, also, Meehan, *The Theory and Method of Political Analysis,* Illinois, Homewood: The Dorsey Press, 1965, 187-226.
19. Ibid., 244.

9

Political Engineering

Everywhere man stands and lives for certain goals and values. He needs to defend these values, human rights and the well being of his near and dear ones under a suitable form of governance. Every nation, religion, community, political party, or group claims to uphold them, but often fails to carry out its proclaimed mission. In Political Science, it can be called as lack of 'political engineering' approach.[1]

Engineering is the application of scientific and technical knowledge to solve human problems. Engineers use imagination, judgment and reasoning to apply science, technology, mathematics, and practical experience. The result is the design, production, and operation of useful objects or processes. Its dictionary meaning for us is to lay out, construct, or manage as an engineer. It is to contrive or plan out usually with more or less subtle skill and craft.

However, it is not a call to 'technocracy', which is a trend that came into being in the USA on the strength of the ideas of the economist T. Veblen. It gained popularity in the 1930s. Technocratic societies had sprung up in a number of countries. Adherents of technocracy claim that anarchy and instability of contemporary capitalist society are the result of the administration of state affairs by politicians. They hold that the ills of capitalist society may be cured provided that economic life and state administration are taken over by technical experts and businessmen. They want direct subordination of the state machinery to the industrial managers. The contemporary scientific and technological revolutions have revived some ideas of technocracy with theories of 'industrial', 'post-industrial', and 'technotronic' societies. There is rise of 'managerism', a doctrine of the leading role of managers or 'managerial revolution' (*J. Burnham*). In the 1970s, came the notion of meritocracy which pretended to replace bureaucracy and technocracy for a 'society of knowledge'. Political engineering stands differently from them. It comes forward as a defence-mechanism of liberal democracy. It declines to support authoritarian rules. Its basic philosophy, values and goals originate from the tenets of liberal democracy.[2]

Liberal Democracy

Liberal democracy operates normally in peacetime[3] but requires knowledge and practice of political technologies to run it effectively and efficiently, particularly, amid crises and challenges from non-liberal ideologies, movements and organisations.[4]

In a liberal democracy, there is combination of free-market economy with which universal adult franchise came up. Conflicting claims of the capitalists and the masses are accommodated under the ideology of 'welfare state'. Procedures and institutional arrangements stand by its new principles. Principles of liberal democracy include: (a) government by consent, (b) public accountability, (c) majority rule, (d) recognition of minority rights, and, (e) constitutional government. Its mechanism includes democratic institutions and procedures. Accordingly, there should be more than one political party freely competing for political power. Political offices should not be confined to any privileged class. Periodic elections based on universal adult franchise should be held regularly. Civil liberties should be protected and granted to all citizens. Independence of judiciary is a must to maintain them.[5]

Waste of Experience of Operating Democracies

After about 100 years of operating constitutional democracies, the rulers and the ruled regularly find themselves standing on the crossroads. Leaders, often times, lack the will and strategy to face critical situations. But the people have to pay a very heavy price for their leaders' ignorance and follies.[6] There exists a powerful consensus that liberal democracy launched in a country as a whole and its units must somehow be defended, protected and made vibrant so as to enable it to tide over internal and external challenges.[7]

One of the major causes of the increasing number of problems and difficulties of the developing political systems has been the lack of learning and transmitting the experiences of the outgoing political rulers by the incoming political rulers. At this level, both sets of them with people as mute spectators remain segregated, isolated, and even hostile to each other. Each set of rulers or political leaders in government is conducting the affairs of the country in a trial and error fashion. At the end of their term or even early, the rulers happen to add more and more problems like increasing poverty, unemployment, insecurity, and discontentment among the people etc. etc. Again the new hands also go on conducting the governance in the same hit-and-run manner. There is no way of learning from the experiences of outgoing rulers. The experience they gained goes with them. Some of these rulers even fail to introspect within and learn from their own experiences. Often problems remain where they were. Problems require solutions borne out of their own experience, which is hardly gained and applied, and transferred to the successors of the contemporary members of fragile democracies. Exploiting their failures and incapacities, usually the army commanders or civilian dictators take over.

As this experience has hardly been analysed and conceptualised in some institutionalised form, stored and effectively learnt by political leaders, the people continue to grope in dark. Barring a few, most of the political leaders and the people do not know why, when, how and what particular action was taken up by the policy-makers, and why it did not come out in an anticipated manner. The total neglect and waste of this experience keeps both the rulers and the ruled ignorant of the realities of each other's activities.[8] The gap existing between the ideals of the Constitution and the realities prevailing in the country remains as ever.

Some of these polities continues to have western model of governance without devising appropriate mechanism and tools to apply them it in a proper manner. A country survives as a democracy but remains weak, soft and insecure. Therefore, the multifarious problems cropping up in a weak democratic system demands, firstly, the objective identification of her past experience of democratic governance, secondly, a context-free conceptualisation of that experience in the form of 'political technologies', thirdly, the processing and updating them in view of changing needs and requirements of the political system, and, lastly, correlating these political technologies with specific problems of the democratic polity. All this has to be done as part of democratic political engineering.

Objectives

Therefore, the objectives of 'political engineering' would be

(a) to formulate, develop and operationalise the concept of 'political technology' suitable to meet the needs and demands of the democratic systems;

(b) to identify political technologies out of experiences gathered by the political leaders during the last five decades of democracy;

(c) to process and update these identified political technologies (IPTs) for use to strengthen, defend and protect the democratic system;

(d) to relate particular political technologies to some specific problems areas so as to empower democratic politicians to be more effective for delivering goods to the people; and

(e) to make these 'political technologies' available to the people.

For this purpose, some areas mentioned below can be earmarked to identify and process political technologies for use by the political leaders of the Third World countries, and also in some advanced countries:

1. Areas of social justice and democratic participation.
2. Clash between the nation-state and globalisation.
3. Internal subversion coming from fundamentalism and violent societies.
4. Restraining a permanent minorities to trample over the legitimate rights of another permanent minority or majority and *vice versa*.
5. Protection of natural, democratic, and fundamental rights of an individual *qua* other individuals and groups or against one's own group, party, religious dispensation, communal teachings, and claims of culture and tradition.

Its long-term perspective would be to envisage the formation of political technologies for democratic governance irrespective of specific culture, ideology, country, religion and language and others. This can be only a distant theoretical goal. The urgent need of the hour is to serve the cause of the weak, still-young, fragile, endangered democracies of the developing countries.

Conceptual Framework of Political Technology

It may be pointed out that the concept of 'political technology' is different from many other forms of politics, which often are long or short-term, legal, ephemeral, specific, secretive and vague like strategy, policy, diplomacy, manipulation, technique, appeal, and other several similar expressions. They may, however, be observed as various forms of 'political technologies' in making.

Future research on them will encompass both an evolving philosophy and a range of techniques. Its primary objective will be to assist decision makers to understand better the potential consequences of present Social Sciences.[9] This concept has to be expanded further.[10]

The proposed concept of 'political technology' is made of two terms, viz., 'technology' and 'politics'. Politics usually is the art or science of government or governing, especially the governing of a political entity, such as a nation, and the administration and control of its internal and external affairs. It includes the activities or affairs engaged in by a government, politician, or political party, and also the methods or tactics involved in managing a state or government. In a broad liberal-moderate way, politics also is the regulation and government of a nation or state. It also means the preservation of its safety, peace, and prosperity, the defense of its existence and rights against foreign control or conquest, the augmentation of its strength and resources, and the protection of its citizens in their rights, with the preservation and improvement of their morals. Pejoratively, it also means intrigue or manoeuvring within a political unit or a group in order to gain control or power, often internally conflicting interrelationships among people in a society.

Politics, in its non-pejorative sense, is a specific kind of activity concerning 'Who gets, What, When and How?' It pertains to power, influence, and control or activities relating to governing of man by man. When broadly viewed, it is an ensemble of certain types of activities within, and related to a political system, including the environment in which the latter operates.

The concept of 'Political technology' directly relates to politics wherein power is generated and employed to gain rewards, and through which the interests of broad segments of population are affected. 'Technology', in human terms, is a relational activity including interpersonal relationships to realise certain goals and values. It is knowledge and a pattern of activities used to manipulate physical environment in order to achieve desired practical ends. It is generally used in some rational, settled and dispassionate manner. Political technology means mastery and utilisation of the *art* of politics for directing political operations and manipulating political methods. It implies systematic application of knowledge to practical tasks. But political technology, as such, is different from 'technique', which is a personal skill. It is a method of doing something expertly for realising a given end. Techniques are learned, and require the acquisition of specialised skills.

Political technology concerns political goals and values, related to power relationships and/or deals with specific forms of interpersonal activities relating to politics. On the basis of past and present experience, and in view of changing goals and objectives, it prepares and applies new patterns of relationships or triggers off appropriate sets of activities. It involves interest-relationship between two or more ends of political actors or groups. Conceptually, at its bare minimum, each political relationship has one end, on the left hand, and the other end, on the right hand. As a cluster of interest-relationship, it can also have many ends or hands. Interest-relationship connects one with the other. This relationship can be concrete or abstract. It may appear in the form of human, moral or material interests. A wider concept of political technology involves three types of relationships. One is the player or actor, second is that which is played or acted upon, and the third is the connection or relation emerging out of the two. When there are three ends or hands in a political relationship, the third one can be called as the connecting or interpersonal relationship, bond, link or engagement operating in a cluster of interrelationship. The person or the user, who has the need of having a political technology, can be seen as the client, operator, customer, player, receiver, and political leader or simply as an activist. However, for all of these persons, the term 'political leader' (PL) has been used here.

Concept of Political Technology

The concept of 'political technology' contains seven clusters of variables and each cluster contains many variables or attributes:

1. *Traits of Political Leader*: In the cluster, *the Personality of the Political Leader* plays the key-role. Its traits can further be divided in two groups:
   (a) Knowledge of mass psychology, specialisation in anticipating public responses, skill in maintaining public relations, and timely use of political technologies; and,
   (b) Political personality: Charisma, spirit of making self-sacrifice, attributes of divinity, high social status, strong will-power, willingness to tolerate/adjust with others, attitude towards opponents and the like.[11]
2. *Values and Goals*: These include temporal as well as other worldly objectives, identification with some god, religion, sub-religion, nation, nationality, race or ethnicity, caste, colour, norms and mores, ideology, hero or superman;
3. *Type of Instruments and Tools:* Solidarity among members of association or relationship, socialisation and training of followers, discipline, number, span of discretion and direction, speed and style, use of non-coercive, coercive or Gandhian technologies;
4. *Issues, Demands and Problems:* Their nature, impact, quantum of pressure – immediate and distant, situation, coverage – national, regional or local;
5. *Patterned or Repeatable Use*: Political technology should be a repeatable or patterned affair;
6. *Power-sharing:* Those who are part of a political technology should have a feel of some power-sharing; and,
7. *Resources at Hand* (on either side of input and output-ends): These can briefly be stated as:
   (a) Material goods: Sociability and size of the collectivity, status, property (land, money, building, business, industry etc.),
   (b) Leadership, type and quality of organisation, management skills, including communication and control over media; legitimacy,
   (c) Friends and allies: Open, secret, links with bureaucrats, mafia, middlemen and contractors, and
   (d) Closeness to potential resources and chance factor

   The number of variables in each cluster can increase or decrease.

As 'political technology' is manoeuvrable interpersonal human relationship aiming to bring about some desired political change or action, it has to be conceptually *separated* from (i) some constitutional/legal obligation or arrangement, (ii) personal or selfish affair, and (iii) functions required under constitutional superstructures or moral compulsions. The first one is the function, which has to be under the power of sanctions, and has to be performed under compulsions of law. The second one is done to serve one's own personal interests, sometimes at the expense of others. The third type of functions are performed under the heavier weight of constitutional structures or moral compulsions. They have to be especially separated from the concept of 'political technology'.

Operational Process of Political Technology

A 'political technology' is manoeuvrable interpersonal human relationship aiming to bring about some desired political change or action. A man can act on his own based on his drives, motives or understanding. However, many other devices can activate him also. Besides political technology, there are other tools also used for inducting political change: such as, (i) invoking authority of constitutional structures, (ii) enforcement of statutory laws, (iii) use of coercion and (iv) appeal on moral and spiritual grounds. Their separation and relationship with political technologies should be made out clearly.

Constitutional Structures

Normally a Constitution is an agreed form of the exercise of social and political power. Each Constitution provides many structures of power and gives in some cases details of their working by which power is generated, exercised, transformed, transferred and devolved. These structures and procedures attached with them aim at making of a particular form of polity. The Constitutional Structures are captioned here as '*Basic Structures*', 'Basic Technologies' or 'Basic Political Technologies' (BTs and BPTs). A constitution can be considered as the storehouse of such commonly 'accepted', 'agreed', 'legitimised', 'constitutionalised', 'basic', or 'first-level' political technologies. Inclusion of these Basic Structures in the Constitution provides form, structure, location, distribution and direction to the power of State. The Constitution provides many legitimate, neutral and non-political structures along with their processes, viz., Government, Supreme Court, Reserve Bank, Election Commission, Armed Forces etc. Behind them, there is consensus of the people who render tacit obedience to them, even accept their coercive and non-coercive sanctions as normal.

Nevertheless, these structures also require and necessitate the prescription of mode, way and form of *exercising* that power. This is done through and by providing *Next* or *Next-to-next Level Structures* or some specific technologies in the Constitution itself. It can be seen in the unified structure of judiciary or bureaucracy. In some cases, procedural details to operate Basic or Next-level structures are also given in the Constitution. But, the selection of type, style, mode, and method of their exercise is left in the hands of *political leaders*. The latter determine the mode, method, and direction of the exercise of the power of basic and next-level structures. In a democracy or rule of law government, they operate over and above every type of political technology.

Statutory Laws

Below Basic Structure level, there are *statutory* laws passed by the Legislature. They are subordinate additions to the above-mentioned constitutional structures made by the ruling political party or group of political parties in a coalition government. Often they are made in terms of promises stated in its agenda or election manifesto. Laws passed according to an established constitutional procedure, are not considered part of active or day-to-day politics. They become part of impersonal laws of governance. However, they are outcomes of majority voting on the floor of the House, and a new majority after the formation of another government can change or modify those laws. Until that moment arrives, those laws continue to display people's consensus and represent legitimacy of the regime.

These Basic and Next-level Structures are found in the Constitution of every country. Statutory laws passed by the Parliament are separate from *political technologies*. They are different from political technologies as those permanent or basic structures, which were originally 'political', but had gone out of the field of active politics, rivalry and opposition. They largely attained legitimacy earned on grounds of consensus and common acceptance over a long period of duration. Now they happen to control *modes of politics*.

Nevertheless, politics can demote a Basic political structure or a Next-level structure or statutory laws again to the level of political technologies. It can also promote the latter two to upper levels. All the four: Basic Structure, Next-level Structures, Statutory Laws and Political Technologies may clash against or co-operate with each other from time to time around demands of politics.

Gaining more and more consensus, the number of Basic or Next-level structures, due to deference of the people to them, may increase. Their number would decrease with the spread of dissent, dissatisfaction, estrangement and rebellion. Even maintenance and continuation of Basic technologies (BTs) depends upon availability and proper exercise of political technologies. Ignorance, lack of knowledge, experience and skill, neglect and misuse of political technologies may ultimately result in the erosion of the effect of basic structures of a Constitution, and weakening of the democratic system. However, Basic and Next-level structures of the Constitution and Statutory laws are not permanent fixtures of a democratic system, and their form, scope and authority can change under pressure of politics.

Politics is largely the result of exercise of free will and influence. However, coercion and morality also play the role in the operations of democratic politics. Political technologies may make use of any one of them or all together.

Use of Coercion

In order to ensure compliance on a continuous basis, political leaders both motivate the people, and also advance allurements and deprivations to them in many ways. There can be milder or harsh forms of threats and coercion. All political technologies, exercising mild or severe form of coercion in favour of democratic values, are considered 'political'. Conventionally, when the form of coercion is either absent or is mild, it comes under the category of 'Political' technology. However, there can be 'coercive' or 'coercion-based' political technologies. Quantum of coercion in them is comparatively more harsh or severe. Still their use is considered political and permissible in democracies. In democratic systems, the use of Non-coercive Political Technologies (NPTs) and Coercive Political Technologies (CPTs) are found subordinate to the demands of popular opinion and democratically elected institutions. Therefore, after exhausting all political and legal avenues, sometimes even before that, the use of force or power is considered permissible within the parameters of the democratic system. Coercion in democracy can be used, with the approval of the consent-giving majority, against the hostile and non-complying elements.

Appeal on Moral and Spiritual Grounds

Identification with common grounds of mores, norms or values also activate humans, including a deep desire to tread on the path of salvation. Gandhi, in the pre-independence era, created such technologies based on his understanding of metaphysics and his sense of morality, which he regarded as a way to salvation.[12] In this sense, his technologies of 'satyagraha' appear 'moral' and 'apolitical' or 'non-political'. He claimed to have developed a science of 'satyagraha'.[13] However, his ultimate goal was to be realised by launching those technologies to attain Swaraj (Self-Government), for redressal of the grievances of the peoples of South African colonies, and, for the people of India against the British Rule. The Goal of independence was attained in his lifetime. Therefore, all the Gandhian methods are put here under the category of either 'Non-coercive Political Technologies' or 'Gandhian political technologies'. They have been discussed in a separate chapter.[14]

After spelling out the concept of 'political technology' and ascertaining its relationship to and difference from other tools of political operations, it can be feasible to identify political technologies out of the raw material of past politics of the developing countries, including India. For this, we have to make search for raw material, devise a plan to make and apply them, and calculate the cost of investment.

Making, Calculation, and Application of Political Technology

Owing to the very nature of politics, the calculation of the cost of 'political technology' would always be tentative.

There are four components of calculating the cost of making and applying a political technology (PT):

(i) Sources,
(ii) Handling Style,
(iii) Stake or Investment, and
(iv) Outcome.

Sources

Sources make up the ground on which political fight is carried is on. One is big or small in terms of one's storehouse of sources. But they are meaningless unless one makes use of them. Sources broadly are inputs of politics in possession or control of a political leader. These are of three types: (a) personal, (b) formal, and, (c) non-formal. *Personal* resources relate to the personal control of an individual political technology. They are material and political. Material resources include building, money, income, physique, stamina etc. Political resources include the number of followers, their organisation, deference to him in areas that can be wide or narrow. It can again be *positive* when his directives are carried out, and *negative* when the same followers or some of them stand against him. *Formal* resources are available as a result of control over the state machinery. Their abundance depends upon nature, size and form of the state. All political leaders contrive for having control over the state machinery. *Non-formal* resources are accumulated beyond and besides the state, i.e., caste, community, relations, voluntary organisations and so on. It may include many other factors of power accretion and its exercise.

Rest of the three components are used in actual political fight.

Handling Style

Sometimes it means a lot when a *political technology* is used abruptly, demonstratively or peacefully. Each type of handling brings in specific response from the concerned people.

Stake or Investment

Investment is putting the resources or a part thereof in winning over the game of politics. One may fight with totality of his resources. Spending of sources appears in the form of actual action. They are used while in confrontation with or facing opposition from the adversaries. Money, manpower, reputation, time, position etc. are put to stake. In this direction, investment has to be deducted from sources. Besides this venture, there can be wastage, loss, routine expenditure and cheating.

Outcome

Outcome or result is the output of the whole political venture. It may be satisfactory or unsatisfactory, adequate or inadequate or desirable or undesirable. In case, it is not satisfactory, it may have to be repeated or more resources have to be spent over the whole venture.

Calculation Programme

For an easy understanding of the Calculation Programme, every factor contributing to a political outcome has been allocated cost in terms of (Indian) money.

In order to calculate the cost of a political encounter of a very big size, (only for understanding the role of main contributory factors), its cost has been approximated to Rs. one lac (Rs. 1,00,000). A big event can cost more, say, from Rupees 10 to 50 lac. This cost can further be distributed against the cluster-variables of the concept of political technology in the manner mentioned below:

	Items of Investment	*Approximate Cost Rs.*
1.	Personality traits of the political leader	
	(a) Knowledge, specialisation, skill etc.	10,000.00
	(b) Charisma, status, will power etc.	40,000.00
2.	Values, goals and objectives	20,000.00
3.	Instruments and Tools	20,000.00
4.	Issues, demands and problems	1,000.00 each
5.	Resources at hand	
	(a) Material goods	2,000.00
	(b) Leadership	2,000.00
	(c) Friends and allies	2,000.00
	(d) Closeness to potential resources and	2,000.00
	(e) Chance factor	1,000.00

Values of these variables are mutually or exclusively transferable, convertible and multipliable and magnifiable. In the process of application of a political technology, any one of them can turn big or small in size, impact and speed.

First of all, we have to identify political technology applied in a particular field of politics. For *identification* we have to conduct (a) survey of specific patterns of political operations, (b) delimitation of the search areas, (c) identification by applying the concept of 'political technology', and (d) classification of identified political technologies. All these steps have been elaborated further.

Making and Identification

Political technologies, as conceived here, are not readily available. They have to be searched, surveyed and discovered and further processed for use. If they are not available, the user has to identify and process them keeping in view the current needs and requirements of the political situation. Such political technologies can come out of the experience, confrontation, and searching solution of the problems. This source can prove to be a laboratory to test and explore the newer ones and turn out finished and final goods of 'political technology' after processing them in adequate manner.

'Identification' means ascertaining of particular patterns of goal-oriented political operations and behaviour. They should be dispassionately observed, studied and discerned for future use. Identification of political technologies should not be person, place and time specific. Identification or discovery does not mean that they were already available to the original users in the past or were manufactured by them in a final and finished form. In fact, in the past, the operators of these technology-like acts, the rulers or governing elite, might not have consciously created them, or have had openly sought help and guidance from political scientists, engineers, and scholars. The users of technologies might have overlooked many other factors. In some cases, the leaders of the ruling coterie might have imitated blindly the acts or steps of their predecessors. In other cases, the genesis of the political technologies may not have been as transparent as was in case of Mahatma Gandhi. He instead of imitating others liked to act upon his 'inner voice' and fabricate a large number of new political technologies. Hundreds of leaders now make an attempt to follow him earnestly.

Political technologies come out of patterns of specific political activities or operations. Only those activities, which fit in or stand within the parameters of the concept of 'political technology' can be considered as such. The seven cluster-variables elaborate this concept. From this point of view all other political variations such as policy, strategy, tools, technique and methods are different from political technology. The latter is not problem or person specific. In a political technology there is a sense of power sharing.

Political technology, besides the above, is a four-directional patterned operation. On the *left*, there is the context of some political problem or demand. On the *right*, there is adversary or opposition. While going on *front* side, there stand your own resources and personality variables. On the *back*, there is the outcome, success or failure. It may be pointed out that the items of the cluster-variables, including the variables of a cluster are interchangeable. A political leader may invest his resources equitably or proportionately. He might put in only one or two types of resources and spend them all. It could be his all-out operation.

Determination of the Form of a Political Technology

At this juncture, culture and values of the parties concerned also form the ground of selection of political technologies. Culture and values often bind or move the hands of the user of the political technology. Usually they determine the type, mode or form of political technology. It could be either non-coercive, coercive or Gandhian, or a mix of them, political technology. General characteristics of these various groups of political technologies can be stated briefly as:

(a) *Non-coercive political technologies* operate on the role of fervent speeches, appeal to inborn factors like caste, sub-caste, religion, sub-religion, ethnicity, geographic affiliation, language or dialect etc., all forms of propaganda, press and media.

(b) *Coercive political technologies* are historically known. However, in democracy, they are used only within the constitutional framework and other statutory laws. Citizens enjoy fundamental rights with right to self-defence and have political power to form and control the government directly and through their representatives. With such a mandate, the government enjoys sovereignty (now supremacy) over every other organisation, group, denomination and similar entities. It gets authority to employ police, para-military and military forces to uphold law and the constitution. As per the procedure of law and verdict of courts, it can rightfully restrain, imprison, and even take away the life and freedom of an individual. It does not permit any one else to exercise these rights and immunities.

(c) *Gandhian political technologies* are based on the *spiritual and moral* experience of the 'political leader' and his faith and confidence in the people that they would feel like him. As this anxiety, more or less, is ever-present in all human beings, he invokes it through appeal, prayer, fasting and various forms of self-suffering. He eschews all forms of violence. When the people are socialised in these values, they can be mobilised even for political goals.[15] Almost all religions do believe in and advocate them to their followers, therefore, remain unable to oppose such non-violent move. As these acts relate to inner world of one's heart and mind, they do not fall within the arena of violation of law.

Political technologies can have varying scopes or sizes of operation: macro, micro and mixed. Political technologies of macro or mega size have special features like bigger geographical area, long term operation, favouring a whole tribe, caste, religion or ethnicity, increase of cost in term of its size and so on. Micro political technologies often operate within the boundaries of mega problems and often are used by local or regional political leaders. Mixed political technologies stand in between the two.

Classification of Identified Political Technologies

Political Technology is a tool of activation of man by man. The holistic or generic concept of Political Technology includes all types of political technologies. Hundreds of political technologies have been utilised in the past, but they are neither known nor readily available. Having been used in different contexts and times, they may not be readily suited to the requirements of each and every type of democracy. All political technologies have to be discovered and 'identified'.

On the broad basis of the use of moral means, all such 'identified' political technologies can, at first level, be divided as (a) conventional political technologies, and, (b) Gandhian political technologies. The *conventional* political technologies can further be classified as (i) non-coercive, and, (ii) coercion-dominating political technologies. Similarly, the Gandhian political technologies too have many forms and styles. First, we should take up *conventional political technologies*.

Non-coercive Political Technologies (NCPTs)

Political leaders, in democracy, move and motivate other persons on grounds of (i) his personality; (ii) his own or others' needs and interests; (iii) gaining higher status, position, property and power; (iv) attainment of bliss, here and after, by living according to certain moral and spiritual values; and, (v) probable exercise of threat and coercion including force. Accordingly, the conceptual scheme of political technologies involves levels from *persuasion* to *force or coercion*. Politics appears when there is need of generating compliance in a particular direction. People are made to act in a particular manner and volunteer compliance preferably on the basis of consent, participation and faith or legitimacy. To practice them on a continuous basis, political leaders advance allurements and deprivations in many ways. All this involves, to a certain extent, mild exercise of threat and coercion. Political technologies operating within this arena are christened as 'Non-coercive'.[16]

During normal times, it is usually found that only political and Gandhian political technologies are put to use for solving many types of problems, including in dealing with opposition and other dissatisfied elements. In a democratic state, persons or political parties who take over power in terms of the periodically held free and fair popular elections and remain responsible to the people, use such technologies. Till this condition is fulfilled, it is expected that individuals, groups and people would render obedience to those regimes. However, difficulties arise when some problems, issues and crises are not settled in normal ways, even by use of non-coercive political technologies. Some people do not accept norms or 'rule of law' of democracy. Such persons either do not permit the use and functioning of political technologies or oppose the verdict of elections or decisions of the legally appointed bodies and their officials.

Coercive Political Technologies (CPTs)

Generally, 'technologies' involving human control, influence or powers over others under milder form of coercion are considered 'political'.[17] A large number of people do render compliance on those grounds, but many others do not. In order to ensure compliance in important areas, greater amount of coercion is applied through legal provisions. At times, even the use of normal political technologies may not be allowed to operate or even tolerated. The exercise of usual political technologies may prove void and may not render any result. The basic mechanism or values of the democratic system may be threatened or endangered. As it is the foremost duty of the political leaders to defend and protect the democratic system, they may be compelled to use coercive political technologies. They have to be willing and remain ready to defend the system, otherwise display their lack of commitment to have and save democracy.

During normal times, in democracies, political technologies are faced or responded to by political technologies only. However, when there is some fatal attack from non-democratic or undemocratic side, like, autocracy, dictatorship, rabid communalism, terrorism, internal subversion, or external aggression, a democratic system, under the present conceptual framework of 'political technology' is bound to counter it by effective coercive political technologies.

Almost all democracies in their constitutions enshrine provisions for handling such difficult situations and emergencies. When their existence is at stake, democracies are equipped with the extraordinary rights to use coercive means and methods. In all democratic political systems, under critical circumstances, exhausting all political, legal and non-coercive avenues, sometime even before their actual occurrence, the use of force of power, i.e., coercive political technologies (CPTs) is permissible within the parameters of the democratic system.

It may be pointed out that coercive political technologies can be used both by a democracy and an authoritarian system. Main difference between the two uses lies in goal or value. In the past, monarchies, autocracies, and dictatorial rulers have been using them against other States at will, and even against their own people, with the sole objective of maintaining and upholding their personal rule. Democracies too use them, but they do so after exhausting all forms of legal, political and non-coercive means.

Gandhian (Moral) Political Technologies (GPTs)

There are many peculiarities of Gandhian Political Technologies (GPTs). First of all, they were used in pre-independence era and were never known before. Secondly, they were largely based on Gandhiji's own personality – his understanding of metaphysics and his sense of morality, which, in sum, was his own way of attaining ultimate salvation. In this sense, his technologies to a person like him would appear 'apolitical' or 'non-political'. They, in fact, were the means (*satyagraha*, non-violence or *Ahimsa*) to realise the Truth (God or *Satya*). Thirdly, notwithstanding the spiritual and moral basis of the Gandhian technologies, their immediate and ultimate goal was political, e.g., attainment of Swaraj (Self-government) for the people of India against the British Rule through change of heart by undergoing self-suffering. Therefore, all the Gandhian methods are put here under the category of 'political technologies'. Using them, Gandhi was able to mobilise millions of the people under his leadership to fight for India's independence.[18]

Processing of Political Technologies

It has already been pointed out that all political interventions, acts, decisions, tactics, techniques, styles, strategies etc. operated by political leaders, successful or failure, are not political technologies in the strict sense of the term examined earlier. To bring them within the parameters of 'Political Technology', a lot of work has to be undertaken. Till it is done, they can be nominally treated as 'Political Technologies under Consideration' (PTsUC). Processing of 'Political Technologies involves refinement, repair, renovation and modification for their present and future use in a context-free sense. This work is very necessary to update them for use to current political affairs. Thus, the task of merely identifying political technologies is not enough. Political operations and programmes undertaken in the past, can not be considered as 'political technologies' unless they are properly tested, refined, reformulated and redesigned as such. Politics and political scenario always undergo minor or major change. As such, political technologies, applied in the past, have to be renewed and reoriented in view of changed political situations. However, discovery and identification of old and 'under consideration' political technologies presents us an opportunity to restructure and redesign the older ones suitable to newer situations.

Application of Political Technologies

Processing of political technologies is updating them. It is taking them from 'context' to 'problem'. Problem-specific political technologies always look towards ends and goals. A political technology is a kind of race or 'run' from problem to its goal. In its run all relevant factors such as time, events, concerning persons, cost and others have to be calculated and pointed out.

Finalisation takes places after political operations, experiences or activities are 'identified' under the concept of 'political technology'. In it, identified political experiences are separated from their specific context, and generalised as problem-oriented political technologies. This process undergoes certain stages:

(a) The relation between the political experience and the persons while solving certain problem or responding to certain demand is depersonalised.

(b) Non-essential factors are removed, and essential factors and features are retained.

(c) If it is found necessary, in view of its earlier inadequacies, deficiencies or weaknesses new factors, elements or additions or alterations are made.

(d) Thereafter, the impugned identified or under-consideration political technologies are tagged with particular categories of problems and demands.

(e) In view of new circumstances, they are further processed.

This process of processing goes on till identified political technologies are recognised as full-fledged and workable political technologies. Process of refinement can go on for long.[19]

Identified political technologies that have proved useful or successful in the past may not appear viable for solving present or future problems. They can suffer from several limitations. Processing or updating identified political technologies is a calculated attempt to remove these limitations. After undergoing this process, political technologies may look ready for application. Processing of identified political technologies presents us an opportunity to restructure, redesign and apply them to newer situations.

Many political leaders now feel that a political academy should be set up.[20] It is essential to nurture political management as a new discipline and to devise appropriate curriculum for training the politicians. The proposed political management courses at the academy can also aim at producing experts in this new discipline of democracy. An academy may be of interest to business houses and all concerned citizens who wish to understand and use the political system for their own benign benefits. There could be both public as well as private initiative. Only after accumulation of a stock of political technologies it would be possible to build up an Engineering wing of Political Science. The latter might open vistas of research, trade and job opportunities.[21]

Thus, one can undertake the task of solving problems found in any areas: of (a) social justice and democratic participation, (b) nation-state and globalisation, and, (c) internal subversion coming from communalism, fundamentalism and terrorism. In fact, an ocean of political experience lies ahead to be fathomed out of different nation-states, regional organisations, and inter-state and global community.[22]

Notes

1. Giovanni Sartori, "Political Development and Political Engineering", *Public Policy*, 17 (1968), 261-98. He highlights 'political engineering' by political parties in the sense that they both 'pre-suppose' and 'produce' political cleavages in society. They make devices to deal with them in their favour.
2. See, infra, Ch. 11. Contrary to democratic or political technologies, there can be 'criminal technologies'. In a village 'Chakmasan', in sub-division 'Suryagadha', of district Lakhisaraya of Bihar, the intelligence police found a mini-university engaged in teaching and training all types of crimes like dacoity, norcotics, murder etc. to its graduate and under-graduate inmates. It had a vice-chancellor, namely Manzur Alam and faculty consisting of male and female lecturers who were regularly paid salaries, even a laboratory preparing drugs to make the victims unconscious. *Rajasthan Patrika*, July 3, 2003.
3. Ibid.
4. See, Chapter 13 "Globalization", and Chapter 16 "Theory of Contemporary Terrorism".
5. Macpherson, C.B. *The Life and Times of Liberal Democracy*, New York: Oxford University Press, 1977
6. See, in India, 15 MPs and 658 MLAs had cases registered against them. Political parties rejected the Supreme Court's directive empowering the Election Commission in 2002 to seek details about a candidate's assets, criminal antecedents and educational qualifications. *Times of India*, July 14, 2002. Now they have to submit all such information with an affidavit.
7. Ishiyama, John T., *Ethnopolitics in the New Europe, Colorado,* USA: Lynne Rienner Publishers, 1998.
8. To counter these deficiencies, former Chief Election Commissioner of India started 'MIT School of Governance"from Aug. 20, 2005, in Pune, Maharashtra. Its aim is to teach technologies, strategies, contesting elections, and all other lessons of politics and award a graduate degree in lieu of an annual fees of Rs. 2.75 lac for teaching and Rs.75,000 for hostel facilities. *Rajasthan Patrika*, July 17, 2005.
9. Clarkson N. Potter and James M. Perry, *The New Politics: The Expanding Technology of Political Manipulation*, 1968. The Head of STOA unit of the Directorate of the European Parliament, Manchester, publishes appraisal

reports of technologies for political control, as reported by EUROPA, August 2, 2001.

10. These political technologies can further be refined on lines used by the Indian Standards Bureau, and award standards of quality like ISO 9000, ISO 14000, IS 18001 etc.
11. Verma, M.M., *Gandhi's Technique of Mass Mobilization*, New Delhi: R.K. Gupta & Co., 1990: "Leadership", 106-11.
12. Vinay Lal, "Gandhi is not history", *Hindustan Times*, September 8, 2006.
13. Verma, M.M., op. cit. 209.
14. See, infra, Ch. 17.
15. Verma, M.M., op cit.
16. See, supra, Ch. 3.
17. See, supra, Ch. 3.
18. See, infra, Ch. 17.
19. In this way, almost all the political parties prepare their own blueprints to win polls. *Rajasthan Patrika*, December 12, 2002.
20. Vijay Goel, "Study the Craft", *Hindustan Times*, May 8, 2003: A full course at the academy may be for a year with participants staying at the campus. Besides, there may be short term orientation programmes – seminars, roundtables, briefing sessions etc. of duration ranging from two days to two months.
21. See, Giovanni Sartori, *The Theory of Democracy Revisited*. Chatham, N.J.: Chatham House, 1987, and *Comparative Constitutional Engineering*. Basingstoke: Macmillan, 1994.
22. In Russia, there is a Center for Political Technologies (CPT) to study growing interest among private entrepreneurs to develop governmental relations programs and, in general, to improve their awareness of political and social trends in the society. In response to this perceived need the CPT intends to utilise its expertise acquired in recent years and to establish a semi-commercial consulting service for businessmen. It is expected to become commercially viable and will not require external financing after a small seed investment. See for details Center for Political Technologies (CPT), 2nd Frunzenskaya St., 8 "C", 119146, Moscow, Russia.

10

State Supremacy

Since ancient times, thinkers have viewed the 'state' in many ways. It has been seen and observed by them in several ways which have often made it partial, limited and parochial. A few them have wished to do away with it replacing it with their own utopias. Some writers define the state as essentially a class-structure, others regard it as the one organisation that transcends class and stand for the whole community. Some interpret it as a power-system, others as a welfare-system, some view it entirely as a legal construction. A few identify it with the nation while others regard nationality as incidental, unnecessary or even falsifying element. Some consider it no more than a mutual insurance society, some statists own it as the very texture of life. Pro-liberty thinkers treat it as a necessary evil, or an evil that is or will some day be unnecessary or done away with. Some put it in the order of 'corporation', while many find it indistinguishable from society itself.

David Easton observed in 1953 that one person sees the state as the embodiment of the moral spirit, its concrete expression; another, as the instrument of exploitation used by one class against others. One thinker defines it as simply an aspect of society, distinguishable from it only analytically; another, as simply a synonym for government; and still another, as a separate and unique association among a large number of other associations such as the church, trade unions, and similar voluntary groups. Most of them looked at it in a partial, limited and parochial manner.

Some sort of political organisation existed since ancient times, yet the concept of the 'state' is comparatively modern. Barker has pointed out that 'The word 'state' when it came into use in England during the sixteenth century, brought with it from Italy the idea of a high 'state; or stateliness (state) vested in some one person or some one body of persons'. *The Concise Oxford Dictionary of Current English* gives us as many as thirteen different meanings of the term 'state'. Volume 2 of the *Shorter English Oxford*

Dictionary gives eight varieties of meaning and volume 9 of the *Oxford New English Dictionary* gives forty types of meaning. One author claims to have collected one hundred and forty-five separate definitions. Modern state owes its origin to Machiavelli (1469-1527) as 'the power which has authority over men' (*The Prince*, 1513). Max Weber (1864-1920) found it as 'a human community that (successfully) claims the monopoly of the legitimate use of physical force within a given territory.' R.M. MacIver in his *The Modern State* (1926) distinguished it from other kinds of associations. It embraces the whole of people in a specific territory and has the special function of maintaining social order. He defines it saying, 'The State is an association which, acting through law as promulgated by a government endowed to this end with coercive power, maintains within a community territorially demarcated the universal external conditions of social order.'[1] According to him, 'to identify the social with the political is to be guilty of the grossest of all confusions. Garner's definition finds it as 'a community of persons, more or less, numerous, permanently occupying a definite portion of territory, independent or nearly so of external control, and possessing an organised government to which the great body of inhabitants render habitual obedience.' However, power or right to use force or employing violence remains central. Giddens defines it as 'a political organisation whose rule is territorially ordered and which is able to mobilise the means of violence to sustain that rule.[2] The state as the body that is the sole legitimate user of force is a common theme. But the recourse to violence is rare. The state-systems can maintain legitimacy through force for only a limited length of time. However, it remains existent, in express or tacit manner, all the time.

Pluralists, corporatists and Marxists have contributed towards contemporary theories of state. They throw light on the origin and nature of state: the social contract, historical, Marxist and others. Some others discuss nature and functions of state. Among them liberal, Marxist, socialist, totalitarian, theocratic, revolutionary, Gandhian, libertarian and communitarian theories are prominent. Others are pluralist, corporatist, statist, and neo-Marxist theories. On the basis of functions, Deutsch classified the state as regulation, *laissez-faire*, planning, welfare, revolutionary and adaptive. He makes a distinction between the state and the political system.[3] Most modern thinkers treat state as different from other units, such as, associations, governments, nation, civil society and others. State is unique and unlike all others. It is false to identify it with any other units or collectivities. However, two among them, *civil society* and *nation* must be specifically separated from it.

Civil Society

State and civil society stand in closer proximity and yet they are different from each other. In the beginning, 'civil society' and 'political society' were used as coterminous. 'Civil society' was synonymous with 'state'. Initially, the Roman thinker Marcus Tullius Cicero (106-43 B.C.) used the term 'civil society' in the sense of the state. Civil society was not merely the external structure of the state, it connoted a society whose members lived together as citizens, abided by the civil laws and led a civilised, cultural and dignified life. The then barbarian communities were not civil societies. Presently, it is the sphere of society in which individuals freely associate in relationships, actions and organisations that are not dependent on state's intervention, institutions or regulations. 'Civil society' connotes those areas of social life – the domestic world, the economic sphere, cultural activities and political interaction – which are organised by private or voluntary arrangements between individuals and groups outside the direct control of the state.[4]

The concept appeared in sixteenth-century English political thought. In today's context, we might conceive of it as a political space, or arena, where self-generated associations of citizens seek, from outside political parties, to shape the rules that govern social life. Civil society groups bring citizens together non-coercively in deliberate attempts to mould the formal laws and informal norms that regulate social relations. Civil society associations assemble people who share concerns about a particular policy issue. It may include anti-poverty campaigns, business forums, pro-democracy groups, environment movements, professional bodies, relief organisations, women groups etc. They can have many forms, constituencies, capacity levels, geographical scopes, ideological persuasions, strategic visions and campaign tactics. Their power, force, influence, pattern of organisation, number, resources etc. may be different and varying. Civil society activity unfolds in relation to a governance apparatus. In the days of statism, when governance was confined only to government, civil society functioned in relation to the state only. But in the context of transplanetary and supraterritorial connectivity and rise of intense of globalisation the role of civil society has largely transformed.[5]

Nation-State

Modern state has grown out of the tribal state, the oriental empire, the Greek city-state, the Roman world empire, the feudal state and the *modern nation-state*. The last one, the nation-state has been the focus of two conflicting ideologies – nationalism and internationalism. *Nationalism* denotes a sentiment as well as an ideology. The former involves an individual's attachment to his nation. It accords primacy to his national interest over all other interests. In the beginning, this sentiment is called 'nationality' which when aspires to be an independent political entity, it attains the status of 'nationhood'. Nationality is a 'nation-in-making'. However, it may or may not like to be a 'nation'. Attachment with or commitment to territoriality is 'nationism'. It is a concept more secular and non-communal than 'nationalism'. Analytically 'nationalism' and 'nationism'[6] are two separate concepts. Nationalism postulates that its political organisation should be founded on nationhood.

When a community grows national consciousness but its territory is occupied by a colonial or imperial power, it often organises itself for the struggle of independence. This struggle is known as 'national movement'. Nationalism pays highest importance to one's loyalty and commitment to one's nation. People are taught or indoctrinated to die and fight for it.

But there are many difficulties with the making of nation-states. Some communities are scattered over different parts of the world. They have a sense of unity on the basis of common culture, common language, common religion and display national consciousness on some of these grounds. But they are unable like the Kurds to organise as a single state. Many ethnic groups live together but are unable to assimilate themselves into one nation. The former USSR, Yugoslavia, Czechoslovakia and Ethiopia entertained such disruptive tendencies and could not unite. Many people like the Chinese migrate to other countries in search of job opportunities, and become naturalised citizens of those countries but remain deeply attached to their mother-country on the basis of their language, culture, faith and customs. Some communities are too small to be treated as nations. Other big communities like the Muslims and the Christians are too big and cannot be treated as one nation owing to divisions prevailing among them.

Presently, the nation-states are in view of growth of nuclear weapons unable to provide security to their residents. They could do so only in the past. Disposal of the industrial waste is not confined to the boundaries of the nation-states. There are problems like limitless consumption of petrol and diesel by the developed nations causing immense harm to the global atmosphere, cutting of forests and denuding of mountains for fuel, timber, lime stone and hydro-electric power and the like. These are not confined to one particular nation-state. Information technology revolution has eliminated distance among nations: telephones, internet, e-mail, fax etc. Satellites have enabled different nation-states to transmit television programmes simultaneously in all parts of the world, and converting it into a 'global village'. Advancement in the means of transport and communication has resulted into globalisation of economy and culture.

Internationalism

In this way there is fast growth of 'internationalism'. It does not regard nation-state as the centre of political organisation. It does not accept it as the object of individual's undivided loyalty. It stands for the growth of larger organisations to achieve some higher objectives. Human interests should be given higher precedence. Earlier it believed in international cooperation in military, commercial, educational and cultural fields. Now United Nations Organisation calls upon to maintain world peace and to eradicate hunger, disease, illiteracy and backwardness from the entire globe. The institutional structure of internationalism is meant for the entire globe. It draws attention towards the problems of environmental pollution, terrorism, drug-trafficking, global warming and disarmament.

Under these circumstances, a new model of state like the European Union (EU) has come up[7] in between 1947 to 1995. It is still growing. However, it is more a Regional Integration. Such is a process by which states in particular regions of the world come to bring together some of the aspects of their economies and politics. Such developments emerge from preferences of states and because of the operation of powerful dynamics beyond the control of nation-states. The European Union has travelled all along from inter-governmentalism to supranationalism. In supranationalism there is development of executive and binding authority at levels other than the nation-state. Still it is not the end of the former nation-states or growth of a super-state.[8]

Emergence of New Elements in Advanced States

In place of ideological commitment, states of advanced countries presently bank more upon elements like industrialisation and subsequent modernisation. Max Weber in the early twentieth century discovered that all modern societies were having a 'legal-rational' model of bureaucracy. Later, James Burnham (1907-87) tried to show in *Managerial Revolution,* 1942, that the managerial class was common to all forms of economies. This symbolised the shift of power from the legal owner of the state to the effective managers. W.W. Rostow (*The Stages of Economic Growth*, 1960), J.K. Galbraith (*The New Industrial State*, 1964) and Simon Kuznets (*Economic Growth and Structure*, 1965) pointed out that economic growth constitutes a uniform process involving definite stages in all industrial economies. There is uniform logic underlying this process. Marion J. Levy, Jr. (*Modernization and the Structure of Society*, 1966) and Talcott Parsons (*The System of Modern Societies*, 1970) sought to identify some common tendencies of development in all 'modernising' societies: modernisation, expansion of education, occupational prestige and mobility patterns, falling birth and death rates, electronic communication networks, universalism, individualism and rationalism. These theorists project 'market society model' as the universal model of development. Daniel Bell, a votary of 'end of ideology' thesis (*The Coming of Post-Industrial Society: A Venture in Social Forecasting*, 1974) holds that the character of social-economic organisation of a country is determined by the level of its industrial development, and not by its ideology.[9] In other words, state has included many new elements in its structure and operation. State now has to be understood from the view of its changing elements.[10]

State in Constant Flux

Thus, the evolution of state, both in the developed and the developing countries, clearly shows that its nature, contents, goals, ambit etc. have always been changing. It is futile, therefore, to cling to the 4-element paradigm of the state which was upheld for long for the purpose of stability and unity of a particular community in the 18th and 19th centuries. It hardly conforms to the realities existing at the end of 20th and the beginning of the 21st centuries. No one can construct the edifice of the modern state on the basis of that imagery. State-building everywhere has been undertaken in a chaotic and haphazard manner. It does not help people in understanding what is what, and what for the state or its constituents or variables are operating at a given point of time. All concerned are now interested in knowing the important structures, operations, and changes found in the modern state. This cannot be comprehended unless one knows the interrelationships existing among the variables or constituents of the modern state. At this point, a conceptual framework of state is being proposed for understanding the operations of the post-war state-system operating for the last sixty years.

State and the State-System

The state is a collectivity of human beings existing at a particular point of time. It is specific, static, structured and fixed in the minds of most of the people. Disciplines like History, Law, Sociology, Geography and some others regard it as sovereign entity made for ever. They know it through the visible bureaucracy, the police and the army, the judiciary, legislatures, central and provincial governments, law, departments etc. However, accepting such state as point of reference or some 'ideal-type' model, scholars of Political Science like to see it more as a 'state-system'. Unlike other social institutions, it is made of certain elements, attributes, constituents, variables or forces. It does not operate in vacuum. It is a dynamic process or a huge live entity in which all these constituents interact with each other. Its reality or power lies in the interaction processes found among those constituents. It is manifested in its various institutions. Power is exercised by people and their leaders who have leading positions in these institutions. Thus, the concept of state-system is wider than the state (see Diagram 1).

However, both state and state-system operate within the ambit of political system of each society.[11] From a general point of view, society as a whole makes up the social system, which contains many subsystems. Political system is one of these subsystems.

Diagram 1

Proposed Elements of State in the Political System (2006)

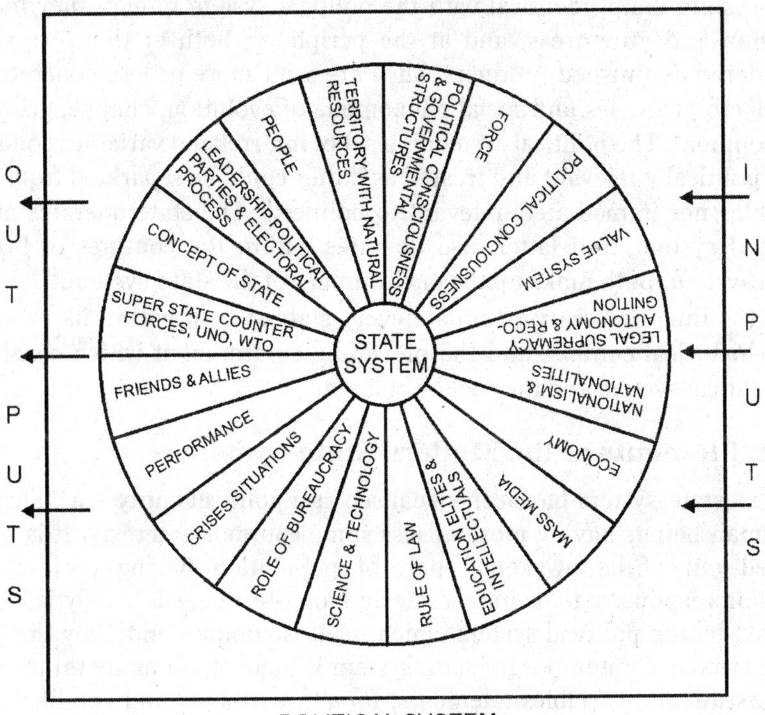

State-System Embedded in the Broader Political and Social Systems

Earlier David Easton had rejected the 'state' and stood for 'political system' as unit of analysis. Accordingly, he wrote, "Political system is a part of the total social system concerned with the authoritative allocation of values in the society."[12] In his later works, he held that the political system is composed of a variety of structures as well as various processes.[13] These structures are formed by such elements as interest groups, formal governmental arrangements, and various political groupings, such as, elites versus masses, party and the like.[14] These structures are to be seen as the determinants of the state and the state is studied as a structural object. Broader political system includes traditional structures like kinship ties, caste groupings, and anomic phenomena such as assassinations, riots and demonstrations. But it is closely concerned with the interactions which affect the use or threat of use of legitimate physical coercion. However, it is operated by the state-system essentially made of legislature, judiciary, administrative agencies, and other political structures like political parties, interest groups and media or communication.

The present framework makes use of the concept of 'state-system'. The state-system is not identical with the political system though they meet in common and grey areas, and at the periphery. Both of them cannot be considered as finished products. They are a bit more or less concrete, and are macro processes and social phenomena of evolution, change, growth or development. The political system is a set of interrelated variables conceived to be politically relevant and treated as if they could be separated from other variables not immediately relevant to politics.[15] The state operates amidst political system, and latter also operates within the confines of broader social system. Both make up the environment of the state-system.[16]

It is thus necessary to situate every state-system within its particular socio-historical context, and the prevailing environment which consists of the political system and the society at large.

Main Elements of the Modern State-System

Modern state-system has been visualised as a political entity – a collectivity of human beings having more or less some common interests. It is mostly formed out of its awakened part of population having socio-cultural cohesion responsive to its immediate and long-term needs. Analytically, it is covered by the political system which itself is comprehended by the larger social system. Contemporary state-system is made up of many things called as constituents, variables, elements, forces, attributes and the like. All of them can be divided into three categories – A, B and C, captioned respectively here as essential, accompanying and intervening constituents (see Diagram 2).

They may be mentioned as below:

(A) *Essential Constituents*

1. Concept of state as an entity made of common sense morality, humanity and political ideals with a will or wish to enforce them;
2. Leadership based on political parties and electoral process;
3. People (individual, groups and classes) with stratification and cohesion with some sense of freedom;
4. Territory with natural resources;
5. Political organisation and governmental structures – levels, divisions and autonomy; and
6. Force – military, police and popular, weapons, and skill to use them, and

(B) *Accompanying Constituents*

7. Political consciousness of individuals and groups;
8. Values, goals and ideology;

Diagram 2

Levels of Elements Constituting the State-System (2006)

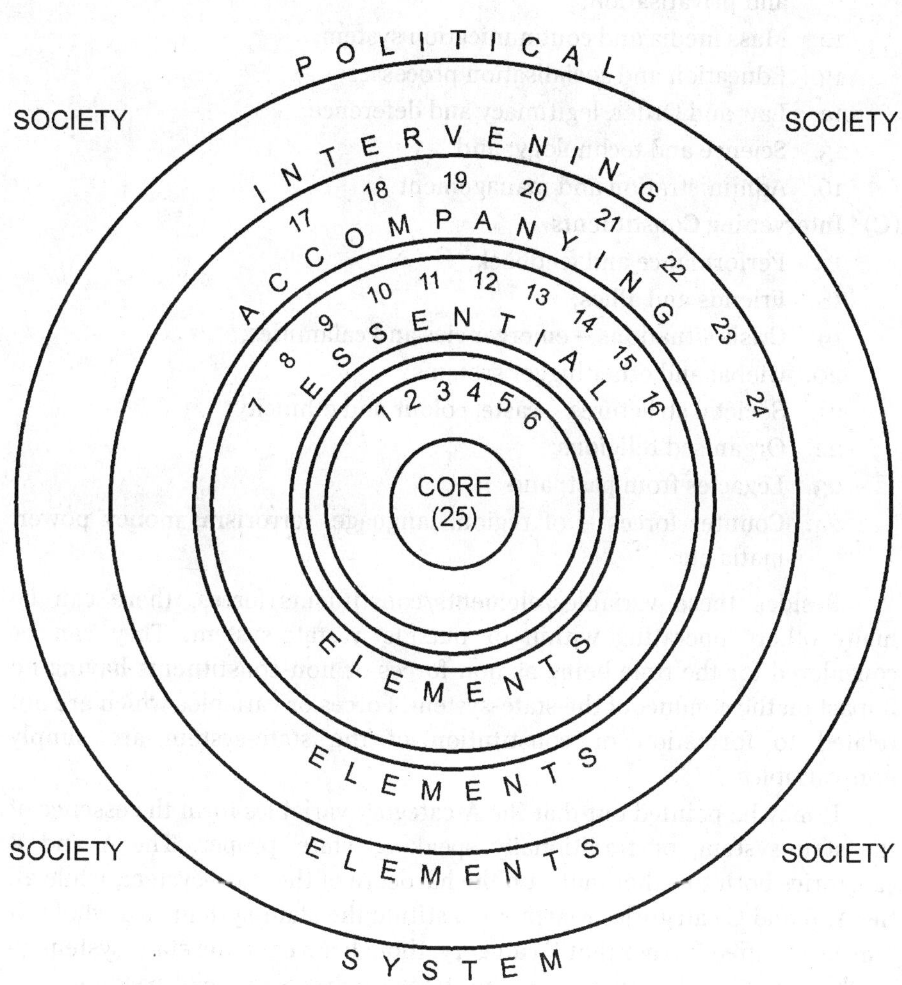

ESSENTIAL ELEMENTS

1. Concept of state
2. Leadership, political Parties & electoral process.
3. People.
4. Territory with natural resources
5. Political organisation & Governmental structures.
6. Force

ACCOMPANYING ELEMENTS

7. Political consciousness
8. Value system.
9. Legal supermacy autonomy recognition.
10. Nationalism & Nationalities.
11. Economy
12. Mass media
13. Education, elites & intellectual.
14. Rule of law.
15. Science & Technology.
16. Role of bureaucracy

INTERVENING ELEMENTS

17. Crises situations.
18. Performance.
19. Friends & allies.
20. Super state (UN)
21. Societal structures
22. Organized Religions
23. Legacy from the past
24. Counter forces

9. Legal supremacy, autonomy and recognition;
10. Nationalism and nationalities;
11. Economy, economic resources and industrialisation – planning and privatisation;
12. Mass media and communication system;
13. Education and socialisation processes;
14. Law and Order, legitimacy and deference;
15. Science and technology; and
16. Administration and management

(C) Intervening Constituents

17. Performance and feedback;
18. Friends and allies;
19. Crisis situations – emergencies and calamities;
20. Global and other bigger systems;
21. Societal structures – caste, colour and ethnicity;
22. Organised religions;
23. Legacies from past; and
24. Counter forces – of region, language, terrorism, money power, mafia etc.

Besides these variables/elements/constituents/forces, there can be many others operating within or outside a state-system. They can be considered for the time being as non-forces or non-constituents having no impact on the conduct of the state-system. Forces or variables which are not related to formation or constitution of the state-system are simply non-variables.

It may be pointed out that the A-category variables form the essence of the state-system, or traditionally speaking 'state' proper. The A and B categories both together make up the hardcore of the state-system, while all the A, B and C categories together constitute the state-system as a whole. It may be clarified further that C category, though a part of the state-system go on changing their locations from the state or political to social systems.

'Essential' constituents are basic elements or variables of the state and are located in the critical areas of the state-system. A constituent is 'essential' if its absence makes the state largely non-existent or renders it ineffective. For example, people or political/administrative organisations come under this category. 'Accompanying' constituents are necessary and remain closely related to the 'essential' constituents for making them more viable, such as, a vibrant or stagnant economy offers legitimacy or acceptability of the people at large. However, the 'intervening' variables are not so important. The 'core' or pivotal element remains concerned with them only in an indirect manner. It may or may not leave them free to operate.

'Intervening' constituents often operate at the periphery of the state-system, and sometimes in the grey areas of political systems. Any element at a time may be 'essential' or 'accompanying' or 'intervening'. The status of an element is often related with the nature or act of the 'core' or pivotal element.

Centrality of the 'Core'

Most important of these 24 constituents is the 'core', pivotal or central constituent. It is the critical or deciding element and may be regarded as the 25th. Basically, it reflects intense, dynamic and motivating course of human interactions. In fact, it is new but comes out of the 24 elements, and it can be single or group of elements that mobilises or organises the rest of the elements at different levels. It may be political leadership, military takeover, organised religion, ethnicity, bureaucracy or economy. When the core changes or is replaced by another 'core', the whole setting of elements at various levels in the state-system undergoes transformation. Its nature, role, cause and consequences change. For example, political leadership as 'core' makes a state-system democratic whereas military takeover as 'core' subordinates every other element of the state-system.

This conceptual framework is simply an analytical tool to find out the actual or real state-system existing in a developed or developing society. It may be reiterated that this conceptual framework presents the state-system as an ideal-type. It reflects the needs, necessities and contents of the modern state required by any society. The number of the variables or constituents may increase or decrease. So can be the number of variables falling in each one of the categories. The number may cross over 24 or be reduced to 10 or 15 in a particular society. This conceptual framework is simply an analytical tool to find out the actual or real state-system existing in a modern society.

When India wrested freedom from the British Raj, she herself did not have the 'state' on these lines. Some scholars do not agree to the statement that India was even a state from August 15, 1947 to January 25, 1950. During that period, India perhaps lacked even the legal-juridical concept of the state. During that transitional period, it was hardly possible to ascertain the really existing number of constituents and put them in A, B and C categories of Essential, Accompanying and Intervening variables or constituents.[17]

Now it is necessary to look into the operating principles of these constituents or elements

Some of the very important *operating principles of the constituents of the state-system* are mentioned under:

(a) The framework presented here is a tentative one and is subject to further modifications. All of its variables included in the state-system are equally viable. They are classified into three categories on the basis of their relative importance and efficacy in a democratic state-system like India. Only a factual analysis or empirical investigation of the state constituents would reveal whether they can be placed under the category of 'essential', 'accompanying' or 'intervening' elements.

(b) In general, all variables or constituents have equal importance. However, when a particular element acquires more importance, its role, efficacy and space also broadens.

(c) Any one of the constituents can become 'core'. A 'core' can operate successfully only when it is adopted, guided and directed by the total concept of the state-system. This concept (element 1) dominates as a form of philosophy, ideology or theory suggesting the ways and means of activating the rest of the constituents. It operates in the form of morality, humanity and similar political ideals with a will to enforce them.

In democracies much depends on the 'core' of political leadership which assigns order, arrangement and roles to these various constituents. In other state-systems the 'core' or the centre of polity can be replaced by any other 'core'. The political system and the society also make an indirect contribution to that change. Absence of 'core' leads to lack of discipline among the 24 elements, rendering the role of most of elements dysfunctional.

(d) The number of constituents in the three categories is not fixed. It can go on increasing or decreasing. Many of these elements have evolved and have been added afresh even to the formation of state-systems. A careful analysis of the evolution of state shows that sometime very important elements have gone out of use or disappeared, such as, kinship and Church lost into oblivion of history. Similarly, if in a particular case, there were elements considered 'essential' for a particular state, in other states 'essential' elements were found to be 'accompanying', or even 'intervening'. In the same state-system, the status of elements may go on changing at different points of time. In fact, the state as a collectivity is not a monolith but has varying degrees and contours of cohesion and operational efficacy.

(e) The ideal-type of classification of elements which have been hypothetically suggested here is applicable to a normally well-developed state operating during peace time. However, empirical studies of actual state-systems would display some varying settings of these constituents/elements operating in a kaleidoscopic manner. They can be seen, displayed and studied as a map showing stars, planets and other heavenly bodies in the solar sky. However, the present conceptual framework cannot be thrust upon from above but has to be applied in a heuristic, inductive and empirical way.

(f) The state-systems, with this conceptual framework, can be studied with many fruitful insights. The study of elements individually and in the form of their settings can reveal their comparative importance in varying historical situations. Their knowledge may be useful for their respective societies. Changing nature of a state-system can be indicated by the variations of settings of these elements falling in A, B and C categories.

If all these changing elements of state are properly discovered and analysed and their role and inter-relations evaluated in different contexts, the clusters of elements would show particular outcomes under relevant 'core'. Such study would have many theoretical implications for use and applications to practical politics.

Thus, there are many gaps between the theory of conventional state and the scenario prevailing in the twentieth and twenty-first centuries. David Held has pointed out five gaps between them. They pertain to (i) the world economy; (ii) hegemonic power and power blocs; (iii) international organisations; (iv) international law, and (v) the end of domestic policy. Forces of Liberalisation, Privatisation and Globalisation (LPG) are filling these gaps in newer ways.

Political activity is being conducted across national boundaries. The Red Cross, Amnesty International and Greenpeace create politics of human rights or of ecology – are not tied to specific territories, histories or cultures. It is a 'multi-centric' world.[18] Thus, transnational forces and globalised market economy have limited hitherto freehand of state in its domestic and foreign policy areas. Enormous differences between states have appeared in terms of elements during changing historical times. At international level, many organisations have constrained its autonomy and transformed its classical 'sovereignty' into 'supremacy'. Some of them are United Nations Organization, International Monetary Fund (IMF), Uruguay Round of the General Agreement on Tariffs and Trade (GATT), and World Trade Organization (WTO). The character of the state should be examined from a fresh outlook.

Nation-State under Globalisation

Presently, there is a growing trend to reduce the role of the state and hand over many state concerns to the world-market. The nation-state is in trouble and may not survive the growing pressures from within and without.[19] The nation-state today is in disarray. It is ceasing to be the central mechanism of the nation and is in the process of acute fragmentation, multiple polarisations and likely disintegration. Both the retreat of the state and erosion of the nation are going hand in hand. Autonomy of civil society is declining. Retreat of state in domestic field has resulted in its decline in the international field also. Increasing dominance of new world order is strengthening authoritarian structure of governance. Masses are alienating from the ruling strata. The number of *'dharnas'*, strikes, rebellion and *'bandhs'* against the government is on increase. Culture of violence is growing. The concept of one world is moving to 'one worldism'. This one Worldism has been hijacked by global capitalism. All these call for new theoretical reconsiderations on relationships among power, ideology and institutions.[20]

Some other major consequences of globalisation have been (i) the dislocation of traditional religions and belief systems; (ii) the beginning of the disintegration of the traditional social fabrics and shared norms by consumerism, cyber-culture, newfangled religions and changing work ethics and work rhythms; (iii) the fast spreading anomie forcing an ever increasing number of individuals to fall back upon the easily accessible pretentious religious banalities; and (iv) religion related creation and acceleration of extremist, fundamentalist and terrorist tendencies in the third world countries.[21]

Earlier, the state had statism. Statism entails governance that is for all intents and purposes reducible to the state.[22] Owing to transplanetary and supraterritorial connectivity and half a century of accelerated globalisation statist conditions no longer exist. Governance now involves suprastate (regional and transworld) regimes that operate with some autonomy from the state. Many substate, municipal and provincial governments engage directly with spheres beyond their country. The Westphalian sovereign state did not share governance over its realm with any other party. Globalisation has made that sovereignty obsolete. The state is unable to exercise control over so many things like electronic mass media, global trade, global currencies, transworld ecological development, etc. Transworld bonds on lines such as class, gender, profession, race, religion etc. have overridden national boundaries. The world has moved into 'the twilight of sovereignty' or 'beyond sovereignty'. Sovereignty is no longer sacrosanct and it has lost much of its significance. It has become obsolescent but has not ended. There is 'partial' or 'shrunken' sovereignty as states have surrendered their prerogative in certain areas. States enjoy 'limited', 'qualified' or 'shared' sovereignty. Some have recommended 'enlightened sovereignty', where states presently cede control in areas subject to universally agreed norms and values. Clearly, the statist conditions to which sovereignty referred in the past are gone. States are impotent in the phase of contemporary globalisation. They can only shape the effects of globalisation on their territories and populations.

However, it does not mean the end of state. It survives despite dismemberment and fragmentation. Its territorialism has passed away but its territoriality remains. In fact, it has never remained fixed. It has been perpetually in motion, evolving, adapting and incorporating. Now it has to address global matters such as ecological change, electronic finance, human rights and transworld production, transworld telecommunications, superterritorial mass media operations etc. There is pressure on its welfarism, such as, provision of education, health care, housing, pensions and the like. Globalisation has undermined the fiscal capacities of states.[23] Globality has reduced some incentives for interstate warfare. There is little focus on territorial conquests. The latter no longer give control over the internet, electronic finance, transworld production chains, global consumer markets, transplanetary ecological trends, or global governance regimes. The recent 'war on terror' has involved satellite remote sensing, monitoring of bank accounts, and hacking into computers along with armed combat. Defence, trade and foreign ministry officials from different states collaborate in non-proliferation export regimes. They engage as members of the nuclear suppliers group and the missile technology control regime in respect of materials that could be used to produce weapons of mass destruction. Similarly, officials are now more and more busy to deal with the problems of disease control, asylum and refugees on a global scale. The MOUs (memorandum of understanding), in contrast to treaties, do not require ratification by legislative bodies, so that transstate relation can easily become technocratic networks that operate outside democratic oversight. States have entered the era of macro-regional and transworld governance.

State and Governance

Governance is a category with a normative and a prescriptive dimension. UNDP defines 'governance' as the exercise of political, economic and administrative authority in the management of a country's affairs at all levels. It comprises the complex mechanisms, processes and institutions through which citizens and groups articulate their interests, mediate their differences and exercise their legal rights and obligations. Good governance has many attributes. It is participatory, transparent and accountable. It is effective in making the best use of resources and is equitable. It promotes the rule of law. Governance includes the *state*, but transcends it by taking in the private sector and civil society. All three are critical for sustaining human development. The state creates a conducive political and legal environment. The private sector generates jobs and income. Civil society facilitates political and social interaction – mobilising groups to participate in economic, social and political activities. Because each has weaknesses and strengths, a major objective of our support for good governance is to promote constructive interaction among all three. Governance can no longer be considered a closed system. Changes in the world's economic, political and social systems have brought unprecedented improvements in human living conditions. But these changes also bring new uncertainties and challenges. The state's task is to find a balance between taking advantage of globalisation and providing a secure and stable social and economic domestic environment.

From State to Global Order

The state under the pressure of global order is getting transformed in the following lines:[24]

(i) There is a shift from relatively discrete national communication and economic systems to more complex and diverse enmeshment at regional and global levels, and from government to multilevel governance.

(ii) New forms of multilateral politics have been established involving governments, intergovernmental organisations (IGOs) and a wide variety of transnational pressure groups and international non-governmental organisations (INGOs).

(iii) Extensive political interconnectedness has produced many international policy making fora – the UN, G7, IMF, WTO, EU, APEC (Asia-Pacific Economic Cooperation) etc.

(iv) Foreign and domestic policy areas have become chronically intermeshed.[25]

(v) There are changes in the world military order. Few states except perhaps the US and China can now contemplate unilateralism or neutrality as a credible defence strategy. There is collectivisation of national security.[26] The way military hardware is manufactured has also changed.

(vi) Political communities are enmeshed in complex structures of overlapping forces, relations and networks.

(vii) Governance is becoming a multilevel, intricately institutionalised and spatially dispersed activity, while representation, loyalty and identity remain stubbornly rooted in traditional ethnic, regional and national communities.

(viii) Cultural nationalism remains central to people's identity.

However, state still holds, and stays on its own ground. But it carries only 'supremacy', not 'sovereignty'. The days of sovereign state and statism are gone for ever.

Notes

1. R.M. MacIver, *The Modern State*, Oxford University Press, 1926, Paperback, 1966, 22.
2. A. Giddens, *The Nation-state and Violence*, Vol. 2 of *A Contemporary Critique of Historical Materialism*, Cambridge: Polity, 1985.
3. Karl W. Deutsch, "State Functions and the Future of the State", *International Political Science Review*, Vol. 7, No. 2. 1986, 209-221.
4. David Held, *Political Theory and the Modern State*, Cambridge: Polity, 1989, 6.
5. Infra, see, Chapter 13.
6. S.L. Verma, *Federal Authority in the Indian Political System*, RBSA Publishers, Jaipur, 1987, Introduction.
7. Barrie Axford et al., *Politics-An Introduction*, London: Routledge, 1997, 306-10, passim. Institutions of the EU are: the European Commission, the Council of Ministers, the European Council, the European Parliament and the European Court of Justice. For all purposes in international relations it has gained the status of a 'state'.
8. A.S. Milward, *The European Rescue of the Nation State*, London: Routledge, 1992.
9. On line of the "withering away of the state", many Western writers had visions of a stateless future as in Rudyad Kipling's *The Night Mail* and H.G. Well's novel *Men Are Like Gods*. Karl W. Deutsch, "State Functions and the Future of the State", *International Political Science Review*, Vol. 7, No. 2. 1986.
10. To illustrate the changes in the nature, contents and constituents of the (Indian) State, see, Rajni Kothari, *The Hijacking of the Indian State, Express Magazine*, August 14, 1988; and the issue of *Seminar*, 367, March, 1990, on "*Politics of the State-a symposium on the state in its different dimensions*".
11. P.E. Alexander, *The Notion of the State: An Introduction to Political Theory*, Oxford Press, 1967, 2.
12. Easton, David, *The Political System: An Inquiry into the State of Political Science*, 2nd edn., New York, A.A. Knopf, 1977, p. xi.
13. Easton, David, *The Analysis of Political Structure*, Routledge, New York, 1990, 30-31.
14. Ibid.
15. Wood, D M, "Comparative Government and Politics" in Wasby Stephen L., *Political Science: The Discipline and Its Dimensions*, Starenden Press, Oxford, p. 492.
16. Kaplan, A Morton, *Systems and Process in International Politics*, New York, 1957, p.4
17. See Chapter 13; and, Upmanu, Shailja, *State in Indian Political System*, Rawat, 1997.
18. There are transnational organisations, transnational problems, transnational communities and transnational structures.

19. Rajni Kothari, "Under Globalization-Will Nation State Hold?", *Economic and Political Weekly*, Vol. XXX, No. 26, July 1, 1995, 1593-1603.
20. Ibid., 1600-1.
21. P. Radhakrishnan, A paper presented at the international conference on 'Religion and Globalisation', held at Payap University, Thailand, from July 27 to August 2, 2003.
22. Scholte, Jan Art, *Globalization: A Critical Introduction*, second ed., Palgrave: 2005, 186.
23. For effects of globalisation and global governance, see, Chapter 13 and 14.
24. See, 'from statism to polycentrism', Chapter 14, 4-6.
25. In the middle of the nineteenth century, there were only two or three inter-state conference per annum, presently there are several thousand annually. National governments can barely monitor them.
26. Clark, I. *The Post Cold War Order*, Oxford: Oxford University Press, 2001.

11

Democracy in the Twenty-First Century

The last twentieth and the present twenty-first century are the 'Age of Democracy'. Democracy has displayed its strength in two world wars. It has triumphed over all forms of dictatorship, including the Soviet Super Power along with its camp-followers. Everyone likes himself to be called a 'demophil', lover or supporter of democracy. Still, surprisingly, only a limited number of people understand it properly.

Democracy: Power of the People

The word 'democracy' is made of two Greek words *'demos'* and *'kratos'* which respectively mean 'people' and 'power'. It is a government where people are powerful. This is a form of government wherein power remains with the people. It is the rule of people or masses, but ironically, we think it a guarantee of the freedom of the individual. This term was not used for the last 2000 years. Its use, for the first time, was by the dreaded Robespierre in February, 1784, and made it hateful. For its support of the 'right of people' within no time, it became a worldwide phenomenon – almost religion or ideology of common man.

Concept and Clarification

The word 'democracy' ever since the time of Herodotus, according the Bryce, denotes that "form of government in which the ruling power of the state is vested not in a particular class or classes, but in the members of the community as a whole." In democracy as a government, "every one has a share " (Seeley), or "the governing body is comparatively a large fraction of the entire nation," (Dicey), or "the majority of the whole nation or community partakes of the sovereign power" (Lewis), or "Public opinion has control" (Hall), or "which shall rest on active consent of the governed" (Strong), or "by those who have greatest concern for and the greatest awareness of the interests and rights of the people generally" (Coker).

The most popular definition is that of the American President, Abraham Lincoln, "Democracy is a government of the people, for the people and by the people.' (Gettysberg speech). It is that form of government in which the mass of population possess the right to share in the exercise of sovereign power." (Gettell) But there are many other aspects or forms of democracy.

Broadening its meaning and application, Giddings has stated that, "Democracy may be either a form of Government, a form of State, a form of Society or a combination of the three". Still its scope remains narrow. Democracy has not only political and social aspects, but also moral and economic dimensions. Miss Follet considers it 'a spiritual ideal.' It can be studied as – (a) a form of government, (b) a form of state, (c) a way of life, or philosophy, (d) an ethical value system, and (e) a system of economy.

Democracy (a) *as a form of government* regards the people as the base or source of power of government. They exercise power directly or indirectly. The government remains responsible to the people. In ancient times Plato, Aristotle and Cicero, and, later, Henry Maine, Lowell, Lincoln etc. held this view. But none of them have explained how do the people come to hold power or run the government. Operationally, only a few people held power which is exercised to benefit them. Hardly, such government is of the people, by the people and for the people. Its apparent features, viz., popular sovereignty, adult franchise, free elections, majority rule, responsibility of the executive to the legislative rarely vests the people with actual exercise of power; (b) *as a form of state* democracy presents 'a mode of appointing, controlling and dismissing Government' (Hearnshaw). Sovereignty resides in the general will of the people. The form of government and important policies are finally determined by the people; and (c) *as a form of society* is studied as a social philosophy and a lifestyle. Liberty, equality and fraternity are its basic values. Everyone is entitled to lead his life according to his will. Man is an end in himself, and never a means to others (Kant). Everyone is counted for one and no one more than one (Bentham). Family becomes a school of these values.

Value of equality involves eschewing all forms of discrimination based on caste, wealth, social status etc. The American Declaration of Independence makes it very clear: we hold these truths to be self-evident, that all men are created equal; that they are endowed by their Creator with certain inalienable right; that among these rights are Life, Liberty, and the pursuit of Happiness. The Declaration of the Rights of Man and Citizen also runs in similar terms. This equality has four aspects: political, civic, economic and social. Unless equality pays respect to merit and personality, it turns into some 'monstrous fiction' (Burke), 'indefeasible proposition' (Coleridge) or an 'anarchic fallacy' (Behtham).

Liberty is another key element of social democracy. It has two, negative and positive, aspects. Negatively it means absence of restraints. Positively, it involves creation of conditions in which one may find himself to be the best. Fraternity emphasises a sense of brotherhood. Sense of brotherhood brings about voluntary cooperation among human beings. (d) *as a way of life* it reflects special attribute towards life. It expects special nature and social behaviour from man. "Do not do unto others that you do not want to be done to yourself." Democracy has overtones of (e) *an ethical value system* which considers a moral ideal that can be realised only by leading a spiritual life. It is an all-round development of human personality: Man is an end. He is a spiritual being. He should never be treated as means. Democracy is universal preference of Brecht. It is the end-value of Dahl, Easton, Lasswell and the whole of the West. It assimilates even isms like nationalism. Presently, it is also advocated as (f) *a system of economy*. Accordingly, the whole society should have control over means of production. There should not be unbridgeable gap between the haves and the have-nots and yet democracy has survived where the rich exploit the poor. Economic democracy does necessarily mean the end of private property, total nationalisation, or public employment. The state should cater for the minimum needs of the people.

All these aspects can again be subsumed under various schools of thought:

1. Classical democracy
2. Liberal democracy
3. Elitist democracy
4. Plural democracy
5. Participatory democracy
6. Marxist democracy
7. Gandhian democracy
8. Radical democracy
9. Cosmopolitan democracy
10. Teledemocracy

1. *Classical democracy* has had a long tradition. Some of its features are: (a) equal participation by all freemen in the common affairs of the polity; (b) participation as an essential instrument of good life; (c) public decisions in an atmosphere of free discussion; (d) general respect for law and for the established procedures; (e) majority opinion determines legislation (Dicey: *Law and Opinion in England*, 1905); (f) people expressed their sovereign will through majority votes; (g) test of government is the welfare of the people; and (h) participation is the 'essence' of democracy (Bryce: *Modern Democracies*, 1921).

2. *Liberal democracy*, until the 19th century, was not at all democratic. Much of it was antidemocratic. The individual has the right to unlimited acquisition of property and to the capitalist market economy. It implied inequality in the political spheres also. It insisted on property qualifications for the right-to-vote. This was contrary to the democratic principles. This classical liberalism fostered capitalism responsible for large-scale industrialisation and urbanisation. There was concentration of workers in large industrial cities. They were forced to live under sub-human conditions created by competitive economy. This class became conscious of its strength and insisted on its rights. In this way the liberal state was forced to accommodate democratic principles in order to save its own existence. A combination of free-market economy with universal adult franchise came up. Conflicting claims of the capitalists and the masses were accommodated under the ideology of 'welfare state'. Procedures and institutional arrangements stood by the new principles (C.B. Macpherson: *Democratic Theory: Essays in Retrieval*, 1973). Principles of liberal democracy include: (a) government by consent, (b) public accountability, (c) majority rule, (d) recognition of minority rights, and, (e) constitutional government. Mechanism includes institutions and procedures. Accordingly, there should be more than one political party freely competing for political power. Political offices should not be confined to any privileged class. Periodic elections based on universal adult franchise should be held regularly. Civil liberties should be protected and granted to all citizens. Independence of judiciary is a must to maintain them.[1]

3. *Elitist democracy* relates to elitist theories which come from sociology. Gaetano Mosca (*The Ruling Class*, 1896) and Robert Michels (*Political Parties: A Sociological Study of the Oligarchical Tendencies of Modern Democracy*, 1911) found the society divided into two groups: the rulers and the ruled. The former control most of the wealth, power and prestige. The ruled remain to replace them. Vilfredo Pareto (*The Mind and Society*, 1915-19) used the terms 'elite' and 'masses' which are respectively superior and inferior groups of a society. Michel observed 'iron law of oligarchy' in every organisation, which is rule of the chosen few. The 'elite' show highest ability in every field while masses feel safe in following the direction of the elite. Karl Mannheim (*Ideology and Utopia: An Introduction to the Sociology of Knowledge*, 1929) reconciled elite theory with democratic theory. According to him, society does not cease to be democratic by entrusting the shaping and making of policy to the elites. The masses cannot directly participate in the government. They can only make their aspirations felt at certain intervals. This is sufficient for democracy. The people can always act to remove their leaders and force them to take decisions in their interests. Selection of leaders is made on merit. Joseph A. Schumpeter (*Capitalism, Socialism and Democracy*, 1942) stood for

market-theory of democracy. According to him democracy is 'an institutional arrangement by which individuals acquire power of decision-making on the basis of competitive struggle for people's votes'. He insists on methods of appointment and dismissing the makers of law and policy. Political decisions are taken by the 'leadership' and there is a free competition among the leaders for winning people's votes. Rulers are different from the common people. The people choose their leaders from the competing elites. This arrangement does not allow the leaders to grab absolute power. Political leaders have to earn larger support of the voters than their opponents. The initiative remains in the hand of the leaders while the people simply respond to policies offered by them. Raymond Aron (*Social Structure and the Ruling Class*, 1950) draws attention on the general system of checks and balances and *plurality* of the elites. The elites are divided in a liberal democracy. Plurality of the elite makes government a business of compromise. This makes them sensitive to public opinion and conscious of the opposition. They have to change seats with the opponents in due course of time. Initiative remains in the hands of the elite. Masses keep limited to choosing the ruling elite and to put pressure on them in their functioning. Giovanni Sartori (*Democratic Theory*, 1958) is more realistic. His views on democracy are similar to Schumpeter. Sartori finds most definitions of democracy half-truths and misleading. They limit democracy to 'government' only. Sartori makes a distinction between democracy as (i) an ideal, (ii) an illusion, and, (iii) a reality. One should keep these three aspects of democracy separate, though the first and the third interact. The three ideals of democracy: (i) popular sovereignty, (ii) equality, and (iii) self-government contradict each other, and make democracy an illusion. One has to be realistic. Everyone likes to have the 'ideals' of democracy. This is so till democracy is accepted as ideal. After its acceptance, when we begin to execute the ideal, it turns into an 'illusion.' In countries, having several crores of people, there cannot be 'rule by the whole people.' Any self-government by them is impossible. If a few are to be governor, and the rest are governed, then the aspect of 'equality' suffers. If self-government is extensive, it cannot be intensive, and *vice versa*. Excessive democracy ultimately tends to kill itself. Power to all means power to none, or some charismatic leader (later dictator) would take over, leading it to dictatorial form of government.

In reality, the people themselves do not rule. They do condition the democratic system or create environment for it. The people elect, influence and control the group of governors. This group is often a political party or some parties. There are many such groups or parties. Thus, democracy, instead of being a self-government, is a polyarchy. A political party selects its leaders. But the people select political party or parties to govern. This selection is an election by the people. It has to be done in a fair, free and independent manner. In practice, democracy is the government only by and of the people. In democracy, power remains with 'active demos,' who actually are minorities or small groups. Their dominance in this system is treated as 'democratic' because entry in them is 'open' or un-restricted. All are free to participate or not to participate. None is coerced for doing so. Therefore, only active citizens have power in democracy. Democracy is rule of the leading elite: or leading minorities. This is the reality of democracy. However, the use of the word 'democracy' must be retained as it represents an ideal or a set of popular aspirations. It opposes the very idea that democratic government can ever be the rule of one person or group. The role of the elite does not suggest any imperfection of democracy. It is the core of the democratic system. Governance is the business of competent leaders. The people exercise their right to govern only at elections. Danger to democracy emanates not from the existence of leaders but from the absence of leadership. In that case masses would be exploited by anti-democratic counter-elites. Leaders also educate public opinion. Sartori says that, 'Actually, I am taking sides for, but against the inconsistency of the many who refuse with one hand what they demand with the other, who refuse the means and yet want the ends.'[2]

4. *Pluralist democracy* appears in two forms: (i) the elitist-democratic, and (ii) the group theories. The former regards, on lines of Karl Mannheim and Raymond Aron, plurality of the elites as the foundation of modern liberal democracy. The latter finds democracy as a process of bargaining among autonomous groups. These groups form the character of the polity pluralistic. A.F. Bentley (*The Process of Government*, 1908) and David Truman (*The Governmental Process*, 1951) find the game of democracy played by a great variety of groups. The task of government is to make policies which reflect the highest common group demand. It is the focal point for public pressure groups. A democratic society is a pluralist or differentiated society. The management of public affairs is shared by a number of groups. Robert A. Dahl (*A Preface to Democratic Theory*, 1956) developed a model of *polyarchy*. It is similar to the models of Bentley, Truman and Latham (*The Group Basis of Politics*, 1952). Their analysis of the nature of democratic society is pluralistic. It is done in the sociological sense. It is sociological explanation of the political process. They find it as different from the elitists in that the bargaining process among the relatively autonomous groups is highly decentralised. There is interaction among all such groups in claiming upon or showing interest in a particular issue. A group will get its way on the basis of its strength and the intensity of participation.[3]

The pluralist theory stands apart from the liberal theory as well as the elitist theory. In it law and policy making is the product of group interaction. It does away with the role of the representatives or a coherent majority or of the autonomous and unrepresentative elite. In this way the form of government becomes redundant. Public policy reflects only the interests of the more organised and vocal groups. Interests of producers dominate over the interests of consumers. The former are usually more organised than the latter. The pluralists repudiate the authoritarian basis of policy-making in a democracy. However, both elitist and pluralist theories favour maintenance of the status quo. They justify the phenomenon of domination either on grounds of certain outstanding inborn qualities of persons or on better organisation of certain interests.[4]

5. *Participatory democracy* maintains that the ultimate authority of governance rests with the people themselves. Bachrach, Bay, Hayden, Lynd, Kariel, Kenniston, Pateman and others stand for it.[5] In representative democracy people become inactive and passive after electing their representatives. In big countries, democracy expands geographically. Distance between the people and their representatives widens. Few citizens are able to contact with their representatives. According to the elitist theorists citizen participation is not a necessary condition of democracy. Citizens only vote for their leaders at the time of periodic elections. Polyarchy of Robert Dahl reconciles democracy with a low level of citizen participation. Both Schumpeter and Dahl treat democracy as a mechanism to maintain equilibrium. They consider it as a competition between two or more elite groups for gaining power. They desire only a low level of citizen participation. Participatory theory regards political participation as the basic principle of democracy. Individuals and groups actively take part in the governmental processes affecting their lives. They play an active role in the process of formulation and implementation of policies and decisions. Political participation includes voting, contesting elections, campaigning, canvassing, celebrating national festivals and functions and the like. Political participation also includes opposition – signing petitions, peaceful demonstrations, organising protest marches, passive resistance, *satyagraha* and the like. Jean Jacques Rousseau (*The Social Contract*, 1762) was pioneer of participatory democracy. He claimed that sovereignty originates in the people. It is retained by them even after the transition from the state of nature to civil society. It can neither be represented nor alienated. Representatives are mere agents of the people. Government is only an instrument to execute the instructions of the general will. The latter is the real will of all members of a community. It reflects the true interest of each individual as well as the common interest of the whole community. The people constantly deliberate on public issues and issue instructions to the government. The government cannot depart from these instructions. If it fails to implement, it can be revoked and replaced forthwith by another set of executives.

Presently, the people have little knowledge and understanding of political problems. Majority of them do not vote and do not discuss. Representatives avoid public accountability. There is rampant corruption and abuse of power. Political participation can remove most of these problems. This can be realised through a decentralisation of administration, b. use of referendum on a wider scale. In this manner, it can prove useful on (i) instrumental, (ii) educational, and, (iii) communitarian grounds. Many socialist countries had also adopted political participation as a counter-measure to elitism and dominance of capitalism. They call their governments as 'people's democracy' or 'people's democratic republic'. But in practice, their attempts merely hide reality. In fact, advocates of participatory democracy are overoptimistic. Excessive political participation may prove harmful. Ordinary people cannot make correct assessment of the situation and concerning issues. They may exaggerate their grievances and demands and resort to streets demonstrations, indiscipline and anarchy.

6. *Marxian democracy* stands on totally different grounds. Marx found matter, productive forces, or modes of production as the basic material. His materialism is scientific and dynamic which grants no place to soul, God or Creator. It is matter-in-motion that operates in a dialectical process – thesis, anti-thesis and synthesis. Modes of production or social existence makes up the basic economic structure, the rest is the political superstructure. Political power or state is a handmaid of economic power. In order to derive legitimacy, political institutions of liberal democracy elections, voting etc. pay only lip-service to the principle of 'sovereignty of the people'. Representative institutions, equal political rights etc. are only ideological misconceptions. Liberal democracy grants only formal equality. The workers who have right to vote with other dominant classes are led to believe that they have an equal share in governance. This type of political system simply lends legitimacy to the prevailing property relations. Liberal institutions do not provide an effective mechanism for transforming the property relations to serve the common interests, particularly, of the workers. Marxian democracy stands for a violent revolution by forcibly taking over the means of production through organisation of workers. It establishes the dictatorship of the proletariat. It implies a stage where there is complete 'socialisation of the major means of production', and planning of all the material production to serve the social needs, and grant rights to work, education, health and housing for the masses. There is fuller development of science and technology to multiply material production to realise greater social satisfaction. The dictatorship of the proletariat is 'concrete democracy'. It is coercive power of the majority over the minority. Exercise of domination and coercion is necessary to contain the forces of capitalism and of counter-revolution. Lenin called it 'democratic decentralisation'.[6] This democratic dictatorship was to remain in force for a transitional period. All property or the means of production will be socially owned. Along with classes, the state would gradually wither away. The power of the state will be 'transformed into simple administrative functions' (Karl Marx: *Capital*, Vol. 3).

It will be "people's democracy" and a classless society. The state will represent uniform interests of all the workers. Marx anticipated that bourgeois democracy would be replace by 'commune system'. In communes, the members own everything in common, including the product of their labour. They would manage their own affairs, elect their delegates for the larger administrative units. The larger units would elect their delegates for the still larger administrative areas, such as, national administration. This system is described as 'pyramidal structure of direct democracy'. All delegates would be bound by the instructions given by their electorates or their committees. In case of violation, they would be removed or recalled. Both Soviet Union (1917) and China (1949) tried this model in their own ways but failed miserably. In fact, in the usage of "people's democracy", the term "people's" is tautological, because democracy means 'the rule of the people'. However, Marxian democracy rules out the existence of democracy itself. It does not include middle and upper classes. It is committed to a particular set of interests. After the ushering of the 'communist' revolution, social conflicts do not end as was witnessed in Soviet Russia and China. Still competition for power, sharp political rivalries and suppression of political opponents broke out. Abolition of classes was negated by occupational grading forming a ruthless pyramid of power. Antonio Gramsci (*Prison Notebooks*) has pointed out that the ruling class in capitalist society now rules not only by force, but also through the consent of the ruled and derives its legitimacy from the cultural and intellectual orientations of the people. The dominant economic class does not exercise its coercive power through the state and governmental apparatus alone.

7. *Gandhian democracy* claims to be the best of all democracies. Whereas all other democracies stand only for welfare relating to this world, it caters to the needs of man living here and hereafter. It means man at all levels, local, regional, national and global, and in all matters, moral, social, personal, religious, economic and political. All it does on the basis of its metaphysical and religious ethos. Accordingly, there is all-pervading Reality of God or Truth. Spiritual freedom finds God or Truth everywhere. The Gandhians ask human beings to look beyond, and rise above temporal present. The goal of life is realisation of 'moksha' or God. This can be attained through faith, meditation, prayers, ascetic life, good will and self-suffering. One has to live by doing disinterested performance of duties and obligations. As God is everywhere and in all living beings there is no room for violence anywhere and in any form. Practice of non-violence, being related to faith in God, generates power. There is power of creed-based non-violence which they regard it as invincible and unfailing. Another is power of policy or expediency based non-violence. If one is not able to obtain first form, as Gandhi himself could not, they would like to employ the second form. It emerges out of organisation, discipline, demands and vast number of protesting satyagrahis. The Gandhians claim to bring about any political, social, economic and moral change by using power of non-violence.

Both of them are ultimately based on self-suffering. But their goal remains the same: realisation of 'moksha' or God. According to them, if that goal is adopted by men, women and communities world over, there would not be any cut throat competition, conflict, hatred, war and violence.

They believe in freedom of soul, and want to fight against all forms of authoritarianism, coercion and violence. To obtain this goal they adopt means and methods of satyagraha. To them only the individual has soul. The state has no soul. Individual is at the root of all progress. Individual, State and society are separate. For men of non-violence, there is no need of sate. Till the individuals reach that ideal stage or 'Ram Rajya', they are not in favour of eliminating the state. Presently, state and political power both are necessary. However, the scope of state activities could gradually be reduced to minimum. In the Gandhian state, everybody is to have 'swaraj' that is to be his own ruler. There would be no need of army, navy, air force, police, courts and laws. It would be a democracy based on non-violence.

They would launch election and representative system on the basis of unanimity and consent. The candidates contesting elections must be unselfish, able, and have self-control. They oppose Western form of parliamentary democracy and repose their faith in statements of the *Hind Swaraj*. The basis of right to vote must be physical labour, and not the possession of property or social status. The Gandhians, preferring 'Gram Swaraj' want to conduct all social construction and welfare activities on voluntary basis.

They want to restructure the present world order on principles of Gandhian economy, such as, (a) non-possessions; (b) opposition to industrialisation; (c) support to cottage and rural industries; (d) trusteeship and personal property for moral upliftment and ending economic exploitation; and (e) class co-operation. They say adoption of these principles would lead to solution of all current problems. They are totally against the prevailing global economic order.

Their ethos of religion usher a new social revolution. They adoption does not permit any kind of racialism, casteism, gender discrimination, untouchability etc. They Gandhians propose to take up many programmes of uplift, social reform and reconstruction as part of their treading on the path of dispassionate performance of duties to realise goal of attaining 'moksha'.

8. *Radical democracy* has been advocated by C.B. Macpherson (1911-87) in his *Democratic Theory: Essays in Retrieval*, 1973. In 1966 (*The Real World of Democracy*) he made clear that only universal suffrage, plurality of political parties and civil liberties do make democracy. Democracy can be existing even when there is intraparty democracy and an open bureaucratic system. Prevalence of mass-enthusiasm in developing countries also makes them democratic. For the classical theorists democracy was founded upon moral foundations to emancipate humanity. For the elitist-plural theorists it was a mechanism to maintain market equilibrium. Radical democracy wants to emancipate human beings from the constraints of prevailing competitive capitalist order. It believes in 'creative freedom'.

Western democratic theory operates on (a) the principle of utility-maximisation, and (b) the principle of power-maximisation advocated respectively by Bentham and J.S. Mill. In the latter sense, man is a doer and creator as well. However, Macpherson makes a distinction between two types of power: developmental power and extractive power. First is man's ability to use his own capacities creatively to realise his own goals, and, the second is his power over others to extract benefit for himself. In capitalism non-owners of property enjoy negligible amount of developmental power. Extractive power remains the sole preserve of the owners of land and capital. In a simple exchange economy an individual is the owner of the means of production as well as the means of labour. In capitalist economy the means of labour are detached from the means of production. Labour is regarded as a commodity which can be bought and sold in an open market. The means of production are owned by the capitalists. They operate them solely for earning profit, having no regard for human values. They indulge in possessive individualism.

9. *Cosmopolitan democracy:* There is rise of the new elites in the global order. These elites include experts and specialists, senior administrative personnel, and transnational business executives, politicians and intellectuals. They constitute a distinct minority whom Held calls 'cosmopolitans'.[7] According to Held, unlike political nationalism, cosmopolitanism registers and reflects the multiplicity of issues, questions, processes and problems that affect and bind people together, irrespective of where they were born or reside. Cosmopolitanism discloses the cultural, legal and ethical basis of political order in a world where political communities and states matter, but not only and exclusively. But cosmopolitanism is multidimensional.[8] Cosmopolitanism grows on three principles: one, the ultimate units of moral concern are individual human beings, not state or collectivities; two, individuals carry the status of equal worth with reciprocal recognition; and, three, each person enjoys impartial treatment of their claims. Cosmopolitanism endures only when it leads to a cosmopolitan democracy. Held stands for cosmopolitan democracy at global level.

For the first time its principles found expression in the legal and institutional initiatives taken after World War II. These can be seen in the UN Declaration of Human Rights and the subsequent 1966 Covenants of Rights.[9] Acceptance of the equal worth of all human beings is found in the laws of war and weapons diffusion.[10] Recognition of democracy is found in the International Bill of Human Rights, new codes of conduct for IGOs and INGOs and the many other regional treaties. Existing international laws generate a new structure of cosmopolitan accountability and regulation. The 'sovereign rights of states' are affirmed alongside more and more cosmopolitan leanings.

All this is proposed to be done by transforming a club-driven and executive-led multilateralism to a more transparent, accountable and just form of governance. Held calls it as 'cosmopolitan multilateralism'.[11]

The proposed cosmopolitan polity would have a division of powers and competences at various levels of political action and interconnectedness. It would embrace diverse and distinct domains of authority, linked reciprocally in both vertical and horizontal manners. States and agencies would be committed to cosmopolitan principles and rules. The UN system has to live up to the UN Charter. This would ensure enforcement of prohibition on the discretionary right of states to use force. There must be a basis for the UN system to generate political resources of its own with an autonomous decision-making centre.

Cosmopolitanism involves the development of administrative capacity and independent political resources at regional and global levels as a necessary complement to those in local and national polities. Therefore, it has to create, on lines given below, an effective, and accountable administrative, legislative and executive capacity both at regional and global levels:

(a) Creation of regional parliaments and governance structures to meet with problems and challenges which states alone cannot resolve;
(b) Establishment of an authoritative assembly of all democratic states and agencies as a reformed General Assembly of the United Nations or stand as a complement to it. It would work out rules, standards and institutions to realise cosmopolitan values and priorities;[12]
(c) Opening of important international organisations to public examination and agenda setting. They would be open and accessible to public scrutiny;
(d) Arrangement of general referenda concerning contested cosmopolitan priorities and their implementation. There can be many kinds of referenda involving a cross-section of the public, and of targeted groups in particular policy areas; and
(e) Development of a cosmopolitan law-enforcement and coercive capability, including peacekeeping as well as peacemaking. There would be provisional deputation of a proportion of a nation-state's military to the new regional or global authorities. These authorities could also establish a permanent independent force recruited directly from among individuals belonging to all countries. The use of force would always be the last resort.[13] A cosmopolitan polity does not call for a diminution *per se* of state power and capacity across the globe. It wants to develop new institutions as a necessary complement to those at the level of the state.

10. *Teledemocracy:* 'Teledemocracy' (literally "democracy at a distance"), is attracting a lot of attention of the democratic elite. It makes use of new communications technologies. Its advocates and contends that innovative forms of electronic discourse can remedy many of the shortcomings of representative democracy of contemporary mass society. The prevailing form of deliberative democracy is mainly founded on the principles of reasoned dialogue and deliberation. The rationale for teledemocracy is consistent with an approach to political theory variously

termed as "rational choice", "negative liberalism", or "the logic of collective action". It is founded on a marketplace conception of the political world in which interests conflict and compete. By contrast, deliberative democracy is rooted in the ideal of self-governance in which political truths emerge not from the clash of preestablished interests and preferences but from reasoned discussion about issues involving the common good.[14] This model is known as "collective rationality", "unitary democracy", or simply "deliberative democracy".

Political thinkers, dating back to ancient Athens, have stressed the importance of public discourse and debate. In the fourth century BC, Pericles, the orator and statesman recognised discussion among the citizens of the *polis* as an "indispensable preliminary" to political action. In the *Nicomachean Ethics*, Aristotle articulated an extensive philosophical rationale for the importance of this process, noting that "the art of legislation" was impossible without reasoned dialogue and deliberation. Modern philosophers, such as Jean-Jacques Rousseau and John Stuart Mill, have reflected on the importance of public discourse. Rousseau deemed it essential to the formation of a "general will". In his work *On Liberty*, Mill outlined a philosophical rationale for something he called "government by discussion." The US Supreme Court Justice, Louis D. Brandeis also observed,

> Those who won our independence believed that the final end of the state was to make men free to develop their faculties; and that in its government the deliberative forces should prevail over the arbitrary .... They believed that ... the greatest menace to freedom is an inert people; that public discussion is a political duty; and that this should be a fundamental principle of American government.

The advent of new technologies such as the telephone, mobile, radio, and television, has radically changed the nature of public discourse in the twentieth and present century. Today political communication has mutated into something the ancient, and even, modern scholars, could scarcely have foreseen. The voluntary associations, public spaces, local newspapers, and neighbourhood assemblies of their day have given way to computer bulletin boards, satellite television, tele-conference and radio call-in programmes.

Kinds of Democracy

From the point of view of formation of government, democracy is of two kinds:

(i) Pure or direct democracy.
(ii) Representative or indirect democracy.

In direct democracy all adult population, remaining present in the form of assembly, takes part in decision-making and exercise of power. It does not delegate its powers to any other person or representatives. Ancient Greek city-states had direct democracy. In modern times, only some cantons of Switzerland have such direct popular assembly, known as *Landsgemiende*.

Still some devices of direct democracy are available: (1) Referendum, meaning referring some important issue, policy or decision to the people, such as, amendment of the constitution. Rendering opinion by the people can be (i) compulsory, or (ii) voluntary. (2) Initiative implying that the people or a certain portion of the citizenry can take initiative to get certain law of its choice passed. They can send the proposal to the legislature which may enact it on usual lines. (3) Recall. By this device, the people of a constituency, by their majority can ask the legislature to send back their representative, and, thus, cancel his membership. Many states of the United States empower their people to do so. (4) Plebiscite indicates that the people are directly consulted on questions of political importance. In 1935, the people of Saar were asked to express their opinion whether they wanted to remain in Germany or not. The people of Junagarh (Saurashtra-Gujarat) were asked to give opinion whether they wanted to remain in India or in Pakistan.

Indirect democracy: It is also called representative democracy. In this form of democracy, people instead of directly taking any part in government, do so by and through their elected representatives. Crores of people of a country cannot assemble at one place and discuss matters and make law. Now all adults elect their representatives at regular intervals. Indirect democracy too has many forms: (i) Parliamentary or Cabinet Form; (ii) Presidential Form; (iii) Unitary Form, and (iv) Federal Form. There are many mixed forms of indirect democracy.

Necessary Conditions for the Success of Democracy

Everywhere democracy does not succeed. To make it a success, certain conditions are necessary.[15] In the absence of these conditions, democracy may not survive as it happened in many developing countries, e.g., Egypt, Iraq, Pakistan, Burma (Myanmar), Afghanistan etc. These are:

(a) The people should have faith in democracy that it can deliver goods to the people.
(b) Vigilance is the price of democracy. The people should remain 'watch dogs' and aware that it is not misused by corrupt politicians, mafia or bureaucrats. They should not remain passive, and fiercely criticise injustice and mismanagement, thinking themselves to be 'masters,' not slaves.
(c) Democracy needs ideal citizens, having virtues, civic sense, morality and spirit of sacrifice. The dying speech of Lord Buddha's to Anand reflect the importance of such virtues.

(d) The people are to have education so that they may know their rights and duties. Education can enable citizens to be good law-makers and administrators, and also compel the rulers to act honestly.

(e) Social and economic equality is basic to political, democracy. There should be no discrimination based on caste, sex, language, region, sect or status. Communalism in all its forms is enemy of democracy.

(f) Effective public opinion is the base as well as guide to democracy. The media should be free and fearless. Its role must be constructive. Yellow journalism, control of money-bags and permissiveness must be avoided.

(g) No democracy can survive unless the people put their country over and above everything – party, religion, language etc. They must be imbued with a sense of national and emotional integration. It would free them from all kinds of parochialism and age-long loyalties.

(h) Political parties are considered 'invisible government' by Finer. They are lifeblood of democracy. Their organisation, goals and functions must be people-oriented. Only lawful means should be adopted by them.

(i) Spirit of toleration is a part of the democratic culture. Majority and minority must be fluid, based on opinion, and not on ethnicity, caste, religion or language. A minority has right to become majority, therefore the latter has no right to eliminate the minorities.

(j) Organisation of government has to be based on constitution. It should have provisions for strong, and responsible executive, separation of powers, independence of judiciary, decentralisation etc. Its basic structure must not be easily amendable.

(k) Rule of law has now been accepted as the basis of democracy. It connotes government of law, not of man. All should be treated equal before law.

(l) Local Government like corporations, municipalities, *panchayats* etc. are regarded as primary schools or training grounds of democracy. These encourage public awareness and create a sense of responsibility towards public functions. Alfred Smith has rightly observed that, "All the ills of democracy can be cured by more democracy." It means there should be decentralisation of power to the largest possible extent.

(m) Atmosphere of freedom makes democracy a success. Press and platform are to remain free. The government has to operate strictly within limits.

Vitals of Democracy

Democracy promotes patriotism, a deep and abiding sense of love for the country. Order and peace go together. It strives for welfare of the people. It has to operate according to the public opinion and honour the pledges or oaths made to them.

Democracy being based on general will or public opinion is the best form of government. It operates on the consent of the governed. It is a value-based government. These values are widely accepted, such as, liberty, equality and fraternity. "In a complete democracy no one can, complain that he has not a chance to be heard" (Lowell). A democratic government exists for the individual, not the individual for it. Only democracy ensures intellectual, moral and personal development of man. Every citizen feels himself sovereign. He is an end in himself. The Rigveda declares 'Yatemahi Swarajye' (5/66/6): We strive for self-rule.

The goal of democracy is welfare of the people. It ensures it without any discrimination. It exists for the greatest happiness of the largest number. Democratic government imparts political education to its citizens. They learn toleration, dutifulness, mutual sympathy, and confidence, generosity etc. by participation in public affairs. C.D. Burns has stated that, "A government is a method of education, but the best education is self-education. Therefore, the best government is self-government which is democracy."

Elections, press, media, public discussion etc. "encourage intelligence, self-reliance, initiative and social sense of freemen by placing the ultimate responsibility for government on the citizens themselves" (Appadorai). It produces the best type of citizens, owing to freedom and spirit of competition. Garner finds increase of efficiency in democracy because of popular election, popular control and popular responsibility. People or their representatives themselves run the government. Democracy infuses love for one's country and prepares himself for making sacrifice to any extent. In such governments, "Popular election, popular control and popular responsibility are more likely to ensure a greater degree of efficiency than any other system of government" (Garner).

Democracy produces popular and stable government. There are elections after fixed intervals. People bring about government of their choice. Such government "is not likely to be revolutionary" (Gilchrist). "The whole people or some numerous portion of them, exercise governing power through deputies periodically elected by themselves" (J.S. Mill). Rules are changed without making use of violent and revolutionary methods. People wait till next elections.

Limitations of Democracy

Admirers and critics of democracy have always been numerous. Plato, Aristotle and others considered it as a "perverted form" of government. Others have called it as 'mobocracy', 'drunken clown', an aristocracy of blackguards' (Tallyrand) etc.

H.G. Wells, Henry Maine etc. have found in democracy *a cult of incompetence and ignorance*. According to Lecky, "it is the government by the poorest, the most ignorant, the most incapable, who are necessarily the most numerous." Such people, on the one hand, do not understand the nature of public affairs, on the other hand, they elect their representatives, not on the basis of merit, but for number. Hartman is right when he says that it is "the paradise of the striker, babbler, word-spinner, flatterer, and tuft hunter". It is a rule of the demagogues.

A few scholars have regarded political parties as bane, not boon of democracy. They encourage hollowness and insincerity, create cleavages in the life of the nation, debase normal standards, and distribute the spoils (*Bryce*). They investigate people by spreading hatred, communalism, and parochialism. The whole system is the government by the inexperienced people. It is a government by the majority which may be of 51 per cent only. It tends to trample over the minority rights. Freedom of individual is lost before the brute majority. Freedom, in fact, is strangulated.

A probe would expose the *myth* that there is rule of majority in democracy. All voters never cast their votes. Owing to multiparty system, a small minority of voters elects the representatives. Leaders elected by say 10 or 20 per cent of voters rule over the country in the name of democracy. Again, half of the representatives sit in opposition. Often class-conflict and class-struggle are encouraged. The moneybags often buy the voters, representatives, bureaucrats and ministers. It is ironically said that democracy is the government **off** the people, by **buying** the people, and remains **far** from the people.

Lecky and Maine find it as enemy of culture, civilisation and science. The majority, favouring the status quo and backward looking, would hardly have allowed progress of mankind, "The thrashing machine, the powerloom, the spinning jenny and possibly the steam engine would have been prohibited." Power actually remains with a disorderly crowd. Hardly anyone feels responsibility. Irresponsibility prevails over.

Democracy suffers from hollow idealism. Equality and liberty both are missing. It is difficult to bring out any major socio-economic change. Number rules, not merit. Merit quality, efficiently and ability find no place. Mediocrity prevails over. Masses have a tendency to worship demagogues as their heros. For example, Hitler in Germany, and Napolean in France rose to power by demagogy.

Democracy is the most expensive form of government. Regular and irregular elections at many levels, prolonged and futile discussions and debates, constitution of several committees, salaries, allowances and pensions of the representatives etc. cause heavy burden to tax payers. It inclines to kill truth, integrity, allegiance etc. and tends to indulge in falsehood, abuse, rumour-mongering, horse-trading, deceit etc. The voice of the majority usurps the office of morality. In fact the very principle of equality is unacceptable. As men are not equal, but unequal, therefore, should be treated accordingly. The one man one vote principle puts merit and mediocrity, the honest and the corrupt, the good and the evil at par.

Often democracy is the rule of the rich or plutocracy. The rich spend money and purchase everything. Money manages to purchase power in democracy. Politics instead of service, turns into profession, trade and investment. There is no way to reduce huge and unnecessary expenses. Integrity, efficiency, skill, ability, honesty and other human values are at stake. Only number counts. Political parities kill individual freedom and right to dissent. Instead of political parties, they are in fact colluding groups under false ideologies and slogans. They disturb social peace and harmony. Their sole aim is to capture power by hook or crook, and often resort to *gherao, bandh, dharma,* fasting, street fighting, arson, murder and terrorism in various forms.

Renovation of Political Democracy

It has been rightly observed that nation-states of the twenty-first century, owing to the prevalence of Liberalisation, Privatisation and Globalisation (LPG), are fast passing from transitia to industria and post-industria. But the most of the political institutions, structures and theories are built upon the experiences of nineteenth and mid-twentieth centuries. All political institutions and systems have grown out-of-date and wasteful. The old pattern of political leadership, which were attractive and useful in the past, are proving a failure to understand and solve the problems of the twenty-first century. Many of the political leaders do have control over nuclear weapons supersonic warplanes, super-computers and the fastest means of transportation and communication. But they too stop and wait for at several levels and seek divergent consultation from different leaders. There is little room for unity of command, hierarchy, authoritarianism or monopoly. Neither a saint nor a hero or a supremo works. The leader is confined to the boundaries of nation-state. National economies are becoming part and parcel of world-economy. It is beyond the control of any one particular nation to solve the problems of inflation, shortage of petrol, nuclear waste, environmental degradation, global warming and the like. Ambit and knowledge of these problems are indivisible but governments, their ministries, departments and corporate bodies operate in a divided, split and competitive manner. Till prime ministers and presidents through their inter-departmental bodies arrive at decisions, it is often too late in dealing with the problems, which demand immediate attention and decision. The procedures are old and out-of-date. Change is so fast that the leaders and governments are taken aback.[16] Even within a single constituency, it is difficult to deal with different groups, local leaders and varying patterns of problems. Making of rules, sub-rules, issuing immediate order, staging flag-march, imposition of 144 under Cr.P.C., distribution of loans and other concessions do not work.

In fact, legislatures in general have turned useless, incapacitated, delaying, war-mongering and helpless. They are hardly built up on the majority of electorate. The majority is a misnomer as it carries only 25 to 30 per cent voters with it. In the absence of a full and adequate discussion, they operate through committees and sub-committees. A large part of budget is passed without any discussion. Government may be of any political party, or a coalition or a national one, plight of the people continues. Bureaucrats go on taking decisions and action in their own apathetic manner. Legislatures are losing legitimacy or people's faith in them. Groups and organisations bank upon their own armies, security arrangements, monetary resources and private connections with the high ups.

People at large, are so past-oriented that they do not like any change or reform in their constitution, governmental structures and working procedures. Their leaders appear ready to commit *harakiri*. All appear ready to stick to the status quo. Their past decides the formation of their present as well as future. Most people worship their leaders on the basis of their past acts and expect them to repeat them in identical manner, forgetting that by now they have turned out-of-date, anachronistic, corrupt, inefficient and untrustworthy.[17]

Democracies should now venture to renovate themselves. It should learn to operate in the context of IT revolution, global village, and emergence of post-industrial societies, mass automation, nuclear families, concentration of wealth, energy and power. Man's ideas on time, space, reason and causality have basically changed. Economics and morality have joined hands. This is a quantum jump in History.[18] Workers, consumers and citizens are crying for direct participation. They want on spot and at once decisions leading to more and more decentralisation and devolution of power. The world is adopting the culture of electronics, computers, internet, e-commerce, and highly efficient calculators. Progress of technology has crossed all limits creating wonders of genetic engineering and parenthood. Ethnicity and fanaticism would become a thing of the past. World Bank, IMF, WTO and ADB have taken over state-market and other local economies. Computer-conferencing, mobiles, video screens, fax etc. have reduced distances of time, place and direct contact.

The basic unit of democracy, the man or individual is now living in a totally new environment. Meaning of child, young, adult, old and woman is changing. Individual requires more respect, multi-centric attention, privacy and special care. Hardly anyone wants old, anachronistic, chaotic and time and energy consuming representative institutions. Most of the legislators are ignorant, selfish, inefficient, corrupt and money spent on them is a waste. They hardly get any majority over any particular issue. All governments are in practice minority governments. People have lost respect for them. Society now, is made of innumerable interest groups. These groups meet in changing size, manner and style. So should the legislatures be constituted accordingly. Leaders and representatives should be selected, nominated and elected on different grounds and for different purposes. Now governance would be 'a minority based twenty-first century democracy'.[19]

New political set-up of democracy has to evolve hundreds of instrumental bodies to bring about constant contact and links of negotiation between the rulers and the ruled. Through them the people can easily share responsibility of governance – executive, legislative and judicial. People, including their different groups formed on the basis of varying interests, have a right to send their deputies to the legislature. This can be done on a short-term basis and for specific purposes. Present representative governments or their legislature have to be replaced by direct contact, consultation or opinion of the voters through mobile or fixed phones, thus, making it a 'direct democracy'. This would reduce arrogance of political leaders, party bosses, ministers and senior bureaucrats. Democratic government would operate at several levels further divided segmentally, horizontally and vertically. They would have to constitute new institutions to become part of transnational, interstate and global systems. Growth of multinational corporations (MNCs) has taken place everywhere. Hardly would there remain any important matters lying with the states to deal within their exclusive sovereign areas. All their leaders would have to be adept in the use of information technologies.

Global Democracy

Globalisation has set people to think afresh about the political institutions, such as, state, democracy and civil society. David Held, in search of a supra-national democracy at global level, observes it as a new international order involving the emergence of a global economic system which stretches beyond the control of a single state (even of dominant states); the expansion of network of transnational linkages and communications over the particular states have little influence; the enormous growth in international organisations which can limit the scope for action of most powerful states; the development of a global military order, which can reduce the range of policies available to governments and their citizens. One can witness a crisis of global civilisation. It involves a counterrevolution of the powerful against the weak. In much of the Third World the processes of urbanisation and economic decline have gone with social chaos, anomie and nihilism.

With the weakening of inter-state borders, threats to environment are increasing. With the resistance of US and Australia and indifference of Russia and China towards Kyoto Protocol (to enforce emission norms for prevention of green house effect) and Copenhagen Protocol (to ensure ozone layer protection from chloro-fluoro carbons), the ecosystem is under grave threat. Globalisation has led to a new world trade market in environmental waste. The state finds it difficult to balance the trade-off between economic growth and environment preservation. Its leaders in theory are accountable to the governed, in practice, they are accountable to market forces, most notably debt structures and structural adjustment programmes. Their major problem is how to make economic revitalisation compatible with democratisation. The international funding institutions such as the World Bank, the IMF and the ADB pressurise the recipient countries for removal of subsidies even on essential sectors like health, education, water, irrigation, agriculture, electricity and free use of public infrastructure such as roads. There is the question of quality versus quantity. The fundamental challenge of globalisation to the state and governance is to become accountable and responsible to the ruled and also to the global institutions.

Democratic Vision for the Twenty-First Century

Outlining deficiencies of Hyperglobalist (Kenichi Ohmae, Fukuda Parr, Kaplinsky etc.) and Sceptics' (Hirst and Thompson, Ruigrok and Tulder, de Soto, Leys etc.) theories, Held et al. have proposed an advanced theory of Political Globalisation. Propounding 'transformational' theory, Held believes in the emergence of a world government.[20] As the new global order has apparently escaped the control of democratic institutions located at the national level, the 'democracy has to become a transnational affair'. He suggests that strategic priority must be given to the key groups, agencies, associations and organisations of international civil society. Their capacity as agencies of democratic control must be extended through an appropriate recasting of territorial boundaries of systems of accountability, representation and regulation and fortified by entrenched transnational bill of social, economic and civil rights.[21]

Problem of Terrorism

It may be stated for the democrats that faith in liberalism or human rights or democracy is important but much more necessary for them is to have a plan of action to deal with fundamentalism of the Islamic world. Democracies should have the ability to encounter all brands of non-democratic ideologies. But it is not clear how would they like to deal with them. As far as terrorism is concerned, for their own survival they may have to prepare themselves in advance of its lethal attacks. In a democracy, there is the rule of majority, which has to uphold fundamental rights of citizens given in a particular constitution. Minorities are to be given proper respect and share in governance. Minority of today can become majority tomorrow. But the question arises: What type of minority is to be respected and given a share in power? If a minority or a substantial part of it is committed permanently to an ideology, authority, *guru*, holy book etc. over and above the constitution, law, fundamental rights or basic structure of a polity, it is not a minority or a part of the polity. It is rather a group of anti-polity or anti-society people who cannot claim to be treated at par with other citizens. They cannot be considered as 'minority' in the normal sense of the term.

It may be suicidal to keep and treat that anti-social group at par with other citizens. If it is mistakenly done so or under some inside or outside pressure, that polity is likely to lose its unity and integrity. Persons belonging to that group at the most may be called as 'non-minority organisations'.

It may be pointed out that even law-abiding minorities, after some time owing to several reasons may go astray and adopt anti-polity identity. Terrorism also relates to poverty, illiteracy and backwardness of the people who are often made into tools for political use by their ruling elites. The ruling elite and the vested interests of these people do not, to make them tool, permit them to learn that there cannot be any covenant of God to particular people or community to kill or abuse. Such an assumption or belief, in fact, puts limitations on powers of the Almighty and makes Him biased. Even if there were commandments of God, they were addressed to specific people belonging to a particular time and place. In spite of these facts, if some of the followers of a particular religion commit acts of terrorism, they are nothing but criminals of the first order as they pretend to commit them in the name of God and His commandments. This makes fundamentalism related to religion or some Holy Books more dangerous than other forms of terrorism. A democracy, owing to their fanaticism, cannot deal with democratically. Only an army trained to fight with appropriate mind, means and weapons, against the terrorists, can overpower and eliminate them.

Citizens of a vibrant democracy can also prevent and eliminate occurrence of terrorism.

Notes

1. Macpherson, C.B. *The Life and Times of Liberal Democracy*, New York: Oxford University Press, 1977.
2. Sartori, Giovanni. *Democratic Theory*, 1958, 465.
3. Kann, Mark E. "A Standard for Democratic Leadership". *Polity*, Vol. xii, No. 2, Winter, 1979, 202-224.
4. Lijphart, Arend, *Democracy in Plural Societies: A Comparative Exploration*, New Haven: Yale University Press, 1977.
5. Cook. T. and Morgan, P. (eds.), *Participatory Democracy*, San Francisco: Canfield, 1971.
6. It implies, (a) that the membership of each body in the political hierarchy (whether of party or state) was to be decided by the vote of the lower body, and, (b) that although free discussion on policy matters was to be allowed at the initial stage, any decision reached by the highest body was to be imposed rigidly at all lower levels in the hierarchy. V.I. Lenin.
7. Held, David, ed. *Taming Globalization: Frontiers of Governance*, 166 and 173.
8. Held, David, *Democracy and the Global Order: From the Modern State to Cosmopolitan Governance*, Cambridge: Polity, 1995, chapter 10.
9. Infra, chapter 18.

10. See, the Nuremberg and Tokyo war crimes tribunals (1945-6, 1946-8), the Torture Convention (1984) and the statute of the International Criminal Court (1998).
11. Held, David, ed. *Taming Globalization: Frontiers of Governance,* 166 and 173.
12. It would be an outcome of a global constitutional convention involving states, regional organisations, IGOs, INGOs, eminent jurists, citizen groups and social movements.
13. Deployment of force would be justified only after all other forms of negotiation and sanction are exhausted.
14. Scott London, "Teledemocracy vs. Deliberative Democracy: A Comparative Look at Two Models of Public Talk", *Journal of Interpersonal Computing and Technology,* Vol. 3, No. 2, April 1995, pp. 33-55.
15. Pennock, op. cit. x-xxii.
16. Toffler, Alvin. *The Third Wave*, London: William Collins & Sons, 1980, 421-28.
17. Ibid., 411.
18. Ibid., 428.
19. Ibid., 431-40.
20. Bryane Michael has deconstructed Held et al. in his article, 'Theorising the Politics of Globalization: A Critique of Held et al. "Transformationalism", *Journal of Economics and Social Research*, 4(2), 3-17; Held, D., A. McGrew, D. Goldblatt, and J. Perraton, *Global Transformations: Politics, Economics and Culture*, 1999.
21. P. Radhakrishnan, A paper presented at the international conference on "Religion and Globalisation", held at Payap University, Thailand, from July 27 to August 2, 2003.

12

Political Ideologies and Political Cultures

POLITICAL IDEOLOGIES

Modern era still is an 'Age of Ideology'. Understanding of 'ideologies' is essential to know and assess the impact, behaviour, goals, means and activities of various political parties, events, inter-relations between states, groups and leaders. Mannheim calls this era as 'idea-struck age' or 'ideocracy'. People talk of 'end of ideology' but there is 're-ideologisation' also. The world today is a place of fast-changing ideologically. If we are to understand the modern world as we approach the twenty-first century, we must know something about the nature and influence of these ideologies.[1] Ideology is first of all concerned with values; that is, how we ought to treat each other and live together in society. Roucek observed: "Thought control is one of the most important weapons of modern declared and undeclared wars, and much is being said these days – and properly so – concerning the war of ideologies."[2] Ideological movements and social changes are closely related. Ideology is a value or belief system that is accepted as fact or truth by some group. It is composed of sets of attitudes toward the various institutions and processes of society. It provides the believer with a picture of the world both as it is and as it should be, and in doing so, it organises the tremendous complexity of the world into something fairly simple and understandable.[3]

Ideology: Conceptual Clarification

"Ideology is a disputed concept; its meaning is not transparent". (Gary K. Browning) It is used as a system of political, legal, ethical, religious and philosophical views and ideas. It can be a set of empirically derived scientific statements or a programme based on certain principles or goals, or a loose statement of certain ideas, goals and ends with means to realise them. An ideology is that set of ideas and beliefs which seeks to articulate the basic values of a group of people – what they cherish for themselves and for others. Ideologues are related to interests, but in a complex and uncertain manner. Ideologies demand partisanship, i.e., involvement in the struggle for power, and not mere commitment to the pursuit of ideas as an end in itself.[4]

The concept was first used in the 17th century by Destutt de Tracy (1754-1836) of France as 'ideologie' (*French*) or 'ideology' (*English*) which meant 'science of ideas.' Condillac defined it as 'study of ideas based on sensory experience'. Since then it has carried many meanings. Napolean and Jeremy Bentham used it in a pejorative sense and scoffed at it. German philosophers like Kant and Hegel used it in a broader philosophical sense as 'theory of knowledge'. Marx and Engels considered it as a by-product of false consciousness. For Minogue, it was an escape from the realities of practical life to imaginary utopias.[5]

In its neutral sense also there is no unanimity. Social scientists find it as 'a set of symbols' (Lasswell), 'crecenda and miranda' (Merriam), 'myth' (Sorel), 'political formula' (Mosca), 'derivations' (Pareto), 'a culture system' (Apter), etc.

R.M. McIver observes it as, "any scheme of thinking characteristic of a group or class". Dahl defines it as" a set of more or less persistent, integrated doctrines that purport to explain and justify leadership in the system". Louis Wirth appreciates it as "complexes of ideas which direct toward the maintenance of the existing order". Lymàn Tower Sargent examines it as "a value or belief system that is accepted as fact or truth by some groups". Meehan includes in the term:

(a) a pattern of belief relating to some particular aspects of social, political or economic life,
(b) a programme of action, and,
(c) element of irrationalism or absolute faith.

It is now used in a social-scientific sense. It refers to a more or less coherent set of ideas that provide the basis for some kind of organised political action. In this sense all ideologies (i) offer an account or critique of the existing order, usually in the form of a 'world view'; (ii) provide the model of a desired future, a vision of the 'good society'; and (iii) outline how political change can should be brought about. Ideologies thus straddle the conventional boundaries between descriptive and normative thought, and between theory and practice. In sum, it is a set of ideas which are adopted by a group to motivate it for the achievement of some predetermined goals.

In the tradition of Karl Mannheim, William Conolly has argued that it was time that ideology be neutrally defined and its applicability generalised to encompass all political interpretation, from radical polemics to orthodox and scientific treatises in Political Science.[6] He defines it as "a set of empirical claims not fully tested, and for practical purposes not fully testable, which functions both to orient political activity and to preserve from destruction of values and higher level beliefs cherished by its authors and supporters".[7]

Eugene J. Meehan deals with characteristics of ideology in his study of British foreign policy.[8] According to him, ideologies have direct and immediate relation to international affairs. They play a vital role in human behaviour of groups. Ideologies appear different from each other. Externally, they relate to the area of human behaviour, which they affect, demands made upon the supporters and complexity of doctrines. They depend on absolutes which often provide solutions to the insoluble. For this they restrict their discussions on the first principles. Each one of them passes through (a) initial statement of principles by the founder; (b) their elaboration by specific group of disciples, and (c) development of priesthood to apply them to all problems. The process of interpretation goes on constantly. Ideology turns important only when it becomes a social force carrying mass acceptance. Followers both support and control those who accept the ideology. There are three levels: (i) masses, (ii) secondary group consisting of individuals who accept the basic principles and programme of action, and (iii) concentration of authority in the hands of a relatively small number of persons. For seeking approval of the masses, level of complexity is lowered to a common denominator. To create 'we-feeling', there are simple answers and widespread use of symbols. Value judgements are not necessarily based on facts. Any means justifies the end when the end is an absolute postulated by the ideology.

According to Dahl, development of an ideology is an essential feature of all political systems. Leaders in them usually espouse a set of more or less persistent and integrated doctrines that purport to explain and justify their leadership in the system. They develop it to endow their leadership with legitimacy and convert their influence into authority. It is more economical to rule by means of authority than by means of coercion. The leaders usually espouse an ideology that justifies not only their own leadership but also the political system itself. An official or reigning ideology usually contains standards for appraising the organisation, policies and leaders of the system. It often gives an idealised description of the way in which the system actually works and should work. When a reigning ideology is widely accepted, its leaders would endanger their legitimacy if they violate its prescribed norms. Ideologies vary enormously from one system to another. Even when it is entirely integrated or internally consistent, it may not be necessarily static. New situations need new explanation and emphasis on newer goals. Sometimes unrelated and inconsistent elements creep in. Sometimes ambiguities may prove positive as they permit flexibility and change in the system. It is also a fact that even a reigning ideology is not

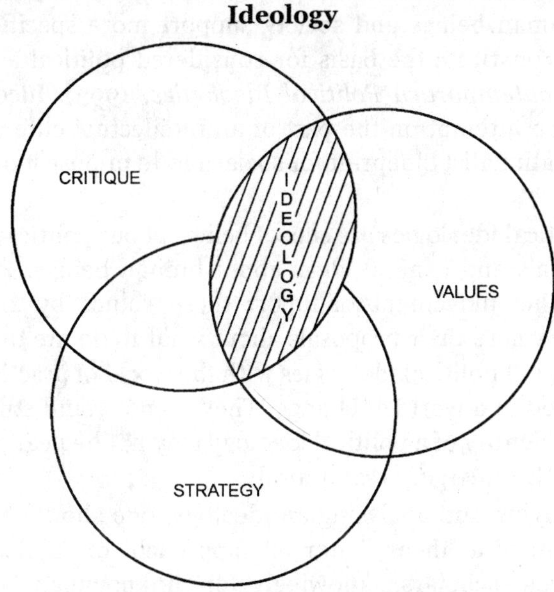

uniformly accepted by all members of an organisation. Most of its members have only the most rudimentary knowledge of the ruling ideology. Many others have their own private views. Some of its members may reject it or adhere to rival and conflicting ideologies and create a crisis of legitimacy. Ideologies have their rise and fall. A revolutionary or opposing ideology may emerge as reigning ideology after some years.

Contents of Political Ideology

During the Cold War period, it was viewed as an officially sanctioned belief system that claimed a monopoly of truth, making a spurious claim to be scientific. Conservative thinkers like Michael Oakeshott treat ideologies as elaborate systems of thought that orient politics towards abstract principles and goals and away from practical and historical circumstances.

William E. Connolly elaborates it as "a set of empirical claims not fully tested, and for practical purposes not fully testable, which functions both to orient political activity and to preserve from destruction, values and higher level beliefs cherished by its authors and supporters." Broadly, "it covers all intellectual positions, surrounding a subject, from the speculations of the crisis to the claims of practitioners' (Menaud). However, it may be made clear here that ideology is not philosophy, theory or approach. Still, today it encompasses a wide variety of thought. However, there are many approaches emphasising particular ideologies.[9] Political ideologies are seen as sets of political beliefs involving programmes of political action which draw large-scale views about human nature and/or historical development.

They represent frameworks of thought about politics in which large-scale ideas about human beings and society support more specific ideas about politics which constitute the basis for considered political action (Eatwell and Wright: *Contemporary Political Ideologies*, 1993). Ideologies essentially embody an attempt on the part of an intellectual elite to construct a dogmatic and rationalist blueprint for social and to impose it on the pluralist social life.[10]

Thus, political ideologies are sets of beliefs about politics incorporating specific proposals and general ideas about human beings. Political ideologies make value judgements, support these values by argument in a practical world where their proposals about what to do are taken seriously. The involvement of political ideologies with the world of practice means that they are involved in a world of change. They do not stand still, and change over time. The identity of a political ideology may not be near and timelessly tidy. It constantly undergoes reappraisal.

While studying and analysing an ideology, one should be careful that ideology is neither a 'theory,' nor an 'approach' or 'philosophy'. Often ideologues, even scholars, knowingly or unknowingly present their 'ideology' as though it were, both philosophy and theory. Held finds such cases as a 'political religion'. But it may be a mix of many things-rational as well as irrational. "The men of power abstract out of the books of political theory words and phrases, and use them in the defense of an actual set of political arrangements or to justify a call for political change." As this process takes place, however, the original theory ceases to be a theory. The abstracted portions are now an ideology which has been put to work for some practical purpose." (Andrew Hecker). When ideology is used to defend an existing system or to advocate a limited or a total change in that system, it becomes a part of politics. It lends legitimacy to the ruling class or may involve an urge for revolution. In many cases political ideologies are presented as political theories such as liberalism or socialism. But political ideology is closely related to politics while political theory involves a disinterested search for a better society. Its goals are under constant investigation and critical examination. Political Science calls for impartial observation of political and social reality.

Liberal democracy, according to Sartori, is the product of 'idea-struck age' and ideocracy. But its theory is besmeared with the tactics of ideologies of Marxian variety, or sociology of knowledge of Mannheim. The latter has become a trend now. It explains a theory 'in terms of its psychological or economic social sources and functions'. It pretends to become super-rationalism. But no sociology of knowledge can explain Marx or Mannheim. It can only explain the success of Marx and Mannheim.[11] The thesis of sociology of knowledge blunts the distinction between receiver and creator of knowledge. It is, according to Sartori, neither an epistemology nor a logic. It cannot tell us either whence the creativity of thought springs, or how to judge the correctness of thought. To know how our present knowledge is conditioned or determined, no longer adds to our present knowledge. With it our knowledge remains where it started, rather takes a step backwards. Accordingly, ideas are to be understood and not unmasked, and our first task remains 'to inquire whether they are true or false, verifiable or unverifiable, consistent or contradictory'.[12]

As a *science of ideas* ideology has been described either as 'sociology of knowledge' (Karl Mannheim) or 'critical theory' (*Frankfurt School).* These views analyse causes of distortion in ideologies. The first view thinks that our knowledge is determined, conditioned or distorted by our social background. It stands for the best form of society and government, as a matter of faith. It thinks with a closed mind and demands subordination to authority. For such people, ideology is an instrument of politics. The second view maintains that human society has not yet evolved a rational form of existence, which is still to be achieved. All social institutions and behaviour should be analysed from the perspective of their deviation from a rational form. It is science of ideas which sees how ideas are formed and distorted. This is done by critical examination with an open mind. It allows individuals to question authority. It is engaged in disinterested search for better society. Thus, it moves in the direction of political theory.

Karl Marx (1818-83) wrote on the nature of ideology. According to him, it is a manifestation of false consciousness. In the process of social development material needs of people advance, but their social consciousness lags behind. This distorted consciousness is reflected in their ideology. Dominant class makes use of ideology to maintain its authority. Both Marx and Engels (1820-95) hold that it is an instrument of protecting the interests of the dominant class. The bourgeoisie or the capitalist class needs ideology to maintain itself in power. A classless society does not need any ideology. But V.I. Lenin (1870-1924) held that ideology is not necessarily a distortion of truth to conceal the prevailing contradictions. To him, it is a neutral concept, which refers to the political consciousness of different classes. The proletariat need an ideology – the ideology of scientific socialism for their guidance, lest they would be overpowered by the bourgeois ideology. Georg Lukacs (1885-1971) in his *History and Class Consciousness (1923)* proposed a theory of dependence of thought on social life which primarily consisted of class relations of material production. Ideology refers both to bourgeois and proletariat consciousness without implying a necessary negative connotation. Marxism itself is the ideological expression of the proletariat. Bourgeois ideology is false, not because ideology itself is 'false consciousness', but because the bourgeois class situation is structurally limited. Bourgeois ideology is deplorable because it dominates and contaminates the psychological consciousness of the proletariat.[13]

Karl Mannheim (1893-1947) in his *Ideology and Utopia* (1929) rejected Marx's theory of ideology on three grounds: (a) there is no direct correlation between consciousness of a group and its economic interests; (b) all thought is shaped by its social background: Marxism itself is the ideology of a class; and (c) other social groups also have a significant influence upon consciousness. The false consciousness may be manifested in two forms: ideology and utopia. Ideology represents conservatism or maintenance of status quo. Utopia represents impetus to change. Marxist vision of a classless society was a utopia. Thus, the relative character of all knowledge makes knowledge of objective truth extremely difficult. Only 'free-floating stratum' of intellectuals between the contending classes can achieve disinterested knowledge. Mannheim identifies these intellectuals as social scientists. They should be given the authority to rule.

Another school of thought relates ideology with totalitarianism. Ideology as an instrument of motivating people for the achievement of predetermined goals comes close to totalitarianism. Karl Popper (1902-94) in his *The Open Society and Its Enemies* (1945) writes that a totalitarian society claims that it has already found the absolute truth, and strives to implement it ruthlessly. It is a tool which enables the rulers to mobilise manpower and other resources for a goal which is declared to embody the absolute truth. They do not allow anyone to oppose or criticise the public policy, which is exclusively determined by the ruling group. Hannah Arendt (1906-1975) in her *The Origins of Totalitarianism* (1951) defined totalitarianism as a system of total domination characterised by ideology and terror. Ideology of totalitarianism was evolved in early twentieth century to describe the dictatorial way of working of communist regime of the Soviet Union till the end of the Stalin era (1953) and the Fascist regime of Italy (under Mussolini) and the Nazi Germany (under Hitler) till the end of Second World War.

Format and Functions of Ideology

Ideology has been described above either as reflection of false consciousness or as an instrument of totalitarianism. In actual practice, these also exist as sets of ideas and vehicles of value systems held by different groups. They are used for motivating people to achieve the goals cherished by their advocates. Some groups use them to convince others regarding their rightful claims. They are not exclusively domains of the dominant classes. Oppressed classes or castes also have their own ideologies. They cannot be set aside as false or distorted consciousness. They serve as meeting ground for the like-minded people and do not confine themselves to their tribe, religion, region and the like. They also reflect changing social consciousness on crucial issues. Some cause strong social movements for the emancipation of oppressed sections of society. Many of them present a futuristic vision.

An ideology consists of an assortment of interrelated sets of statements that satisfy the following criteria:

1. They all have concern with the same category of societal or interpersonal relationships; personal involvement is the criterion of depoliticisation;
2. Some of them indicate desirable values to be realised in these relationships (the core values of the ideology);
3. Some of them seek to diagnose deficiencies (injustice, suffering, and so forth) in these relationships as seen from the vantage point of such values (the diagnostic component of ideologies);
4. Some of them seek to explain how these deficiencies have come about (the explanatory component of ideologies);
5. Some of them offer cures or policies supposed to eliminate or reduce the deficiencies (the policy component of ideologies);
6. Some of them consist of appeals to people to believe in the diagnoses, and explanations to apply the policy or take the necessary action (the agitational or propagandist component of ideologies);
7. Some of them describe an ideal state of affairs that supposedly can be arrived at as a result of the cure or the action, and which represents a realisation of the core values of the ideology (the utopian component of ideologies).

But some of the statements also indicate ideology when several of the various types of statements mentioned above are missing. Some types of statements mentioned are necessary and some are optional components of an ideology. Necessary components are either (2), that is, statements expressing the core values of the ideology, or (7), that is, statements expressing an ideal state of affairs to be attained. The simultaneous presence of both types of statements is not necessary.

Thus, ideology is 'a structured assortment of explicit or implicit beliefs and appeals concerning deficiencies, and/or causes, and/or policies and action, and/or ideals relating to some delimited kind of societal or inter-personal relationships, and to some minimum set of explicitly held values applying to these relationships'.[14] In the light of this elaboration, depoliticisation means (a) simply the development of ideological consensus; (b) that the impact of ideology in practical politics is becoming weaker; (c) there is separation of functions of ideological statements and of practical politics; and, (d) there is decreasing saliency of manifest ideological statements which become purely factual, economic or technical. The impact of ideology is measured by the degree of discrepancy between manifest ideological structure and specific policy decisions.

Political ideologies still perform many important functions.[15] They formulate and pick suitable goals for political action. An ideology provides ground of legitimacy through which party leaders express symbolically the identity and unity of the party and help grow loyalties among them. It is a source of emotional gratification of the individual members, which provides language, style, common culture and goals to them. It gives guideline for the formulation and implementation of many concrete political proposals and policies. Often an ideology happens to be the basis of justification of holding power and crushing opponents. It lessens pressures of narrow interests, pressures of caste, class, creed and region, and widens and deepens community feelings. It is instrumental in bringing about cultural homogeneity, redistribution of social welfare, equality and discipline. It has played a vital role in the development of the third world countries.

In sum, the debate and its latest version are designed to project the supremacy of liberal-democratic system in theory as well as in practice. In the 21st century, the spread of Liberalisation, Privatisation and Globalisation (LPG) the thesis still appears to be gaining ground. However, it needs a closer scrutiny. Western democracies are not epitome of justice and morality. Human emancipation is a complex venture. There are no ready-made solutions to all human problems. Richard Titmuss, C. Wright Mills, C.B. Macpherson, Alasdair MacIntyre and others have severely criticised the end of ideology thesis. It supports the monopolistic concentration of economic power and advocates the status quo. Macpherson finds its failure in solving the problem of equitable distribution within the market society. According to Alasdair MacIntyre it is itself the ideology of a particular time and place.

End of Ideology

The concept of 'end of ideology' debate implies that at the advanced stage of industrial growth, a country's social-economic organisation is determined by the level of its development, and not by any political ideology. Edward Shils reported it as 'The End of Ideology'.[16] This has been argued on two occasions. The first occasion was in the 1950s when an argument was put forward as the 'end-of-ideology' thesis. The second occasion has produced the 'end-of-history' thesis which first appeared in 1989, and is still the subject of fierce debate.[17] The best known proponents of 'end-of-ideology' thesis are: Seymour Martin Lipset (1922-) (*Political Man, 1959)* and Daniel Bell *(The End of Ideology*: *On the Exhaustion of Political Ideas in the Fifties,* 1960) For the first time, Lipset offered the version of 'end-of-ideology' thesis that was later espoused by Daniel Bell, Edward Shils, and Raymond Aron. For Lipset, post-war societies in the West eliminate the *functional* need for ideologies since they have solved the fundamental political problems of the industrial revolution that generated these ideologies. Daniel Bell pointed out that in the Western World 'there is today rough consensus among intellectuals on political issues: the acceptance of a Welfare State; the desirability of decentralised power; a system of mixed economy and of political pluralism. In that sense too the ideological age has ended.' Ralph Dahrendorf found that formerly capitalist societies have become 'post-capitalist societies'. In these societies conflicts are confined within the borders of their proper realm, and do not influence politics and other spheres of social life. Daniel Bell in his *The End of Ideology* (1960) asserted that they are prone to similar development irrespective of their ideological difference. In his *Political Man: The Social Bases of Politics* (1960) Seymour M. Lipset observed that 'democracy is not only even primarily a means through which different groups can attain their ends or seek the good society; it is the good society itself in operation'.[18] Intellectuals now realise that they no longer need ideologies or utopias to motivate them to political action. W.W. Rostow, in his *The Stages of Economic Growth: A Non-communist Manifesto* (1960) built a unidimensional model of economic growth which was applicable to all countries irrespective of their political ideologies. J.K. Galbraith, in his *The New Industrial State* (1967), identified certain characteristics of advanced industrial societies which corresponded to the thesis of end of ideology. These are: centralisation, bureaucratisation, professionalisation and technocratisation. Every country's techno-economic structure is shaped by the level of its industrialisation. The bureaucratic and technocratic elite have merged in the advanced industrial societies.

In some advanced countries, politics is boring. Politics seemed to have been transformed from vivid clash over ideology to dull technical discussion about means for promoting goals questioned by none.[19] This process is often referred to as "the end of ideology" or as depoliticisation of politics. Depoliticisation implies a transformation of political ideologies into a set of more or less distinct administrative technologies based on a widespread consensus as to what kind of goals one should try to attain. Even if ideological differences are de-emphasised in a depoliticised political community. Idea of depoliticisation was spread by Herbert Tingsten between 1946-1960. Whether depoliticisation prevails in a country depends upon a clear-cut notion of ideology.[20]

Within a few years, with the advent of the New Left, the theory looked doubtful. There was no more revival of ideology, but the most well-off and privileged youth of the richest Western countries demanded an end of materialism which was the essence 'end-of-ideology' thesis. The modern version of the end-of-ideology thesis does not argue that all ideology had come to an end, but claims that one ideology, the 'right' one, has finally, absolutely and permanently, won the conflict of ideas and would dominate human thinking in perpetuity. This view is known as the 'end-of-history' thesis. It has been put forwarded by Francis Fukuyama (*The End of History and the Last Man*, 1992).

The End of History

The end of history is the end point of mankind's ideological evolution and the universalisation of Western liberal democracy as the final form of human government. The whole idea of history having an end is taken from Hegel. Hegel believed that human history had passed through a series of necessary stages of civilisations. Each of them developed internal conflicts or 'contradictions' that undermined it and could only be resolved in passing on to a new and more advanced civilisation. History ends when it reaches a form of society where all conflicts have been resolved and humanity will have discovered the form of society best suited to its nature. He misread Hegel in thinking that Hegel has recognised liberal democracy as the ultimate society. Francis Fukuyama (1952-) thought that liberal democracy had to contend with a series of rivals and had won fascism in the Second World War and defeated communism at the end of Cold War. It is a specific claim about the triumph of Western liberal capitalism over Soviet Communism. It is history in the specialised sense of a single, coherent, and progressive process that has reached its finishing point. 'With those gone there is no serious challenger to modern capitalist liberal democracy. There is religious fundamentalism and nationalism, but Fukuyama insists these present no adequate alternative'.[21] He believes that free market liberal democracy is the society which alone can provide humanity with maximum satisfaction and fulfilment.[22]

But there are many objections to the end-of-history thesis. The great economic successes of countries like South Korea, Singapore, Taiwan and Hong Kong are not the result of liberal democracy. There is combination of free market with various degrees of authoritarian rule. The values of community and loyalty are strong in Asia. To them the Western model presents a questionable ideal. There are over one billion Muslims in the world that reject the West and push their own alternative. This might mean rise and triumph of religious fundamentalism. Michel Foucault and Jacques Derrida known as post-modernists claim that there are a multitude of differing ways of looking at the world each with its own kind of truth. We simply do not have the means of judging between these different versions of what is true. All truth is relative, not merely to different historical periods and cultures but to different theories, religions, outlooks, fashions and even ideologies. Fukuyama's ideas look rather naïve and simplistic.

The British sociologist and influential theorist of the 'third way' politics, Anthony Giddens (1938-)[23] offers a different and more unsettled version of the claim that the ideological traditions are exhausted. Particularly, three traditions of sociological developments in particular have emptied ideological credibility: (i) globalisation; (ii) emergence of post-traditional social order; and, (iii) expansion of 'social reflexivity'. A different and bleaker response to liberal triumphalism has appeared in form of Huntington's vision of 'clash of civilisations'.[24] He accepts that ideological and economic conflicts are on decline on the world level. But there is reconfiguration of global politics on principally cultural lines. Conflict is not being superseded. Rather alignments defined by ideology and superpower relations are giving way to alignments defined by culture and civilisation. The principal conflicts of global conflicts will take place between nations and groups of different civilisations. New alignments would be made of primordial religious affiliations, nation, and ethnicity. Conflicts on these lines would be more dangerous than conflicts based in ideologies.

Religion as Ideology

Religion as Ideology has played its role in history several times, and still continues to do so. Colton has rightly remarked that 'Man will fight for religion, write for it, fight for it, anything but live it'. But is also equally true that in many cases it is religion, which has made man to do so. But one should differentiate between religion as 'religion' and religion as ideology which political leaders still like to call it their religion.

Usually, the central contents and items of 'religions' are regarded abstract, unverifiable, non-empirical and subjective. They may be real or non-real or fantasy. Nothing can be said with certainty about the existence or non-existence of the contents of the 'religion', definiteness of particular ways and means to know them, or about the outcome of knowing them. Hardly anyone can confirm the experiences of a person that one has attained such realisation. Most of these things or ways and means to realise them are based on subjective knowledge, faith and belief of the claimant. When a claimant announces his experience as the best and highest goal of life of man and society, and calls upon others to attain it by and through living a particular way of life, adopting specific form of worship, and unite as a community of believers, he transforms his 'religion' into an 'ideology'. It is an ideology to the believers. When these claimants, founders, prophets, seers, and teachers (*gurus*) of that religion or their successors or nominees apply, propagate and spread teachings and rules of prescribed behaviour among common people, and use means to motivate them, it turns into an ideology of religion.

It may be pointed out that there have been, from time to time, many claimants of 'religions'. There have been many religions. Owing to the very nature of a 'religion' and claims made about it which, no other claimant or non-believer can contradict, owing to subjective nature of religious experiences, or oppose the experiences and expressions of the other claimant. In due course of time, power gained this way by religions becomes irresistible as well as unchallengeable. The claimed experiences stand beyond reason or above every kind of controversy. Millions of believers or followers stand by them and are found to fight and die for it. Thinkers, scholars and rulers have been concerned with this use of religion. It proves to be a powerful engine for operating a government, society and community. Important writers who have recognised the use of religion as ideology have been Machiavelli, Hobbes, Locke, Rousseau, Montesquieu, Pascal, Hegel and some others. Kant regarded three beliefs necessary to make man moral and happy: in God, in the freedom of the will, and immortality of the soul. Marx regarded religion as fantasy of the alienated man.

Religion, used in this way, is a form of false consciousness or an ideology. Political leaders use religion as ideology, as in religion man sees himself as subject to higher beings. Religion confirms his experience that he is not yet his own master. He has not yet learned to adapt his environment to his needs and is the victim of circumstances as yet beyond his control, but he has aspiration to be his own master. It reinforces prevailing morality by promising rewards and threatening punishments in an afterlife, but make man willing to suffer during this life. Undergoing incessant suffering men tend to propitiate malevolent spirits and to invoke the help of benevolent ones. Communities, social groups and political parties resort to religion as an ideology as a system of beliefs regardless to its truth. It is an effect of ignorance and curiosity. It consists of fantasies that give the illusion that men have knowledge where they in fact lack it. It allays fears and gives an outlet to men's inability to control the forces of nature, society and economy. Communities and groups hold together in unity on the basis of its declared sacred character. It reinforces men's motives for observing social rules on threat of punishment by some other-worldly being or beings more powerful than man. Religion provides man with a conception of himself and of his place in the world that satisfies him.[25]

Culture as Ideology

In the wake of modernisation the world over, global politics is reconfiguring along cultural lines. Peoples and countries with close cultures are coming together. Ideology-defined alignments and super-power relations are giving way to alignments defined by culture and civilisation. Political boundaries are now being drawn to coincide with cultural ones: ethnic, religious, and civilisational. Cultural communities have replaced Cold War blocs. The fault lines between civilisations have become the central lines of conflict in global politics.[26] Cultural identity is the central factor in shaping a country's associations and antagonisms. It defines the state's place in world politics, its friends and its enemies. In coping with identity crisis, blood, belief, faith and family are counted. The European powers make it clear that they do not want a Muslim state. The Russian army is fighting Muslim fundamentalists in Tajikistan and Muslim Nationalists in Chechnya. The two Koreas are moving hesitatingly, but meaningfully, toward unification. Political leaders of the concerned countries invoke and publicly identify with 'greater' cultural communities that transcend nation-state boundaries, such as, 'Greater Serbia', 'Greater China', 'Greater Turkey', 'Greater Russia', 'Greater Albania', 'Greater Iran', 'Greater Nagaland' (India), and so on. Cultural commonality facilitates cooperation and cohesion, and, also cultural differences promote cleavage and conflicts.[27] Differences in intra and extra civilisational behaviour stem from:

1. feelings of superiority toward people who are perceived as being very different;
2. fear of and lack of trust in such people;
3. difficulty of communications with them as a result of differences in language and civic behaviour; and
4. lack of familiarity with the assumptions, motivations, social relationship, and social practices of other people.

Improvements in transportation and communication have produced more frequent, more intense, more symmetrical, and more inclusive interactions among people of different civilisations. Thus, civilisational identities have become increasingly more salient. The French, Germans, Belgians, and Dutch increasingly think of themselves as European. There is ubiquity of conflict. It is natural for humans to hate. For self-definition and motivation people need enemies: competitors in business, rivals in achievement, and opponents in politics. The 'us' versus 'them' tendency is almost universal. The end of the Cold War has not ended the conflict but has rather given rise to new identities rooted in culture and to new patterns of conflict among groups from different cultures which at the broadest level are civilisational. Common culture also encourages cooperation among states and groups in the form regional associations and the like. Culture can also be seen as 'ideology'. Even after looking at the claims of Fukuyama, Giddens and Huntington (1927-) it can be said that ideological debate is not on the wane.[28]

On 'ideology' Michel Foucault, Ernesto Laclau and Chantal Mouffe take a different line. They sum up:

The End of Ideology means 'socialism is dead'.

The End of History means 'We are all liberals now'.

For Fukuyama, the end of history is the end of political events. It is the triumph of liberalism over other competing ideologies in the march of history towards its goal. He himself has pointed out that the notion of the end of history is not an original one. Although its most famous proponent is Marx. Two factors lead to the cessation of history and to the attainment of liberalism. The first is natural science and the second, the human struggle for recognition.[29]

Foucault Contra Althusser

Althusser has set out his account of ideology and science in *For Marx* (1969). Ideology for Althusser is a 'system (with its own logic) of representations (images, myths, ideas or concepts, depending on the case) endowed with a historical existence and role within a given society. The crux of the difference between ideology and science concerns the functions that each performs. Ideology is 'a matter of the *lived* relation between men and their world'. It has a 'practico-social' function, in contrast to the 'theoretical' function of science. Ideology is, additionally, 'an organic part of every social totality, a structure essential to the historical life of societies. It has an indispensable role to play in all societies'.[30] What is more, ideology is not merely, or even mostly, conscious; it is in great part unconscious. People are largely unaware that their activities and beliefs are ideological. It does not describe reality. It determines the real historical conditions of people's lives, their beliefs and how they experience the world.

But Althusser's former pupil, the French philosopher, Michel Foucault (1926–1984) differs. Foucault offers three reasons for rejecting ideology: first, because ideology is seen as the opposite of truth or science; second, because of its link with the subject; and finally, because it relies upon the base-superstructure model of Marxism. He rejects the pairing of ideology and science. He presents an alternative scheme of 'identity'. In some other way, Laclau and Mouffe offer 'hegemony' in place of ideology. They draw this concept from the Italian Marxist, Antonio Gramsci (*Prison Notebooks,* 1929-35) Hegemony, or 'political leadership' operates not simply by coercion or the direct imposition of ruling ideas on the subordinated groups, but also crucially by winning the active 'spontaneous' consent of the dominated. Hegemony is best understood as the *'organisation of consent'*. This means it can be maintained only to the degree that the ruling bloc is able to frame the way in which reality is defined for the majority of people, such that the power of the bloc seems to be natural and legitimate. Ideologies are sets of ideas, meanings, and ways of behaving, furnishing practical rule to live by; what he calls 'common sense'. Ideologies can take different forms. But no hegemony is ever secure but rather always unstable. It has to be continually maintained. To Gramsci it is 'a continuous process or formation and superseding of unstable equilibria'. The Marxist account of ideology is economically determined. But the post-Marxist account of ideology, by Laclau and Mouffe in their book *Hegemony and Socialist Strategy,* is contingent and discursive. They reformulate Gramsci's idea of hegemony by eradicating all class elements from it. For them, hegemonic activity is not tied to class, but articulates different subject positions and identities into a common political project.

POLITICAL CULTURE

Political consensus on values is a must for a political system to survive and confront pressures, conflicts and crises emerging from time to time. It relates to political culture which is a sub-structure of each political system. Political culture affects the political system at all levels and supports it. It decides boundaries of politics and the political system, providing measures of legitimacy. All political processes, roles, problems of participation and matters of contentions fall within its purview. It reflects subjective realm of a political system. Max Weber, Parsons, Mannheim, Pye, Verba[31] and many others have accepted role and importance of political culture to analyse political behaviour. However, the concept of *political culture* has to be separated from *civilisation, culture, and political culture.*

Civilisation, Culture and Political Culture

Samuel P. Huntington has argued that the defining characteristic of the 21st century will be a clash of civilisations. Conflicts between civilisations will supplant the conflicts between nation-states and ideologies that characterised the 19th and 20th centuries. Civilisation is the culture of a complex society, not just the society. Every society has a specific set of ideas and customs, and a certain set of items and arts, that make it unique. Civilisation, by nature, seeks to spread, to have more, to expand, and to possess the means by which it has to do this.

Civilisations are basic. They comprise deep-rooted values and institutions that provide different answers to life's great questions. They are also the "broadest" and "most comprehensive" cultural entities, binding smaller sub-cultures to a shared world-view. They adapt and change. Civilisations endure by virtue of powerful "structuring ideas" that shape the identity of individuals and communities over centuries. Often religion is a central defining characteristic of civilisations. Recognising that their boundaries are rarely clear-cut, Huntington identifies a limited a number of "true" civilisations: the Western, Latin-American, Islamic, Sinic, Hindu, Orthodox, Buddhist, and, with some caveats, African and Japanese.

Culture has been called "the way of life for an entire society." As such, it includes codes of manners, dress, language, religion, rituals, norms of behaviour and systems of belief. Culture or civilisation includes knowledge, belief, art, morals, law, custom, and any other capabilities and habits acquired by man as a member of society. It consists of four elements that are passed on from generation to generation by learning values, norms, institutions, and artifacts. Difference is basic. Values and beliefs are a second source of conflict. Western concepts differ fundamentally from those prevalent in other civilisations.[32] Some countries have a fair degree of cultural homogeneity but are divided over whether their society belongs to one civilisation or another.[33]

Culture and political culture are closely related. By 'culture' we mean those historically created selective processes, which channel men's reaction, both to internal and external stimuli' (Clyde Kluckhohn and William H. Kelly). Culture includes, in a member as a member of society, knowledge, belief, art, ethics, traditions and other capacities. According to Wiseman, culture is common orientation between two or more persons. It carries wider connotation, and has deeper roots in our life. It reflects in our mind, thinking, feelings and behaviour.

Political culture is inseparable part of common culture. To stabilise, expand and survive, culture requires the support of political and administrative structures. These structures along with their processes interact on physical environment which begins to change in some manner. Political culture, in comparison to culture can be progressive or conservative. Both can appear different at horizontal as well as vertical levels – regional and central. One cannot overlook non-political cultural elements coming from different groups, pressures of interests, associations and communal parties and organisations. An individual should learn to have knowledge and feelings grown around historical context of politics. Every generation, in a way, after absorption of political culture also makes improvement and brings about a change in it. In this way, conflicts between old and new or tradition and modernity go on. Such conflict is very acute in all developing societies.

A political system is influenced by and pervades the forces of political culture. The latter directs as well as restricts it, making it dynamic or static. No analysis can be complete without learning the extent, direction and depth of the influence of political culture on a political system and its leaders. Often this helps in understanding political behaviour of a political system. One can understand rule of law, form of democracy, bases of legitimacy, ideology, nationalism etc. only in the light of its political culture. It moulds values and goals, civic training, modes of public opinion, political obligations, and responses of citizens of political system. Even similar political systems operate differently owing to different impact of political cultures. Political culture relates both to political and non-political elements, and exposes their connectedness and continuity. Political development depends on the support of a favourable political culture. Otherwise, Political development has to reform and reformulate political culture itself.

Political culture is both the cause of stability and turbulence. Bob Jessop has given a framework for studying 'political culturology'. Most of the people employ it 'as a mere catchword or residual category for all sorts of influences that are neither legal or institutional and include both structural and orientational factors'.[34] The concept has been treated in an arbitrary fashion. They merely re-describe it and do not submit a casual explanation. It is not necessary to assume that ideas, norms, beliefs etc. necessarily result in actions. Actions can take place on account of other factors also. No such causal relationship exists. Jessop believes in the logical possibility of establishing causal relations between political culture and political action.

Political culture is the set-up of attitudes, beliefs, and sentiments which give order and meaning to a political process and which provide the underlying assumptions and rules that govern behaviour in the political system.[35] It is the set of values, beliefs and attitudes within which a political system operates.[36] According to Almond and Powell, a political culture is 'a distribution of political attitudes, values, feeling, information, and skills'. As people's attitudes affect what they will do, a nation's political culture affects the conduct of its citizens and leaders throughout the political system.[37] According to Dennis Kavanagh it is 'a shorthand expression to denote the set of values within which a political system operates. Almond and Verba defined it as the 'pattern of orientations to political objects among the members of the nation'.[38] By 'political objects' they mean parliaments, political parties, political history and the like. It encompasses both the political ideals and the operating norms of a polity. It manifests in an aggregate form of the psychological and subjective dimensions of politics. A political culture is the product of both the collective history of a political system and the life histories of the members of that system, and is thus rooted equally in public events and private experiences. Almond and Verba after studying political cultures of Great Britain, USA, Germany, Italy and Mexico reached the conclusion that a political system is a bundle of specific orientations and attitudes of individual roles. It is made of cognitive, affective and evaluative elements. Though the concept came up in 1956 with the comparative studies of political systems made by Gabriel Almond, Ulam Beer took it up in 1958. However, it was not a totally unknown concept. Herotodus, Plato, Aristotle etc. in the past, and De Tocquivelle, Bryce, Emerson, Mead, Fromm etc. in modern times, in their own manner thought about and used it. Psychoanalysis and cultural anthropology further elaborated it. all modern concepts have come under its spell. For Almond and Powell, it is a set of propensities and attitudes.

Comparatively, it is a recent term. It explains explicitly all concepts like political ideology, national ethos, spirit, national political psychology, and the fundamental value of the people. It is more inclusive than political style or elite behaviour, but is restrictive than public opinion and national character. The theory of political culture represents a significant advance in the direction of integrating psychology and sociology with Political Science to produce a richer and fuller understanding of politics.[39]

Nature

Scholars have held varying views regarding its nature, growth and process. For Almond it is 'orientation'. Beer calls it 'political culture'. Easton observes as 'environment'. For Spiro it is 'political style'. Almond and Coleman empirically applied the concept for the first time while studying developing societies. It is collective expression of subjective and psychological dimensions of the political. It is a joint product of collective history of political systems and life history of a political system. In other words, it comes out of both individual and public events, and forms a special property of every society. It has, according to Almond and Verba, some common features of democratic systems. Nathan Leeds sees it as syndromes found between political culture and personalities. At the political level, political system brings about uniformity among members of a polity. Common aspirations, needs, pressures and compulsions produce such uniformities. They become part of values, beliefs, habits and dispositions. Still political culture does not completely determine or regulate human behaviour. Political culture itself is dynamic and changing. In political culture, an individual stands eclectic when he prefers elements conducive to his own universal values. One should analyse both collective elements as well as subjective ethos appearing in a political culture. Often uniformities stand for conservative values whereas specific ethos call for progress and change. Orientation of an individual relates to many interconnected factors. In them, historical, geographical, conceptual and socio-economic factors are more important. Stories of attaining victories and defeats make up historical base of a political culture. History stands as a source of inspiration, sure witness and a guide. Mountains, rivers, planes, etc., help citizens' head to hold high and nurture them. The land is treated either as 'mother' or 'father'. Climate, topography, mines, flora and fauna, birds, animals, rains and air all mould physical features of political culture. So is the social structure which proves a motherly lap for them. All its communities, castes, social groups, languages and dialects, traditions and taboos form part of its civic life. Along with its economic structures and processes, all of them provide rock like life to society. Dynamism is added to them by ideologies, educational system, press and the media. The latter have produced even upheavals and revolutions in many countries. Inner and outer environment of a political system plays an important role. Wars, innovations in science and technology, and ideas cause major turning points in them.

Processes and Identification

Political culture is educative and transmissible, though its speed is often slow and indirect. It is taught and communicated through socialisation. Non-political culture and events too contribute in its making. Family, society, economic system, religious institutions, great personalities etc. also determine its shape. They undergo change while meeting new political experiences. Man is compelled to learn new political ethos and values. Expectations and predictions about them radically change. New images and dreams take over. It changes little in developed countries. But undeveloped and developing countries change beyond expectations. Change in them is very painful. Transition in them becomes unbearable.

It is very important to identify the form and extent of a particular political culture. Some areas are important for their identification: (i) often values operating at national, regional and local levels can be seen as a hierarchy; (ii) rules of game determine the type of organisation ana their processes; (iii) the constitution or the basic law provides a concrete, visible and valid location; (iv) values reflect acts of governance, planning, conflicts and struggles among political parties, and positive and negative expectations and responses of the people; (v) provisions of participation, equality and liberty; (vi) ethos, allegiance and commitment make sound and solid foundation of civic life; (vii) symbols, idols, ideals, celebrations, festivals. Even studies of urbanisation, density, per capita income, GDP etc. have been considered important to know political culture.

Kinds and Forms

Political cultures have many forms. They can be based on several factors. A political culture can have many sub-political cultures. These sub-political cultures, in the context of specific political institutions and their processes, generate different political attitudes and values. When sub-political cultures dominate political culture, a political culture suffers crises after crises, as it has been happening in Ireland and Sri Lanka. On the basis of number and power, political culture takes two forms – elitist and mass based. Even a mass political culture has many variations and grows heterogeneous. However, their values can be complementary to each other. A political culture decides in what way the members belonging to masses would be recruited and taken into the elite groups. Their different socialisation processes too influence each other. When cleavages between them is too deep and wide, or general political culture goes weak, political system suffers from increasing conflicts, disintegration and ultimate dismemberment. A third level between them also exists. It is the middle class which has gained strength everywhere. A powerful middle class happens to hold balance among different sub-political cultures. Its presence lessens violent conflicts. Aristotle in the past, and most of the modern liberal political thinkers stand for it. On the basis of continuity, cultures can be conservative or modern or most modern or postmodern. Almond and Coleman find most of cultures as 'mixed'. W.F. Riggs calls them 'prismatic', 'developing' or 'transitional'. From the viewpoint of speed, cultures can be static, slow or revolutionary. It is difficult to determine their indicators. Political culture, on the basis of ideologies, can be communist, socialist, democratic, authoritarian or fascist. Some scholars have found political cultures as hilly, plane, oceanic, north or south polar. They have been related to ethnicity, colour or race: yellow, black, brown, white etc. Huntington, recently, has connected them with civilisations.

On the bases of congruence or uniformity, Wiseman, has pointed out three in their pure or ideal forms, and, other three as their mixed forms:

Kinds of Political Cultures on the Basis of Congruence

Pure or Ideal Forms	*Mixed Forms*
1. Parochial	1+2
2. Subject	2+3
3. Participant	3+1

Norms of congruence are allegiance, apathy and alienation. They indicate orientation of citizens towards the political system. Orientation relates to inputs and outputs of political systems. It can be positive (+) and negative (–). Orientation towards them can be different in congruent political cultures:

Kinds of congruence based

Political Cultures	*Inputs*	*Outputs*
1. Parochial	–	–
2. Subject	–	+
3. Participant	+	+

S.E. Finer puts political cultures into four categories: (i) mature; (ii) developed; (iii) low; and (iv) lowest. He saw pre-revolutionary France as the lowest political culture. According to Almond, political cultures connected with particular political systems, can be categorised into four groups:

1. *Anglo-American Political System*: Its political culture is homogeneous. It combines modern, transitional and secular outlooks. Mostly its political culture is plural, free, libertarian, rational and experimental. Both political ends and means are clearly defined. Sometimes, a few groups prefer one particular value at the expense of others. On other occasions, all groups urge for one particular value or goal. Role of political parties, individual leaders and other associations is publicly recognised. Plurality of political, civic, economic and cultural life finds place in different pressure groups which respect each other's existence.
2. *Continental European Political System*: It has few traits of uniformity. In some areas there is polarisation of political cultures, some of its elements are traditional whereas others are rational. Imbalance among sub-political cultures causes tension and generates conflicts. Secularisation succeeds in a limited way. Secular political culture exists only in some modern and industrial sectors. Existence of differing ideologies

also causes sharp cleavages and political alienation among several sections of people. Political leaders have less deference toward law-making bodies and elections. Instead of using public forum for exchange of ideas, discussion, negotiation and arriving at consensus, leaders rather use them to teach, preach, warn and bargain. Their roles are deeply rooted in sub-political cultures. In place of law, sub-political cultures dominate the scene. Bureaucracy holds the keys of decision and policy making structures.

3. *Non-Western Political System*: In this group of countries, modernity of a political system resides in cities only. Attempts are made to usher it in rural areas also. Form of authority is charismatic, which leads to instability, indecision and subjectivity. Narrow political interests prevail, though underground. Their operation leads to sporadic violence and bloodshed. Communication channels are secretive, sectarian and slow. Bureaucracy is backward and insensitive.
4. *Totalitarian Political System*: It is fully monolith, organised and authoritarian, which permits no alternative or free institutions, There is complete control over press and media. Consensus is imposed on all matters. Dissension is crushed. It often goes underground. Modern technologies are used for serving narrow and personal ends. However, it develops expertise in maintaining monopoly over the whole system. Fascist Italy, Nazi Germany, Stalinist Russia etc. have profusely illustrated this type of political culture.

However, many political scientists have not accepted Almond's above-mentioned structural classification. Political culture is an independent, or at the most an intervening variable. It is not subservient or subordinate to political system. It has its own existence. It does influence a political system directly or in a definitive manner, and influences its decisions and policies in some indirect manners.

Civic Culture

The behavioural study of political culture was done by Gabriel Almond and Sidney Verba. It was done in *The Civic Culture* (1963). It was a report on an extensive survey carried out in USA, UK, Italy, Germany and Mexico. They identified three ideal types of political culture: (i) parochial; (ii) subject; and (iii) participant. They regarded these types of political culture as the properties of both individuals and political systems as a whole. They concluded that all the three types would be unsatisfactory for a stable democracy. They argued that the best sort of political culture for a stable democratic system would be a mix of subject and participant elements. This mixture was called as 'the civic culture'. Citizens possess high levels of knowledge about the political process and feel empowered as political actors. They recognise the legitimacy of the elites to make decisions on their behalf. The elites are sensitive enough to the preferences of the masses. But their view suffers from ethnocentrism. But all stable political systems do not possess qualities associated with the civic culture. Arend Lijphart noted that explicitly non-consensual political cultures were also able to achieve democratic stability.[40] He calls this as 'consociational democracy'. There is existence of a segmented society, whose segments are largely autonomous. Political elites share executive power. These institutions ameliorate the impact of political culture upon the political system. For Lijphart there is no direct connection between the shape of a political culture and the stability of the government. Consociational democracy depends upon a coalescent elite political culture. To him culture is a derivative of institutions. On the contrary, Almond and Verba found democratic stability as being determined by political culture. C. Pateman saw interdependence of culture and structures and found them mutually reinforcing.[41]

Alternatives to Political Culture

There are some alternatives to the Political Culture approach directly. They are (1) Ideology, (2) Sub-political cultures, (3) Political Identity, (4) World culture, and (5) World cultures.

1. *Ideology*: On the basis of the concept of 'ideology' many Marxist and neo-Marxist thinkers have thought about differently on the operations of politics. Marx and Engels regarded the dominant ideas of any historical epoch as an expression of the interests of the most powerful social groups. All political and cultural ideas are rooted in the prevailing power relationship. The class which controls economic life dispenses throughout society its attitudinal patterns and belief systems. But it is understood in two ways: (a) as false consciousness that masks 'real interests' of the bulk of society. Real interests lay in the overthrow of capitalism and its replacement by communism; and, (b) as expressions of material circumstances, such as, attitudes, beliefs, ideologies etc. rooted in the structure of production relations in any given society. Antonio Gramsci (1891-1937), while in prison, questioned why there had not been a successful communist revolutionary overthrow of a regime in the advanced capitalist countries?[42] He found the cause in the ability of advanced capitalist regimes to rule by *consent* rather than by *coercion*. This was its intellectual and moral leadership rather than military and police repression. It was termed as *hegemony* used to describe the non-coercive aspects of domination, the diffusion throughout society of the value and knowledge systems of a ruling group. Louis Althusser, the French structuralist Marxist thinker, elaborated it further.[43] He highlighted the way in which hegemony actually

worked. The state has two key components: repressive and ideological state apparatuses (ISAs). The former functions via coercion in the last instance while the latter work ideologically. The list of ISAs included Religion, Education, Family, Law, Politics, Trade Unions, Communications and Culture. The ideological supports of state power are deeply embedded in society. The ISAs may also operate as sites of resistance to the dominant knowledge and attitudinal patterns associated with capitalism. Robert Cox and Stephen Gill, both neo-Gramscians, have dealt with the power of knowledge and ideas in the global political economy. Its organising principles come from neo-liberalism which stands for the sanctity of free markets, avoidance of state intervention, free capital movement and efficient allocation of resources on a global scale.

2. *Sub-political Cultures*: Many sub-political cultures co-exist within a political system. There is interaction among these sub-political cultures. Political system as a whole comes under this interaction. Sub-political culture stands for a particular identity of a societal group. Sub-political culture makes it a group of people that possesses a distinct and consistent set of attitudes, beliefs and orientations to political objects. Sub-political cultures become irreconcilable, as in case of Ireland and Tamil Tigers in Sri Lanka. It may also rise like the Asian Tigers. But the European Union is showing the way to negotiation, mediation, reconciliation, and integration. Dennis Kavanagh[44] gives four bases of these sub-political cultures: (1) The elite versus mass culture; (2) Cultural divisions within the elites; (3) Generational subcultures; and, (4) Social structure.
3. *Political Identity*: The components of identity include a series of common assumptions, attitudes, dispositions and beliefs. The boundaries between political identity and political culture are not very clear. However, 'identity' is endemic to the human condition. Calhoun says, 'We know of no people without names, no languages or cultures in which some manner of distinctions between self and other, we and they are not made'.[45] There are many possible bases for political identity and each person is made of multiple identities. Some identities seem to prevail over others.[46] There are many rationalist, constructivist and power approaches to identity.
4. *World Culture*: There are many makers and developers of world culture: intergovernmental organisations, transnational corporations, states, and individuals. Individuals include scientists, policy advisors technical experts, organisational consultants, activists, and so on.[47] Much of world culture is embedded in national and local structures to such as extent that it is simply taken for granted. State sovereignty is there. Yet institutions like the ICC (International Criminal Court) transcends state sovereignty, relying on a principle of individual

responsibility for one's actions and the presumed capacity of individuals to follow their consciences in choosing good over evil. They are obliged to behave as world citizens. Yet critics of neoliberalism, opponents of radical Islamism and defenders of national identity oppose this phenomenon. According to Lechner and Boli, 'In the twenty-first century, world culture will be a fact of life. Its content will change; its influence may rise or decline. But in many respects, the world works the way it does because world culture has grown as it has.'[48]

5. *World Cultures or Civilisations*: There are many world cultures or civilisations. All tend to clash. Huntington opines that the fundamental source of conflict is not primarily ideological or primarily economic. The great divisions among humankind and the dominating sources of conflict are cultural. Nation-states still remain the most powerful actors, but the principal conflicts of global politics would occur between nations and groups of different civilisations.

There is worldwide Islamic opposition to World Culture. World Culture, in fact, stands presently for Western Culture. But Islam considers itself to be the World Culture. As such, it opposes every other culture, civilisation or ideology appearing as World Culture. In their revolt against the dominant world order, the Islamists aim to create a new kind of civilisation. Islam is a world religion. It is centred on the universal declaration of the freedom of man on the earth from every authority except God's. Its call to freedom may be confined by geographic or racial boundaries but is valid for all humanity. Most of the aggressive militants have increasingly focussed on the linchpin of world culture (the chief oppressor of Muslims): the United States of America or the "Great Satan". The entire earth must be subject to the religion of Allah by all means.

Clash of Civilisations

Huntington (1927 –) argues that cultural differences are likely to be at the heart of future global conflicts. All cultural alternatives will collide with each other. Modern information and communication technologies make people more mobile and reveal deep cultural differences among them. Each one of them claims to be invincible.[49] The main axis of confrontation will be relations between "the West and the Rest". Across the world run civilisational fault lines, each liable to erupt in violence as the cultural plates collide. The most dramatic collisions, Huntington feared would occur along Islam's "bloody borders", from Nigeria to Chechnya to Kashmir.[50] With the demise of the Soviet Union, there is decline of significance of ideology. Therefore other kinds of conflict have come to the fore. Increasingly, nation-states are shaped by cultural identities and enmeshed in distinct civilisational blocs. As ideology and nationalism recede, the cause of civilisations takes over. This applies especially to Islam. For the West, the underlying problem "is not Islamic fundamentalism. It is Islam, a different civilisation whose people are convinced of the superiority of their culture.

The Kin-country Syndrome

These civilisations become caught up in conflict, among groups along their fault lines and among their leading states, because the values they contain matter so much to so many. When the stakes are highest and groups face their greatest troubles, he implies, they are most likely to fall back on what is most "basic, enduring, and comprehensive." This is precisely what happened in the "Islamic resurgence": faced with the traumas of modernisation, in states that let basic needs unmet, Muslims found identity and loyalty in religious community.

Groups or states belonging to one civilisation that become involved in war with people from a different civilisation try to rally support from other members of their *own* civilisation. H.D.S. Greenway has termed it as "kin-country" syndrome. It replaces political ideology and traditional balance of power considerations as the principal basis for cooperation and coalitions. Conflicts and violence can occur between states and groups within the same civilisation. Such conflicts are likely to be less intense and less likely to expand than conflicts between civilisations. Common membership in civilisations reduces the probability of violence in situations where it might otherwise occur.

Evaluation of Civilisational Clash Theory

Civilisational clash intensifies because there is no universal civilisation to contain it. Westerners assume that there is a universal civilisation that contains their values – beliefs in individualism, market economies, and political democracy. They mistake it for a global culture. In fact, the very concept of a universal civilisation is a "distinctive product of Western civilisation". It is a false, immoral, and dangerous form of wishful thinking. The behaviour of the West fuels the clash. As Westerners made their way into the world, they uprooted local traditions, claimed control over territory, and exploited the resources of others. They aggressively asserted the universal validity of their ideas. Thus, both Islamists and Huntington perceive a world made up on irreconcilable blocs, with religion as the basic source of identity. Both foresee intensifying struggles in a multipolar world. Unlike Islamists, he wants the West to survive and civilisations to coexist, but even his recommendations, such as urging the West to have greater faith in Western values, parallel those of Islamists, who advocate the same approach on their side of the divide.[51] Huntington's view of world culture is mistaken about the world affairs. He envisions a grand alliance of the "rest" against the West. He underestimates the strength of cross-civilisational ties and downplays the virulence of intra-civilisational struggles, such as the Iran-Iraq war, the Gulf War, and the Algerian civil war, which have cost more Muslim lives than the supposed clash of civilisations. Fault lines have appeared within Islam and even within countries. His overall arguments about civilisations are misleading. To him, civilisations are tight bundles of beliefs and value, not loose grab bags.[52] He mistakes an abstract category for existential reality. Civilisations are not neatly organised wholes. Real civilisations are composites, cobbled together from long histories and complex exchanges with others. Civilisations are so complex that they provide no certain answers to new problems. They may inform and give meaning to social life. Modern societies have much in common. Huntington misinterprets world events, misjudges Islam, misunderstands civilisations, and misprizes world culture. In fact, they all make parts of world culture, in all its various aspects.

Toffler predicts that future divisions of the world would be not between the East and the West or the North and the South, but between the "fast" and the "slow". The control of knowledge will be the crux of tomorrow's worldwide struggle for power in every human institution. This would be the fast-arriving civilisation of the twenty-first century.[53]

Political Culture Approach and Its Theory

Political culture approach has been very popular for conducting comparative studies and making empirical analyses of transitional societies. Scholars have liked to investigate political behaviour and processes in the context of their political cultures. Almond, Verba and Pye have been its pioneers.

Borrowing concepts from Sociology and Anthropology, Almond has developed a methodology for comparative studies of political cultures. He believes that all political cultures can be comparatively studied on that basis. For Almond, political system is a system of roles which can be empirically observed and understood scientifically. He studied, besides legal-institutions, family relations, mass-behaviour, electoral system, power, influence and the like. The basis of his classification and analysis of the political systems is their structures and cultures. Both are related to each other. Political culture of a society is deeply influenced by its structures, and vice versa. For explaining relationship between them he picked up orientation of roles and political actions. All political activity reflects attempts made to attain maturity. Attitudes, feelings and preferences are their indicators. To him, political system is an interactive set of roles or is a structure of roles. In some societies, degree of differentiation of role is more, while it is less in others.

The boundaries within which a political system operates to attain its goals and purposes make space of its culture. He discovered three models of political systems, which reflect attitudes of individuals towards political activity. They are like Weberian ideal-types. He measures political culture of a society on the basis of its orientation towards political action and political structures. Orientation of an individual involves cognitive understanding of political objects, events, acts and disputes; his emotional attachment; and methods and rules of evaluation. An individual's objective knowledge usually stands on undermentioned four grounds:

1. *Understanding* of the whole system;
2. *Input processes* which are connected with transforming structures like political parties, bureaucracy etc.;
3. *Output processes* include acts of executive offices, judiciary, bureaucracy etc.; and
4. *Self* which involves matters of personality, such as, rights, powers, possessions and obligations.

One can know political culture on the basis of these grounds.

There is close relation between political culture and political system. Political culture is the basis of survival of all old and modern political systems. A political community, even without having 'state', can exist as a polity or political system. Whatever be the form of a political system – developing or developed, it does possess some form or pattern of political culture. Stateless political systems like the United Nations Organisation (UN), many international and regional organisations, are more or less, operating on the basis of some form of political culture.

Observing important and role of political culture for a political system, many scholars at advanced stage of theoretical sophistication, are trying to move ahead from political culture 'approach' to political culture 'theory'. However, their attempts are being severely criticised. It has been observed that political culture is a new name for an old existing concept. Hardly there is consensus on its variables, indicators and methods of study and measurement. One can know a lot about the political culture of a political system on the basis of his own insight or intuition. Political culture continues to grow, turn complex and appear more and more subtle. When it is said that political culture is the directing and determining element or force of political structures, and is also an outcome of cultural values, the whole argument looks circular. In fact, political culture approach is a by-product of modernisation and development theories. It is not certain whether they regard it independent variable or dependent variable, e.g., cause or effect. As such, the whole perspective happens to become conservative, static and anachronistic. When looked from this view, 'civic culture' of Almond and Verba suffers, centring on the political cultures of USA or

Great Britain, from bias and prejudice. Arendt Lipzart has pointed out that prevalence of homogeneous values is not an essential element of political cultures of Germany and Italy. He found institutional participation of the elites much more relevant. He calls them as 'consociational democracy'. Pateman too does not accept cause-effect relations between stability of a democracy and its political culture. D. Kavanagh finds the role of sub-political cultures as more important. In the past, Almond and Powell had also tried to rescue themselves from this plight by resorting to the concept of 'secularisation'. Thus, no final conclusion comes out.

Notes

1. Ian Adams, *Ideology Today,* Manchester University Press, 2002.
2. Roucek, Joseph S., ed., *Contemporary Political Ideologies,* London: Vision Press Ltd., 1961.
3. Sargent, Lyman Tower, *Contemporary Political Ideologies, A Comparative Analysis,* Illinois: Homewood: The Dorsey Press, 1969, 1.
4. Beteille, Andre, "Ideologies: Commitment and Partisanship", *L'Homme, 1978, 18, 3-4,* July-Dec., 47-67.
5. Plamenatz, John, *Ideology,* Macmillan: 1970, 15; and, Larrain, Jorge, *The Concept of Ideology,* New Delhi: B.I. Publications, 1979, Indian edition, 1980, 17.
6. Connolly, William E., *Political Science and Ideology,* New York: Atherton Press, 1967, viii.
7. Ibid., 49.
8. Meehan, Eugene. J., *The British Left Wing and Foreign Policy, A Study of the Influence of Ideology,* New Jersey: Rutgers University Press, 1960.
9. Dyke, 172.
10. Festensten, Mathew and Kenny, Michael, *Political Ideologies,* Oxford: 2005, 431.
11. Sartori, *Democratic Theory,* op. cit., 458.
12. Ibid., 460.
13. Larrain, Jorge, *The Concept of Ideology,* op. cit., 201.
14. Ibid., 69.
15. Plamenatz, John, op. cit., 143.
16. Edward Shils presented the report held on "The Future of Freedom" held in Milan in 1955 and published it in *Encounter* under this title.
17. Adama, Ian. *Political Ideology Today,* Manchester & New York: Manchester University Press, 1993, 348.
18. Lipset, Seymour Martin, *Political Man: The Social Bases of Politics,* London: Mercury Books, 1959, Reprint, 1966, 403. His other books are: *The First New*

Nation: The United States in Historical and Comparative Perspective, 1963; and, *American Exceptionalism: A Double-Edged Sword, 1996.*

19. Ulf Himmelstrand, "Depoliticization and Political Development-A Theoretical and Empirical Approach", in Erik Allardt and Stein Rokkan, eds., *Mass Politics: Studies in Political Sociology,* 1970.
20. Ibid., possim.
21. Ian Adams, op. cit. 350.
22. Fukuyama, Francis, *The End of History and the Last Man,* Penguin Books, 1992. His other books are: *Trust: The Social Virtues and the Creation of Prosperity, 1995,* and *State-Building: Governance and World Order in the Twenty-First Century, 2004.*
23. Giddens, Anthony. *From Beyond Left and Right: the Future of Radical Politics,* Polity Press, 1994. His other important books are: *The Third Way, 1998,* and *The Global Third Way, 2001.*
24. Huntington, Samuel. *The Clash of Civilizations and the Recasting of World Order,* Touchstone Books, 1998. His other books are: *Who are We? The Challenges to American National Identity,* 2004.
25. Plamenatz, op. cit., 84-92.
26. Festenston, Mathew, and Kenny, Michael. *Political Ideologies, Oxford: 2005,* 447.
27. Ibid., 450-51.
28. Gamble, Andrew. *After Politics,* Polity Press, 2000; Lyotard, J.F. *The Postmodern Condition,* Minnesota: 1979; and Shtromas, A., (ed.). *The End of 'Isms',* Basil Blackwell: 1993.
29. From Maya Llyod, *'The End of Ideology?', in Eccteshall,* Robert; Kenny, Michael; Finlayson, Alan; Geoghegan, Vincent; Kenny, Michael; Lloyd, Maya; Mackenzie, Ian; and Welford, Rick. *Political Ideologies: An Introduction,* Second Edition, Routledge: London, 1994, 220-225.
30. Ibid., 226.
31. Pye, Lucian W. and Verba, Sidney. *Political Culture and Political Development,* Princeton: Princeton University Press, 1965.
32. Western ideas of individualism, liberalism, constitutionalism, human rights, equality, liberty, the rule of law, democracy, free markets, the separation of church and state, often have little resonance in Islamic, Confucian, Japanese, Hindu, Buddhist or Orthodox cultures. Huntington, Samuel P. 'The Clash of Civilizations', *Foreign Affairs,* 72(3), 1993.
33. Ibid., Huntington calls them as 'torn countries', such as, Mexico, Turkey, Russia and others.
34. Jessop, Bob. *Traditionalism, Conservatism and British Political Culture,* London: George Allen & Unwin Ltd., 1974, 17.
35. Pye, Lucian W. *"Political Culture", International Encyclopaedia of the Social Sciences,* 12, 218.
36. Axford, Barrie; Browning, Gary K.; Rosamond, Ben; Turner, John. *Politics, An Introduction,* Ben Rosamond, 'Political Culture', 75-105.

37. The authors have compared aspects of political culture in different nations, and tried to understand the propensities for present and future behaviour. Almond, Gabriel A. and Powell, G. Bingham Jr., General Editors, *Comparative Politics Today: A World View,* 4th ed. Glenview, Illinois: Scott, Foresman & Co., 1988, 40-1.
38. Almond, G.A. and Verba, Sidney. *The Civic Culture: Political Attitudes and Democracy in Five Nations,* Princeton: Princeton University Press, 1963.
39. Pye, op. cit. 224.
40. Lijphart, A. *Democracy in Plural Societies: A Comparative Explanation,* New Haven, CT: Yale University Press, 1977.
41. Pateman, Carole. "Political Culture, Political Structure and Political Change", *British Journal of Political Science,* 1(3), 1971.
42. Gramsci, A. *Selections from the Prison Notebooks,* London: Lawrence & Wishart, 1970.
43. Althusser, L. *Lenin and Philosophy and Other Essays,* London: New Left Books, 1971.
44. Kavanagh, Dennis. *Political Culture,* 1972 in Ben Rosamond, op. cit., 87-91.
45. Calhoun, Craig. "Social Theory and the Politics of Identity", in C. Calhoun (ed.) *Social Theory and the Politics of Identity,* Oxford: Blackwell, 1994.
46. Smith, A.D. *National Identity,* Harmondsworth: Penguin, 1991.
47. Lechner, Frank J. and Boli, John. *World Culture: Origins and Consequences,* Blackwell, 2005, 234-35.
48. Ibid., 240.
49. Huntington, Samuel P. "The Clash of Civilizations", *Foreign Affairs,* 72(3), 1993; *The Clash of Civilizations and the Recasting of World Order:* Touchstone Books, 1998, 125-30.
50. Huntington, op. cit. 254.
51. "A Confucian-Islamic military connection has thus come into being, designed to promote acquisition by its members of the weapons and weapons technologies needed to counter the military power of the West." Huntington, op. cit.; See also, Huntington: *Who are We? The Challenges to America's National Identity,* 2004.
52. Op. cit., 205
53. Alvin Toffler, *Power Shift: Knowledge, Wealth, and Violence at the Edge of the 21st Century.* Bantam Books, 1990.

13

Theory and Ideology of Globalisation

Globalisation[1] is a notion that is poorly understood. Globalisation is not only an economic phenomenon. It should not be equated with the emergence of a 'world system'. It is really about the transformation of space and time.[2] Globalisation does not only concern creating large-scale systems. but also the transformation of local, and even personal, contexts of social experience. Our day-to-day activities are increasingly influenced by events happening on the other side of the world. Conversely, local lifestyle habits have become globally consequential. Globalisation is not a single process but a complex mixture of processes, which often act in contradictory ways, producing conflicts, disjunctures and new forms of stratification. Globalisation is a super-transnational force. Global governance is its manifestation as well as management.

Globalisation is the emergence of a complex web of interconnectedness by which our lives are increasingly shaped by events that occur, and decisions that are made, at a great distance from us. It means geographical distance is of declining relevance, and that territorial boundaries of the nation-states are becoming less significant. It is the deepening as well as the broadening of the political process.[3] Anthony Giddens considers it as the intensification of worldwide social relations. Kenichi Ohmae finds it as a 'borderless world'. It is linked to the growth of 'supra-territorial' relations between people, where territory matters less because an increasing range of connections have a 'trans-world' or trans-border character. There is a single increasingly integrated and universalised world economy largely operating across state frontiers and also beyond the frontiers of state ideology and state-controlled mechanisms.

The Concept

Globalisation is used to refer to a process, a policy, a marketing strategy, a predicament, even an ideology. But it is not a single process but a complex of processes, often overlapping and interlocking processes, but also, at time, contradictory and oppositional ones. Globalisation can be defined as a complex set of distinct but related processes – economic, cultural, social but also political and military – through which social relations have developed global reach and significance. In this sense globalisation includes the development of transnational relations of many kinds as well as specifically global forms.[4]

Briefly, it stands for (i) cross-border relations or internalisation e.g. movement of goods, investments, people, capital, communications, ideas etc. (ii) removal of regulatory barriers to international trade, travel, financial transfers, transactions and communications, i.e., liberalisation; (iii) increase of trans-border relations making out a 'global village'.

New Globalisation

The term 'globalisation' was not coined until the second half of the twentieth century.[5] Some theorists have presented globalisation as the focal point for an alternative paradigm of social inquiry. Yet ideas of globalisation remain as elusive as they are pervasive. According to Anthony Giddens there are few terms that we use so frequently but which are so poorly conceptualised. It is a malleable catchall term that can be invoked in whatever way the user finds convenient. To make its meaning more explicit, the term should be distinguished from internationalisation, liberalisation, universalisation and westernisation. Internationalisation refers to a growth of transactions and interdependence between countries. Hirst and Thompson see globalisation as an intense form of internalisation. But the term is politically objectionable as it finds world social relations in terms of country units, state governments, and national communities. Liberalisation denotes a process of removing officially imposed constraints on movements of resources between countries in order to form an open and borderless world economy. Globalisation as liberalisation opens no new insights. Globalisation as universalisation is assumed to entail standardisation and homogenisation with worldwide cultural, economic, legal and political convergence. In this sense, 'global' means 'worldwide' and 'everywhere'. This conception too opens no new and distinctive insight. This statement can have unhappy political consequences. Cultural protectionists oppose it. Globalisation in many ways can promote cultural diversity, revival and innovations. As westernisation it represents particular social structures of modernity (capitalism, industrialism, rationalism, urbanism, individualism etc.) In this sense, globalisation is interpreted as colonisation, Americanisation, westoxification, unipolar hegemony, neo-imperialism and the like. But westernisation, and also modernisation and colonisation have a longer history than contemporary intense globalisation. The two are not coterminous.

Following eclectic approach, Scholte identifies globalisation as the spread of transplanetary and supraterritorial connections between people. In this approach the words 'global', 'transplanetary' and 'transworld' are synonyms. He prefers the word 'globality' or spatiality which says something about the *arena* and the *place* of human action and experience: the *where* of social life. Globality in the broader sense of transplanetary relations refer to social links between people located at points anywhere on earth. The global field is in these cases a social space in its own right. Distinctiveness of recent globalisation involves more than the quantity, frequency, scope and depth of transplanetary social links. Qualitatively much of today's global connectivity is different. Unlike earlier times, contemporary globalisation is marked by a large-scale spread of supraterritoriality. 'Supraterritorial' relations are social connections that substantially transcend territorial geography. Global connections have qualities of *transworld simultaneity and transworld instantaneity* as seen in telecommunication networks, global mass media, global finance etc. Territoriality has lost its monopoly hold. Earlier periods did not know jet travel, satellite communications, Internet, television broadcasts, intercontinental production chains, global credit cards etc.

Elements of Non-globalisation

Globalisation based on rise of transplanetary and supraterritorial connectivity does not mean that territorial space has ceased to matter. Contemporary history has witnessed the end of *territorialism*, but there is no end to *territoriality*. Territory is still important. Territorial production arrangements, territorial governance mechanisms, territorial ecology and territorial identities remain highly significant, though territoriality does not monopolise the situation as before. The end of territorialism has not marked the start of globalisation. Contemporary globalisation has been closely connected with certain forms of *re*territorialisation like the rise of micro-nationalist politics, urbanisation and the growth of globally connected cities. Reterritorialisation is accompanied by fast growing regionalisation. Thus, there is no globality that exists independently of territorial space. However, the relative simplicity of a territorialist-statist-nationalist world is fading. Globality is not a discrete concrete condition. The global is not a domain unto itself, separate from the regional, the national, the provincial, the local and the built environment. One should not think in terms of opposites or dichotomies like the global and the local, old and new, here and there. People can have intimate relations with both of them. Globalisation should not be associated with some kind of cultural homogenisation. Transplanetary and supraterritorial connectivity does not automatically reduce cultural diversity. Globalisation can increase cultural pluralism as well. To Robertson, globalisation is also localisation. It can have heterogenising as well as homogenising effects. Globalisation is also not the other name of universalisation. It has not touched all of humanity to the same extent. Globalisation is also not apolitical or neutral.[6] Human geography like culture and economics is not politically neutral. It is illusory to think that globality can be divorced from issues of power and justice. There are power relations between social structures, age groups, classes, races, civilisations, genders and the like. The growth of transplanetary and supraterritorial connections empowers some people and disempowers others. As a political process, globalisation is about contests between different interests and competing values. Multiple globalisations are also possible. There is nothing inevitable about the scope, speed, direction and consequences of this trend.

Theories of Globalisation

All theories of globalisation have been put hereunder in seven categories: liberalism, political realism, Marxism, constructivism, postmodernism, feminism and eclecticism. Each one of them carries several variations.

Theory of Liberalism

Liberalism sees the process of globalisation as market-led extension of modernisation. At the most elementary level, it is a result of 'natural' human desires for economic welfare and political liberty. As such, transplanetary connectivity is derived from human drives to maximise material well-being and to exercise basic freedoms. These forces eventually interlink humanity across the planet. They fructify in the form of (a) technological advances, particularly in the areas of transport, communications and information processing, and, (b) suitable legal and institutional arrangement to enable markets and liberal democracy to spread on a transworld scale. Such explanations come mostly from Business Studies, Economics, International Political Economy, Law and Politics. Liberalists stress the necessity of constructing institutional infrastructure to support globalisation. All this has led to technical standardisation, administrative harmonisation, translation arrangement between languages, laws of contract, and guarantees of property rights. But its supporters neglect the social forces that lie behind the creation of technological and institutional underpinnings. It is not satisfying to attribute these developments to 'natural' human drives for economic growth and political liberty. They are culture blind and tend to overlook historically situated life-worlds and knowledge structures which have promoted their emergence. All people cannot be assumed to be equally amenable to and desirous of increased globality in their lives. Similarly, they overlook the phenomenon of power. There are structural power inequalities in promoting globalisation and shaping its course. Often they do not care for the entrenched power hierarchies between states, classes, cultures, sexes, races and resources.

Theory of Political Realism

Advocates of this theory are interested in questions of state power, the pursuit of national interest, and conflict between states. According to them states are inherently acquisitive and self-serving, and heading for inevitable competition of power. Some of the scholars stand for a balance of power, where any attempt by one state to achieve world dominance is countered by collective resistance from other states. Another group suggests that a dominant state can bring stability to world order. The 'hegemon' state (presently the US or G7/8) maintains and defines international rules and institutions that both advance its own interests and at the same time contain conflicts between other states. Globalisation has also been explained as a strategy in the contest for power between several major states in contemporary world politics. They concentrate on the activities of Great Britain, China, France, Japan, the USA and some other large states. Thus, the political realists highlight the issues of power and power struggles and the role of states in generating global relations. At some levels, globalisation is considered as antithetical to territorial states. States, they say, are not equal in globalisation, some being dominant and others subordinate in the process. But they fail to understand that everything in globalisation does not come down to the acquisition, distribution and exercise of power. Globalisation has also cultural, ecological, economic and psychological dimensions that are not reducible to power politics. It is also about the production and consumption of resources, about the discovery and affirmation of identity, about the construction and communication of meaning, and about humanity shaping and being shaped by nature. Most of these are apolitical. Power theorists also neglect the importance and role of other actors in generating globalisation. These are substate authorities, macro-regional institutions, global agencies, and private-sector bodies. Additional types of power-relations on lines of class, culture and gender also affect the course of globalisation. Some other structural inequalities cannot be adequately explained as an outcome of interstate competition. After all, class inequality, cultural hierarchy, and patriarchy predate the modern states.

Theory of Marxism

Marxism is principally concerned with modes of production, social exploitation through unjust distribution, and social emancipation through the transcendence of capitalism. Marx himself anticipated the growth of globality that 'capital by its nature drives beyond every spatial barrier to conquer the whole earth for its market'. Accordingly, to Marxists, globalisation happens because transworld connectivity enhances opportunities of profit-making and surplus accumulation. Marxists reject both liberalist and political realist explanations of globalisation. It is the outcome of historically specific impulses of capitalist development. Its legal and institutional infrastructures serve the logic of surplus accumulation of a global scale. Liberal talk of freedom and democracy make up a legitimating ideology for exploitative global capitalist class relations. The neo-Marxists in dependency and world-system theories examine capitalist accumulation on a global scale on lines of core and peripheral countries.[7] Neo-Gramscians highlight the significance of underclass struggles to resist globalising capitalism not only by traditional labour unions, but also by new social movements of consumer advocates, environmentalists, peace activists, peasants, and women. However, Marxists give an overly restricted account of power. There are other relations of dominance and subordination which relate to state, culture, gender, race, sex, and more. Presence of US hegemony, the West-centric cultural domination, masculinism, racism etc. are not reducible to class dynamics within capitalism. Class is a key axis of power in globalisation, but it is not the only one. It is too simplistic to see globalisation solely as a result of drives for surplus accumulation. It also seeks to explore identities and investigate meanings. People develop global weapons and pursue global military campaigns not only for capitalist ends, but also due to interstate competition and militarist culture that predate emergence of capitalism. Ideational aspects of social relations also are not outcome of the modes of production. They have, like nationalism, their autonomy.

Theory of Constructivism

Globalisation has also arisen because of the way that people have mentally constructed the social world with particular symbols, language, images and interpretation. It is the result of particular forms and dynamics of consciousness. Patterns of production and governance are second-order structures that derive from deeper cultural and socio-psychological forces. Such accounts of globalisation have come from the fields of Anthropology, Humanities, Media of Studies and Sociology. Constructivists concentrate on the ways that social actors 'construct' their world: both within their own minds and through intersubjective communication with others. Conversation and symbolic exchanges lead people to construct ideas of the world, the rules for social interaction, and ways of being and belonging in that world. Social geography is a mental experience as well as a physical fact. They form 'in' or 'out' as well as 'us' and they' groups. They conceive of themselves as inhabitants of a particular global world. National, class, religious and other identities respond in part to material conditions but they also depend on inter-subjective construction and communication of shared self-understanding. However, when they go too far, they present a case of social-psychological reductionism ignoring the significance of economic and ecological forces in shaping mental experience. This theory neglects issues of structural inequalities and power hierarchies in social relations. It has a built-in apolitical tendency.

Theory of Postmodernism

Some other ideational perspectives of globalisation highlight the significance of structural power in the construction of identities, norms and knowledge. They all are grouped under the label of 'postmodernism'. They too, as Michel Foucault does strive to understand society in terms of knowledge power: power structures shape knowledge. Certain knowledge structures support certain power hierarchies. The reigning structures of understanding determine what can and cannot be known in a given socio-historical context. This dominant structure of knowledge in modern society is 'rationalism'. It puts emphasis on the empirical world, the subordination of nature to human control, objectivist science, and instrumentalist efficiency. Modern rationalism produces a society overwhelmed with economic growth, technological control, bureaucratic organisation, and disciplining desires. This mode of knowledge has authoritarian and expansionary logic that leads to a kind of cultural imperialism subordinating all other epistemologies. It does not focus on the problem of globalisation *per se*. In this way, western rationalism overawes indigenous cultures and other non-modern life-worlds. Postmodernism, like Marxism, helps to go beyond the relatively superficial accounts of liberalist and political realist theories and expose social conditions that have favoured globalisation. Obviously, postmodernism suffers from its own methodological idealism. All material forces, though come under impact of ideas, cannot be reduced to modes of consciousness. For a valid explanation, interconnection between ideational and material forces is not enough.

Theory of Feminism

It puts emphasis on social construction of masculinity and femininity. All other theories have identified the dynamics behind the rise of transplanetary and supraterritorial connectivity in technology, state, capital, identity and the like. Biological sex is held to mould the overall social order and shape significantly the course of history, presently globality. Their main concern lies behind the status of women, particularly their structural subordination to men. Women have tended to be marginalised, silenced and violated in global communication.[8]

Theory of Transformationalism

This theory has been expounded by David Held and his colleagues.[9] Accordingly, the term 'globalisation' reflects increased interconnectedness in political, economic and cultural matters across the world creating a "shared social space". Given this interconnectedness, globalisation may be defined as "a process (or set of processes) which embodies a transformation in the spatial organisation of social relations and transactions, expressed in transcontinental or interregional flows and networks of activity, interaction and power." While there are many definitions of globalisation, such a definition seeks to bring together the many and seemingly contradictory theories of globalisation into a "rigorous analytical framework" and "proffer a coherent historical narrative". Held and McGrew's analytical framework is constructed by developing a three part typology of theories of globalisation consisting of "hyper-globalist," "sceptic," and "transformationalist" categories. The Hyperglobalists purportedly argue that "contemporary globalisation defines a new era in which people everywhere are increasingly subject to the disciplines of the global marketplace". Given the importance of the global marketplace, multi-national enterprises (MNEs) and intergovernmental organisations (IGOs) which regulate their activity are key political actors. Sceptics, such as Hirst and Thompson (1996) ostensibly argue that "globalisation is a myth which conceals the reality of an international economy increasingly segmented into three major regional blocs in which national governments remain very powerful." Finally, transformationalists such as Rosenau (1997) or Giddens (1990) argue that globalisation occurs as "states and societies across the globe are experiencing a process of profound change as they try to adapt to a more interconnected but highly uncertain world". Developing the transformationalist category of globalisation theories, Held and McGrew present a rather complicated typology of globalisation based on globalisation's spread, depth, speed, and impact, as well as its impacts on infrastructure, institutions, hierarchical structures and the unevenness of development.[10] They imply that the "politics of globalisation" have been "transformed" (using their word from the definition of globalisation) along all of these dimensions because of the emergence of a new system of "political globalisation." They define "political globalisation" as the "shifting reach of political power, authority and forms of rule" based on new organisational interests which are "transnational" and "multi-layered." These organisational interests combine actors identified under the hyper-globalist category (namely IGOs and MNEs) with those of the sceptics (trading blocs and powerful states) into a new system where each of these actors exercises their political power, authority and forms of rule. Thus, the "politics of globalisation" is equivalent to "political globalisation" for Held and McGrew. However, Bryane Michael criticises them. He deconstructs their argument, if *a* is defined as "globalisation" (as defined above), *b* as the organisational interests such as MNEs, IGOs, trading blocs, and powerful states, and *c* as "political globalisation" (also as defined above), then their argument reduces to *a* . *b*. *c*. In this way, their discussion of globalisation is trivial. Held and others present a definition of globalisation, and then simply restates various elements of the definition. Their definition, "globalisation can be conceived as a process (or set of processes) which embodies a transformation in the spatial organisation of social relations" allows every change to be an impact of globalisation. Thus, by their own definition, all the theorists they critique would be considered as "transformationalists." Held and McGrew also fail to show how globalisation affects organisational interests.

Theory of Eclecticism

Each one of the above six ideal-type of social theories of globalisation highlights certain forces that contribute to its growth. They put emphasis on technology and institution building, national interest and inter-state competition, capital accumulation and class struggle, identity and knowledge construction, rationalism and cultural imperialism, and masculinism and subordination of women. Jan Art Scholte synthesises them as forces of production, governance, identity, and knowledge.

Accordingly, capitalists attempt to amass ever-greater resources in excess of their survival needs: accumulation of surplus. The capitalist economy is thoroughly monetised. Money facilitates accumulation. It offers abundant opportunities to transfer surplus, especially from the weak to the powerful. This mode of production involves perpetual and pervasive contests over the distribution of surplus. Such competition occurs both between individual, firms, etc. and along structural lines of class, gender, race etc. Their contests can be overt or latent. Surplus accumulation has had transpired in one way or another for many centuries, but capital*ism* is a comparatively recent phenomenon. It has turned into a structural power, and is accepted as a 'natural' circumstance, with no alternative mode of production. It has spurred globalisation in four ways: market expansion, accounting practices, asset mobility and enlarged arenas of commodification. Its technological innovation appears in communication, transport and data processing as well as in global organisation and management. It concentrates profits at points of low taxation. Information, communication, finance and consumer sectors offer vast potentials to capital making it 'hypercapitalism'.

Any mode of production cannot operate in the absence of an enabling regulatory apparatus. There are some kind of governance mechanisms. Governance relates processes whereby people formulate, implement, enforce and review rules to guide their common affairs.[11] It entails more than government. It can extend beyond state and substate institutions including suprastate regimes as well. It covers the full scope of societal regulation. In the growth of contemporary globalisation, besides political and economic forces, there are material and ideational elements. In expanding social relations, people explore their class, their gender, their nationality, their race, their religious faith and other aspects of their being. Constructions of identity provide collective solidarity against oppression. Identity provides frameworks for community, democracy, citizenship and resistance. It also leads from nationalism to greater pluralism and hybridity. Earlier nationalism promoted territorialism, capitalism, and statism, now these plural identities are feeding more and more globality, hypercapitalism and polycentrism. These identities have many international qualities visualised in global diasporas and other group affiliations based on age, class, gender, race, religious faith and sexual orientations. Many forms of supraterritorial solidarities are appearing through globalisation. In the area of knowledge, the way that the people know their world has significant implications for the concrete circumstances of that world. Powerful patterns of social consciousness cause globalisation. Knowledge frameworks cannot be reduced to forces of production, governance or identity. Mindsets encourage or discourage the rise of globality. Modern rationalism is a general configuration of knowledge. It is secular as it defines reality in terms of the tangible world of experience. It understands reality primarily in terms of human interests, activities and conditions. It holds that phenomena can be understood in terms of single incontrovertible truths that are discoverable by rigorous application of objective research methods. Rationalism is instrumentalist. It assigns greatest value to insights that enable people efficiently to solve immediate problems. It subordinates all other ways of understanding and acting upon the world. Its knowledge could then be applied to harness natural and social forces for human purposes. It enables people to conquer disease, hunger, poverty, war, etc., and maximise the potentials of human life. It looks like a secular faith, a knowledge framework for capitalist production and a cult of economic efficiency. Scientism and instrumentalism of rationalism is conducive to globalisation. Scientific knowledge is nonterritorial. The truths revealed by 'objective' method are valid for anyone, anywhere, and anytime on earth. Certain production processes, regulations, technologies and art forms are applicable across the planet. Martin Albrow rightly says that reason knows no territorial limits. The growth of globalisation is unlikely to reverse in the foreseeable future. However, Scholte is aware of insecurity, inequality and marginalisation caused by the present process of globalisation. Others reject secularist character of the theory, its manifestation of the imperialism of westernist-modernist-rationalist knowledge. Anarchists challenge the oppressive nature of states and other bureaucratic governance frameworks. Globalisation neglects environmental degradation and equitable gender relations.

Forms and Contents

Globalisation takes many *forms*: political, economic, cultural, and the like.

(1) *Political* globalisation is appearing in erosion of national sovereignty and growing intervention and importance of international organisations and non-state actors. Some of them are: UNO, NATO, European Union (EU), the World Bank, the International Monetary Fund (IMF), the World Trade Organization (WTO), the Organization for Economic Cooperation and Development (OECD) and the like. Nation-State is being taken over by inter-governmentalism, supra-nationalism and transnationalism.

(2) In *economic* globalisation there is a shift from a world of distinct national economies to global economy in which production is internationalised and financial capital flows freely and instantly between countries.

(3) *Cultural* globalisation is the process whereby information, commodities and images that have been produced in one part of the world enter into a global flow that tends to 'flatten out' cultural differences between nations, regions and individuals. It is sometimes seen as a process of McDonaldisation.

Thus, globalisation is linked to homogenisation of cultural, social, economic and political diversities in which all watch the same television programmes, buy the same commodities, eat the same food, support the same sport and celebrities.

Consequences

Critics argue that globalisation has pronounced neo-liberal or free-market ideological character. They find it as global capitalism, which is sure to generate new forms of misery, exploitation and injustice. The Third World critics of globalisation feel it as a new method of old colonialists to exploit the developing countries. This neo-colonialism is more dangerous than the earlier ones as in this process the industrialised powers exploit the developing counties without responsibility. To increase profits, the multi-national corporations/enterprises (MNCs/ MNEs), employ business outsourcing (BPO), medical transcription etc. in the developing countries. Emanuel Wallerstein and Samir Amin have observed that globalisation favours the West, and impoverishes the developing countries. It is defined as the process of enriching the rich and impoverishing the poor. Globalisation provokes men's desire for materialistic life and to satisfy these he is instigated to borrow and the borrowing entraps him in a vicious circle. As a result, inequality between 'core' and 'peripheral' countries increases gradually.

As a reaction to globalisation, there is the rise of localisation, regionalisation and multi-culturalism. When allegiances based on national and cultural nationalism fade, they are replaced by local community, or region, or religious and ethnic identity. As such, it is also perceived as a form of imperialism which provokes cultural and political resistance reviving interest in declining languages and minority-cultures. There is emergence of anti-capitalist and anti-free trade union and social movements.

Globalisation generates risk, uncertainty and instability. Economic decision making is gravely influenced by global financial markets which are inherently unstable, as it happened in Mexico, South Eastern nations and some others. It creates 'a risk society' characterised by individualism and weakening of tradition, community and established institutions. There is environmental degradation beyond repair.

Role and Claims of US Supremacy

After the collapse of the bi-polar system, the United States claims that it has won the Cold War, and being a victor state, it has legitimate right to re-shape and re-redesign the post-Cold War international scenario. As such, there is the phenomenon of intervention which has become a fact of international life. On the pretext of self-defence or under the garb of issues like human rights, non-proliferation, weapons of mass destruction, intellectual property rights etc. for ideals of globalisation, liberalisation and privatisation (LPG) the powerful states are employing the weapon of intervention to serve their interests against powerless states like Serbia, Afghanistan and Iraq. Kofi Annan had previously expressed his deep concern against the doctrine of 'pre-emptive military intervention' warning that it could set the stage for a 'lawless use of force' neglecting the UN and without any credible justification.[12]

Bogey of Inevitability

Petras and Veltmeyer have dismissed the 'inevitability bogey'. As both, a description of widespread, epoch-defining developments, and, a prescription for action, globalisation has achieved a virtual hegemony, it is presented with an air of inevitability that disarms ominous apprehensions and prevents the thought of and action towards a systemic alternative, for more just social and economic order. The "inevitability" of globalisation is a critical issue. But a more critical issue, perhaps, is what the discourse on globalisation is designed to hide and obfuscate. This is the form taken by imperialism in the current, increasingly worldwide capitalist system for organising economic production and society.

The "inevitability" of globalisation and the adjustment or submission of peoples all over the world to free market capitalism depends on the capacity of the dominant and ruling classes to coerce people to their will, and convince them that their interests are the people's interests. They make them see the interests of capital as their own. It also depends on the capacity of these dominant classes and their ideologues to undermine the growing resistance to the model of free market.

The two authors have also exposed the class project behind globalisation, namely, "the attempt to obfuscate rather than accurately describe what is going on worldwide", and "the attempt to throw an ideological veil over the economic interests of an emerging class of transnational capitalists". According to them, globalisation is little more than imperialism in a new form, yet another phase in the long historical process of imperialist expansion. Their reasoning is that globalisation was created by deliberate policies put in place by powerful states under the control of dominant classes to divert attention away from the resurgence of imperialist powers, and it is not a structural part of the capitalist system. Thus, it is an ideological smokescreen used to divert attention away from the resurgence of imperialist powers.

Globalisation is not merely an economic phenomenon. It has multiple manifestations such as political, social, cultural, and religious. These manifestations are ghastly and gruesome, especially in the developing countries. The political dimension is evident from the global "super-cop" stalking the world, making countries of lesser might live in insecurity. The other manifestations have begun to unfold particularly in the developing countries, where societies have begun to disintegrate under the invasion of consumerism, culture, and social fads.

In the ultimate analysis, globalisation is not global integration by breaking the barriers across and among the nations through a global compact for turning the world into a 'global village'.

It is common knowledge that the UN is often unable to exert an effective influence on global economic and political issues of critical importance. This is due to what may be called as 'democracy deficit', which prevents effective multilateralism, a multilateralism that is based on a democratically evolved global consensus. Therefore, reform and restructuring of the United Nations system can alone provide a crucial link in an expanding chain of efforts to refashion international structures, imbuing them with a greater degree of participatory decision-making, so as to make them more representative of contemporary realities.[13]

Globalisation, according to Robert Woog and Vladimir Dimitrov, in their article "Globalization: Democracy in Decline", presents many faces to many different observers. The most general and the most negative are those dealing with the process of economic globalisation. The ugly face of globalisation has become the huge transnational corporation with a relentless drive to create a consumer dominated global middle class.

The Ugly Face of Globalisation

The thesis of Robert Woog and Vladimir Dimitrov is that 'the wider the process of economic globalisation, the narrower the circle of those who benefit from it. The free, global market has begun to appear less and less free. Both trade and investment seem to be governed by more and more complicated laws and procedures in favour of monstrously rich economic and financial corporations, the real beneficiaries of the free global market. With the passing of each day, these unaccountable corporations, with unlimited life, size and power, are taking ever increasing control over national economies, largely to the detriment of the individual consumer, worker, neighbour and citizen. One can find much evidence that corporate-led globalisation negatively affects the environment, financial stability, equity, security, food safety, health and cultural diversity of millions of people.

Some of the observable *facts* are:

(1) The number of the countries classified as the 'most poor' in the world has doubled in the last several years. There is a tendency for the governments in the Western 'free' democracy to act as the 'armed' militia for the large financial corporations and banks.

(2) Most international trade is still between the rich counties of Western Europe, North America and Japan, where less than 15 per cent of the world's population is located. Also, whilst foreign exchange may be highly mobile, land and infrastructure are usually immobile, and even factories are expensive to move. Moreover, whilst there is deregulation in certain areas of economic life, elsewhere new regulations have been introduced, and the old ones are rigorously enforced.

(3) Patents, copyrights, franchises, business secrets and tariffs shield major western corporations, and agriculture in the US and the European Union is heavily protected. Further, whilst, what Pierre Bourdieu calls, the 'left hand' of the state, has been in decline, its 'right hand', that which tends to benefit big capital, remains strong.

Worldwide, between 1960 and 1995, the gap between the income of the wealthiest 20 per cent of the world's population and the poorest 20 per cent increased from 30: 1 to 82: 1. In the four years to 1998, the net worth of the world's richest 200 people more than doubled, to reach over $1 trillion, a figure so great that, if they all provided a yearly donation of just one per cent of their wealth, it could be possible to provide universal access to primary education. The combined assets of the top three – which included Bill

Gates – were greater than the combined Gross National Product (GNP) of the 48 least developed countries (which provided a home for some 600 million people) (UNDP, 1999: 37, 39).

In the US itself by 1997 the top 1 per cent owned over 40 per cent of all US assets, more than 94 per cent of all other Americans combined. The bottom 90 per cent of Americans no longer share in the continued prosperity of America.

Joseph Kruth[14] presents four core issues of the 21st century in the following manner:

1. Environmental Degradation of Life Support Systems
2. The Growing Divide: Increasing Concentration of Wealth and Income
3. The Enormous Growth of Corporate Power
4. Learning to become Citizens of the 21st Century

It is hardly possible that individuals may educate themselves about how these financial systems work, who they benefit and how they can be changed? The real state of our society continues to be interpreted to obscure these facts by a media largely owned by corporations benefiting from these policies. Education should develop primarily to encourage the ability to discriminate among offered alternatives. Presently, it does not build the capacity to question basic assumptions and think of new alternatives.

Globalisation as Ideology[15]

Looking from a Marxism-inspired viewpoint, Graham Harrison evaluates the present orthodoxy of globalisation as an 'ideology'.[16] The orthodox notion of *globalisation* provides an ideology used to obscure the political and ideological purpose behind neo-liberal reforms that cannot be controlled. The world is not a commodity. Globalisation is an elite process, driven by a small clique of transnational managers, intellectuals, bureaucrats and politicians. Harrison stands for counter-globalisation that can be ushered in by adoption of positive nationalism, cosmopolitan democracy, global governance and global social movements, and global civil society. It asserts not only the existence and inevitability, but also the desirability of an increasingly integrated and deregulated world economy. National boundaries are seen insignificant as if nation states had little power to control the forces of global capital. The orthodox view exaggerates that the nation-state is losing power. It glosses over the damaging effects of intensified international competition both on environment and on the majority of the world's population. Globalisation is a story not of success, but of unemployment, malnutrition, poverty or extreme uncertainty about the future.

But Harrison does not want to abandon the concept of globalisation. He insists that globalised capitalist economy remains dependent upon workers to produce surplus. This dependency lies at the heart of global capitalism. It means that it is not untouchable. Labour can also organise globally and bring about radical transformation. The United States does not provide the only possible model for capitalism. People can identify opportunities for resistance and struggle through new forms of democracy and civil society. Globalisation does not spell the end of the national stage or the end of politics.

David Held has outlined a model of cosmopolitan democracy, which involves: regional parliaments, transnational referenda, more open intergovernmental organisations, and a reformed United Nations. There will be new forms of authority within the global system. It will be within formal intergovernmental organisation such as the United Nations and the World Bank and with the private and civic spheres. It would lead not to global government or a global superstate but to democratically effective global governance. 'A globalised labour movement presents the possibility not only of re-embedding globalisation-from-above, but by transforming it.'[17]

Supporting the Marxian ideology, Gail Omvedt observes that opposing "liberalisation, globalisation and privatisation" has become such a *mantra* of the Left.[18] In fact, the whole depiction of globalisation as "neocolonialism" is in many ways against the very spirit of Marx, who proclaimed the immense creative-destructive forces of capitalism with the intention not of preventing their growth, but of moving through them, going beyond history to the establishment of a socialist society. For Marx , capitalism was the final stage of class society and it lays the basis for socialism in two ways – first by creating the productive forces, the technology that could produce a truly wealthy existence, and second by creating the human beings, the "proletariat", who could manage this technology. Marx was a resolute internationalist; "independent" or nationally-based capitalist development as opposed to global development was never his concern. Socialism; for Marx, had to be based on a scientific and realistic understanding of the potentialities of the society of the time, not on dreams. What has been lost today in the political programme of the Left is precisely this vision of a position that is not simply negative but moves towards socialism, that can use and harness the immense development of human productive powers that capitalism, with globalisation, represents. Marx viewed the historical process as one of contradiction and exploitation; unlike conventional social scientists he did not see it as ending with capitalism. With all of this, though, he still believed that capitalism produced growth, that this was transmitted through market relations and foreign investment, and that there was no road directly from feudalism to socialism. Capitalism, to Marx, meant not simply exploitation, which had existed in all pre-capitalist class societies, but specifically the rapid advancement of the forces of production, the overturning of old ways of life and the increasing integration of the world. All these factors he saw not as negative, but as laying the basis for socialism. Success of globalisation through transplanetary capitalism leads to victory of socialism the world over. Omvedt clarifies that imperialism was the "highest stage", because the concentration of capital and development of production it represented was the immediate stage before socialism, creating new productive forces and laying the basis for the proletarian capture of power. Capitalism, for Lenin, also was not simply a demon to be resisted, but rather an aggregation of opportunities for human society to move ahead.

Challenges to Democracy and Globalisation

Some of the underlying principles of democracy are: (i) people take, after deliberation and negotiation, democratic decisions collectively, together, as a group; (ii) all qualified persons do so on equal footing, having equal opportunities of involvement; (iii) people engage in democratic activities as autonomous agents; (iv) democracy is conducted in an open and transparent manner, wherein everyone can see what decisions are taken, how and why; and (v) democracy is a responsibility as well as a right. In an ideal type of democracy, the public should shape its own destiny. But such democracy is rarely available. However, a society not striving for it happens to be less worthy and also dangerous to live in. Practice of democracy is culturally and historically contingent. Globalisation has brought significant shifts in the mode of governance. Democracy and globalisation both presently are at odd with each other. Both suffer from several inherent deficiencies. The conventional liberal democracy based on a territorial state is not an adequate formula for rule by the people. On other side, the decision-taking processes that govern globalisation suffer from shortfalls of public participation and accountability. Besides these inadequacies, there is widespread ignorance among citizens, the media and legislature about globalisation. This has severely restricted the possibilities of democratic regulation of governance of transplanetary relations. Deeply entrenched structural inequalities hardly permit citizen involvement in the governance of globalisation. There is a great need of evolving a variant of postterritorialist and poststatist democracy.

Already there are many limits of statist liberal democracy. Contemporary globalisation has further weakened liberal democracy grown around state. Democracy came up when people grouped themselves as distinct nations living in discrete territories, ruled by sovereign states made them subject to popular control. Globalisation pushed statist democracy to over 117 countries by 1998. But there have been other forces like the student activists, NGOs, rebellion etc. But democracies in many of these countries are only skin-deep and lack real credentials. In many countries, democracies have not proved culturally appropriate. Formal democracies are inherently deficient. Democracy requires more than multiplicity of political parties, periodic elections, legal provisions of civil rights, or neutral bureaucracy. All these are low-intensity democracies. Territorially grounded democracy cannot serve a state where many social relations are substantially supraterritorial. Global democracy requires to be more than a democratic state. It cannot control its jurisdiction's involvement with global flows. It needs ideational transformation. The contemporary 'public' of a country is not more confined to the nation-state. The 'public' or the 'people' have many sides, domestic and outside. Globalisation has undermined conventional frameworks of liberal democracy. Its mode of governance has moved from statism towards polycentrism.

A people unaware of this situation cannot pursue meaningful self-determination. They are ignorant of the issues, concepts, principles, policies and the working of globalisation. They know little about globality and it governance. Even the activists confuse the IMF with the World Bank. Formal education at lower and higher levels has no provision for teaching the students on globalisation. School and university curricula have generally prepared young people poorly for global citizenship. Universities still neglect globalisation and its polycentric governance. 'Global studies' are usually put along with 'international studies'. Print, audio and visual journalism do try to raise citizen awareness in these matters. Big conferences on major global challenges find a passing mention in the media. Journalists themselves are poorly educated on global mattes. Only the globally organised big business exploits liberalisation and privatisation in the communication sectors. They give prominence to news opposite of globalisation. Only Internet is making some positive contribution, but its approach is still very limited. Civil society associations have certainly made efforts for the common man to understand the global problems and policies related to them. They organise teach-ins, lectures, symposia, colloquia, workshops discussion groups, round tables, artistic performances and road shows. In some countries, they have built up publicly accessible libraries and documentation centres. These have been done only in modest proportions. They lack resources to sustain long-term programmes of large-scale citizen education on global affairs.[19] Rulers have a democratic duty to educate the governed about their governance: what policy decisions are taken on global issues, at what time, where, by whom, from what options on what grounds, with what expected results and with what supporting resources. Citizens should have ready access to all such information. Elements of confidentiality and secrecy must be minimum. The IMF and the WTO have launched elaborate websites, along with huge arrangement for press releases, newsletters, reports, pamphlets, audio-visual productions, in-person contacts, and public exhibitions. However, governments remain tight-lipped about their dealings with global governance agencies and global corporations. Transgovernmental relations stand outside of public eye. They hardly know that many private regulatory schemes are important for various aspects of global communications, global finance, global investment and global trade. Many governance agencies fall short of effective transparency with respect to their dealings on globalisation. Documents released by governance institutions are opaque for the uninitiated owing to their overwhelming use of technical terms, obscure acronyms, professional jargon and other specialised vocabulary.

Global governance has been suffering from democratic deficit. Democracies are poorly equipped with tools, techniques and measures to deal with transplanetary and supraterritorial connectivity and globalisation. Democracies lack processes to conduct polls of the affected public. There are sample public opinion surveys by polling agencies, but have no place in activating democratic participation in global politics. Official public referenda do not figure, save in Switzerland, in the governance of globalisation. Questions of globalisation find so mention in parliamentary and presidential elections. Most of the suprastate institutions operate without elected popular representatives. Macro-regional parliamentary organs, NATO, ASEAN, IMF or WHO, are not directly elected. Technical means to conduct transplanetary ballots are currently not available. Even global political parties, like the Socialist International, are not equipped to launch intercontinental electoral campaigns. Even various private regulatory mechanisms in the governance of globalisation have operated without any kind of public polls.[20] Elected representative legislative institutions also do not exercise democratic oversight of the governance of globalisation. Only some members of parliaments monitor certain aspects of the regulation of global relations. Often legislative assemblies escape their duties and overlook global matters. Devolution of governments has not yielded greater democratic oversight of global governance. Regulation of global regimes does not come in treaty form, and thereby it escapes the need for legislative approval. Governments take decisions on global questions without consulting the legislatures. It is difficult to obtain official documents on global subjects. Few parliamentarians bring personal expertise to do their job on global issues. There are few professional researchers and advisers to help and guide them. There are some instances of increased legislative activism concerning globalisation: the Global Legislators Organization for a Balanced Environment (GLOBE), 1989, Parliamentarians for Global Action, 2004, Parliamentary Conference on the WTO, 2000 etc. However, such bodies lack number, influence and regularity. Rules to govern transplanetary connections have proliferated without involvement from popularly elected assemblies.

On the judicial side, avenues to obtain justice are generally not available in the governance of global issues. Citizens normally cannot take grievances regarding global affairs to their national and local tribunals. Courts cannot pronounce on the activities of the state outside its territory or on the activities of suprastate authorities. Global courts are either absent or unavailable for direct citizen's petitions concerning the governance of globalisation. The International Court of Justice in the Hague considers cases brought only by states. The same holds true for the WTO Dispute Settlement Mechanism. There are no official avenues even for public inspections, independent evaluations, and investigations by authorities. Accountability remains modest. Open, outside, independent, published assessment of the performance of the global bodies is lacking.

Civil society associations encourage citizen participation in policymaking on global issues, both from the inside and from the outside, but their activism remains modest. These groups have sometimes fallen short of democratic standards of participation and accountability in their own practices. Only a small proportion of the world's population participates in citizen mobilisation. These civil society organisations have small membership and nominal involvement (payment of subscription only). The larger public rally behind a campaign only on a short-term and ad hoc basis. NGOs are mostly the preserve of relatively small number of full-time professional activists. They lack democratic credentials in their own behaviour. They are run on top-down managerial authoritarianism. In some cases, their jet-setting staff has little touch with their notional beneficiaries as they fly from one global conference to the next elsewhere. They rarely hold regular, independently monitored elections of their officers. They do not publish independent evaluations of their actually conducted activities. Some of them are not public interest organisations, but fronts for governments, political parties and corporations. There is lack of transparency about who they are, what objectives they pursue, where their funds originate, how they reach their policy positions, how they happen to continue etc. However, some of their leaders do challenge their own democratic practices. Their critical voices demand more participation, transparency and accountability in their own ranks.

Technocracy wins over democracy in the governance of globalisation. Regulation of global affairs often rests with bureaucrats who are largely insulated from public inputs and public controls. Some officials cherish 'depoliticisation of global governance' at their own levels. They consider themselves as objective experts who operate global regimes most efficiently without ill-informed public interference. However, some civil society consultation has been built into a number of global policy-making processes. Accredited organisations do participate in many global governance convocations and inject citizen voices into policy processes on global issues. Some of the activists accept invitations to join state delegations to such events. Civil society associations also arrange public meetings where citizens can express concerns and make proposals regarding globalisation. Other meetings take the form of noisy rallies, marches, petitions, campaigns and boycotts.

Structural Inequalities

One of the inescapable consequences of globalisation is a massive concentration of wealth and power in the remote bodies beyond the reach of political accountability, making it problematic for nation-states and local communities to shape their economic, social, and environmental development.[21]

Effective operation of democracy requires suitable education, institutions and social structure. Its education relates to citizen awareness and mobilisation, institutions permit public participation and accountability, and social structure admits equal opportunity of involvement for everyone. All the three are closely interconnected and mutually determining. The former two depend on social structures of equality. Social inequalities present a major barrier to full democracy. They all throw major challenges to democracy in globalisation.

Inequality between countries constitutes one of the principal bases of dominance and subordination in contemporary globalisation. Governments of subordinated countries have less opportunities for involvement and influence in global regulatory processes. North America and Western Europe have greater say in the governance of global affairs.[22] In comparison to G8, the Southern groups of G24, or G77 exercise negligible influence. Only five states have the arbitrary privilege of permanent membership and veto power in the UN Security Council. Innumerable proposals for more democratisation of the UN have not gone beyond the commission report. Besides WTO and IMF, structural inequality of countries also extends to civil society activities. Even the best resourced civil society actors of the South do not match the North based academic, business, labour, NGO, professional and religious bodies. Northern elements generally hold positions in transworld civil society organisations. Critics dismiss so-called 'global civil society' as neocolonial affair. *Class inequalities* also place major structural impediments in the way of democratic governance of global relations. Financiers, industrialists, professionals and people with inherited wealth have more chances to shape the governance of globalisation than their fellow citizens. There is 'corporate rule': rule by the elite or the business people. Small number of transborder enterprises dominate most sectors of global economy. There is no market-democracy. Only a minority has the opportunity to own big shares. The main shareholders have been large trusts, pension funds and insurance companies who usually have little contact with the everyday lives of the common man. Even governance agencies are more concerned about business interests and investor confidence. Many states happen to reduce the capacities of organised labour to promote worker interests. Large majorities of elected officeholders and top bureaucrats come from advantaged classes who, adept in English, dominate global and regional civil services. This managerial class moves within closed social networks of education, recreation, status, past background and aspiration. Civil society associations too involve only university-educated, computer-literate and propertied persons. Many NGOs draw their personnel and members from elite quarters. In poor countries, NGO jobs are highly coveted where only the privileged people obtain large share of the NGO funds. The underclass people lack the funds, language frequency and organisational capacities required for effective participation in global civil society. Opportunities for them are severely limited. Many other *cultural, gender and age inequalities* also prevail to obstruct democratic working in the global governance. Most of the rules of global governance reflect norms of the dominant civilisation. They are secularism, anthropocentrism, instrumentalism, and techno-scientist rationalism. No place is given to non-Western, non-modern and native ways of being and believing. Regulators of contemporary globalisation have neither understood nor have time to understand them. Usually aboriginals and indigenous peoples are sidelined. No non-Western religion or civilisation, Hindu, Sikh, Islam, or Bauddha, their spirituality or appeal to transcendent forces, is given opportunity to influence or guide globalisation. Native peoples have only marginal involvement in global civil society activities. As transplanetary and supraterritorial connections threaten their values, they look for ways to express their concerns and protect their way of life. Contemporary globalisation leaves very limited possibilities for cultural pluralism and intercultural negotiation. Hierarchies also prevail on gender lines.[23] Globalisation has largely a masculine agenda. A large number of women is participating in the ranks of NGOs and social movements. Males at the top often dominate them. Women provide the bulk of administrative support. Social hierarchies based on age, race, urban-rural location, disability and the aged also prevail. Structural inequalities have produced far more dominance than democracy. Contemporary globalisation has no time or mood to deal with them.

In sum, contemporary globalisation has very weak democratic credentials. Its polycentric governance of global affairs has very low level of participation from and accountability to the people at large. The people on the whole have been uninformed and uninvolved, particularly, when it comes to life and death questions like global climatic change, global financial crises, global militarisation, or global terrorism. Global governance has come down to a kind of minority rule without rights to majority. Regulation of transplanetary and supraterritorial connectivity lacks democratic legitimacy. Its authority can be legitimate only when the governed acknowledge that the reignholders of global governance have a right to rule over them. They conduct global affairs more on the basis of ignorance, apathy, neglect, exploitation, and coercion of the large proportions of the global population, and less and less on consent. To render globalisation more humane, Scholte has proposed to enhance human security, social equality, and democracy by exploiting all the available possibilities.[24] These possibilities pertain to enabling technological and organisational development, greater public awareness of global problems, larger transworld solidarities among people, popular mobilisation on global issues, and increased receptiveness among elites to reform policies on globalisation. All this has to be done in view of challenges posed by intensely rising globalisation. Briefly they are: (i) continuing substantial force of neoliberalisation; (ii) large power of big capital; (iii) resistance of the dominant US state to global public policy; (iv) persistent attachment to myths of (Westphalian) sovereignty; (v) underdeveloped institutional capacities to formulate and implement global public policies; (vi) limited popular constituencies for far-reaching policy innovations; and, (vii) inexperience with ethics of interculturalism, particularly among western modernists.

Notes

1. The inventor of "globalisation" and former editor of *Harvard Business Review* Dr. Theodore Lewit passed away on July 7, 2006.
2. From Festenston, Mathew, and Kenny, Michael. *Political Ideologies,* Oxford: 2005, 443, in Anthony Giddens, *Beyond Left and Right: The Future of Radical Politics*: Polity Press, 1994, 3-11.
3. B.M. Sharma and Roop Singh Bareth (eds.), *Good Governance, Globalisation and Civil Society*, Jaipur: Rawat Publications, 2004, 10.
4. Martin Shaw, "The global revolution and the twenty-first century: from international relations to global politics", in Stephen Chan and Jarrod Wiener, eds., *International History and the Twentieth Century*, London: IB Taurus, 1999.
5. Ibid., passim.
6. Infra, p. 355.
7. Supra, Chapter, 7.
8. For details, see, Chapter, 11.
9. Held, D., A. McGrew, D. Goldblatt, and J. Perraton. *Global Transformations: Politics, Economics and Culture*. Polity and Stanford University Press, 1999.
10. Held and McGrew (1999) do not label their theory as "transformationalist." However, Held and McGrew (2001) do cite their 1999 work under the rubric "An Intermediate Way: the Transformationalist Analysis" thus explicitly label their theory as a transformationalist theory and explicitly seek to place it analytically "in-between" hyper-globalist and sceptic theories.
11. For details, see, Chapter 14.
12. Address of Kofi Annan, Secretary-General to General Assembly on 23.9.03.

13. Quoted by Pantich, L. "Rethinking the Role of the State" in J.H. Mittesiman (ed.), *Globalisation: Critical Reflections*, London: Lynne Rienner, 1996, 83-113.
14. Joseph Kruth, *Entering the Age of Transformation: Choosing The Destiny of Humanity in the 21st Century*, 1999.
15. On "ideology", see, Chapter 12.
16. Graham Harrison, "Globalization" in Georgina Blakeley and Valerie Bryson, *Contemporary Political Concepts: A Critical Introduction*: London: Pluto Press, 2002, 14-33.
17. Harison, op. cit. 29.
18. Gail, Omvedt, "Marx and globalization", from http://www.the-hindu.com/2001/03/01/stories/05012524.htm; Referred by: Sashi Kanth, published on: March 5, 2001.
19. However, some civil society associations at their own or in collusion with some vested interests have discouraged public learning about globalisation. They spread inaccurate information and biased views.
20. The Forest Stewardship Council (FSC) is an exception in having chambers to represent different stakeholders, although the people involved have been largely self-appointed.
21. Volodin in Harshe, Rajen, ed., *Interpreting Globalization: Perspectives in International Relations*, Jaipur and New Delhi: Rawat Publications/Indian Council of Social Science Research, 2004
22. See, Chapter 14 on "Global Governance", WTO and IMF.
23. For details, see, Chapter 15.
24. Jan Art Scholte, *Globalization: A Critical Introduction*, Second Edition, Palgrave, 2005, 422-3.

14

Understanding Global Governance

Understanding 'Governance'

According to Samuel M. Makinda 'there is no universally accepted definition of 'governance', but this term is often used to refer to interpretations of order, stability and politico-economic management.' 'Governance' is said to be the process whereby public institutions conduct public affairs, manage public resources and guarantee the realisation of human rights. 'Governance is the sum of the many ways individuals and institutions, public and private, manage their common affairs. It is a continuing process through which conflicting or diverse interests may be accommodated and cooperative action may be taken. It includes formal institutions and regimes empowered to enforce compliance, as well as informal arrangements that people and institutions either have agreed to or perceive to be in their interest.' This concept of "governance" is not new. It is as old as human civilisation. It simply means: the process of decision-making and the process by which decisions are implemented (or not implemented). Governance can be used in several contexts such as corporate governance, international governance, national governance and local governance. Since governance is the process of decision-making and the process by which decisions are implemented, an analysis of governance focuses on the formal and informal actors involved in decision-making and implementing the decisions made. It means formal and informal structures that have been set in place to arrive at and implement the decision.

Governance is a new paradigm. It denotes something more than 'government' which refers to a set of instruments through which people govern themselves by means of laws, rules and regulations enforced by the state apparatus. Sometimes it connotes reform in government and its relations with other societal institutions. Some find it closer to the concept of 'New Public Administration',[1] 'Public Choice School',[2] 'Reinventing Government',[3] and 'New Public Management'.[4]

But to the present author, 'governance' is 'dynamism' of political system. It is thinking, deciding and action-taking part of a polity. Governance means undertaking of leading, running, moving, maintaining and protecting a people or political community amid flux of changing environment. This environment consists of other systems and subsystems which may be opposing and challenging that system. Apparently, 'governance' is non-aggressive. It may be democratic or non-democratic. As a 'neutral' concept, its variables can be ascertained and operationalised. With this view, its 'structures' and 'functions' can be empirically determined. The concept can further be improved or reformulated to realise specific goals and values. It can also be looked at as a series of decision-making processes.

After ascertaining the empirical form of 'governance' in terms of requisites and variables, we can explain and examine any other existing form of 'governance'. We can also observe this 'empirically ascertained form of governance' as a 'scale' or an instrument or device of measurement. With this scale we can measure the type, size, quality of any type of 'governance' and evaluate it on merit. Deficiencies of that particular set of 'governance' can be booked for reform. Various forms or sets of 'governance' can be compared with one another on the basis of this scale. This scale can indicate various steps to a polity to improve its governance to realise specific goals.

Rosenau finds 'governance' consisting of "systems of rule at all levels of human activity – from the family to the international organisation – in which the pursuit of goals through the exercise of control has trans-national repercussions." According to the Commission on Global Governance (1995), 'Governance is the sum of the many ways individuals and institutions, public and private, manage their common affairs. It is a continuing process through which conflicting or diverse interests may be accommodated and cooperative action may be taken. It includes formal institutions and regimes empowered to enforce compliance, as well as informal arrangements that people and institutions either have agreed to or perceive to be in their interest.

According to Samuel M. Makinda, the concept of global governance, as distinct from 'good governance', refers to formal and informal sets of arrangements in global politics. It implies that states alone cannot manage global affairs, and therefore, it accords roles to international governmental organisations (IGOs), non-governmental organisations (NGOs) and multinational corporations (MNCs).

Taking the concept a step further and perhaps bringing it closer to earth, Finkelstein defines it as "governing, without sovereign authority, relationships that transcend national frontiers. Global governance is doing internationally what governments do at home".[5] World Bank defines governance as the traditions and institutions by which authority in a country is exercised for the common good. This includes (i) the process by which those in authority are selected, monitored and replaced, (ii) the capacity of the government to effectively manage its resources and implement sound policies, and (iii) the respect of citizens and the state for the institutions that govern economic and social interactions. Rosenau conceives it as system of rules as the purposive activities of any collectivity that sustains mechanisms designed to insure its safety, prosperity, coherence, stability and continuance. These activities are undertaken by organisations other than governments, but governments specialise in them; so whilst governance occurs without government, government cannot be there without governance.

Governance and Good Governance at Global Levels

The World Bank and the International Monetary Fund, on the other hand, use 'good governance' to refer to a particular type of political and economic order. For them, 'good governance' is associated with the spread of democracy and transparency in governments and free markets. 'Good governance' is the opposite of arbitrary and self-seeking rule, corruption and cronyism, which have been endemic in some Third World societies. However, the World Bank and IMF's version of 'good governance' has been expansive to Third World peoples. Although the World Bank and the IMF started to emphasise different priorities following the crises in East Asia in the late 1990s, their 'good governance' is still associated with reduction in public expenditure, emphasis on exports and less charges in hospitals and schools. Any 'governance' can turn out to be 'good' or 'bad', 'efficient' or 'efficient', or 'effective' or 'ineffective'. In order to make governance 'good', certain variables, attributes or functions are ascribed to it. For World Bank or the UN Funding Agencies, governance is 'good' if it accepts tenets of LPG and liberal democracy. But it can assume any form of its own liking. However, in order to be effective and viable, it has to be popular, participative and inclusive, though these attributes or qualities may tell upon 'governance', in terms of speed, cost, effect and efficiency. Remedy lies in having good governance, not in cosmetic palliatives or plastic surgery. 'Good governance' is essentially free from abuse and corruption, and with due regard for the rule of law. Good governance is a process which enables an organisation, structure or institution to anticipate and prevent problems and to take readily all steps to solve them effectively and efficiently when they arise. The true test of "good" governance is the degree to which it delivers the goods in the form of the promise of human rights: civil, cultural, economic, political and social rights. The key question is: are the institutions of governance effectively guaranteeing the right to health, adequate housing, sufficient food, quality education, fair justice and personal security? The concept of 'good governance' has been clarified by the Commission on Human Rights. In its resolution (2000/64) the Commission identified the key attributes of good governance as: (1) transparency; (2) responsibility;

(3) accountability, prompt and effective action, learning and use of knowledge; and (4) participation. To bring about structural change and reforms in their favour, they extend or attach aid, grants, donations on condition of replacing their old democracy and administration in some form.

An another analysis of 'good governance' exemplifies eight major characteristics: (1) participation; (2) rule of law; (3) transparency; (4) responsiveness; (5) consensus oriented; (6) equity and inclusiveness; (7) effectiveness and efficiency; and (8) accountability. Major donors and international financial institutions are increasingly basing their aid and loans on the condition that reforms that ensure "good governance" are undertaken.

Andrew Taylor has proposed that a state pursuing good governance would (i) actively fight corruption and the use of public office for private gain; (ii) enhance democratic procedures, institutions and principles; (iii) institute limited terms for key public offices; (iv) reduce government in size and function; (v) remove economic controls; (vi) privatise state and parastatal enterprises; (vii) establish and enforce a code of conduct; and (viii) promote independent and effective judiciary.[6]

Global Governance

At the global level, governance has been viewed primarily as intergovernmental relationships, but it must now be understood as also involving non-governmental organisations (NGOs), citizens' movements, multinational corporations, and the global capital market. Interacting with these are global mass media of dramatically enlarged influence.

Globalisation[7] evolves its own methods, means and mechanism of Global Governance. Still Global Governance is not world government. But it is moving toward a form of World Government mainly dominated by G-7. David calls this process as 'transformationalism' (David Held, A. McGrew, D. Goldblatt, and J. Perraton, *Global Transformation: Politics, Economics and Culture*, 1999).

From Statism to Polycentrism

Contemporary large-scale and accelerated globalisation has rendered the *statist* mode of governance non-viable. It has encouraged the emergence of *polycentric* regulation. 'Statism' refers to a condition where societal governance is more or less equivalent to the regulatory operations of territorial bureaucratic national governments. All occurs directly through the state and inter-state relations. Macro-regional and global regulatory mechanisms are small in scale. Local governments have no significant autonomy from central governments regarding national questions. They lack authority to engage directly with the wider world outside their state. Owing to transplanetary and supraterritorial connectivity statist conditions no longer mark governance today. Governance now involves suprastate regimes that enjoy some autonomy from the state. It has become multilayered and trans-scalar. No single 'level' reigns over the other. This situation of governance is called 'polycentrism'. Other terms used for it are: 'empire' (Michael Hardt and Antonio Negri), 'cosmocracy' (John Keane), 'new medievalism' (Bull), 'new multilateralism' or 'plurilateralism' (Cerny, Cox, and Schechter), 'mobius-web governance' (James Rosenau) and some others. But *polycentrism* is a better term. It both captures the multi-sited character of current governance and invites an exploration of the interplay between sites.[8]

Polycentrism involves:

1. *The obsolescence of statism*: Accelerated globalisation and the rise of transplanetary and supraterritorial connectivity have made Westphalian construction of state sovereignty obsolete.[9] However, sovereignty has not ended, but has taken new forms to fit poststatist conditions. It has not marked the end of state power. Governments can shape the effects of globalisation on their territories and populations. State is not the same. It is changing on four counts: one, it has to serve global as well as national constituencies; two, state provisions of social welfare are being readjusted; three, warfare has undergone total transformation; and, four, regulatory processes are busy with increased transstate connections, as with, G7/8, G20, G24, G77 (133) and the like. Global concerns and connections have loosened the cohesiveness of the state.
2. *Multi-scalar public governance*: Governance does not end with the state. Globality is diffused from states to other sites 'above' and 'below' the country government. Public-sector governance has dispersed in three ways: (i) As country based statist regulation has become impractical, institutions at municipal, provincial, macroregional and transworld levels have come into action to fill the gap in effective governance; (ii) In dealing with the issues of global health, global environmental changes etc. substate and suprastate agencies have comparative advantage over states; and (iii) Growth of global communications, global travel, global organisation, global finance, global law and global consciousness have equipped substate and suprastate authorities with more tools to sustain their operations even bypassing states. Many substate authorities have developed direct transborder contacts with parties abroad. Some provincial governments have bypassed the central state to develop direct links with suprastate agencies.

Globalisation has encouraged a trend of macro-regionalisation among states, such as, GATT, the League of Arab States, the Organisation of American States, NATO, ASEAN, EU, SAARC etc. But suprastate governance involves more than regional arrangements. HIV/AIDs, the Internet, air travel, refugee movements, transplanetary money flows, climate change, etc. cannot be effectively regulated without global regulation and structures. Global governance is unavoidable and indispensable in the twenty-first century. Global arrangements like IMF, UNDP, World Bank etc. are a 'must' today.

3. *Privatised governance*: There is also the spread of private, non-statutory frameworks of rules. Formulation, implementation, monitoring and enforcement of societal rules is also occurring through nonofficial channels of market-based agencies and society organisations. Globalisation encourages them in two ways: (a) a number of private regulatory arrangements fill regulatory gaps left in suprastate governance. Unprecedented growth of transworld and macro-regional regimes has yet not come under regulatory global relations. Therefore, non-governmental actors are stepping in. The private agencies are constructing the necessary standards and norms to enable increased global relations to develop; and (b) the prevailing neoliberalist approach is also promoting the rise of private regulations. They have gone far beyond the past arrangements. Some maintain 'corporate social responsibility' (CSR), such as, the UN Centre for Transnational Corporation, WHO Framework Convention on Tobacco Control etc. Illustrations of some other CSR arrangements are: Global Reporting Initiative, 1997, Amnesty International, 1998, Forest Stewardship Council, 1993, etc. Global companies handle their disputes through private arbitration like the International Court of Arbitration of the International Chamber of Commerce, the London Court of Arbitration, etc. The New York Convention on the Recognition and Enforcement of Foreign Arbitral Awards, 1958, stipulates that national courts cannot review the judgements of arbitrators on core issues. Others are: the World Federation of Exchanges, the Derivatives Policy Group, the International Federation of Accountants, the International Telecommunication Union, the Internet Corporation for Assigned Names and Numbers, the International Air Transport Association, the World Tourism Organization, and the like. There is 'contracting out' of the delivery of public services to private providers to non-profit organisations like the CARE International, the World Vision International, and so on.
4. *Global civil society*: The character of civil society has changed with the rise of globalisation. Civil society associations have redirected their operations from states to other sites, networks of governance and

global regulatory arrangements. There is 'multilateralism' of civil society associations. There are many transnational social movements, supraterritorial advocacy networks, and global citizen action societies. Their range, scope and number is much more today. Contemporary civil society has gone global in *seven* directions: (i) about transplanetary problems – arms control, climate change, cultural protection, debt relief, gender equity, HIV/AIDS, human rights, labour standards, religious revivalism, and specific trade agreements. There is rise of activism against globalisation itself, popularly known as anti-globalisation, alter-globalisation, or counter-globalisation; (ii) about UN agencies, the World Bank, the IMF, and the WTO. The ICFTU, the Institute of International Finance, the Oxfam etc. maintain offices closer to the headquarters of the IMF and the World Bank; (iii) convening of global meetings alongside the official global governance conferences; (iv) global organisations like the Geneva-based World Economic Forum, the Brussels-based ICFTU, and others; (v) civil society developments helped by global finance, e.g., the Ford Foundation supports many NGOs throughout the world; (vi) transterritorial organisations based on sentiments of transplanetary solidarity related to age, class, disability, gender, profession, race, and religious faith; and (vii) cooperation of civil society associations in areas of transworld regulatory activities, such as, World Bank Structural Adjustment Policy Review Initiative, the Ethical Trading Initiative, and the like. Environmental NGOs are particularly prominent in these areas.

At times, civil society associations have also blocked global governance initiatives. They have also worked to press changes in state policies, particularly on budget allocation, economic planning, environmental laws and justice. Dispersion of regulatory activities does not entail a diffusion of power. As a result, the contemporary globalising world faces crises from time to time and confronts critical democratic deficits in the globalisation framework as a whole.

Theoretical Context

Global governance has a conceptual approach to describe how the world works politically in an era when focus on the nation-state does not suffice.[10] There is purpose in the global order, and while no actor seems to control the outcomes, there are enough patterns of influence to suggest that some form of management occurs. John R. Mathiason identifies five functions that are performed by this international sector: regime creation, mobilisation of information, direct provision of certain public services, norm enforcement and internal management. Each covers a wide variety of tasks and objectives.

Samuel M. Makinda in his essay 'Recasting Global Governance' demonstrates that global governance can be understood from several *perspectives*. This he does by focusing on three themes: *state sovereignty, globalisation* and Western hegemony. He explains briefly the theoretical approaches, and describes how the global 'interpretive community' has sought to influence perceptions of global governance. He also analyses how sovereignty has evolved.

As *global governance* is a multifaceted process, studying it requires theoretical framework that goes beyond a single paradigm. Makinda employs a *pluralist* approach that is informed by insights mainly, but not exclusively, from *realist, liberal* and *constructivist* research programmes. There are several variants of realism, liberalism and constructivism. Moreover, even when taken together, these three paradigms cannot shed light on every facet of global life. They go a long way in explaining power, order, norms and change. As Stephen Walt has argued: 'The "complete diplomat" of the future should remain cognizant of realism's emphasis on the inescapable role of power, keep liberalism's awareness of domestic forces in mind, and occasionally reflect on constructivism's vision of change'.

Realist accounts of global politics tend to emphasise how states use power to maximise their national interests. They posit that the most important international actors are sovereign states, which are rational and operate in an inherently competitive, anarchic and self-help environment. Realists assume that sovereignty makes states functionally similar. They also emphasise strategies that states devise in efforts to improve their standing in international economic competition, influence weaker states or compete for international prestige. Thus, realists focus on military balancing and 'positional competition' in economic, technological and other non-military matters. They acknowledge the existence of globalisation, civil society and transnational forces, but they give no room to these in their analyses. While realism may be helpful in highlighting the role of power and self-interest in global governance, it discounts the function of ideas, culture, institutions and norms, except as instruments in power politics.

At a glance, *liberalism* would appear to be the most appropriate approach to use in the study of global governance because, as Michael Doyle has observed, it is identified 'with an essential principle, the importance of the freedom of the individual'. Liberalism would adequately explain the interactions of states, civil society, MNCs and IGOs in global governance. The liberal perspective on global politics posits that there 'is at the minimum a heterogeneous state of peace and war' which could 'become a state of global peace, in which the expectation of war disappears'. Liberals believe that IGOs, such as the UN, play a vital role in world politics. They acknowledge that 'states live under international anarchy', but they argue that 'states are inherently respectful of international law' and that 'they do not experience a general state of war'. Liberals reject the realist claim that states are functionally similar units. Doyle, for example, has argued that states 'are inherently different "units", differentiated by how they relate to individual human rights'. In general, liberals believe that the interests of states extend beyond security and include the protection of human rights.

Constructivism is concerned with the way norms, rules and institutions constitute the identities and interests of states and other international actors. It claims that the structures of human association, including the international society, are determined primarily by shared ideas and culture rather than material forces. While realists claim that it is the distribution of capabilities that determines the nature of the international system, constructivists argue that those capabilities have meaning only because of the ideas we attach to them. Constructivists claim that it is the distribution of ideas and culture that determines the shape of the international system. As constructivism focuses on the roles of norms, ideas and culture in constructing international structures, it would have plenty to say about how global governance is constituted. As already indicated, global governance is about norms and power. It is constituted by ideas, culture and material forces. It also helps generate norms, ideas and culture. Global governance involves states and non-state actors, and it affects life from the local to the global levels.

Role of the Interpretive Community

Global governance, essentially a product of liberal thinking, concerns so-called global values, norms, standards and rules. The majority of values that are considered global are Western and so global governance basically facilitates and reflects *Western hegemony*. Western hegemony here refers to the dominance of Western institutions, interests, standards and NGOs. The 'global civil society' is based on Western mores. In global governance, non-Western states and NGOs have had to redefine their interests and identities in relation to Western norms and power. Severe socio-economic problems have delivered the Third World political leaders and NGOs into the hands of the West, thereby making Western hegemony appear like an 'empire by invitation'.

The dominance of Western institutions is partly due to the function of an *'interpretive community'* that constantly explains, promotes, advocates and justifies global governance. The 'interpretative community' has been extremely successful in portraying Western ideas, values and preferences as *global*. The term 'interpretive community' refers to any group of people who are committed to providing justification and legitimating principles for particular institutions, values or practices. Members of an 'interpretive community' may come from different professional backgrounds, such as scholars, journalists, international civil servants and NGO workers. They may also be recruited from different countries and might not even be aware that they operate as a part of a global 'interpretive community'. What they have in common is a conviction that they are interpreting reality, when, in fact, they may be only expressing aspirations. Sometimes the ideas of an 'interpretive community' may influence practice. In the post-Cold War era, members of the global 'interpretive community' have converged on several themes, including a new world order, globalisation and new forms of sovereignty and security. For example, in December 1988, Soviet President Mikhail Gorbachev used the phrase 'new world order' in his address to the UN to underline the new strategic thinking and the global restructuring which he envisaged, but the 'world' simply ignored it. However, when the US President George Bush used the same phrase two years later, the 'world' took notice. In condemning Iraq's invasion of Kuwait in August 1990, Bush talked of a new world order 'where the rule of law supplants the rule of the jungle, a world in which nations recognise the shared responsibility for freedom and justice'. This liberal aspiration contrasted sharply with the realist logic of power politics, in which war between states is always considered a possibility. It was no more than a wish for a different type of international system in the post-Cold War era, but other world leaders, scholars and journalists subsequently started talking of a new world order, as if it was a reality. Bush's aspiration did not spell an end to power politics; instead it gave impetus to a re-thinking of norms in world politics, and this, in turn, energised efforts to portray Western values, standards and institutions as global norms.

It was in this intellectual climate that the Commission on Global Governance issued a report which defined sovereignty as an institution that is ultimately derived from the people: 'It is a power to be exercised by, for, and on behalf of the people of a state'. This report implies that sovereignty should be respected, only if the people of a state have had an opportunity to exercise their political, economic and cultural rights. The report also argues that 'the principle of sovereignty and the norms that derive from it must be further adapted to recognise changing realities'. Furthermore, 'global security extends beyond the protection of borders, ruling elites and exclusive state interests to include the protection of people'. The Commission was simply expressing aspirations that may become practice one day. At about the same time, a former Australian Foreign Minister Gareth Evans argued that the concept of security, 'as it appears in the [UN] Charter, is as much about the protection of individuals as it is about the defence of the territorial integrity of states'. Earlier in April 1991, a former UN Secretary-General Javier Pérez de Cuéllar had argued that state sovereignty needed to be reassessed in response to 'the shift in public attitudes towards the belief that the defence of the oppressed in the name of morality should prevail over frontiers and legal documents'. Similarly, his successor, Boutros Boutros-Ghali, argued that the time of absolute and exclusive sovereignty had passed

The former UN Secretary-General, Kofi Annan, went further in redefining sovereignty, when he told the General Assembly in September 1999 that his interpretation of the UN charter was that it aims 'to protect individual human beings, not to protect those who abuse them'. Annan argued, in his speech to the General Assembly in 1999, that sovereignty had been 'redefined by the forces of globalisation and international cooperation', and that the state was the 'servant of its people, and not vice versa'. The conclusions of the Commission on Global Governance and those of the UN secretaries-general and other analysts in recent years suggest that the re-thinking of norms has given rise to an interpretive community which is ready to argue for changes in the practices of sovereignty. By arguing for liberal interpretations of the UN charter, they have promoted a particular view of global governance. However, the views of an 'interpretive community', without changes in the practices of the majority of international actors, cannot constitute a shift in the meaning of sovereignty. According to some analysts, it was not possible in the 1990s to see a clear-cut turn in state practices. As Adam Roberts has observed, while idealists have hoped that 'the sovereignty of states would take second place to human rights', humanitarian action in the 1990s 'owed much to political considerations that were often tinged with an element of *realpolitik*'. It is such interpretations that set the stage on which 'NGOs and IGOs grope, sometimes cooperatively, sometimes competitively, sometimes in parallel towards a modicum of global governance'. What these interpretations do not say is that global governance links together 'global civil society', individuals, the state and market forces. It is also about the generation of, and the response to, 'shared' values and institutions, which give rise to a process to identify issues, form an agenda, and arrive at outcomes and make arrangements to implement them. In this way, global governance has definite implications for interpretations of sovereignty.

Ideology of Global Governance

Governance is not a neutral description of an inevitable process. It is an ideology that justifies the neo-liberal state. Much of its activity is directed towards creating a business-friendly environment and managing the tensions caused by globalisation.[11] Presently, governance is a value-judgement about the nature and purpose of government which should be reduced in size and scope. Small government is 'good' governance. It legitimises neo-liberal ideas on government's 'correct' functions and is presented as a rational, technical and inevitable adjustment to new political conditions created by globalisation. Governance emphasises the complexity of the political process and the variety of actors and is often silent on the quality of the state-society interactions, but does concede unequal participation and that some interests are more important that others. It allocates the state key roles but the state has its own interests and enjoys relative independence from those who empowered them (Engels 1890: 685-6). 'Only the state can give meaning, objectives and direction to governance.'[12] The state provides a strategic overview, determines priorities, and retains substantial economic and coercive resources. Governance is a process, not an end. The state still balances and reconciles competing and contradictory demands with accumulation.

Agencies of Global Governance

WTO

Global governance is related to the key multilateral economic institutions like the IMF, the World Bank and the WTO. It varies from TRIPs, TRIMs and agriculture to services, market access and dispute settlements. Many people are unaware of the World Trade Organization (WTO), yet it makes decisions which affect the future of everyone. Established in 1994 (Marrakech Agreement) and located in Geneva, the WTO makes rules and regulations about health, safety and environmental standards worldwide. Member-states commit themselves (with no reservations allowed) to alter their national statutes and procedures to comply with suprastate laws. Advice of the DSB (Dispute Settlement Body) is binding unless every state party to the global trade regime votes to overturn the advice. Its standards are often based on industry requests, with little, if any, input from consumers. The WTO, successor of GATT, divides global governance by means of various trade-related agreements, which are both technical as well as all-compassing general instruments.[13]

It operates on the basis of one vote per member state. But core global trade negotiations occur between the USA and the EU. Nearly one-third of the member governments lack the resources to maintain a permanent delegation in Geneva to monitor and intervene in its day-to-day affairs of the WTO. Most of the states of the South and the East have no representation whatsoever in decision-making at the OECD.

The WTO has final authority over all of its decisions, and is more powerful for trade matters than any nation, including the US. All however is not bleak. On the positive side, over 600 non profit organisations worldwide used the Internet to prevent adoption of one of the most offensive treaties, the Multilateral Agreement on Investment (MAI). The World Bank and the IMF have charted out a course of action for parties in dispute with each other. It makes up a remarkable instrument of governance. Corporate power globally is enormous and growing. It is hard to imagine that more than half of the top 100 economies in the world are now private businesses. Corporate power also grows significantly through international treaties.

IMF

In 1946, the Washington-based IMF held a modest attempt to establish and then manage the Bretton Woods regime of fixed exchange rates. However, since the 1970s the Fund has intervened more intensely with its client governments.

At the IMF, governments of the G7 control 45 per cent of votes on the Executive Board. The African 44 states have less than 5 per cent of the total votes. According to a prevalent convention, a West European is always Managing Director of the IMF, while a citizen of the USA is always President of the World Bank.[14]

Since then, the IMF has undertaken comprehensive and detailed surveillance of economic annual performance of its 184-member states and of the world economy as a whole. The IMF supplies major training and technical assistance services, largely to poorly equipped states. The IMF Institute has 21,000 officials the world over. The Fund has gone beyond its traditional stabilisation measures to sponsor wide-ranging economic restructuring programmes in 80 countries. It plays a pivotal role in responding to crises in global finance, including emergencies occurring everywhere. It has acted as something like a suprastate central bank. It has developed some general principles for overseeing global commercial banking , such as, capital adequacy ratios, payment and settlement systems. The World Bank has given considerable attention to reforming state and substate governance in areas such as the civil service, the judiciary and labour legislation.

OECD

The OECD (Organization for Economic Cooperation and Development) also illustrates the contemporary growth of global economic governance. With a Paris based secretariat consisting of 2,300 people, the OECD convenes some 200 committees, working parties, and expert groups. Its recommendations has multiplied more than tenfold. Its measures have especially addressed the environment, taxation, and transworld investments. Like the WTO and the IMF, the OECD has acquired a significant role in policy surveillance.

It is essential to understand that humanity is engaged in a contest over who will determine its future. Will the business and financial world define and dominate human societies and relationships with little consideration for individuals, communities and nations? Even the *New York Times* reported this as the "inevitable clash between the power of government and the power of markets … . In Russia, Malaysia, and even Japan, the United States is insisting on reforms that would essentially give power to investors to move their money across borders at will, instead of to governments seeking to control their own destinies." We should understand that these "reforms" do often conflict with the ability of nations and peoples to control their destinies.

Sovereignty and Global Governance

State sovereignty is like a living organism; it casts off its meanings as it evolves in response to the demands of global governance. In simple terms, sovereignty can be described as a principle that legitimises internal political organisation and serves as a mechanism for enhancing international order. It is, therefore, linked to both internal and global governance. Thomas Biersteker and Cynthia Weber have argued, state sovereignty is 'a political entity's externally recognised right to exercise final authority over its affairs'. With regard to internal political control, sovereignty revolves around population, territory and recognised authority. To this Alan James has added a constitutional dimension, claiming that 'sovereign states are those territorially-based entities which are independent in terms of their constitutional arrangements'.

The present author makes a distinction between *three* types of sovereignty. The first is *external* or *juridical* sovereignty, which is based on the notion that theoretically 'the state has over it no other authority than that of international law'. The second is *internal* or *empirical* sovereignty, which is based on the view that states have the right (and capacity) to control the people, resources and institutions within their territories. The third is *individual* or *popular* sovereignty, which is predicated on the claim that all people are entitled to fundamental freedoms and that states exercise control over them only with their consent. Empirical sovereignty and juridical sovereignty accord states rights and responsibilities that other no international actors do have.

The concept of *global governance* implicitly questions some understandings of sovereignty because it is based on the assumption that states and non-state actors are partners in the management of global affairs. Realists, who claim that states are the most important international actors, would regard global governance as a diminution of sovereignty. The realist view of sovereignty is that theoretically each state is free to pursue its domestic and external affairs without outside interference. Hence there appeared Hans Morgenthau's definition of sovereignty as 'a centralised power that exercised its law-making and law-enforcing authority within a certain territory'. On the other hand, liberals, who subscribe to the view that transnational forces play important roles in world politics, regard global governance as a necessary process of addressing anarchy in the absence of central authority. Liberals believe that sovereignty gives states the right to exercise control within their territories, but that this control is to be exercised with some degree of consent and legitimacy from society. For this reason, liberals associate empirical sovereignty with popular sovereignty. Constructivists, who consider sovereignty to be socially constructed, regard global governance as a part of the social construction and reconstruction of international society.

The assumptions that underpin sovereignty date back to the Peace of Westphalia, which inaugurated a new 'international' legal order for Europe. The Westphalian regime, which brought about a break from the previous religious order, is best remembered for making the territorial state the cornerstone of the modern international system. Since then, the development and reinterpretation of sovereignty has closely mirrored the evolution of the state and the prevailing norms of global governance. However, sovereignty has not always been honoured. In Europe, sovereignty was occasionally subverted with a view to maintaining the balance of power. This is partly why Stephen Krasner has claimed that breaches 'to the Westphalian model have been an enduring characteristic of the international environment'. Krasner has more recently written of sovereignty as 'organised hypocrisy'. Others have suggested that sovereignty can be understood only with reference to particular historical periods. Sovereignty has undergone various transformations in accordance with the prevailing norms of global governance. Whenever serious crises undermine the legitimising principles of sovereignty, new norms are negotiated, and these norms often reflect the preferences of the hegemonic states. It is the processes of negotiating the rules for sovereignty which Biersteker and Weber had in mind when they argued that sovereignty was socially constructed. They posited that it is 'the practices of states and non-state agents [that] produce, reform and redefine sovereignty and its constitutive elements'. In such social interactions, all participants help, in varying degrees, to shape, and are also shaped by, the structure of the system. A global structure that is characterised by power politics and secret diplomacy is likely to favour the notion that sovereignty resides with governments. However, a global order, which is committed to the promotion of democracy and human rights, would favour popular sovereignty. Thus, it is the norms, values and institutions which underpin global governance that determine the nature of sovereignty.

The UN and the Future of Global Governance

Globalisation and global governance will go on with or without the UN. Global governance has so far reflected mainly the interests of Western societies, but the UN, a confederation of 192 states (by June 28, 2006), has the potential to make it truly global. It has the potentiality to ensure that the ideas, norms and rules, which underpin global governance, reflect the diversity of values and interests in the world. The UN needs to work out its programmes in such a way that, wherever possible, racial, gender, cultural and economic inequalities are taken into account.

At the hands of the UN, global governance has also grown as an instrument of conflict management. In this direction, the UN has undertaken over 30 peace-keeping operations since 1956 and several humanitarian interventions in 1990s. A global Nuclear Non-proliferation Treaty (NPT) has been administered through the International Atomic Energy Agency (IAEA) since 1970. Other global arms control regimes have addressed biological and chemical weapons. There is a suprastate governance in respect of human rights, labour laws, concerning torture, racial discrimination, protection of children etc. Hardly any state now invokes the domestic jurisdiction clause of the UN Charter. Global human rights governance has brought even individuals to justice after World War II and in the 1990s. A permanent International Court of Justice (ICJ) has been established in Rome in 2002, although its statute has not been ratified by states like China, Russia and the USA. The UN has undertaken direct administration of Bosnia, Cambodia, East Timor, Haiti, Kosovo and South West Africa (Namibia). The construction of governance institutions has not been a one-way affair.

In 'gazing beyond the horizon', the Deputy Secretary-General, Fréchette has emphasised three broad imperatives for the UN: legitimacy; instruments and institutions; and effectiveness. These are very important factors, but they are more complex than they first appear. This is because the UN means different things to various groups. Makinda briefly looks at how realists, liberals and constructivists view the legitimacy of the UN and finally suggest that the UN 'managers' need to reinterpret the charter consistently.

The UN appears to straddle the borderline between realism and liberalism, and it has lasted thus long partly because it has been perceived by both realists and liberals to have been in their interest. Realists care about the legitimacy of the UN, but for them this legitimacy is derived from the UN serving as an *instrument* of state interests. A UN without the potentiality to serve as a device through which states use their power to pursue national interests, has little legitimacy for the realists. There is no doubt that some organs of the UN, especially the Security Council, serve as a platform for power politics. What generally concerns Third World states is that most of the power within the UN is held by Western countries, which dominate the international system politically, economically, technologically and militarily. Western countries also have the means to promote their values and norms more effectively than the non-Western states. That is why Samuel Huntington has argued: 'The West in effect is using international institutions, military power and economic resources to run the world in ways that will maintain Western predominance, protect Western interests and promote Western political and economic values'. Other realist scholars have made similar claims in relation to Western states' control of the UN and other international organisations. For example, John Mearsheimer has argued: 'The most powerful states in the system create and shape institutions so that they can maintain their share of world power, or even increase it'.

If the UN is to remain acceptable to the majority of people around the world, it has to erase the perception that it serves as a mechanism through which the values of powerful states are imposed on the weaker ones.

If realists have been mainly interested in the exercise of power and the pursuit of national interests, liberals have been interested in the UN's *universalist* and *progressive* character. Liberals believe the UN has put power politics under check and facilitated the collective management of global public goods. From some liberal perspectives, the UN derives legitimacy from its inclusiveness and its potential to bring about human progress. As Ramesh Thakur has argued: 'The greatest strength of the United Nations is that it is the only universal forum for international cooperation and management. It must continue to play a central role in establishing a normative order which strikes a balance between the competing demands of equity and political reality'.

On the issues of democratisation and participation, some liberals have argued that the UN has neglected non-state actors for too long. Hence the increasing calls for the UN to involve the 'global civil society' more deeply in global governance. There is no doubt that a good number of NGOs have achieved phenomenal success in specific issue-areas. However, agreeing on a mechanism for their participation with the UN in global governance is likely to raise difficult questions. NGOs have the capacity to do a great deal, but they have no obligation to do anything. Voluntary organisations are not accountable, even in theory, to those whom they serve. The UN requires great ingenuity to pursue democratisation without compromising the effectiveness and universal acceptability of its action.

For constructivists, the legitimacy of the UN is derived largely from its *constitutive* and *transformative* character. The UN is both a product, and producer, of ideas, norms and state interests and identities. The world's leading constructivist in the International Relations discipline, John Ruggie, is a senior adviser to the UN Secretary-General. Ruggie has said his transition from academia to the UN 'went surprisingly smoothly because it quickly became apparent that creative leadership in international organisation is social constructivism in action'. The UN has been an agent of transformation. It has generated numerous ideas on such issues as development, the environment, human rights, women's rights and peace-keeping. In this respect, the UN has become a very important norm-setting organisation. As the interests, preferences and identities of member states are neither fixed nor exogenously given, the UN has participated, however marginally, in influencing the way they are defined and redefined.

However, there is a perception in the Third World that the UN's transformative power has been harnessed by the West and works to the detriment of non-Western interests. If the UN were to make a difference to global governance, it would need to address more seriously the imperative for democratisation in its agencies, taking account of growing demands for transparency and popular participation. Greater openness cannot be achieved without creative efforts to recast sovereignty. Thakur argues that the 'partial erosion of the principle of national sovereignty is rooted today in the reality of global interdependence', but there is a general perception that this 'erosion' is too slow and too minimal. For example, in discharging their responsibilities in the human rights area, UN secretaries-general have often been constrained by the UN charter, especially Article 2(7) that prohibits intervention 'in matters which are essentially within the domestic jurisdiction of any state'. This part of the charter has previously been interpreted in a manner in which it has indirectly shielded dictators from the international scrutiny of their human rights records. However, in his address to the General Assembly in September 1999, Kofi Annan had said 'Nothing in the charter precludes a recognition that there are rights beyond borders'. This line of re-thinking should be stretched further. With the rapid changes brought about by globalisation, what was 'essentially' within the domestic jurisdiction of states in 1945 may not remain so in present millennium. Therefore, it is incumbent upon the UN 'managers' to reinterpret the charter to reflect the new global realities. It would be a travesty of trust if the UN charter were to serve as a hindrance to the evolution of state sovereignty. The community is to reinterpret the charter consistently.

The UN has the potential to make it truly global.

It has the potentiality to ensure that the ideas, norms and rules, which underpin global governance, reflect the diversity of values and interests in the world. The UN needs to work out its programmes in such a way that, wherever possible, racial, gender, cultural and economic inequalities are taken into account.

Programme and Achievements

Global governance refers to transnational networks, institution building, norm entrepreneurship, regime creation and the management of global change. It covers many issues, such as women's rights, human rights, development, democratisation, the environment, security and investments. It has worked out some recent achievements include the treaty banning landmines, the Kyoto climate convention, the international criminal court, the World Trade Organisation, and the 'new generation' UN peacekeeping operations. In a nutshell, global governance describes regimes or systems of rule, embracing both formal and informal regulatory mechanisms. Underlying global governance is tolerance and a willingness to manage differences and reconcile self/other, us/them and inside/outside. This can take place only where there is a common set of values, norms, beliefs, ideas and institutions. As these values evolve, the nature of global governance has necessarily to change. Global governance is a broad, dynamic, complex process. It is constantly evolving and responding to changing circumstances. However, it is power that determines whose interests, rules and standards become 'global'. Thus, while global governance requires tolerance and accommodation of conflicting interests across national, racial, class, gender and ethnic boundaries, it is often the preferences of the most powerful actors that are accommodated.

Globalisation and global governance will go on with or without the UN. But global governance has so far reflected mainly the interests of Western societies.

Threat to Nation-States

Both Globalisation and Global Governance go together. They are proving a threat to the nation-states.

It should be accepted that both of them have made some positive and fruitful contribution to the entire world. But there is also a great need to overcome and remove the evils caused by it. The world has to be made safe and livable. If Globalisation aims at dismantling nation-states and democracies, it has got to be opposed in every possible manner.

Success of a nation-state depended on correct mixing of (a) identity, (b) legitimacy, and (c) security.[15] All of them began to erode during the era of globalisation. Both Soviet Union and the US exercised the right of intervention in many sovereign countries. Few members and fewer votes from the developing countries find a place on the boards of the IMF and the World Bank. Subscribing to the triad of human rights, free markets and democracy has been put as a condition precedent to them. Owing to expansion the TNCs (Transnational Corporations) and NGOs (non-governmental organisations) legitimacy of nation-states has lost their former shine. Global business has neutralised national boundaries. A part of power and identity has shifted upwards from the nation-states to the global agencies. About 90 per cent of foreign news and information in the print media is controlled by four news agencies located in the North.

The 'spectre of globalisation' haunts the earth. It has raised doubts about the relevance, role and even the need for nation-states at the end of the twentieth century.[16] If this trend continues, there would be neither 'state' nor 'nation' at least in developing countries.

Threat to Democracies

Globalisation is undermining democracy. Global governance concentrates economic power in the hands of a few individuals and corporate bodies. GATT/WTO, IMF, OECD (Organization for Economic Cooperation and Development), World Bank (International Bank for Reconstruction and Development), United Nations Conference on Trade and Development (UNCTD) and other financial institutions manage global political economy. The World Bank, IMF and WTO are expected to work in a coherent manner for it. Every member of the WTO has to accept in its entirety a common set of rules and disciplines covering goods, services and intellectual property. The WTO has legal and institutional foundation for enforcement of its decisions on disputes in the areas of goods, services and the protection of intellectual property rights. Its General Council makes appropriate arrangements for effective cooperation with other intergovernmental organisations that have responsibilities related to the WTO.[17] Other international organisations and agencies mentioned below also operate in regulating the global economy:

1. World Intellectual Property Organization;
2. International Organization for Standardization (IOS);
3. Coadex Alimentarious Commission;
4. International Office of Epizootics; and
5. International Plant Protection Office.

All political power and capacity to decide on behalf of global community is with the western world because of the 'unequal' nature of distribution of economic power among the nation-states, including making of important appointments on these bodies.

Global inequality has become quite acute. Structural inequality of power between the few developed centres of capitalism and a large majority of peripheral developing states has changed the whole agenda of contemporary discourse where the very relevance of nation-state as a centre of decision-making for national management has become questionable. According to the Pearson Commission this gap has been further widened because of the concentration of finance capital in a 'few capitalist countries'.[18]

Globalisation has set people to think about the political institutions, such as, state, democracy and civil society. David Held, in search of a supra-national democracy at global level, visualises a new international order involving: (i) the emergence of a global economic system which stretches beyond the control of a single state (even of dominant states); (ii) the expansion of network of transnational linkages and communications; (iii) the enormous growth in international organisation which can limit the scope for action of most powerful states; and (iv) the development of a global military order can reduce the range of policies available to governments and their citizens. One can witness a crisis of global civilisation. It involves a counter-revolution of the powerful against the weak. In much of the Third World the processes of urbanisation and economic decline have gone with social chaos, anomie and nihilism.

Its leaders in theory are accountable to the governed, in practice, they are accountable to market forces, most notably debt structures and structural adjustment programmes. Their major problem is how to make economic revitalisation compatible with democratisation. The international funding institutions such as the World Bank, the IMF and the ADB pressurise the recipient countries for removal of subsidies on even essential sectors like health, education, water, irrigation, agriculture, electricity and free use of public infrastructure such as roads. There is the question of quality versus quantity. The fundamental challenge of globalisation to the state and governance is to become accountable and responsible to the ruled and also to the global institutions.

However, to counterbalance these trends, Henry Kissinger, the former US Secretary of State has suggested steps to make major progress in the emerging international order by involving all key nations to say to themselves that this is our system. This is not an American system or anybody's system. This is something we participated in creating it and we have an interest in maintaining it.[19]

Threat to Environment and Culture

With weakening inter-state borders, threats to environment are increasing. With the resistance of the US and Australia and indifference of Russia and China towards Kyoto Protocol (to enforce emission norms for prevention Green House effect) and Copenhagen Protocol (to ensure ozone layer protection from chloro-fluoro carbons), the ecosystem is under grave threat. Globalisation has led to a new world trade market in environmental waste. The state finds it difficult to balance the trade-off between economic growth and environment preservation.

Some other major consequences of globalisation have been (i) the dislocation of traditional religions and belief systems; (ii) the beginning of the disintegration of the traditional social fabrics and shared norms by consumerism, cyber-culture, new-fangled religions and changing work ethics and work rhythms; (iii) the fast spreading anomie forcing an ever increasing number of individuals to fall back upon the easily accessible pretentious religious banalities; and (iv) religion related creation and acceleration of extremist, fundamentalist and terrorist tendencies in the Third World countries.[20]

Challenges of Globalisation

There are many other challenges to globalisation:[21]

1. Contemporary processes of globalisation and regionalisation create overlapping networks of power that put pressure on, and strain, a world order designed in accordance with the Westphalian principle.
2. The locus of effective political power does not reside with the national governments. Effective power is shared and bartered by diverse forces and agencies. Some of the most fundamental forces and processes, which determine the nature of life chances, are now beyond the reach of individual nation-states.
3. There is a distinction between the domestic and the international, and between territorial and the non-territorial.
4. It highlights the richness and complexity of the interconnections which transcend states and societies in the global order.
5. A large number of transnational policy issues cut across territorial jurisdictions and existing alignments.
6. Nations, peoples and organisations are linked by many new forms of communication, which establish virtually instantaneous worldwide links.
7. The new communication systems have created new experiences, new modes of understanding and new frames of political reference independently of direct contact with particular peoples, issues or events.
8. Differences over boundary matters were resolved by pursuing 'reason of state' and ultimately by coercive means. Now issues stand beyond those means, such as, resource depletion, environment degradation etc.
9. Powerful states make decisions not just for their peoples but for others as well. There is the problem who should be accountable to whom, and on what basis.
10. There are crucial regulatory and political gaps: jurisdiction gap, who is responsible for them; participation gap, and incentive gap.

There is also the 'moral gap' This gap is displayed by a world in which over 1.2 billion people live on less than a dollar a day; 46 per cent of the world's population live on less than $ 2 a day; and 20 per cent of the world's population enjoy 80 per cent of its income.[22]

Recasting Global Governance

Outlining deficiencies of Hyperglobalist (Kenichi Ohmae, Fukuda Parr, Kaplinsky etc.) and Sceptics' (Hirst and Thompson, Ruigrok and Tulder, de Soto, Leys etc.) theories, Held et al. have proposed an advanced theory of Political Globalisation. Propounding 'transformational' theory, Held believes in the emergence of a world government.[23] As the new global order has apparently escaped the control of democratic institutions located at the national level, the 'democracy has to become a transnational affair'. He suggests that strategic priority must be given to the key groups, agencies, associations and organisations of international civil society. Their capacity as agencies of democratic control must be extended through an appropriate recasting of territorial boundaries of systems of accountability, representation and regulation and fortified by entrenched transnational bill of social, economic and civil rights.

Global governance is not, and it shows no sign of becoming global government. Globalisation is not leading to the creation of a centralised world-state. Regulation in today's globalising world occurs in a polycentric manner. It is being done through macro-regional, state and substate authorities as well as global arrangements. These global governance frameworks have very limited and fragile legitimacy in public eye. Most citizens are barely aware that transworld regulatory arrangements exist.[24]

Anne-Marie Slaughter asks us to completely rethink how we view the prevailing political world. It is not a collection of nation states that communicate merely through presidents, prime ministers, foreign ministers, and the United Nations. Nor is it a clique of NGOs. It is governance through a complex global web of "government networks." It is a world in which government officials, police investigators, financial regulators, even judges and legislators exchange information and coordinate activity across national borders to tackle crime, terrorism, and the routine daily grind of international interactions. National and international judges and regulators also work closely together to enforce international agreements more effectively than ever before. These networks, which can range from a group of constitutional judges exchanging opinions across borders to more established organisations such as the G8 or the WTO, make many good things happen. But they stand under-appreciated and, worse, underused to address the challenges facing the world today.[25] For this a blueprint can be prepared with democratic accountability. But it would be not a new world order with some "world government" enforcing global dictates.

Notes

1. Frank Marini, Dwight Waldo, Nigro and Nigro etc. belong to this school.
2. See, Ostrom, *The Intellectual Crisis in American Public Administration*, 1974; and, *The Political Theory of Compound Republic*, 1987.
3. David Osborne and Ted Gaeblet, *Reinventing Government: How the Entrepreneurial Spirit is Transforming to Public Sector*?, Reading, Addison Wesley, 1992.
4. *Indian Journal of Public Administration*, Vol. XLIV, No. 3, 1998, 15-17.
5. Finkelstein, Lawrence S. "What is Global Governance?" *Global Governance* 1, No. 3 (Sept-Dec 1995), p. 369.
6. Andrew Taylor, "Governance", in Georgina Blakeley and Valerie Bryson, ed. *Contemporary Political Concepts: A Critical Introduction,* London: Pluto Press, 2002, 38.
7. The inventor of "globalization" and former editor of *Harvard Business Review* Dr. Theodore Lewit passed away on July 7, 2006.
8. Scholte, Jan Art. *Globalization: A Critical Introduction,* second ed., Palgrave: 20005, 187.
9. Also, see, infra.
10. Vijay Joshi and M.D. Little, *India's Economic Reforms:* 1991-2001, New Delhi: Oxford University Press, 1997.
11. Andrew Taylor, "Governance", in Georgina Blakeley and Valerie Bryson, ed. *Contemporary Political Concepts: A Critical Introduction,* London: Pluto Press, 2002, 35.
12. Pierre, J. and Peters, B. G. *Governance, Politics and the State,* London: Macmillan, 2000, 198.
13. Krueger, Anne (ed.), *The WTO as an International Organisation,* University Press, New York and Oxford, 1998.
14. Matters are better at the BIS, where over 30 states of the South and the East have become members. The BIS has opened its representative offices in Hong Kong and Mexico City. However, the main BIS operations remain centred in Basle.
15. Pandav Nayak, "Globalisation and Nation-State Today", in Mohan Lal Sharma, op. cit. 315-328; Jain, R.B., *Public Administration in India-21st Century Challenges for Good Governance,* New Delhi: Deep & Deep Publications Pvt. Ltd., 2001.
16. Quoted by Pantich, L. "Rethinking the Role of the State" in J.H. Mittesiman (ed.), *Globalisation: Critical Reflections*, London: Lynne Rienner, 1996, 83-113.
17. Ibid.
18. Ibid.
19. Henry Kissinger spoke to Manoj Joshi during the two-day HT Leadership Initiative Meeting in New Delhi on the principal threats of the age. *Hindustan Times*, 9.11.04.

20. P. Radhakrishnan. A paper presented at the international conference on 'Religion and Globalisation', held at Payap University, Thailand, from July 27 to August 2, 2003.
21. Held, David, and, Mathias Koenig, ed. *Taming Globalization: Frontiers of Governance,* Archibugi, Polity, 2003, 162-64.
22. Ibid., 163-4.
23. Bryane Michael has deconstructed Held et al. in his article, 'Theorising the Politics of Globalization: A Critique of Held et al.'s "Transformationalism", *Journal of Economics and Social Research*, 4(2), 3-17; Held, D., A. McGrew, D. Goldblatt, and J. Perraton, *Global Transformations: Politics, Economics and Culture*, 1999.
24. Scholte, op. cit. 213; Amartya Sen, *Development as Freedom,* Oxford, 1999.
25. Anne-Marie Slaughter, *A New World Order*, 2004.

15

Feminism and Its Impact on Future of Political Theory

Feminism is a house divided. It is a house within which there are now many mansions, whose occupants are engaged in a series of dialogues over the means of resolving the wrongs perceived to afflict women.[1] According to the core principles of feminism, Delmar defines a feminist who holds that women suffer discrimination because of their sex, that they have specific needs which remain negated and unsatisfied, and that the satisfaction of these needs would require a radical change in the social, economic and political order. Feminism is an 'umbrella ideology'.

Emergence and upsurge of feminism has several stages, levels and waves. Its beginning in ancient times stopped with Plato who emancipated women in his *Republic* only to join the ruling class. Background for liberation of women was prepared by the natural rights theory of John Locke and Rousseau. But they did not put woman at par with man. Only after the French Revolution, there was insistence that natural rights applied to man as well as woman. Since then, feminism begins to play an independent role.

Stages of evolution of feminism have been observed as 'waves'. Each 'wave' incorporates several shades, schools and forms of feminism. In all, there are three waves: first, second and third.

First Wave of Early Liberal Feminism

The first wave continues from the late eighteenth to the 1920s set within a predominantly liberal tradition.

Edmund Burke's *Reflections on the Revolution in France* in 1790 provoked the first major feminist work. Mary Wollstonecraft's (1759-97) *A Vindication of the Rights of Women* (1792) pleaded liberal values and arguments for the women's cause. Women's nature was primarily human. A woman was a rational being, therefore, was entitled to the same rights of liberty and self-determination as a man. If they could be properly educated, enjoyed full civil rights, be legally independent of their husbands and exercise their talents in any occupation, then they would be full members of society and fit companions for men. Wollstonecraft expected only a minority of exceptional women would pursue independent careers. The majority would find fulfilment in their roles of wife and mother. Similar arguments were put forward by a range of both male and female liberal theorists, such as, John Stuart Mill during the course of nineteenth century. Early liberal feminism was wedded to the achievement of formal legal equality for women. In the works of Harriet Taylor (1807-58) and her second husband John Stuart Mill (1806-73) there was call to obtain suffrage and widening opportunities for employment. Mill was a utilitarian liberal, rather than an exponent of natural rights of women like Wollstonecraft. He spoke about the benefits that would accrue to society from implementation of equal rights.

The result was a steady extension of women's civil rights, including the right to hold property within marriage, and access to higher education and the professions. After a series of militant campaigns, such as that the Suffragettes in Britain, it was extended to political rights mostly after World War I.

Utopian Socialist Feminism

Utopian socialists focused more upon the material inequalities intrinsic to a class-based society. They were William Thompson (1775-1833), Anna Wheeler (1775-?), Robert Owen (1771-1858), Charles Fourier (1772-1837), and Henri Saint Simon (1760-1825). They understood women to be doubly oppressed, not only within the public sphere but also in the family.

Women's cause was further taken up by some utopian socialists and Marxists. Charles Fourier saw the status and treatment of women as the critical indicator of progress. The higher their status and the greater their liberty, the more advanced the stage of civilisation. The restrictive family would be abolished in the ideal society of co-operative communes. Women would be able to develop themselves fully. When that happened, women would outshine men both in qualities of character and performing any activity that did not depend on physical strength. Both the family and monogamous marriage were oppressive to women. Men and women would choose their partners at will. There would be a 'hotel system' with private accommodation and common services. Children would be cared communally by those who specialised in the work, while still leaving room for the exercise of parental affection. He was unusual in rejecting monogamous marriage. In socialist society, marriage would be a genuine partnership of equals. The utopian socialists differed from the early liberals in two important respects: (i) they stressed the economic dimensions of equality; and, (ii) they drew a distinction between women's and men's natures. Owen and the followers of Fourier gave practical application to some of their ideas as part of a genuinely egalitarian society.

Marxist Feminism

Marxists dismissed the ideas of the utopian feminists as 'unscientific'. Marx (1818-1883) himself wrote little on feminism leaving it to his collaborator Friedrich Engels (1820-1895) and the German social democrat August Bebel (1840-1913).[2] Both exhorted women to throw in their lot with men in the common struggle to achieve a classless society, free from the exploitative relations intrinsic to capitalism. Neither Marx, nor Engels nor Bebel was opposed to marriage, but each contended that only in a socialist society would this relationship be based upon love and without male domination. Engels wrote his *The Origin of the Family, Private Property and the State* in 1884. It was based on the speculations of the American anthropologist Lewis Morgan. Accordingly, before the rise of private property, there was matriarchy, group marriage and descent through the female line. Emergence of private property brought the dominance of the male who wished to pass his property to his recognised heirs. Thus came up monogamy and descent through the male line. Engels saw this as a world-historical defeat for the female sex. It was followed by millennia of domination and oppression of women by men. The modern bourgeois family, supposedly based on love, is in fact based on a form of unpaid and constant prostitution in which a woman sells herself into domestic slavery to survive. The man has all the economic power. Within home, man is the bourgeois while the wife is the proletariat. To him, the family is an economic unit and its whole existence is bound up the property. The communist revolution, abolishing private property would eliminate the economic basis of the monogamous bourgeois family. There would be public provision for housekeeping and childcare. Marriage would be genuinely based on love and mutual respect. The family and not marriage was the obstacle to women's liberation and her full entry into society. Women's freedom and equality was bound up with the emancipation of humanity and realizable only through a communist revolution. The new Soviet state, after the success of the Bolshevik Revolution in 1917 began to implement laws giving women a new status and new freedom from the shackles of conventional family. However, within a few years, the policy was changed and women were exhorted during the Stalin's (1879-1953) regime to be good mothers and maintain the family. In a way, they were worse off in that women were now expected to be full-time workers and also perform all their traditional duties, having only an easy divorce. The attempt to associate patriarchy with a particular economic system did not convince other feminists. Radical feminists accused Marxism of sex-blindness.

During this era, unmodified liberalism was rejected.[3] Liberal feminists during the era of late nineteenth and early twentieth centuries secured many important rights for women: removal of many legal disabilities, access to education and the professions, the right to vote etc. New Zealand was the fist modern state to give women the right to vote in 1893. Britain enfranchised all women of thirty years of age in 1918. American women got the vote in 1920.

Second-Wave Feminism and Radical Critique

The second wave gathered momentum in the mid to later 1960s. It was preoccupied with differences between women and men.

It is also called as 'modern feminism' or 'radical feminism'.

There was formal equality for women with men in the 1950s and 1960s. There was also disillusionment with growing affluence for the overwhelming majority of people in the West. Despite the gains, the world was still male-dominated and women were heavily discriminated in almost every walk of life. Two writers particularly articulated these feelings. Simone de Beauvoir (1908-1986) in *The Second Sex* (1952) and Betty Friedan in *The Feminine Mystique* (1963) caught the imagination of a generation of women. Both of them are seen as percusors of the feminist movement launched in the late 1960s.

The Second Sex of de Beauvoir bridges over the apparent gap between the first and the second waves of the feminist movement. She gives a long and penetrating account of women's plight. It argues that women have always been defined in terms of their feminine nature. Men, on the other hand, are defined as free, independent beings, and not in terms of their relationship with women. This asymmetry expresses man's domination over women. Women are defined in terms of their sex and not their human rationality and freedom, thus, treated as and classified as incomplete human beings. Men subordinate women in order to guarantee their freedom, but this creates dissatisfactory relationship. Their 'otherness' has been imposed upon them by men. But the women have internalised this condition themselves. This signifies the psychoanalytic aspect of her ideas. She resolutely rejected the proposition that women's anatomy, or Freudian penis-envy theory, defined their destiny. Women must realise their own capacity for self-awareness, make their own choices and celebrate their own deeds. They should avail themselves of contraception and abortion to have control over their bodies. 'One is not born but rather becomes a woman.' Her encouragement of women to take control of their bodies was consistent with radical feminism's later concern with the politics of sexuality and reproduction.

There is great impact of existentialism in Beauvoir's analysis. It reflects the influence of Jean-Paul Sartre, her lifetime partner. But she is not a pessimist like Sartre. She believed that the difference between men and women are more than merely physical, still women can assert their freedom and transform their lives. They can achieve satisfactory relationship with men on the basis of equality.

In *The Feminine Mystique* (1963), Betty Friedan (1921 –) changed the direction of liberal feminism. Her book is a key text of the second wave feminism. It is in line with the liberal tradition of equal rights feminism. It exposed the image of the happy contented housewife as a disabling myth. She asked women to achieve educational qualifications and to re-enter employment as the means of escape from the gilded cage of domestic life.[4] She flatly rejected the taken-for-granted assumption that women are different, and had basic characteristics that especially fitted them only for home, and just needed formal equality of status. This was not good enough. She exhorted that the differences, symbolised in the so-called 'feminine mystique' were overrated. Women wanted to get out of their traditionally given world. There was a great need to have careers and compete with men on equal footing.

Both Simone de Beauvoir and Betty Friedan contributed a lot to feminism. But it was in the late 1960s that modern feminism, also known as 'Second Wave' Feminism, took off. During this period, growing discontentment felt especially by young women was articulated in terms of the concepts and categories of the New Left. The late 1960s 'new wave' of feminism, or 'Women's Liberation', appeared with a new ideology. The first wave feminist theory was an extension or special case of one of the more extensive ideologies. The Second Wave feminism came with the development of radical feminism. Radical feminism was a new strand feminism in its own right. Prominent among them are: Kate Millet, Germaine Greer, Shulamith Firestone etc. Shulamith Firestone represents the radical wing of the Women's Liberation movement.

There are four arenas of the second wave feminism: (i) reproduction; (ii) patriarchy; (iii) lesbianism; and, (iv) identity.

'The man problem' became increasingly prominent within the second wave feminism. There were and are feminists who cast men as the unremitting enemies of women. Men become wholly redundant in women's lives.

In its undiluted form, patriarchy is understood in ahistorical and universal terms: that men always have been, are, and always will be, motivated to dominate women and will employ both subtle and unsubtle means to exert their control. It extends both to public and private spheres. Patriarchy as an analytical category was deployed as shorthand for describing the conditions of inequality and disadvantage experienced by women in the public and private realms.

Kate Millet and Juliet Mitchell: Patriarchy

Kate Millet's (1934-) book *Sexual Politics* (1970) the first second wave text to elaborate upon the concept of patriarchy. She was influenced by New Left ideas: domination, repression and alienation, and the use of psychoanalytic concepts. She raised the question why all important decisions are made by men when and where in a free society women do have full range of civil and political rights, and have all possible educational opportunities. She used the concept of 'patriarchy' to explain women's subordination and oppression. Patriarchy worked by brainwashing women from childhood into accepting a role that was constructed for them by men. It was reinforced by law, tradition, language, social 'science', media and magazines. The main stereotype was the 'wife' and 'mother': passive, caring, and emotional. All preoccupied with domestic matters and personal appearance.[5] The other stereotype, though not socially approved, was (whore and temptress) the 'prostitute' who were independent and dangerous, but were meant for the benefit of men. Women internalised their sex-role stereotypes and came to accept them as 'natural'. Those women, who did not see their fundamental role as domestic and rejected the stereotype, tended to be derided as 'unnatural'. Thus, there was pressure on women to conform to the stereotype. In this way women were kept in subjection with no overt coercion employed upon them.

Millet developed the notion of 'sexual politics', by arguing that even in the most personal relations between men and women, it was men who controlled the sexual relations. Men took the initiative and defined and restricted female sexuality in terms of their own needs, leaving women often unfulfilled. This situation was termed as 'political' as it was a power relationship: a relationship of domination and subordination, where subordinate exists for the sake of the dominant. It was a dimension of 'patriarchy'. This was the root cause of the feminist slogan. 'The personal is the political'.

Juliet Mitchell (1940-) argued that women's oppression could not be explained solely in material terms. It should also be understood in psychological and cultural terms. Family engendered women's and men's roles. It transmits their respective social identities as male and female sex, setting a higher value on the latter. But she rejected determinism of family or patriarchy. She presents patriarchy as a socially constructed value system. It could be challenged and defeated.[6] In place of accepting that women were only materially oppressed in the home and the economy, Mitchell pleaded that they were also psychologically oppressed. The site of that oppression was the family, an agency of patriarchy, through reproduction, the socialisation of children, and sexuality. A psycho-cultural revolution, led by women, was therefore crucial to the elimination of patriarchy.

There was a general reaction against the notion of women as being 'different': that they had 'different' emotions; that they valued 'different' things; that they had 'different' ways of thinking; that they had 'different' needs, including sexual needs. This question was raised by Germaine Greer in her book *The Female Eunuch* (1970). She argued that the traditional conception of female sexuality as being soft and passive was in fact a stereotype. It was imposed by men, which satisfied them but left women unfulfilled. Women's true sexuality was distorted and repressed to the point of effectively rendering them 'castrated' and sexless, mere 'sex-objects. Greer was influenced by Herbert Marcuse's analysis of contemporary society as repressive and in need of sexual liberation, applied particularly to women.[7] Women now insisted on being treated as 'persons' and not 'sex-objects'. They oppose on being patronised and put into categories and told 'all women think like this'. To demonstrate the 'stereotyping' of women, there was public practice of 'bra-burning'. It was a symbolic act by the feminists who rejected the stereotyped image of the ideal woman as being of a certain shape which all women were supposed to try to achieve in order to please men. It went along with attacks on pornography and beauty contests.

Other Aspects of Patriarchy

Many other aspects patriarchy are found in language, history, literature, art, social and political theories. All talk in terms of 'man': 'man in society', the 'nature of man', 'all men being equal ...', 'from each according to his need' etc. etc. God always being presented as male, chairman, history and so on. The global nature of this exploitation is summed up in the 1980 United Nations report that women constitute one half of the world's population, perform nearly two thirds of its work hours, receive one tenth of the world's income and own less than one hundredth of the world's property.[8]

Lesbianism

A society of androgynes did not appear to radical lesbian feminists. They understood heterosexual relationships to be essentially about power. Women in such relationships were accused of collaborating in their own oppression. In effect, they were sleeping with the enemy. For them, 'Feminism is the theory, lesbianism the practice'. They rejected men both as sexual and political partners. Lesbianism was classified as 'unnatural'. It was condemned by society as part of a general denigration of any female behaviour that did not conform to the male-imposed stereotype. Women were forced to conform in order to keep them subservient. In this respect, all feminists made a common cause with gay men, who were also engaged in challenging the sexual stereotype of their own sex. They worked for founding a society that was 'androgynous', that is, where men and women were not expected to behave differently and have different role. They stand for a society where a woman's 'masculine' characteristics, such as, ambition and aggression, and a man's 'feminine' characteristics, such as, gentleness and caring, were not suppressed. Men and women would, therefore, be 'themselves', thus, be 'natural', instead of trying to achieve some socially constructed ideal version of self.

Shulamith Firestone: Anti-'men'

Manifesto issued by the New York (1969) group said:

> Women are an oppressed class. Our oppression is total .... We identify the agents of our oppression as men. Male supremacy is the most basic form of domination .... All men receive economic, sexual and psychological benefits from male supremacy. All men have oppressed women .... We will not ask what is 'revolutionary' or 'reformist', only what is good for women.[9]

Radical feminists like Shulamith Firestone (1945-) are uncompromising in their insistence that the cause of women's oppression is not 'class' or 'socialisation' or any other social structure or process, but simply, directly and emphatically 'men'. Men are the enemy. It is not enough to give women more of the important jobs or facilities for easing the burdens of childcare, or to change the social structure like family or marriage. Women's oppression goes much deeper. Its end requires more drastic change. It is the oppression of women by men that is most fundamental. Other oppressions, of class or race or whatever, are special cases or extensions of the basic sexual oppression. This view finds place in her book *The Dialectic of Sex* (1970). She argues that Marx's historical materialism is correct in form but incorrect in substance. It does not recognise that the root of inequality and of oppression is that of women by men. Class domination and exploitation begins with 'sex class'. Economic class comes later. The origin of this exploitation and oppression is 'biological'. Women are vulnerable and exploited because of women's role in reproduction, and its consequent dependence on men. Women's oppression is built into the biological family. Therefore, the key to revolution is sexual revolution. She wrote, "... unless revolution uproots the basic, social organisation, the biological family ... the tapeworm of exploitation can never be annihilated. We shall need a sexual revolution much larger than – inclusive of – a socialist one to truly eradicate all class systems" (*The Dialectic of Sex*). To accomplish biological revolution, Firestone puts her faith in science. By means of 'artificial reproduction', and by socialising childcare, that is, by sharing the work among all members of society, women's physical and psychological responsibility for reproduction would be eliminated, and make their liberation possible. A society freed from sexually assigned roles would flourish.[10]

All radicals do not accept Firestone's analysis in full, still less her prescriptions, but they share the belief that the basic problem is men, and not society. Sexual oppression is the most basic oppression. The emancipation of women is the necessary precondition for the emancipation of humanity from other forms of oppression. Beyond this common outlook, there is much controversy over a wide range of issues.

Third-Wave Feminism: The Supremacists

The third wave moves around differences among and between women, reflecting the current concern with subjectivities and identity politics. It is motivated by the politics of recognition of black women, Muslim women, lesbians, and disabled women. However, it gave no thought to the women of the Third World.

Some radicals still stick to Engels' view of a matriarchal golden age as a convenient morale-raising myth. But few take it seriously. Neglecting the historical origins, a common view is that women's oppression is being reaffirmed and reproduced over generations. It operates at economic, legal, psychological and physical levels. However, there is controversy over the root cause of oppression.[11]

Others differ on the nature and importance of 'feminine characteristics'. For them, the so-called feminine characteristics is a myth or a set of idealised characteristics. These were submissiveness, domesticity, caring, love, sympathy etc. For diehard feminists these mythmakers were simply betraying their 'sisters'.

But there has been some change of heart among feminists of all variety. Now they discard denigration and denial of most women's experience. They feel that the career and public role option smacked too much of having to 'be like men'. 'Women characteristics' are now being accepted as the stuff of women, sources of value, a desirable moral vision and so on. They are willing to celebrate 'feminine qualities' and uphold women's experience like caring and co-operation, whatever be their origin. They want to recover women's history and achievements. All of them provide an alternative approach valid and arguably superior to the claims of some of the 'masculine characteristics' of women.

A minority of feminists boldly stand for the 'masculinity' of women. Characteristics of women, masculine or feminine, are not the result of any socialisation. These are natural and inherent, and have biological origin. In this way, they reject the central tenet of the modern feminist movement. They insist upon the superiority of feminine characteristics, women's values and the female sex in general. To them, women are morally superior to men. The world would be safe and civilized only when women rule it. Feminine theories of this variety are called as 'supremacists'. Important supremacist writers are Mary Daly, Andrea Dworkin and Dale Spender. Supremacists abjure dealing with men. Some of them are lesbians, or 'political lesbians'. Political lesbians insist that women should strive to fulfill all their needs, including emotional and sexual, from among themselves. Inspite of a woman's personal preference, a man is not essential for woman for sexual or emotional fulfillment. Any woman may choose to be a lesbian as a political act. Women who choose to have male partners are necessarily incomplete women. They are 'man-identified' as they allow themselves to be defined in terms of a man. Only 'woman-identified' women can be autonomous and complete.

But lesbianism, pure or political, is not a precondition of a supremacist (or isolationist) approach. As women's psyche is so damaged by millennia of male domination, women, before again having dealing with men, have to live apart for some time until recovered. To achieve this goal, some organisations (especially in the USA) have raised all-women communes. These communes try to live with as little contact with men and male dominated society as possible.

Some less extreme organisations only exclude some pro-man elements. They exclude women having permanent relationships with men. Some exclude men even if they are sympathetic to the cause of women. However, small groups of women share experiences and give support to each other while upholding women's cause.

Barbara Arneil describes the 'third wave' of feminism as

> Third wave feminism(s) are characterised by a commitment to beginning one's analysis from women's own perspective: that it, a recognition of 'difference' in perspective, both between women and men and *among women.*[12]

Opposition and Revision

The socialist feminists disliked political correctness of lesbianism as a sexual practice along with separatism as a political strategy. They argued that it isolated women from their potential allies. Both of them were ideologically wedded. But they had no reply to the centrality of patriarchy causing women oppression. The campaign for the Wages for Housework also created split among them. Many socialist and non-socialist feminists objected to the idea of paying women for domestic work because it legitimised rather than confronted the prevailing division of labour within the family. Heidi Hartmann also argued that it was in the material interests of men to perpetuate the sexual division of labour.

Apart from opposing settled ideas of different forms of feminism, some of the prominent feminists appear revising their known views. Some of them have begin to perceive motherhood as a means of empowerment and fulfilment for women. This is 'maternal revivalism'. For Jean Bethke Elshtain, Betty Friedan, Germaine Greer and Sara Ruddick motherhood is compatible with feminism. They seek to rehabilitate maternity. By 1984, in *Sex and Destiny,* Greer came to expound a version of pro-family feminism, rejecting the numbing isolationism and lovelessness of nuclear family. She advocated plural childcare within a transgenerational 'stem family' and therefrom the recovery of sexual energy by women. Friedan in *The Feminine Mystique* and *The Second Stage* also represented a *volte-face.* She now presented family as one form of relationship within which women could satisfy their emotional needs. Elshtain in *Public Man, Private Woman* (1981) defended the privacy of child-centred family and celebrated mothering as 'a complicated, rich, ambivalent, vexing, joyous activity which is biological, natural, social, symbolic and emotional'. An another form of 'pro-woman' feminism is ecological feminism. It refers to the relationship between women and nature. Eco-feminism accepts the connectedness of human and non-human nature, and insists upon the integrity of all living things. Pro-womanism and eco-feminism stress difference between women and men on an essentialist basis. But gynocentric feminism elevates women's qualities above those of men, and rejects both androcentrism and androgyny. Woman's attributes are seen to derive from their innate closeness to nature, to their bodies and nurture. A more radical expression pro-womanism is found in the work of cultural feminists like Mary Daly (1928-). She advocates withdrawal into a woman-only culture untainted by patriarchal constructions of femininity. The celebration of motherhood and essentialism has also provoked criticism from many other feminists. Post-modernism also stood against it.[13]

Summary and Conclusions

Feminism as a movement has spread the world over. But it has not appeared in the form of national or international organisations. Feminism is much more diffuse and intangible in its goals and priorities. Most of the feminists are locked into their pre-existing ideological outlooks with their deep-rooted antipathies. There are many forms of feminisms. Even one form of feminism has several groups within it. Often they are at odds with each other.

Liberal feminists want women to have their proper share within existing society. They are best organised and most political and campaign for more representation, child-care and other issues. But they have to face difficulties when accompanied by the lesbians and other radicals. The National Organization for Women (NOW) fell foul of fellow feminists when they refused to back the abortion campaigns of other feminists for fear of losing support for ERA (Equal Rights Amendment) from the Catholic Church and other organisations.

Socialist feminists determine to overthrow existing society. They see the achievements of liberal goals as merely benefiting middle-class women.

Radical feminists reject traditional formal politics altogether. They see it as a male-centred political game. Various 'separatists' and 'supremacists' find the male power politics as the root-cause of all wrong in the world. They do not want any organisation with men in it.

The 1980s witnessed slackening of the women's liberation movement. Its earlier supporters revised their thoughts. Betty Friedan in her book *The Second Stage* (1982) and Germaine Greer in *Sex and Destiny* (1985) were tolerant on the virtues of domesticity and motherhood. They were sharply criticised by the radicals as 'betrayal'. There was backlash against the general radicalism of the 1960s and 1970s. All this reflected in the intellectual and political successes of the New Right. There was insistence on 'traditional values'. the virtues of family life, and conventional feminism. This trend opposed abortion, blamed working mothers for appearance of adolescent crime, and several other maladies. Elections were contested in favour of 'family values.'

Women's movement in the 1980s also felt exhausted because of its successes and achievements. Attitudes of the people had changed a great deal. Anti-discrimination laws had been passed everywhere. The male majority was more aware of the problem and was sensitive to sexist assumptions and language. Scope of study and research on women's problems widened. Women were generally turned more confident of challenging male dominance in many areas.

Post-Feminism

The term 'post-feminism' connotes the idea that women are now the full co-equals of men, able to exercise their unfettered autonomy in making choices about their lives, public and private.[14] Post-feminists assert that, however defined, feminism has outlived its usefulness. Women now have it all. The future is female. But Greer identifies a host of disabling disadvantages that confront women today, both at home and at work. She ridicules the notion that an egalitarian, post-feminist world has been achieved in which women do 'have it all'. She insists that 'to be feminist is to understand that before you are of any race, nationality, religion, party or family, you are a woman'.[15] She also holds the idea of female essentialism which depicts the notion of a basic difference between women and men. For her, liberation struggles are not about assimilation but about asserting difference between sexes.

Neglect of Other Forms of Women Oppression

Western feminism, in general, has neglected many other forms of women oppressions. Concentrating on all-White middle class feminism, it suffers from ethnocentrism. It is culpable of some kind of cultural and ideological imperialism. It has neglected oppressed women of third world societies. It has neglected race, class and colour.

> The women's movement has never taken up the question of racism in any real way ... [this] has ensured and will continue to ensure that the women's movement as a whole is irrelevant to the needs and demands of most black women.[16]

Protest and Ideology of Feminism

There is the emergence of 'Humans' or the 'New Man'. He has shed the automatic assumptions of male superiority. The male person now is sensitive to women's needs. He recognises the 'feminine' elements in his own nature, and accepts domestic responsibilities on the same basis as his partner. As things perceptibly improved, crusading zeal and sisterly solidarity among women looked less assertive. The majority of women do not want to overthrow existing society, or like to live in lesbian communes. There is a great variety and considerable overlapping. At the grassroots of the feminine movement, a good deal of eclecticism prevails. It includes elements from different theories and traditions. The liberal preoccupation with rights has tried to make them a reality.[17] Socialist feminists support such campaigns, but they are more for working women and for the causes of black women. The liberal feminists seek a change in women's situation within an accepted liberal-capitalist framework, socialist feminists see women's liberation as part of a more general liberation following the abolition of capitalism. According to them, women suffer a double oppression, men and capitalism combined. This view rejects the traditional Marxist-feminist belief that the overthrow of capitalism is sufficient for women's emancipation. Radicals stand more for small group structures, 'consciousness raising', and shared experiences. They look like anarchists as they prefer leaderless movements, grassroots, federal organisations, without formal national structures. To them conventional state and party power structures are essentially masculine. They are more innovative and theoretically more interesting.

Bryson concludes that in some ways, 'the situation of women in Western societies has obviously improved, and many of the issues for which feminists have fought in the past are now part of the 'common sense' assumption'.[18] The very diversity of modern feminist politics is itself a source of strength. It keeps issues alive and ensuring. We can identify areas of agreement that must form the basis for any feminist political theory in the twenty-first century. The starting point of such a theory is an expanded concept of politics based on power relations between men and women. These relations are not confined only to the 'public' worlds of law, the state and administration and economics. They pervade all areas of life. Family, reproduction and sexuality are also included in political analysis. The perception that 'the personal is political' forms part of that theory. Liberty and equality to women requires changes in the family as well as in the law and public life. Okin in her new theory of justice rejects the public/private dichotomy and treats justice within the family as central.

Feminism challenges the conclusions as well as content of traditional political theory. The existing concepts and values are not gender neutral. They frequently reflect the limited perceptions of man. As such, they cannot be used as ready-made tools for feminist analysis. They have to be criticised, modified and elaborated for better use.

Values of existing political theory are inadequate. There is no agreed goal. Some of the differing goals are: a communist revolution, evaluation of womanly virtues to be learned by man, replacement of men by sperm-banks or pathogenesis for production etc. Postmodernists reject the whole idea of identifying agreed feminist goals as 'a totalitarian enterprise that denies the diversity and specificity of women's experiences.'[19] Radicals believe that gender divisions are biologically ordained, therefore, they see lesbianism as the only solution. A large majority hopes that men are not beyond redemption and a sexually egalitarian society is in principle possible. All these views draw closer when their protagonists formulate the theory on the basis of women's lives and struggles.

Liberal feminists hope to change only gender relations keeping all other social structures intact. Their ideas have far-reaching and subversive implications. Socialist feminists do not press for an imminent revolution, and, like radical feminists, want to defend existing legal rights and reforms. All seem to agree that in ideal society gender inequalities would end and women would be able to realise their full potential in all areas of life. In such a society, activities traditionally associated with women would be more highly valued. They might see child-rearing as a potentially fulfilling aspect of life that can be shared with men or professionally trained carers. Socialists would also understand the importance of domestic work. Bearing and rearing of children can be made more compatible with other activities. Thus, mothers can be fully active citizens and workers. This would involve flexible working practices, collective provision of childcare, shared parenting with men, or all together.

Feminine Political Theory proposes many practical avenues. It looks into the opportunities and problems involved in achieving a sexually just society. It would provide form, format and activities of such society in general, and family in particular. This is necessary because men as a group are privileged by existing gender inequalities, and like to sustain them. Structures of society also support their interests. The key institutions like the state and the education system are not neutral. They reflect the perceptions, interests and priorities of the men who happen to control them. Attention to them allows women struggle to be based on a realistic assessment of the opposition that they are likely to face. Mere rationality and rightness of the demands of women are not enough to ensure their success. Some men do support feminist goals, either because they are persuaded that they are just, or that they too would also gain from the desired feminist change. A feminist theory would distinguish between the structures and agents of women oppression. Every individual man is not necessarily 'the enemy'; on the contrary, he may prove as potential ally. Women would frequently choose to organise autonomously, treating male support with great caution, but would not reject support and cooperation automatically.

The conflict is not only between the vested interest of men and the feminist demands. Gender inequality serves the needs of capitalism and the ruling class.[20] The whole of the dominant economic system supports it. Liberal feminists do not wish to challenge the capitalist system, but forget that equal pay legislation, elimination of sexism in education, and monitoring of the employment practices demand state intervention and planning. Liberal feminism in itself cannot provide good quality childcare and full participation of all men and women in child-rearing along with pursuit of a career.

It does not mean that no feminist goals can be met unless a full-scale revolution succeeds. Gender division is not the only source of social inequality. Race and class are also the perennial source of women oppression. Invoking a spurious sisterhood simply reflects the cause of white middle-class women which is not a unitary group. It is racism and elitism. A worldwide feminism should be based on that understanding and on an enormous diversity of needs and experiences of variety of women. One should not indulge in reductionism, that is, concentrating attacks only on the prevailing economic system. Multiplicity and interconnectedness of social forces maintain present inequalities. This finding should not lead to a sense of helplessness and a paralysis of political will. There must be flexibility and plurality in forms of feminist political activity. All actions are not valid. A good feminist political theory must make effective political choices.

Unfortunately, the present feminist political theory is a product of experiences of the white women of Western middle class, and it has little concern with the non-Western societies, Black, Gray and Yellow.[21] It must guard against the kind of self-referential elitism that furthers academic careers, but is cut off from common ground. To formulate a holistic and good feminist political theory is not easy and it would be needlessly obscure, devoid of collective action and understanding.

Formulation of a Feminine Political Theory

Diversity of feminist thinking is apparent. A taxonomy of contemporary feminism includes not just liberal, socialist and Marxist feminists but, among others, exponents of differing lifestyles, standpoints, cultural, ecological, postmodern, lesbian, radical and 'black' feminisms. Such diversity is self-defeating. Its complexity implies political cost. There is something of a division of labour within the contemporary women's movement. Liberal feminists press for legislative and policy change and operate in the mainstream of politics, while others, such as cultural feminists operate on the margins of politics discourse, creating their own, separate responses to the wrongs they perceive to afflict women. All feminists do share the status of social critics. One cannot reconcile the views of those who emphasise sameness with those who stress difference(s), between women and men and among women.

To conclude, there is no explanatory political theory of feminism. So far it has reached the level of a diffuse, scattered and multi-dimensional ideology. Its scope appears to be unlimited, but subject matter is unclear, fuzzy and floating. Feminists, except the supremacists, are not clear on their goals and methods of action. What do they want to achieve? How and who would like to rule and control over the other, men with enhanced rights to women, women with men as subordinate, both as equal partners, or womenocracy separate from men at every step? Feminists so far have remained unable to determine the commonality of both women and men. The feminist scholars are yet to discover and analyse the nature of this commonality. Feminists, to formulate an explanatory political theory, despite their different persuasions, must examine their own specific concepts. They have to contemplate the form and nature of society, community, institutions of law and state. Where would they place family, production, children, their caring and rearing, education, marriage, safety and protection, pleasure and livelihood. How and what would they like to run and manage economy, public and private? Hardly any feminist has proposed a plan to accommodate diversities of race, culture, language, levels and stages of development, political ambitions and amount of civil rights. These problems are less with the liberal feminists as they propose to go ahead in close cooperation with the other sex. But socialist and Marxist feminists want total change in the capitalist system, and propose to bring about 'revolution'. Their stand on patriarchy and family overlook the demands of radical feminists who stand for psycho-cultural change. Radicals want society and government without men, institution of marriage, childcare and production.[22]

Obviously, it is very difficult to have a coalition government inclusive of main elements of different feminisms. Who would lead the rest of them? What would be the role of men in their feminist dispensation? The feminists so far should unable to answer these questions.

In sum, it is very difficult to formulate a valid and workable feminist political theory which might guide the feminist to run democratic government. Few feminists would be able to work upon it. Till the feminists of different persuasions are able to formulate an agreed political theory of feminism, they would have to bear with an improved model of liberal political theory.

Notes

1. Eccteshall, Robert, et al., *Political Ideologies: An Introduction,* Third edition, London: Routledge, 1994, 183.
2. Bryson, Valerie, *Feminist Political Theory: An Introduction,* US edition, New York: Paragon House, 1992, 121.
3. Bryson, Valerie, op. cit., 181.
4. In order to win equal rights for women enshrined in the 1964 Civil Rights Act, Friedan co-founded the National Organization for Women (NOW). She urged enforcement of laws against sex discrimination, demanded equal educational opportunities for women, child-care centres and the right of women 'to control their reproductive lives'. Rick Wilford, "Feminism", in Eccteshall, Robert, et al., *Political Ideologies: An Introduction,* op. cit., 202.
5. Bryson, Valerie, op. cit., 185.
6. Rick Wilford, op. cit. 206.
7. There prevailed something of a fashion in the late 1960s for having heterosexuality and a rejection of the passive image.
8. Bryson, Valerie, op. cit., 197.
9. Crow Barbara, ed. *Radical Feminism: A Documentary Reader,* New York: New York University Press, 2000, 223-35.
10. Bryson, Valerie, op. cit., 213.
11. Susan Brownmiller in her book *Against Our Will* (1976) exposes that the ultimate threat of rape keeps women in subjection and under oppression. A man rapes a woman on behalf of his whole sex and keeps her submissive. Adams, op. cit., 307.
12. Arneil, Barbara, *Politics and Feminism,* Oxford: Blackwell, 1999, 9.
13. Bryson, Valerie, op. cit., 225-29; Pateman, C., *The Sexual Contract,* Polity, 1988.
14. Rick Wilford, "Feminism", in Eccteshall, Robert, et al., *Political Ideologies: An Introduction,* Third edition, London: Routledge, 1994, 185.
15. Greer, Germaine, *The Female Eunuch,* 1971; *The Whole Woman,* London: Doubleday, 1999, 7.
16. Parmar, Pratibha, 'Other kinds of dreams', *Feminist Review,* 31: 55-56.
17. But the British Parliament with a woman Prime Minister had only 56 women out of 631 MPs in 1992; Mueller, C., *The Politics of the Gender Gap,* 1988.

18. Bryson, Valerie, *Feminist Political Theory: An Introduction,* US edition, New York: Paragon House, 1992, 261.
19. Ibid., 263; also, Bryson, Valerie, *Feminist Debates: Issues of Theory and Political Practice,* Basingstoke: Macmillan, 1999.
20. Squires, Judith, *Gender in Political Theory,* Cambridge: Polity Press, 2000.
21. Mohanty, Chandra Talpade et al., eds., *Third World Women and the Politics of Feminism,* Bloomington IN: Indiana University Press, 1991.
22. Code, Lorraine, ed. *Encyclopaedia of Feminist Theories,* London: Routledge, 2000; Stephan K. White and Donald Moon, ed., *What is Political Theory?*, Sage, 2004.

16

Theory of Contemporary Terrorism

Terrorism is the most important phenomenon found today in a large number of Muslim and non-Muslim states. It broke out in the late 1980s and overshadowed the beginning of 21st century. Terrorism can be seen as a 'theory' of violence. But it is being practiced as an 'ideology' of special war by many organisations and governments. Both are interrelated. But few know them fully. A proper understanding of contemporary terrorism requires to know: (a) Basic Tenets of Terrorism (b) Evolution of Islamic Fundamentalism (c) *Sunni* and *Shia* Fundamentalism; (d) From Islamic Fundamentalism to Contemporary Terrorism; (e) Theory of 'Terror'; (f) Making of Terrorism; (g) Offshoots of Contemporary Terrorism; and (h) Existential Challenges.

There are many sources and forms of terrorism. It may be Islamic, Christian, Jewish, Maoist, Hindu, Naxalite and so on. It may come out on grounds of religion, sub-religion or sect, ethnicity, colour, culture, or chauvinism. All have made their presence from time to time. But its most potent, prevalent and dangerous form today is Islamic or Jehadi terrorism. It has appeared as the next and final phase of Islamic Fundamentalism. Islamic Fundamentalism stands for the adoption, restoration, and rejuvenation of Islam eliminating all pseudo-Islamic or non-Islamic governments, religions and cultures. Terrorism is the next phase of Islamic Fundamentalism. A follower of Islam has to have full faith in many tenets of his religion. Those who want to lead the Muslims to war, revolution, rebellion or large-scale conversion make fervent use of these tenets as their weapons.

Some of the important tenets are given below:

1. Allah has very kindly made revelation, given commands and directions to the community at the appointed time and place.
2. These commands and directives were given by Allah to the Prophet or Messenger who declared them to be obeyed by all persons irrespective of time and place.

3. The Message delivered in form of the Holy *Quran* after its revelation to the Prophet is the last and final one. It can never be amended, revised or changed by any human being.
4. Allah or His Messenger in that revelation has authorised the believers to bring all others to that faith, by all means.
5. One can attain Bliss, Grace, Heaven or Divine Favour only when a follower himself acts on or compels others to accept and follow these teachings. He is assured of all pleasures here and hereafter.
6. Those who do not obey are liable to be punished by the followers of Islam or the Islamic courts or the rulers of the Islamic state.
7. Islam demands complete faith, total surrender and strict adherence to it in letter and spirit.
8. Islam claims to envelop all the followers of the world as its community, and does not permit any other institution like state, nation, constitution or creed to stand before or run parallel to it. It demands undivided loyalty to it.
9. The rest of the social, legal, political and ritual set up is also ordained to be the part of the Holy *Quran*. It has to be accepted by all irrespective of differences of race, caste, colour, social status, language and culture except slaves, non-believers, women and animals.
10. Islam literally means peace, but it permits the use of force or violence. In this respect, Prophet Mohammed has asked the followers to learn from his life and actions.

Thus, most of the tenets make up and generate the basic spirit of Islam. Islam being the best and the last revelation has to be adopted by mankind. A believer is authorised to pursue all peaceful and violent means and bring out the rule of Allah or the Holy *Quran*. Critics of the Holy Book have no right to exist. All other laws and institutions are subordinate to the Islamic injunctions. With this spirit, the Muslims and their leaders have tried to spread Islam throughout the whole world. The ideology that prompts to realise them vigorously is known as 'Islamic Fundamentalism'.

Rise and Spread of Islamic Fundamentalism

Close commitment to religion is called as 'Fundamentalism'. Terrorism is a special form of Fundamentalism. Strong commitment to Islam is named as 'Islamic Fundamentalism'. There are many other forms of Religious Fundamentalism, but their influence, goal etc. are not so deep, widespread and problematic. None others has been able to withstand and replace the operations of Islamic Fundamentalism. Islam has always been the most political of the world religions from its very beginning.[1]

All branches of Islam are devoted to its propagation. But there are two main branches of Islam: the Sunni and the Shia. Both have tried to spread

Islam as Islamic Fundamentalism. Both branches have undergone the various phases of Islamic Fundamentalism. The Sunnis constitute about 85 per cent of the world's one billion Muslims. The other 15 per cent are Shias. Yet the Shia Fundamentalism has been much more spectacular and aggressive. However, both have been violent and expansive forms of Islamic Fundamentalism.

The two branches of Islam parted company at an early stage over the succession to the Prophet. Shias were the followers of Ali, the son-in-law of the Prophet. Ali had refused to become Caliph on the terms offered to him. Eventually, he had become Caliph on his own terms. One of Ali's sons, also revered by the Shias, chose to suffer martyrdom rather than renounce his claim to the caliphate. This self-sacrifice and sticking to principle became characteristic of Shiaism. The Shi'ites tend to be more puritanical, more fundamentalist and more devoted to martyrdom, to holy war and to the fusion of religion and state than the Sunnis. Shiaism tends to be more anti-establishment form of Islam, and puts greater emphasis on social justice. It appeals strongly to the poor and dispossessed. The Sunnis are the followers of the *Sunna*, the beaten path or Tradition. Sunnism is usually the pro-establishment religion. In most states, its religious leadership is part of the establishment. Law, education and preaching are all practiced under the aegis of the state. The *ulamas* receive state salaries. The Sunni clergy have often acted as the mouthpiece of the state. The Shia clergy, even in Shia states, have a separate organisation from the state and have traditionally performed a more critical role. Shiaism has a messianic dimension that Sunnism lacks. It believes that there will be a restoration of the rule of the Prophet with the return of the 'hidden Imam' who will one day lead the Islamic community to a final paradise. All injustice will be banished and the oppressed will inherit the earth. Sunnis believe a *caliph* to be merely a fallible interpreter of the Quran, whereas, Shias believe that a true *caliph* is an *Imam*, a divinely inspired and therefore infallible religious leader in true descent from the Prophet and Ali. The true descent of the Prophet has been lost, but, Shias believe, one will eventually be found again.

Prophet Muhammad (670-732), the founder of Islam, is known to have direct revelation of Allah. He gave directions to him on all matters – cosmos, religion, politics, society, family, economy and duties of a believer. Basically, they were pivoted on non-idolatry, equality and fighting for the cause of religion. With these teachings, he founded the first Islamic State and led its expansion by fighting and winning over the Arabian tribes. In this manner, the founder of Islam was a *political* and *military*, as well as a *religious*, leader. He gave the weapon of Islamic Fundamentalism or of Absolute Faith and Belief to his followers to spread his Message. It did not so happen in case of the founders of other religions. Most of the founders of non-Muslim religions were devoted to self-realisation of God, and kept themselves confined to preaching and religious living only. All other matters were secondary to them. In terms of temporal power and influence, they stand no match to Islam.

The Islamic ideal has been the unity of political authority. It has always been a conquering and proselytising faith. It began with the domination of the Arabian Peninsula. Within a couple of centuries of its foundation, Islam possessed an empire stretching from Spain to India. It crushed and trampled over all other non-Muslim dynasties, cultures, religions, communities and economies. It was victorious everywhere. Towards the end of the Middle Ages, the leadership of Islam passed from the Arabs to the Turks. The Turks, with the Sword of Islam, succeeded in conquering much of Europe.

The Sunni Fundamentalism

Islamic thought on politics did not centre around the state but around the idea of the community of all Muslims led by the *Caliph* or successor of the Prophet, who then made himself the leader and religious ruler of the entire Islamic community. The *Caliph* ruled with the advice of the *ulama,* the body of religious scholars. The latter were experts on the *Sharia,* or the divine law found in the Quran (direct word of Allah revealed to the Prophet). Further guidance was to be sought from the sayings and deeds of the Prophet.

When the Ottoman Turks dominated the Islamic world, the Turkish ruler, the Sultan, also became the *Caliph,* and claimed the loyalty of all Muslims (from Morocco to southern China). Arab Muslims did not have much choice since the Turks had conquered their lands. Muslims of India and beyond also began to look to the Turkish Sultan for leadership as they became increasingly subject to European control.

The Turks remained powerful during the sixteenth and seventeenth centuries. But Islamic thinking under the Turkish rule was extremely conservative, traditionalist and introvert. Muslims lagged behind the Europeans. They changed little for a thousand years. Turkey became weak and vulnerable as 'the sick man of Europe'. After that Europe began to dominate the world economically and militarily. Europe underwent three major intellectual movements – the Renaissance, the Enlightenment, and the democratic and nationalist ideas of the French Revolution. European conquests of large parts of Islamic Asia, North Africa, and Turkey, provoked fresh thought, which fructified during the nineteenth century. This change was resented by the Muslims who regarded their own civilisation and culture as far superior to that of the Europeans. They thought that they were lazy and slack, and neglectful of their powerful, divine and true religion. They accepted only the nation-state from the Europeans and gave up the idea of recreating the worldwide Islamic community as a single political entity led by a *Caliph*. But they kept it alive as an ideal. In all other matters, the Muslims chose to resort to Islamic Fundamentalism and launch the tenets of the Holy Koran.[2]

The Muslim leaders chose to turn existing national states into Islamic states. They stood for the unity of religion and politics. The Prophet and his immediate successors tried to maintain balance between religious and political authorities, but, in practice, everywhere, the political was made subordinated to the religious. Islamic Fundamentalism claimed to restore the balance, but it could not do so. The choice before them was to westernise or Islamicise.

Under Kemal Ataturk (1881-1938), the Turks moved decisively towards the creation of a modern Western nation-state. He overthrew sultanate and abolished caliphate, thus, ended the traditional fusion of political and religious authorities. The Turks introduced Western law, emancipation of women, socio-religious reforms, and suppressed many elements of the Islamic traditionalism. Thus, Ataturk successfully showed the way of modernism to the Muslims.[3]

But the traditionalists also moved towards a modern territorial, centralised nation-state, but one inspired by Islamic ideals based on divine law. This has been the chosen field of Islamic fundamentalism. But they did not adopt the modern political methods. They opted to work with the methods characteristic of the Middle Ages and the methods of the Prophet himself. However, for the first time, the protagonists of modernism launched a political party seeking power in the nation-state of Egypt in the late 1920s.

Abdul Ibn Saud belonged to the Sunni sect. He actually was the hereditary leader of one of the tribes of the Arabian Peninsula. Since the eighteenth century, it had been the home of puritanical version (Sunni) of Islam. Following the Prophet, Ibn Saud, a charismatic leader, united the tribes around him. By a mixture of political manoeuvring and force of arms, Saud conquered the Arabian peninsula and declared himself King. His New Kingdom included the two most holy sites of Islam, Mecca and Medina. Ibn Saud claimed the guardianship of the Holy Places as well as of the whole of the Islamic world. The combination of oil and pilgrimage made the Saudis richest ever since. It was the duty of all Muslims to go on a pilgrimage (the *Haj*) to these holy places at least once during their lifetime. The Muslims continue to abide by that injunction.

Ibn Saud made Saudi Arabia a deeply religious country. Islamic practices are strictly observed there. The *ulamas* control the religious police who enforce Islamic laws. Saudi society is extremely conservative. Saudi Arabia is still an absolute monarchy with no political parties. The unusually large royal family amounts to a party on its own. However, despite its strict adherence to Islamic codes, the Saudi royal family has been subjected to criticism by the fundamentalists. Some of the grounds of their criticism are: close alliance with the USA, the lifestyle of the royal family, avoiding of their religious duties at home, living of royal princes in the fleshpots of the West, etc.

The Iranians (Shias) since their revolution in 1979, vilified the Saudi royalty as corrupt and un-Islamic. In 1979, a group of fundamentalists (the Iranian Shia fundamentalists) reached there and captured the Great Mosque at Mecca. The Saudis took several days in removing them and a great deal of bloodshed occurred. Those captured alive were subsequently beheaded in various public places. Thus, there was an open and public clash between two types of Islamic Fundamentalism: the Shias fought against the Sunnis and vice versa.

A third form of Islamic Fundamentalism appeared in the Islamic (Sunni) Brotherhood in Egypt in 1928. Egypt at that time was under the British control with a subservient king. It was the most westernised of the Arab countries. Western dominance was much resented by the Muslims, the modernising nationalists and the traditionalists. One of the traditionalists, Hassan al Banna, founded a youth movement, known as the Islamic Brotherhood. In the 1930s, the Islamic Brotherhood became the first full-fledged fundamentalist political party.

Hassan al Banna, the founder of the Islamic Brotherhood, believed that the Islamic world was corrupted by the Western ideas and needed to be purified. A restored or purified faith must be put at the centre of the nation's life. The *Sharia* must be given its central authority, and Islamic principles be applied to all aspects of social and economic life. It should be an Islamic society neither socialist nor capitalist. It would be possible only by resorting to a *jehad* or holy war. They would destroy the colonial power and liberate Egypt, and the rest of the Islamic world.

Increasing instability and violence by the Brotherhood helped by army colonels caused the overthrow of the monarchy. One of the colonels, Nasser, eventually took over control of government. In the beginning, the Brotherhood co-operated with Nasser's modernising nationalist government. Later on, it stood in opposition. Nasser cracked down severely on them, and many of them went into exile. The Brotherhood continued to spread Islamic Fundamentalist ideas throughout the Arab world. However, the catastrophic defeat of Egypt by the Israelis in the six-day war of 1967 forced Nasser to compromise with them. He attempted to appear a good Muslim, and allowed the Brotherhood to operate to a certain extent. Many recruits of the Brotherhood returned from exile. Anwar Sadat, the successor of Nasser, had closer ties with the Brotherhood fundamentalists. He was hailed as the 'believer president'. In order to attract American investment, Sadat allied himself with the Americans. He permitted considerable commercialisation of Cairo. The outraged fundamentalists of the Brotherhood took to rioting and destroyed Cairo's night-clubs in January, 1977. They were further outraged by Sadat's peace treaty with Israel signed in 1979. Many more extreme groups besides the Brotherhood emerged, and one of them assassinated President Sadat in 1981. His successor President Hosney Mubarak (since 14 October, 1981) had to make many concessions to the fundamentalists.

The Brotherhood and its offshoots are found in many countries:

In Syria, President Hafiz al-Assad, despite leading a secular Ba'ath Party, had to put down the fundamentalist uprisings with considerable bloodshed, but ultimately had to make concessions to them.[4] In the same way, Sudan and Pakistan had become 'Islamic'. In Algeria, the National Liberation Front (FLN), after Algeria became free from the French rule in 1962, had to give up the path of modernisation abruptly and surrender to the fundamentalists in 1991. Morocco and Tunisia both fear their own Islamic fundamentalists. In Libya, a country of Sunni Muslims, the position of Colonel Quadhafi since September 1, 1969, was no better.[5]

The Shia Fundamentalism

Hostility between state and the Islamic leadership had a long history in Iran. After the World War I the Shah, backed by Britain, stripped Iran's religious leadership off much of their financial, legal and educational powers, and launched a vigorous programme of westernisation. He forbade many Shia rituals, such as, self-flagellation, and forbade the pilgrimage to Mecca. Aytollah Khomeini, the hero of the religious masses, fiercely attacked the Shah's acts. His arrest in 1963 was followed by massive riots. Khomeini was sent into exile. From his base in Iraq where there is majority of Shias, he launched bitter and vituperative attacks on the Shah and the whole concept of monarchy. He argued that the *ulama* should not just give advice on laws and government actions, as has been their traditional functions, but should actively participate in the overthrow of repressive governments and lead the regimes that replace them. The ideal Islamic state was theocratic state. The Shah fled into exile in January 1979 and Ayatollah Khomeini returned in triumph. He established his legitimacy by holding a referendum on the creation of an Islamic republic, and became its ultimate ruler for life. There was a council of 'experts' whose task was to choose a successor to the leader. It also had to ensure that whatever the Islamic republic did was 'in conformity with the will of Allah. The *Sharia* or 'divine law', as found in the Koran and the works of the Prophet, was incorporated into the constitution. The leader (Khomeini) appointed a Council of Guardians, composed of religious scholars, to make sure that the parliament passed no law that was contrary to divine dispensation. As time went on, the regime became more clerical, more intolerant and totalitarian. Enforcement of Islamic law became more vigorous. Iran was isolated, even within the Islamic world.

Having created an Islamic republic, Khomeini assumed that Iran was now the leader of not only of Shia Muslims, but the entire Islamic world.[6] It condemned other regimes and encouraged Muslims to overthrow their leaders, particular of Saudi Arabia and Kuwait which were pockets of the hated America, 'the Great Satan'. In 1987, he sent a large number of Iranian pilgrims chanting political slogans and waving pictures of the Ayatollah.[7] The Saudi police killed them all, and the rest were publicly executed. After the death of Khomeini, President Rafsanjani tried to rebuild Iran following a long destructive war with Iraq. But the fundamentalists continued to obstruct his ways.

Iranian influence is visible in a number of important places. There is Shia presence in the southern republics of former Soviet Union and Iraq. So far the Sunnis ruled in Iraq, Shias 60 to 65 per cent and Sunnis 32 to 37 per cent, now after the fall of Saddam Hussein, the Shias have formed government there. In Lebanon, the Lebanese Shias look to Iran for inspiration. After the 1979 revolution, the Iranian fundamentalists living there are engaged in a holy war against the Israelis. Their suicide attacks on the Israelis and against the peacekeeping forces of America and France there shocked the world. (300 US marines were killed in an incident in 1983). The Western hostages were kept there as prisoner and ill-treated for six years. The Shia militias saw, blessed by the Khomeini, the West and Israel as the same. They started a holy crusade to liberate the Islamic city of Jerusalem from the Zionists. Death in this struggle was declared martyrdom and promised instant access to heaven. The Lebanese Shias (the Hezbollah and other groups) have continued guerilla war against the Israelis.[8]

The whole history of Islamic Fundamentalism, identified with extremism or fanaticism, shows that it had been activated by the teachings and directives of the Holy Books.[9] In order to restore supremacy and purity of Islam, the fundamentalists have resorted to fratricide, rebellion, bloodshed and violence against defaulting Muslims and non-Muslims. In order to advance Islam, they have crushed, destroyed and trampled over non-Muslim population even if there was no grievance against them. In right earnest they obliterated alien cultures, art, literature, ways and structures of worship, enslaved and converted them to Islam in millions. The fanatics and fundamentalists did not spare even liberal Muslims and followers of middle or mixed path. They rejected all liberal values and stood for traditional Islamic values like patriarchy, four wives, sexual morality, anti-usury, blind faith *namaj* (prayer) etc. Throughout centuries of advancing Islamic Fundamentalism, their issues have remained almost the same except anti-Americanism, elimination of Israel, occupation of Jerusalem, and holding petrol as weapon.

However, one is not considered as fundamentalist or extremist if he believes in religious tenets, observes rituals or worships God in form he likes, or spreads teachings at his individual conscience level and without hurting others. When they give shape to those teachings in the form of action, organisation, community, identity and influence, they do reflect their religion. It is without recourse to material interests, power and politics.[10]

Slow-down of Islamic Fundamentalism

Fundamentalists were powerful till 90s. They made Islam the world's largest religion after Christianity. But advance of Islamic Fundamentalism, except in Muslim-dominated territories, has been stopped. Muslim nation-states now mostly lack unity, modernity and progress. The USA and other European nations have complete mastery over science, technology, industry, nuclear energy, electronics and media. The West dominates most of the global institutions, diplomacy, international relations, UN and its agencies, and armament. The Islamic countries have, apart from Islam, the only weapons of oil, which too cannot be used in an arbitrary manner. Muslim countries now are not free to expand their territories, convert non-Muslims on a large scale, launch war and use WMDs. Islamic Fundamentalism cannot so easily touch the survival of different religions, cultures, architecture, and institutions of worship and higher learning.

From Islamic Fundamentalism to Contemporary Terrorism

Under these pressing circumstances, owing to disabilities of Muslim countries and constraints imposed on them by big powers, authority of Security Council, and others, the Islamic fundamentalists are compelled to resort to the use of Terror as their only weapon. This Weapon of Terror is much more fatal, subversive, devastating and beyond the reach of enemy. It operates on lines of their past history.

This fatal weapon was used in September 11 terrorist attacks on the US World Trade Centre and the Pentagon. Since then the world under the US leadership and the UN surveillance appears to have determined to eliminate it in every possible way. To realise this objective, the world has amassed immense sources through diplomatic means, made military deployment and placed intelligence all over the globe for fighting this menace. Terrorism has been now accepted with one voice more dangerous than a conventional or a nuclear war.[11] To eradicate it, every time, soon after the occurrence of some terrorist attack, the relevant bodies of the UN and groups of nations pass resolution after resolution to destroy its remnants. But havocs perpetrated by the terrorists do not stop. Most of the world leaders fully know the names, forms and areas of various terrorist organisations, but remain unable to eradicate them. They only declare them 'illegal' and make the list of terrorist organisations lengthier.[12] Security forces and intelligence agencies do take action, kill and catch hold of some of terrorists here and there, but their real godfathers, preachers and trainers remain unhurt, protected, and continue to operate terrorism as usual. Terrorists are caught and killed, but 'terror' remains. In fact, world leaders, including the political leaders of the country concerned, talk only about the 'terrorists' and their terrorist acts. They look at the outcome of 'terror' or 'terrorism' only. They do not go to the form and making of 'terror' itself. One has to understand the 'theory' of terror. To know it one has to discover the factors, causes, elements and attributes of 'terror'. Their understanding will tell us who, what and why of 'terror' itself. 'Terror' is the key or core element, while 'terrorism' is its practice, planning and ideology. Both operate together. One cannot exist without the other. Often people consider them as identical, one and the same. They are two close but different concepts.

Theory of 'Terror'

Terrorism is defined as "The threat of violence, individual acts of violence or campaign of violence designed to instill fear to terrorise" (M. Jenkins). Its key element is 'terror'. *Terror* literally means 'extreme fear'. But in actual practice it stands for all acts committed to create 'terror' in the minds of people. This is done by committing heinous crimes like murder, arson, blasting of public utilities and the like. It is naked, blatant, cruel and inhuman act of killing of innocent people.

Terror is an aftermath, a creation, or outcome or result of certain acts. It is produced by killing some innocent or unaware persons, burning and destroying property, or blasting bridges, buildings and public utilities. Some trained persons who use deadly weapons for killing harmless persons create terror. By doing so the killers or the arsonists intend to invoke terror in the minds the people. The terrorised 'people' include both the rulers and the ruled. By doing so they intend to force change the government, faith or ideology of the people, destroy economy, occupy territory and make life miserable.

There are many kinds, forms and varieties of 'terror'. Thus, in the production of *jehadi* or contemporary 'terror', there is (i) a person/s with intuition or divine direction to commit acts of terror; (ii) a firm belief in the specific tenets of his religion, particularly, to kill non-believers; (iii) existence of motivation that he is selected and trained by senior clerics/terrorists to kill, blast and destroy others and bring about terror around this great mission; (iv) non-believers or opponents of religion would not change or convert to his beliefs, therefore, to be killed by him; (v) already fixed targets for killing, and burning, (v) availability of guidance and directions, and protection of his family by the mentors, (vi) an environment of utmost faith for performing such missions, acts of fanaticism and making of sacrifice, (vii) bestowal of public honour and guarantee and security of members of the family of the killer, and attainment of heaven on being killed (martyrdom), (viii) avoidance of direct and open fight with the enemy, and, (ix) support and connivance of the members of his community within the country and outside. Theory of 'Terror' involves religion, philosophy and rationale of realising the mission by killing others. It also keeps the doer ready to die during the encounter gladly.

In terror, the killer operates like a human bomb. Human bombs have no face, but doubles up in power as a bomb. It is often unfailing and more destructive than a nuclear bomb. The individuals operating as human bombs have no fear. They just have an obsession that drives them through hell (this world), in search of heaven. They feel proud of their act even when are caught or imprisoned.

While using the term 'terror', common man understands little about the real event. The victim does not know that he is being killed as a means to intimidate or coerce a particular society or a government. He is totally ignorant of this unbelievable fact that there are persons who turn so intolerant on the basis of their understanding of some sacred books or religion that they kill everyone not holding views like them. They have been taught to do such planned killings as a result of some uncompromising policy and ideology developed by the mentors. To the victims of terrorism, they are but murderers, killers, inhuman demons, ferocious beasts etc.

Those who commit such acts are known as '*terrorists*'.[13] Religion-based terrorists call themselves 'jehadis', 'mujahedeens', 'warriors of their religion', 'soldiers of Islam' etc., but they are 'terrorists': murderers and killers. All acts of 'terror' are totally against law, human rights, morality and democracy.

In the practice of terrorism, a terrorist is encouraged to think himself as a hero, superman and martyr. That feeling makes him to die for the cause. Blind faith prompts him to kill others. Terrorists are ruthless killers of the worst type. They embody nothing but hate and revenge. Terrorists are anti-God, anti-man, anti-culture and enemy of the family, state and society. They do not allow any other view to prevail. The whole world, particularly, the hostile nations have to abide by them. Their words and actions are the final verdicts upon earth. State laws everywhere consider them as *terrorist acts.*[14]

Those who commit the acts of terrorism are not individuals or scattered persons. They are well-organised, equipped, trained, and financed by governments and non-governmental organisations. This makes, every kind of big and small terrorism, a kind of war on non-conventional lines.

If a terrorist is compelled to live in a state, or a nation or a community different from his own, he stands at war with it. Even in a Muslim state, which is not run according to the tenets of Islam, he feels himself at war with it. He may keep patience and show forbearance till the opportune moment arrives to transform that polity into the version of their religion.

Thus, *jehadi* terror provides a perfect theory of action built up as a kind of Divine Dispensation. This equips terrorists with an unfailing weapon to get success here and hereafter. It is enabling many Islamic states and organisations to fight against any kind of state howsoever big and resourceful it might be. Terror can use any strategy, means, method, style, tactic or pause to realise its goal. Operators of Terror find themselves fully authorised to acquire and use WMDs, including nuclear weapons.

As the number of terrorists and terrorist organisations increases, it becomes more dangerous and more devastating to humanity and world peace. Even the Islamic countries where the terrorists operate, have begun to fear them. In fact, terrorism wants and plans to have its influence and control over the ruling elements of each and every government, including its army. Improvement in the quality of education, training, quality of weapons, and strategy brings the terrorists closer to success. With the advancement of science, IT, and military hardware, terrorists are able to choose their targets at will. Of late, their hands are in search of crude or latest technology of nuclear bomb. It is reported that they are able to buy, steal or smuggle technology of nuclear weapons. They function with overt and covert support of their governments, its army and intelligence, community, and disgruntled elements of hostile countries. As Muslims having sympathy to them are scattered over in all developing and developed countries, the terrorists get local support and shelter quite easily. As terrorism can be maintained at a very low cost, it is used as a common tool by the terrorists almost everywhere.

Terrorism as Ideology of Terror

So far, no attempt has been made for ascertaining the common elements or features of various forms of terrorism so that they may be made the basis of law or objective criteria to determine, define and declare particular acts as 'terrorism'. To escape from the charge of bias or hostility against a particular religion, all forms of terrorism, such as, Sunni, Shia, Catholic, Palestinian, Jewish, Maoist, Naxalite, ultra nationalistic and the like should be taken into consideration. This should be in the agenda of the UN and the patterns of action against it be decided by the world body in advance.

'Terrorism' is an ideology which stands for the ideas, policies, planning, organising, collecting arms and money, preaching and training persons, using media and publication towards creation of 'terror'. Terrorism is justification, advocacy, planning, and motivation, procuring weapons and using them for killing innocent and unconcerned persons for creating terror. It is conducted to realise the desired goals. It is a war by proxy launched by some interested group, community, party, state or nation. Terrorism is an advanced stage of extremism, fanaticism and fundamentalism. Terrorism is the mental make up of a terrorist.

The term 'terrorism' also comes out of the root word 'terror'. It does not spell out what actually it is. Its use hides all ugly, inhuman, heinous and bloody acts committed by killers and murderers of human beings. Plainly speaking, terrorism should be outrightly spoken of as 'killerism' and 'murderism'. It is simply and directly killing of innocent human beings.

Terrorism is not new. What is new is the combination of terrorism, fanaticism and the technological capability to wreck vast and inhumane devastation, whether by act of terror or any other means. For understanding and explaining Terrorism, one needs to know the making of Terrorism.

Distinction between Religious Fundamentalism and Terrorism

Although the basis, ground, methods and goals of Religious Fundamentalism and Terrorism happen to look alike, still they are different. Terrorism, in the present context, can be seen as an outcome of Religious Fundamentalism. Still they are not identical. In Religious or Religion-related Fundamentalism, state government, its army or intelligence takes part with the larger goal of overpowering their adversary. Its goals are total rule or governance on line of the Holy Books. It acts in an all-out, open and direct manner. The targets of terrorists are limited to creating 'terror' by committing specific killing, blasting and destroying the enemy and his people. Only a few, trained and entrusted persons take part in it. They operate secretly and suddenly. Hardly their adversary or the human targets know anything about their attacks in advance. Their mentors – political leaders, military rulers or others fix up targets for them. Whereas religious fanaticism and fundamentalism prompts them to launch war, indulge in rioting or setting fire, the terrorists are not always concerned with religion. They can kill, if need be, the followers of their own religion or ideology. Religious fundamentalism fights against both (deviant) Islamic and non-Islamic elements. It goal is the total subjugation of the enemy, its people, culture, and community. Targets of terrorism are only specific persons, groups and places of worship and buildings and monuments. On comparison, acts of terrorism are much less expensive, less time consuming and much more effective than that preparation of war made by religious or religion-related fundamentalism.[15]

Making of Terrorism

Both as concept and practice, 'terrorism' is wider than 'terror'. It is ideology, ethos, practice, planning, strategy and politics motivating the operations of terror. Inclusive of the elements of 'terror' and the 'terrorist', making of terrorism (see diagram below) can be explained as follows:

Perfect, Fighting and Proselytising Religion/Ideology

As Terrorism is extreme and strategic form of launching Religious Fundamentalism, it builds on the foundation a Perfect, Fighting and Proselytising Religion/Ideology. Terrorists believe in a religion (*jehadi*) or an ideology (Maoist or Naxalism) fanatically. They entertain the idea that God has made revelation, given commands and directions to them either directly or through some Prophet or Messenger. As such, they have to be obeyed by all persons irrespective of time and place.

All non-believers and renegades have to be brought to that faith, by all means. Everyone can attain Bliss, Grace, Heaven or Divine Favour when he himself acts on and compels others to follow these tenets. The believer is assured of all pleasures here and hereafter. Those who do not obey are, in larger interest, liable to be punished by them. Their faith or ideology demands complete faith, total surrender and strict adherence. It requires undivided loyalty to it. It has to be accepted by all irrespective of differences of race, caste, colour, social status, language and culture. To give a concrete

Terror, Terrorism and Terrorists

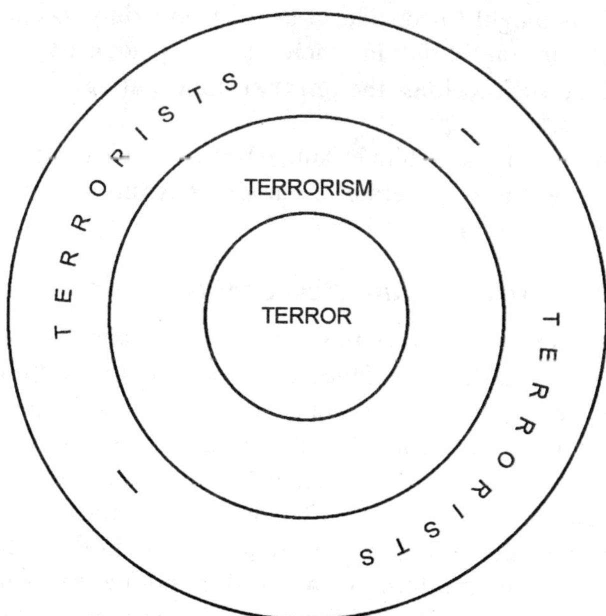

reality to their faith, use of force or violence is taught in various type of terrorist camps.[16]

Strong History, Large Community, and Local Support

Usually terrorism carries a very strong past in which their forefathers have been rulers of vast territories and possessed robust cultures.[17] Their number is usually over millions and millions inhabiting many states and countries.[18] On this basis they are able to establish links, where the terrorists commit acts of terrorism, with the local people, get support, intelligence, and information from fellow-believers. Elements of some Islamic governments and their armies also help and direct them.

Religious/Ideological Call and Training

There must be abundance of human resources. Availability of a large number of persons, particularly young, poverty-stricken and illiterate is necessary.[19] They should be willing to undergo training in terrorism. This training is imparted as part of religion or ideology.[20] It is actually conducted under the cover of religion. Senior terrorists, actually militiamen train the youngsters in various *madarsas*, training camps and institutions to die for the (cause) religion or mission.[21] Preachers train non-believers and elements hostile to their religion or ideology. Senior leaders are authorised to shoot immediately any hesitant, renegade or disobedient terrorist. No person is permitted to seek shelter of a *guru*, prophet or preacher from any other different religion. If someone so dares he can be killed on the spot. Every terrorist is taught to consider it as his prime duty to kill the person raising doubt or objection in their goals, guidance and training. Overwhelmed by such feelings the terrorist unhesitatingly engages him in the job of killings.[22]

Osama bin Laden found him ordained by the Holy *Quran* to target even the citizens. Being the taxpayers of a particular tyrannical government he considers them as potential combatants.[23]

Terrorism as Ultimate and Best Strategy

Use of terror or terrorism is now the only strategy available to the religious fundamentalists. It is the only alternative available to the fundamentalist people and governments. They cannot exercise religious fundamentalism in old ways. They resort to terrorism as they find themselves to be incapable, constrained and ill equipped to launch an 'open' war for the cause of religion. Extremists among them do not have big armies, heavy weapons, legitimacy to rule, and sources to engage the enemy in the battlefield. The world community, under international law does not permit them to launch fighting. They are also constrained by their own governments if they operate for them. Such governments for various reasons and as a matter of policy avoid direct confrontation or war with the enemy, which may be a nation, state or community living in adjacent area. Supporting governments of such terrorists either lack resources or avoid using WMDs for fear of sanctions from international community.[24] In place of conducting a full-fledged war, they find use of terrorists and terrorism much cheaper, easier, more effective and efficient in outcome.

Political Goals

In all acts of terror, the perpetrators, also known as militants and *jehadis*, kill innocent persons who are totally unknown to the havoc being inflicted on them. Innocent people are killed, their public or private property destroyed, women and girls raped and buildings blasted. All these acts are considered by the political leaders and administrators as simple 'killing' of innocent people. But the use of term 'terror' for such heinous acts is deceptive as it creates confusion and deceit. It hides the failure and irresponsibility of persons, the security force and rulers in not protecting the victims of terrorism. These terrorists, therefore, must be clearly and openly called as murderers and killers, arsonists, vandals and the like. They are criminals of the first order, and need an outright condemnation and elimination.

Their acts are not simply acts of 'terror' or of violence, but in fact, by proxy, are *political* acts and war. Theirs are 'heinous crimes' operated by the political leaders or their military commanders through the terrorists to realise specific goals. The terrorists kill men, women and children not out of grievance against them but to warn the attacked people or their government that they have to do what the terrorists want and demand, or leave their people, territory, and governance to them. Through the acts of terror, they make attempt to compel enemy-governments to change policy, planning, disrupt economy, and cause communal riots and bloodshed. The 'government' includes local, provincial or central governments, including their security agencies, police, and military and civil officers. These terrorists are supported, prompted and helped by their governments, communities, groups, and organisations. The people who live in neighbouring and other countries, but submit to their ideology, religion and nationality give intelligence, financial, and material support to the terrorist outfits. They also get recruits from them.

Non-state Actors: Beyond the Purview of UN

Mostly the terrorists are non-state actors spread over in different parts of the world. Before the world community the governments sheltering, guiding and protecting them refuse to accept the responsibility for their heinous acts, even their presence or residence in their territory. Links or connections with them are kept secret. Funds, material, weapons, etc. are made available to them through covert agencies. The terrorists make use of the most sophisticated weapons.[25] In fact, they are in search of nuclear bombs and WMDs. Some of the governments like Iran are on the verge of making them, and the other like Pakistan, is already in possession of them with mindset to use them.[26] Obviously, no people or their army can fight against this type of terror: the human bomb. Timing, place, mode of attack and type of weapons being used are not known beforehand. One cannot prepare oneself in advance. Islamic diehards residing almost everywhere render sympathy, shelter, and help to them.

Guidance from Fraternal Government, Intelligence Agencies and the Army

The terrorists are supported, guided and protected by the ambitious political leaders and military rulers.[27] The latter operate the wires of terrorism. They manage to send them to kill innocent people, set their houses on fire, cause disturbance, spread communal tension and the like. The terrorists are asked to do so at times in the name of freedom or avenge some injustice or in the national interest. Their government manages to dispatch them as infiltrators, human bombs, fifth columnists and terrorists. In view of the worldwide call to fight against terrorism, it is not possible for them to enter into an open, large-scale and all out war. Islamic governments or organisations often use terrorism as a political weapon. Under international pressure, ambitious political leaders and military rulers resort to it under the cover of defending religion, seeking Justice or realising Freedom.[28]

At home, when the mission of terrorism is realised, the terrorists are given a warm welcome and treated like heroes and martyrs. They are given blessings that they would be rewarded with entry in heaven.[29] Verses from the Holy Books are recited to support and boost their deeds in large gatherings.

Financial Sources for Use of Sophisticated Weapons

The terrorists are not short of funds, weapons or manpower.[30] They get recruits from all over the world[31] Terrorism is fully motivated and taught by preachers of 'Terror', and, practiced by the terrorists. Islamic terrorism, earlier, was financed by are three Saudi princes, seven banks and eight charitable groups. Some of the charitable groups are the International Islamic Relief Organisation, the Muslim World League, the SAAR Foundation and the World Assembly of Muslim Youth.[32] Bin Laden has prepared an encyclopaedia for the terrorists of Al Queda to fight the holy war by spreading terrorism and use all means. Bin Laden claims Islamic rights over Pak N-bombs also: "We supported the Pakistani people and congratulated them when God was gracious enough to enable them to acquire the nuclear weapon. We regard this as one of our rights, our Muslim rights." He is actively looking to pile up more nuclear weapons as well as chemical and biological weapons. His intended targets usually are the US, Britain and Israel. In fact, all states, openly or clandestinely, using Terrorism, are engaged in this venture. A few of them do not even fear or care for total annihilation, as they consider it divinely ordained. The terrorists now claim to be ready to repeat many 9/11 blasts in US, UK, and many European countries. India has been their victim several times.

Youth, Poverty and Ignorance

After profiling more than 50 Muslim suicide bombers, serving in the Hezbollah, Hamas and the Palestinian Islamic Jehad, Ariel Merari, a Tel Aviv University psychologist concluded that there is no single psychological or demographic profile of suicide terrorists. "Intense struggles produce several types of people with the potential willingness to sacrifice themselves for a cause. Their motives range from religion, patriotism, hatred of the enemy to a profound sense of victimisation." A BBC report states that suicide bombers are typically unmarried men in their late teens and 20s. They act on the belief that they will go straight to paradise after the deed is over. Recruits are picked from mosques, schools and religious institutions and are reassured that their families will be looked after.[33] The mentors of Terrorism exploit utter poverty, ignorance and fanatic faith of the youth and downtrodden people of Muslim communities.

Exploitation of Public Grievances, Legal Flaws and Ineffective Judicial Process

An another requisite and source of Terrorism is abundance of Public Grievances, Legal Flaws and ineffective, expensive and dilatory Judicial Process in the enemy country. The ordinary common laws of a country provide ample opportunity for conducting war of terrorism. It is very difficult to apprehend the terrorists, both before and after they commit the crime of terrorism. Their methods are slow, dilatory, costly and ineffective. By the time the case is decided the terrorist may commit several fresh terrorist acts. After a few years of judicial proceedings, one terrorist might be sentenced to death. But before that happens, his accomplices would have killed hundreds of innocent men, women and children. Loopholes of ordinary law are fully exploited by the terrorist links. September 11 bomb attacks terrorised the American mind and changed the country for ever.[34] Terrorism is able to play havoc because of weaknesses and malfunctioning of democratic governments. Countries like India often like to wait and wait, and owing to lack of courage or fear of Muslim reaction avoid taking action. They have information and sources to deal with it but refrain from taking action in right direction. Both war against terrorism and implementation of ordinary laws and human rights as means to prevent it hardly go together. Containment of terrorism demands full or partial sacrifice of some rights, conveniences and privileges in varying degrees.

Terrorists already know the inability of some states to govern their societies, handle their security and military measures, and protect their territories from serving as sanctuary to terrorists and criminal organisations.

At the international level, even legal action becomes more difficult in view of absence of extradition treaties, sovereignty of states, administrative incapability and lack of cooperation from concerned governments.[35] The terrorists know all these weaknesses of national and international communities, and exploit them fully.

Terrorism as War

Fight against terrorism must be treated not only as proxy war but a kind of special 'war' launched for the realisation of religious and political goals. It is not 'merely terrorism' as such. It is intermixed with religious fundamentalism. There are two ways to fight terrorism. Firstly, it has to be met by force, if possible, before its occurrence, otherwise after it. The second way provides long term solution. It requires separation of religion from fundamentalism. In place of religion one may also have absolute or fanatic faith in some ideology. Separating religion from religious fundamentalism or fanaticism is much more difficult. This separation has to be defined, accepted, supervised, enacted and properly implemented. Still few countries have understood the true nature and tactics of Terrorism, and suffer from utter lack of means and tools to eliminate it. Presently, they are fighting against it without proper arms and armies able enough to defeat Terrorism.

Offshoots of Contemporary Terrorism

There are four offshoots of contemporary terrorism: (a) Invincibility of Terrorism; (b) Failure of Liberals, (c) Solution through Law, and (d) Existential Challenges.

Invincibility of Terrorism

Few people realise that terrorism is invincible. It cannot be eliminated either by force, propaganda of human rights or spread of liberal education. Terrorism is *'jihad'* or religious duty committed in the name of Allah, Guru, Prophet, Holy Books or their Preachers. For instance, internally the whole of Islam may not be teaching or preaching terrorism. But there must be some statements in the Holy Books that authorise the terrorists to indulge in terrorism.[36] It might be done just to obey the divine directives or punish the non-believers or propagate it by deeds of violence. Thousands of terrorists claim to act, either at their own will or on the direction of their mentors, or on these divinely ordained statements.[37] Terrorists are doers and others are passive onlookers. The terrorists do not consider these passive onlookers as believers of Islam. They see the whole world as anti or non-Muslim. Therefore, in the name of Islam they commit any kind of violence. They are taught or trained to make any sacrifice. No power on earth can, particularly, when they are supported and guided by the leaders of their own government and community, stop them. Weapons, diplomacy, technology and politics are unable to restrain terrorists. The terrorists and their mentors are trying to possess nuclear bombs. The moment they succeed they would be invincible. Islamic rulers, dictators and political leaders make full use of their commitment to Islam.[38] No other religion or ideology has been able to stand up to face this encounter. Terrorists know this position of all other peaceful religions or ideologies well. Terrorism is treated as an unfailing weapon of religion. Religions that thrive on teachings of peace, toleration, otherworldly bliss and non-violence simply have either to surrender to them or keep dispassionate, introvert and listless silence. Doggedness of terrorism has disabled the nation-state, viability of democratic systems and protection of well-equipped standing armies.

A large number of scholars, intellectuals and leaders, in the past, already knew the power of Islam, but only a few realise that presently it is also a perennial source of terrorism in the modern world. They fail to face the reality for the sake of their own survival, fear of widespread communal disturbances, dependence on goodwill of the Muslims for protecting their vested interests and sustenance of fragile polities. The killing sword of Islamic terrorism continuously hangs over their head. Muslims and non-Muslims all suffer from this threat. Any attempt to analyse or discuss the mystery, or casting doubt, criticising or suggesting correction, reform or remedy in the tenets of Islam is likely to result in severe punishment, humiliation, amputation, destruction and death of the person or persons engaged in such acts. Islam authorises every believer to stop and punish non-Islamic acts. A believer, in fact, has no discretion to keep himself away.

Contemporary terrorism has a perennial human source. Out of one billion Muslims, there is likelihood of a few million of Muslims to continue to operate as fundamentalists or terrorists. Under the circumstances, terrorism becomes an all-weather weapon to fight against the enemies, particularly, the US, Israel, and the European Union. The Islamic countries like to push the frontline of terrorists to tread only on the road of terrorism.[39] Islamic teachings provide a perennial and readymade source of manpower to them. Military rulers and political leaders of the Muslim states cunningly and knowingly make use of them to realise their political goals. This they do by transforming their political and military goals as the part of teachings of Islam. After the conversion of their politics into religion, there appears no power on earth, which can distract them from their assigned mission.

Whether one is Muslim or a non-Muslim, one has to accept the Holy Book as the last and final word of God. None is allowed to discuss, criticise and object to it. One cannot raise any objection to statements made in it. If someone dares to do it he can be killed on spot. Every Muslim as a soldier of Islam considers it his prime duty to kill the person doubting or objecting to those holy statements. Developed nations and their citizens foolishly complain that the Islamic extremists in the name of *jihad* are attempting to mould the whole world into their ideology. They forget that they are doing what they are directed to do. There is no way to advise them to live like good and peaceful citizens.

Their main difficulty is that they all, including the liberals, are, at heart, blind followers of Islam. They have absolute faith in the teachings of the *Quran* and the *Shariat*. The Muslims, as a community of faith, know well that the secret of their strength lies in keeping belief in Islam, in tact. Even if they like to, they cannot change themselves. They have learnt that theirs is the last, final and universal faith. They have to appear diehard, and there is no way out. Being the last message of Allah, the Holy *Quran* stands over and above everything. There can be no change in it. It has to be obeyed by the whole of Ummah (the community of the believers) spreading the world over in millions. It is the final Law over and above every other law.

Islam is a product or creation of a non-state and non-nation society. It does not recognise entities like state, nation and rule of citizenship, which would bind a believer, or follower of Islam. Islam is global by nature. No state, nation or world-body can claim to stand over and above it. A Muslim in terms of the Holy *Quran* can live and follow his tenets only when he lives in a community without having a state or nation. However, if he is compelled to live in a state, or a nation or a community different from his own, he stands at war with it. He can be at peace only in a society of Islam. Muslims tactically can keep patience and show forbearance, or cool down non-Muslims by making liberal interpretation of terror-oriented tenets of Islam, till the opportune moment arrives to transform that polity or community into the version of their orthodox religion. The orthodox believers are to operate as extremists, insurgents and rebels. There is no way to persuade the diehard terrorists to live like good citizens.

Launching war, gunning down or imprisoning them, making sophisticated weapons, outlawing their organisations, stopping aid and shelter to them, and the like does not deter or discourage them.[40] It may slow down their speed of action and its effect. In fact, all killings, pains and tortures to them rather make their will and acts much stronger and deadlier.[41] It is almost suicidal to imagine or expect that these terrorists would ever change at their own.

However, invincibility of Terrorism invites reaction, counter-action and challenge from the side of opponents. There are two ways to overcome the threat of contemporary Terrorism: one, the Turkey way, and, two, of emergence of more powerful counter-religion or ideology. Turkey has shown the way that Islamic Terrorism can be met even by the Muslims themselves, provided they are able to throw off their orthodox and conservative Islamic mettle under some powerful leadership. This has to be supported by a strong, modern and secular military. The second way is either the emergence of one another more powerful, organised and strong religion/ideology or reformulate some already existing virile religion/ideology. It has to inherit another Revelation directly from God covering tenets on all matters of life, commandeering to destroy and eliminate every other form of religion, past and present, of similar *jehadi* nature. Being based on the universal principles of Justice, Reason and Equality, the new religion can claim itself to be the Last and Final Message of Man. Such religion would deny all civil, political, financial and existential rights at global level to the differing perpetrators of violence and terrorism in the name of God or holy books. From this point of view, it looks futile to bank upon the Religions of Peace and Piety, or Gandhianism[42] for riding mankind of from the scourge of terrorism. Surely, such powerful message superior to hitherto obtained from God Himself would consider itself concerned more to save innocent men, women and children from being killed in the name of Islam. It would prove a final attempt to stop fanaticism, fundamentalism and terrorism appearing to be defender of God and His Revelation. Any emancipator of humanity from the scourge of terrorism can vehemently claim Revelation from God, the Almighty. Unfortunately, such invention or recovery of another Religion, based on some kind of revelation directly or through some Prophet, Messenger or Avatar is not likely to happen. Even if it is made to happen, it would not be acceptable to the men and women of 21st century.

Failure of Liberals

Another offshoot comes from the liberals. Liberals both Muslims and non-Muslims everywhere are in majority. But they are unable to stop the terrorists from committing such heinous crimes. Particularly, Muslim liberals, fail to reject *jihadis'* claims that the terrorists cannot be judges unto themselves and have divine sanction to use force. Terrorism happens to be the ideology of the super-sovereigns. It depends only on the individual understanding, training and education of the terrorists that to what extent they would, in the prevailing manner, fight for the cause of religion. But, unfortunately, as supporters of use of force and violence for religion, all stand along with the terrorists. Inability of liberals and non-Muslims to oppose *jihadi* or religious terrorism is very much prominent in the field of supremacy of state. Forgetting the role of modern state, they consider the non-believers, even sympathisers of the West, US, Israel, Hinduism etc. as criminals and connive at the acts of the terrorists. Even the liberals do not accept that state now is the supreme, secular and sovereign organisation, claiming monopoly of obedience of all citizens. The liberals too maintain that state has to be subordinated to religion. They do not like to permit state to stand over and above all individuals, groups and organisations. They regard only divine law as superior to all other laws. In the field of international relations, states are placed next to the United Nations Organization – an effective confederation of 191 states. They claim even the UNO subordinate to Islam.

Because of their innate commitment to the religious fundamentals, the liberals remain unable to isolate orthodox Muslims from supporting *jihadi* terrorism and eschew their indirect support to terrorists. Most of the liberal interpretations of Islam have largely been to justify the use of violence by the individual believers on old lines. This results in permitting the continuation of terrorism and breaking of civil laws. These liberals fruitlessly continue to permit *jihad* (war) when it is no more permissible to do so. As the liberals can be declared as renegade or *kafir*, they cannot tell the believers that now no individual or organisation or community has the right to exercise force and violence except in a very narrow area of 'self-defense'. They are unable to inform or educate the terrorists that now state has taken over all of their earlier functions; under the universal 'rule of law', democracy has evolved means and methods to redress injustice, oppression and exploitation; anyone using violence stands against the 'rule of law' and the constitution; and, a practitioner of violence can, therefore, be treated as a criminal, rebel or insurgent. If they muster courage to do so, they rightly fear that conservative *kazis* and *mullas* would declare them as anti-religion, renegades and *Satan* (evil). Unfortunately, the liberals also forget that maintaining apathy or silence amounts to providing moral and religious support to the terrorists. Thus, the liberals, because of the basic call of Islam and their submission to them, cannot go in a different direction.

Solution through Law

For this purpose, the UNO can prove to be the most appropriate body to solve this problem. The Security Council can pass a resolution and constitute

a high power body which would, upholding the principles of democracy, freedom and human rights, be authorised to appoint two expert committees of scholars. Its success would lie in finding out suitable and impartial persons to do the job of separating pure and simple religion from religion-related fundamentalism. The First Expert Committee consisting of scholars and practitioners of various religions would be formed to trace out portions, parts, sentences, sayings or statements of the holy books which the extremists and fundamentalists claim to have authorised them to resort to terrorism for divine goals. They should be able to find out and explain the correct meaning and application of controversial divine directions that are maligned by the fundamentalists for their cruel ends. The Second Expert Committee would collect literature, books, leaflets, newspapers and speeches of the leaders of the fundamentalists and terrorist organisations and compare and contrast them with the original statements of the Holy Books. It would determine the places and point out where the terrorists go beyond the permissible limits of law, society and government. Such exercise would help them to ascertain criminality of the acts and intentions of the terrorists, their trainers and supporters. Conclusions drawn by these two expert committees would be reported to the high power body which would forward it to the UN. Their reports would be discussed and a resolution passed by majority in the General Assembly. It would be the responsibility of the Security Council to get the resolution implemented through the member-states, various UN organs and organisations including recognised NGOs.

On the basis of that resolution, the UN, and later on, other international bodies can declare that such commandments, directives etc. and their teaching excite and encourage terrorism, therefore, are *illegal* and against International Law, Human Rights, Democracy and Freedom. The member-states would be requested to frame, repeat, and reformulate laws accordingly, and implement them in letter and spirit. The Security Council Resolution no. 1373 and others already show the desired way.

Laws framed in this direction by a state or the world body would prevent, restrict and disallow every kind of preaching, inciting, training and encouraging people to indulge in spreading extremism, fundamentalism and terrorism. In that situation even the local authorities of the states, big and small, would be able to prevent and stop terrorism of all kinds. In this way, all terrorism in the making can be intercepted before it comes into existence. The huge task of eradication of worldwide terrorism, thus, would be decentralised and effectively implemented at different levels.

It should be propagated, recommended and reiterated again and again that none of the tenets of any religion inciting terrorism in any form, past or present, will be permitted to stand against the fundamentals of Human

Rights. In fact, acceptance of Universal Declaration of Human Rights does not leave any room for existence and operation of Terrorism. But it lacks the teeth to fight against and eliminate it.[43]

These provisions can be given a concrete shape by denying citizenship or entry into a country to a person if one does not subscribe to an anti-terror oath, to be prescribed by each and every state.

Existential Challenges

To eliminate contemporary Terrorism, all orthodox Muslims in general, and fundamentalists and terrorists in particular, and the Islamic diehards should be motivated and encouraged to question and reconsider their basic tenets of Terror.[44] The Islamists may not allow any other to do that. Those who do this are likely to meet *fatwas* of death, torture and imprisonment. But, as human beings, they should be asked to listen to others. All of them are to be somehow told that if Allah is the Almighty, He can do everything for man and his cosmos directly. Why should He supposedly act through some Messenger? God is not helpless or powerless without pronouncing some Message. He does not need to depend on the doings of own creation, the humans. For the Almighty there is no need to make revelation either at His own will or at man's request through some human agency. The specific event of divine revelation, in effect, downgrades the status of the Almighty, who is All-pervading, Just and All-creating. He is disabled and made partisan that way. Why can He not do it so by using other own and natural means so as to benefit all men equally upon earth. Presence of some fanatic followers is not necessary to prove His Existence or the truth of His Revelation. Such assumption automatically deprives the rest and posterity from getting similar messages from Him for all time to come. Obviously the whole arrangement is to establish superiority of Islam over all other religions making them redundant, ineffective or invalid. Plurality of religions disappears or dies in the Islamic manifesto.

If God (or Allah) is everywhere, and is all powerful, there is no need of His dependence on some people – extremists, fundamentalists and terrorists, to prove His Existence by killing and destroying others. God does not require proving that He granted Revelation/Special Message to a particular community, much less through some Incarnation, Prophet or Messenger. Acceptance of the need of any Incarnation, Prophet or Messenger to learn Divine Discipline makes Him powerless, limited, and dependent. It is an insult to God to attribute to Him that He himself felt need to do so. No person can claim to know timings, place and need of God's desire or feeling to make Revelation. The Almighty God as Impartial Judge and Controller of Creation cannot make a particular revelation for a particular people. Knowledge of such a God or Revelation cannot be confined to a particular place, in a particular language, addressed to and through a particular person or community, and meant for some particular Objective or Mission. A Message as such can never be the last, final and irreversible. Creation by Him does not stop. God cannot be bound by His own Message. How an intelligent man can be sure that somewhere, some such Message or Revelation took place. How can one believe without some valid proof that the Revelation has that particular Form, specific Contents and hidden or open Meaning. Who would witness that God Himself uttered that particular Revelation? Would God not have been God without making that Revelation?

Even if God made that Revelation, the utterances of God or Prophet appearing in the past cannot be right for the man of today. Therefore, a man should not accept all that what has been said and written in the Holy Books by order, threat or teaching thrust upon in childhood or thereafter. Why is there no room for the use of reason or arguments or modernity in religious matters? Intuition cannot compel others to obey its bidding.[45]

Why should a man, community or group of people of today accept a particular Revelation: the *Quran*, the *Bible*, the *Gita*, and others? Why and how should they believe that it had happened in the past at a particular time and place and among the members of some particular community and made in a particular language and is useful, last and final one? On this questionable basis, a terrorist has no authority to compel others to do what he likes. A Revelation cannot be acceptable to or be thrust on others even if a large number of fanatic followers believe in it. If some followers of any Religion feel and do like that, why should others feel and like to do the same? What would happen if some other people claim Revelation in the same manner and determine to execute its teachings in the manner of Islamic terrorists or *jehadis*?

Under the prevailing form of democracy, rule of law and world community, no one can be equipped with the divine, even civil, right to use force in 'self-defense' and fight against oppression anywhere in the world. Under UN Charter no one can have any divine injunction to wage wars and convert peoples and communities.[46] No such right can be legitimised for liberating a people in this nuclear age even if they have been oppressed and tyrannised. They have to seek redressal through courts and parliaments.

Coming under the control and command of the terrorists or fundamentalists simply means elimination of other religions and communities. This eliminates plurality of religions world over. Hardly anyone would like to see such Revelation to be the only religion of the world. A country may not like to permit citizenship, even residence, to any brand of fanatics who consider themselves to be at war, when living in Non-Islamic states, till they are ruled over by Islam.

In fact, Islam of terrorists and the Modern State cannot go together.[47] No modern state can be organised and operated on the tenets of Terrorism and vice-versa. That is not possible within a democratic set up. The believers are asked to bring non-Muslims to their faith. On particular occasions, they are allowed to harass, punish, torture and kill the non-believers, particularly the idolaters. Some religions require absolute faith in religion and do not allow supremacy of state, law and other regional and global arrangements.

A large number of orthodox Muslims indulging in contemporary Terrorism do not consider themselves bound by the Constitution or Judiciary as it clashes with the teachings of the *Quran*. Their Faith of Violence is not ready to accept and implement the 'rule of law' in the modern sense of the term. Most of the Islamic states do not like to abide by international laws and implement the resolutions of the UN. It is also a mistake to think that terrorism can be guided by the US and Europe, or even by the sponsor states.[48]

There is little doubt that 'the world is facing a dangerous escalation of violence by extremists and fundamentalism who are the self-proclaimed enemies of free and democratic family of nations. The key for world peace and security cannot be left in the hands of terrorist organisations and their sponsor states who publicly proclaim their evil strategy.'[49]

Some scholars feel the need to focus on ideas, and the need to alter the 'dynamics in the minds of men' that legitimise the use of indiscriminate violence. The latter has, according to them, arisen out of the policies of western powers as well as authoritarian rulers of Islamic states who use extremism in Islam as an instrument of strategy.[50] Huntington advises the 'West to maintain the economic and military power necessary to protect its interests in relation to these (Confucian and Islamic) civilisations. It will also, however, require the West to develop a more profound understanding of the basic religious and philosophical assumptions underlying other civilisations and the ways in which people in those civilisations see their interests.'[51]

But this is not enough. Perhaps, for their survival and safety, liberal democracies, and their leaders will have to take steps towards "Anti-Terrorism". They will have to repudiate all concepts, ethos, strategies, and goals of terrorism. The world community or the UN will have to, irrespective of the claims, origins, grievances, and preparations of the terrorist outfits, attack, destroy, and eliminate, fiercely and forcefully, all elements – men, material, and weaponry, including teaching and training camps. Wherever they are, and, whatever be their colour, creed, ethnicity, identity, origin and culture, they have to be done away with. In no case, the terrorists and their sponsors, should be permitted to possess WMDs and nuclear weapons.

Contemporary terrorism, practiced in the form of ruthless 'violence', has to be earmarked, targeted, and attacked. Objects of attack include specific contents of terrorist teachings, its teachers, trainers, organisation and weapons of terror. Its supporters and financiers also stand on the same footing. But the programme "Fight against Terrorism" cannot be undertaken unless the Fighters undertake their task in a more serious and effective manner. The outcome of the war between the Terrorists and these Fighters would depend ultimately on the superiority of will, weapons, action, and organisation of science and technology.[52] Future survival and progress of mankind will depend on the achievements of these anti-terrorist Fighters in their war against Terrorism. For this everyone will have to make resolve, act and go ahead more effectively than the forces of Contemporary Terrorism.[53]

Notes

1. Adams, Ian, *Political Ideology Today*, Manchester University Press, 1993, 324.
2. Supra, see, above, 1.
3. It had many intermittent military coups (1960, 1971, and 1980). In 1997, the military again helped engineer the ouster – popularly dubbed a "post-modern coup" – of the then Islamic-oriented government. In 1964, Turkey became an associate member of the European Community; over the past decade, it has undertaken many reforms to strengthen its democracy and economy, enabling it to have associate membership within the European Union.
4. Hafiz al-Asad died July, 2000; his son, Bashar al-Assad was approved as President by popular referendum in 2000.
5. Libyan support for terrorism decreased by 1990s. Libya agreed to reveal and end its programmes to develop weapons of mass destruction.
6. Iran has been designated a state sponsor of terrorism for its activities in Lebanon and elsewhere in the world. There are Shi'a Muslims 89 per cent, and Sunni Muslims 9 per cent. President Mahmud Ahmadi-Nejad (since 3 August 2005) is the Head of Government.
7. In 1989 he had issued a *fatwa* (judgement) condemning Salman Rushdie to death for his allegedly making offensive references to the Prophet in his novel *The Satanic Verses*. He died the same year, but nobody could dare to revise the *fatwa*.
8. The United States, the United Kingdom, Australia, Canada, and the parliament of the European Union all designate Hezbollah as a terrorist organisation, and not without some evidence. It is Lebanon's militant political group Hezbollah (Party of God). Hezbollah likes to see Lebanon become a theocratic state in the model of one of its primary funders and supporters. Therefore, it is the only faction in the country allowed to keep weapons, ostensibly as a buffer against Israeli incursions. "Fighting the Israelis is not a picnic; it's blood spilled. It's not a reward in a festival,"

Hezbollah says, with emphasis. "No one can take that mission unless he has faith – extreme faith and loyalty to this country." The UN security council unanimously approved a resolution calling for an end to the conflict (broke out from July 12 to Aug. 13, 06) in Lebanon on 12.8.06 and deployment of up to 15,000 UN peacekeepers in Southern Lebanon, to help Lebanese armed forces take control as Israeli troops withdraw. Hezbollah has promised to cooperate with Lebanese and UN troop. But the Shia Muslim group (Hezbollah) has made it clear it will not disarm or leave the south. Nor has it pledged to remove the rocket launchers it used to bombard Israel during the conflict. *Hindustan Times*, 18.8.06.

9. Kushwant Singh, *Unholy Warriors*: In all three countries, India, Pakistan and Bangladesh, nurseries that preach exclusiveness and hatred of other religions are flourishing. If you do not believe it, take a look at Edna Fernandes' "Holy Warriors: A Journey into the Heart of Indian Fundamentalism": Viking. *Hindustan Times*, 15.4.06.
10. Asghar Ali Engineer, a liberal writer, writes, 'Fundamentalism should not be confused with fundamentals of religion. Those who believed that every word of the Bible is literally divine word were called fundamentalist. (Ali uses this logic) To follow Islam or Hinduism should not be described as 'fundamentalism'. Even to follow orthodox traditions of religion should not be dubbed as 'fundamentalism' though one may not agree with orthodox practices.' *Secular Perspective: Fundamentalism and Terrorism,* Vol. VI, No. 1, Jan. 1-15, 03.
11. In Bombay, there were seven terrorist blasts occurred on July 11, 06. In all 200 persons were killed and over 714 wounded. Four terrorist blasts also occurred on the same day in Srinagar which took toll of 8 persons dead and 23 wounded. *Patrika*, 12.7.06.
12. Some of the terrorist underworld includes Al-Qaida, Hamas, Hezbollah, Islamic Jihad, Jaish-e-Mohammad in remote jungles, deserts and in the centres located in large cities. In his annual report to the US president and the Congress Rumsfeld attributed the emergence and growth of Jaish-e-Mohammad and other terrorist outfits to the conditions prevailing in some states, including some with nuclear weapons where there are no capable or responsible governments. The wide areas of Asia, Africa and the Western hemisphere are fertile grounds for non-state actors to engage in terrorism, acquisition of NMC (nuclear, biological and chemical) weapons, illegal trafficking, or other illicit activities across state borders. He perceived inability of some states to govern their societies, safeguard their military armaments and prevent their territories from serving as sanctuary to terrorists and criminal organisations.
13. The draft prepared by the Law Commission of India defines a terrorist act. See, infra, 9.
14. If the terrorist act results in death, it is punishable with death or imprisonment for life and liable for fine. Any other crime is punishable with a minimum imprisonment of three to five years. This could be extended to life term and shall be liable for fine. Proceeds of terrorism: Properties and assets acquired by terrorist acts are liable to be forfeited.

15. After four defeats in open wars against India, Pakistan finds terrorism as the most suitable as well as manageable weapon to realise her political goals. The terrorists are commandeered to kill innocent persons, political leaders, pilgrims, police and security men, and make all attempt to create communal tension. In encounters with the security and police forces, the terrorists are caught and killed, and their dead bodies along with huge cache of arms and ammunition are publicly displayed to the people.
16. There are three kind of terrorist camps. The first kind imparts training in different forms of terror and combat tactics. A second set of camps offers indoctrination lessons. Powerful video films, extolling the valour of Muslim warriors and promising martyrs an eternity in *Jannat*, are shown to young recruits. The latest videos show footage of the Iraq war and the 9/11 attacks. The third set of camps, close to the LoC (Line of Control, India-Pakistan) operate essentially as launching pads, where the trained terrorists wait to cross over to India. Arun Joshi, "Teaching the basics", *Hindustan Times*, 9.8.06; Kuldeep Kumar, "Comment-Secularism contested": Use of coercion continues to remain a legitimate means to convert non-Muslims into Islam. The secular historians should read Iqbal's Shiqwa (Complaint to the God) to see how much pride he displays in the Sword of Islam and how bitter he is about Allah rewarding the Kafirs instead of the Muslims ignoring their services to the faith. In an entry in his diary, Iqbal wrote: 'All nations accuse us of fanaticism. I admit the charge. Fanaticism is patriotism for religion.' *Seminar* 550 March, 2006, 59-60.
17. See, supra, 2-7.
18. For example, Muslims are about 450 million spread over in India, Pakistan and Bangladesh. They are over one billion in the entire world, mostly found in 57 Islamic countries.
19. In a Pakistani religious school called the Haqqania madrasa, Osama bin Laden is a hero, the Taliban's leaders are famous alumni and the next generation of mujahedeen is being militantly groomed. In Jeffrey Goldberg's *The Education of a Holy Warrior,* photographs by Laurent Van Der Stockt. Arun Joshi continues that young recruits are taught how to fire guns, launch rockets, hurl grenades and the techniques of guerilla warfare in jungles, mountains and urban areas. Hostage taking is also part of the training. For the last two years, the trainees are also being taught Indian languages, Hindi in particular, to help them masquerade as Hindus. They are also trained in use of computers, laptops and are equipped with satellite phones and palmtops and mobile phones. Arun Joshi, "Teaching the basics", *Hindustan Times*, 9.8.06.
20. Mohammed Amir Rana, *Gateway to Terrorism,* London: New Millennium, 2002.
21. *Jehadi* indoctrination begins early in Pakistan. The evidence is in the curriculum of the mainstream schools of Pakistan where *jehad* is still taught as a subject, not just in the *madrasas*. Vikram Sood, "Securing the State", *Hindustan Times*, 2.7.06; Most of these camps are in Bhawapura in Pakistan and in the mountains and jungles of PoK (Pakistan occupied Kashmir). Pakistan had dismantled 18 camps after 9/11. But 59 of them have been recon-

structed and are currently functional. Arun Joshi, "Teaching the basics", *Hindustan Times*, 9.8.06.

22. This has been Osama bin Laden's basic ideology and Islamic faith.
23. In the 7,000-page guide, titled *Encyclopaedia of Jehad,* provides an insight into how terrorists from Osama bin Laden's Al-Qaida network operate.
24. The birth of contemporary suicide terrorism began from October 23, 1983 when Muslim extremists drove into the barracks of the US and the French contingents of the multinational peacekeeping force in Beirut and detonated bombs with no intention of escaping. Ramadan Salah, Secretary General of the Palestinian Islamic Jehad states: "Our enemy possesses the most sophisticated weapons in the world and its army is trained to a very high standard. We have nothing with which to repel killing and thuggery against us except the weapon of martyrdom. It is easy and costs us only our lives .... Human bombs cannot be defeated, not even by nuclear bombs." Ibid.
25. The ringleader of Al-Quada, a deadliest terrorist organisation having over sixty branches and links with two hundred similar organisations, Osama bin Laden claimed the right of Islam over Pakistan's nuclear bombs, which he claimed to have financed, and supported it. He perceived inability of some states to govern their societies, safeguard their military armaments and prevent their territories from serving as sanctuary to terrorists and criminal organisations. He claims Islamic right and direct them to do what he (Islam) says. He even threatens to inflict serious consequences if they fail to do so.
26. China, and some other countries, nursing hostility, envy, and enmity against India, are encouraging Pakistani terrorists to go faster in that direction.
27. The Pakistani army openly commands their followers to a *jehad* against Jews and Hindus. Vikram Sood, "Securing the State", *Hindustan Times*, 2.7.06.
28. See, footnote 9 supra.
29. One Islamic *Jehad* school taught the boys the benefits of becoming suicide bombers. Boys between 12-15 years of age are told to draw pictures of themselves with explosives strapped to their bodies. "We are teaching the children that suicide bombing is the only thing that makes the enemy very frightened. Furthermore, we are teaching them we have the right to do so." The reward of suicide terrorism, according to a teacher, is: "A place in heaven where the martyrs will be greeted by 70 virgins." – Nikhat Kazmi, "How to handle human bombs", *Times of India*, 7.10.01.
30. Hamid Gul, the former ISI chief had described the Lashkar-e-Tayyeba as Pakistan's frontline soldiers in Kashmir. Vikram Sood, "Securing the State", *Hindustan Times*, 2.7.06.
31. Arun Joshi, "Pak terror camps gun for West too": There were about 60 terrorist-training camps, run by Al Qaeda, Lashkar-e-Tayyebba (LeT), Jaish-e-Mohammad, and Harkat-ul-Mujahideen, in Pakistan. They all are members of the Al Qaeda led International Islamic Front (IIF). While most of these are laboratories for anti-India strikes, a few are training people from the West, Bangladesh, Indonesia, Egypt and Sudan – for striking targets in Europe and the US. The sources said, the anti-West terror cells were small and

men were trained not in guerrilla warfare but in making bombs and in detonating them in airports and trains. Bangladeshis, Indonesians, Egyptians and Saudis are trained to target western interests elsewhere like ships, banks and tourists. The men speak English and can easily pass off as ordinary tourists from the West. They are even taught to speak against terrorism in measured tones at restaurants and while commuting and shopping. The idea is to provide them with a perfect cover of a westernised lifestyle. *Hindustan Times*, 9.8.06.

32. *Times of India,* August, 02.
33. An MSN survey tells that 47 per cent of suicide bombers have an academic education, 83 per cent are single and 64 per cent are between the ages of 18-23. Nikhat Kazmi, "How to handle human bombs", *Times of India*, 7.10.01.
34. Over 6,000 persons were killed at one stretch and property worth billions of dollars was destroyed with prestige of the US knocked down. Court judgement relating to the Bombay blast committed in 1993 has been announced after 13 years, *Hindustan Times*, 15.8.06.
35. The UN resolutions passed in 1999 and 2000 called for freezing of bank accounts and assets of 146 Taliban officials, 10 Arabs including Osama bin Laden, and three Afghan entities. No action was taken by the member-states. For years the 189 members of the United Nations have wrangled over the formal definition of 'terrorism'. It is unable to differentiate between terrorism and the rights to self-determination. Although the effort to combat terrorism is embodied in several treaties and two UN resolutions adopted in the wake of September 11, there is no world tribunal currently empowered to try terrorist cases. Some proposed that they should be brought before the International Criminal Court (ICC) but some other countries and US have expressed reservations.
36. Arun Shourie has indicated that there are 1000 verses in the *Quran* which say, 'Spread Islam, have nothing to do with these kafirs, kill them, they are untrustworthy, they are unclean', then? The Hadith is full of this. There are rewards for killing the kafir. If this is to be a good Muslim, then a multi-religious society in India would become impossible.' Quoted from "More secular than thou", Kushwant Singh, *Hindustan Times*, 26.2.05.
37. Millions of Islamists apparently do not appear to agree with them. But few come forward openly to denounce, boycott or oppose them. Hardly do they organise to stop these fanatics from finding terrorism in the Holy Books, and acting fanatically.
38. It is said that Al-Qaeda people have access to crude nuclear bombs. George Tenet former CIA Director finds Pakistan's father of Pakistani Nuclear bomb A Q Khan is at least as dangerous as Osama-bin-Laden. *Hindustan Times*, 25.11.04. A Q Khan had been running a private company for the dissemination of nuclear weapons' know-how, blueprints, technology and equipment. He did it with Libya and Iran. P.N. Khera, "Weapons of Choice", *Hindustan Times*, 30.11.04.

39. Scheur, *Imperial Hubris: Why the West is Losing the War on Terror*, Anonymous, Brassey's Inc: The author recommends ' a long, ruthless bloody war against the Islamists' but forgets that Osama does not like to be the leader of the defensive *jehad* (though by focusing Muslim anger against America that is what he had become), but rather act as an inciter for all Muslims to fulfil their religious obligation of defending the faith.
40. Manoj Joshi reported in *Hindustan Times* (May 15, 2005) that: Tariq Mehmood, an Al-Badr militant after his arrest in Srinagar declared, "I have no regrets. On the contrary, I am happy since I have come to fight for the path of Allah." Married and with two small children he was a registered medical practitioner and a Jamaat-e-Islami activist from Pakistan's Gujarat district. What drives such fanaticism is a special "culture of death" that terrorist groups foster. When a militant is killed in Kashmir, there are elaborate funeral rites, complete with the burial of an empty coffin in his village in Pakistan. The parents of the "*shaheed*" are made to sit on a pedestal and feted by the local elite. Emotional speeches detail the "*shaheed's*" valour. With emotions at the highest pitch, volunteers are called for, and not surprisingly, anywhere between 80-100 young men register.
41. The Hamas, a terrorist organisation which won the elections in the Palestinian Territories recently, has made no secret of the fact that it is part of the global *jihad* movement, based upon an extremist religious ideology, whose goals include, as a priority, the annihilation of the State of Israel. Hamas declared that it will continue using violence to further its goals. Respect for human life runs counter to Hamas' *jihadi* philosophy of using human bombs to kill as many civilians as possible. The covenant of the Hamas states: "Israel will exist and will continue to exist until Islam will obliterate it. Just as it obliterated other before it .... There is no solution for the Palestinian problem except by *jihad*. Initiatives, proposals and international conferences are all a waste of time and an exercise in futility." *Hindustan Times*, 5.2.06.
42. See, infra, Ch. 17.
43. See, infra, Ch. 18.
44. See, supra, 418-19.
45. Dr. Wafa Sultan bitterly criticises the Muslim clerics, holy warriors and political leaders who she believes have distorted the teachings of Muhammad and the *Quran* for fourteen centuries. The world according to her was not witnessing a clash of religions or cultures, but a battle between modernity and barbarism, a battle that the forces of violent, reactionary Islam are destined to lose. *Hindustan Times*, 12.3.06.
46. Ibid.: "Only the Muslims defend their beliefs by burning down churches, killing people and destroying embassies." It is clash between a mentality that belongs to the Middle Ages and another mentality that belongs to the 21st century.
47. The idea of an Islamic state is a misnomer. An Islamic state can only be brought into being through state terrorism, observes Saleem M.M. Qureshi in

Kukeraja, Veena, and, Singh, M.P., eds. *Pakistan: Democracy, Development and Security Issues,* Sage: New Delhi, 2005

48. Vir Sanghvi, "Why the War on Terror was Lost", *Hindustan Times*, 20.8.06.
49. David Danieli, "Unsettling Terror", *Hindustan Times*, 18.8.06.
50. K. Subrahmanyam and Jasjit Singh in John, Wilson, and, Parashar, Swati, eds., *Terrorism in South East Asia: Implications for South Asia*, New Delhi: Pearson Education, 2005.
51. Samuel P. Huntington, "The Clash of Civilizations?", *Foreign Affairs* (Summer 1993), 49.
52. In this case, see, 'Israel vs Hezbollah', *Hindustan Times*, 2.8.06.
53. S.L. Verma, *Beyond Hindutva*, Jaipur: Rawat Publications, 2007.

17

Truth Behind Gandhian Political Technologies

The more man is coming under the threats of war and weapons of mass destruction (WMD), more he is seeking shelter of Gandhi and his non-violence. Witnessing the success of non-violence in the freedom movement of India, leaders and scholars, India and outside,[1] appear earnestly in search of proper understanding and use of non-violence, particularly against the fear of nuclear warfare. In this respect, Gandhi appears to be relevant to them.[2] Even against the might of an all-powerful state, Gandhi's weapon of non-violence has come closer to their hearts. His real contribution consists in his research in the possibilities of *Ahimsa* in all walks of life.[3]

Outside India too, the world acknowledges the power of techniques and methods of non-violence, captioned here as Gandhian political technologies or GPTs.[4] Some of these GPTs have also been practiced outside India even before and after the assassination of Mahatma Gandhi.[5] But a few political leaders and scholars find them no more useful for the people of India, particularly after the attainment of independence, adoption of a self-made comprehensive constitution and launching a democratic form of government. Apart from such thinking many other questions arise. Should India adopt and practice the whole of Gandhism or apply only a useful part of it? Would GPTs prove viable and effective even in the absence of Gandhi? What is that reality lying behind these GPTs which, apart from the presence of Gandhi, made them viable? What type of GPTs would be acceptable and applicable to solve some of the problems of the people of different countries? Do conditions and circumstances still exist, as were earlier, for their fruitful use in India and outside?

Before other questions are taken up, the last question may be answered in the affirmative. GPTs require a religion-prone environment, and the people of India are still religious since time immemorial.[6] All major religions of India – Hinduism, Jainism, Buddhism, Christianity, Sikhism, Islam etc. uphold non-violence or *Ahimsa* as one the highest values or goal of life. Religious communities as such pay highest regards to their godmen, religious leaders, priests, saints, gurus and preachers. Masses, traditionally, appreciate their way of giving up all worldly comforts, undergoing all kinds of sufferings, observing strict moral codes[7] for their upliftment and living a life of renunciation.

Need of Gandhian Political Technologies

There is still great need of practicing Gandhian political technologies. India and many other countries have democracy but power is concentrated, despite political parties, periodic elections and adult franchise, in the hands of a few governing elites. About forty per cent voters do not have time, energy and means to reach the polling booths. Out of sixty per cent, hardly twenty to twenty five per cent of them cast votes on their own. Every citizen has fundamental rights, and courts are there to hear them in case of violation of these rights. But most of them owing to poverty and illiteracy are unable to reach them. Bureaucracy, police and other regulatory organisations care little for the woes of the common man. All these compel the masses to pin their hopes again in some Gandhi-like leader that might represent and lead them and fight for their cause by means and methods known to them. There must be someone to show them amid the murky darkness of privatisation and globalisation the way to go in right direction. Other acute crises relate to pollution and lethal and nuclear weapons likely to cause an instant death of the earth itself.[8]

Therefore, it is necessary to know, apart from faith-based and ideological claims of the Gandhians, the actual power and form of these Gandhian ways and means or GPTs. What is the extent of their power? What are those political technologies? Which type of problems can be solved by them? What type of leaders is required to use them? What role non-violence occupies to make up these technologies? Is that role truly non-violent?[9]

Sources and Bases of the Gandhian Non-violence

Gandhi was essentially a man of Religion or *Dharma* (different from sectarian religions). All the fundamentals of Gandhian philosophy and thought came down from Religion.[10] He believed in God or an omnipresent fundamental spiritual reality or an all-embracing living Light called *Brahma*, *Rama*, or Truth etc. He put emphasis on the moral value of man as spirit. All religions are founded on the same moral laws which bind men all over the world. He accepted Hinduism as its spiritual and moral values were commonly found in all the great religions of the world. He declared that he was essentially a religious man in quest of *moksha*. He, following the teachings of the *Gita*, engaged himself in the disinterested pursuit of obligations and duties.[11] Truth was what the voice within tells us. God at times became his 'inner voice'. He claimed to have the ability to hear and obey the 'inner voice'.

To him God, Creativity or *Brahma* is an all-pervading spirit. It underlies all human activities. As such, there was no politics devoid of religion. Politics bereft of religion is a death-trap which kills the soul. It has to subserve religion.[12] He declared his aim to spiritualise political life and institutions of the country. He made it clear that 'I could not be leading a religious life unless I identified myself with the whole of mankind and that I could not do unless I took part in politics.' He identified God with *Sat* that which exists. The term *Satya* (Truth) is derived from *Sat*, which is the source of all eternal and universal values. Truth or *Satya* is only a part of the wider *Sat*. The universe reflects *Sat* or Absolute Truth. *Satya* is realisable as well as attainable.

In view of this understanding of an all-pervading *Sat* or God, means and ends became convertible terms for him. He regarded them to be the two sides of the same coin. Truth is the end, and non-violence or *Ahimsa* is the means. But he put more emphasis on purity of means. If we take care of the means, we are bound to reach the end sooner or later. He stood for the enlightened non-violence or non-violence of the brave: the highest and purest level of non-violence. It is pure non-violence. It pervades every sphere of human life and does not calculate or bend. Total *Ahimsa* is a state of mind. As this world is a creation of all-pervading God, there is no room for any ill-will, hatred or injury to anybody. If there was purity of means, even one step was enough. Non-violence was all-in-all for him, both in negative and positive sense, non-injury as well as love.

This non-violence proved to be a great power during India's freedom movement. The people of India began to believe in its invincibility. On the basis of purity and effectiveness, Gandhi put it at three levels:

Level I: Non-violence based on creed

Level II: Non-violence based on policy and expediency, and

Level III: Non-violence based on cowardice

Power of Non-violence as Creed: Initial Formative Power (IFP)

Gandhi regarded pure non-violence as the most powerful one. It was non-violence of the brave *satyagrahi*. He called it as soul or spiritual force (Spiritual Power SP) which is invincible and never-failing. It could move mountains, transform life and flinch from nothing in its unmistakable faith.

It has the unique capacity of winning adherents, building up morale and invoking sacrifice, arousing public opinion and weakening the adversary. He was so much convinced of its potency that he advised many allies during the Second World War to fight aggression by non-violence alone. A votary of such non-violence or *satyagrahi* had to observe very strict discipline. One had to take vows like *rishis* (seers) of ancient India and undergo a comprehensive moral and spiritual discipline to adopt total *Ahimsa*.[13]

Gandhi himself, while in South Africa and later India, transformed himself step by step, from common man dressed in English clothes to a saint, a *rishi* or a *mahatma* by appearance, word, thought and deed: 'My earthly possessions consist of six spinning wheels, prison dishes, a can of goat's milk, six homespun loin clothes and towel and my reputation, which cannot be worth very much.'[14] He believed in the ideal of non-possession. Very soon he attained the stature of an *avatar* (incarnation), and wherever he went, people cried, '*Mahatma Gandhi ki jai*' (Hail to the Mahatma). Village folks began to revere him like a god, prophet, *avatar* and godman. The number of his followers, accepting this line, was not very large. Only a few men had full faith in his non-violence as a creed. There were millions of men and women who in line with India's religious traditions, praised, sympathised and backed up the sayings and doings of the Mahatma without subscribing to his creed. All this made him a 'super-power' unto himself.

But Gandhi's non-violence of the brave was more a wish, possibility or imagination. Most of those statements were made merely as eulogy or poetry to attract people at large. According to the traditional *Shastras* the power of non-violence of the brave (Spiritual Power SP) was supposed to dawn on a satyagrahi only after he attained perfection of soul,[15] which none of the satyagrahis could do so. Gandhi continued to strive to attain non-violence of the brave, but actually could never reach that stage. He continued experimenting with his search of Truth till the end of his life. Therefore, it is not possible to conclude that he ever attained the ordained power of non-violence of the brave.

According to him, the real secret of non-violence of the brave was 'self-suffering'. It was the unfailing instrument of a non-violent *satyagrahi* to evoke the best in the opponent. In inflicting suffering on the *satyagrahi*, the opponent helps in his own defeat. The *satyagrahi* thrives on repression inflicted on him by the opponent, and no amount of violence can crush the soul in him. *Ahimsa* is the most efficacious in face of the greatest '*himsa*' (violence). There is no such thing as defeat or failure in non-violence because in *satyagraha* to suffer is to win. The struggle may be slow or long-drawn-out but he regarded it as the wisest way for it was the surest. For him it touched and strengthened the moral fibre of those against whom it was exerted. Use of non-violence benefited even the opponent. It touched the people most for whom that non-violent struggle was launched. In fact, all these are tall claims and personal wishes of Gandhi as *Mahatma*.

However, owing to their religious background, the masses continued to believe, despite Gandhi's own rebuttals,[16] that the Mahatma had mastered non-violence of the brave, and was able to attain all goals claimed by him.[17] The people were so eager to see the image of their Mahatma as real that they, overlooking the role of so many national and international events, concluded that the realisation of India's freedom was the result of the power of non-violence alone. The tragic assassination of the Mahatma, and the propaganda made by the post-independence leadership, the Congress party and the press reinforced this impression.

At many places, Gandhi himself had made it clear that by perfection in non-violence, he meant the perfection of 'striving', and not of actual attainment. He himself believed that perfection was unattainable. His perfect non-violence was impossible as long as man in human body was living. He, perhaps, stood at the theoretical level of pure non-violence, but often operated at the level of non-violence as policy or expediency: 'Mine is a struggling, striving, erring, and imperfect soul.' That non-violence did not prove unfailing. Gandhi's winning over the adversary, even on the basis of his long self-suffering, could not become a reality.[18]

However, because of Gandhian leadership, non-violence did flourish in India. There were many favourable conditions permitting the conduct of Gandhian movements. The Government of India was operating under the charge of the British parliamentary democracy which wanted to keep up the show of 'rule of law' ongoing. Non-violence could also flourish owing to the British understanding of law and justice. Courts, big and small, while punishing a culprit looked into the existence of evil intention underlying a particular act. In the absence of evil intention, the result, outcome, effect or consequence related to satyagraha acts did not remain very important to the rulers or courts. The pattern of Gandhi's non-violence of the brave operated on this ground only. Movements under leaders committed to pure non-violence were likely to remain peaceful. The eventual transfer of power to India also remained peaceful.

Thus, the power of non-violence of the creed was actually not the most effective one as Gandhi has thought and claimed. It was rather the power of the people who thought Gandhi to be the most powerful leader because of his non-violence. This power appeared to be increasing because of the sufferings of the *satyagrahis* which attracted their sympathy and identification owing to their faith in common values. Gandhi infused values around non-violence of the brave, and organised the people into a mass-movement. It was rather the *Initial Formative Power* of Gandhian non-violence, not an actual power. Non-violence as 'creed' did not form an independent source of power despite all tall claims.

Non-violence as Policy and Expediency (APPP): Actual Physical Power of the People

Philosophically, Gandhi came down to the second level non-violence through his concept of Relative Truth. Relative Truth lies in the acceptance of the need for a corrective process of experimentation with our own experience and to learn from errors. He always wished to propagate non-violence as a creed though as a politician he also tried to justify it as a policy. He was equally convinced that if he had accepted men of pure non-violence only, he would have stood all alone. Thus, non-violence was adopted as a measure of expediency and sound policy in some spheres of political life. He considered it non-violence of the weak or passive non-violence of the helpless. If non-violence is accepted as policy, Gandhi thought it to be capable of achieving results to a certain extent. It is based on expediency and not on the belief in the infinite moral worth of the brave. It had power, not owing to its declaration of non-violence but on the basis of large number of followers, their unity of purpose and of organisation, programme and discipline. It is this power which lies behind 'policy' or 'expediency' non-violence. It has been captioned here as *Actual Physical Power of the People* (APPP).

The second level of non-violence permitted the use of men as means. He advised the Congress to adopt this form of non-violence as policy: 'I placed it before the Congress as a political method, to be employed for the solution of political questions .... As a political method, it can always be changed, modified, altered, even given up on preference for another .... If I have carried the Congress with me all these years, it is in my capacity as a politician.' He could not try his personal creed stated in the *Hind Swaraj* even in the South Africa. He devoted his corporate activities to the attainment of parliamentary *Swaraj* so much discarded earlier. He in exceptional cases also gave concessions to the users of non-violence.[19] According to him, a nation or an individual could exceptionally choose violence as against non-violence and cowardice. In 1947, he approved violence when Indian troops were flown to Kashmir to repel Pakistani aggression.

Gandhi rose to political power only when a large number of people developed faith in him that he was a man of non-violence of the brave.[20] Some of the people began to emulate or follow his directions earnestly. Gandhi assiduously trained, organised and led some of them in the Indian National Congress. The British Government finding a lack of 'evil' intentions (which had no place in the concept of non-violence) could not oppose it.[21] This strategy enabled him to launch three mass-movements and lead the country closer to freedom.

Presently, too, in India, religion and spirituality, if used properly for a public cause is surest road to power, as the Indian people still have great respect for their godmen, saints, *gurus* and *mahatmas*. Such leaders have to lead a simple and ascetic life and apparently live for the spiritual and material goods of others. On undergoing suffering or being oppressed for their good acts or ideas, the number of their followers and sympathizers is likely to increase. The actual power of policy-non-violence lies in the number of followers, size of organisation and sources in their possession. This is 'actual physical power' (APP) of the people, not of non-violence. It may be organised or unorganised, and act or operate in a peaceful or violent manner. However, under the leadership of a Gandhi-like leader subscribing faith in non-violence as creed, it would largely remain nonviolent and peaceful.[22]

On making a comparison, one would find that the number of true satyagrahis following non-violence of the brave remains always less than the crusaders of non-violence as policy or expediency. But the adversary or the government fears more the power of policy-non-violence. However, under this dispensation, the latter, non-cooperators or civil resisters, could if circumstances permitted or they themselves made up their mind, resort to the methods of violence. Obviously, the government is likely to have fear from the power of non-violence as policy more than the power of the non-violence of the few brave. When the *satyagrahis* are put unnecessarily under torture, oppression or suffering, the situation is likely to become more provocative. Again, it is the number of people whose physical power is being challenged. One has to see that the number of persons on the ruling side remains much smaller than the non-cooperators and their sympathizers.

But this could be possible only when scholars, leaders, and people are able to see the underlying power of (ii) Non-violence as Policy and Expediency. This is Actual Physical Power of the People (APPP). This Actual Physical Power of the People (APPP) has three other non-visible forms.

Like the Actual Physical Power of the People (APPP) underlying the (ii) Non-violence as Policy and Expediency, these forms of power have also remained hidden from the eyes of the common man.

When a leader finds no support of the APPP, he becomes helpless, and carries little political weight.[23] Gandhi had lost such power after the failure of the Cabinet Mission Plan.[24]

The non-visible forms of power of the people (APPP) are: (a) Probable Potential Power of the People (PPPP), (b) Counter Power (PCF), and (c) Non-Power (NP). These are explained below:

Probable Potential Power of the People (PPPP)

It is the third hidden but real power underlying operations of non-violence as policy or expediency. This power has never been discussed and analysed or paid attention to by any Gandhian scholar. In a way real power often remains invisible. In case of non-violence, it rests with the probable reaction of the non-participant people which can cause immense loss to all concerned.[25] Where the size of the ruling elite remains very small, the vast number of non-cooperators or non-taxpayers means organisation of physical force of a considerably large of masses. It can cause loss of material and financial resources to the government. When exercised on a mass scale, this power consists in depriving the government of its revenue, generating alienation and dissatisfaction among the people, causing law and order problem and preparing the ground for spread of anarchy and hatred towards it.[26] On taking action against non-violent popular movements, the government, on the other hand, will have to bear heavy financial loss, administrative load and erosion of legitimacy. No democratic government would like to put its military and police forces into action against the people.

A government out of its prudence, compulsion or present or future policy may like to yield to the demands of satyagrahis either at (i) Initial Formative Power (IFP) or Creed Level, or (ii) Policy-non-violence (APPP). Apparently, it may also yield to the Non-violence at Creed Level, if this is supported by APPP, or PPPP or both. The outcome may be the acceptance of the demands of the satyagrahis by the adversary. But it is no more a moral transformation or 'change of heart' by the adversary. It would at the most be treated as change of policy by the government made out of political compulsion or under threat from the power of the people.

Counter Power (PCF)

But the adversary, cherishing values different from the *satyagrahis*, does not yield to their demands so easily. It deals with them in terms of power, APPP or PPPP. On such occasions, the adversary invites counter-adversaries to join it, and encourage them against the *satyagrahis*. It would be found that many groups, minorities, and political parties, on their own or on instigation, stand by the government or against the non-violent movement. They may also keep aloof or become a third party to bargain. From time to time, the British rulers tried to enlist the counter power of minorities, jamindars, princely states, capitalists and other vested interests to turn the power of Gandhian non-violence into non-power.[27] Any adversary can do that to cow down a non-violent leader and his peaceful movement.[28]

Non-Power (NP)

Thus, non-power is the denial or nullification of every type of power available with the *satyagrahis* by enlisting co-operation from their adversaries. When followers leave the leader or their number dwindles, the leader becomes powerless.[29]

Non-violence Under the Cover of Cowardice (NUCC)

Gandhi, in fact, was not clear about the third level of non-violence as cowardice. On the basis of his utmost commitment to non-violence he regarded all men of 'violence' as 'coward'.[30] Gandhi has severely criticised this third level of non-violence. As it was the passive non-violence of the coward and the effeminate, he did not like to call it non-violence. According to him a coward flees from danger instead of facing it. Cowardice is impotence worse than violence. The coward desires to take revenge, but being afraid to die and fight, he looks to others to do that work, including his own defense. Gandhi preferred violence to cowardice. But he did not suggest any plan or training programme to make use of that violence. He forgot that in a civilized democratic polity, violence is not permitted, even if it is done under the garb of non-violence. When violence is resorted to, it has to be authoritatively quelled by police and military forces. A movement launched by cowards would disappear at the very appearance of the police and other authorities. Such movements consisting of cowards do not bring about any fruitful result.[31]

Operation of the Power Process under Gandhian Non-violence

For using GPTs, the operation of the power process of Gandhian non-violence should be understood in a comprehensive manner. The power-process of nọn-violence consists of five stages or forms:

Spiritual Power or Soul-force (SP)

When a person realises soul, God, Truth, *Brahma* etc., he, as proclaimed by the *Shastras*, attains real spiritual power. Gandhi aspired to have that power.[32] This power enables one to change the heart of his adversary even without self-suffering. But the *satyagrahi*, as part of Universal Spirit through self-suffering invokes the souls or spirits of all human beings, including the adversary, and gains sympathy for his cause. As the people believe in the goals and values of their leader gather together on his call, they feel that the leader has the power of non-violence of the brave. In fact, it is the organisation and number of followers gathered around him that makes him look powerful.

Spiritual or soul-force alone cannot be considered as power in the sense of interpersonal influence. Soul-force remains confined to the 'person' of the individual concerned. It attains attributes (not real) when that individual considers himself to be in possession of that mystic, abstruse or enigmatic power, or the people alike him or those who are under his influence, credulously believe that he holds power of non-violence in his person. In this manner, he becomes the source of power. This power is lost when followers leave him alone.[33]

Initial Formative Power (IFP)

Soul-force, whatever be the number of admirers or followers, remains confined to the leader. When the latter attracts and gathers a large number of people for a purpose on the basis of faith in some 'common moral values/principles', power begins to generate. This moral power has no political goal.[34] Common values initiate or generate 'corporate' power. It can be named as *Initial Formative Power,* which resides in that spiritual or saintly person and also his followers. When that person takes up some public or political cause, and organises a large number of people, his *Initial Formative Power* (IFP) is converted into 'direct physical power'. Issues of morality and conscience are converted into concrete 'formative' power. Both soul-force and formative power of moral principles take shape around some issue, demand or claim of a large number of people.

Actual Physical Power of the People (APPP)

The man-of-religion or a leader like Gandhi employs[35] various tools and techniques like *hartal*, picketing, demonstration etc. The followers usually remain peaceful till they remain behind their non-violent leader. But under the leadership of a man of non-violence, they are expected to be peaceful. In his absence, they may be organised or unorganised, violent or non-violent and constitutional or unconstitutional. Direct or actual physical power appears in the form of a large number of people organised by the leader making a claim or demand. It is this concrete reality which stands before the adversary or the government. In this way, *Initial Formative Power* (IFP) is translated into *Actual Physical Power of the People* (APPP). It is actual operating power of the agitating people. The number of agitators increases when the leader is put under greater and greater suffering like beating, imprisonment, confiscation of property, fast unto death, and other threats to life.

Probable Potential Power of the People (PPPP)

This power rests with the people who do not take part in the movement. They live in the countryside, away from the scene of the struggle, and may remain apathetic, dormant and inactive. This dormant power does not operate in accordance with the wishcs or directives of the non-violent leader. Their power is probable but irresistible. When it is active, it can compel the adversary to relent and concede the demands. Every large group, community or organisation invariably possesses *probable potential power* even without displaying its actual physical power. It is a condition precedent of all sorts of power including assumed or actual power.[36]

When the government with the help of the police and army tries to crush their non-violent movement, a large number of people join it. As these people are not trained and initiated in the methods and techniques of non-violence, they act and operate as insurgents and rebels. All of them together release or make up this '*probable potential power*' of the people. It is this power which a government keeps in mind. By its neglect, the government might be facing riots, rebellion, anarchy and armed struggle. Potential power of the people remains dormant, silent and apathetic till their basic values and interests are not at stake. When some leader of their liking calls on them or puts his life in danger, the whole community stands up in defense.[37]

Gandhi or Gandhi-like leadership, on the basis of moral values like non-violence, initiates power by gathering people around those values. But those values only do not make up power. Power consists in the number, organisation and goals of those people. This has been labeled as their *Actual Physical Power of the People*. It becomes much more effective when if is supported by *Probable Potential Power of the People*. Devoid of APPP and PPPP no non-violence can prove to be effective. Even fastings by a satyagrahi leader appears effective only when they are propped up by APPP and PPPP.[38] But neglecting the real source of power behind this fasting, a leader may make moves, which happen to not be relevant to the situation.[39]

Influence of the votary of non-violence of the brave dwindles if the bond of common values and goals existing between the leader and his followers disappears. Non-violence of a leader turns powerless when it is supported neither by *Actual Physical Power* (APPP) nor by *Probable Potential Power* (PPPP).[40] When larger issues are involved, more and more people come out to join the *satyagraha* movement.

However, the Probable Potential Power of the People (PPPP) has to face the Power of Counter-Forces (PCF), and, sometimes, is rendered into Non-Power (NP) if the Probable Potential Power is split and weakens.

Of course, invoking some other common values, a leader belonging to some form of Counter-Force (PCF) can simultaneously seek help from both APPP and PPPP of his community.[41] It was so done by M.A. Jinnah of the Muslim League. It can also be successful if supported by the powerful Adversary. The British Raj had helped the Muslim League against the Indian National Congress and granted partition. In a way, it was more successful than the non-violence of Gandhi at all the three levels. There can be more than two or three such leaders. If one group, under Gandhian type of leadership, sticks to non-violence without the support of APPP or PPPP, and the other does not resort to non-violence of any type, the former has have to surrender to the demands of the latter. If the Gandhian movement too comes down to the latter level, there could be anarchy, insurgency or rebellion.

Thus, the operational process of non-violence moves normally from (a) assumed power of spirit or soul of a Gandhi-like leader to (b) initial formative power of a few followers to (c) actual physical power of the people taking part in the movement, but they also carry with them (d) potential physical power of the whole people or community which may burst out when the adversary appears to cross all limits. However, owing to close moral bonds between the saint-leader and the people at large, the former while sacrificing his life for them through 'fast unto death' or otherwise, also can directly invoke the probable potential power of the people.

A government can always invoke the power of other counter-forces like minorities, caste and class groups, unions and other vested interests to transform of the power of a movement into *non-power*.

Conditions and Requisites of Using GPTs

The Gandhian Political Technologies or GPTs are organisational and institutional devices to gather and organise masses to fight non-violently for realising higher values of life. As such, they cannot be used by anyone for any purpose. Therefore, it is necessary to spell out essential conditions and constraints for using them.

Some of them are mentioned below:

(a) The leader must represent and reflect his closer connection with God, Truth, *Brahma* or the Almighty, and operationalise that connection in form of non-violence. Practice of non-violence displays apparent power of the Almighty in favour of the satyagrahi leader.[42]

(b) They can be used only for higher values and goals of life, such as, independence, justice, equality etc. Their goals and objectives are limited.

(c) Both the *satyagrahis* and their adversaries must cherish some common values. GPTs may not be used if the adversary totally rejects human values, basic tenets of democracy, and respect for human life. The government must be democratic, operating on rule of law and grant some fundamental rights to its people.

(d) There must be some Gandhi-like leader. It is not necessary that he practices only non-violence of the brave or pure non-violence. It is enough that he has faith in superiority of non-violence and is committed to observe non-violent means only. This would provide him the good ground of having good intentions only. In that case, no authority of the government would be able to implicate him or his followers in some criminal offence.[43] For people, his image or impression that he is a man of non-violence is enough.

(e) He lives like a saint or simple man. He must be aware of and be deft in using the media.[44] He must have arrangement of teaching the principles of satyagraha or his mission to his followers in some *ashram* like institution.[45]

(f) The leader and his close followers must be ready to undergo all types of sufferings, from loss of property to sacrifice of life. Sufferings generate sympathy in masses. The more he suffers the more popular he is. Witnessing sufferings, millions of people are likely to come forward to make sacrifice for him, including participation in the movement.

(g) The leader must have masses with him. The number of his followers must always be many times larger than the number of persons with the adversary; otherwise non-cooperation or civil disobedience would have no effect and lose all meaning. Only the large number would prove that his movement is capable of invoking the probable potential power of the masses. The number of his followers shows that he has the capacity to deprive the adversary of revenue, legitimacy and obedience. If their demands are not met, there can be, in case of imprisonment or exile of the leader, law and order problem, breakdown of administration, and even chaos and anarchy. The state must be made to feel that it can neglect probable potential power of the people only at its own peril. The adversary could be compelled to realise that his survival depends upon cooperation of the people at large.

(h) GPTs would prove effective and successful only when they are used in favourable and demanding environment. They should be resorted to when all other individual, legal, political and administrative avenues are exhausted. There must be a large number of people willing to act upon the directives of a Gandhi-like leader.

Limitations

Conditions given above for using GPTs indicate also their constraints. Still there are some limitations as under:

(i) There are many limitations when the country upholds a 'secular' polity. Therefore, politics cannot be made a part of or subordinate to religion, even in its broadest connotation. Every religion claims to be divine and claims to cover the whole humanity. Techniques of politics or adoption of GPTs may not be intended as instruments for realisation of God or Truth. One can speak now in term of religion of humanity or civility only.

(ii) All people do not believe in the fundamentals of one particular religion. Some of them may not have faith in the tenet of spirituality. A few may disagree that violence has no place in life. One may have second thought that undergoing self-suffering was not violence or its voluntary adoption causes conversion of heart of one's adversary. In case the latter is committed to a cause, he may not change his heart or mind at all. Rather he may ask the Gandhi-like leader to change his mind.

(iii) In this age of free press, open media, right to information etc. one may not accept the logic of 'inner voice'. One may find it as sectarian and mythical. Very few of his followers would accept it.[46] In a democracy, operating on the principles of fundamental rights, periodic free elections, free press, free and independent judiciary, egalitarian society and responsible government, hardly is there any place for the dictates of 'inner voice'.

(iv) Often a society is divided on the basis of castes, sub-castes, religions, sects, cultures, languages etc., therefore, the people hardly organise and unite on mystical and controversial grounds. As soon as a Gandhi-like leader begins to raise some value-laden issue, there would be many other groups to oppose him. These counter-forces are likely to make his power of non-violence as non-power.

(v) In view of the nature and paradigm of a secular democracy, one may like to give up all other mega goals of the Gandhian philosophy, such as, no-state, trusteeship, village self-government, bread-labour, spiritualisation of politics etc. Liberal democracy of 21st century refuses to accept them as its goals.

Gandhi was concerned with the role, power, nature and scope of non-violence of the brave and evolved several types of tools and techniques of *satyaghraha*. But he actually could use them only in the policy areas of non-violence. On this account, the GPTs can still be used.

Classification, Features and Selection of GPTs

Under the then prevailing circumstances, Gandhi had formulated, developed and applied many kinds of political technologies. They can, however, be useful only by a Gandhi-like leader.

The Gandhian GPTs can be used by a leader only under certain given conditions:

1. If there is some mega value-problem, such as, realisation of independence, bringing basic changes in society, rooting out widespread evils like corruption, communalism and the like;
2. When there is one or more than two or three leaders, widely known for their high moral character;
3. He or his close kith and kin must not be holding position of power, or should not have express or secret goal to grab power;
4. He must show absolute faith in the efficacy of non-violence as creed or policy and peaceful means and remain willing to undergo travails of all kinds of sufferings; and
5. He must keep himself away from all narrow considerations of class, caste, creed, region, culture and the like.

Classification of GPTs

In order to connect GPTs to their general use and objects, it is necessary to classify them. In all, there are approximately fifteen broad forms of GPTs.

Out of the available GPTs, some of them like exile or *hizrat* are considered beyond national and international laws. Their use is now no more constitutionally feasible. Therefore, they are kept apart. Remaining GPTs are mentioned below:

I Demonstration
II Protest March or Rally or *padyatra*[47]
III Picketing or *dharna*
IV Burning or giving up symbols of oppression
V Silence, Prayer, Fasting and Fast Unto Death[48]
VI Strike or *hartal*
VII Social ostracism
VIII Spinning Wheel (*charkha*)
IX Boycott
X No-tax movement
XI Non-cooperation
XII Civil Disobedience
XIII Constructive Programme and *ashrams*[49]

The GPTs may be put into four groups: A, B, C, D and E. A-Group GPTs, from I to V, reflect protest or opposition on moral grounds. They cause no loss to either party. The B-category GPTs, from VI to VIII, end up in some social reform or achievement: better conditions of work, increase of status or honour, render services to the community, earning bread etc. Group: C GPTs, from IX to XI, are negative, cause loss to other party. Group: D GPTs–XII, is revolutionary. Group E GPTs-XIII, is both evolutionary and revolutionary. It brings about total change. The GPT of Fasting belongs to Group: A, but it is undertaken by a great leader who goes to the extreme of sacrificing life, the result can be as revolutionary as that of Civil Disobedience. On the basis of goals and objectives, they can be placed in five groups:

Group A: Demonstrative GPTs from I to V
Group B: Constructive GPTs from VI to VIII
Group C: Alienating GPTs from IX to XI and
Group D: Revolution-oriented GPTs – XII
Group E: Acceptable GPTs – XIII

All GPTs in their ultimate analysis involve the back up of probable potential power of the people (PPPP) via actual physical power (APPP). PPPP is the possible reactive power of the masses. The adversary or the government is directly concerned with the efficacy, extent, intensity and nature of PPPP. Group A and B GPTs demonstration, picketing, protest march, short term fasting etc. display direct or actual physical power of the people. Group B and C GPTs not only demonstrate actual physical power of the people (APPP), also put the adversary to financial, administrative, psychological and material loss. Strike and social ostracism may cripple the opponent in a serious manner. Non-cooperation, if it is taken to the extreme, can make the government standstill. Civil Disobedience is more offensive as it encourages breaking of specific laws leading the people ultimately to take over. When the police (government) begins to beat, crush and imprison the *satyagrahis* or protestors, confiscate their property or harass the members of their families, they unwittingly invite the wrath of the PPPP of the people. The non-violent movement may turn from defensive to offensive, as it happened in 1942.

Political Technology of Constructive Programme

In 1937 assumption of office by the Congress helped it to give legislative effect to Gandhi's constructive programme.[50] Gandhi had immense faith that the constructive programme allied with non-cooperation and civil disobedience, it would lead to the establishment of a parallel *satyagrahi* government. He believed that this combination would be miraculous enough to transform relationship ending in a peaceful transfer of power.[51] The *constructive programme* constituted the most objective, practical and laudable aspect of Gandhi's satyagrahic mission. It was a common bond, between *satyagrahis* and those who did not believe in non-violent direct action. It was ever significant that in spite of much criticism, no practical alternative to it was suggested. In Gandhi's words it could be 'construction of *Poorna Swaraj* or Complete Independence by truthful and non-violent means.' Several times he revealed the inseparable link between political activity and socio-economic effort. In 1942, he wrote, "If he or she is unable to offer civil disobedience, the alternative is to pursue the items of the constructive programme."[52] Gandhi equated Constructive Programme with Civil Disobedience.

These GPTs classified as A, B, C, D, and E can be connected to different types of micro and macro problems. Smaller problems belong to Group A. As they are short term, e.g. neglect of slums, lack of potable water, absence of medical and health services, torture of women and the like, their solution would also require smaller efforts. Group B demonstrate power of the people to the rulers that they can also manage their affairs. Resort to them displays their power to compel the rulers to deliver goods to the people. GPts under Group C demonstrate the power of non-cooperation. If cooperation is withdrawn, the government may not exist for long. The D Group leads to total rejection of the existing social, economic and political set up. Power behind them is that of non-violence as policy. It carries the impression of having the power of non-violence, but actually stands on the grounds of number, organisation, demands and style of the movement. However, the power of fasting is unique. Its motivating power resides in the will of the leader to die for a cause. But the real power is related to the threat of the reactionary and revolutionary behaviour of the followers concerned with the death of their leader. Group E GPT is related with total reconstruction of the country and its people.

Feasibility of Use of GPTs in Newer Areas

It may be stated that so far GPTs have been used only in some specific and conventionally known areas. Gandhi wanted to experiment with them in areas of international wars, education, economy, gender equality, *gram-swaraj* (autonomy of village) etc. but he could not do so especially because of his immediate concern for realising India's independence without partition. Apart from these untouched areas of Gandhian era, there are many new areas where GPTs, as claimed by the Gandhians, can be used to bring about major socio-economic and political change. Some of the GPTs can perhaps be used to confront the evils of prevailing forces of privatisation, liberalisation and globalisation appearing since 1991. GPTs, they say, if someone makes a proper use of them can compel unwanted MNCs to turn out of a country. A collective organisation of non-nuclear states can ask the nuclear states to put their nuclear arsenals under the supervision and control of a democratically elected world-*panchayat*. The problems of pollution, corruption, waste, inequality, racism, exploitation of women and children and the like are not beyond the remedy of GPTs. Some peace foundations pronounce that they have the capability to attract the probable potential power of the majority of world population, and also majority of the states of world community. Gandhi need not be kept confined to the awakening of a people for some freedom movement only.

Gandhian Non-violence for State and Society

After ascertaining the truth or reality of Gandhian Political Technologies (GPTs), it is desirable to analyse its role in the organisation of State and Society. As actual field of practicing GPTs is State and Society, it is incumbent on us to determine the impact of Gandhian non-violence on them. Gandhi claimed to have made "The Science of Satyagraha", which was a result of the hardest labour a human being is capable of.[53] By use of non-violence, he proposed to bring about total change in man and society.

Often all praise is showered on the power of spiritual and moral elements of non-violence, by relegating material and potential aspects of the problems.[54] Neglect of reality underlying the Gandhian non-violence as

Table

Application of Gandhian Political Technologies

Group	*Pattern of Behaviour*	*Objectives or Goal*	*No. of persons (app.).*	*Extension of People's Faith in NV*	*Duration of movement*	*Cost/ Investment*	*Adversary and his Power*	*Supportin g Groups*	*Action by Adversary*	*PPPP Distance*	*Achieve-ment*
1	*2*	*3*	*4*	*5*	*6*	*7*	*8*	*9*	*10*	*11*	*12*
A	Individual or Group centered-wearing protest indicators, absenting voluntary service, short term fasting, rallies, banners, slogans etc.	Protest against small oppres-sions	a. A few – 100-4000 b. Some – 5000-20000 c. Mass – 20000 and above	NV IIa NV IIb NV IIc	From one to 15 days	Mandays* no. of persons	Individual/ group or unit/local/ total unit/part of law/ sanctions/ union etc.	All leaving a few exciting rival groups	Explanation, suspension, break in service, sect. 144 lathicharge, tear gas etc.	Too long people's apathy	Goals may/may not be realised
B	Strike, social ostracism, constructive work	Moral pressure showing power of organisa-tion	As above a. b. c.	As above NV II a, b and c	From one To four weeks	Mandays* no. of persons+ future gains	Total organisa-tion	Ruling groups & classes, divide and rule	removal	Distant	Power of self-and partial success

Contd...

Contd...

C	Boycott, ltd. non-coope-ration, gradual, total-non-cooperation, non-pay-ment of taxes, long fast	Show dependence on protesters, causing loss of revenue, manpower, accept sufferings jail etc.	As above a. b. c.	Same as above NV IIa NV IIb NV IIc	About one month	Confisca-tion of property+ loss of job +mandays* no. of persons & families	Total adminis-trative set up & govern-ments-local, regional or national	Decreasing no. of groups and classes with action by police & para-military	Imprison-ment, confiscation, torture	Impact of sufferings and common cause, Sympathy	Acceptance of all major demands citizen empower-ment fearlessness
D	Fast unto death, breaking of selected laws, parallel govt.	Invoking APPP and bringing total change or revolution	Top leader selected few, or masses	NV I NV I NV I & NV II	Max. 3 weeks	Immense sufferings & loss upto death	Total govern-ment/ society	Senior bureaucrats & use of military	Criminal proceedings, fine, imprison-ment and the like	Mass-awakening, joining the movement in millions	Replace-ment by better set up and values
E	Engagement of masses	Long-term goals of masses for take over	All people	NV I NV II	No limit	nil	Idleness & apathy	All commu-nities	No action	Distant	Mass awakening

Asteriks show approximation.

creed, and treating it as Power-in-itself has resulted in immense loss to the cause of Knowledge and sustenance of State and Society at large. It is forgotten that absolute faith in and dependence on the *power of non-violence as a creed* results in (a) neglect of making adequate preparations to fight violence by violence, and, (b) dismantling the structure of state and society, and (c) indulging in *apolitics* for personal spiritual gains at the cost of community interests. Scholars, leaders and people are also required to see its side effects on polity.

'Power' versus 'Non-violence'

Gandhi in his notion of 'non-violence' replaces all forms of 'power' by 'non-violence'. Gandhi fails to appreciate the phenomenon of 'power' and does not distinguish between 'power' and 'violence'. He based all faith and confidence in his creed of non-violence. He put all forms of power – coercion, force, influence, might or sanctions behind law under the category of 'violence', and denigrated all of them and by putting them at par with 'violence' and considered them 'immoral'. Violence is hurting others with evil intentions. But hurting of one's own self or body has not been considered 'violence' by him. For Gandhi, violence is using coercion with evil intentions. But use of coercion or hurting others without evil intentions is use of 'force', a form of power, and is not violence.[55] Use of physical power is exercise of force, and is not 'violence' till it is done with immoral or evil intention. Use of legitimate force or sanctions by civil and security authorities cannot be considered as 'immoral'. He failed to appreciate that if a *satyagrahi* by use of non-violence fails to rescue people from large-scale oppression or exploitation, and still continues his *satyagraha* on the basis of his faith that non-violence never fails, his non-violence results into violence to the aggrieved people. He caused people suffer owing to his treating such 'non-violence' as 'non-violence' even if it resulted in violence.[56]

Non-violence in Complex Conditions

Gandhi overlooked many existing complex conditions. He at times allows the use of "violence," but does not recommend the need of its preparation and training for its proper and effective use. The Government of India in 1948 as usual, kept military Forces in alerted condition. Otherwise how Gandhi could have permitted the use of "violence" (use of armed personnel) to repel the aggression. Violence or Army also like non-violence requires discipline, preparation, and training. Few would agree that all "violence" (power) is used out of cowardice. He always declared that non-violence always wins or never fails. But it is a widely known fact that both types of non-violence, i.e., non-violence of the brave as well as non-violence of policy or expediency failed to deliver the goods, i.e., 'Swaraj within one year' (1920) and 'Complete Independence' (1930). Even after the use of these two types of non-violence, the society was left unprotected. Evidence is nowhere available that a few non-violent persons are ever able to turn out the aggressors after the latter forcibly entered and settled down in a country. Non-violent measures undertaken later often fail to stop their misdeeds, and, expel them from the land. Similarly anti-social elements finding non-violence as ineffective or powerless often perpetrate much more violence to society than a limited use of force by some trained armed persons which would do some hurting and killing, but defend the larger segments of society in a disciplined and legally permissible manner. What would happen if there were no civilised or liberal government available to permit the use and spread of violence? Would a society or community like to leave their fate in the hands of a leader for whom the realisation of independence is not an end, as was in case of Gandhi, but a means for the realisation of God? Can a leader like Gandhi be allowed to treat defence and protection of the whole nation as means to realise his own personal end: the *moksha* (salvation). To achieve independence of India was not the central theme and ultimate goal of his techniques.[57]

The use of non-violence perhaps is simple when there is only one opposing party confronting a Gandhian movement as was during the days of freedom movement. That too must be alien or foreigner, a small minority, not residing in the country. Difficulties would arise in case it was to be conducted against one's own countrymen. There can be equal number or a substantial majority of adversaries standing against the *satyagrahis*. In such a situation, it is not easy to determine the 'truthfulness' of the issue or outcome of the conflict even if a large number of *satyagrahis* make sacrifice of lives on both sides. Similarly, there can be more than three or four parties to the conflict. One or two of them may not be believing in practicing non-violence. In such a situation, the fate of 'non-violence' would hang in balance. A country, divided badly into differing big religious, cultural or ethnic communities, when resorts to *satyagraha* movement may fall prey to separatism, partition or civil war.

It can not be denied that even with his largely or partially known truth and non-violence and its practice in many areas, Gandhi could awaken and move the masses in millions. It could be possible only when repression and violence did not crush the movement. It also needed a leader having religion-oriented personality and people's religious faith in what the leader said about the power of non-violence. There should be some other factors contributing to the success of the movement, like the limits of a liberal government along with crises of great economic depression and the events of World War II occurring at the time of freedom movement.[58] There may be hundreds of Gandhian diehards committed to save and enhance the status of their leader and his non-violence.

In case the religious values are not common or not very effectively ingrained in the minds of the people, non-violent movement might either not happen or cause dissension or separatism, as it did in case of other communities particularly Muslims and Sikhs.

Treating the Gandhian non-violence of creed as a total reality or the only source of power is to do immense harm to the cause of knowledge. It weakens the fabric of the state and society. It has resulted in the neglect of factors and forces making the state viable. It also demoralises the armed forces, which make up the spine of the state. Such attitude slackens the defense preparedness of governments.

The security persons, the police and the armed forces are recruited to use force and arms for the protection of society. It is almost a suicidal teaching that permits the aggressors enter the country, later to be persuaded to get out of it by use of *satyagraha*. There is every likelihood that once a country is at war with its enemy; the latter likes to take over and settle soon after its gives up weapons and turns non-violent.

Democracy, operating on the principles of fundamental rights of the individual, periodic free elections, free press, independent judiciary, political parties, egalitarian society, welfare state and responsible government, has hardly any place for the dictates of 'inner voice' and anarchic devices like fasting, non-co-operation or civil disobedience.[59] A person, group, community or a party, claiming to have attained any height of spirituality, cannot be permitted to be the only repository of truth. A votary of absolute non-violence, in public life, often appears to regard himself greater than God. God has not been able to operate the world on total non-violence, but can a leader dare claim to do so and create a totally non-violent society?

Promise and provision of non-violence in pure form for the society as a whole is misleading as well as suicidal. Even a great man like Gandhi could not adopt it successfully and always found himself in an 'experimental' stage. Neither the non-cooperation nor civil disobedience movements succeeded to the extent of his satisfaction, nor his venture of Hindu-Muslim unity could witness its complete realisation. Ordaining non-violence to one segment of society and allowing the rest to exercise their own choice amounts to put the former at the mercy of violence-prone communities and persons. Men of non-violence like Gandhi are often devoted to self-realisation or their identity with God. For them politics is a means to achieve their religious goals. They do not care much even if others do not follow them and go on indulging in their own misdeeds. Such godmen have little time for the reorganisation of society and state on realistic basis. By the time, a good number of people begin to develop absolute faith in them, they happen to disappear from the scene leaving the society in a vacuum, rather in worse condition. At many times, non-violence in some cases becomes a cover for their cowardice, imbecility, servility, weakness and ignorance.

Often 'intention' of the leader is considered to be the core element of non-violence. But a pious wish or faith in peace is not enough. Society is largely concerned not with mere intentions or motives, but also with short and long term results, outcomes and consequences of non-violence.

Gandhi's Apolitics

Gandhi was unable to see, find and tell about the political forces lying behind and beyond non-violence. It was because of his never-failing desire to realise his ultimate goal of self-realisation or *moksha* (salvation). Religion exemplified as God, Truth or Morality was everything for him. Politics, social reform, social service etc. were treated as part of his concept of non-violence, which was the only means to his ultimate goal. In this sense, the total thrust of his ideas and action was *apolitical* or *non-political*, even *anti-political*. He could not appreciate that politics is a worldly activity and it stands to make life better here and now through collective human efforts made and based on human reason. Therefore, Gandhi is more useful only for those who want to live closely to religion, morality or spirituality and resort to non-violence at all costs.

It also means that there is no place for non-believers. Followers of Gandhi have to adopt his brand of faith either by reforming his own conventional religious conceptions or abandon some of them for good. In practice, his teachings were mostly addressed to the Hindus who identified him as a great *avatar*, godman, *mahatma* and saint. Others also who were alike the Hindu followers accorded similar respect to him. Most of them could not visualise that Gandhi's apolitical ethics struck at the roots of their own total philosophy, social fabric and political interests as a community.

At the individual level, perhaps his religious and spiritual precepts are good for obtaining *moksha* or self-realisation. But one may not be permitted to realise them at the cost of interests of a nation, group or others. Clearly the power to fight against injustice, colonial rule or exploitation did not reside in those precepts, and their practice at the individual level. Gandhi instead of understanding the other forms of power, such as, actual physical force or probable potential power of the people, exhorted the people to see non-violence as the only source of power. Thus, he always put emphasis on *apolitical* or *non-political* things of spirit, ethics and religion. Sometimes, he was ready to sacrifice even the country and the Congress for the sake of *Ahimsa* or non-violence. Earlier he had clearly declared that he entered politics as he "could not be leading a religious life unless I identified myself with the whole of mankind and that I could not do unless I took part in politics". By and by, he adopted the saintly lifestyle in full, and regarded his moral means as an end itself. He began to be guided by his "inner voice" and prayers: he said that "This ability to bear and obey the "inner voice" gives me whatever power I may have and has enabled me to render some little service to the country". This small voice within was the final arbiter when there was a conflict of duty. His testamentary wish was, 'if someone killed me and I died with prayer for the assassin on my lips, and God's remembrance and consciousness of His living presence in the sanctuary of my heart, then alone would I be said to have had the non-violence of the brave.'

He claimed to be working for the formation of a society utterly decentralised, stateless and non-violent where individuals like him would lead an ascetic, simple and self-sufficient life to attain salvation. As wars involved killing, he stood for non-violent action against an alien aggression. When change of heart through self-suffering in other fields did not bear fruit he was ready to permit use of law and some strictly very limited use of force, but his main thrust was to rely on soul-force or non-violence of the brave. Thus, Gandhi was apolitical rather non-political. Politics was not an end for him, but a means to subserve religion: realisation of God, Truth or *moksha*. He made it several times clear that, 'I could not be leading a religious life unless I identified myself with the whole of mankind and that I could not do unless I took part in politics.' He rejected the possibility of any conflict between political expediency and moral principles derived from religion. He always claimed to engage himself in devoting to pure and selfless service thereby gaining real power. In the ultimate analysis, he stood for *non-politics* or *apolitics*, and had his faith, heart and mind, in the world of religion and morality.

Therefore, while using the GPTs, and non-violence as an independent source or power, one should not stop at the gates of soul-force or much praised non-violence of the brave. They should rather directly deal with the actual physical power of the agitating sections of masses, and also the probable potential power of the people, that lay behind them. All GPTs are ultimately based on power. Democratic politics is an interplay of probable potential power, direct physical power wielded by groups and parties, and counter-power of the opposing groups. Morality, religion and soul-force appear only as initiating formative power, which ultimately operates on the basis of direct physical power or probable potential power. A state would neglect probable potential power of the people at its own peril. Consideration of non-violence as power-in-itself without reference to the actual or potential power of the people is to mistake half or partial truth as full truth. Gandhian non-violence to a certain extent is only a background, initiative or formative part of the power of the people engaged in some moral or just struggle. The ideal of non-violence does not tell the whole truth about the sources of its actual power. Its praise provides only a cover for the other two forms of power: APPP and PPPP. Non-violence turns effective only in the context of PPPP and APPP.

The partial truth of Gandhian non-violence so far has resulted in an imbalance among societal forces. Smaller segments of society not adopting non-violence become more powerful and dominant than bigger segments believing in non-violence. The latter continue to grow weaker and turn helpless. The former often refuse to adopt non-violence at latter's cost. In order to maintain balance and harmony, both state and society, including their leaders, would have to concentrate on actual physical force and probable potential power of the people, and act sagaciously.

Notes

1. Vinoba Bhave, Jaiprakash Narain, Dada Dharmadhikari, Ram Mahohar Lohia, R.R. Diwakar, Martin Luther King (Jr.), and other leaders of peace movements in Europe, Latin America, and Africa.
2. Verma, M.M., *Gandhi's Technique of Mass Mobilization*, New Delhi: R.K. Gupta & Co., 1990, 238.
3. Ibid., 24, 208.
4. For the concept of 'political technologies', see, supra, Ch. 9.
5. For use of Gandhian non-violence and satyagraha, see, Hardiman, David, *Time and Ours: The Global Legacy of his Ideas,* London: C. Hurst & Co. Publishers, 2004; S.L. Verma, *Gandhi: Use, Abuse and Misuse*, 2008.
6. S.L. Verma, *On Grounds of Gandhian Polity*, Jaipur: RBSA Publishers, 1990, p. 3; Verma, M.M. op, cit., 208; V.R. Mehta, *Ideology, Modernization and Politics in India*, New Delhi: Manohar Publications, 1983, p. 135; Louis Fisher, *The Life of Mahatma Gandhi*, London: Harpers, 1983, p. 93.
7. Verma, M.M., op. cit. 226.
8. See, Chapter 13 and 14.
9. 'Non-violence coerces as well as violence, sometimes ever more terribly' by Nehru, Jawaharlal, *An Autobiography,* London: The Bodley Head, 1955, 539.
10. *Dr. Babasaheb Ambedkar, Writings and Speeches*, Vol. 3, Mumbai: Education Department, Government of Maharashtra, 1987, pp. 3-90; M.K. Gandhi, *My Religion*, Ahmedabad: Navajivan Publishing House, 1955, p. 3.
11. कर्मण्येवाधिकारस्ते मा फलेशु कदाचन–गीता
12. V.R. Mehta, *Foundations of Indian Political Thought*, Delhi: Manohar, 1992, p. 213; Raghvan Iyer, *The Moral and Political Writings of Mahatma Gandhi*, Oxford: Clarendon Press, 1986, p. 7.
13. Verma, M.M., op. cit., 87, 99-105.
14. Verma, M.M., op. cit. 106-11.
15. (All enmity disappears when a person enters the vicinity of a seer having won over Non-violence) अहिंसा प्रतिष्ठायां तत्सन्निधौ वैरत्यागः –महर्षि पतंजलि
16. Ashutosh Lahiry, *Gandhi in Indian Politics*, Calcutta: Firma KLM Pvt. Ltd., 1976, p 47; Mehta, op. cit., p. 180; Nirmal Kumar Bose, *My Days With*

Gandhi, Calcutta: Nishana, 1953; The net result of Gandhian non-violence was not necessarily love and affection from the adversary – Churchill, Linlithgow, even Wavell besides Jinnah and others. See, Padma Ramkrishnan, *Gandhi and Indian Independence*, New Delhi: Blaze Publishers & Distributors Pvt. Ltd., 1994.

17. Verma, M.M., *Gandhi's Technique of Mass Mobilization*, op. cit., Conclusion.
18. Ibid., 20, 184, and 202: He failed in 1920, 'Swaraj in one year', in 1930, 'now or never', and in 1942, 'do or die'. Tara Chand writes, Gandhi's release from detention on May 5, 1944, 'marked the end of the Gandhian era'.
19. At times, he permitted abandonment of non-violence. When we kill the mosquitoes, according to him, we destroy their lives to sustain our bodies. If a lunatic runs amuck killing everyone on the road, and there is no possibility of capturing him alive, we have to kill him and thus save the community. Similarly, when a man or an animal suffers the unbearable torture of slow death, and there are no means to rid him of the agony, the final remedy would be to take the life. He suggested these remedies despite their being against his concept of non-violence.
20. Iyer, op. cit., p. 34. In the context of Hindu dominated majority of Indians, pure non-violence got him the prestige of a 'Mahatma' to the maximum by 1930, thereafter Gandhi wanted to convert the whole Congress with his creed of non-violence. When he could not he left the Congress by October 1934, but the aura of being a Mahatma, because his creed, continued, and he carried the mass following. Most votes for Congress candidates in 1937 were a vote for Gandhi. Padma, op. cit., pp. 20-71.
21. R.R. Diwaker, *Saga of Satyagraha*, Bombay: Bhartiya Vidya Bhavan, pp. 1-47; Hiren Mukerjee, *Gandhiji: A Study*, Calcutta: National Book Agency, pp. 141-43; and, Glorney Bolton, *The Tragedy of Gandhi*, Delhi: Modern Publishers, 1986, passim.
22. Asha Rani, *Gandhian Non-Violence and India's Freedom Struggle*, Delhi: Shree Publishing House, 1081, passim; Verma, *Gandhi: Use, Abuse and Misuse*, 2008.
23. Verma, M.M., op. cit. 179-81.
24. Ibid., 204-06.
25. R.C. Majumdar, *History of Freedom Movement in India*, Vol. III, Calcutta: Firma KLM, 1963, p. 62; Pattabhi Sitaramayya, *The History of the Indian National Congress*, Vol. I, Bombay: Padma Publishing House, 1964, p. 199; Rajni Palme Dutta, *India Today*, 2nd rev. ed., Bombay: 1948, pp. 314-54; Iqbal Singh, *The Indian National Congress: A Reconstruction* 1919-23, Vol. 2, New Delhi: Manohar Publications, 1988, pp. 314-42; and, Coupland, *India: Restatement*, London: Oxford University Press, 1954, p. 119.
26. Judith M. Brown, *Gandhi's Rise to Power in Indian Politics*, London: Cambridge University Press, 1972; Aloo J. Dastur, "Salt Satyagraha", *Political Science Review*, Vol. 9, Nos. 1 & 2 (Jan.-June, 1970), pp. 1-11; R.C. Majumdar, op. cit., p. 338; S.C. Bose, *Indian Struggle*, Part II, Calcutta: Thacker Spink & co., 1948, p. 255; and, Lahiry, *Gandhi in Indian Politics: A Critical Review*,

Calcutta: Firma KLM, 1076. Gandhi disowned any responsibility for the 1942 violence.

27. At the time of the Cabinet Mission Plan, the British rulers enlisted the support of Muslim League, and others.
28. According to Gandhi the four pillars of the British Indian Empire were: the European interests, the army, the princes and the communal elements. The native states constituted a network of friendly fortresses to the British Raj. Consequently, the All India States Peoples Congress formed by the Congress in Poona in 1927 was declared outcaste by all the princes till 1945. Under the Government of India Act 1935, they were given 1/3 seats in the lower house, 125 out of 275, and 2/5 in the upper house, 104 out of 260. Thus the rulers constituted a conservative counterweight to the Congress. They represented 24 per cent population only and were under the complete control of the British officers and agents. Similarly, by conceding the principle of partition, the Cripps Scheme strengthened the Muslim League as a political force and rival of the Congress. Pakistan had advanced one stage further. Communal tension was intensified in many provinces as communal organisations began to organise local defense volunteers. Thus, the British gave veto power to the Muslim League.
29. During the final phase of his life, Gandhi seemed to withdraw as into a shell, so far his involvement in politics is concerned. He wrote in Oct. 1946, "I know that mine is today a voice in the wilderness." *Harijan*, Oct. 6, 1946. He was helpless and now could only make politically impractical suggestions, like that Jinnah should be the prime minister. Ultimately he assumed the role of a saintly mission. Padma, op. cit. pp. 217-8 and 224. He said at the prayer meeting in Delhi on April 1, 1947, "My writ runs no more". Verma, M.M., op. cit., 204-06.
30. See, infra, 'Power' and 'Violence', 21.
31. Few scholars and critics have been able to appreciate that the third level of Gandhian non-violence makes all movements led and organised by Gandhi as 'movements of cowardice' as they died down before the brute force of the British rulers.
32. Many times Gandhi claimed that "God had chosen him as His instrument for presenting non-violence to India. And his mission was to convert every Indian and finally the world, to non-violence for regulating mutual relations whether political, economic, religious or social". *Harijan*, March 11, 1939, vol. VII, 46.
33. See, footnote 29.
34. "What I want to achieve that I have been striving and pining to achieve these thirty years – is self-realisation, to see God face to face, i.e., to attain *moksha*". See his *Autobiography*.
35. Verma, M.M., op. cit., 85.
36. M.K. Gandhi, *Harijan* (March 30 and June 1, 1940), Sir Reginald Maxwell, Home Member of the Central Executive Council, Statement, September 17, 1942; *Legislative Assembly Debates*, Vol. III, No. 2, pp. 41-51; Government of India, *Congress Responsibility for the Disturbances*, Home Department

(February, 1943); Pyare Lal, *Mahatma Gandhi, The Last Phase,* Vol. I, Ahmedabad: Navajivan Publishing House; Leonard Mosley, *The Last Days of the British Raj,* London: Wiedenfeld & Nicolson, 1961, pp. 368-95; Ashok Mitra, "The Great Calcutta Killings of 1946, What Went and After", *Economic and Political Weekly,* Vol. XXV, No. 5 (February 3, 1990), pp. 273-85.

37. Gandhi was ready to face death for the cause he had undertaken: B.R. Nanda, "Face to Face with Death", *Times of India,* 1 February, 1987.

38. Gandhi held his epic fast while he was a prisoner in the Agha Khan palace for 21 days from Feb. 9, 1943. It caught and held the moral imagination of the Indian people. It had an electrifying effect on the people. Gandhi had demonstrated to the world the righteousness of his cause. Gandhi, thus, was strongest when he was behind bars and his strength lay in fasting. Padma, op. cit. p 250; also, Verma, M.M., op. cit., 142-44.

39. When Gandhi was left alone in the aftermath of the acceptance of the Cabinet Mission Plan, he began to talk of appointing Jinnah as the prime minister, and even rejecting independence at the price of partition. Ibid., pp. 224-7.

40. When Gandhi started 'individual satyagraha', the British rulers remained unruffled for it lacked both APPP as well as PPPP. According to Gandhi himself it was no more than a 'token protest'. According to a Government report, in some areas it was limping along, in others it was moribund and in others again it seemed to be dead. File No. 4/8/41, NAI, Home Political Files, Nos. 18-10-41.

41. Jinnah made full use of the power of the Muslim population under his concept of Islam. Jawaharlal Nehru was invited on 6th Aug. 1946 to form the Cabinet of 14 members. But he was unable to do so. The Muslim League resorted to 'direct action' followed by widespread massacres in Calcutta. When it joined it wrought greater havoc by coming into the government than staying out of it. The outside fight was carried over into government circles and there was 'direct action' in another form, covert and subdued, but dangerous nevertheless. The British Raj had abdicated its role. Democratic norms were made impossible to operate. The League had converted its PPPP to APPP and won the battle. Within ninety-six hours of joining office, Nehru wrote to Wavell that it was not possible to continue in government. Padma, op. cit. pp. 196-211.

42. 'A man or woman who is saturated with ahimsa has only to will a thing and it happens'. *Harijan,* 18 August, 1940, vol. VIII, 254; 'Non-violence is a universal law acting under all circumstances. Disregard of it is surest way to destruction'. *Harijan,* 15 July, 1939, vol. VII, 201.

43. An 'offence' under the Indian Penal Laws requires evidence of evil intention or motive or an act committed willfully.

44. Verma, M.M., op. cit., 121.

45. Ibid., 129-32.

46. Verma, M.M., op. cit., 105-6.

47. Ibid., 121.

48. Ibid., 142-44.

49. Ibid., 124-28 and 129-32.
50. Ibid., 124-28.
51. *Harijan*, 17 Feb. 1946.
52. Padma Ramkrishnan, *Gandhi and Indian Independence*, New Delhi: Blaze Publishers & Distributors Pvt. Ltd., 21.22, Prakash Apartments, Ansari Road, New Delhi, 1994, p. 144.
53. Shukla, Chandrashankar, *Conversations of Gandhiji*, Bombay: Vohra & Co., 1949, 41.
54. S.L. Verma, *On Grounds of Gandhian Polity*, Jaipur: RBSA Publishers, 1990, p. 3; Geoffry Ashe, *Gandhi: A Study in Revolution*, Bombay: Asia Publishing House, 1968, p. 144; Purshottam Mehra, 'Politician as Saint', *The Hindustan Weekly*, (20 October, 1974).
55. See, supra, Ch. 6.
56. Nehru, *An Autobiography*, op. cit. 539.
57. Verma, M.M., op. cit., 234.
58. Raghvan Iyer, *The Moral and Political Writings of Mahatma Gandhi*, Oxford: Clarendon Press, 1986, p. 13; Michael Edwards, *The Myth of Mahatma*, New Delhi: UBS Publishers, 1986, pp. 179, 191, 203, 215, 224 and 250; and also see, Bhikhu Parekh, *Colonialism, Tradition and Reform: An Analysis of Gandhi's Political Discourse*, New Delhi: Sage Publications, 1989, and, *Gandhi's Political Philosophy: A Critical Examination*, London: Macmillan, 1989, p. 248.
59. In the Constituent Assembly of India, B.R. Ambedkar had declared them as 'grammar of anarchy'; S.L. Verma, *Beyond Hindutva*, op. cit.; also, *Gandhi: Use, Abuse and Misuse*, 2008.

18

Theoretical Aspects of Human Rights

It was the religions in ancient and medieval times, and major ideologies in the modern age that have made claims upon man's surrender to them. Religions, as such, could be put into two categories: one, religion of God as the only Reality, Truth, and Existence. World to them was ephemeral, temporary and unreal. Man's duty was total surrender and total submission to, and total identification with, God, eschewing all worldly matters. The other category of religions ordained to follow Directives or Commandments of God revealed for man directly or through some Messenger, Prophet, *Guru* or Seer. Men and women obtained discipline how to pursue them to worldly and otherworldly lives. They had to follow them literally and faithfully. The third category of ideologies, such as, Socialism, Communism or Individualism, catered for total change through the role of individual, nation, revolution and radical reform. Man was a simple tool or an instrument for the realisation of their 'ideal' world. Only the fourth category stands for 'man' and only for 'man', his family and community. To realise this goal, it empowers man and women with 'rights'.

Almost everywhere, in ancient times, there were no 'rights' as such. There were only duties and obligations. Man, considered as part of God's Creation, Cosmos, Energy, *Brahma* etc., had to learn only humanity, non-violence, brotherhood, love and so on. He was part of God's Huge Machinery and had to perform only the given role. His role was to commit 'total surrender'. But that too was neglected: from where would he learn this role; who, how and why would someone teach this role? It was not thought out how and who would build up a peaceful socio-economic and political environment conducive to learn and act on that role? Can one pursue that role without minimum arrangement of bread, housing, clothing, health and safety? What steps would be taken to protect this conducive milieu? Who would confront and subdue the violators of peace? What would be done to those who teach differently and compel others to follow them against their wishes? What would happen to their children, the sick, and the disabled? As all these problems remained unlooked for, performing of 'duty' remained almost mandatory. Therefore, it is very important to know how it has come about as 'right'. Man had the only role of performing his religiously ordained 'duties'. Only that was obligatory while the rest were voluntary. The concept of 'right' emerged to change his plight.

Evolution of the Concept

In the beginning, it is necessary to point out that the concept of 'Human Rights' is different from that of 'Humanism'[1] and 'Humanitarianism'.[2] By the term 'Human Rights', we mean availability of conditions or opportunities in which a person feels free to do or not to do certain things, or acts for oneself. The concept of Human Rights is based on certain universalistic moral perspectives. It claims that there exists a rationally identifiable moral order. Legitimacy of this moral order precedes all social and historical conditions and that it applies to all human beings everywhere and at all times. Moral beliefs and concepts are capable of being objectively validated as fundamentally and universally true. The individual is the bearer of certain 'natural' rights. He has inherent and equal moral worth being a rational human being. He is a member of a universal moral community comprising all human beings.[3]

These ideas began with Aristotle and the Stoics like Cicero and Seneca. According to Aristotle, there is a natural moral order. It provides a set of criteria for evaluating the legitimacy of actual 'man-made' legal systems. Being 'natural' it has the same validity everywhere and does not depend upon acceptance. Thus, the criteria for determining a truly rational system of justice preexist social and historical conventions. The exercise of reason helps in determining the form and content of natural justice. For Cicero and Seneca morality originated in the rational will of God. His ethically universal code imposed upon all of us carries a duty to obey the will of God. It formed a universal moral community of Christianity. However, the contemporary idea of human rights clearly emerged in the 17th and 18th centuries in form of 'natural law'.

Natural law coming from John Locke (*Two Treatises of Government,* 1688) believed in the existence of a natural moral code. It pre-existed all actual and political systems. It is based on the identification of certain fundamental and objectively verifiable human goods. Basic goods are necessary for human enjoyment. Enjoyment of these basic goods depends on our possession of equally fundamental and objectively verifiable natural rights. Individuals possessed these natural rights independent of society or polity. They are valid irrespective of the recognition given by any political ruler or assembly. These natural rights are possessed independently of, and prior to, the formation of any political community. Natural rights flowed from natural law. Natural law originated from God. Accurate discerning of the will of God provided us with an ultimately authoritative moral code. Each of us owes a duty of self-preservation to God. This can be done if an individual is free from threats to life and liberty. Basic positive means for self-preservation is personal property. Thus, the duty of self-preservation to God requires the existence of basic natural rights to life, liberty and property. The principal purpose of the investiture of political authority in a sovereign state is the provision and protection of individuals' basic natural rights. It was the sole justification for the creation of a government. These natural rights also set clear limits to the authority and jurisdiction of the State. Individuals are morally justified in taking up arms if the ruler fails in his duty to secure these rights to individuals. Locke provided establishment of legitimate political authority upon the foundation of natural rights but it had an appeal to the authority of some superhuman entity.

Immanuel Kant emancipated human rights from the concept of superhuman entity or God. Kant did this on the ideals of equality and the moral autonomy of rational human beings. He believed in a potentially universal community of rational individuals who autonomously determined the moral principles for securing the conditions for equality and autonomy. He justified human rights within the authority of human reason. In place of 'human goods', he made an appeal to the formal principles of ethics, which lead to a correct determination of the formal properties of human reason. An attempt has to be made to identify these principles or reasoning that can be applied equally to all rational persons, irrespective of their own specific desires or vested interests. This is 'categorical imperative': 'act only on that maxim through which you can at the same time will that it should become a universal law'. This is his basic condition of universality. It should determine the moral principles for governing human relations. It is necessary for the moral autonomy and fundamental equality of all rational individuals. The categorical imperative is self-imposed. It is so accepted by morally autonomous and formally equally rational persons. The exercise of reason is the distinguishing characteristic of humanity and the basis for justifying human dignity. Reason must satisfy the test of universality. Human rights that we give to ourselves we do as autonomous and formally equal beings. Such rights originate in the formal properties of human reason, not out of the will of some superhuman being.

Ideas of Locke and Kant have dominated the era of Enlightenment during the 17th and 18th centuries. Ideals such as natural rights, moral autonomy, human dignity, and equality made up the normative bedrock for attempts at reconstituting political systems. They were enshrined in the United States' Declaration of Independence (1776) and the French Declaration of Rights of Man and Citizen (1789). In the 19th century, similar ideas were further reflected in Mary Wollstencraft's *Vindication of the Rights of Women*. The Constitution of Soviet Russia (1917) also embodied them.

Concept of 'human right' came very late. It came up with the emergence of the concept of 'natural rights'. Later, the idea was taken to other fields. Harold J. Laski spoke of rights as 'those conditions of social life without which no man can seek in general to be himself at his best.' The concept of 'universal right' was used by Thomas Paine, J.S. Mill, Henry David Thoreau and some others. Thoreau was first to use the term 'human rights' in *Civil Disobedience*. Concept of 'human right', in modern sense, is totally new. Franklin Delano Roosevelt first used it in 1941 in the context of *Four Freedoms*. Churchill also stood for 'enthronement of human rights'. A full declaration of human rights finally occurred during the 20th century during the World War II, particularly after the making of United Nations Organization (UNO) on Oct. 24, 1945. UN Declaration of Human Rights (UDHR) was adopted on Dec. 10, 1948, birthday of Alfred Nobel.[4] UDHR has further been supplemented by documents as the European Convention for the Protection Human Rights and Fundamental Freedoms (1953), the International Covenant on Economic, Social and Cultural Rights (1966) and many others. Aspirations of these documents have further been reinforced by innumerable other Declarations and Conventions. All these make up the Theory of Human Rights.

Thus, there are four stages of the growth of the theory of human rights: (i) in form of life, liberty, property and political participation; (ii) Universal Declaration of Human Rights (UDHR), 1948; (iii) socio-economic rights: rights to welfare, education, and leisure; and (iv) rights like the right to self-determination, a clean environment, and the rights of indigenous minorities.

Human Rights can be analysed as a phenomenon having many elements:

Better than Natural Rights

In the opinion of James Nickel,[5] the contemporary concept of human rights goes beyond that of natural rights in three ways: one, it is far more concerned to realisation of equality, as it requires positive action by the state; two, whereas advocates of natural rights conceived of human beings merely as individuals, human rights recognise the importance of family and community in individuals' lives; and, three, human rights are more 'internationalist' in scope and orientation than are natural rights. Human rights demand international action and concern.

Nature of Human Rights

More Moral Less Legal

Human rights are moral claims, and not legal rights. Legal rights exist within legal codes and enjoy recognition and protection of the law. It cannot be said to exist prior to its passing into law. The limits of its validity are set by the jurisdiction of the body passing that law. Moral rights claim to exist prior to and independent of legal rights. Their existence and validity is dependent upon the actions of jurists and legislators. A belief prevails that human rights may or may not have received legal recognition, still stands valid and morally compelling. They are 'fundamental' to man. Man cannot live without having them. They are fundamental to his existence, survival and progress. Human rights are meant to apply to all human beings everywhere. It does not matter whether they have received legal recognition by all countries. They are valid as fundamental rights. The universality of human rights as moral rights lends greater moral force to human rights. Still human rights should be identified with moral rights. They should be thought both as moral rights and legal rights. The legitimacy of human rights is tied to their status as moral rights. However, the practical efficacy of human rights is largely dependent upon their developing into legal rights.

More as Claims

Most of the rights in UDHR expressed as 'liberty' rights are in fact 'claims' rights. Claims rights owe duty to help the holder of this right to perform his duty. A claims right is a right one holds against another person or persons who owe a corresponding duty to the right holder. Claims rights one holds to some specific good or service, which some one other has a duty to provide. Negative claim rights are rights one holds against others' interfering in or trespassing upon one's life or property in some way. Liberty right is a right to do as one pleases. With it one is not under an obligation, grounded in others' claim rights, to refrain from so acting. Liberty rights provide for the capacity to be free, without actually providing the specific means by which one may pursue the objects of one's will. They consist of those actions one is not prohibited from performing. In contrast to claim rights, liberty rights are primarily negative in character.

Varying Order of Priorities

There are different categories of substantive rights: rights to life; rights to freedom; rights to political participation; rights to the protection of rule of law; and, rights to fundamental social, economic, and cultural goods. Some rights depend more on the existence of various claims rights. It requires the positive provision of the objects of such rights. Often people consider these rights having equal importance. But all rights are not equally important. Therefore, conflict between rights can and does occur. Developing countries have severely limited financial and material resources. They are incapable of providing resources for realising all of the human rights for all of their citizens. Some rights are more absolute and fundamental. Therefore, a morally correct action for a government is to prioritise these rights. It requires the existence of some more ultimate criteria against which one can 'measure' the relative importance of separate human rights. It is also important to know who and how one would do this?

Agencies for Securing Rights

Human rights are to be possessed equally by everyone. Everyone has a duty to protect and promote the rights of everyone else. The onus for securing human rights typically falls upon national governments and international and intergovernmental bodies. Moral burden for securing human rights falls disproportionately upon institutions as some are best placed and most able to effectively perform this task. Non-governmental organisations and some private citizens also have an important role to play to protect human rights. National governments are held responsible for the adequate provision of their own citizens' human rights. They have to ensure that all individuals have the opportunity of leading a minimally good life. The goal of human rights is to secure 'minimal levels of decent and respectful treatment'. However, this goal cannot be limited by national boundaries. The more affluent and powerful nation-states have to provide sufficient assistance to the countries currently incapable of adequately ensuring the protection of their own citizens' basic human rights. Even the briefest survey of the extent of human suffering and deprivation in many parts of the world today demonstrates how the world is far away from realising even this 'fairly minimal standard of living'.

The goal of the creation of opportunities for all individuals to lead a 'minimally good life' should not be equated to creating a 'morally perfect society'. Even the aspirations of leading a minimally good life is far from being realised in the world. The actual aspirations of human rights are quite modest. But the force of human rights is intended to be *near* absolute. Even *all* the opportunities to lead a minimally good life cannot be realised. However, considerations of human rights' claims must take priority over other considerations.

Basis of Justification: Interests versus Will

Human rights require validity, i.e., justification. Mere factual existence or their recognition is not enough. They have to be proved on the basis of 'oughtness' or norms. This is usually done on the basis of (a) interests theory, and, (b) will theory. Interest theory argues that the principal function of human rights is to protect and promote certain essential human interests. It is necessary to identify the social and biological prerequisites for human beings to lead a minimally good life. John Finnis[6] argues that human rights are justifiable on the grounds of their instrumental value for securing the necessary conditions of human well-being. He identified seven fundamental interests: life and its capacity for development; the acquisition of knowledge as an end itself; play, as the capacity for recreation; aesthetic expression; sociability and friendship; practical reasonableness, the capacity for intelligent and reasonable thought processes; and religion, or the capacity for spiritual experience. These are essential prerequisites for human well-being, which serve to justify our claims to the corresponding rights.

The interests-based approach provides a justification for respecting, and even positively acting to promote the interests of others. James Nickel argues that each individual, due to his prudential reason, owes a basic and general duty to respect the rights of every other individual. The basis for this duty is not mere benevolence or altruism, but individual self-interest. This necessitates the establishment of a co-operative system. But the fundamental aim of this co-operative system is not to promote the common good, but the protection and promotion of individuals' self-interest. This theory appeals to human commonality, to those attributes we all share. It also resolves some of the potential disputes, which can arise over the need to prioritise some human rights over others. But the theory banks upon some account of common human nature. Appeals to human nature have proven to be highly controversial. They resist achieving the degree of consensus needed for establishing legitimacy of any moral doctrine. Indian economic philosopher, Amartya Sen has argued that determining the minimal conditions for a decent life are socially and culturally relative. It cannot justify the claims of universal human rights. Interests cannot be predeterminants of human moral ends like freedom and love.

The will theory proposes to establish validity of human rights often upon a single attribute: the capacity for freedom. H.L.A. Hart writes that all rights are reducible to a single, fundamental right: 'equal right of all men to be free'. But Henry Shue argues that many of these rights imply more than mere individual liberty. He grounds rights upon liberty, security and subsistence. Alan Gewirth[7] finds rights in 'capacity for rationally purposive agency'. Rights are necessary means for rationally purposive action. Every human action is done for some reason. There exists an absolute right to life possessed separately and equally by all of us. The right to life is absolute and cannot be overridden under any circumstances. Will theorists further attempt to establish the validity of human rights upon the ideal of personal autonomy. Rights are a manifestation of the exercise of personal autonomy. However, this theory neglects marginal cases of human beings that are temporarily or permanently incapable of acting in a rationally autonomous fashion. It also excludes human beings that act out of sympathy, and have a general emotional concern for others. However, each theory suffers from certain limitations. It yields conclusions that limit or undermine the full force of human rights. Therefore, plurality of theories or approaches is the only way out.

John Rawls[8] writes that only an international order, no nation by itself can realise human rights. Human rights in but one land are a contradiction. Jurgen Habermas[9] argues that human rights are not accepted because of good consequences such as knowledge of the Absolute. They are accepted as presuppositions of inquiry for the sake of inquiry.

Foundations of Human Rights

Supporters of human rights are often committed to a form of *moral universalism*. Human rights are considered to be universally valid. Disagreeing with them, moral relativists argue that universally valid moral truths do not exist. They view morality as a social and historical phenomenon. Moral beliefs and principles are socially and historically contingent. They are valid only for those cultures and societies in which they originate and within which they are approved. One can find a wide diversity of fundamental moral beliefs, principles, and practices. Contemporary societies are pluralist and multicultural in character. In respect of human rights, relativists focus upon such issues as the presumed individualist character of the human rights. They are unduly biased towards morally individualist societies and cultures. They do so at the expense of moral complexion of many Asian and African societies. They appear to be positively harmful to them. If fully implemented, they replace the fundamental values of one civilisation with those of another, thereby perpetuate a form of cultural and moral imperialism.

But merely pointing to moral diversity and the presumed integrity of individual cultures and societies does not prove the truth of relativism. Relativism is not a sufficient critique of universalism. Relativism can be incompatible with human rights. Still a relativist does not actually forgo his possession of human rights. Relativism also, like Nazism and Communism, makes an attempt to illegitimately justify oppressive political systems. Against this, the third and fourth stages of evolution of human rights take care of rights of minorities and communal land rights. Human rights today are no more 'culture-blind'.

In search of an objective basis of human rights, one can object to the inherently subjective character of moral rights. Richard Rorty[10] argues that human rights are based not upon the exercise of reason but a sentimental vision of humanity. He insists that human rights are not rationally defensible. Moral beliefs and practices emanate from a sympathetic identification with others. Morality originates in the heart, and not in the head. Existence of human rights as a 'good and desirable thing', something whose existence we all benefit from. They are better served by emotional appeals to identify with the unnecessary suffering of others, than by arguments over the correct determination of reason. An emotional identification with others is a legitimate concern. But Michael Freeman has pointed out that Rorty confuses *motivation* and *justification*. Sympathy is an emotion. Whether the action we take on the basis of our emotions is justified depends on the reason advanced for the action. Rorty eliminates reasoning itself. He explicitly rules out the validity of appealing to the independently verifiable criteria. He fails to give an independent reason for accepting his conclusion. Human rights are founded upon the claim to moral objectivity. Underlying them there may be appeal to interests or will or both. They are best thought of as potential moral guarantees for each human being to lead a minimally good life. The contemporary world has to institute a morally compelling order based upon human rights.

Ideology of Human Rights

As stated above, the International Bill of Rights includes (i) Universal Declaration of Human Rights (UDHR) (1848), (ii) International Covenant on Civil and Political Rights (1966), and (iii) International Covenant on Economic, Social and Cultural Rights (1966). However , the Universal Declaration of Human Rights provides the base of all Human Rights. Human Rights, in fact, set a common standard of achievement for all peoples and all nations. It contains one Preamble and 30 Articles. The Preamble along with Art. 1, 6, and 30 provide its ideology. Its ideology is imbued with many postulates. Accordingly, Human Rights are 'man' (human beings) centred. They relate to the commonality of human beings, and there life and living, here and now. Human rights do not cater for life after death or for supposedly next birth. In this sense, human rights are limited to man's present life.

Man under Human Rights is different from the 'man' of religion, philosophy and Holy Books. Whatever he is supposed to have, he has in this life. His status and existence is substantive and real. It recognises that man has inherent dignity and equal and inalienable rights. He has all these rights because he is born as man. He is a member of human family. They are not given, bestowed and granted by any other external authority. Man himself is the *source* of these rights. Basic beliefs and postulates about man are: (i) All human beings are born free and equal in dignity and rights; (ii) They are endowed with reason and conscience; (iii) They should act towards one another in a spirit of brotherhood being members of human family; and (iv) Everyone has the right to recognition everywhere as a person before the law.[11] It is the basic assumption of the United Nations Organization (UNO) that these rights are 'the foundation of freedom, justice and peace in the world' (Preamble). They would lead to promote social progress and better standards of life of men and women in larger freedom. A common understanding of these rights and freedoms would promote the development of friendly relations between nations and their cooperation with the United Nations.

These rights have some very special features. They are closely connected with freedoms and their goal is enjoyment of life. One has to enjoy them at his own will. Only in this way, they promote social progress and better standards of life in larger freedoms. There is no hierarchy, stratification, privileges or immunities in the possession of these rights. Everyone is entitled to all the rights and freedoms without distinction of any kind, such as race, colour, sex, language, religion, political or other opinion, national or social origin, property, birth or other status. It does not accept any distinction made on the basis of the political, jurisdictional or international status of the country or territory to which a person belongs, whether it be independent, trust, non-self-governing or under any other limitation of sovereignty.[12] This position has universal recognition and is supported by international force. All these rights can be put into categories.

Right to Life

It can be elaborated positively as (i) right to life, liberty and security of person, and negatively as (ii) total rejection of slavery in any form; and (iii) total discarding of torture, cruel, inhuman and degrading treatment or punishment, and (iv) denial of any arbitrary arrest, detention or exile.

Right to Equality

It speaks of all persons as equal before the law. They are entitled without any discrimination to equal protection of the law. All are entitled to equal protection against any discrimination in violation of these rights.

Right to Justice

The UDHR gives guarantee to free, fair and impartial justice: (i) It entitles everyone in full equality to a fair and public hearing by an independent and impartial tribunal in all legal matters; (ii) Everyone charged with a penal offence is given the right to be presumed innocent until proved guilty according to law; (iii) There has to be a public trial at which every person has had all the guarantees necessary for his defence; (iv) For holding a person guilty of any penal offence, it is necessary that the said offence constitute a penal offence, under national or international law, at the time when it was committed; (v) It is further stated that the penalty imposed must be in force at the time offence was committed.[13]

Right to Non-interference

Every person has been granted protection from arbitrary interference with his privacy, family, home or correspondence, or to attacks upon his honour and reputation. Everyone has the right to the protection of the law against such interference or attacks.

Right to Freedom of Movement, Residence, and Nationality

The UDHR confirms that everyone has the right to freedom of movement and residence within the borders of each state. A person can not be discriminated or confined in his own country. Another very important right it has granted to individuals is the right to leave any country, including his own, and to return to his country.[14] A similar right to persons is to seek and to enjoy in other countries asylum from persecution. However, this right may not be invoked in the case of prosecutions genuinely arising from non-political crimes or from acts contrary to the purposes and principles of the United Nations. In practice, it is severely limited almost everywhere.[15]

Everyone, under the Human Rights, has the right to a claim nationality. It means no one can be arbitrarily deprived of his nationality nor denied the right to change his nationality. An individual can assert, be a renegade or adopt any particular nationality.

Social Rights

Among these rights is the right to marry and to found a family without any restriction of race, nationality or religion. Men and women are given equal rights as to marriage, living in marriage and its dissolution. It further explains that marriage has to happen only with the free and full consent of the intending spouses. This right makes a new and unusual declaration that "(3) The family is thc natural and fundamental group unit of society and is entitled to protection by society and the State."[16]

Another tool in the hands of the individual is that everyone has the right to own property alone as well as in association with others. No one can be arbitrarily deprived of his property.

Righl lo Freedom of Expression, Assembly and Association

Enjoying freedom of speech and belief has been proclaimed as one of the highest aspiration of the common people. For this, the Declaration grants that everyone will have the right to freedom of thought, conscience and religion; this right includes freedom to change one's religion or belief, and freedom, either alone or in community with others and in public or private, to manifest his religion or belief in teaching, practice, worship and observance. It makes no mention of compulsion or violence in matters of religion. Apart from religion everyone has been given the right to freedom of opinion and expression. This right includes freedom to hold opinions without interference and to seek, receive and impart information and ideas through any media and regardless of frontiers.

This right has been given a concrete form by granting right to everyone to organise peaceful assembly and association. However, no one can be compelled against his will to belong to an association.

Right to Economic Security and Cultural Protection

These rights are indispensable for a person's dignity and the free development of his personality. For this, everyone has been given the right to work, to free choice of employment, to just and favourable conditions of work and to protection against unemployment. At par with it, everyone, without any discrimination, also has the right to equal pay for equal work.

The UN community desires that everyone who works has the right to just and favourable remuneration. It should ensure for himself and his family an existence worthy of human dignity, and supplemented, if necessary, by other means of social protection. However, everyone also has the right to rest and leisure. For this his working hours should be reasonably limited and he should have periodic holidays with pay. In order to make this right a concrete reality all have been given the right to form and to join trade unions for the protection of their interests.[17]

However, all these rights are not mercy or pity shown to persons in the way the employer likes at will. The latter has to see that every person enjoys the right to a standard of living adequate for the health and well-being of himself and of his family, including food, clothing, housing and medical care and necessary social services. One has to have the right to social security in the event of unemployment, sickness, disability, widowhood, old age or other lack of livelihood in circumstances beyond his control. The states of motherhood and childhood are entitled to special care and assistance. All children, even if they are born in or out of wedlock, should enjoy the same social protection.

Right to Compulsory and Humanist Education and Knowledge

To equip a person mentally and morally with education everyone shall enjoy the right to education. Education shall be free, at least in the elementary and fundamental stages. Elementary education shall be compulsory. Parents are given a prior right to choose the kind of education that would be given to their children. Technical and professional education are to be made generally available and higher education shall be equally accessible to all on the basis of merit. The goal of education would be the full development of the human personality and to the strengthening of respect for human rights and fundamental freedoms. It would promote understanding, tolerance and friendship among all nations, racial or religious groups. In this way, it would work for the maintenance of peace.

In the field of culture, everyone will have the right freely to participate in the cultural life of the community, to enjoy the arts and to share in scientific advancement and its benefits. A persons has the right to the protection of the moral and material interests resulting from any scientific, literary or artistic production of which he is the author.

Right to Participation in Governance

It is the most important right granted by the UN. It is the right to make and unmake one's fate to participate in governance. Accordingly, every person is given the right to take part in the government of his country, directly or through freely chosen representatives.[18]

"(3) The will of the people shall be the basis of the authority of government; this will shall be expressed in periodic and genuine elections which shall be by universal and equal suffrage and shall be held by secret vote or by equivalent free voting procedures." At the level of administration, everyone has the right of equal access to public services in his country. Thus, they have been given the right to realise a social and international order in which the rights and freedoms set forth in the Declaration are fully realised.

Limitations and Duties

The UDHR also exhorts that everyone has duties to the 'community' in which alone the free and full development of his personality is possible. An individual, therefore, is bound by certain duties and limitations. In the exercise of rights and freedoms, everyone has been put to limitation and restrictions that are determined by law. But their purpose should be of securing due recognition and respect for the rights and freedoms of others. They should meet the just requirements of morality, public order and the general welfare in a democratic society.

It has been made clear that these rights and freedoms may in no case be exercised contrary to the purposes and principles of the United Nations. It has further been clarified that nothing in this Declaration may be interpreted as implying for any State, group or person any right to engage in any activity or to perform any act aimed at the destruction of any of the rights and freedoms set forth therein.[19]

Resources, Tools and Instruments of Implementation

The preamble of the Universal Declaration of Human Rights (UDHR) provides the international sources of implementation of human rights. It also indicates tools and instruments to launch the Declaration in actual practice. Accordingly,

(1) human rights have to be protected by the *rule of law through states*;
(2) they have to be promoted through the development of friendly relations between nations;
(3) to implement them member-states have pledged to act in cooperation with the UN;
(4) a common understanding of these rights and freedoms is necessary for the full realisation of the Declaration;
(5) launching of Human Rights has to be striven by teaching and education;
(6) it has to be realised in degrees by progressive measures, national and international, to secure their universal and effective recognition and observance, among the peoples of member states themselves;
(7) the main tool of providing effective remedy would be by the competent national tribunals constituted for acts violating the fundamental rights granted to persons dealing with gross violation of Human Rights by the constitution or by law; even the UN has constituted International Court of Crimes (2002), and
(8) In case these instruments fail, man has the right to have recourse, as a last resort, to rebellion against tyranny and oppression, that is in case of utter neglect of human rights.

Role of UN and Other International Organisations and Agencies

Human rights are said to be possessed equally by everyone. A corollary of this claim is that everyone has a duty to protect and promote the human rights of everyone else. They can be enjoyed only when there are suitable social, cultural, economic and political conditions within the state and outside. But most of the Third World states do not have structures and resources to provide and maintain those conditions. In practice, thus, the onus of for securing human rights falls upon national governments and international and inter-governmental bodies. The moral burden for securing human rights, under these circumstances, falls disproportionately upon these institutions precisely because only some of them are best placed and most able to perform that task effectively. Non-governmental organisations and MNCs also have an important role to play. But the primary burden falls on relevant national and international institutions: the governments of the nation-states and the UN and the World Bank. Global inequalities in the distribution and possession of wealth undermine the ability of the poorer counties to grant these human rights to their people. Both nation-states and their legal set-up and cooperation of nation-states within international institutions require securing the requisite global conditions for the protection and promotion of everyone's human rights. Without this kind of arrangement, the UN or the politically active rich nations, international agencies like IMF and the World Bank cannot expect the poorer nations to implement the human rights. Even the 'minimal levels of decent and respectful treatment' cannot be a matter left to national governments. The problem is not limited to national boundaries. The more affluent and powerful nation-states should provide sufficient assistance to the countries incapable of adequately ensuring the protection of their citizens' basic human rights. Only then all individuals can be treated in an equal and like fashion in respect of provision of fundamental human rights.

Thus, the problem of protection and enforcement of human rights at the national and international levels requires serious attention of the scholars and leaders.

Enforcement of Rights

Active faith in teachings of *Dharma* (religion), morality, rationality and humanitarianism and education do play a voluntary role in spreading Human Rights. But the most effective way of upholding of Human Rights is that either the state's basic laws incorporate them or the state or UN declare legal support to them and make them 'justiciable'.

The first concrete support to Human Rights comes of from the constitutional and legal set up of a particular country, often from fundamental rights enshrined in a State Constitution. In some areas, the State Constitution includes many more rights than provided by the UDHR. Sometimes, the fundamental rights are given under the Constitution and its statutory laws grant rights more than that of the Declaration. Often the rights given by the State Constitution and other ordinary statutory laws (a) are more specific with all available details; (b) there is well organised machinery, judicial and administrative, to implement them; and they are applicable only to the citizens and persons living in a country.

The rights under the UDHR are written as general statements addressed to all individuals, groups, organisations, nations and states. In a way they are 'charter against states'. For their protection, the weapons with the UN are: moral appeal, education, supervision and political reporting. Their realisation, unlike fundamental rights and state laws, is gradual, time-consuming and uneven.

The normal process to deal with the violation of Human Rights is informally outlined at the UN level.

On receipt of a complaint of human rights violation by the UN, the UN Secretariat passes on the matter to the Committee of Human Rights.[20] This complaint is considered in closed session. The complaint is admissible if it is (i) not anonymous; (ii) not against a state which has not accepted the Optional Protocol; (iii) is not an abuse of the procedure (false or propaganda); (iv) concerned with the violation of one of the rights laid down in the Covenant; (v) not under the consideration of any other international procedure or agency; and lastly, (vi) the complainant must have exhausted all domestic remedies open to him.

When all these steps have been taken, the Secretary General presents the matter to the UN bodies for consideration and action, i.e., General Assembly and the Security Council. The defaulting state, organisation or party is reminded again and again on these developments and invited to present its view before the appropriate body. Suggestions are made and action is proposed by the UN in general and as well as specific terms. Before going into the actual nature of the verdict by the UN, one should keep actual status of Human Rights in mind.

Actual Status of Human Rights

Status of Human Rights can be seen from many angles:

Sufficient and Adequate for Men

As far as 'man and his family' is concerned, the ideology of Human Rights appears sufficient and adequate. It takes all aspects of man as man in view and stands by him. It stops at human concerns, and does not attempt to propose restructuring state and UN systems. At levels above the concerns of man, they may adopt any ideology, prefer a form of structure suitable for them.

Dominance of State Sovereignty

The concept of state sovereignty hangs heavily over UDHR. Human Rights cannot claim to override state sovereignty. Owing to their attitude, both China and United States were not voted onto the UN Human Rights Commission in 2002. US had refused to vote for the landmine restriction and withdrew from the Kyoto Protocol of global warming. China's record of human rights was poor on the Thianamen Square massacre of 1989.

Lack of Universalism

Human rights so far appear more on paper, and look more theoretical. Universal Declaration of Human Rights (UDHR) remains sacrosanct and a document of veneration. At many places, its articles are conflicting and lack precision. Genocide, ethnic conflicts, exploitation, casteism, child labour, atrocities on women etc. prevail that shows lack of universalism in the acceptance of human rights.

Arrogance of Religions

Human rights are often challenged by religions like Islam, Christianity, Hinduism, Judaism and the like. They often mix up state and religion. State is subordinate to demands of religion. Maintaining their religion as ultimate Message of God, they subordinate human rights to their teachings. They stand for the otherworldly goals, and neglect the demands of present life. The individual is only a tool and an instrument of religion. Equality is applied only to their followers. Hardly do they permit liberty to the individual. Individual rights undercut Confucius ethics. In Asian societies, community, society and law and order are regarded superior to human rights.

Counter-ideologies of Ultra Nationalism and Fundamentalism

Human rights are often identified with Western cultural imperialism. It is challenged by ultra-nationalism emerging in many developing countries. It has so happened in Yugoslavia, Rawanda, Sri Lanka, Serbia, and others. There is rise of religious fundamentalism or Islamism, particularly, in Iran, Iraq, Pakistan, Turkey, Sudan, Indonesia, etc. People there are segregated as damned and saved. The damned part of population is hated, tortured and killed. There is *ethnic cleansing* in many parts of the world.

Despite dubious, fuzzy and indeterminate status of UDHR, Human Rights is definitely a 'move forward' in the field of culture, political development, world peace and progress of mankind. It shall have a penetrating impact like that of the theory of natural rights. Its realisation remains incomplete. But even in its incomplete form it would 'revolutionise' every walk of individual and community life. In due course of time, most of the bonds, inhuman laws and traditions, inequalities, disparities etc. would be done away with. Man would become an end and instrument unto himself. as a result of gaining capacities at par with each other. Human Rights would bring about total democratic and liberal change in form of polities. Universality of Human Rights would rationalise the operations of Liberalisation, Privatisation, and Globalisation (LPG) ushered in the Twenty-first Century. It is expected that its understanding and application would incarnate new culture and civilisation of Humanity. For some applications of Human

Rights, it would be a turning point towards humanism if a scale for measurement of Human Rights is devised.

Measurement of Human Rights Cluster

With the help of ten categories of Human Rights under the Declaration, a 'scale' can be proposed hypothetically to measure quantum or extent of protecting Human Rights in a culture or polity.[21] These categories can be treated as variables also. The number of these categories can further be increased in the present context. Each proposed category has been allotted here value of 20 marks. However, a particular category owing to its greater importance can be allotted marks from 20 to 50. As such, it makes up a scale of 200 marks. It is proposed to measure Human Rights found in different systems, organisations and ideologies. A 'guidelines for measuring Human Rights Cluster or Human Rightism' is proposed hereunder.[22]

Scale Proposed for Measuring Human Rightism

Item of Measurement	*Assigned Value*
Right to Life	20
Right to Equality	20
Right to Justice	20
Right to Non-interference	20
Right to Freedom of Movement, Residence, and Nationality	20
Social Rights	20
Right to Freedom of Expression, Assembly and Association	20
Right to Economic Security and Cultural Protection	20
Right to Compulsory and Humanist Education and Knowledge	20
Right to Participation in Governance	20
Total	200

Such a Scale of Measuring Human Rightism would be useful in knowing span of Human Rightism found in a particular political system, political party, government, organisation or community. The scale may be applied to know the extent of Human Rightism prevailing in the whole world or any part or region thereof. This scale can be applied to measure Human Rightism irrespective of particular ideology, structural system, faith or religion. It can be done so on the basis of the concept of 'minimal good life' to be brought about by Human Rights. One can, thus, neglect the preference of the West and the US for making civic and political rights compulsory and the Eastern societies upholding requirements of society as a whole. The scale of Human Rightism, overriding them both, can evaluate them. The proposed scale can give an estimate of Human Rightism found in an ideology, religion or school of thought. With its help, one can find out the gap or extent of difference between 'theory' and 'practice' of Human Rightism claimed by a particular political party, system, organisation or institution.

It can report as well as compare the quantum of Human Rightism found in different political systems, cultures and ideologies during a particular century, historical stage or era. It can be done so both horizontally as well as vertically: Human Rightism existing in different states during medieval period or in Hindu states for the last two centuries.

Each type of comparison, analysis, or evaluation can predict guidelines to increase Human Rightism further. After ascertaining guidelines, one can formulate programme of reform, agitation and struggle to realise the needed quantum of Human Rightism, and arrive at an estimate of the cost, in terms of men, money and material, to be incurred for launching that programme. This cost can be reduced by resorting to peaceful means like generating consensus, procuring consent, seeking mutual cooperation, and entering into friendly deliberation. The leaders or managers can divide their programme into several segments and stages. Some separate board, commission, corporate body, tribunal, bureau or organisation can be constituted for the purpose of its proper implementation and reporting of the programme. Every society, community, caste or group can determine its own path of human progress from minimum to maximum Human Rightism. One can also anticipate the hurdles, difficulties and challenges coming in the way of survival or existence of a system struggling to increase Human Rightism.[23]

However, it may be concluded that Human Rights do not stand on strong footing of their own. They depend on care and mercy of the nation-states and the UN bodies, and ultimately on the might of dominating powers. Recourse to them is not very safe for man. Nowhere and none of the human rights provide strength to man to overcome effectively the forces, organisation and *jehadi* teachings to forgo their claim to practice violence openly against innocent persons, security forces and peace loving persons. There are Human Rights bodies like Amnesty International (1961), Human Rights Watch (1978) and so on that stand by the victims of human rights violation, but lack courage, skill, aptitude and manpower to stop violence of the violators of Human Rights: Extremists, Fundamentalists and Terrorists.

Notes

1. Humanism is 'a doctrine, or way of life centred on human interests or values; *especially*: a philosophy that usually rejects supernaturalism and stresses an individual's dignity and worth and capacity for self-realisation through reason'.

2. It is the doctrine that people's duty is to promote human welfare.
3. Vadkar, Praveen, *Concepts, Theories and Practice of Human Rights,* Delhi: Rajat, 2000, passim.
4. It was adopted by 48 vs zero voting with eight abstentions. It consists of a Preamble and 30 articles.
5. Nickel, James, *Making Sense of Human Rights: Philosophical Reflections on the Universal Declaration of Human Rights*, Berkeley: University of California Press, 1987.
6. Finnis, John, *Natural Law and Natural Rights,* Oxford: Clarendon Press, 1980.
7. Gewirth, Alan, *Reason and Morality*, Chicago: Chicago University Press, 1978.
8. Rawls, John, "Justice as Fairness: Political, not Metaphysical", *Philosophy and Public Affairs,* vol. 14, 287.
9. Habermas, Jurgen, *Moral Consciousness and Communicative Action,* trans. C. Lenhardt and S.W. Nicholson, Cambridge, MA: MIT, 1990, 197.
10. Rorty, Richard, "Human rights, rationality, and sentimentality", in S. Shute and Hurley (eds.) *On Human Rights: the Oxford Amnesty Lectures 1993,* New York: Basic Books, 1993.
11. Universal Declaration of Human Rights (UDHR), 1948, Art. 1 and 6.
12. Ibid., Art. 2.
13. Ibid., Art. 10 and 11.
14. However, this right is severely restricted in every country by state laws.
15. UDHR, Art. 13 and 14.
16. Ibid., Art. 16.3.
17. Ibid., Art. 22, 23 and 24.
18. Ibid., Art. 21.
19. Ibid., Art. 29 and 30.
20. Such matters are dealt with by the Office of the High Commissioner for Human Rights, 8-14 Avenue de la Paix 1211Geneva, 10, Switzerland.
21. There can be 25 or 30 or more categories (variables) in a proposed scale.
22. The concept 'Human Right Cluster' is abbreviated as 'Human Rightism'.
23. At one time in 1985 India had human rights rating of 70 per cent when average rating of countries all over the globe was 58 per cent as done by the World Human Rights Guide; See, Joseph Benjamin, *Human Rights in Indian Situation*, Indian Social Institute, 2007.

Epilogue

It is now clear that many new emerging national and international forces have transformed conventional Modern Political Theory into Advanced Modern Political Theory. Still, so far it is not much comprehensive, explanatory, and action-oriented.

In the previous chapters, we have observed, analysed, and evaluated some of the emergent force of Globalisation, Global Governance, Feminism, Human Rights, and Contemporary Terrorism, but still they have not matured enough to provide explanatory political theories. So far their studies appear confined more to some kind of analyses or explanations. We have talked of Fundamental Human Rights, but not about real nature and goals a man likes to pursue. Man is actually not confined to 'this-worldly' only, and does a lot in the light of what he believes in and regards it to be otherworldly, godly, or Truth. In the absence of a wider perspective, inclusive of both this and that world, an *advanced modern political theory* cannot be holistic, and closer to human heart and mind and his basic needs. With such lame, broken and limited political theory, we may not comprehend political phenomena in their totality.

Owing to Several limitations and restrictions, it has not been possible for us to take up issues like Survival of the Earth as a community, Justice for every ethnic, racial, cultural, or other group, etc. There are many other Life-and-Death issues: global warming, ecological warnings, predictions about animal, plant, and human health risks from increases in deforestation, global fresh water shortages, climate changes, depletion of the protective ozone layer etc. The effects of our industrial practices and standards on the Earth's flora and fauna are important dimensions, of public relationships. Humans have accumulated enough technical ability to befoul the planet on a wholesale level. Therefore, we have to develop a theory of political ecology within the ambit of an Advanced Modern Political Theory to relate it to environment.[1] This has to be a fast-track priority. It is not much useful to ponder over a political culture that will allow us only to remain healthy and alive. People cannot afford to think what constitutes an optimal state of affairs for man. Dead people will have no need to consider any political values. We analyse and prescribe liberties to use natural resources. The environmental clock is ticking very fast and we have to hurry before we are too late.

An another life-and-death issue relates to the problem of war and peace. The ability of modern nuclear, chemical, biological, and other kinds of weapons to end life is beyond imagination. A large-scale nuclear war would make growing of crops impossible and create a fatal nuclear winter for rest of population, if any. Biological and chemical weapons would have similarly, lethal effects on a global scale. Even a very large conventional war would be many times more destructive than that of the last world war. Smaller wars constantly take place and kill many thousands annually. Nations and groups collectively spend trillions of dollars on weapons in peacetime. Research, development, purchase, and maintenance of modern weapon systems constitute a massive cost for a polity. All this makes resources unavailable for health care, food, housing, social security and other basic human needs. Military preparation mobilise many of the best brains and research facilities for weapons development and leave little for the civilian sectors.

Organisation of the present international system is also not morally neutral. The contemporary global system is partially the cause of many major wars. It lacks a central authority to settle disputes or enforce international laws or norms. The United Nations lacks sufficient political and military resources to deter major powers from destroying each other and endangering world peace. Future international politics requires to meet the needs of all global citizens. Advanced Modern Political Theory has to be more pro-active on arms control and disarmament issues. Arguments about 'just' wars have to be re-examined in the light of the consequences and dangers of modern warfare. Theologians, political leaders, social reformers, piece activists and scholars should discuss which wars under what circumstances can be just. Similar dialogue should take place among the arms control and disarmament experts on issues like the causes and prevention of war, morality of various arms control proposals, alternative settlement of disputes, development of crisis management centres and the like. Scholars, citizens and political theorists have to learn more about the processes of international political conflict, role of, peace-maintaining institutions, and political technologies.

Use and application of Science and Technology has also revolutionised domestic and international politics.[2] Development in information technology is a matter of concern both the governments and citizens. It must not be distorted or co-opted by those who would manipulate it for their own advantage. We have to educate citizens and future leaders about the potential for distortion and manipulation that co-option of these powerful avenues of information represents. Knowledge is power. This power is both an end and a means that needs to be examined and used responsibly to serve the public interest. Alwin Toffler predicts that future divisions of the world would be not between the East and the West or the North and the South, but between the "fast" and "slow". The control of knowledge will be the crux of tomorrow's worldwide struggle for power in every human institution. Knowledge would make up the essence of the fast-arriving civilisation of the twenty-first century.[3]

In the making of an advanced Political Theory, there is an opportunity to influence direct and divert the future course of public affairs. There is a lot to contribute with cogent analyses, explanation and working theories, for speaking truth to power that be, and thus, to act morally. They will be serving public interest if they use techniques of critical political thinking and make technologies for bringing about changes for the better.

With these concerns, the Advanced Modern Political Technology has to go a long way. It has to comprehend various theories and political technologies to know their ambit, impact, and force, and their vital control points for correction and better application.

Notes

1. Fowler, Robert Booth, and Orenstcin, Jeffrey R., *An Introduction to Reinvention of Political Theory*, Harper Collins, 1997, Ch. 19–'Agenda before Advanced Modern Political Theory', 189–216.
2. See, Supra, Chapter 13.
3. Toffler, Alvin, *Power Shift: Knowledge, Wealth, and Violence at the Edge of the 21st Century*. Bantam Books, 1990.

Author Index

Subject Index